Cognitive Phenomenology

Cognitive Phenomenology

EDITED BY
Tim Bayne and Michelle Montague

OXFORD
UNIVERSITY PRESS

Great Clarendon Street, Oxford OX2 6DP

Oxford University Press is a department of the University of Oxford.
It furthers the University's objective of excellence in research, scholarship,
and education by publishing worldwide in

Oxford New York

Auckland Cape Town Dar es Salaam Hong Kong Karachi
Kuala Lumpur Madrid Melbourne Mexico City Nairobi
New Delhi Shanghai Taipei Toronto

With offices in

Argentina Austria Brazil Chile Czech Republic France Greece
Guatemala Hungary Italy Japan Poland Portugal Singapore
South Korea Switzerland Thailand Turkey Ukraine Vietnam

Oxford is a registered trade mark of Oxford University Press
in the UK and in certain other countries

Published in the United States
by Oxford University Press Inc., New York

British Library Cataloguing in Publication Data

Data available

Library of Congress Cataloging in Publication Data

Data available

Typeset by SPI Publisher Services, Pondicherry, India
Printed in Great Britain
on acid-free paper by
MPG Books Group, Bodmin and King's Lynn

ISBN 978–0–19–957993–8

1 3 5 7 9 10 8 6 4 2

Contents

List of Contributors

TIM BAYNE is University Lecturer in Philosophy of Mind at the University of Oxford and a Fellow of St. Catherine's College, Oxford

PETER CARRUTHERS is a Professor of Philosophy at the University of Maryland

TERRY HORGAN is a Professor of Philosophy at the University of Arizona

URIAH KRIEGEL is a Professor of Philosophy at the University of Arizona

JOSEPH LEVINE is a Professor of Philosophy at the University of Massachusetts Amherst

MICHELLE MONTAGUE is a Lecturer in Philosophy at the University of Bristol

DAVID PITT is an Associate Professor of Philosophy at the California State University, Los Angeles

JESSE J. PRINZ is a Distinguished Professor of Philosophy at the City University of New York

WILLIAM S. ROBINSON is a Professor of Philosophy at Iowa State University

CHRISTOPHER SHIELDS is Professor of Classical Philosophy at the University of Oxford and a Fellow of Lady Margaret Hall

CHARLES SIEWERT is a Professor of Philosophy at Rice University

MAJA SPENER is a Lecturer at the University of Oxford and a Junior Research Fellow at St. Catherine's College, Oxford

GALEN STRAWSON is Professor of Philosophy at the University of Reading

MICHAEL TYE is a Professor of Philosophy at the University of Texas at Austin

BÉNÉDICTE VEILLET is an Assistant Professor of Philosophy at the University of Michigan-Flint

DAVID WOODRUFF SMITH is a Professor of Philosophy at the University of California, Irvine

BRIGGS WRIGHT is a graduate student in Philosophy at the University of Texas at Austin

Cognitive Phenomenology: An Introduction

Tim Bayne and Michelle Montague

1 Introduction

Consciousness is rich. There are experiences in the five familiar sensory modalities: vision, audition, olfaction, gustation, and touch. There are bodily sensations of various kinds: itches, tingles, cramps, pains, and experiences of hunger, thirst, and drowsiness. There are the conscious states associated with emotions and moods, such as feelings of elation, despair, boredom, fear, and anxiety. Each of these kinds of conscious state has a distinctive phenomenal character; there is 'something it is like' to be in such states. Although no one would pretend that we have a fully adequate conception of these forms of consciousness, it seems fair to say that we have a respectable grip on how they ought to be characterized. We know—at least in rough and ready terms—what it is that a theory of perceptual and sensory consciousness must account for.

But our conscious lives are not limited to perception, bodily sensation, and affect. With the possible exception of moments in which one is immersed in physical exercise, musical performance, or some form of meditation, the stream of consciousness is routinely punctuated by episodes of conscious thought. We deliberate about what to have for lunch, we remember forgotten intentions, we consider how best to begin a letter or end a lecture, and we puzzle over the meaning of a friend's remark and the implications of a newspaper headline.

In contrast with the amount of attention that has been devoted to perceptual and sensory consciousness, conscious thought has been woefully neglected. This neglect might be understandable if conscious thought were well understood, but even the most cursory acquaintance with recent philosophy of mind reveals that that is very far from being the case. The disagreement surrounding conscious thought is not limited to its details or fine-grained structure, but concerns its fundamental nature.

Simplifying somewhat, we can distinguish two very different conceptions of conscious thought. One approach holds that although sensory states—broadly construed to include images, moods, and the feelings associated with emotions—have a distinctive 'phenomenal character' or 'what it's likeness', conscious thoughts do not. Here are some representative examples of this position:

Bodily sensations and perceptual experiences are prime examples of states for which there is something it is like to be in them. They have a phenomenal feel, a phenomenology, or, in a term sometimes used in psychology, raw feels. Cognitive states are prime examples of states for which there is *not* something it is like to be in them, of states that lack a phenomenology. (Braddon-Mitchell and Jackson 2007: 129; original emphasis)

Should we include any mental states that are not feelings and experiences on the list of phenomenally conscious states? Consider my desire to eat ice cream. Is there not something it is like for me to have this desire? If so, is this state not phenomenally conscious? And what about the beliefs that I am a very fine fellow? Or the memory that September 2 is the date on which I first fell in love? . . . It seems to me not implausible to deal with these cases by arguing that insofar as there is any phenomenal or immediately experienced felt quality to the above states, this is due to their being accompanied by sensations or images or feelings that are the real bearers of the phenomenal character. (Tye 1995: 4)

Our thoughts aren't like anything, in the relevant sense, except to the extent that they might be associated with visual or other images or emotional feelings, which will be phenomenally conscious by virtue of their quasi-sensory status. (Carruthers 2005: 138–9)

Neither the *believing* nor the *consciousness* that one oneself is believing *feels* like anything, if by 'feels' one means some sort of phenomenal or phenomenological state. It is only because we take sensations and sensation-like states as our paradigms of consciousness that we think that any state about which we are conscious must have phenomenological properties. (Nelkin 1989: 424; original emphasis)

We will refer to this as the 'conservative' conception of conscious thought—conservative because it conceives of sensory phenomenology, broadly construed as above, as the only kind of phenomenology there is. On this view, conscious thoughts lack any kind of distinctive non-sensory or non-imagistic phenomenology. There are two main varieties of the conservative view. The first grants that conscious thoughts may possess phenomenal character, but that they do so only in virtue of the sensory states with which they are associated or embedded. The second and more radical version of conservatism holds that there is a non-phenomenal kind of consciousness, and that thoughts are conscious only in a non-phenomenal sense. (Some may regard reference to non-phenomenal consciousness as incoherent; we will return to this point in §3.)

Until recently, conservatism was orthodoxy within the philosophy of mind. (At least, within so-called 'analytic' philosophy of mind.) Prominent textbooks in the subject would state the position without argument—indeed without even acknowledging that the view might be controversial. But controversial it is, for running alongside it is another—and increasingly influential—view, according to which conscious thoughts do possess a 'distinctive' and 'proprietary' phenomenology. This phenomenology—'cognitive phenomenology', as it has come to be called—can initially be defined negatively as a kind of phenomenology over and above sensory phenomenology. We will call this the 'liberal' conception of conscious thought—liberal because it sees the domain of phenomenology as extending beyond the sensory.[1]

Here are a few recent expressions of this liberal view:

[T]he experience of seeing red and the experience of now seeming to understand this very sentence, and of thinking that nobody could have had different parents . . . all fall into the vast category of experiential episodes that have a certain qualitative character for those who have them as they have them. (Strawson 1994: 194)

. . . generally, as we think—whether we are speaking in complete sentences, or fragments, or speaking barely or not at all, silently or aloud—the phenomenal character of our noniconic thought is in continual modulation, which cannot be identified simply with changes in the phenomenal character of either vision or visualization, hearing or auralization, etc. (Siewert 1998: 282; emphasis suppressed)

In addition to arguing that there is something it is like to think a conscious thought, I shall also argue that what it is like to think a conscious thought is distinct from what it is like to be in any other kind of conscious mental state, and that what it is like to think the conscious thought that p is distinct from what it is like to think any other conscious thought . . . (Pitt 2004: 2)

Intentional states have a phenomenal character, and this phenomenal character is precisely the what-it-is-like of experiencing a specific propositional-attitude vis-à-vis a specific intentional content. Change either the attitude-type (believing, desiring, wondering, hoping, etc.) or the particular intentional content, and the phenomenal character thereby changes too. (Horgan and Tienson 2002: 522)

The aim of this book is to take stock of the debate between the advocates of these two conceptions of conscious thought—what we call the 'cognitive phenomenology' debate. Our contributors attempt to identify just what the cognitive phenomenology debate is about; they present arguments for and against the existence of cognitive phenomenology; and they wrestle with the question of what might be at stake in this debate.

The aim of this introduction is to set the stage for the chapters that follow, and to provide newcomers to this debate with a map by means of which they might orient themselves. We begin in §2 with a brief—and no doubt opinionated!—overview of the historical backdrop to the debate. In §3 we consider some of the terminological challenges posed by the current literature. §4 distinguishes various ways in which the commitment to cognitive phenomenology might be understood. In §5 we turn our attention to arguments for and against the existence of cognitive phenomenology. We conclude in §6 by considering some of the potential implications of the cognitive phenomenology debate.

---

[1] In this volume Siewert distinguishes 'inclusivist' from 'exclusivist' conceptions of consciousness; Robinson distinguishes 'liberal' from 'frugal' views; and Prinz distinguishes 'restrictive' from 'expansive' conceptions of consciousness. These distinctions correspond, at least in broad outline, to our distinction between 'liberal' and 'conservative' views of consciousness.

2   Some historical context

One of the striking features of the cognitive phenomenology debate is that it exists at all. Why do some theorists (the 'conservatives') hold that there is no distinctive phenomenal character to thought, whilst others (the 'liberals') hold that there is? After all, it is widely held that one is—or at least can be—aware of the phenomenal character of a given mental state just in virtue of being in that mental state. In light of this, explaining why there is such deep disagreement about the nature of conscious thought poses something of a challenge. (Compare the cognitive phenomenology debate to debates about the sensory-phenomenological character of perception, which are not typically about whether sensory phenomenology exists but about how best to explain it.)

In order to understand the current discussion of conscious thought, we need to appreciate its historical roots. As theorists, we come to the study of consciousness with particular expectations and distinctive vocabularies in which to express those expectations, and our opponents may share neither our expectations nor our vocabulary. Although we cannot hope to provide a full 'genealogy' of the current cognitive phenomenology debate here, we do want to draw attention to some of the more influential historical moments that have helped shape the contemporary landscape.[2]

Because René Descartes has been such a central figure in the philosophy of mind, it seems fitting to begin with him. Consider Descartes's definitions of 'thought' and 'consciousness':

By the term 'thought' I understand everything which we are aware of as happening within us, insofar as we have awareness of it. Hence, *thinking* is to be identified here not merely with understanding, willing and imagining, but also with sensory awareness. (1644; 1.195 *Principles* 9)

Thought [cogitatio]. I use this term to apply to all that exists within us in such a way that we are immediately conscious of it . . . thus all the operations of the will, the intellect, the imagination and the senses are thoughts. [1641: 2.116 *Second Replies*]

Part of what is significant about these remarks is that Descartes is introducing a term that applies to all mental states in virtue of something they have in common. To this extent, therefore, he is treating the concepts THOUGHT and in turn CONSCIOUSNESS as unitary concepts. All mental states of which we are consciously aware fall under the same concept—what Descartes is here calling 'thought' ('cogitatio'). The property that unites all mental states that are part of the conscious field is our being immediately conscious of them. We find the same idea, expressed in different terms, in Locke, Berkeley, Hume, and Reid, among many others.

Franz Brentano (1874) also possessed a unitary conception of consciousness. According to Brentano, mental phenomena must be studied from the first-person

---

[2] See the chapters by Prinz, Siewert, and Smith for further discussion of the historical context to the cognitive phenomenology debate.

perspective, a method that he called 'phenomenology'. Franz Brentano (1874) also possessed a unitary conception of consciousness. He proposes to use the word 'conscious-ness' as 'synonymous with "mental phenomenon" or "mental act"' (1874: 102), holding accordingly that all mental phenomena are conscious and must be studied from the first-person perspective (a method for which he coined the name 'phenomenology'): 'every idea or presentation which we acquire through sense perception or imagination is an example of a mental phenomenon... furthermore, every judgment, every recollection, every expectation, every inference every conviction or opinion, every doubt is a mental phenomenon' (1874: 78–9).[3] There is no indication that Brentano thought of conscious-ness as taking one of two forms—a phenomenal form and a non-phenomenal form.

A similar conception of consciousness can arguably be found in Edmund Husserl, one of the central proponents of the phenomenological method. Husserl had a very inclusive theory of what the discipline of phenomenology covered—of what was *experienced* by the subject:

> ... percepts, imaginative and pictorial representations, acts of conceptual thinking, surmises and doubts, joys and griefs, hopes and fears, wishes and acts of will etc., are ... 'experiences' or 'contents of consciousness'. (1900–01: V. 2)

Husserl here endorses the view that acts of conceptual thinking are just as much experiences as percepts and pictorial representations. Kant had earlier expressed much the same point: 'experience consists not only of feelings, but also of judgements' (1788: Preface, *Critique of Practical Reason* Ak. 5:14).

This inclusive conception of consciousness can also be found in the writings of the very person to whom we owe the notion of the 'stream of consciousness'—William James:

> We ought to have some general term by which to designate all states of consciousness merely as such, and apart from their particular quality or cognitive function ... 'Feeling' has the verb 'to feel,' both active and neuter, and such derivatives as 'feelingly,' 'felt,' 'feltness,' etc., which make it extremely convenient. But on the other hand it has specific meanings as well as its generic one, sometimes standing for pleasure and pain, and being sometimes a synonym of '*sensation*' as opposed to '*thought*'; whereas we wish a term to cover sensation and thought indifferently ... In this quandary we can make no definitive choice, but must, according to the convenience of the context, use sometimes one, sometimes another of the synonyms that have been mentioned. *My own partiality is for either* FEELING *or* THOUGHT.' (1890: 1.186–7)

Moving closer to the present day, some have argued that we can also find a commit-ment to cognitive phenomenology in the work of G. E. Moore. Although Moore rejected the view of the British Empiricists, such as Locke, Berkeley, and Hume, that understanding involves internal imagistic goings-on, he did not think that it is

---

[3] Of course, it is a further question whether the immediate awareness that Descartes and Brentano think that we have of our conscious states should be understood in *phenomenal* terms, but many are inclined to think that it should.

altogether devoid of experiential character. Rather, he argued that it involves a certain sort of cognitive experience:

I will now utter certain words which form a sentence: these words, for instance: Twice two are four. Now, when I say these words, you not only hear them—the words—you also understand what they mean. That is to say, something happens in your minds—some act of consciousness— over and above the hearing of the words, some act of consciousness which may be called the understanding of their meaning.... [B]esides the mere hearing of the words, there occurs another act of consciousness—an apprehension of their meaning....(Moore 1910/1953: 57, 59)

Taken as a whole, these quotations suggest a widespread commitment to what we have called the 'liberal' conception of consciousness. From Descartes to Moore, we find authors who possess a common commitment both to the claim that the concept of consciousness is unitary, and to the claim that the concept of experience applies just as firmly to thought— episodes of judging, entertaining, and understanding—as it does to sensory episodes.

Just as today's liberals can find anticipations of their position in earlier writers, so too can today's conservatives. One influential figure in this tradition is C. I. Lewis. Although C. S. Peirce (1866) coined the term 'quale' (plural: 'qualia'), it was Lewis's (1929) use of it that left an abiding mark on the philosophy of mind. Lewis did not explicitly deny the existence of cognitive phenomenology, but he did contrast 'qualia', the subjective elements given in immediate experience, with the interpretational/ conceptual elements of thought:

Qualia are subjective; they have no names in ordinary discourse but are indicated by some circumlocution such as 'looks like'; they are ineffable, since they might be different in two minds with no possibility of discovering that fact and no necessary inconvenience to our knowledge of objects or their properties. All that can be done to designate a quale is, so to speak, to locate it in experience, that is, to designate the conditions of its recurrence or other relations to it. Such location does not touch the quale itself; if one such could be lifted out of the network of its relations, in the total experience of the individual, and replaced by another, no social interest or interest of action would be affected by such a substitution. What is essential for understanding and communication is not the quale as such but that pattern of its stable relations in experience which is what is implicitly predicated when it is taken as the sign of an objective property. (1929: 124–5)

We are presented here with a dichotomy between what is experiential and non-conceptual on the one hand, and what is conceptual and non-experiential on the other hand.

Another figure who can be placed in this conservative tradition is Gilbert Ryle. Although Ryle himself had no theoretical use for such notions as the stream of consciousness or sensation, he does make the following striking remark:

Whatever series of sensations an intelligent person may have, it is always conceivable that a merely sentient creature might have had a precisely similar series; and if by 'stream of conscious-ness' were meant 'series of sensations', then from a mere inventory of the contents of such a stream there would be no possibility of deciding whether the creature that had these sensations was an animal or a human being; an idiot, a lunatic or a sane man...(1949: 204–5)

These comments suggest a fairly radical version of conservatism, insofar as they would reduce the stream of consciousness to a series of sensory states, none of which have any substantive connection to thought. A similar view seems to be implicit in the following passage from J. J. C. Smart:

. . . for a full description of what is going on in a man you would have to mention not only the physical processes in his tissues, glands, nervous system, and so forth, but also his states of consciousness: his visual, auditory, and tactual sensations, his aches and pains. (1959: 142)

Hilary Putnam takes up this general train of thought, suggesting that there is a deep divide between the way in which concepts feature in our mental lives and the way in which images, sensations, and feelings do:

When we introspect we do not perceive 'concepts' flowing through our minds as such. Stop the *stream of thought* when or where we will, what we catch are words, images, sensations, and feelings . . . to attribute a 'concept' or a 'thought' to someone is quite different from attributing any mental 'presentation', any introspectible entity or event, to him. Concepts are not mental presentations that intrinsically refer to external objects for the very decisive reason that they are not mental presentations at all. (1981: 17–18, emphasis added)

One recurring feature in the writings of the authors just discussed is the idea that sensory features are 'directly' experienced in a sense in which thoughts and their constituent concepts are not. According to this tradition, thoughts feature in the stream of consciousness only indirectly—by way, perhaps, of structuring those sensory elements which themselves make up the contents of consciousness. Those who reject cognitive phenomenology—'conservatives' in our terms—might not want to endorse all of the various claims expressed by Lewis, Ryle, Smart, and Putnam, but it is possible to see them as the heirs to this intellectual tradition.

3 Terminology

We turn now from the historical background of the cognitive phenomenology debate to the terminology in which it is conducted. Perhaps the central question here is whether the key terms that are employed in discussions of conscious thought—'phenomenology', 'phenomenal character', 'what it's likeness', 'experience', 'qualia'—are used in the same ways by the various parties to the discussion. As we will see, there is reason to doubt whether this is so.

At the centre of the current debate, in addition to the core term 'phenomenology', we find the expression 'phenomenal consciousness' and its cognates 'phenomenal property', 'phenomenal character', and so on. The widespread usage of 'phenomenal consciousness' owes much to Ned Block (1995). Block denied that the term could be defined as such, but he did suggest that 'phenomenal consciousness' could be regarded as a synonym for 'experience'. He also contrasted phenomenal consciousness with what he called 'access consciousness'. A mental state is phenomenally conscious (or 'P-conscious') just in case there is 'something it is like' to be in that state, whereas a mental state is access conscious (or 'A-conscious') just in case its content is available for free use in reasoning and the rational control of action. Finally, Block also provided examples of states that he took to be paradigms of phenomenal consciousness and access consciousness respectively:

The paradigm P-conscious states are sensations, whereas the paradigm A-conscious states are 'propositional attitude' states such as thoughts, beliefs, and desires, states with representational content expressed by 'that' clauses. (1995: 232)

By contrasting phenomenal consciousness with access consciousness, and by suggesting that sensations, rather than thoughts, are the paradigms of phenomenal consciousness, Block arguably encouraged the view that thought has no distinctive phenomenal character. However, Block did not deny that thoughts have a distinctive phenomenal character (nor, for that matter, did he deny that sensations can be access conscious). Indeed, Block expressed some uncertainty about what the phenomenal character of thought involves: 'One possibility is that it is just a series of mental images or subvocalizations that make thoughts P-conscious. Another possibility is that the contents themselves have a P-conscious aspect independent of their vehicles' (1995: 232).

The standard way in which the notions of phenomenal consciousness and phenom-enology are introduced is by appeal to the phrase 'what it's likeness'.[4] Phenomenal states, it is said, just are states that there is something it is like for the subject of experience in question to be in. Not only can we distinguish phenomenal states from non-phenomenal states by appeal to the notion of 'what it's likeness', but—so the thought goes—we can also distinguish phenomenal states of different types from each other by reference to what it is like to be in them. What it is like to taste ripe strawberries differs from what it is like to smell lavender, and both of these experiences differ in turn from what it is like to feel the touch of silk. But what exactly does 'what it's likeness' amount to?

One obvious point is that 'what it's likeness' must be understood in terms of what it is like *for the subject* itself to be in the relevant states (see e.g. Levine 2001; Strawson 1994). This qualifier is needed because there are all sorts of entities—shoes, ships, and sealing wax—that lack phenomenal states but for which the question 'What is it like?' is perfectly well formed. Although there is a sense in which there is something it is like to be (say) a shoe, there is nothing that it is like for a shoe to be a shoe.

[4] To the best of our knowledge, the phrase was first used in print by Farrell (1950) and then Sprigge (1971). It also occurs in Wittgenstein's *Remarks on the Philosophy of Psychology, Vol. 1.*, although Wittgenstein's remarks were not published until 1980. We owe the current influence of the phrase to Nagel (1974). See Lormand (2004) for a detailed analysis of the use of the phrase in the current literature.

We should also note that there are uses of the phrase 'what it's like' that do not even purport to pick out phenomenal states. Consider the claim that there is something that it is like to live in Hull (grow up in the circus; spend a winter at the North Pole, etc). Presumably no one would use this expression in order to make the claim that there is a particular phenomenal property—a particular 'what it's likeness'—that is uniquely associated with living in Hull. Instead, reference to what it's like to live in Hull (grow up in the circus; spend a winter at the North Pole) is presumably intended as a convenient way of identifying a messy collection of phenomenal states that those who live in Hull (grow up in the circus; spend a winter at the North Pole) might enjoy.

Although it is widely assumed that there is a notion of 'what it's likeness' that is sufficiently well-behaved to function as the starting point for theorizing about consciousness, this assumption is far from universally granted.[5] Lycan, for one, has described the phrase as 'worse than useless', claiming that its use 'sends the struggling mind of even the most talented philosopher into yet another affect-driven tailspin of confusing a welter of distinct issues' (Lycan 1996: 77).[6] Few theorists have endorsed Lycan's pessimism, but a significant number have argued that there is more than one sense of 'what it's likeness' at play in contemporary philosophy of mind. Georgalis distinguishes a restricted sense of 'what it's likeness', which includes bodily sensations and perceptual states but not thoughts, from an unrestricted sense that includes not only sensory states but also propositional attitudes and their contents (Georgalis 2005: 69). Carruthers (1998, 2000) distinguishes what he calls 'worldly what it's likeness' from 'mental state what it's likeness', where the former concerns what the world (or the state of the organism's own body) is like for an organism and the latter concerns what the organism's *representations* of the world (or its own body) are like for the organism. Rosenthal (2002) argues for a similar distinction, couched in terms of a contrast between what he calls 'thin phenomenality' and 'thick phenomenality'. Indeed, Lycan (2008) himself distinguishes what he calls 'first-order what-it's-likeness' from 'second-order what-it's-likeness', where the former is an apparently monadic property inhering in a mental state, and the latter is a higher-order property of the apparently monadic property. Clearly, any account of whether there is 'something that

---

[5] There are also theorists who hold that the notion of 'what it's likeness' can come apart from that of phenomenal consciousness. Consider the following passage from Kim's *Philosophy of Mind* (2nd edn): '... it is evident that there are conscious mental states with no special phenomenal character. In general, mental occurrences that we call 'experiences' appear to be those that possess phenomenal properties. If this is so, the idea of phenomenal character and the idea of there being something that it is like come apart. For it certainly seems that there is something that it is like to believe something, to suspend judgment about something, to want something, and so on. But as we saw, at least many instances of these states don't have any phenomenal, sensory quality' (1996: 159).

[6] Consider also Papineau's claim: 'There are many ways of being, from those of humans who make phenomenal judgments about their own states, through cats who can attend but not introspect, down to amoebas and plants with simple sensorimotor systems. Why suppose that the phrase "like something" draws a line across this spectrum?' (Papineau 2002: 227). See also Hill (2010) and Snowdon (2010) for further worries about the utility of the phrase in discussions of consciousness.

it is like' to have an occurrent thought needs to reckon with the charge that there is more than one notion of 'what it's likeness' at play in discussions of consciousness.[7]

What about the notion of experience? On one use of the term 'experience', there is a natural contrast between experience and thought. In this sense of the term, to experience an object is to be acquainted with it in perception rather than thought. It is this notion that is operative when we ask someone whether they have experienced vegemite (skiing; ballroom dancing; Paris) or whether they know about it only on the basis of testimony. In this sense of the term, thoughts are by definition non-experiential. Some of our contributors have this sense of 'experience' in mind. For example, Carruthers and Veillet announce that the purpose of their chapter is to 'defend the view that phenomenal consciousness is exclusively experiential (or non-conceptual) in character', assuming that if they can establish that consciousness is exclusively experiential, then they will have thereby shown that thought has no distinctive phenomenal character. But as we saw in §2, there are also uses of the term 'experience' according to which thoughts might qualify as experiential. In this broader sense of the term, an experience is any element or component of the stream of consciousness—any element that constitutes what it's like to be the creature in question. To deny from the outset that thoughts can be experiential in *this* sense of the term would beg the question against the advocate of cognitive phenomenology.

Let us turn now from 'experience' to 'qualia'. Perhaps no term in the study of consciousness carries with it more conceptual baggage than 'qualia'. One important contrast is between those who take it that qualia are by definition non-intentional states or 'raw feels', and those who leave open the possibility that qualia can be understood in intentional terms. Those in the second camp hold that to recognize the existence of (e.g.) colour qualia is not to take a position on whether colour experience can be captured in intentional terms, whereas those in the first camp hold that colour qualia exist only if it is not possible to capture colour experience in intentional terms. In light of this, the assertion that there are cognitive qualia is ambiguous. On the one hand, it could simply mean that conscious thought has an experiential or phenomenal character—a character that cannot be captured in sensory terms. On the other hand, it could mean that conscious thought has an experiential or phenomenal character that cannot be captured in intentional terms. This contrast is important, because the latter claim is considerably more controversial than the former.[8]

Leaving that issue to one side, one might think that qualia must in any case be aspects of sensory or perceptual experience, and that the notion of cognitive qualia is something of a contradiction in terms. Perhaps there are uses of 'qualia' for which that might be the case, but there are also other—and venerable—uses that allow for the possibility

[7] See Byrne (2004) for an illuminating discussion of this literature.
[8] See Langsam (2000) for an argument for the existence of qualia in the second sense of the term based on the need to distinguish conscious thoughts with a certain content from conscious perceptions with the same content.

of cognitive qualia. According to C. S. Peirce, there is 'a distinctive quale to every combination of sensation . . . a distinctive quale to every work of art—a distinctive quale to this moment as it is to me—a peculiar quale to every day and every week—a peculiar quale to my whole personal consciousness . . .' (1866: para 223). In the more recent literature, Flanagan distinguishes between a narrow sense of 'qualia' that is limited to sensations and a broader sense 'under which fall all types of experience with subjective, first-person, phenomenological feel'. He goes on to say that 'beliefs, thoughts, hopes, expectations, and propositional-attitude states generally, as well as large narrative structures, are qualitative (or have qualitative components) in this sense' (Flanagan 1992: 67).

This brief survey of the terminology in which the cognitive phenomenology debate is conducted has raised the question of whether central aspects of the debate might not be 'merely verbal'. Perhaps those who advocate the existence of cognitive phenomenology have something rather different in mind by that phrase than those who deny its existence. We won't develop this theme here, but the reader might want to keep it in mind. Whether or not the cognitive phenomenology debate is 'merely verbal', one thing the preceding discussion clearly demonstrates is just how difficult it is to break out of a fairly narrow circle of terms: 'phenomenological', 'what it's like', 'qualia', 'experiential'. One can perhaps define each of these notions in terms of the others, but finding a stable place to nail down the entire cluster of concepts remains an ongoing challenge.

4 The varieties of cognitive phenomenology

In §2 we distinguished a liberal conception of the nature of conscious thought, according to which conscious thought possesses a distinctive phenomenal character, from a conservative conception, which denies that that is the case. We turn now to the task of providing a more detailed characterization of what separates the liberals from the conservatives. We should note at the outset that providing a characterization of this debate is no simple matter. Different contributors conceive of the debate in different ways, and it is not entirely clear that there is a single claim that might separate all of those who endorse 'cognitive phenomenology' from those who reject it. The aim of this section is to distinguish some of the many positions that might—and arguably do—trade under the 'cognitive phenomenology' label.

We start with a point that is common ground among all parties to the debate: dispositional or unconscious states have no phenomenological character. As such, reference to the phenomenology of beliefs, desires, intentions, and other thoughts should be taken to refer to occurrent or conscious tokens of such states ('events', if you prefer). Readers who hold that beliefs (desires, intentions, and so on) cannot as such be occurrent but are necessarily dispositional should take reference to conscious beliefs (desires, intentions, and so on) as shorthand for the analogues of these states that can—by the lights of such readers—be occurrent. Reference to thoughts ought also to be understood in terms of token mental acts or states—particular, dated instances of thinking such-and-such—rather than thoughts considered as types.

4.1 First approximations

At the heart of the cognitive phenomenology debate is the question of whether conscious thought possesses a non-sensory phenomenology. As we read them, most of those who see themselves as advocates of cognitive phenomenology answer this question in the affirmative, whereas those who see themselves as opponents of cognitive phenomenology answer it in the negative. The contributors to this volume refer to non-sensory phenomenology as 'pure' cognitive phenomenology (Levine) and as a kind of phenomenology that is 'proprietary' to thought (Pitt, Prinz).

Some theorists reject the existence of a kind of cognitive phenomenology that is 'pure' or 'proprietary', but nonetheless hold that there is a sense in which thoughts 'possess' a distinctive phenomenal character. There are two ways in which one might develop this idea. On the one hand, one might hold that thought always and essentially involves, or is somehow 'realized in', a sensory medium of some sort, such as inner speech. On this view, a particular thought will be 'carried by' a phenomenal state, but the phenomenology of that state will be exclusively sensory. On the other hand, one might hold that thought (and the deployment of concepts more generally) has an impact on the structure of the subject's sensory manifold. For example, one might argue that judging something to be (say) meat as opposed to soy changes the phenomenal character of the way that it tastes, or that recognizing someone changes the phenomenal character of one's visual perception of them. Levine refers to these phenomena as examples of 'impure' cognitive phenomenology; one might also refer to them as instances of 'non-proprietary' cognitive phenomenology (see also Nes, in press).

It is an open question whether impure or non-proprietary cognitive phenomenology ought to be regarded as a genuine form of cognitive phenomenology. Although we recognize that there is something to be said for an inclusive conception of cognitive phenomenology that would bring such states within its ambit, we prefer a narrower use of the phrase, according to which cognitive phenomenology is by definition 'pure' or 'proprietary'. In our view, the label 'cognitive phenomenology' is best reserved for a class of phenomenal properties that are non-sensory. One consequence of this stipulation is that it is possible for someone to reject the existence of cognitive phenomenology whilst holding that conscious thought necessarily has a (sensory) phenomenal character. Indeed, one could even reject the existence of cognitive phenomenology but hold that the phenomenal character of a particular thought-type was unique to tokens of that type on the grounds that a certain cluster of sensory phenomenal properties is possible only in the context of a particular thought.

It is sometimes said that the cognitive phenomenology debate is about whether phenomenal character is 'individuative' or 'constitutive' of thought (e.g. Pitt 2004; Lycan 2008; Carruthers and Veillet, this volume; Tye and Wright, this volume). We can distinguish two ideas behind such claims, one stronger than the other. The stronger—and perhaps more natural—reading of this claim is that there is a necessary relationship between phenomenal state types and thought state types, such that it is not possible to be in a certain thought state without being in a certain phenomenal state. For example, one might hold that there is some particular phenomenal property (or cluster of phenomenal properties) P that characterizes the thought ⟨fish swim⟩, such that one thinks ⟨fish swim⟩ if and only if one instantiates P. Tye and Wright (this volume: 338) seem to have this idea in mind when they claim that the phenomenology of thought thesis requires 'that there be a unique phenomenology that goes along with any token thought with the one content'.

A weaker notion of what it means to claim that the phenomenology of thought is individuative or constitutive applies to thoughts considered not as types but as tokens. On this reading, to claim that phenomenal character is individuative or constitutive of thought is to claim that for any subject, S_1, S_1's thought of a certain type (t_1) has a phenomenal character that sets it apart from S_1's thought of a distinct type (t_2). This thesis allows that there may be another subject of experience, S_2, whose t_1-type thoughts have a different phenomenal character from that which S_1's t_1-type thoughts possess. It is important to note that on neither of these two readings is the claim that the phenomenology of thought is individuative or constitutive entailed by the claim that there is a pure or proprietary phenomenology of thought. In other words, one could coherently claim that thought possesses a non-sensory phenomenal character but deny that this phenomenal character is individuative or constitutive of it.

4.2 Attitude

Within the sensory realm we can distinguish a vast variety of sub-types of phenomenal states. Not only are there obvious differences between experiences in different perceptual modalities, there are also many distinctions to be made within perceptual modalities. What it's like to smell a piece of mouldy Camembert differs from what it's like to smell a freshly baked apple pie, and each of these experiences differs from what it's like to smell wet grass. Is there a similar kind of richness and diversity within the phenomenology of thought? If so, what are the central dimensions in terms of which it might be structured?

Following Bertrand Russell (1918/1919, 1948), it is common to think of thoughts as attitudes to propositions. On this model, judging that fish swim is to be understood as taking up the attitude of judgment to the proposition ⟨fish swim⟩. Similarly, desiring to visit Asmara is to be understood as adopting the attitude of desire to the proposition that ⟨one visits Asmara⟩. Our interest here is not in the question of whether (all) thoughts can be understood as propositional attitudes, but in the question of whether this approach to thought might give us a useful framework for considering the structure of its phenomenology. Arguably it does: we can ask whether cognitive phenomenology is structured in terms of propositional attitudes, and we can ask whether it is structured in terms of propositional content. We examine these two questions in this and the following section respectively. (Both questions, of course, are premised on the assumption that there is something worth calling 'cognitive phenomenology'.)

Are there distinctive phenomenal characters corresponding to different attitude types (Peacocke 1998)? Russell himself appears to have great sympathy with this view, claiming that believing P feels different from remembering it, expecting it, disbelieving it or doubting it (Russell 1921: 176, 250). On this view, judging that P will have a phenomenal element in common with judging that Q, even if their *overall* phenomenal characters may differ; similarly, desiring that P and desiring that Q will share that phenomenal element which is in common to all occurrent desire. (Of course, each of these states might be characterized by a generic phenomenology of thought that sets them apart from sensory and affective states.) One might think of the phenomenal characters of particular attitude types on the model of the phenomenal character of the various perceptual modalities. Just as visual experiences have a phenomenal character that distinguishes them from auditory experiences, so too merely cognitive (non-evaluative) judgements have a distinctive phenomenal character that distinguishes them from desires. Indeed, one could hold that phenomenal character marks fine-grained attitudinal contrasts between thoughts, such that there are distinct phenomenal characters associated with (say) the strength of one's belief in a given proposition or the degree to which one desires that a certain state of affairs obtain (Klausen 2008).

One question raised by attitudinal phenomenology is whether it might play a role in the individuation of thought types. In his contribution to this volume, Shields argues that it does. A less demanding position—one that Shields considers and rejects—is that attitudinal qualia are merely associated with particular propositional attitudes, rather than essential to them, and that the individuation of propositional attitudes is fixed by (say) the functional roles of the propositional-attitude states. A third possible view would be that although attitudinal qualia are required in order for thoughts to play certain functional roles, it is those functional roles (rather than the qualia themselves) that make it the case that a thought is (say) a belief rather than a desire.

What do conservatives make of attitudinal phenomenology? In their contributions to this volume, Prinz and Robinson allow that thoughts do possess a distinctive 'what it's likeness' on the basis of their attitudinal character, but they argue that attitudinal phenomenology should be thought of as sensory in a suitably broad sense of the term. They suggest that attitudinal phenomenology should be grouped together with that of emotions and epistemic feelings, such as curiosity, novelty, and confusion (see §4.4). On this view, the phenomenology associated with one's desire to win the race may be explicable in terms of nervous anticipation, and the phenomenology associated with doubting that one will win the race may be explicable in terms of feelings of uncertainty.

In addition to the phenomenology of thoughts, some would argue that we ought also to recognize a phenomenology that is distinctive of *thinking*. Thoughts can occur as isolated events, but they are more usually tokened within the context of trains of thought. Sometimes, the members of such trains are linked with each other only on associative grounds; at other times, one thought leads to the next on the basis of inferential considerations. One might put together the thoughts 'Today is Monday' and 'I have a faculty meeting on Monday', and as a result token the thought 'I have a faculty meeting today'. Examples like this encourage some theorists to hold that there are phenomenal states associated with certain kinds of transitions between thoughts. For example, one might argue that there is something that it is like to grasp the fact that one thought entails another (see, classically, James 1890: ch. 9; also Chudnoff 2010).

4.3 Content

A second dimension along which positions within the cognitive phenomenology debate can be located concerns the *content* of thought. At one end of the spectrum there are theorists who deny that the content of thought has any direct impact on its phenomenal character; at the other end of the spectrum are those who hold that every distinction between thought contents brings with it a distinction in phenomenal character. In between these two poles are theorists who hold that only certain kinds of distinctions between thought contents are reflected in phenomenal character.

There are, of course, multiple conceptions of intentional content. Some theorists conceive of intentional content in terms of objects and their properties, others conceive of it in terms of states of affairs or sets of possible worlds, and still others take content to involve modes of presentation. Complicating matters further is the fact that many philosophers allow that thought and perception can have multiple layers of content. In the same way that it is an open question which kind(s) of content might best capture the phenomenology of perception (Chalmers 2004; Pautz 2009; Thompson 2009), so too it is an open question which kind(s) of content might best capture the phenomenology of thought (if such there be).

A central question here is whether the kind of content that varies with phenomenal character is internal ('narrow') or external ('wide'). This issue can be illuminated by contrasting the phenomenal states of a person on Earth with those of their 'twin' on Twin Earth (Putnam 1975). The twins are, let us suppose, both consciously thinking thoughts expressed by the sentence 'water is wet' in their respective languages. If both of their 'water' thoughts can have the same cognitive-phenomenological character, then cognitive-phenomenological character must be associated with internal ('narrow') content. If, on the other hand, their two 'water' thoughts cannot have the same cognitive-phenomenological character, such character must be associated with external ('wide') content.

Although both proponents and opponents of cognitive phenomenology have usually assumed that cognitive phenomenology must be narrow, it is not obvious that this assumption should be granted. After all, it is somewhat controversial whether perceptual phenomenology must be narrow, with a number of theorists arguing that it is wide (Dretske 1996; Lycan 2001). If it can be plausibly argued that perceptual phenomenology is wide, then perhaps it can also be plausibly argued that cognitive phenomenology is wide. (Of course, if it can be argued that cognitive-phenomenological content is narrow, then perhaps one could adapt such arguments to show that perceptual-phenomenological content is also narrow.)

A further question about cognitive-phenomenological content is whether it is structured. It is very plausible to suppose that *perceptual* phenomenology is structured. What it is like to see a dog involves a state whose phenomenology is in some way 'built up' out of phenomenal states that concern its various features—its shape, its colour, its spatial location, and so on. Is the phenomenal character of thought similarly structured? Consider the thought ⟨apples are sweeter than lemons⟩. Just as its intentional content is built up out of the concepts APPLES, LEMONS and IS SWEETER THAN, so too one might argue that its overall phenomenal character is built up out of the phenomenal characters of its constituent concepts. Of course, this view is not a forced move, and advocates of cognitive phenomenology might argue that the structure of the phenomenal character of thought content is somewhat independent of its conceptual structure.

A final but particularly important question to be addressed here is whether phenomenal properties might *ground* or *determine* the content of thought. This possibility is raised in Kripke's seminal discussion of meaning in *Wittgenstein on Rules and Private Language*. In an attempt to address the question of what might fix the meaning of the concept PLUS, Kripke considers the following proposal:

> Why not argue that 'meaning addition by "plus"' denotes an irreducible experience, with its own special quale, known directly to us by introspection? ... I refer to an introspectible experience because, since each of us knows immediately and with fair certainty that he means addition by 'plus', presumably the view in question assumes that we know this in the same way we know that we have headaches—by attending to the qualitative character of our own experiences. Presumably the experience of *meaning addition* has its own irreducible quality, as does that of feeling a headache. (1982: 41, see also p. 43)

Although Kripke went on to reject this proposal, a number of theorists have argued that there is a form of intentionality—often dubbed 'phenomenal intentionality'—which is wholly constituted by phenomenology alone (see e.g. Farkas 2008; Horgan and Tienson 2002; Kriegel 2007; Loar 2003). A radical form of this approach holds that phenomenal intentionality tells the full story about intentionality—that phenomenal intentionality is the only genuine form of intentionality (see e.g. Farkas 2008). A less radical version of this position holds that although phenomenal intentionality is the fundamental form of intentionality, there are modes of intentionality that are fixed by non-phenomenal relations (see e.g. Horgan and Tienson 2002).

Whichever of these two views they adopt, advocates of phenomenal intentionality need to account for the apparent existence of unconscious intentionality. Kriegel addresses this challenge in his contribution to this volume, arguing that it can be met by adopting what he calls 'interpretivism'. His proposal is that a state possesses unconscious intentionality just in case an 'ideal' interpreter would interpret it as having the relevant content. Kriegel argues that since interpretation is a conscious activity, interpretivism entails that unconscious intentional content is grounded in cognitive phenomenology. Whether or not Kriegel's arguments are persuasive, they are a further reminder of how close the question of cognitive phenomenology is to issues that lie at the heart of philosophy of mind.[9]

4.4 Emotion, perception, and epistemic feelings

So far we have focused on the question of whether thoughts—instances of judging, entertaining, desiring, intending, and so on—have a phenomenal character. In this section we examine three other domains of mental activity in which there is some reason to think we can find cognitive states that possess a distinctive phenomenology: the domain of emotion; the domain of categorical perception; and the domain of epistemic feelings.

There is no doubt that emotional states often (if not invariably) involve phenomenal properties. There is something that it is like to experience sadness about the death of a loved one, jubilation about the success of a friend, or anger at a perceived injustice. The question is whether the phenomenal character of emotions can be captured in purely sensory terms. On some accounts, emotions are to be understood as nothing more than 'perceptions of changes in our respiratory, circulatory, digestive, musculoskeletal, and perhaps endocrine systems' (Prinz, this volume: 180; see also Prinz 2004). Other accounts hold that emotions have cognitive components, but they regard the cognitive element(s) of emotions as independent of their phenomenal character. For example, on some views emotions are composites of a cognitive state (such as a judgment) and a non-cognitive sensory feeling. Such views would be of a piece with 'conservative' conceptions of phenomenology.

There are, however, conceptions of the phenomenal nature of emotions that might support liberal treatments of phenomenology. For example, Gunther (2004) argues that various types of emotional states (anger, joy, and so on) are characterized by distinctive, and non-sensory, phenomenal properties. More recently, Montague (2009) has argued that emotions should be understood as *sui generis* intentional attitudes, and that part of their distinctiveness is to be explained by their phenomenological character, and in particular by what she calls their 'evaluative or affective phenomenology', which she takes to be non-sensory.

Categorical perception or 'perceiving as' provides us with a second domain in which we may find cognitive states that possess a distinctive phenomenology. Consider the claim that one can see something as a pine tree, smell the odour in the air as that of overripe bananas, or hear a sequence of notes as the opening of Schubert's *Unfinished*

---

[9] For further discussion of the idea that intentionality (including all dispositional intentionality) can and perhaps must be grounded in consciousness see Searle (1992: ch. 7), Fodor and Lepore (1994), Strawson (1994: ch. 7; 2008) and Kriegel (forthcoming).

Symphony (Wittgenstein 1953: II. ix; see also e.g. Siegel 2005; Bayne 2009; Masrour, in press; Smith, this volume). Do such acts of 'high-level' or 'categorical' perception possess a distinctive phenomenal character? Many have been tempted to think so. After all, we do describe objects as (e.g.) looking like pine trees (smelling like overripe bananas; sounding like the *Unfinished Symphony*). However, it is controversial whether such talk is to be understood in phenomenal terms, and a number of authors have argued that such claims are true only in a non-phenomenal sense of the relevant appearance terms (see e.g. Lyons 2005; Tye 2000).

Suppose, however, that it can be plausibly argued that high-level or categorical content does enter into perceptual phenomenology—what bearing would this have on the cognitive phenomenology debate? It may not provide direct evidence for cognitive phenomenology, for one could argue that high-level perception is quite distinct from thought. At the same time, it is not implausible to suppose that the existence of categorical phenomenology might provide indirect evidence for cognitive phenomenology (in our sense of the term). At the very least, one might argue that if 'perceiving as' involves conceptual content—as many theorists have argued—then the phenomenology of categorical perception shows that there is no inconsistency between the possession of conceptual content and the possession of a proprietary phenomenal character. One might also argue that some instances of 'perceiving as' ought not be regarded as purely perceptual but are intermediate (or perhaps 'hybrid') states that straddle the divide between thought and perception. The notion of a perceptual judgement, which some of the contributors to this volume appeal to (see Smith), can perhaps also be regarded as a state that is neither purely perceptual nor purely thought-based.

A third domain of mental activity in which we may find cognitive states with a distinctive phenomenal character is that of 'epistemic feelings'—feelings of knowing, tip-of-the-tongue experiences, experiences of familiarity, experiences of understanding, and so on (Clore 1992; Koriat 2000; Trout 2002). The distinctive phenomenal character of these states seems to be intimately related to their cognitive content. Indeed, Goldman appeals to tip-of-the-tongue experiences as evidence for the existence of non-sensory phenomenology:

When one tries to say something but cannot think of the word, one is phenomenologically aware of having requisite conceptual structure, that is, of having definite . . . content one seeks to articulate. What is missing is the phenomenological form: the sound of the sought-for word. The absence of this sensory quality, however, does not imply that nothing (relevant) is in awareness. Entertaining the conceptual unit has a phenomenology, just not a sensory phenomenology. (1993: 24)

Not everyone has been persuaded by Goldman's conception of tip-of-the-tongue phenomenology. Drawing on Jackendoff (1987), Lormand (1996) argues that such experiences can be accounted for solely in sensory terms. According to him, there is a void associated with the absent phonological representation, and there is something it is like, sensorily speaking, to experience this void (akin to what it's like to 'hear' silence). Tip-of-the-tongue experiences involve a sense of effort, but according to Lormand this too is sensory, akin to what it is like to sense physical effort. So, a question remains as to whether tip-of-the-tongue experiences—not to mention the other examples of 'epistemic feelings'—are states with a distinctive cognitively-structured phenomenology.

We have examined three domains in which there is some reason to posit states with a non-sensory phenomenal character. How might this bear on the question of whether thought itself has a phenomenal character? One possibility is that these states might function as a kind of bridgehead for the advocate of cognitive phenomenology: if the cognitively-structured states seen in emotion, categorical perception, and epistemic feelings possess a distinctive phenomenology, why shouldn't thoughts also possess a distinctive phenomenology? Establishing that these three domains furnish us with examples of cognitive states that possess a distinctive phenomenology might not demonstrate that thought too possesses a distinctive phenomenology, but it might undermine certain objections to that thesis. For their part, those who reject cognitive phenomenology will either want to resist the claim that emotion, categorical perception, and epistemic feelings do involve states with a distinctive non-sensory phenomenal character, or they will want to draw a principled distinction between these 'thought-like' states and thoughts proper. Whether either of these tasks can be successfully executed is a task we leave for readers to explore.

5 Argumentative considerations

Having distinguished various conceptions of cognitive phenomenology, we turn now to some of the central arguments for and against its existence. These arguments differ in their ambitions. Some of them are relatively modest, aiming to establish only that we enjoy—or, as the case may be, do not enjoy—cognitive phenomenology. Others are bolder, purporting to show either that cognitive phenomenology is in some way necessary for thought or, alternatively, that it is impossible. We will start with some of the less ambitious arguments.

5.1 Introspection

The most straightforward argument for the existence of cognitive phenomenology involves a direct appeal to introspection. Just as (say) emotional or perceptual phenomenology is introspectively discernible as such, so too—say the advocates of cognitive phenomenology—there is a type of phenomenology distinctive of thought that is also introspectively discernible as such. As Horgan and Tienson put it, 'attentive introspection reveals that both the phenomenology of intentional content and the phenomenology of attitude type are phenomenal aspects of experience, aspects that you cannot miss if you simply pay attention' (Horgan and Tienson 2002: 522–23). Perhaps few advocates of cognitive phenomenology would put things quite as boldly as this, but the idea that cognitive phenomenology is introspectively manifest enjoys widespread support. In the current volume, endorsement for this view can be found in the chapters by Horgan, Kriegel, Montague, Pitt, Shields, Siewert, Strawson, and Smith.

Needless to say, conservatives have not been persuaded. Here, for example, is Wilson:

> In the spirit of Horgan and Tienson's appeal for a reader to 'pay attention to your own experience', I have just done the decisive experiment: I thought first that George Bush is President of the United States, and had CNN-mediated auditory and visual phenomenology that focused on one of his speeches. I then took a short break, doodled a little, wandered around the room, and then had a thought with that very same content and . . . nothing. (2003: 417)

In a similar vein, Nichols and Stich describe the view that there is a distinct feel or set of qualia for every type of propositional attitude and content as 'crazy':

> As best we can tell, believing that 17 is a prime number doesn't feel any different from believing that 19 is a prime number. Indeed, as best we can tell, neither of these states has any distinctive qualitative properties. Neither of them feels like much at all. (2003: 196)

This position is echoed by a number of contributors to this volume. Robinson claims that there is nothing it feels like, phenomenally speaking, for one to have a particular belief or desire (see also Robinson 2005); Tye and Wright trace the primary source of resistance to cognitive phenomenology to its 'introspective unfamiliarity'; Prinz comments on the 'introspective elusiveness' of purely cognitive qualities; and Carruthers and Veillet claim to be unable to detect anything in the contents of their introspection that might qualify as cognitive phenomenology.

It is possible to distinguish at least two ways in which introspection has been used to motivate the case for cognitive phenomenology. Most straightforwardly, some theorists have argued that there are conscious thoughts which are not clothed in any kind of sensory or imagistic 'garb', and hence that the 'what it's likeness' of such thoughts must be non-sensory (see e.g. Siewert 1998; Pitt 2004). As Prinz notes in his chapter, the question of whether non-imagistic thought exists is not a new one but has been around since the late nineteenth century. In fact, this question was at the heart of one of the most important debates in the history of introspection (Boring 1953; Lyons 1986; Ogden 1911). On one side were Titchener and his followers at Cornell, who claimed that introspection provides no evidence of non-imagistic thought. On the other side were the members of the Würzburg school—notably Külpe, Ach, and Bühler—who claimed to have discovered introspective evidence of non-imagistic thought. The debate between these two positions was extremely heated. As one observer put it,

> one is left with the feeling that the case is largely reduced to mere assertion, and denial, occasionally to vituperative recrimination. It seems to be largely a matter of 'It is!' or 'It isn't', adorned with such adjective as taste may dictate and capacity afford. (Angell 1911: 305)

The debate surrounding the existence of non-imagistic conscious thought continues in this volume, although hopefully with less 'vituperative recrimination'.

Even if it should turn out that all conscious thought is clothed in sensory form, one might still argue that it is possible to introspectively discern non-sensory elements within a thought's overall phenomenal profile. On this view, 'what it's like' to consciously judge (say) that guavas are fruit might involve distinctively cognitive elements in addition to whatever sensory elements it might have, such as those associated with inner speech. One way to develop this claim would be to argue that even if every tokening of the thought <guavas are fruit> is accompanied by *some* sensory phenomenology or other, it is far from obvious that there will be any sensory elements in common to all such tokenings. And yet—the liberal might argue—introspection reveals the existence of a common phenomenal element running through all conscious tokenings of this thought.

Can a liberal reasonably hold that cognitive phenomenology only ever occurs in conjunction with sensory phenomenology? Prinz (this volume) suggests not, arguing that if there are non-sensory phenomenal qualities, then we ought to be able to experience them in isolation from their sensory brethren. After all, he argues, given that it is possible to experience various components of sensory consciousness in isolation from each other, there is no reason why it shouldn't also be possible to experience the elements of cognitive phenomenology (if they exist) in isolation from each other and from the various elements of sensory phenomenology. He concludes that the case for cognitive phenomenology may require advocates of the view 'to come up with a clear example of a cognitive experience that occurs without any sensory experiences, or at least without any sensory experiences that are related to the cognitive act' (Prinz: 193). Some liberals will think that Prinz's demand is easily met. Others may argue that whether or not it is easily met, it is not a reasonable demand: they might either challenge Prinz's assumption that the various components of sensory consciousness *can* be experienced in isolation from each other, or they might challenge his assumption that cognitive phenomenology must share the 'atomistic' structure that allegedly characterizes sensory phenomenology.

Let us return to the two forms of the introspective argument for cognitive phenomenology. As we have seen, both arguments are problematized by the fact that conservatives fail to discern in their own experience the kinds of states that liberals claim to find. There is disagreement both about whether thought is ever non-imagistic, and about whether imagistic thought might contain non-sensory elements. Each of these disagreements is deeply puzzling. If non-imagistic thought exists, why are some theorists unable to detect it? If it doesn't exist, why do some theorists claim to be able to detect it? If imagistic thought contains non-sensory elements, why are some theorists unable to detect them? If it doesn't, why do some theorists claim that it does?

In her contribution to this volume, Spener grapples with the implications of these disagreements. She argues that they undermine the introspective warrant that each side of the debate claims for its own position: introspection neither counts for nor against the existence of cognitive phenomenology. Whether or not Spener's case is persuasive—and we suspect that her arguments will convince neither liberals nor conservatives—she makes a powerful case for the claim that the cognitive phenomenology debate raises questions about the trustworthiness of introspection (see also Schwitzgebel 2008).

5.2 Phenomenal contrast arguments

Faced with the dialectical impotence of direct appeals to introspection, advocates of cognitive phenomenology have often resorted to indirect appeals. Such appeals involve what are known as phenomenal contrast arguments. Contrast arguments are so-called because they involve the presentation of two scenarios that allegedly differ in phenomenal character but not in sensory or perceptual features. One kind of case concerns two subjects who hear the same sounds but have different overall experiences, because one of them experiences the sounds as words that they understand and the other does not (see e.g. Moore 1910/1953: 58–9; Strawson 1994: 6–7; Siewert 1998: 275–6). Another class of contrast arguments concerns high-level perceptual content (§4.4). Siegel, for example, argues that learning to recognize pine trees can change the way that they look—in the phenomenal sense of 'look' (Siegel 2005; see again Wittgenstein 1953: II.ix). The claim is that since the sensory phenomenology is unchanged by perceptual learning, we must appeal to the cognitive components of such states to explain the change in phenomenal character that occurs. We can think of phenomenal contrast arguments as a species of inference to the best explanation: since there is no sensory difference between the two scenarios, the phenomenal contrast between them can be accounted for only by appealing to some form of non-sensory phenomenology.[10]

Broadly put, there are three ways in which conservatives can respond to contrast arguments. Most obviously, the conservative can simply deny that the particular scenarios in question do involve any *phenomenal* contrast. As we previously noted (§4.4), although we do describe objects as (e.g.) looking like pine trees, it is controversial whether such talk is to be understood in phenomenal terms. Those who hold that such descriptions are true only in a non-phenomenal sense of the appearance terms might hold that learning to recognize a class of objects on the basis of perception involves no distinctively phenomenal change to the subject's point of view.

A second response to contrast arguments allows that the scenarios concerned do involve phenomenal contrasts, but holds that such contrasts can be fully explained in sensory terms. For example, Tye and Wright (this volume) point out that the contrast between hearing a language that one understands and hearing an unfamiliar language involves differences in the way that one processes the auditory stream, which in turn leads to differences in auditory phenomenology. In a similar vein, Carruthers and

---

[10] See Siegel (2007) for discussion and defence of the phenomenal contrast method.

Veillet (this volume) claim that although a subject's concepts do not directly enter into or constitute the subject's phenomenal states, they do have a causal influence on their phenomenology. Similarly, Levine (this volume) holds that although thoughts have no 'proprietary' or 'pure' phenomenal character, they do affect the structure of the subject's sensory manifold. Finally, Prinz (this volume) attempts to account for a range of contrast cases by appealing to the phenomenal effects of prototypicality, verbal labelling, the generation of images, and the allocation of attention to category-relevant sensory features. In each case, the conservative's claim is that phenomenal contrasts can be accounted for by appealing to differences in sensory phenomenology. Note that this line of reply doesn't attempt to establish that contrast scenarios don't involve differences in cognitive phenomenology, but only to undermine the thought that contrast scenarios *require* us to posit a distinctively cognitive phenomenology.

A final response allows that contrast arguments do establish the existence of high-level *perceptual* phenomenology, but holds that they do not provide any evidence for the existence of cognitive phenomenology in the sense in which we have been using the term—that is, for the claim that *thought* has a distinctive phenomenal character. For example, one might take Siegel's arguments to show that such properties as *being a pine tree* can be encoded in visual phenomenology, but deny that they provide any reason to think that thoughts about pine trees possess a distinctive phenomenology. Insofar as it is unclear just where (and how) to draw the line between thought and high-level perception (see §4.4), it will also be unclear whether a particular contrast argument would establish the existence of 'cognitive phenomenology' even if successful. Consider, for example, what Strawson calls 'understanding experience' or 'meaning experience'. Opinions might differ as to whether understanding speech qualifies as a form of perception or thought. Our intention here is not to pronounce on this issue, but merely to draw attention to the fact that certain contrast arguments inhabit the murky zone between categorical perception and thought.

5.3 Self-knowledge

A third argument for cognitive phenomenology appeals to the role that cognitive-phenomenological properties might play in accounting for the kind of epistemic access we have to our conscious thoughts. It is quite plausible to suppose that knowledge of one's own bodily sensations and perceptual experiences involves direct acquaintance with their phenomenal properties. The suggestion is that we can extend this account of self-knowledge from knowledge of sensations and perceptual experiences to knowledge of cognitive states. Alvin Goldman (1993; although see Goldman 2006) was an early advocate of this position, arguing that we know what propositional-attitude states we are in on the basis of their phenomenal character. Central to his argument for this position is the claim that awareness of one's own mental states must involve properties that are both intrinsic (non-relational) and categorical (non-dispositional), and that the only properties that might meet these conditions are phenomenal properties. A more recent defence of the self-knowledge argument for cognitive phenomenology can be found in the work of David Pitt (2004; this volume), although his version of the argument focuses only on knowledge of the contents of one's own thoughts.

The self-knowledge argument has not met with much enthusiasm in the literature. Some theorists deny that we have introspective access to our propositional-attitude states, and hence that there is no problem that phenomenal properties need be invoked in order to solve. Carruthers (2010) defends a version of this view, arguing that we have no direct or privileged access to our conscious judgments or conscious intentions (see also Gopnik 1993). Other theorists allow that we have introspective access to our thoughts, but deny that such access as we have involves the detection of phenomenal properties. Phenomenal properties may play a role in explaining how we know our sensations and perceptual states, but—say such theorists—they play no such role in accounting for knowledge of one's own thoughts (see e.g. Nichols and Stich 2003; Prinz 2004; Schwitzgebel, forthcoming).

The self-knowledge argument for cognitive phenomenology is discussed by a number of contributors to this volume, with Pitt's (2004) version of the argument being singled out for particular attention. Tye and Wright claim that Pitt's argument depends on a (discredited) perceptual model of introspective awareness, and that even if introspective awareness of thought did involve phenomenal properties, these properties would not be possessed by thoughts themselves. Levine also criticizes Pitt's phenomenological account of self-knowledge, and develops an alternative model of self-knowledge in its place. Drawing on a broadly Fodorian (1975, 2008) account of thinking, according to which propositional attitudes involve distinctive functional relations to 'mentalese' sentences, Levine argues that what it is to have knowledge of one's thoughts involves tokening a higher-order mentalese sentence that expresses what one is thinking. This counts as 'immediate self-knowledge' because the higher-order state is reliably caused by the first-order state and some functionally defined internal monitoring process. In his own contribution to this volume, Pitt defends his phenomenological account of self-knowledge and argues against some of the leading alternatives to it.

5.4 Grounding content

The three lines of argument for the existence of cognitive phenomenology that we have examined so far are all modally weak in that none attempts to establish that phenomenal character is in any way essential to the nature of thought. However, a fourth kind of argument for cognitive phenomenology would, if successful, provide a deep link between thought and phenomenal character. Philosophers have different strategies for making this link, but the central idea is that we must appeal to phenomenological considerations in order to ground the intentional content of thought. We might refer to these arguments as 'content-grounding' arguments (see e.g. Goff, in Press; Horgan and Tienson 2002; Horgan and Graham, in press; Kriegel, this volume; Loar 2003; Strawson 2005, 2008).

One content-grounding argument concerns the determinacy of thought. At least since Quine (1960) and Kripke (1982), philosophers have worried that the apparent determinacy of intentional content might be an illusion. Put most broadly, the worry is that the determinacy of thought—the fact that we can think about particular properties and objects as such—must be grounded in something, and yet there seems to be no viable account of what that ground might be. Since no purely functional or physical relation could underwrite the determinacy of content, thought cannot—despite appearances to the contrary—really have determinate content.

Horgan and colleagues have argued that even if no purely functional or physical relation can underwrite the determinacy of thought, it doesn't follow that the determinacy of thought is an illusion (Horgan and Tienson 2002; Horgan and Graham, in press). Rather than being grounded wholly in physical or functional relations, the determinacy of thought—they suggest—might be partly grounded in its phenomenal character. Given that what it is like to think *that rabbits have tails* is distinct from what it is like to think *that collections of undetached rabbit parts have tail subsets*, we can appeal to this difference in 'what it's likeness' to explain why these two states have different intentional contents. More generally, the proposal is that we can appeal to the phenomenal character of a thought—together, perhaps, with facts about the environment in which the thinker is situated—to explain why it has the particular content that it does. And since we need to appeal to cognitive phenomenology in order to secure the determinacy of content, we have here an argument for the existence of cognitive phenomenology.

A second content-grounding argument can be found in Strawson (2008), who argues that cognitive phenomenology is needed in order to solve what he calls the 'stopping problem'. Consider a subject, Lucy, who is perceiving or thinking about Mandy the moose. Assuming that Lucy has the appropriate causal connections to Mandy, how does Lucy's experience or thought manage to be about Mandy the moose, rather than about the set of Mandy-caused photons impacting on her retinas, or certain other sets of causes on the causal chain leading to the experience? How does Lucy's thought manage to stop precisely at Mandy rather than at some other location on the causal chain? Strawson rejects Dennettian 'interpretationist' solutions to this problem, and argues that the answer must appeal to cognitive phenomenology: Lucy's experience contains a certain (fully internalistically specifiable) conception of what particular kind of thing her experience is about, and this conception, which is part of the cognitive-phenomenological content of her experience, is an essential part of what enables her experience (or thought) to be specifically about Mandy, given her causal relations to Mandy.

Content-grounding arguments have been subject to two lines of criticism. Some critics have raised concerns about just how phenomenal properties might ground intentional properties. After all, it is not entirely clear *how* phenomenal properties might underwrite the determinacy of thought or solve the stopping problem. Others have argued that the advocates of this argument have been too quick to dismiss the possibility that non-phenomenal properties might be able to ground the determinacy of thought. Dennett (1982) and others would argue that our interpretative practices and the behavioural patterns that underlie them can fully account for the kind of determinacy our thoughts possess. Millikan (1984) and others would argue that our evolutionary heritage bestows a sufficient degree of determinacy on thought. And Fodor has argued that the determinacy of thought can be secured by what he calls the strategy of 'counterfactual triangulation' (Fodor 2008). Just where these three lines of response leave the grounding argument is an issue for further discussion.

5.5 The ontology of thought

For the most part, the opponents of cognitive phenomenology have been on the defensive. Rather than provide positive arguments of their own, they have tended to focus on responding to the arguments of their opponents. However, it is possible to discern a couple of arguments against the existence of cognitive phenomenology in the literature. One such argument can be found in the contribution that Tye and Wright make to this volume.[11] Drawing on the work of Geach (1957) and more recently Soteriou (2007, 2009), Tye and Wright argue that thoughts are not the kinds of entities that *could* enjoy phenomenal character.[12] Their argument involves two claims. Firstly, anything that figures in the stream of consciousness must 'unfold over time'; in other words, it must be an event or a process rather than a state. Secondly, thoughts are states, and as such they do not unfold over time. To use their example, in thinking the thought 'The claret is delightful' one does not first grasp the noun 'claret', and then the copula 'is', and finally the adjective 'delightful' in a successive process. Instead, they claim, the entire thought arrives 'all at once'. According to Tye and Wright, it is only the various phenomenal goings-on that *accompany* thoughts—for example, linguistic sub-vocalizations and images—that unfold over time. Thoughts themselves do not, and as a result they cannot feature in the stream of consciousness.

There are two general lines of response that advocates of cognitive phenomenology might adopt in response to this argument. On the one hand they might argue that even if the stream of consciousness is limited to events and processes, it by no means follows that there can be no phenomenology of thought, for at least some thoughts do unfold over time. We certainly describe ourselves as thinking through a problem or deliberating about what to do, and it is far from obvious that such occurrences lack a temporal structure. A more 'confrontational' response to the objection would be to take issue with the claim that the stream of consciousness is limited to events and processes. One way to put pressure on that assumption would be to argue that not all elements of *perceptual* experience are processive. Consider, for example, perceptual recognition.

---

[11] Carruthers and Veillet (this volume) also provide arguments against the possibility of cognitive phenomenology, one of which we mention in §5.6.

[12] This position is often associated with the work of the later Wittgenstein (1953).

Although perceptual recognition might be (necessarily) embedded in processes that unfold over time, it is not clear that the 'act' of recognition itself unfolds over time. The experience of seeing an assortment of dots as (say) a Dalmatian or recognizing a sequence of notes as comprising a particular tune appears to arrive 'all at once'. Whatever the merits of these responses, it is clear that there are important points of contact between the cognitive phenomenology debate and questions concerning the temporal structure and the ontology of consciousness.

5.6 Epistemic challenges

We bring this section to a close by considering a cluster of arguments that centre on the epistemic challenges that are closely associated with consciousness. Three such challenges can be identified. Firstly, there is the famous 'explanatory gap' between phenomenal properties on the one hand and neural (or functional) properties on the other (Levine 1983). We are certain that there is an intimate relationship between the brain states that underlie phenomenal consciousness, but we lack an adequate explanation of the relationship between brain states and phenomenal states. Secondly, there is Jackson's (1982) knowledge argument, the upshot of which purports to be that no amount of physical (or functional) knowledge of the brain and its operations suffices for knowledge of phenomenal properties. As Jackson's celebrated example has it, Mary can know everything there is to know about the neurophysiology of the visual system but she won't know what it's like to see red. Thirdly, there are 'zombie' intuitions: it seems conceivable that there might be creatures that are physically and/or functionally and behaviourally identical to us but lack phenomenal properties (Kirk 1974; Chalmers 1996).

Our interest here is not in these epistemic challenges per se, but in the question of what light they might shed on the cognitive phenomenology debate. One possibility is that these challenges might function as criteria or markers for the presence of phenomenal properties.[13] In other words, one might argue that the case for cognitive phenomenology turns on whether conscious thought poses an explanatory gap, or whether it is possible to construct a thought-based version of the knowledge argument, or whether certain kinds of cognitive zombies are conceivable. Let us consider these ideas in more detail by examining how some of our contributors develop them.

In their chapter, Carruthers and Veillet argue against the existence—indeed, the very possibility—of cognitive phenomenology on the grounds that there is no explanatory gap for thought. Their focus is on the conceivability of inverted-experience scenarios. They argue that inversion scenarios are not conceivable for conceptual states on the grounds that inversion scenarios require the deployment of conceptually isolated phenomenal concepts, and that there are no such phenomenal concepts when it comes to conceptual content. They conclude that since conscious thought

---

[13] For further discussion of this proposal see Block (2002), Goldman (1993), and especially Kriegel (2009).

would give rise to an explanatory gap if it had a distinctive phenomenal character, the lack of any such gap is evidence that it has no such phenomenal character.

In his chapter, Horgan uses the epistemic puzzles associated with consciousness to argue for precisely the opposite conclusion. His focus is not on the explanatory gap but on the conceivability of partial zombies. Partial zombies are creatures who are functionally identical to us despite the fact that they enjoy only certain aspects of our overall phenomenology. Horgan's particular interest is in the conceivability of cognitive zombies: creatures who share our sensory phenomenology but not our cognitive phenomenology. He argues that since such creatures are robustly conceivable, there must be more to the nature of conscious thought than its functional role: it must also possess a proprietary phenomenal character.

It is clear from the foregoing that there is no settled view in the literature concerning whether the epistemic challenges associated with consciousness might also apply to conscious thought. A more fundamental question is whether it is indeed legitimate to treat the epistemic puzzles associated with consciousness as markers of phenomenal consciousness. There is reason for caution here, for such puzzles appear to be more closely connected to certain aspects of perceptual phenomenology than others. It is noteworthy that discussions of the explanatory gap, the knowledge argument, and zombies almost always invoke the experience of secondary properties (colours, flavours, tastes, and so on) and rarely appeal to the experience of primary properties (shape, motion, spatial relations, and so on). Perhaps one reason for this is that the epistemic puzzles associated with phenomenal consciousness are more pressing with respect to experiences of secondary qualities than they are with respect to experiences of primary qualities. Despite this fact, there is little doubt that experiences of primary qualities do have a robust and proprietary phenomenal character. The upshot of these reflections is that question marks surround the use of the epistemic puzzles associated with phenomenal consciousness as general markers of phenomenal consciousness.

6 Implications

We bring this introduction to a close by sketching some of the ways in which the cognitive phenomenology debate might inform our understanding of consciousness and of the mind more generally.

We have already noted one issue that arises from the cognitive phenomenology debate: the trustworthiness of introspection. If there is cognitive phenomenology, then conservatives are guilty of overlooking a range of phenomenal states that they enjoy. If on the other hand there is no cognitive phenomenology, then liberals are guilty of positing a range of phenomenal states that they don't enjoy. Either way, the failure of theorists to converge on a shared conception of the phenomenal character of thought calls into question the reliability of introspection. Of course, introspective disputes are not confined to discussions of cognitive phenomenology, but this introspective dispute seems particularly worrying (Schwitzgebel 2008; Bayne and Spener 2010; Spener, this volume).

The cognitive phenomenology debate also has the potential to constrain and inform accounts of the nature and functional role of consciousness. Some accounts of consciousness are at odds with the existence of cognitive phenomenology. Consider, for example, accounts that identify phenomenal states with representational states that have either analogue content (Dretske 1995) or non-conceptual content (Tye 1995). Such accounts would appear to be in trouble if thought has a distinctive phenomenal character that attaches to its content, for the content of thought is neither analogue nor non-conceptual. If, on the other hand, it can be shown that there is no distinctively cognitive phenomenology, then this might provide something in the way of indirect evidence in favour of such accounts.

A third issue raised by the cognitive phenomenology debate concerns the question of what positive characterization of conscious thought conservatives might be able to provide. In the first section we mentioned two main conservative views of conscious thought: one view grants that conscious thought possesses phenomenal character, but only in virtue of the sensory states with which it is associated or embedded; the second claims that thought is characterized only by a non-phenomenal kind of consciousness. Each of these proposals raises questions. With respect to the first proposal, one might ask exactly how the possession of sensory phenomenology accounts for the fact that the thought itself is conscious. Given some particular conscious thought, does there have to be a particular kind of sensory phenomenology that makes it conscious, or will any sensory phenomenology suffice? With respect to the second proposal, one might ask for a more thorough analysis of non-phenomenal consciousness. Is it possible to characterize it in purely functional terms, or—like phenomenal consciousness—is it a form of consciousness that appears to resist functional analysis? Cases of blindsight give us a sense of what unconscious awareness might be, but a *non-phenomenal yet conscious* sense of awareness is an entirely different matter.

Fourth, the cognitive phenomenology debate has implications for our view of the relationship between 'the phenomenal mind' and the 'intentional mind'. These two features of the mind have often been regarded as metaphysically independent, with many theorists holding both that some mental states possess phenomenal character but lack intentional content, and that some mental states possess intentional content but lack phenomenal character. Following Horgan and Tienson (2002), one might conceive of such approaches to the mind as forms of 'metaphysical separatism'. Metaphysical separatism has fostered a kind of methodological separatism, with many theorists holding that phenomenality and intentionality can and should be tackled independently of each other. In defence of metaphysical separatism, theorists often point to the fact that thoughts have no (distinctive) phenomenal character. But if the existence of cognitive phenomenology can be established, then this line of argument would no longer be available to the separatist. Of course, this would not itself establish any form of inseparatism, but it would make inseparatist conceptions of the mental that much more plausible (Montague 2010).

Finally, the cognitive phenomenology debate has implications for the broader project of understanding the place of consciousness in nature. Attempts to explain how consciousness comes about as a result of 'irritating nervous tissue' (Huxley 1866: 189) have focused almost exclusively on states of sensory consciousness. Theorists have worried about the gap between what it's like to smell a rose, taste burnt sugar, or feel sharp pain and the neural states underlying such experiences. How might the hard problem(s) of consciousness look if we were to suppose that thoughts too possess a distinctive phenomenal character? There are two possibilities. Pessimists might worry that accepting cognitive phenomenology would mean that the prospects for closing the explanatory gap and solving the hard problem will be that much bleaker than many of us used to think, for conscious thought would no longer be immune to the deep puzzles that surround sensory experience. Optimists, on the other hand, might welcome the establishment of cognitive phenomenology, on the grounds that such a view might provide us with new ways of thinking about the explanatory gap and the hard problem, ways that our fixation on sensory consciousness might have obscured.

The resurgence of interest in consciousness is now into its third decade. There is no doubt that we have made progress on many fronts. We have a better conception of the neural basis of consciousness; we possess a richer set of empirical data against which to test accounts of consciousness; and we have a better understanding of the logical space in which those accounts are located. But for all this progress, the cognitive phenomenology debate is a reminder that our grasp on the fundamental features of consciousness itself remains surprisingly tenuous.[14]

References

Angell, J. R. (1911). 'Imageless thought', *The Psychological Review*, 18 (5): 295–322.

Bayne, T. (2009). 'Perception and the reach of phenomenal content', *Philosophical Quarterly*, 59: 385–404.

——and Spener, M. (2010). 'Introspective humility', in E. Sosa and E. Villanueva (eds), *Philosophical Issues*, 20: 1–22.

Block, N. (1995). 'On a confusion about a function of consciousness', *Behavioral and Brain Sciences*, 18: 227–87.

——(2002). 'Concepts of consciousness', in D. Chalmers (ed.), *Philosophy of Mind: Classical and Contemporary Readings*. Oxford: Oxford University Press, pp. 206–18.

Boring, E. G. (1953). 'A history of introspection', *Psychological Bulletin*, 50(3): 169–89.

Braddon-Mitchell, D. and Jackson, F. (2007). *Philosophy of Mind and Cognition* (2nd edn). Oxford: Blackwell.

[14] We are very grateful to Susanna Siegel, Maja Spener, and Galen Strawson for helpful comments on an earlier version of this introduction.

Brentano, F. (1874). *Psychology from an Empirical Standpoint* (trans. L. McAlister). London: Routledge.

Byrne, A. (2004). 'What phenomenal consciousness is like', in R. Gennaro (ed.), *Higher-Order Theories of Consciousness: An Anthology*. John Benjamins, pp. 203–25.

Carruthers, P. (1998). 'Natural theories of consciousness', *European Journal of Philosophy*, 6: 203–22. Reprinted in P. Carruthers, *Consciousness: Essays from a Higher-Order Perspective*. Oxford: Oxford University Press, pp. 36–60.

——(2000). *Phenomenal Consciousness: A Naturalist Theory*. Cambridge: Cambridge University Press.

——(2005). 'Conscious experience versus conscious thought', in *Consciousness: Essays from a Higher-Order Perspective*. Oxford: Oxford University Press, pp. 134–57.

——(2010). 'Introspection: divided and partly eliminated', *Philosophy and Phenomenological Research*, 80: 76–111.

Chalmers, D. (1996). *The Conscious Mind*. Oxford: Oxford University Press.

——(2004). 'The representational character of experience', in B. Leiter (ed.), *The Future for Philosophy*. Oxford: Oxford University Press, pp. 153–80.

Chudnoff, E. (2010). 'The nature of intuitive justification', *Philosophical Studies*, 126(3): 347–73.

Clore, G. (1992). 'Cognitive phenomenology: Feelings and the construction of judgment', in L. L. Martin (eds), *The Construction of Social Judgments*. Hillsdale, N.J.: Erlbaum, pp. 133–63.

Crane, T. (2001). *The Elements of Mind*. Oxford: Oxford University Press.

Dennett, D. (1982). 'Beyond belief', in A. Woodfield (ed), *Thought and Object: Essays in Intentionality*. Oxford: Clarendon Press, pp. 1–96.

Descartes, R. (1641/1985). *Meditations and Objections and Replies in the Philosophical Writings of Descartes Volume 2* (trans. J. Cottingham et al.). Cambridge: Cambridge University Press.

——(1644/1985). *The Principles of Philosophy in the Philosophical Writings of Descartes Volume 1* (trans. J. Cottingham et al.). Cambridge: Cambridge University Press.

Dretske, F. (1995). *Naturalizing the Mind*. Cambridge, MA: MIT Press.

——(1996). 'Phenomenal externalism or If meanings ain't in the head, where are qualia?', *Philosophical Issues*, 7: 143–59.

Farkas, K. (2008). 'Phenomenal intentionality without compromise', *Monist*, 91/2: 273–93.

Farrell, B. (1950). 'Experience'. *Mind*, 49: 170–98.

Flanagan, O. (1992). *Consciousness Reconsidered*. Cambridge, MA: MIT Press.

Fodor, J. (1975). *The Language of Thought*. Cambridge, MA: Harvard University Press.

——(2008). *LOT 2: The Language of Thought Revisited*. Oxford: Oxford University Press.

——and Lepore, E. (1994). 'What is the connection principle?', *Philosophy and Phenomenological Research*, 54(4): 837–45.

Geach, P. (1957). *Mental Acts*. London: Routledge.

Georgalis, N. (2005). *The Primacy of the Subjective*. Cambridge, MA: MIT Press.

Goff, P. (in press). 'Does Mary know I experience plus rather than quus? A new hard problem', *Philosophical Studies*.

Goldman, A. (1993). 'The psychology of folk psychology', *Behavioral and Brain Sciences*, 16: 15–28.

——(2006). *Simulating Minds: The Philosophy, Psychology, and Neuroscience of Mindreading*. Oxford: Oxford University Press.

Gopnik, A. (1993). 'How we know our minds: The illusion of first-person knowledge of intentionality', *Behavioral and Brain Sciences*, 16: 1–14.

Graham, G., Horgan, T., and Tienson, J. (2007). 'Consciousness and intentionality', in M. Velmans and S. Schneider (eds), *The Blackwell Companion to Consciousness*. Oxford: Blackwell.

Gunther, Y. H. (2004). 'The phenomenology and intentionality of emotion', *Philosophical Studies*, 117(1–2): 43–55.

Hill, C. (2010). *Consciousness*. Cambridge: Cambridge University Press.

Horgan, T. and Graham, G. (in press). 'Phenomenal intentionality and content determinacy', in R. Schantz (ed.), *Prospects for Meaning*. Amsterdam: de Gruyter.

——and Tienson, J. (2002). 'The intentionality of phenomenology and the phenomenology of intentionality', in D. J. Chalmers (ed.), *Philosophy of Mind: Classical and Contemporary Readings*. Oxford: Oxford University Press, pp. 520–33.

——, ——, and Graham, G. (2006). 'Internal-world skepticism and the self-presentational nature of phenomenal consciousness', in U. Kriegel and K. Williford (eds), *Self-Representational Approaches to Consciousness*. Cambridge, MA: MIT Press, pp. 41–62.

Husserl, E. (1900–01/1984). *Logische Untersuchungen II*, Husserliana XIX/1–2. Den Hag: Martinus Nijhoof: *Logical Investigations I–II* (trans. J. N. Findlay). London: Routledge, 2001.

Huxley, T. H. (1866). *Lessons in Elementary Physiology*. London: Macmillan.

Jackendoff, R. (1987). *Consciousness and the Computational Mind*. Cambridge, MA: MIT Press.

Jackson, F. (1982). 'Epiphenomenal qualia', *Philosophical Quarterly*, 32: 127–36.

James, W. (1890). *The Principles of Psychology*. Harvard: Harvard University Press.

Kant, I. (1788/1956). *Critique of Practical Reason* (trans. Lewis White Beck). Indianapolis: Bobbs-Merrill.

Kim, J. (1996). *Philosophy of Mind* (2nd edn). Boulder CO: Westview Press.

Kirk, R. (1974). 'Zombies v. Materialists', *Proceedings of the Aristotelian Society*, supplementary vol. 48: 135–52.

Klausen, S. (2008). 'The phenomenology of propositional attitudes', *Phenomenology and the Cognitive Sciences*, 7: 445–62.

Koriat, A. (2000). 'The feeling of knowing: Some metatheoretical implications for consciousness and control', *Consciousness and Cognition*, 9: 149–71.

Kriegel, U. (2007). 'Intentional inexistence and phenomenal intentionality', in J. Hawthorne (ed.), *Philosophical Perspectives, Vol. 21: Philosophy of Mind*, pp. 307–40.

——(2009). *Subjective Consciousness: A Self-Representational Theory*. Oxford: Oxford University Press.

——(ed.). Forthcoming. *Phenomenal Intentionality: New Essays*. New York: Oxford University Press.

Kripke, S. (1982). *Wittgenstein on Rules and Private Language*. Oxford: Blackwell.

Langsam, H. (2000). 'Experiences, thoughts, and qualia', *Philosophical Studies*, 99: 269–95.

Levine, J. (1983). 'Materialism and qualia: The explanatory gap', *Pacific Philosophical Quarterly*, 64: 354–61.

——(2001). *Purple Haze: The Puzzle of Consciousness*. Oxford: Oxford University Press.

Lewis, C. I. (1929). *Mind and the World Order: Outline of a Theory of Knowledge*. New York: Charles Scribner's Sons.

Loar, B. (2003). 'Phenomenal intentionality as the basis of mental content', in M. Hahn and B. Ramberg (eds), *Reflections and Replies: Essays on the Philosophy of Tyler Burge*. Cambridge, MA: MIT Press, pp. 229–58.

Lormand, E. (1996). 'Nonphenomenal consciousness', *Noûs*, 30: 242–61.

——(2004). 'The explanatory stopgap', *Philosophical Review*, 113: 303–57.

Lycan, W. (1996). *Consciousness and Experience*. Cambridge, MA: MIT Press.

——(2001). 'The case for phenomenal externalism', *Philosophical Perspectives*, 15: 17–35.

——(2008). 'Phenomenal intentionalities', *American Philosophical Quarterly*, 45: 233–52.

Lyons, W. E. (1986). *The Disappearance of Introspection*. Cambridge, MA: MIT Press.

Lyons, J. (2005). 'Perceptual belief and nonexperiential looks', *Philosophical Perspectives*, 19: *Epistemology*, 237–56.

Masrour, F. (in press). 'Is perceptual phenomenology thin?', *Philosophy and Phenomenological Research*.

Millikan, R. (1984). *Language, Thought and Other Biological Categories*. Cambridge, MA: MIT Press.

Montague, M. (2009). 'The logic, intentionality, and phenomenology of emotion', *Philosophical Studies*, 145: 171–92.

——(2010). 'Recent work on intentionality', *Analysis*, 70(4): 765–82.

Moore, G. E. (1910/1953). 'Propositions', in *Some Main Problems of Philosophy*. London: Allen and Unwin.

Nagel, T. (1974). 'What is it like to be a bat?', *Philosophical Review*, LXXXIII: 435–50.

Nelkin, N. (1989). 'Propositional attitudes and consciousness', *Philosophy and Phenomenological Research*, 49(3): 413–30.

Nes, A. (in press). 'Thematic unity in the phenomenology of thinking', *Philosophical Quarterly*.

Nichols, S. and Stich, S. (2003). 'How to read your own mind: A cognitive theory of self-consciousness', in Q. Smith and A. Jokic (eds), *Consciousness: New Philosophical Essays*. Oxford: Oxford University Press, pp. 157–200.

Ogden, R. M. (1911). 'Imageless thought: Résumé and critique', *The Psychological Bulletin*, 8(6): 183–97.

Papineau, D. (2002). *Thinking about Consciousness*. Oxford: Oxford University Press.

Pautz, A. (2009). 'What are the contents of experiences?', *Philosophical Quarterly*, 59: 483–507.

Peacocke, C. (1998). 'Conscious attitudes', in C. McDonald, B. Smith, and C. Wright (eds), *Knowing Our Own Minds: Essays on Self-Knowledge*. Oxford: Oxford University Press, pp. 63–98.

Peirce, C. S. (1866/1935). *Collected Papers Vol. 6*, C. Hartshorne and P. Weiss (eds). Cambridge, MA: Harvard University Press.

Pitt, D. (2004). 'The phenomenology of cognition or What is it like to think that P?', *Philosophy and Phenomenological Research*, 69: 1–36.

Prinz, J. (2004). *Gut Reactions: A Perceptual Theory of Emotion*. New York: Oxford University Press.

——(2004). 'The fractionation of introspection', *Journal of Consciousness Studies*, 11: 40–57.

Putnam, H. (1975/1985). 'The meaning of "meaning"', in his *Philosophical Papers, Vol. 2: Mind, Language and Reality*. Cambridge: Cambridge University Press.

——(1981). *Reason, Truth and History*. Cambridge: Cambridge University Press.

Quine, W. V. O. (1960). *Word and Object*. Cambridge, MA: MIT Press.

Robinson, W. S. (2005). 'Thoughts without distinctive non-imagistic phenomenology', *Philosophy and Phenomenological Research*, LXX: 534–61.

Rosenthal, D. (2002). 'How many kinds of consciousness?', *Consciousness and Cognition*, 11: 653–65.

Russell, B. (1918/1919). 'The philosophy of logical atomism', *The Monist*, 28: 495–527 and 29: 32–63, 190–222, 345–80. Reprinted, in D. Pears (ed.) 1985. *The Philosophy of Logical Atomism*. La Salle, IL: Open Court, pp. 35–155.

—— (1921). *The Analysis of Mind*. New York: The Macmillan Company.

——(1948). *Human Knowledge: Its Scope and its Limits*. New York: Simon and Schuster.

Ryle, G. (1949). *The Concept of Mind*. Harmondsworth: Penguin.

Schwitzgebel, E. (2008). 'The unreliability of naïve introspection', *The Philosophical Review*, 117/2: 245–73.

——(forthcoming). 'Introspection, what?', in D. Smithies and D. Stoljar (eds), *Introspection and Consciousness*. Oxford: Oxford University Press.

Searle, J. (1992). *The Rediscovery of the Mind*. Cambridge, MA: MIT Press.

Siegel, S. (2005). 'Which properties are represented in perception?', in T. Szabo Gendler and J. Hawthorne (eds), *Perceptual Experience*. Oxford: Oxford University Press, pp. 481–503.

——(2007). 'How can we discover the contents of experience?', *The Southern Journal of Philosophy*, 45: 127–42.

Siewert, C. (1998). *The Significance of Consciousness*. Princeton, N.J.: Princeton University Press.

Smart, J. J. C. (1959). 'Sensations and brain processes', *The Philosophical Review*, 68: 141–56.

Snowdon, P. (2010). 'On the what-it's-likeness of experience', *The Southern Journal of Philosophy*, 48: 8–27.

Soteriou, M. (2007). 'Content and the stream of consciousness', *Philosophical Perspectives*, 21: 543–68.

——(2009). 'Mental agency, conscious thinking, and phenomenal character', in L. O'Brien and M. Soteriou (eds), *Mental Actions*. Oxford: Oxford University Press, pp. 231–52.

Sprigge, T. (1971). 'Final causes'. *Proceedings of the Aristotelian Society (Supplement)*, 45: 149–70.

Strawson, G. (1994). *Mental Reality*. Cambridge, MA: MIT Press.

——(2005). 'Intentionality and experience: Terminological preliminaries', in D. W. Smith and A. L. Thomasson (eds), *Phenomenology and Philosophy of Mind*. Oxford: Oxford University Press, pp. 41–66.

——(2008). 'Real intentionality 3: Why intentionality entails consciousness', in his *Real Materialism and Other Essays*. Oxford: Oxford University Press, pp. 281–306.

Thompson, B. (2009). 'Senses for senses', *Australasian Journal of Philosophy*, 87: 99–117.

Trout, J. D. (2002). 'Scientific explanation and the sense of understanding', *Philosophy of Science*, 69: 212–33.

Tye, M. (1995). *Ten Problems of Consciousness*. Cambridge, MA: MIT Press.

——(2000). *Consciousness, Color and Content*. Cambridge, MA: MIT Press.

Wilson, R. (2003). 'Intentionality and phenomenology', *Pacific Philosophical Quarterly*, 84: 413–31.

Wittgenstein, L. (1953). *Philosophical Investigations*. Oxford: Blackwell.

——(1980). *Remarks on the Philosophy of Psychology, Vol. 1*. Chicago, IL: University of Chicago Press.

The Case Against Cognitive Phenomenology

Peter Carruthers and Bénédicte Veillet

The goal of this chapter is to mount a critique of the claim that cognitive content (that is, the kind of content possessed by our concepts and thoughts) makes a constitutive contribution to the phenomenal properties of our mental lives. We therefore defend the view that phenomenal consciousness is exclusively experiential (or nonconceptual) in character. The main focus of the chapter is on the alleged contribution that concepts make to the phenomenology of visual experience. For we take it that if cognitive phenomenology is to be found anywhere, it should be found here. However, we begin with a discussion of the question of cognitive phenomenology more generally, and we close by sketching how our argument might be extended into the domain of non-perceptual thought.

1 Introduction

We take our start from a problem raised by Bayne (forthcoming): how is the debate over the alleged existence of cognitive phenomenology to be adjudicated? On the one hand, there are those who insist that only the nonconceptual contents of experience are ever phenomenally conscious (e.g. Tye 1995, 2000). On the other hand, there are people who declare it to be introspectively obvious that thoughts, too, are *like* something to undergo, in the relevant sense (e.g. Strawson 1994; Siewert 1998). Bayne reviews these debates, arguing that they resist resolution and that our grasp of what is at stake is much less secure than one might initially have thought. We will suggest a way forward. Similarly, Schwitzgebel (2008) uses the apparent irresolvability of the question of cognitive phenomenology to argue for the unreliability of introspection itself. In this, however, he oversteps the mark. For the main point at issue, we will suggest, is whether cognition is implicated in phenomenal consciousness *constitutively* or just *causally*. And this isn't a difference that should always be accessible to introspection, on anyone's view of the latter.

No one denies that thoughts are (sometimes)[1] associated with phenomenal qualities, or that it can be *like* something to entertain a thought. For some thoughts can be expressed in "inner speech" or can be accompanied by visual imagery, where the latter properties are, of course, phenomenally conscious. It is therefore a delicate matter to say precisely how the question of cognitive phenomenology should be formulated. Is it the question whether (some) thoughts possess phenomenal attributes *intrinsically*? We believe not (at least if "intrinsic" means "non-relational"). For it is very much disputed whether *experiences* possess their phenomenal character intrinsically (non-relationally), even amongst those who are realists about phenomenal consciousness. Thus, there are those who think that the phenomenal properties of an experience can be reductively explained in terms of the relations that the state in question bears to other things. (This is true of reductive representationalists about phenomenal experience, for example, whether of a first-order type—Dretske 1995; Tye 1995—or of a higher-order sort—Lycan 1996; Carruthers 2000; Rosenthal 2005.) The same range of options should surely be available to those who believe in cognitive phenomenology.

Is the question then whether the phenomenal characters associated with (some) thoughts are constitutive of those thought-types? If someone entertains a thought with a certain phenomenal character, should our question be whether anyone could count as entertaining *the very same* thought if her thought did *not* have that phenomenal character? This still isn't right. For one could surely believe that thoughts are to be individuated in terms of their content alone (together with their causal role, perhaps) while nevertheless believing in cognitive phenomenology. In which case someone might count as entertaining the very same thought even if its phenomenal properties were different (in something like the way that the very same thought can be entertained in English or in French, for example), or even if its phenomenal properties were absent altogether.

Is the question then whether a thought is (sometimes) a constitutive part of a given phenomenally conscious mental episode? Is the idea that no one could undergo the very same phenomenally conscious episode who didn't entertain the thought in question? Thus, one might claim that no one could enjoy the exact same phenomenology that one does when one says to oneself in inner speech, "Red is a primary color," who did not at the same time entertain the *thought* that red is a primary color. (One might claim, for example, that the phenomenology of a monolingual French speaker rehearsing the exact same sounds would be different.) Would this be enough to demonstrate the existence of cognitive phenomenology? Although this gets us closer, it is still not quite right. For as we will see in more detail later, a thought could be a constitutive part of a phenomenally conscious event without making a constitutive

---

[1] The qualification is needed because most of us will allow that thoughts can occur unconsciously, and that as such they don't possess phenomenal qualities (just as most will now allow that there are access-unconscious *perceptual* states that lack phenomenal attributes).

(as opposed to a causal) contribution to the phenomenal properties of that event. Thus consider the following analogy. When one bakes a cake, one mixes together water, flour, eggs, sugar, and perhaps other ingredients. The result is sweet to the taste. But although the water forms a constitutive part of the cake, it makes no direct contribution to its sweetness. Likewise, it may be that the cognitive content of any given phenomenally conscious state, although a proper part of the latter, makes no direct contribution to its phenomenal qualities.

We suggest that the question before us is this: concerning some phenomenally conscious events, is it true that a thought occurring at the same time (perhaps as a constitutive part of the event) makes a constitutive, as opposed to a causal, contribution to the phenomenal properties of those events? (We intend this formulation to be understood in such a way as to cover any instance where a thought is *identical with* a given phenomenally conscious event, as a limiting case of the constitution-relation.) Those who believe in cognitive phenomenology will answer this question positively. Those who think that thoughts per se lack phenomenal properties will answer it negatively (while allowing, of course, that thoughts are often *associated* with phenomenal properties, and that they will often make a *causal difference* to one's phenomenally conscious mental life).

We should stress that this way of construing the question of cognitive phenomenology is rather different from that commonly found in the literature, and in many of the other chapters in this book. But most writers neglect to draw the causal/constitutive distinction in their arguments. Once that distinction is held clearly in mind, however, it should be plain that what is really at stake in these debates is whether thoughts and concepts make a *constitutive* contribution to the phenomenal properties of events in which they are embedded.[2]

Our construal of the question of cognitive phenomenology might be challenged. If one is to demonstrate the reality of cognitive phenomenology, why shouldn't it be enough to establish that concepts make a *causal* contribution to phenomenology? Who gets to say that the question of cognitive phenomenology has to be understood constitutively and not causally? By way of reply, consider first the debate about the cognitive phenomenology of perception. Here the causal question has never been in dispute. Tye (1995, 2000), for example—who has been one of the main champions of

---

[2] Some contributors to this volume think that the question of cognitive phenomenology is really the question whether occurrent thought has a *proprietary* or *sui generis* phenomenology. Thus, Pitt (this volume) thinks that the question is whether thoughts have a phenomenology that is as unlike auditory or visual phenomenology as the latter are unlike each other. And Kriegel (this volume) thinks that the question is whether thoughts have phenomenal properties that don't reduce to some other, already familiar, forms of perceptual or somatic phenomenology. These characterizations are stronger than ours. For if cognitive phenomenology is *sui generis* (in either of these senses) then it must follow that the thought-content in question makes a constitutive (and not just a causal) contribution to the phenomenal properties of our mental lives. But the reverse doesn't hold: concepts might make a constitutive contribution to phenomenology even if the resulting phenomenal properties aren't *sui generis*. Our critique of the idea of cognitive phenomenology, as we characterize it, will thus apply equally to these stronger understandings.

the claim that phenomenal consciousness is exclusively nonconceptual—has always insisted that concept deployment nevertheless has a causal impact upon phenomenology. Indeed, once the causal/constitutive distinction is duly noted, this seems so obvious as to be barely worth asserting. What is true, however, is that discussions of cognitive phenomenology have often failed to draw the distinction in question explicitly. As a result, theorists will frequently move illicitly from causal claims (or claims that are best interpreted causally) to constitutive ones.

Now consider the debate over the phenomenal properties of non-perceptual thoughts and judgments. It would be foolish to try to make a controversy out of claiming that such thoughts, as well as perceptual experiences, have phenomenal properties (as defenders of cognitive phenomenology characteristically wish to do), unless what is meant is that thoughts make a *constitutive* contribution to our phenomenal lives. For of course *everyone* allows that what one thinks can make a *causal* difference to what one experiences. For depending on what one is thinking about one will direct visual attention in one direction or another, engage in inner speech or manipulate visual images, and so forth, all of which will result in changes in one's phenomenal experience. Hence the claim of cognitive phenomenology, if it is to be at all interesting, needs to be construed constitutively and not merely causally.

Although our ultimate target is the question whether thoughts of any kind make a constitutive contribution to phenomenology, we will mainly focus on a narrower issue (discussed in Sections 2 and 3). This is the question whether or not concepts (or perceptual judgments) make a constitutive difference to the phenomenology of our perceptual experience. At the outset of this discussion we will assume that the question should be framed in terms of the vexed conceptual/nonconceptual distinction, before generalizing to approaches that deny any such distinction. The lessons that we learn in addressing this issue will then carry over to the question of the phenomenal contribution of non-perceptual thought, which will be discussed more briefly in Section 4.

2 Concepts in experience

Tye (1995, 2000) is adamant that experiences possess nonconceptual content, and that *only* states with such content (including bodily sensations, visual and auditory images, and emotional feelings) are phenomenally conscious. He claims, furthermore, that phenomenal consciousness is *exhausted* by such content. If he is correct, then there is no cognitive phenomenology in the sense that concerns us. Carruthers (2000) agrees with the first two of Tye's claims, pointing to the richness and fineness of grain of our perceptual and imagistic states, and arguing that these are the properties that give rise to the phenomenality of experience. Carruthers also argues, however, that our experiences are often imbued with concepts, and that these make an important contribution to the phenomenal content of those experiences. We will briefly review and critique his arguments, together with a more recent argument by Bayne (2009). The result will be a stand-off, which we will attempt to resolve in Section 3.

2.1 Arguments from phenomenal change

One of the arguments in Carruthers (2000) is that concept acquisition can transform the phenomenology of one's experience. This is familiar to common sense, and is also confirmed experimentally. When one first takes up birdwatching, for example, one's experience of the birds that one observes will be comparatively impoverished. One might only see collections of little grey birds on a beach, for instance. But having learned to distinguish knots from plovers from redshanks, one *sees* them as such. And it doesn't seem correct to gloss what takes place in such learning by saying that one's experiences stay the same but are now accompanied by differences in belief. On the contrary, having acquired the relevant concepts, the differences between the birds jump out at one phenomenologically.

In a related set of experiments, Livingston et al. (1998) trained subjects to categorize shapes into *Zofs* and *Gexs*. The differences between the two shape-types were fairly minor, and subjects rarely became explicitly aware of their distinguishing features. Nevertheless, with time, all subjects became quite reliable at recognizing instances of the two concepts. The experimenters collected similarity-ratings at both the start and the end of the experiment. At the start, subjects rated Zofs and Gexs as very similar to one another, but by the end their similarity ratings had been pushed quite far apart. Subjects now *saw* shapes of the two types as dissimilar to one another, even though they couldn't (for the most part) articulate the difference.

Carruthers (2000) also draws attention to the familiar fact that deployment of one or another concept in one's experience can transform the phenomenology of the latter. This is especially clear in the case of ambiguous figures like the famous duck–rabbit. Although the figure itself remains unchanged (and likewise with it, one might be tempted to think, the nonconceptual content of one's experience, representing a particular arrangement of lines on a plane surface) one can dramatically shift the phenomenology of the experience at will. By deploying the concept *duck* one sees the figure *as* a duck, and by deploying the concept *rabbit* one sees it as a rabbit.[3]

These arguments aren't successful as they stand, however. They fail to establish that the phenomenal qualities of a state aren't exhausted by its nonconceptual content. For they don't distinguish between the *causal* and *constitutive* contributions that concepts might make to the phenomenology of experience. When one acquires a new concept one learns to attend preferentially to those features of its instances that are distinctive of them. To recognize a plover, for example, one needs to look for the dark ring around its neck. And to distinguish knots from redshanks one needs to pay attention, *inter alia*, to the length and coloring of the legs. These forms of attention can either be overt, in the form of increased numbers of saccades to the relevant features, or covert, devoting extra processing to information deriving from the relevant portions of the visual field.

---

[3] Throughout we will understand concepts to be individuated by their contents (whether wide or narrow; on this we remain neutral, see section 3.2.), rather than by their vehicles. We refer to them using italics.

And indeed, subjects who wear eye-trackers while viewing ambiguous figures show different patterns of overt attention under the two viewing conditions (Pylyshyn 2003). It is hardly surprising, then, that the phenomenology of one's experience should differ in the two cases. This is because the concepts that one deploys have a causal impact, via patterns of attention, on the nonconceptual contents that result from the normal operations of the visual system.

Opponents of nonconceptualism might attempt to reply to this critique, relying on the assumption that causes cannot be simultaneous with their effects. For the contribution that concepts make to the phenomenology of experience can seemingly be simultaneous with the experience itself. One does not (normally) *first* see a little grey bird on a beach and then (having categorized it as a plover) *see it as* a plover. Rather, one can see the bird as a plover at first glance. It seems to follow that the contribution that concepts make to the phenomenology of experience cannot be causal and must therefore be constitutive. This reply is ineffective, however, because there is every reason to think that concepts do their work in perception unconsciously, in interactions with the incoming nonconceptual representations within the visual system before any representations become conscious (Kosslyn 1994). So the contribution made by concepts to one's perceptual phenomenology can be merely causal even if there isn't any time differential discernable within phenomenal experience itself.

Although an appeal to the non-simultaneity of causation doesn't help, the argument from concept acquisition can seemingly be bolstered from another direction. For similar data exist for the acquisition of color concepts, where it might appear that patterns of attention are unlikely to have any impact (Burns and Shepp 1988). Consider people who view two red cards, one of which is painted a uniform shade of scarlet and the other of which is painted a uniform shade of vermillion. And suppose that at this point subjects only possess the generic concept *red*. Asked to rate the similarity of the two cards, subjects are inclined to place them pretty close to one another on a color similarity-scale. But now the subjects undergo training, and become proficient with the concepts *scarlet* and *vermillion*. Asked to rate the similarity of the same two cards once again, subjects now mark them as less similar to one another than they had done before. This effect can't be explained by changes in patterns of overt attention. For since each of the cards is uniformly colored, the very same data will result for the visual system to process no matter how one saccades over them. Yet what the two cards are *like* for subjects has changed. This might be taken to suggest that concept acquisition can make a constitutive difference to the phenomenology of one's experience.

Unfortunately, these data can't rule out the possibility that changes in patterns of *covert* attention are responsible for the changes in phenomenology. For as is well known, colors can be analysed along three different dimensions—hue, saturation, and intensity. While we have no positive evidence that this is the case, it may be that training in color discrimination, of the sort reported by Burns and Shepp (1988), has the effect of enabling subjects to pay differential attention to (and hence to devote increased cognitive resources to processing) the different dimensions. This would have an effect on the nonconceptual contents that result.

In any case, however, the color data also admit of an alternative explanation. This is that subjects, post-training, judge the two shades to be unlike one another simply because they are thought to belong to two different categories. The phenomenology of their experience of the two colors can be unchanged. Here is how the story would go. If one is asked how similar two shades of color are, where both fall under the only relevant concept that one has (*red*, say), then one might expect the answer to be a confluence of two factors: (1) both are the same insofar as both are red; (2) they are different depending on how far apart they are along the color spectrum. But now if (post-training) one looks at those same two shades, one of which is scarlet and the other of which is vermillion, one will judge them to be categorically distinct, because each falls under a distinct concept. When asked how similar the colors are, therefore, one might express greater dissimilarity than one did previously. But what one is really expressing is one's *belief* that the shades are different in *type* (because they belong to different categories). Consistent with that, the phenomenology of one's experience of the shades might be unchanged. And even if subjects were asked to comment explicitly on their phenomenology (rather than on the colors themselves, as was actually the case in these experiments), and were to express greater dissimilarity following concept-acquisition, this could be dismissed as a case of "cross-contamination" from first-order judgments of difference to higher-order ones.

The arguments from phenomenal change turn out to be inconclusive, then. They don't allow us to determine whether concepts make a contribution to the phenomenology of experience that is constitutive rather than merely causal.

2.2 An argument from vision science

Carruthers (2000) offers a further argument for the thesis that concepts can make a constitutive contribution to phenomenally conscious experience. This depends upon two premises. The first is that phenomenally conscious experience is *co-extensive*, at least, with the global broadcast of perceptual and imagistic information in the brain. There is widespread evidence that this is so (Baars, 2002; Dehaene and Naccache, 2001; Dehaene et al., 2003). Not everyone agrees, of course, that global broadcast per se is sufficient for phenomenal consciousness. Indeed, Carruthers himself will claim that it is only sufficient given the presence of a properly functioning higher-order thought faculty which serves as one of the consumers for the global broadcasts. And many more will deny that it provides a successful reductive explanation of phenomenal conscious-ness. But neither of these sources of disagreement matter for present purposes. Even property-dualists about phenomenal consciousness can accept the co-extensiveness claim (as does Chalmers 1997, for example).[4]

---

[4] That claim will nevertheless be denied by those who, like Block (1995, 2002), think that there are access-unconscious states that possess phenomenal properties. But even Block will accept that globally

The second premise of the argument is that conceptual representations are globally broadcast *alongside* (or rather, *bound into*) the nonconceptual representations that trigger their activity. This is supported by the work of Kosslyn (1994) and others, which suggests the following model of the operations of the visual system. The initial nonconceptual outputs of early vision are monitored by a whole host of conceptual systems, each of which uses a battery of conceptual "templates," attempting to achieve a best match with the nonconceptual data. When one is found, the relevant concept is attached to the nonconceptual representation in question and globally broadcast along with it, for other concept-wielding consumer systems to take note of and draw inferences from.

Now, if globally broadcast percepts and phenomenal consciousness coincide with one another, and if concepts often form a constitutive part of the global broadcast, then that might be taken to imply that phenomenal consciousness, too, is partially constituted by concepts. And so it will turn out that elements of cognition—specifically, concepts—make a constitutive, and not just a causal, contribution to the phenomenology of experience. But this argument, like the argument from concept acquisition, misses its mark. From the fact that a given concept is a constitutive *component* of a phenomenally conscious perceptual state it doesn't follow that the concept makes a constitutive *contribution* to the phenomenal qualities of that state. So far as the phenomenology goes, it might be that perceptual states carve cleanly into two types of component: their nonconceptual content, which is wholly responsible for their phenomenal properties, and their conceptual content, which makes no constitutive contribution to that phenomenology.

2.3 An argument from visual agnosia

Bayne (2009) suggests that pure cases of visual agnosia can be used to support the existence of cognitive phenomenology. Such patients perceive colors and shapes normally. For example, a patient might be capable of accurately copying a drawing of a pipe or a toothbrush. But he will be incapable of recognizing the object as such. The condition is characterized by an inability to apply concepts in one's visual experience of the world (although the concepts themselves, and the semantic knowledge that goes with them, remain undamaged). This appears to have a significant impact on visual phenomenology. For the descriptions that agnosic patients provide of their experience, while they struggle to make sense of the world around them, suggest that their experience is very different from normal (Rubens and Benson 1971; Farah 2004). But there is nothing here, as yet, to demonstrate that the contribution that concepts would normally make to the phenomenology of experience is constitutive rather than merely causal. For it may be that the causal connections between the

broadcast states are de facto phenomenally conscious. That is, although he denies the co-extensiveness claim he will accept the sufficiency claim.

agnosic patient's concepts and the visual system, which would normally be used to direct visual search and visual processing, have been broken.

It might be questioned whether different patterns of attention alone can be responsible for all of the phenomenal differences between associative agnosia and normal forms of visual perception, however. Granted, when an agnosic person looks at an object the nonconceptual content of the resulting experience will differ from that of a normal person, caused by differences in attention and visual search. But there will surely be many more phenomenal disparities here than would occur within the experience of a normal person who first sees an ambiguous figure as a duck and then sees it as a rabbit. Indeed, this is so. But it is far from clear that differences lend any real support for cognitive phenomenology. For the visual world makes little sense to an agnosic patient. He sees colors and shapes, but not tables, chairs, or people. Hence the *world* of an agnosic patient will be very different from normal. But while this difference might *cause* differences in perceptual phenomenology, it is unclear that it itself *constitutes* a phenomenal difference. Moreover, the patient's visual experience will be accompanied by feelings of anxiety and puzzlement, and object-identification, when it occurs, will be slow and effortful. Since these states are phenomenal ones, what it is like to be an agnosic person will be markedly different from what it is like to be a normal visual perceiver. But the differences are ones that appear to be caused by the absence of visual identification from visual experience (and hence by the absence of concepts from visual contents), rather than being constituted by the latter.

2.4 A generalized stand-off

Up to this point we have assumed the existence of a real distinction between conceptual and nonconceptual content. Does the question of the contribution that concepts make to the phenomenology of experience look any different if one denies this distinction? We believe not. Consider McDowell (1994), for example. He thinks that the difference between thought and experience lies not in the presence and absence of concepts (both are equally conceptual), but rather in the comparative *fineness of grain* and *large numbers* of indexical concepts that go to make up experience. The concepts that figure in our thoughts, in contrast, are comparatively coarse-grained, and only a handful can be entertained at any one time. Suppose that some version of the global broadcast story about conscious experience is also endorsed. So suppose that a given phenomenally conscious experience will normally be composed of *both* a large number of fine-grained indexical concepts *and* a few coarse-grained concepts (such as the concept *red*). Does it follow that the latter will make a constitutive contribution to the phenomenology of the experience? It does not. It might be that phenomenal properties are determined entirely by the fine-grained and rich character of the experience, and that any contributions made by the sorts of coarse-grained concepts that can also figure in our non-perceptual thoughts are purely causal.

What we have so far, then, is a stand-off. This closely parallels the stand-off that Bayne (forthcoming) describes between opponents and defenders of the view that thoughts, per se, are ever phenomenally conscious (although we have offered different arguments). It seems that neither side has a decisive case against the other, and it is hard to see how to make progress in resolving the dispute. What we will now argue, however, is that we can, indeed, make progress if we assume that phenomenally conscious features are those that give rise to the so-called "hard problem" of consciousness.

3 Do concepts contribute to the hard problem?

Here is the proposal: concepts should only count as making a constitutive contribution to the phenomenally conscious aspects of experience if they also make such a contribution to the main respects in which phenomenal consciousness is thought to be problematic or puzzling. To get the flavor of how this might go, consider *ineffability*, which has often been thought to be a property of conscious experience. We have difficulty articulating or describing the properties of our phenomenally conscious experience. When we try to say what it is *like* to see red, or smell a rose, or taste coffee, we are reduced to gesturing toward the properties that our experiences are *of*. We say, for example, "It is the experience that I undergo when I see/smell/taste *that*." It is plain, however, that ineffability (insofar as it exists) is a property of the nonconceptual content of our experience *only* (specifically its fineness of grain). For there is no problem whatever in expressing the *conceptual* content of our experience. We can say that it is *of* red, or *of* a rose, or *of* coffee, thereby deploying the very concept that is globally broadcast as part of the experience itself.[5]

The main puzzle about phenomenal consciousness, however, concerns how it can exist in a physical world. This is the so-called "explanatory gap." People find it hard to see how any physical story could fully explain the qualities that we are aware of in our experience. For in respect of any such story that we are offered, we can see in advance that we shall be capable of thinking, "But all of that might be true while *these* qualities of this experience were different or absent." So we need to ask whether any such gap exists with respect to the concepts that figure in our experience.[6]

---

[5] Of course a similar point can be made (with just a few adjustments) from the perspective of those who deny the existence of nonconceptual content. Such people can say that the ineffability of experience is due entirely to the fine-grained indexical concepts that compose it, and owes nothing to the presence within the experience of coarse-grained thought-concepts such as *red*.

[6] We will develop our argument throughout on the assumption that the explanatory gap is real. This is because we believe in conceptually isolated phenomenal concepts (see Section 3.1), and because, given the existence of such concepts, it is plain that the gap-inducing thought experiments really are coherent. We actually believe, however, that a version of our argument could be acceptable to so-called "Type A" materialists who deny the conceivability of the gap. For even Type A materialists allow that there is at least the *illusion*, or *appearance*, of an explanatory gap. As we will see in Section 3.2, however, once the question of cognitive phenomenology is correctly framed, then it is *obvious* that there is no explanatory gap with respect to the conceptual components of experience.

Here, in summary form, is the argument that we will develop:

(1) A property is phenomenal only if it contributes to the hard problem of consciousness, and in particular, only if it gives rise to an explanatory gap.

(2) A property gives rise to an explanatory gap only if we have a conceptually isolated phenomenal concept for it (such as the concept *these qualities* deployed in the thought just quoted in the paragraph above).

(3) So a property is phenomenal only if we have a conceptually isolated concept for it.

(4) We lack conceptually isolated concepts for any cognitive/conceptual properties of experience (that is to say, for experiences individuated in such a way as to include their cognitive/conceptual components).

(5) So cognitive/conceptual properties don't give rise to an explanatory gap.

(6) Hence cognitive/conceptual properties aren't themselves phenomenal ones.

If the conclusion in (6) can be established, then it will follow that concepts make, at best, a *causal* contribution to the phenomenal properties of experience. We take it that premise (1) would be widely agreed upon (although we will return to consider a challenge to it in Section 3.4). We begin (in Section 3.1) with a brief defense of premise (2) before making the case for premises (4) and (5) in Section 3.2. In examining whether cognitive properties give rise to an explanatory gap, we propose to focus on the conceivability of inverted experience. While a number of different thought-experiments have been deployed in defense of the explanatory gap (including black-and-white Mary and zombies, in addition to cases of inverted experience), not all of these are appropriate in the present context, for reasons that will emerge in Section 3.3.

3.1 The role of conceptually isolated phenomenal concepts

It is widely agreed that the explanatory gap depends upon a set of conceptually isolated phenomenal concepts. Indeed, just about everybody in recent debates (both property-dualists and physicalists alike) acknowledges the crucial role that these concepts play in the explanation of explanatory gaps, inverted-experience thought-experiments, and so forth (Loar 1990; Chalmers 1996, 2007; Balog 1999; Carruthers 2000; Tye 2000; Papineau 2002; Stoljar 2005; Carruthers and Veillet 2007; Levine 2007). The dispute between dualists and physicalists is (for the most part) about whether phenomenal concepts can be used to provide an adequate explanation of the gap without appealing to any non-physical properties, not about whether phenomenal concepts are *necessary* for a gap. And the crucial thing about phenomenal concepts is that they should have the right sorts of conceptual isolation from physical and functional concepts, together with bearing the right sorts of immediate relations to their referents. (Perhaps they are indexical and/or recognitional concepts of a certain sort; see Loar 1990; Carruthers 2000; Perry 2001; or perhaps they actually contain, by quoting, the experiences that they are about; see Balog 1999; Papineau 2002. We will explore these possibilities in Section 3.2.) It is this isolation from other sorts of concepts that underpins the conceivability of zombies and inverted experiences, and which means that no amount of physical information can entail a priori that any given phenomenal concept should be applied.

We should stress that we are not here meaning to endorse the so-called "phenomenal concept strategy" for reconciling physicalism with the explanatory gap (Carruthers and Veillet 2007; Chalmers 2007). We are only claiming that conceptually isolated phenomenal concepts are a necessary condition for a gap to obtain, not that they are *sufficient* for explaining it. The phenomenal concept strategy aims to defend the latter thesis (that an appeal to phenomenal concepts is *all* that is needed to explain the explanatory gap). But all we assume here is the former—rather uncontroversial— claim that we need to possess conceptually isolated concepts for thinking about our experiences in order for the explanatory gap to arise. This might be rejected by so-called "Type A" physicalists like Dennett (1991), who think that zombies and the rest are strictly inconceivable. But it is accepted by almost everyone else. Chalmers (2003), for example, allows the existence of phenomenal concepts, and thinks that he must do so. For if our concepts for our experiences *weren't* conceptually isolated, then it should be possible for us to discern entailment relations from physical and functional descriptions to phenomenal ones, and there would be no gap.

Here is another way to make the point: assume that the dualist is right and there are non-physical properties after all. This ontological fact could give rise to the conceivability of inverted experiences or of zombies only if the *concepts* that we use for *thinking about* the non-physical properties are conceptually isolated from our physical and functional concepts. The explanatory gap is, of course, an epistemic one, and depends upon the conceptual isolation of our concepts, even if the dualist is correct that underlying it is an ontological divide. This, we think, establishes the truth of our second premise: that a property will give rise to an explanatory gap only if we have a conceptually isolated phenomenal concept for it. Once again, this isn't to endorse the idea that phenomenal concepts can be used to defend physicalism. Anti-physicalists like Chalmers (2003) *and* physicalists like Stoljar (2005) and Tye (2009) can reject the phenomenal concept strategy, while acknowledging that we possess phenomenal concepts of the sort envisaged.

3.2 No cognitive gap

We now argue that we do not possess conceptually isolated phenomenal concepts for the conceptual components of experience, and hence that cognitive properties do not give rise to an explanatory gap. Central among the well-known gap-inducing thought-experiments that phenomenal concepts make possible are those that dissociate the phenomenally conscious state in question from its intentional content (either *wide*, embracing the worldly properties that it is about, or *narrow*, perhaps characterized in terms of internal cognitive role). This is what happens in an inverted-experience thought-experiment. For example, faced with a particular shade of red, one can think the thought, "*This* experience might not have been about red, or might not have had the content *red*—it might not have been a seeming of red." Of course this isn't the *only* variety of inversion thought-experiment. One can also imagine one's experiences having inverted causal roles, say. But inversion of content is surely the central case. (It is this, for example, that underlies the familiar skeptical question about other minds: "How do I know that what I experience when I see red isn't what you experience when you see green?") It should also be emphasized that what is required for an explanatory gap isn't that experience inversion should be genuinely possible (most representational theorists about phenomenal consciousness will deny this), but rather that it is *thinkable*. Again, the gap that almost everyone agrees upon is an epistemic one.

Consider, then, the thought, "*This* experience might not have been an experience of red, or might not have had the content *red*." In order for this thought to be thinkable, it appears that the phenomenal concept that one deploys must be picking out *only* the nonconceptual content of the experience. For if that concept picked out an experience that contained the concept *red* as a constituent,[7] in such a way as to include immediate reference to the latter, then how could the experience *not* be about red, and how could it *not* be a seeming of red? Let us grant that the experience has both a nonconceptual and a conceptual content. In which case, if both make a constitutive contribution to the phenomenal qualities of the experience, then the phenomenal concept that one deploys must engage with both aspects. Yet if the experience that one refers to with one's phenomenal concept has the content [red_{17}, *red*], then how could one coherently think, of a state with that content, "This might not have been about red"? For the concept *red* will be right there in the content of the state that one's phenomenal concept picks out, and it is of the essence of that concept that it should be about red.[8]

Does this argument presuppose externalism about conceptual content? We believe not. The thought-experiments that give rise to an explanatory gap are generally believed to be independent of any particular theory of content. It is supposed to be *content* (however characterized) that can be pulled apart in thought from *feel*. And the same is surely true here. Instead of the thought, "This experience might not have been about red" one can entertain, "This experience might not have had the content *red*", where content can be characterized internally rather than externally. But if the phenomenal concept *this experience* in such a thought were to pick out both the (narrow) conceptual and the nonconceptual content of the relevant experience, then it will entail, "The concept with the content *red* might not have had the content *red*." This is surely incoherent, on anyone's view, for concepts are individuated in terms of their content.

---

[7] Recall from Section 2.2 that there is evidence that concepts like *red* are globally broadcast in conscious experience along with the nonconceptual contents that give rise to them.

[8] As previously, the same argument will apply *mutatis mutandis* from the perspective of those who deny the reality of the conceptual/nonconceptual distinction.

By way of bolstering this argument, consider an example where the implied contrast will make it clear that one is referring to *both* the nonconceptual *and* the conceptual content of an experience. Suppose that one has been playing with one's perception of a duck–rabbit figure by making it flip back and forth between the two aspects. While one is seeing the figure *as* a duck, we have every reason to think that the concept *duck* is deployed as a constitutive part of one's experience. But one cannot coherently think, "This experience (as opposed to that other one, the rabbit-like one) might not have had the content *duck*, or might not have involved a seeming of duckishness." Nor does it make any sense to ask, "Why does *this* experience (the duck-like one) represent a duck as opposed to a rabbit?" When one refers to an experience in such a way that one's thought designates both its conceptual and its nonconceptual content, one *can't* entertain the sorts of thought–experiments that figure in the hard problem of consciousness. In which case the right conclusion to draw is that the conceptual content of experience doesn't make a constitutive contribution to the phenomenal properties that give rise to that problem.

Let us work through this argument in a bit more detail, once for each of the candidate accounts of phenomenal concepts. Consider the quotational account first (Balog 1999; Papineau 2002). On this view, any thought about a phenomenally conscious experience literally contains that very experience, by quoting it. On such an account the thought, "This experience might not have been about red/might not have had the content *red*" really has the form, "The experience _____ might not have been about red/might not have had the content *red*", where what fills the blank is the very experience in question. But if *both* the nonconceptual *and* the conceptual content of the experience figure within this thought, then it will entail the judgment, "The concept *red* might not have been about red" (if concepts are widely individuated), or it will entail the judgment, "The concept *red* might not have had the content *red*" (if concepts are narrow). Either way, the upshot will be incoherent. Since it denies that the quoted item has a property that is in fact essential to it (being about red, or having the content *red*), it would have the same incoherent status as, "The word 'red' might not have contained three letters."

Now consider an indexical/recognitional theory of phenomenal concepts (Loar 1990; Carruthers 2000; Perry 2001). On such an account it might seem that we *can* explain the conceivability of inverted experience, even if concepts make a constitutive contribution to phenomenal consciousness. For compare: even if it is conceptually necessary that cats are living beings, one can coherently think, "*This* might not be/might not have been a living thing," provided that one is unaware that what one's indexical thought picks out is actually a cat. (One might only be aware of a dark shape in the bushes.) Likewise, then, one might be able to think, of an experience of red, "*This* might not have been about red," provided that one is unaware of the conceptual component of the experience in question.

It is plain that no account of phenomenal concepts that construes them as *pure* indexicals can be adequate, however. (By a "pure" indexical we mean something similar to the indexical "here" in the thought, "I wonder where *here* is," entertained by someone who has been taken blindfolded to an unknown location. These are index- icals that aren't grounded in an awareness of their referents.) For when we think about our own experiences, or entertain the possibility of zombies or inverted experiences and so forth, we surely take ourselves to be *aware* of the experiential state in question, in a way that is both more primitive than, and which serves to ground, the application of our phenomenal concept. Yet if the concept *red* makes a constitutive contribution to the phenomenal properties of the experience and the latter properties serve to ground the application of the recognitional/indexical concept *this experience*, then the content of the former concept would surely figure in our awareness. But in that case the thought, "*This experience* might not have had the content *red*" will be incoherent (however conceptual content is individuated).

It might be replied that one can be aware of an experience in a way that can serve to ground the application of a phenomenal concept without being aware of any of the concepts that are components of that experience. But this doesn't seem right, either. Consider, again, the phenomenon of *seeing as*. What is one aware of when one is aware of seeing a figure *as* a duck? Surely the duckishness of the experience figures in the content of one's awareness just as much as does the nonconceptual experience of a certain pattern of lines and shapes. And then if one's phenomenal concept picks out the entire experience (including its conceptual components), one should be incapable of thinking, "*This* experience might not have been about duckhood," or, "*This* experi- ence might not have had the content *duck*."

The same point would surely hold if it were true that concepts *ever* made a constitutive contribution to the phenomenology of experience. In using a phenomenal concept to pick out those phenomenal properties via awareness of them, one would surely have to be aware of the constituent concepts. For example, if the concept *red* made a constitutive contribution to the phenomenology of one's experience while one looks at a red tomato, then surely the reddishness of the experience would figure in one's awareness just as much as the fine-grained representation of hue, saturation, and intensity. And then (contrary to fact) one should be incapable of thinking, "*This* experience might not have been about red, or might not have had the content *red*."

Suppose one says, then, that phenomenal consciousness is whatever gives rise to the distinctively hard puzzles about consciousness, and one thinks that thought- experiments involving inverted experience and explanatory gaps have a central place amongst those puzzles. And suppose one also accepts that conceptually isolated phe- nomenal concepts are necessary for the puzzles to arise. Then one has reason to say that concepts *don't* make a constitutive contribution to phenomenal consciousness. Although concepts are constitutive of the globally broadcast outputs of our perceptual faculties, and are hence constitutive of our phenomenally conscious experiences, they make no constitutive contribution to the phenomenal properties of those experiences.

The phenomenal properties—the properties picked out by our phenomenal concepts—are constituted by the nonconceptual content of our experiences alone.[9]

3.3 Why inverted experiences?

We have argued that cognitive properties do not give rise to inverted experience thought-experiments, and hence don't contribute to the hard problem of consciousness. But someone might object that the inference simply isn't warranted. We have focused exclusively on inverted experiences, despite the fact that there are other prominent thought-experiments (zombies, black-and-white Mary) that indicate the existence of the hard problem. Our critic might think that cognitive properties will give rise to Mary-like scenarios or to the conceivability of cognitive zombies and will, as a result, contribute to the hard problem after all. We argue here that the critic is wrong.

Jackson (1982, 1986) imagines the case of Mary, who is a famous vision scientist brought up in an entirely black-and-white room, with no experience of color. Many share the intuition that she will learn something new when she leaves the room and experiences red for the first time, suggesting that phenomenal knowledge is something over and above the physical knowledge that she already possesses (which is stipulated to be complete). Can a similar thought-experiment be used to demonstrate that the concepts deployed in our experience likewise make a contribution that seems to defy physical description? Arguably not. (But not, as it turns out, for any reason that counts against the existence of cognitive phenomenology.)

Suppose that Mary is kept in a tomatoless room instead of a colorless one, where she is prevented from ever seeing a tomato (not even a picture of one). Nevertheless, she is given all theoretical knowledge about tomatoes (and about the effects that perceptions of them have on the brain). Will she learn anything new when she is shown a tomato for the first time? Arguably not, but this is because her theoretical knowledge of tomatoes (along with perceptual contact with red things and with roughly round objects) would surely have enabled her to *imagine* what a tomato looks like. So a defender of cognitive phenomenology can continue to insist that the concept *tomato* makes a constitutive contribution to the phenomenal experience of seeing a tomato, despite the fact that Mary learns nothing new when seeing a tomato for the first time. For that contribution will *already* have been made in the tomatoless room, when Mary first imagines a tomato. But equally, the thought-experiment provides no support for such a view.

For rather different reasons the zombie thought-experiment can't be used in support of cognitive phenomenology, either. There are two ways in which such a scenario might be developed: either we imagine a regular zombie who lacks any conscious

---

[9] As previously, the same conclusion can be expressed without commitment to the conceptual/nonconceptual distinction. One could say that only the numerous fine-grained indexical concepts that figure in our experiences but not in our thoughts and beliefs ever make a constitutive contribution to phenomenology.

experience whatever; or we try to imagine one who is zombie-like *only* in respect of the contribution made by concepts to his conscious experience. In the former case, since the zombie fails to have conscious experience at all, it is obvious that we have no way of telling whether the absence of any cognitive contribution to phenomenology is constitutive or merely causal.[10] The second case appears initially more promising. We might imagine a creature physically and functionally just like us, who does have phenomenally conscious *nonconceptual* experience, but for whom there is no phenomenal difference between seeing the duck–rabbit as a duck and seeing it as a rabbit. He experiences just the same pattern of lines on a plane surface in either case, while at the same time being disposed to judge, "It is a duck," on some occasions and, "It is a rabbit," on others. While such a zombie does seem conceivable, it can't help discriminate between the constitutive and causal hypotheses. For we have no way of telling whether the concept-zombie's deficit is that his concepts are incapable of making a *constitutive* contribution to his phenomenal life, or whether they merely fail to have any *causal* impact upon the latter. This leaves us with the explanatory gap itself, together with the associated experience-inversion thought-experiments that were the focus of our argument.

3.4 An attack on the method

Before concluding this section we need to consider an objection raised by Bayne (forthcoming) against the entire strategy of linking phenomenal consciousness to the various problematic thought-experiments. (This is a challenge to the first premise of the argument summarized at the outset of this section.) The objection is that all of these thought-experiments seem to involve secondary qualities like color. But experiences of primary qualities such as shape and movement can surely be phenomenally conscious also. In which case phenomenal properties aren't exhausted by those that give rise to the hard puzzles.

We agree that in connection with primary qualities it can be harder to construct intuitively convincing examples that parallel the thought-experiments involving in-verted color-experiences and so forth. (However, see Thompson 2010, for examples.) In order to provide an example where cube-experiences and sphere-experiences would be inverted with one another, for instance, we would need to construct a highly complex scenario involving worlds where the physical properties of light and reflectance of light are very different, and so on. But this isn't true of *all* primary qualities. In particular, it isn't true of motion. The existence and effects of spatially

---

[10] Of course one can *stipulate* that part of what is missing in the case of a complete zombie is the constitutive contribution that concepts make to phenomenology. And if concepts *do* make such a contribution then they will belong among the elements of mind that give rise to an explanatory gap. But since the zombie thought-experiment is supposed to be pre-theoretically accessible, it is plain that it can't provide any independent support for cognitive phenomenology.

inverting lenses makes it quite intuitive to entertain thoughts like, "*This* experience [as of movement from left to right] might have represented movement from right to left."

In any case, however, even if it is hard to spell out a detailed description of a world that would render the relevant counterfactual true, one *can* nevertheless think, "*This* very [cube-like] experience might not have represented cube-hood." We can coherently entertain the thought that the experience we are undergoing now (a cube-like one) could have had a different functional role and/or a different representational content. No matter how one spells out the different accounts of intentional content (informational, teleosemantic, conceptual role, wide or narrow, and so on) we can see in advance that we will be capable of thinking, in respect of any such account, "I could have had this very experience [a cube-like one] in the absence of the relevant representational state, and vice versa." No matter what functional and/or representational account is provided, one can still think that one could have had the same experiences without the functional and/or representational basis, or could have had the same basis without the experience. And *that* is the explanatory gap.

We conclude, therefore, that our methodology is sound: phenomenal consciousness can be equated with whatever gives rise to the various "hard problem" thought-experiments. And given the soundness of that methodology, it turns out that concepts do *not* make a constitutive contribution to the phenomenal qualities of our experience.

4   Against a phenomenology for thought

We take ourselves to have shown that there is no such thing as cognitive phenomenology in the case of perception. The arguments that have been offered in support of the idea are inconclusive (Section 2), and we have offered what we take to be a powerful argument against it (Section 3). In the present section we propose to sketch how our arguments might be extended into the domain of non-perceptual thought.

4.1 Inconclusive arguments

As we have already noted, everyone allows that there are phenomenal properties associated with and/or caused by our thoughts. The real question is whether cognitive content ever makes a *constitutive* contribution to phenomenology. We think that some combination of the points already made in our discussion of perceptual phenomenology can be deployed to undermine the various arguments that have been offered. For example, the fact that there is a phenomenological difference between hearing one and the same utterance with and without understanding (Strawson 1994; Siewert 1998; Pitt 2004) can be explained in terms of the different patterns of attention to the sound stream that will occur in the two cases (c.f. the duck–rabbit), together with the presence of feelings distinctive of what psychologists call "fluency" in the one case and puzzlement in the other (c.f. visual agnosia).

These factors seem unlikely to play a role in the phenomenal differences that can occur when one adopts one or another interpretation of a single token utterance, however, such as, "He has gone to the bank" (Pitt 2004). But of course there will be differences within what might be called the subject's "total phenomenal field" that either cause or are caused by one or another interpretation. (These might include images of dollar bills or perceptions of a nearby river.) Moreover, there is a danger of "cross-contamination" here, similar to the one we noted when discussing the difference that color-concepts might make to the phenomenology of color experience. If one is asked to report on what it is like to be thinking about a financial institution versus what it is like to be thinking about a riverbank, one's answer may be contaminated by the fact that banks themselves (the financial institutions) are very different from river banks. These are two very different kinds of thing, falling under distinct categories. Since money-banks are quite unlike riverbanks, one might naturally say that thinking about the former is very different from thinking about the latter, even if the two events are *phenomenologically* indistinguishable.

Some people have claimed that it is possible to entertain purely propositional—unsymbolized, imageless—thoughts, and that it is nevertheless *like* something to think such a thought. For example, Siewert (1998) describes how he was once standing in front of his apartment door, with his hand fumbling in an empty pocket where he would normally keep his keys. He says that at that moment he was wondering where he had left his keys, but without any imagery relevant to such a thought passing through his mind. However, the possibility of cross-contamination in judgments of "what is it like" returns in spades with this sort of example. For of course the location of one's keys is a very different thing from any other object or state of affairs that one might be thinking about, such as the likelihood of a pizza dinner. Because the location of one's keys *is* very different from the likelihood of a pizza dinner, one will naturally—and correctly—report that *thinking* about the former is very different from *thinking* about the latter. But for all that, unsymbolized thinking might be wholly lacking in phenomenology.

It is hard to establish whether episodes of propositional thinking in the absence of imagery are genuinely phenomenally conscious. In which case we have another stand-off. Subjects may report their occurrence, of course. That is enough to make them *access* conscious (Block 1995). But it isn't sufficient for phenomenal consciousness.[11] Moreover, it is true that subjects will be dumbfounded if asked to say what it is *like* to be wondering where one's keys are in the absence of any imagery. Very likely, all that they will be able to say in reply is: it is like wondering where one's keys are. And it might be said that this is not unlike the dumbfounding that occurs when people are asked to say what the smell of a rose is like, or the taste of coffee. But this

[11] Someone might object that access consciousness is widely believed to be nomologically sufficient for phenomenal consciousness. But this argument begs the question at issue. Granted, we have reason to think that the access consciousness *of perceptual states* is (via global broadcast) nomologically sufficient for their phenomenally conscious status. But we only have reason to think that this law extends to access-conscious *cognitive* states if such states are likewise phenomenally conscious. And that is just what is at stake in our current discussion.

doesn't amount to evidence in favor of the phenomenal consciousness of the thought, because an equally possible explanation for the dumbfounding is that there *is nothing* that it is like to entertain the thought, except that one knows that one is thinking it.

4.2 Conceptually isolated concepts of thought?

If thought-contents are to be phenomenally conscious, then they should give rise to an explanatory gap. And if they give rise to an explanatory gap, then we should possess some conceptually isolated concepts for them. Could there be *recognitional* concepts for our thought-contents, for example? It is hard to envisage how this could be possible, except via recognition of the phenomenal features of thoughts that happen to be expressed in inner speech or visual imagery. But even if episodes of inner speech were to constitute a kind of thought (which we deny), on no account can the content of the thought be equated with the form of words used. This is because the same sentence can be used to express more than one content, and because many thoughts are only elliptically expressed. So even if we had direct recognitional capacities for the sentences that figure in inner speech, this would not be the same as having a recognitional capacity for the *contents* of those sentences.

In contrast, a quotational account of our concepts of thought-contents looks quite plausible. For numerous authors have pointed out that we can think about our thought-contents via a process of semantic ascent, embedding the content in question within a phrase that effects reference to it (e.g. Evans 1982; Gordon 1996). In particular, one can refer to the content of any given thought *P* by embedding it within the phrase, "The thought _____." Indeed, some have pointed out that thoughts of the form, "I am thinking that P", have the same kind of indubitability and infallibility that have traditionally been associated with thoughts about our own phenomenal experiences (Burge 1996).

Although quotational concepts of propositional content possess some of the properties of phenomenal concepts, it is plain that they don't have the conceptual isolation necessary for the hard problems of consciousness to arise. In particular, one cannot coherently think, "The thought that polar bears are endangered might not have had the content *polar bears are endangered*." (This would be the analogue of an inverted experience thought-experiment.) This is because the content of a thought is an essential, not an accidental, property of it. Nor can one coherently think, "Someone might have all of the right representational and computational machinery, related in the same sorts of ways to features of the world or to other features of our cognition as occurs in ourselves, but without being capable of the thought that polar bears are endangered." This would be the analogue of a zombie thought-experiment.

We have offered only the barest sketch of an argument against non-perceptual cognitive phenomenology, of course. But it does at least suggest that the case made out against the cognitive phenomenology of perception in Sections 2 and 3 is likely to generalize. The detailed demonstration that this is so must be left for another occasion.[12]

References

Baars, B. (2002). "The conscious access hypothesis," *Trends in Cognitive Science*, 6: 47–52.

Balog, K. (1999). "Conceivability, possibility, and the mind-body problem," *Philosophical Review*, 108: 497–528.

Bayne, T. (2009). "Perceptual experience and the reach of phenomenal content," *Philosophical Quarterly*.

——(forthcoming). "The reach of phenomenal consciousness," (submitted).

Block, N. (1995). "A confusion about the function of consciousness," *Behavioral and Brain Sciences*, 18: 227–47.

——(2002). "The harder problem of consciousness," *Journal of Philosophy*, 99: 1–35.

Burge, T. (1996). "Our entitlement to self-knowledge," *Proceedings of the Aristotelian Society*, 96: 91–116.

Burns, B. and Shepp, B. (1988). "Dimensional interactions and the structure of psychological space," *Perception and Psychophysics*, 43: 494–507.

Carruthers, P. (2000). *Phenomenal Consciousness*. Cambridge: Cambridge University Press.

——and Veillet, B. (2007). "The phenomenal concept strategy," *Journal of Consciousness Studies*, 14: 9–10, 212–36.

Chalmers, D. (1996). *The Conscious Mind*. Oxford: Oxford University Press.

——(1997). "Availability: The cognitive basis of experience," *Behavioral and Brain Sciences*, 20: 148–9.

——(2003). "Phenomenal belief," in Q. Smith and A. Jokic (eds), *Consciousness*. Oxford: Oxford University Press.

——(2007). "Phenomenal concepts and the explanatory gap," in T. Alter and S. Walter (eds), *Phenomenal Concepts and Phenomenal Knowledge*. Oxford: Oxford University Press.

Dehaene, S. and Naccache, L. (2001). "Towards a cognitive neuroscience of consciousness: Basic evidence and a workspace framework," *Cognition*, 79: 1–37.

Dehaene, S., Sergent, C., and Changeux, J. (2003). "A neuronal network model linking subjective reports and objective physiological data during conscious perception," *Proceedings of the National Academy of Science*, 100: 8520–5.

Dennett, D. (1991). *Consciousness Explained*. London: Allen Lane.

Dretske, F. (1995). *Naturalizing the Mind*. Cambridge, MA: MIT Press.

Evans, G. (1982). *The Varieties of Reference*. Oxford: Oxford University Press.

Farah, M. (2004). *Visual Agnosia* (2nd edn). Cambridge, MA: MIT Press.

---

[12] We are grateful to Tim Bayne and two anonymous readers for Oxford University Press for their insightful comments on earlier drafts of this essay.

Gordon, R. (1996). "'Radical' simulationism," in P. Carruthers and P. Smith (eds), *Theories of Theories of Mind*. Cambridge: Cambridge University Press.

Jackson, F. (1982). "Epiphenomenal qualia," *Philosophical Quarterly*, 32: 127–36.

——(1986). "What Mary didn't know," *Journal of Philosophy*, 83: 291–5.

Kosslyn, S. (1994). *Image and Brain*. Cambridge, MA: MIT Press.

Levine, J. (2001). *Purple Haze*. Oxford: Oxford University Press.

——(2007). "Phenomenal concepts and the Materialist Constraint," in T. Alter and S. Walter (eds), *Phenomenal Concepts and Phenomenal Knowledge*. Oxford: Oxford University Press.

Livingston, K., Andrews, J., and Harnad, S. (1998). "Categorical perception effects induced by category learning," *Journal of Experimental Psychology: Learning, Memory, and Cognition*, 24(3): 732–53.

Loar, B. (1990). "Phenomenal states," in J. Tomberlin (ed.), *Philosophical Perspectives: Action Theory and Philosophy of Mind*. Atascadero, CA: Ridgeview Publishing Company, vol. 4, 81–108.

Lycan, W. (1996). *Consciousness and Experience*. Cambridge, MA: MIT Press.

McDowell, J. (1994). *Mind and World*. Cambridge, MA: Harvard University Press.

Milner, D. and Goodale, M. (1995). *The Visual Brain in Action*. Oxford: Oxford University Press.

Papineau, D. (2002). *Thinking about Consciousness*. Oxford: Oxford University Press.

Perry, J. (2001). *Knowledge, Possibility, and Consciousness*. Cambridge, MA: MIT Press.

Pitt, D. (2004). "The phenomenology of cognition," *Philosophy and Phenomenological Research*, 59: 1–36.

Pylyshyn, Z. (2003). *Seeing and Visualizing*. Cambridge, MA: MIT Press.

Rosenthal, D. (2005). *Consciousness and Mind*. Oxford: Oxford University Press.

Rubens, A. and Benson, D. (1971). "Associative visual agnosia," *Archives of Neurology*, 24: 305–16.

Schwitzgebel, E. (2008). "The unreliability of naïve introspection," *Philosophical Review*, 117: 245–73.

Siewert, C. (1998). *The Significance of Consciousness*. Princeton, NJ: Princeton University Press.

Stoljar, D. (2005). "Physicalism and phenomenal concepts," *Mind and Language*, 20: 469–94.

Strawson, G. (1994). *Mental Reality*. Cambridge, MA: MIT Press.

Thompson, B. (2010). "The spatial content of experience," *Philosophy and Phenomenological Research*: 80.

Tye, M. (1995). *Ten Problems of Consciousness*. Cambridge, MA: MIT Press.

——(2000). *Consciousness, Color, and Content*. Cambridge, MA: MIT Press.

——(2009). *Consciousness Revisited*. Cambridge, MA: MIT Press.

From Agentive Phenomenology to Cognitive Phenomenology: A Guide for the Perplexed

Terry Horgan

In recent philosophy of mind, a debate has arisen between proponents and opponents of the claim that occurrent intentional mental states such as thoughts and wishes have a distinctive, proprietary, phenomenology—a distinctive "what-it's-like," over and above the phenomenology that accrues to sensory experience. This putative kind of phenomenal character is often called "cognitive phenomenology", with the word "cognitive" here being used for a rubric that is broad enough to subsume conative intentional states such as occurrent wishes.[1]

One common line of argument deployed by proponents of cognitive phenomenology appeals to contrasting forms of conscious experience, where the contrast allegedly involves the presence vs. absence of some form of cognitive phenomenology—for instance, the contrast between the overall experience of someone who is hearing sentences in French and understands French vs. the overall experience of someone who is having exactly the same sensory phenomenology but does not understand French. There is a palpable difference between the two experiences, and the claim is that it should be clear, upon introspective reflection, that this is a *phenomenological*

---

[1] Proponents of cognitive phenomenology include Goldman (1993), Strawson (1994), Siewert (1998), Horgan and Tienson (2002), Horgan, Tienson, and Graham (2004), and Pitt (2004). Explicit opponents include Nelkin (1989) and Lormand (1996). Implicit denial of cognitive phenomenology has been extremely widespread in philosophy of mind during the past sixty years or so, by virtue of the widespread acceptance of what Horgan and Tienson (2002) call "separatism"—roughly, the view that phenomenal mental states are non-intentional, whereas intentional mental states are non-phenomenal. Separatism is clearly manifested in the writings of those philosophers who on one hand are sympathetic to the idea that the essence of intentional mental states is their causal/functional role vis-à-vis other internal states of the cognitive agent and/or external states of the agent's environment, and on the other hand maintain that there are certain non-intentional mental states (often dubbed "qualia") that (i) have an intrinsic "what it is like" essence that cannot be captured by a causal/functional role, and (ii) are non-intentional. Such separatism seems quite clearly presupposed, for instance, in Kim (2005).

difference: although the two experiencers have the same *sensory* phenomenology, only one of them has *language-understanding* phenomenology.

Another common line of argument is epistemological. People normally have special, and especially strong, epistemic access to their own current, occurrent, thoughts and wishes. The claim is that the best explanation of this distinctive form of epistemic access invokes cognitive phenomenology: phenomenal character is *self-presenting* to the experiencing agent, in a way that non-phenomenal internal states are not; and the best explanation of people's special epistemic access to their own occurrent cognitive states is that these states have proprietary, non-sensory, cognitive phenomenology. Since phenomenal character is self-presenting, cognitive phenomenology provides special, and especially strong, epistemic access to one's present occurrent cognitive states.

I am a proponent of cognitive phenomenology, and I myself tend to find such arguments persuasive.[2] But skeptics abound, who claim to be unimpressed by the arguments. They can concede, for example, that there is a big difference in the current mental goings-on—the current *experience*, in a sufficiently broad use of this term—of the person who is hearing spoken French and who understands French, as compared to the current experience of the person who is hearing the same sounds but understands no French. But they are apt to contend either (1) that this experiential difference is entirely a matter of the differences in the non-phenomenal *functional role* of the respective mental states of the respective persons but not a difference in phenomenology[3], or else (2) that any phenomenological differences would consist only in various kinds of non-cognitive, non-proprietary, phenomenology (e.g. emotional-affect phenomenology, sensory-imagistic phenomenology, or the like) that might be caused by the functional-role differences. Not all mental states that are conscious-as-opposed-to-unconscious are *phenomenally* conscious, they will insist; rather, some are merely "access conscious" (in the terminology of Block 1995), with no distinctive or proprietary phenomenal character at all.[4] Hence, not all aspects of experience—where

---

[2] As regards special epistemic access to one's own current, occurrent, cognitive states, what I consider strong evidence for cognitive phenomenology is not such access per se, but rather the fact that virtually nobody gets psychologically gripped by the prospect that one is radically mistaken about what one is now thinking (radical "internal-world skepticism"), whereas virtually everyone who hears about radical external-world skepticism, and who has any philosophical leanings at all, gets psychologically and intellectually gripped by the prospect that one's external-world experience might be radically non-veridical. For an argument that the non-grippingness of internal-world skepticism provides strong abductive support for the reality of cognitive phenomenology, see Horgan, Tienson, and Graham (2006). For a related argument in favor of a form of infallible knowledge concerning the phenomenal character of one's current experience, see Horgan and Kriegel (2007).

[3] I put the point in terms of a *non-phenomenal* functional role because I mean to leave open whether or not phenomenal mental features are themselves a particular kind of functional, or functionally specifiable, feature.

[4] This leaves open whether or not certain kinds of phenomenal character can be *possessed* by a token cognitive state without being distinctive or proprietary of the cognitive state-type that is being tokened. Perhaps, for example, non-proprietary visual-sensory phenomenology can be possessed by some occurrent tokens of a belief-type, especially when the token belief concerns one's visually presented surroundings and

"experience" is used generically enough to cover all aspects of mentality that are conscious-as-opposed-to-unconscious—have phenomenal character. There is such a thing as understanding-experience, all right—but there is no distinctive, proprietary, cognitive *phenomenology* involved. So say the skeptics.

As for the special epistemic access that people have to their own occurrent cognitive states, the skeptics are apt to concede such specialness but then argue that it can be adequately explained without any appeal to such a thing as cognitive phenomenology. They can claim, for instance, that part of what makes cognitive states count as conscious (in the generic sense) is that they reliably tend to cause accurate second-order beliefs about themselves (perhaps sometimes also causing certain accompanying non-cognitive phenomenology, e.g. emotional or sensory-imagistic). The first-order cognitive states are access conscious, after all, and this tendency to cause accurate higher-order beliefs about themselves counts as part of the constitutive functional role of access-conscious states. Thus, there is no need to appeal to cognitive phenomenology in order to explain why beliefs about one's current cognitive states are epistemically special. So say the skeptics.[5]

My aim in this paper is to set forth some considerations that will bolster the case for cognitive phenomenology. My hope is that these considerations will have some persuasive impact on those who profess skepticism, and also on those who find themselves at least perplexed (if not outright skeptical) about the very idea of cognitive phenomenology. The points I will make will not be entirely new, or entirely divorced from the familiar arguments I have mentioned. In particular, my discussion will be similar in spirit to the first of the two kinds of argument mentioned above, involving putative phenomenological differences that can accompany the very same sensory phenomenology. But I will introduce some novel wrinkles, which at the very least will put some serious new dialectical pressure on the skeptics. Maintaining skepticism in the face of these considerations will evidently require the biting of some sizeable-looking bullets.

My approach will be informed by two guiding ideas. First, a promising dialectical path leading to acknowledgment of cognitive phenomenology—or at least acknowledgment that denying it requires implausible bullet-biting—is a path that commences from, and then is continuously informed by, introspective attention to one's agentive experience. (Hence the title of this paper.) Second, the strategy of describing certain kinds of mental-difference scenarios—ones involving agents who have normal sensory phenomenology and are functional duplicates of a normal human, but who nonetheless differ mentally from a normal human—is a useful way of guiding the perplexed

arises directly from one's current visual-sensory experience. The issue concerns whether there are kinds of phenomenal character that are non-sensory and also are proprietary of certain cognitive state-types.

[5] The skeptics also are apt to try to explain the non-grippingness of radical internal-world skepticism in ways that do not appeal to cognitive phenomenology. Various ways of trying to do that are described and criticized in Horgan, Tienson, and Graham (2006).

along the path from agentive experience, with its recognizable and proprietary phenomenal aspects, to the recognition and acknowledgment of full-fledged cognitive phenomenology.

1 Zombie scenarios and phenomenology

Zombie scenarios of various kinds have figured prominently in recent philosophy of mind. It will be useful to distinguish two kinds of zombie. A *complete* zombie is a putative creature which, although it has internal states that play all the same functional roles that are played in humans by mental states of various kinds (and thus is a perfect functional duplicate of an ordinary human), has no phenomenology at all. None of its internal states have any "what-it's-likeness," and thus there is nothing it is like to *be* such a creature. A *partial* zombie, on the other hand, has *some* phenomenology, but lacks certain kinds of phenomenology that are present in the mental lives of ordinary humans—and, once again, is a perfect functional duplicate of an ordinary human.

It is often claimed that one or another sort of zombie scenario is conceivable, and that its conceivability is *robust* in certain ways. Robustness involves, inter alia, the persistence of conceivability under inclusion of arbitrarily greater detail and specificity. Thus, although one can perhaps conceive in some *non-specific* way of someone proving the completeness of elementary number theory—one imagines in a non-specific way someone producing a logically sound proof whose conclusion is the proposition that elementary number theory is complete—one cannot conceive this *robustly*. To do that would be to incorporate into the imagined scenario all the specific details of such a proof—which is impossible, in light of Godel's work.

Thought-experimental scenarios involving complete zombies are very familiar in recent philosophy of mind. It is often claimed that one can robustly conceive a creature who is a complete functional duplicate of an ordinary human being, but who lacks phenomenal consciousness altogether—i.e. a complete zombie. It is also frequently claimed that one can conceive of such a complete zombie who is also a complete *physical* duplicate of an ordinary human, too.

Partial-zombie scenarios are familiar as well—e.g. the thought-experimental case of a creature who is a functional duplicate of an ordinary human but is also a "perfect blindsighter." Such a person would lack visual phenomenology altogether (just as real blindsighters supposedly do), but would rapidly and spontaneously form very detailed, fully accurate, beliefs about what is going on within the immediate front environment—beliefs with the same content as those that would arise in an ordinary human via visual experience. The person's cognitive architecture would have the same functional organization as that of an ordinary person, despite the lack of visual phenomenology.[6] Beliefs triggered by retinal stimulations would arise spontaneously

---

[6] At any rate, this is so for a perfect blindsighter who is also a partial zombie. Visual zombiehood is a matter of (i) having ordinary visual-cognitive architecture that operates normally, while yet (ii) lacking any visual

without accompanying conscious visual experience, while also arising via the operation of normal processing of retinal information by ordinary cognitive architecture—processing that has accompanying visual phenomenology for ordinary humans, but not for the visual blindsighter. This visual-experience deprived partial zombie would behave just like an ordinary person, despite navigating the environment without any visual phenomenology. (Also, this person would have no awareness of having an experiential deficit. On the contrary, the partial zombie would have beliefs expressible by sentences like "I have normal visual experience.")

Such scenarios have been invoked in philosophy of mind for various purposes. For instance, the robust conceivability of complete and/or partial zombies is sometimes put forward as grounds for the claim that these creatures are metaphysically possible—and hence as grounds for the denial of functionalism, at least insofar as phenomenal consciousness is concerned. Likewise, the robust conceivability of complete zombies who are also complete *physical* duplicates of ordinary humans is sometimes put forward as grounds for claiming that they too are metaphysically possible—and hence as grounds for the denial of materialism about the mind. But of course, the inference from robust conceivability to metaphysical possibility is very tendentious here; there are many in contemporary philosophy of mind who concede the robust conceivability of zombies but reject the inference from their robust conceivability to their meta-physical possibility. (There are hard-liners too, who deny robust conceivability itself; but that is a large bullet to bite.)

For present purposes, it does not matter whether or not the inference from robust conceivability to metaphysical possibility is legitimate and correct, in the case of zombie scenarios. Nor does it matter whether or not phenomenal mental properties are in fact identical to certain first-order physical properties (e.g. neurobiological properties) or to certain functional properties. (One recently popular view has it that although phenomenal *concepts* are so different from physical-functional concepts that zombie scenarios are robustly conceivable, nonetheless the *properties* picked out by phenomenal concepts are identical to certain physical or functional properties—and that these property-identities obtain with metaphysical necessity.) Rather, what matters here is this: *the robust conceivability of certain kinds of zombie scenarios can serve as a criterion for the existence of certain kinds of phenomenal character*. Especially relevant will be some thought-experimental scenarios involving robustly conceivable creatures who (i) are complete functional duplicates of ordinary humans, (ii) have the same sensory phenomenology as ordinary humans (and also are the same with regard to any other kind of non-cognitive phenomenology there might be in ordinary humans, e.g. emotional or sensory-imagistic), but (iii) are partial zombies nonetheless. What they are missing are certain kinds of cognitive phenomenology that are present in the mental lives of ordinary human beings.

phenomenology. One can also imagine perfect blindsighters in whom retinally transduced information is processed by cognitive architecture that operates differently than in normal humans.

The dialectical strategy in the discussion below will be as follows. I will focus on the phenomenology of agency—the what-it's-likeness of experiencing one's behaviors *as one's own actions*. I will describe a series of thought-experimental partial-zombie scenarios, each of which involves a hypothetical creature who, despite being a functional duplicate of an ordinary human being and despite having ordinary sensory phenomenology (and any other kind of ordinary non-cognitive phenomenology such as emotional or sensory-imagistic), nonetheless has a specific agentive-experience deficit. Insofar as each of the successive scenarios is robustly conceivable, this will reveal an aspect of agentive phenomenology over and above the uncontested kinds of phenomenology. Some of the scenarios will involve phenomenological deficits, in the envisioned partial zombies, that constitute the absence of one or another kind of cognitive phenomenology that is present in the mental lives of ordinary humans—deficits with respect to elements of *purposiveness* that are present in normal agentive phenomenology but absent in the zombie's phenomenology.

In short, this guide for the perplexed will be a tour through several partial-zombie scenarios, each involving aspects of agentive experience and each being robustly conceivable. The hoped-for result will be a reflective-introspective recognition, on the part of the reader, of the reality of cognitive phenomenology—and also its richness and its variety. Or, failing that, the reader should at least come to recognize that skepticism about cognitive phenomenology can be maintained only at the cost of denying the robust conceivability of partial-zombie scenarios that initially seem strikingly easy to conceive.

2 Methodological preliminaries

Before proceeding, let me make some methodological remarks.

First: The scenarios to be described all involve one or another kind of phenomenology-deficit, relative to ordinary human phenomenology. I suspect that some—perhaps all—of the deficits I characterize actually occur among humankind, perhaps as byproducts of brain damage. Also, I suspect that such deficits in real humans would almost invariably tend to generate abnormal behavior and/or abnormal cognition, detectable by external observers (e.g. psychologists and neurologists in V.A. hospitals). Why, then, yoke the descriptions of the various phenomenology-deficits to *partial-zombie* scenarios? The reason is dialectical: doing so precludes a response that could otherwise be expected from skeptics about cognitive phenomenology—namely, claiming that the pertinent deficits are no more than the lack of certain access-conscious states that occur in normal humans (together perhaps with the lack of certain kinds of non-cognitive phenomenology that such access-conscious states might cause, such as emotional or sensory-imagistic), rather than the lack of cognitive phenomenology. As noted already, the robust conceivability of specific partial-zombie scenarios is a good criterion for the existence of various kinds of phenomenal character—kinds that are present in the mental life of ordinary humans but are absent in the envisioned partial zombies.

Second: Let me clarify the respects of similarity that are to obtain, by stipulation, between an ordinary human on one hand, and the various partial zombies on the other hand. The partial zombies will be functional duplicates of a normal human, in this sense: the zombies and the normal human would exhibit exactly the same *bodily motions* in all actual or potential circumstances, and would do so by virtue of exactly matching internal functional architecture. (This leaves open whether or not action descriptions that apply to the human also apply to a given partial zombie, and also whether or not ascriptions of intentional mental states that apply to the human also apply to the partial zombie.) Also, the partial zombies will have all the same *uncontested* phenomenology as does a normal human—i.e. whatever kinds of phenomenology would be acknowledged by a philosophical skeptic about the existence of cognitive phenomenology. Uncontested phenomenology surely includes *sensory* phenomenal character; beyond that, the category "uncontested phenomenology" is deliberately vague, since those who are skeptics about cognitive phenomenology might also differ among themselves about what kinds of non-sensory phenomenal character exist (if any). They might disagree with one another about whether mental imagery of sensory experience has phenomenal character, for instance, or about whether moods like elation or depression have phenomenal character, etc. (For present purposes, the vagueness of the notion of uncontested phenomenology should not matter.) Let a *core functional-and-phenomenal duplicate* of an ordinary human— for short, a *CFP duplicate*—be a creature who is a functional duplicate of the human (in the sense explained above) and also has all the same uncontested phenomenology as the human.

Third: A CFP duplicate of a normal human being will, of course, undergo various internal states that play functional roles that exhibit all the features needed to qualify as what Ned Block calls "access conscious." I will refer to these as *"access conscious" states* (for short, *"AC" states*), as a nod toward Block's influential terminology. A CFP duplicate of a normal human undergoes, in the course of its life, states that exactly match, functional-role-wise, the conscious states that the normal human undergoes. But I mean to leave open whether or not the CFP duplicate's "AC" states are really *conscious* in any pre-theoretic sense of the term. (Hence the scare quotes.) I also mean to leave open whether those "AC" states in the CFP duplicate are *mental* states at all—and, if they are, what kinds of mental states they are, whether some of them are intentional, and what their intentional content is (if they have any).

Fourth: The process of conceiving a complete or partial zombie can be usefully characterized as comprising three distinct stages—a characterization that will prove useful below. At the first stage, one conceives a creature from the third-person perspective, as instantiating various features involving matters like observable behavior, functional organization of the internal information-processing system, and/or the physical implementation of that functional organization. This stage leaves unspecified certain further facts about the creature—in particular, facts about what the creature's mental life is like from the first-person perspective. At the second stage, one conceives a creature largely from the first-person perspective: one conceives the creature as undergoing specific kinds of "what it's like" states—or, in the limit case, one conceives a creature that lacks any first-person what-it's-likeness altogether. This stage leaves unspecified certain features that were specified in the first stage—in particular, certain aspects of internal functional organization and/or physical implementation. (The second stage might include *some* third-person aspects, however—e.g. facts about the creature's observable behavior.) At the third stage, one imaginatively "fuses" the first two stages: one conceives a single creature as having all the features attributed to the creature conceived in the first stage, and also all the features attributed to the creature in the second stage. These three stages need not be sequential, but instead might all occur simultaneously (or in sequence with stage two preceding stage one); still, they are separate *aspects* of the overall conceiving-process.[7]

3 A fundamental element of agentive phenomenology: Self as source

I will be appealing to the phenomenology of agency, as a way to leverage one's way to a recognition of full-fledged cognitive phenomenology. (Getting one's foot in the door; the camel sticking its nose under the tent; the train leaving the station—choose your metaphor.) So let me make some pertinent observations about agentive phenomenology.

What is it like, phenomenologically, to experience your own behavior as action? At present I want to stress one especially salient aspect of such experience. Suppose that you deliberately do something—say, holding up your right arm with palm forward and fingers together and extended vertically. What is your experience like? To begin with, there is of course the purely bodily motion aspect of the phenomenology—the what-it's-like of being visually and kinesthetically presented with one's own right hand rising with palm forward and fingers together and pointing upward. But there is more to it than that, because you are experiencing this bodily motion not as something that is "just happening," so to speak, but rather *as your own action*. You experience your arm, hand, and fingers as being moved *by you yourself*; this is the what-it's-like of *self as source*.

---

[7] Also, this kind of three-stage conceiving, even when robust, is compatible with the metaphysical impossibility of what is thereby conceived. For example, when one conceives a creature in a stage-one manner that specifies a sufficiently great amount of detail about matters of functional organization and neural implementation, one might thereby be conceiving a creature who possesses, as a matter of metaphysical necessity, a mental life with a specific, determinate, first-person nature—even though one has not conceived the creature *as* having such a first-person nature. (Conceiving-as is an intensional mental act.) If so, then when one does a stage-three fusing of this stage-one conceiving with a stage two that conceives the creature's mental life as having some *other* first-person nature—or, in the case of a total zombie, no first-person nature at all—one thereby conceives of something that is metaphysically impossible. (One does not conceive of it *as* metaphysically impossible, however—again because conceiving-as is intensional.)

The language of causation seems apt here too: you experience your behavior as *caused* by you yourself. Metaphysical libertarians about human freedom sometimes speak of "agent causation" (or "immanent causation"), and such terminology seems *phenomenologically* right regardless of what one thinks about the intelligibility or credibility of metaphysical libertarianism. One does sometimes experience some of one's own bodily motions as mere happenings, rather than as self-produced—e.g. when the doctor taps one's knee with a mallet to check one's "kick-forward" reflex, or when one trips over an unnoticed obstacle and finds one's body falling to the ground. (And Dr. Strangelove, famously, experienced his own involuntary arm-raising motion that way too.) But these kinds of bodily motion experiences are exceptions that prove the rule: they lack the phenomenology of agency—the phenomenal aspect of *self as source*.

This phenomenal feature, I submit, clearly reveals itself to introspection. I should add, however, that although I do claim that the existence of self-as-source phenomenology is introspectively obvious, I do not claim that the *satisfaction conditions* for such phenomenology are introspectively obvious. On the contrary, elsewhere (e.g. Horgan 2007a, 2007b, in press) I have argued that one cannot reliably tell, just on the basis of introspection, what those satisfaction conditions are—i.e. what is required of the world and of oneself, in order to be the kind of self-source of one's behavior that one experiences oneself to be. More specifically, I have argued that one cannot reliably determine, just by introspection, whether or not the satisfaction conditions for agentive experience require one to be a godlike "unmoved mover"—an agent cause of one's behaviors in the metaphysically heavyweight sense of "agent cause" espoused by libertarians about free will. I have also argued that there are powerful reasons to think that the satisfaction conditions for self-as-source phenomenology do *not* require agent causation in the heavyweight sense—although the considerations are mainly abductive rather than introspective.

Now, someone who is skeptical about the existence of full-fledged *cognitive* phenomenology—i.e. the putative, putatively proprietary, what-it's-likeness of occurrent thoughts, occurrent wishes, and the like—might well profess skepticism about agentive phenomenology too. Doubts could be raised that are parallel in structure to the doubts I described (in the fourth paragraph of this paper) concerning the putative phenomenological difference between the person who hears and understands spoken French and the person who hears it without understanding it; i.e. a skeptic could concede that there is a big difference, for example, between the current mental goings-on—the current *experience*, in a sufficiently broad sense of this term—of the person who experiences a particular bodily motion as constituting deliberate action, as compared to the person who experiences that same bodily motion "Strangelove-wise"—i.e. passively, as something that "happens to one's body." But the skeptic could go on to contend that this experiential difference is entirely a matter of differences in what is access conscious in the respective cases, together perhaps with differences in non-cognitive phenomenology (e.g. emotional or sensory-imagistic) that are caused by these differences in access-conscious states—rather than involving any differences in the putative aspect of cognitive phenomenology. Actions are bodily motions that are caused by occurrent intentional mental states that rationalize them (e.g. an occurrent wish together with an occurrent thought about how to achieve that wish); often these states themselves are access conscious when the bodily motion occurs; and thus, the overall "experience of acting" often includes the presence of these access-conscious rationalizing states. Passively experienced bodily motions, however, are caused some other way—maybe by other kinds of access-conscious mental states like excitement (as in Dr. Strangelove's case), or maybe by states that are not access conscious at all. So the difference between experiences of agency and experiences of non-agentive bodily motion is entirely a matter of mere access consciousness, together perhaps with accompanying differences in non-proprietary, non-cognitive, phenomenology—in the case of agentive experience, the presence of access-conscious rationalizing states (together perhaps with accompanying non-cognitive phenomenology, e.g. emotional or sensory-imagistic), and in the case of mere-motion experience, the absence of these. The rationalizing states are *merely* access conscious, lacking any distinctive or proprietary phenomenology. Likewise, agentive experience too lacks any distinctive or proprietary phenomenology; it differs from passive bodily motion experience not phenomenologically, but only by the presence in access consciousness of mental states that rationalize the bodily motion and have no distinctive or proprietary phenomenology themselves. So says the skeptic about agentive phenomenology.

This kind of skepticism too will be something I challenge below, in addition to challenging skepticism about cognitive phenomenology—and by the same dialectical strategy.

4 Agency absence partial-zombie disorder

I am ready now to commence the consideration of partial-zombie scenarios. The first item of business is to describe a scenario that challenges skepticism about agentive phenomenology—including the form of skepticism just described, which alleges that the distinctive features of agentive experience do not involve any such thing as proprietary agentive phenomenology.

Suppose that $Andy_1$ is a normal human being (named Andy), and that his mental life is rich and varied. $Andy_1$ is a philosopher, and has views in philosophy of mind. Specifically, he denies the existence of proprietary cognitive phenomenology, and he also denies that there is anything distinctively phenomenological about agency experience, apart from the sensory aspect of kinesthetic bodily motion phenomenology. What is distinctive of those behaviors that count as actions, says $Andy_1$, is nothing phenomenological but rather this: an action is an item of behavior that is caused by access-conscious mental state(s) that "rationalize" it—e.g. caused by a combination of an access-conscious belief and an access-conscious desire. Although actions sometimes might be accompanied by certain kinds of non-cognitive phenomenology in addition to kinesthetic sensations (e.g. emotional or sensory-imagistic), there is no such thing as the putative phenomenology of "self as source."[8]

The partial zombie I will now describe, and the others to be described subsequently, all have—by stipulation—the same stage-one specification, as follows. Each of them is a CFP duplicate of $Andy_1$. Each of them occupies a global environment that is exactly like the actual global environment that $Andy_1$ himself occupies. Each of them undergoes a trajectory through life which, from an external perspective, is exactly like $Andy_1$'s own life-trajectory; thus, each is a perfect behavioral duplicate of $Andy_1$. I will call this *the common stage-one specification*, since it will be in common across all the scenarios to be described.

The only differences among these thought-experimental zombies will be phenomenological. These differences will figure in different stage-two conceivings, each of which can be imaginatively fused with the common stage-one specification to yield an overall stage-three conceiving of a distinctive partial-zombie scenario. (And remember: all that matters, for my purposes, is whether the scenarios I will describe are *robustly conceivable*; they need not be metaphysically possible.)

I submit that one can robustly conceive a person, $Andy_2$, as follows. Stage one: He is conceived as satisfying the common stage-one specification. Thus, he is a CFP duplicate of $Andy_1$, and follows an exactly similar lifelong behavioral trajectory through the world.

Stage two: He is conceived, in a way that largely involves the first-person perspective, as behaving just like $Andy_1$ while having a mental life that is just like $Andy_1$'s except for the following (quite substantial) differences. $Andy_2$ has no agentive phenomenology at all—in particular, no experiences as-of certain bodily movements emanating from himself as their source.[9] Rather, he always experiences his own bodily movements as just happening, in much the way one experiences one's lower leg extending itself when a doctor taps one's knee with a reflex-testing mallet, or the way Dr. Strangelove experiences his arm involuntarily rising Nazi-style when he's excited.[10]

Stage three: He is conceived as possessing both the stage-one features and the stage-two features. As so conceived, he is a CFP duplicate of $Andy_1$, but is mentally different

---

[8] I know some very smart, very subtle, very well-informed philosophers who profess such views. And I believe that they are sincere, even though I think they are mis-describing their own phenomenology; for more on this, see the Postscript.

[9] Since $Andy_2$ has no agentive phenomenology at all, he has no phenomenology of *mental* agency either. The successive stages of his mental life are experienced passively by him, rather than as mental doings.

[10] $Andy_2$'s kinesthetic sensory phenomenology in such cases is different from the kinesthetic sensory phenomenology associated with experiences as-of one's body's being caused to move *by some force* (either external or internal). $Andy_2$ experiences his body as *just moving by itself*—rather than experiencing his movements either as emanating from himself as their source or as emanating from some external or internal force.

from Andy$_1$, nonetheless. I will call his experiential deficit *agency absence partial-zombie disorder*.[11]

Of course, since Andy$_2$ is otherwise just like Andy$_1$ mentally, Andy$_2$ is consciously aware of many of his occurrent beliefs and desires—including, often, beliefs and desires that rationalize his bodily motions.[12] Nonetheless, he always experiences his own bodily motions passively—as happenings—rather than as actions that emanate voluntarily from himself as their source. In this respect his mental life resembles the mental lives of Galen Strawson's thought-experimental "weather watchers" (Strawson 1994), conscious creatures with lily-pad-like bodies that float on the water, and who lack any capacity to generate their own motions. They have occurrent beliefs and desires (including, perhaps, desires about which direction they would like their bodies to be oriented, with visual input then impinging on them from objects in that direction)— but they have no agentive phenomenology. Andy$_2$ is a "self-watcher," one might say: when various bodily motions of his contribute to the satisfaction of his occurrent wishes, he takes note of this fact, and is pleased about it. He is rarely surprised by such wish-implementing bodily motions, since he has learned from experience that they often occur. He regards this systematic correlation as no accident, but rather as resulting from the fact that occurrent combinations of a belief state and a desire state often *cause* motions that they rationalize. Nonetheless, he utterly lacks bodily behavior agentive phenomenology, the what-it's-like of self as source of one's own bodily motions. Instead, he goes through life experiencing his overt behavior passively as a self-watcher, rather than experiencing himself as an active instigator of voluntary bodily actions.

Since Andy$_2$ is a CFP duplicate of Andy$_1$, Andy$_2$ behaves exactly the same way as does Andy$_1$. This means, inter alia, that in philosophical discussions about agency and phenomenology, Andy$_2$ adamantly utters (just as Andy$_1$ does) sentences like this: "There is nothing distinctively phenomenological about agency experience, apart from the sensory aspect of kinesthetic bodily motion phenomenology." And the striking thing is that in Andy$_2$'s case (but not Andy$_1$'s case), *his utterance is true!*[13]

I myself have no trouble conceiving of Andy$_2$, or in understanding how Andy$_2$'s mental life differs from that of Andy$_1$. I am betting that the same will be true for my readers. Of course, I can't *force* the obstinate skeptic to acknowledge the

---

[11] I intend this label to be understood in a way that leaves open whether or not a creature like Andy$_2$ is in fact an agent. The point is that he does not *experience* his behaviors as actions.

[12] I myself contend that normal conscious awareness of one's occurrent beliefs and desires involves the presence of proprietary cognitive phenomenology, whereas the skeptic about cognitive phenomenology denies this. For my immediate purposes, however, this issue can be set aside. Andy$_2$ is consciously aware of his occurrent beliefs and desires in the same way that Andy$_1$ is—whatever way that is.

[13] One might well wonder whether the sentence uttered by Andy$_2$ actually means the same as the orthographically identical sentence uttered by Andy$_1$, given that Andy$_2$ has learned to use expressions like 'agency' and 'agency experience' without ever having undergone any actual agency experience at all. I myself am inclined to say no, but my present point does not depend on it. Andy$_2$'s utterance is true, whereas Andy$_1$'s is false—whether or not the two utterances have the same meaning.

conceivability of a person like Andy$_2$ and the clear difference between Andy$_1$ and Andy$_2$. But claiming that one finds this thought-experimental malady inconceivable is a very large bullet to bite—as is the claim that phenomenology of ordinary agentive experience is really just Andy$_2$'s phenomenology.

Alternatively, skeptics about cognitive phenomenology could concede the robust conceivability of Andy$_2$, and could concede that this conceivability-fact makes manifest the existence of self-as-source phenomenology as something over and above sensory-kinesthetic phenomenology, and yet still profess skepticism about cognitive phenomenology itself. But the Andy$_2$ scenario is only the first stop on our journey through conceivability space.

5 Language-understanding absence partial-zombie disorder

There is more to agentive phenomenology than the sensory aspects of bodily motion and the aspect of self-as-source. There are also various phenomenological aspects involving *purpose*—both generic on-purposeness and specific purposes for which one acts. And these purpose-related aspects involve matters cognitive—specifically, one's occurrent beliefs and occurrent desires. Purposes are directed toward states of the world one occurrently *wants* to come about, and actions done for a purpose are behaviors that one *believes* will contribute to the coming about of those desired states. Cognitive phenomenology is thus an element of the overall phenomenology of agency.

That is the guiding thought behind what follows, in this section and the next two. I will describe three partial-zombie counterparts of Andy$_1$, each of whom seems robustly conceivable. Each envisioned agent will suffer a deficit in his agentive phenomenology that pertains, at least in part, to purposiveness—and thus reveals an aspect of cognitive phenomenology that is present in Andy$_1$ but absent in the given kind of partial zombie.

I begin with a scenario that is closely connected to examples like the one mentioned in the second paragraph of this paper, involving the putative phenomenological difference between the overall experiences of two people hearing the same spoken French, one of whom understands French and one of whom does not. The skeptic about cognitive phenomenology would respond by saying that this difference is entirely a matter of access-conscious states (together perhaps with certain resulting differences in uncontested kinds of phenomenology, e.g. emotional or sensory-imagistic), rather than a difference involving the presence vs. absence of cognitive phenomenology. I propose to parry that response with a partial-zombie scenario involving a conceivable person who lacks language understanding but who nonetheless behaves just like an ordinary language-understander and also has all the same uncontested phenomenology. The partial zombie's *agentive* phenomenology in so behaving will be quite abnormal, involving peculiar aspects of purposiveness—thereby making vivid the fact that cognitive phenomenology is actually an aspect of agentive phenomenology itself. Since the partial zombie will be a complete functional duplicate of an ordinary language-understanding person, and also will have all the same uncontested phenomenology, the conceivability of the scenario will mean that what's missing in the zombie's mental life can only be proprietary cognitive phenomenology—namely, the what-it's-like of language-understanding.

I submit that one can robustly conceive a person, $Andy_3$, as follows. Stage one: He is conceived as satisfying the common stage-one specification. Thus, he is a CFP duplicate of $Andy_1$, and follows an exactly similar lifelong behavioral trajectory through the world.

Stage two: He is conceived, in a way that largely involves the first-person perspective, as behaving just like $Andy_1$, while having a mental life that is like $Andy_1$'s except for the following (very substantial) differences. The sounds and marks that $Andy_1$ experiences as intelligible language are always experienced by $Andy_3$ as meaningless noises and squiggles—even when he produces them himself. Although he does have agentive bodily behavior phenomenology (unlike $Andy_2$), he never experiences his verbal or written squiggle-producing behavior as *speech acts*, nor does he experience his behaviors prompted by others' noises or squiggles as *responses to linguistic communications*. Rather, his ongoing experience includes frequently arising spontaneous impulses to generate various of these squiggles and sounds in various situations, and to engage in various specific actions upon hearing or seeing such sounds or squiggles that have been produced by others. He routinely acts on these spontaneous impulses, with little or no hesitation. And the people with whom he interacts usually seem friendly and pleasant enough, in response to his behavior in interpersonal or group settings, even though he never experiences either others or himself as engaged in linguistic communication. This fact is something he normally experiences as a massive coincidence, since he never construes the sounds and squiggles as language. So, his agentive phenomenology is quite impoverished in relation to that of $Andy_1$. Even though he behaves in ways that make him appear to other people as someone who understands written and spoken language and engages in ordinary linguistic communication, he has no experience as-of deploying public language or as-of acting for purposes that arise from experiences of language-understanding.[14]

Stage three: He is conceived as possessing both the stage-one features and the stage-two features. As so conceived, he is a CFP duplicate of $Andy_1$. Thus, there are "AC" processes at work in $Andy_3$, parallel in their functional roles in $Andy_3$ to their functional roles in $Andy_1$, such that the functional roles they play in $Andy_3$ are ones

---

[14] Needless to say, the $Andy_3$ scenario is reminiscent of the famous "Chinese Room" scenario in Searle (1980). Especially analogous is a variant of the Chinese Room that Searle describes himself: the agent (who understands no Chinese) memorizes the rules for manipulating symbols in response to combinations of other symbols plus sensory input, and also memorizes the rules for generating various behaviors in response to combinations of other symbols plus sensory input, and then follows these rules when he is out and about among the Chinese population.

that would be appropriate for conscious mental states like *intending to perform a speech act with content p* or *experiencing a spoken or written sign-design as a linguistic expression with content p*. Nonetheless, $Andy_3$'s mental life is quite different from that of $Andy_1$. For instance, when $Andy_3$ instantiates a functional state which is experienced by $Andy_1$ as consciously intending to order a chicken salad sandwich for lunch, in $Andy_3$ this same functional state is experienced as intending to emit such-and-such meaningless-seeming vocal noises. ($Andy_3$ emits those noises, after which—in what seems a happy coincidence—he finds himself being served a chicken salad sandwich.) When $Andy_3$ instantiates first a functional state which is experienced by $Andy_1$ as a request by his wife that he take out the garbage, and then a functional state which is experienced by $Andy_1$ as a desire to comply with that request, in $Andy_3$ the first functional state is experienced as meaningless-seeming vocal noises emitted from her, and the second functional state is experienced as the onset of a spontaneous, seemingly "out of the blue," desire to take out the garbage. ($Andy_3$ acts on that desire, of course.) And so it goes, throughout $Andy_3$'s entire life. ($Andy_3$ is also quite an un-curious person. It never occurs to him to wonder about why and how all his spontaneous behaviors involving meaningless noises and squiggles seem to result in things going so smoothly for him in his life.) I will call $Andy_3$'s experiential deficit *language-understanding absence partial-zombie disorder.*[15]

I myself have no trouble conceiving of $Andy_3$, and I suspect that the same is true for you the reader. Moreover, for me—and I suspect you too—the conceivability of $Andy_3$ is robust: it can withstand any amount of supplementation of the stage-one story about the details of the cognitive functional architecture that $Andy_1$ and $Andy_3$ have in common, or about the details of how that functional architecture is neurally implemented in both of them. The moral of this robust-conceivability fact is that the difference between $Andy_1$ and $Andy_3$ is phenomenological. Furthermore, since they both have the same uncontested phenomenology—the same sensory phenomenology, and any other uncontested, non-cognitive, phenomenology (e.g. emotional or sensory-imagistic)—the difference between them can only be a matter of *cognitive* phenomenology. Specifically, it involves a species of the phenomenological genus that Galen Strawson (1994) calls "understanding experience." $Andy_3$ lacks the kind of understanding experience that figures in language comprehension, whereas $Andy_1$ has such phenomenology. This cognitive-phenomenological difference is present in their respective agentive phenomenology too; agentive phenomenology is itself a species of cognitive phenomenology, by virtue of its purposiveness aspects.

---

[15] I intend this label to be understood in a way that leaves open whether or not a creature like $Andy_3$ in fact lacks language understanding. The point is that he does not *experience* himself as a language-under-stander—and thus he also does not experience his verbal and written behaviors as speech acts, and he does not experience his behavioral responses to others' noises and squiggles as content-appropriate behavioral responses to others' speech acts.

Now, as recently noted, Andy$_3$ does have all the same "AC" states as does Andy$_1$, and these states play all the same functional roles in Andy$_3$ as they do in Andy$_1$. In particular, they mediate the production by Andy$_3$ of noises and squiggles that others he interacts with construe as speech acts, and they mediate those non-linguistic behaviors by Andy$_3$ that others around him construe as manifestations of linguistic understanding. The question thus arises whether it is right to say that Andy$_3$ actually does undergo states of conscious language-understanding, albeit ones that are merely access conscious without also having the distinctive phenomenology of Andy$_1$'s occurrent language-understanding states. Speaking for myself, I do feel some small degree of attraction toward a positive answer to this question—since, after all, Andy$_3$'s disorder would be entirely undetectable by those around him. Nevertheless, I feel a much stronger—indeed, overwhelmingly strong—pull toward the verdict that Andy$_3$ really lacks language-understanding altogether: in him, it seems right to say, the pertinent "AC" states are not language-understanding states, but rather are mere spontaneous impulses to produce his own meaningless noises and squiggles on one hand, and on the other hand to respond in specific ways to the meaningless noises and squiggles that are emitted by others.[16] Perhaps your own judgment-tendencies about this matter will accord with my own. But for present purposes, that doesn't matter. The key points, rather, are that Andy$_3$'s agentive phenomenology is indeed different from Andy$_1$'s, and that this difference involves the presence of language-understanding cognitive phenomenology in Andy$_1$ vs. its absence in Andy$_3$.

6 Ulterior-purpose absence partial-zombie disorder

Ordinary agentive phenomenology is richly cognitive: it is suffused by aspects of purpose, involving occurrent beliefs and occurrent desires. One way to make this manifest to oneself is to conceive of creatures whose agentive phenomenology lacks some of these cognitive features but who otherwise behave like a normal person. Andy$_3$ was a case in point. Let us now push this further in the same direction, by describing a CFP duplicate of Andy$_1$ who is even more phenomenologically impoverished than Andy$_3$.

I submit that one can robustly conceive of a person, Andy$_4$, as follows. Stage one: He is conceived as satisfying the common stage-one specification. Thus, he is a CFP duplicate of Andy$_1$, and follows an exactly similar lifelong behavioral trajectory through the world.

Stage two: He is conceived, in a way that largely involves the first-person perspective, as having the following peculiarities. First, like Andy$_3$, Andy$_4$ has

---

[16] However, I also find it fairly plausible to say that natural-language processing is going on *sub-personally and unconsciously* in Andy$_3$, by virtue of the fact that he is a functional duplicate of an ordinary language-understanding person. The numerous desires that he constantly experiences as arising out of nowhere actually arise from unconscious language processing.

language-understanding absence partial-zombie disorder; i.e. $Andy_4$ lacks language-understanding phenomenology, and thus his agentive phenomenology lacks any aspect of purposively performing speech acts or of purposefully responding to comprehended language. Second, in $Andy_4$ the on-purpose phenomenal aspect of agency is confined to bodily motions as such; i.e. he only experiences himself as moving his body or his body-parts (e.g. mouth and tongue) in thus-and-such way *in order that his body move that way*, and he never experiences any of his actions as having some further purpose either known or unknown. (He constantly experiences sudden desires to move his body or his body-parts in various ways, and normally he spontaneously acts on those desires.) Third, he has no other occurrent-belief phenomenology or occurrent-desire phenomenology, apart from the what-it's-like of the ongoing, spontaneous, bodily motion desires (and accompanying I-can-so-move and I-am-so-moving beliefs) that constantly arise within him and suffuse his agentive phenomenology.

Stage three: He is conceived as possessing both the stage-one features and the stage-two features. As so conceived, he is a CFP duplicate of $Andy_1$. Thus, there are "AC" processes at work in $Andy_4$, parallel in their functional roles in $Andy_4$ to their functional roles in $Andy_1$ (and in $Andy_2$ and $Andy_3$), such that the functional roles they play in $Andy_4$ are ones that would be appropriate to conscious ulterior motives of the sort that $Andy_1$ has. Nonetheless, $Andy_4$ is mentally very different from $Andy_1$ (and also from $Andy_2$ and $Andy_3$). Some of the "AC" states that are experienced by $Andy_1$ as ulterior motives are instead experienced by $Andy_4$ as move-thusly-for-its-own-sake motives; other "AC" states that are part of $Andy_1$'s conscious mental life are phenomenally blank in the case of $Andy_4$. I will call his experiential deficit *ulterior-purpose absence partial-zombie disorder.*[17]

I myself have no trouble conceiving of $Andy_4$, and I suspect that the same is true for you the reader. The agentive phenomenology of $Andy_4$ would be extremely different from that of $Andy_1$, as would the rest of $Andy_4$'s mental life. Since $Andy_1$ and $Andy_4$ are functional duplicates of one another and they have all the same uncontested phenomenology, the differences between them can only involve cognitive phenomenology: $Andy_1$ has lots of it, and it suffuses his agentive phenomenology with numerous aspects of ulterior purpose; but $Andy_4$ has far less of it, and has a vastly impoverished experiential life compared to $Andy_1$. ($Andy_3$ is in between, since his agentive phenomenology has *some* ulterior-purpose phenomenology but none involving language understanding.)

Of course, $Andy_4$ has all the same "AC" states as does $Andy_1$, and they play all the same functional roles—including mediating all the behavior by $Andy_4$ that external observers would construe as intelligent behavior (including linguistic

---

[17] I intend this label to be understood as characterizing a deficit in $Andy_4$'s experience, but as still leaving open whether or not $Andy_4$ in fact has ulterior purposes or in fact acts for ulterior purposes. Also, I here am using "ulterior" not to connote hidden or non-obvious aspects of purpose, but rather to signal aspects of purpose above and beyond the minimal purpose of having one's body move in thus-and-such way.

behavior) explainable by appeal to conscious occurrent desires that constitute ulterior purposes plus conscious occurrent beliefs about how to implement those purposes. The question thus arises whether it is right to say that the pertinent "AC" states in $Andy_4$ are indeed conscious beliefs and desires—albeit ones that are merely access conscious without also having the distinctive phenomenology possessed by those states in $Andy_1$. Once again, I myself feel an overwhelmingly strong pull toward a negative verdict—toward saying that his only conscious desires are body-movement desires, and his only conscious beliefs are simple beliefs about his own bodily motions (e.g. which ones he is capable of producing, and which ones he is currently making).[18] Perhaps your own judgment tendencies will accord with mine. But in any case, the key points are that $Andy_4$'s agentive phenomenology is vastly different from $Andy_1$'s, and that this difference involves cognitive-phenomenological aspects of ulterior purpose that are present in $Andy_1$'s agentive phenomenology but absent in $Andy_4$'s. $Andy_1$'s agentive experience is suffused with the phenomenology of occurrent desires that constitute ulterior motives, and with the phenomenology of occurrent beliefs about how to satisfy those desires behaviorally.

7 Absent cognitive-and-agentive-phenomenology partial-zombie disorder

Return now to $Andy_2$, in light of the robust conceivability of $Andy_3$ and $Andy_4$. $Andy_2$ was conceived as being mentally as much like $Andy_1$ as possible, apart from having no agentive phenomenology. Thus, $Andy_2$ has a rich mental life both cognitively and conatively. He understands language, and he has a rich range of conscious occurrent desires and beliefs. So, despite the fact that $Andy_2$ lacks any agentive phenomenology whereas $Andy_3$ and $Andy_4$ each have some, apart from that the mental lives of $Andy_3$ and $Andy_4$ are greatly impoverished in comparison to that of $Andy_2$.

When one reconsiders $Andy_2$ in light of these non-agentive respects in which his mental life is richer than those of either $Andy_3$ or $Andy_4$, and in light of the fact that all three of them are CFP duplicates of one another, it becomes clear that the comparatively greater richness of $Andy_2$'s mental life can only be a matter of cognitive phenomenology that he possesses but $Andy_3$ and $Andy_4$ do not possess. He possesses language-understanding phenomenology, whereas the other two do not. And he possesses the phenomenology of occurrent beliefs and desires involving matters other than his own bodily motions qua motions, whereas $Andy_4$ does not.

---

[18] However, I also find it fairly plausible to say that richly goal-directed information processing is going on sub-personally and unconsciously in $Andy_4$, by virtue of the fact that he is a functional duplicate of an ordinary person. The numerous move-thusly-for-its-own-sake desires that he constantly experiences as arising out of nowhere actually arise from sub-personal goal-directed information processing.

Bearing all this in mind, a natural question arises concerning the conceivability of a CFP duplicate of Andy$_1$ that is even more phenomenologically impoverished than is Andy$_4$. Indeed, I submit, one can robustly conceive a creature, Andy$_5$, as follows. (I find myself reluctant to call it a *person*, or to apply personal pronouns to it.)

Stage one: It is conceived as satisfying the common stage-one specification. Thus, it is a CFP duplicate of Andy$_1$, and follows an exactly similar lifelong behavioral trajectory through the world.

Stage two: It is conceived, in a way that largely involves the first-perspective, as having no agentive phenomenology, and no cognitive phenomenology at all. Its only phenomenology is the kind that skeptics about cognitive phenomenology are prepared to recognize—sensory phenomenology and other kinds of uncontested phenomenology.

Stage three: It is conceived as possessing both the stage-one features and the stage-two features. As so conceived, it is a CFP duplicate of Andy$_1$. Thus, there are "AC" processes at work in Andy$_5$, parallel in their functional roles in Andy$_5$ to their functional roles in Andy$_1$ (and in Andy$_2$ and Andy$_3$ and Andy$_4$), such that the functional roles they play in Andy$_5$ are ones that would be appropriate to the conscious cognitive states that Andy$_1$ undergoes. Nonetheless, Andy$_5$ is mentally very different from Andy$_1$ (and also from Andy$_2$ and Andy$_3$ and Andy$_4$). Phenomenologically, Andy$_5$'s mental life is a mere *sequence of raw sensations* (plus perhaps raw emotions, raw sensory images, etc.), utterly untinged by any phenomenological aspects of agency, or purpose, or cognitive states like belief or desire. The "AC" states that are experienced by Andy$_1$ as actions are experienced by Andy$_5$ as mere bodily motions; and the "AC" states that are experienced by Andy$_1$ as beliefs, desires, intentions, and other such cognitive states are all phenomenally blank for Andy$_5$. I will call his experiential deficit *absent cognitive-and-agentive-phenomenology partial-zombie disorder*.

Of course, Andy$_5$ has all the same "AC" states as does Andy$_1$, and they play all the same functional roles. So for Andy$_5$ too, the question again arises whether it is right to say that the pertinent "AC" states are indeed conscious beliefs and desires—albeit ones that are merely access conscious without also having the distinctive phenomenology possessed by those states in Andy$_1$. Again I find myself with an overwhelmingly strong pull, even stronger than in the earlier cases, toward a negative verdict—toward saying that this creature lacks altogether any conscious cognitive states, including any conscious beliefs and desires.[19] Perhaps your own judgment tendencies will accord with mine. But in any case, the key points are that Andy$_5$'s phenomenology is vastly different from Andy$_1$'s, and that this difference involves rich and pervasive elements

---

[19]   However, I also find it fairly plausible to say that richly goal-directed information processing is going on sub-personally and unconsciously in the Andy$_5$ creature, by virtue of the fact that this creature is a functional duplicate of an ordinary person. Nonetheless, it seems to me that there is no *person* here, but only an organism whose enormously impoverished conscious mental life is undergirded by remarkably rich sub-personal goal-directed information processing.

of cognitive phenomenology that are ubiquitously present in Andy$_1$'s mental life but are utterly absent in Andy$_5$'s. Andy$_5$'s experience is so utterly bereft of any non-sensory phenomenology that one hesitates to call this creature a person at all.

8 Conclusion

The partial-zombie scenarios I have described here all seem robustly conceivable. Yet, since the partial zombies all are envisioned as being CFP duplicates of Andy$_1$ (and thus of one another), the only differences between the envisioned partial zombies and Andy$_1$, and between the respective partial zombies themselves, are phenomenological. Thus, the robust conceivability of these various scenarios constitutes strong evidence that ordinary phenomenology comprises not only the uncontested kinds of phenomenal character, but further kinds as well. It includes self-as-source phenomenology, as an aspect of agentive experience. And it also includes full-fledged cognitive phenomenology—both as something that suffuses ordinary agentive phenomenology with the aspect of purposiveness, and as an element of one's overall phenomenology even apart from agentive experience. Even someone who insists, implausibly, that all these partial zombies have exactly the same conscious-as-opposed-to-unconscious states as Andy$_1$, should acknowledge that there are various kinds of agentive and cognitive phenomenology that Andy$_1$ possesses but that none of the partial zombies fully possesses.

Someone who persistently denies cognitive phenomenology despite the considerations I have adduced must either deny the robust conceivability of scenarios like those described here, or else must find a plausible, well-motivated, and non-question-begging way of arguing that the robust conceivability of such scenarios is not a suitable test for the existence of cognitive phenomenology. The burden of proof—a heavy one—is now on the shoulders of the skeptics.

Concluding autobiographical and sociological postscript

Why am I unwilling to take at face value the sincere testimony of those philosophers who adamantly deny that they have any proprietary cognitive or agentive phenomenology, rather than accepting their own testimony as accurately descriptive of their own mental lives? (After all, one possibility is that they really do lack such phenomenology, even though I myself have what they lack.) Let me briefly address this question, by citing some autobiographical considerations and also some sociological ones.

Autobiographically, I know from long personal experience what it is like (!) to be in the grip of functionalist orthodoxy concerning intentional mental states like occurrent thoughts and wishes. I believed for many years that the essence of such mental states, qua mental, is their functional role (perhaps "long-armed" functional role that incorporates certain typical-cause connections between internal states of the cognitive agent and aspects of the agent's external environment)—whereas sensory experience is fundamentally different because of its intrinsic phenomenal character. (See, for instance, Horgan 1984.) I now believe that the theoretical attractiveness of functionalist orthodoxy, as a partial framework for a materialistic metaphysic of mind—a framework for "physicalism, or something near enough" (cf. Kim 2005)—was perverting my introspective judgments, an error that was aided by the fact that sensory phenomenology is more strikingly vivid than cognitive phenomenology. (As I recall, I was awakened from my dogmatic slumbers mainly through philosophical conversation with John Tienson.) I strongly suspect that many in philosophy of mind who deny the existence of cognitive phenomenology are making that same error.

Sociologically, I find it noteworthy that my philosophy colleagues who do not work actively in philosophy of mind typically claim to find it quite obvious that there is cognitive phenomenology—often spontaneously citing familiar examples like the phenomenological difference between hearing spoken language understandingly and hearing it non-understandingly. The deniers, by contrast, seem to come largely from the ranks of those who work actively in philosophy of mind and who espouse some form of functionalist orthodoxy. This sociological phenomenon, I suggest, is yet further evidence that the deniers are reporting theoretically perverted introspective judgments.[20]

References

Block, N. (1995). "On a Confusion about a Function of Consciousness," *Behavioral and Brain Sciences*, 18: 227–287. Reprinted in N. Block, O. Flanagan, and G. Guzeldere (eds), *The Nature of Consciousness*. Cambridge, MA: MIT Press (1997), 375–415.

Goldman, A. (1993). "The Psychology of Folk Psychology," *Behavioral and Brain Sciences*, 16: 15–28.

Horgan, T. (1984). "Functionalism, Qualia, and the Inverted Spectrum," *Philosophy and Phenomenological Research*, 44: 453–69.

——(2007a). "Agentive Phenomenal Intentionality and the Limits of Introspection," *Psyche*, 13/2: 1–29.

——(2007b). "Mental Causation and the Agent-Exclusion Problem," *Erkenntnis*, 67: 183–200.

——(in press). "Causal Compatibilism about Agentive Phenomenology," in T. Horgan, M. Sabates, and D. Sosa (eds), *Supervenience in Mind*. Cambridge, MA: MIT Press.

——and Kriegel, U. (2007). "Phenomenal Epistemology: What is Phenomenal Consciousness that We May Know it So Well?" *Philosophical Issues*, 17: 123–44.

——and Tienson, J. (2002). "The Intentionality of Phenomenology and the Phenomenology of Intentionality," in D. Chalmers (ed.), *Philosophy of Mind: Classical and Contemporary Readings*. Oxford: Oxford University Press, 520–33.

——,——, and Graham, G. (2004). "Phenomenal Intentionality and the Brain in a Vat," in R. Schantz (ed.), *The Externalist Challenge*. Berlin: Walter de Gruyter, 297–317.

[20] Thanks to Tim Bayne, Dave Chalmers, Stew Cohen, Helen Daly, Aeyn Edwards, Brian Fiala, Richard Healey, Joe Levine, Eric Schwitzgebel, Mark Timmons, and two anonymous referees for helpful comments and/or discussion.

——,——, and Graham, G. (2006). "Internal-World Skepticism and the Self-Presentational Nature of Phenomenal Consciousness," in U. Kriegel and K. Williford (eds), *Self-Representational Approaches to Consciousness*. Cambridge, MA: MIT Press, 41–61.

Kim, J. (2005). *Physicalism, or Something Near Enough*. Princeton: Princeton University Press.

Lormand, E. (1996). "Nonphenomenal Consciousness," *Noûs*, 30: 242–61.

Nelkin, N. (1989). "Propositional Attitudes and Consciousness," *Philosophy and Phenomenological Research*, 49: 413–30.

Pitt, D. (2004). "The Phenomenology of Cognition: Or What is It Like to Think that P?" *Philosophy and Phenomenological Research*, 69: 1–36.

Searle, J. (1980). "Minds, Brains, and Programs," *The Behavioral and Brain Sciences*, 3: 417–57.

Siewert, C. (1998). *The Significance of Consciousness*. Princeton: Princeton University Press.

Strawson, G. (1994). *Mental Reality*. Cambridge, MA: MIT Press.

Cognitive Phenomenology as the Basis of Unconscious Content

Uriah Kriegel

1 Introduction: Phenomenal intentionality and the question of unconscious intentionality

This paper's title pays tribute to Brian Loar's seminal paper "Phenomenal Intentionality as the Basis of Mental Content." Whereas mainstream analytic philosophy of mind has by and large assumed that the phenomenon of intentionality can be understood independently of the phenomenon of consciousness, Loar's paper (which was circulating since the late nineties) brought to the fore the possibility that all intentional content might be somehow grounded in a kind of distinctively conscious intentionality, which he called "phenomenal intentionality."

One way to precisify Loar's thesis is by appeal to the familiar distinction between derived and underived intentionality. Grice (1957) famously argued that the intentionality of language is merely derivative, in that a linguistic symbol such as c ˆa ˆt is not in and of itself more suited for representing cats than dogs, and ultimately derives its content from speaker intentions, whereas the intentionality of the mental is non-derivative, in that mental states represent what they do in and of themselves. One way to interpret Loar's thesis is as claiming that in reality, only phenomenally conscious states represent what they do in and of themselves, i.e. non-derivatively, while the intentionality of phenomenally *unconscious* states ultimately derives from phenomenal intentionality. (Note well: by "phenomenally unconscious" states I mean states that are unconscious in the phenomenal sense of "conscious"; I do not mean to refer to, or even suggest the existence of, states that are unconscious but nonetheless have a phenomenal character.)

Independently of Loar's exegesis, the emerging thesis is quite important. We may formulate it as follows:

(PI) The only non-derivative intentionality is phenomenal intentionality.

This thesis has been the cornerstone of an approach to intentionality which has been gathering momentum in recent years, in large part due to the work of Loar, as well as of such philosophers as Searle, Strawson, and Horgan, and which we may call the Phenomenal Intentionality Research Program (see Kriegel and Horgan 2011).[1] The central point of this program can be appreciated by contrast to the kind of approach to intentionality that sees it as altogether independent of consciousness.

Since work on intentionality started flourishing in the late 1970s, the dominant research program for understanding intentionality has been what we may call the Naturalist–Externalist Research Program (NERP). There are many ways to characterize this program; here is one back-of-the-envelope characterization: the source of intentionality is a certain natural relation that obtains between internal states of the brain and external states of the world; all other intentionality is ultimately based on this natural relation. Different theories within this research program offer different accounts of (a) the relevant natural relation and/or (b) the way it grounds all other intentionality. Prominent theories are associated with philosophers such as Dretske, Fodor, Harman, and Millikan.[2]

The Phenomenal Intentionality Research Program (PIRP) can be modeled on the same theoretical structure. Here, the rough idea is that the source of all intentionality is the phenomenal character of conscious states, typically construed as a purely internal affair; all other intentionality occurs in virtue of appropriate relations to phenomenally conscious states. Again, different theories within PIRP would differ most centrally on (a) the kind of phenomenal character they take to constitute intentionality (and how it does so) and/or (b) the relation to phenomenal consciousness they take to underlie unconscious intentionality.[3]

Several important questions arise within the framework of PIRP. Perhaps the most central are the following three:

- Why should we believe the thesis that only phenomenal intentionality is non-derivative?

---

[1] See Searle (1991, 1992); Loar (1995, 2003); Strawson (1994, 2005, 2008); Horgan and Tienson (2002); Horgan and Graham (2009). Other defenses of (PI) include McGinn (1988); Horst (1996); Kriegel (2003a, 2007, forthcoming); Georgalis (2006); Bourget (forthcoming); and as far as I can tell Brentano (1874) and Husserl (1900).
[2] See Dretske (1980, 1981, 1988); Fodor (1990); Millikan (1984); Harman (1987). For example, Dretske (1988) combines a teleo-informational account of the all-important natural relation and an intention-based account of the way it grounds other intentionality. The view is that internal states of certain systems are intentional in virtue of being recruited to perform a certain function within the system due to the informational connections they bear to external conditions, and anything intentional that is not intentional for this reason is intentional because we use it with a certain intention (the intention having its intentionality from the relevant natural relation).
[3] Later on I will discuss in passing some of the suggestions that have floated for understanding how phenomenal character grounds intentionality in phenomenal intentionality. For a more thorough discussion, see Kriegel forthcoming ch. 3.

- What is the nature of phenomenal intentionality? In particular, what is it about phenomenal character that endows it with intentional content?
- What is the nature of non-phenomenal intentionality? More specifically, what is the relation a non-phenomenal item must bear to a phenomenally intentional state in order to exhibit intentionality?

What I want to do in the bulk of this paper is pursue this last question. There may arise for some readers legitimate worries about the viability and merit of PIRP, but I propose to set these worries aside here.[4] The reason is partly substantive but mostly methodological. Substantively, it is simply my opinion, for which I argued elsewhere (Kriegel 2003a, 2007, 2011 ch. 1) but will not here, that PIRP is in fact viable and merits pursuit. Methodologically, research programs in both philosophy and science rarely win converts by *a priori* demonstration of their viability and merit; rather, it is when the research program is actively pursued, and its pursuit is shown to be fruitful and productive, that it flourishes and attracts proponents and exponents. Actually pursuing PIRP is therefore central to making the case for its viability and merit.[5,6]

[4] Proponents of NERP are typically mystified by the notion that phenomenal character can blossom into intentionality: they allow that there may be a sense in which a phenomenal character can "fit" an external object, but suspect that it would also fit any qualitatively indistinguishable object. However, a parallel worry about the sources of intentionality also animates many proponents of PIRP, who are equally mystified as to how external connections can blossom into intentionality: such relations can perhaps "connect" an internal item to an external object, but presumably they would connect it to any perfectly collocated external item. (For example, they would connect the internal item just as well to the fusion of the external object's undetached parts. For this consideration, see Loar 1995; Horgan and Tienson 2002; Georgalis 2006.) These foundational challenges strike me as tremendous for both research programs, and although some insightful work has already been done by way of addressing them, few philosophers are satisfied that the challenges have been fully met. At the same time, few philosophers take this as reason to suspend research within NERP, and the same attitude should attach, I contend, to PIRP.

[5] Thus, I find that PIRP has been hurt by its underdog status inasmuch as insufficient energy has been channeled toward its pursuit individually and regardless of the prospects of other research programs. Much more energy has been devoted to arguing that it *should* be pursued than to pursuing it. This is perhaps an understandable predicament for an ascendant research program in the initial phases, but there also comes a time where the program has to actually be pursued.

[6] Furthermore, proponents of NERP and PIRP have tended to be quite confrontational, assuming that the two programs are in competition with one another and only one of them can be viable, but there are also ways of being more conciliatory. One way is to hold that a general theory of intentionality will have to incorporate elements from both programs. For example, according to Horgan and collaborators (2002, 2004), the kind of intentionality which can be the basis for all other intentionality must involve both a phenomenal character and a natural relation to external items. A different way to be conciliatory, which I prefer, is to hold that there are in fact two distinct properties, each with its legitimate claim on the term "intentionality," such that one behaves roughly the way indicated in NERP and one roughly the way indicated in PIRP. Thus, in his response to Searle's (1991) claim that intentionality depends essentially on consciousness, Davies (1995) argues that dependence on consciousness characterizes some kinds of aboutness but not others; which kinds of aboutness should be called "intentionality" may then be a merely verbal matter. My own inclination would be to call the NERP-ly property *representation* and reserve the term *intentionality* for the PIRP-ly property (the point of PIRP could then be put as the rejection of a "representational account of intentionality"). But if this labeling policy is deemed insufficiently neutral, I would be perfectly happy to use the labels "intentionality$_1$" and "intentionality$_2$" instead.

Our central agenda is thus to seek a satisfactory account of unconscious intentionality within the PIRP framework. Call this the *unconscious intentionality question*:

(UIQ) For any phenomenally unconscious item *x*, such that *x* has intentional content, what makes it the case (i) that *x* has the intentional content it does and (ii) that *x* has an intentional content at all?

In §2, I propose an answer to UIQ, an answer that takes its cue from Dennett's (1971, 1981, 1987) interpretivist approach to intentionality. On the account I offer, what makes a phenomenally unconscious item have the intentional content it does, and an intentional content at all, is (very roughly) that it is profitably interpreted to have that content. For reasons we will see in §4, an upshot of this account is that all phenomenally unconscious intentionality derives ultimately from a certain type of cognitive phenomenology, a notion I will introduce and motivate in §3. The upshot, then, is that without cognitive phenomenology there would be no unconscious intentionality. I will close with more general remarks on the crucial role of cognitive phenomenology in the relationship between mind and world.

2   Interpretivism

(PI) implies that all unconscious intentionality derives from conscious intentionality.[7] Interestingly, there is a NERP-ish approach to intentionality that takes *all* intentionality to be derived. The idea of this section is to adopt this approach but restrict it to unconscious intentionality (in an independently motivated way).

The approach I have in mind is Dennett's interpretivist "intentional stance" theory.[8] On this view, there is a web of intentional concepts, such as belief and desire, that we can use to produce a rough-and-ready interpretation of conspecifics and other creatures in real time and "on the go." When we use this web of intentional concepts, we take a stance toward our targets of interpretation that involves conceiving of them as intentional systems; this is the intentional stance. The intentional stance produces a kind of interpretation that is a good enough approximation of the truth to make it useful, but not good enough that we can take it at face value. If we operated without constraints on the employment of time, energy, and other resources, we could produce a much more accurate theory of conspecifics' behavior, in principle a fully accurate one; but this other interpretation would deploy a web of neurophysiological and

---

[7] I say "implies" because although (PI) states that only conscious intentionality is underived, and this entails that all unconscious intentionality is derived. It would strictly *follow* that all unconscious intentionality derives *from* conscious intentionality only on the assumption that all derived intentionality derives *from* underived intentionality. This assumption is not tautologous, however, as far as I can tell. Thus, Bourget (forthcoming) seems committed to its denial.

[8] The approach is naturalistic in that it denies that intentionality is a supernatural phenomenon and attempts to cast intentionality as part of the natural order, with its relatively familiar ingredients. It is not, however, comfortably classified as an instance of NERP as the latter was characterized in §1.

broadly physical concepts, not the web of intentional concepts we use in everyday life. In everyday life, the most cost-beneficial balance between resource expenditure and interpretative accuracy happens to be that provided by the intentional stance.

On this picture, it is not so much because certain intentional facts hold that certain interpretations become possible as that because those interpretations are possible that the intentional facts hold. Thus, for someone to believe that p just is for the best exercise of the intentional stance to assign to them the belief that p. As Dennett (1981: 72) puts it, "all there is to really and truly believing that p is being an intentional system for which p occurs as a belief in the best (most predictive) interpretation." On this interpretivist view, for an internal state to have intentional content C is for the state's subject to be best interpreted (within the framework of the intentional stance) as being in an internal state with C.

Interpreting someone to be in a certain intentional state is itself an intentional act, however: the act whose content is that someone is in some intentional state. Therefore, Dennett's interpretivism entails that the intentionality of each intentional state derives from the intentionality of some *other* intentional state, namely, the relevant interpretive state (whose own content presumably derives from that of a second-order interpretive act). It is thus an upshot of Dennett's view that all intentionality is derived (see Dennett 1988, 1990).

An immediate difficulty with this position is that it leads straightforwardly to infinite regress: an item x can acquire the content C only if there is an item y with content $C^\star$, where $C^\star = <x$ has C>, but for y to have that content, there would have to be an item z with content $C^{\star\star}$, $C^{\star\star} = <y$ has $C^\star>$, and so on *ad infinitum*.[9] The only way to stop the regress is to posit a class of privileged intentional states, such that (i) their intentionality does not derive from interpretation and (ii) they have interpretive acts as a subset.[10]

My suggestion is to designate phenomenally conscious intentional states as that privileged class, with phenomenally conscious interpretive acts as the requisite subset. Some independent story would have to be told about what endows phenomenally *conscious* intentional states with their intentional content; for that, see Kriegel forthcoming chs. 2, 3. But once they do, and assuming some of them are phenomenally conscious acts of interpretation, we can account for the intentionality of phenomenally unconscious states as derived from theirs. To a first approximation, the resulting answer to UIQ would be this: what makes an unconscious item have the intentional content it does, and to have one at all, is that the best exercise of the intentional stance would

---

[9]   It is possible to avoid this infinite regress simply by advancing interpretivism as a non-reductive (or non-constitutive) account of intentionality (Child 1994). But the kind of interpretivism I want to offer as an account of *unconscious* intentionality is reductive, so I focus in this discussion on the reductive version. Anyway, a non-reductive interpretivism is not really an *account* of intentionality—it is more like a *comment* on it.

[10]   For a paper-length development of the point made in this paragraph, see Kriegel 2010a.

produce an interpretation according to which that item has the intentional content it does, and has one at all.[11]

Note that in the first instance, the relevant interpretation need not itself be phenomenally conscious. However, if it is not, then as noted above, it must have its own (interpretive) content in virtue of being interpreted by some second-order interpretation, and that second-order interpretation would itself be either conscious or interpreted by a third-order interpretive state, and so on. Ultimately, this regress of interpretations would have to end with a conscious interpretive act. In other words, the relevant interpretations need not be conscious, but they must be part of (potentially one-stepped) chains of interpretations that are capped by conscious interpretations.

We can simplify somewhat the formulation of this interpretivist account of unconscious intentionality by construing unconscious intentionality as the right sort of *response-dependent property* (Kriegel 2010a). These are properties characterized in terms of their disposition to elicit certain responses in certain respondents under certain conditions.[12] Since we are dealing here with the *best* exercise of the intentional stance, we can think of the relevant respondents, in the first instance, as *ideal interpreters*, that is, subjects who exercise the intentional stance perfectly under all conditions. The thesis is then that for any unconscious intentional state, there is *some* possible ideal interpreter who, under *some* conditions, produces an intentional interpretation of that state, and moreover does so *consciously*.[13] If so, we may formulate interpretivism relatively economically as follows:

(A) For any unconscious item x and intentional content C, x has C iff x is such as to elicit in ideal interpreters under some conditions a conscious intentional state with the content $<x$ has C>.

Or perhaps more rigorously:

(A1) For any unconscious item x and intentional content C, x has C iff there are a possible conscious item y, a possible ideal interpreter N, and possible conditions K, such that (i) y has the content $<x$ has C> and (ii) x is such as to elicit y in N under K.

I will now offer some clarifications (see also Kriegel 2010a)—in particular, concerning the nature of interpretation, ideal interpreters, and ideal conditions—and then suggest that this view is superior to the alternatives.

I start with clarification of the nature of interpretation. There are, in fact, several possible views on the nature of interpretation, and different versions of interpretivism

---

[11] I mention something like this account as an option in passing in Kriegel (2003a and 2010a), and expand on it in a more endorsing mode in Kriegel (2007).

[12] See Johnston (1989) for a more precise characterization. The key is this formula: "x is C iff x is such as to produce an x-directed response R in a group of subjects S under conditions K" (Johnston 1989: 145). When this biconditional holds *a priori*, then C is a response-dispositional property.

[13] That is, for any unconscious intentional state, there is some ideal interpreter and some circumstances, such that the hierarchy of interpretations that state induces in that interpreter under those circumstances is capped at the first step. Thus, we can conceive of an ideal interpreter all of whose mental states are conscious (but who does not have fewer mental states for that).

will differ in adopting different views on that matter. In the literature on interpretation, three main theories seem to compete (Goldman 1989): theory theory, simulation theory, and rationality theory.[14] According to theory theory, intentional ascription is based on something like inference to the best explanation from the behavior (including verbal behavior) of the target of ascription, the kind of inference characteristic of theorizing in general. According to simulation theory, intentional ascription is based on the off-line tokening of the very intentional states ascribed, by way of simulation of the target of ascription's internal goings-on. According to rationality theory, intentional ascription is based first and foremost on the application of a principle of charity that casts the target of ascription as a rational agent whose intentional states are by and large justified. In addition to these three "pure" theories that assume all intentional ascription is carried out by a single mechanism, there are also "impure" theories that combine two or three of the above mechanisms. If the above are the *only* three interpretive mechanisms, this would mean that there are seven possible views of how interpretation works.[15]

For my part, although I cannot argue for this here, it seems to me that a simulation mechanism is most plausible for the ascription of phenomenal states, including phenomenally intentional states. So it would not be relevant as much for the ascription of phenomenally *unconscious* states, including unconscious intentional states. For those, my view is that interpretation involves the cooperation of a theory mechanism and a rationality mechanism. More specifically, ascription of unconscious intentional states proceeds in two phases: first, inference to the best explanation produces a number of possible ascriptions fully consistent with the behavioral explananda; then, the principle of charity is used to pick among them the single ascription that casts the target of interpretation in the most rational light.[16] Thus, my version of interpretivism appeals to a combination of theorization and rationalization as the elements of the relevant kind of interpretation.

It may be objected that this view cannot account for altogether non-mental intentionality, such as we find in language, traffic signs, representative art, etc., since it is unclear what the behavioral data for inference to the best explanation are supposed to be. The interpretivist has two options here, it seems to me. One is to insist on theorization-cum-rationalization for non-mental intentionality, but offer different data for the relevant inferences to the best explanation. Another, perhaps more promising option is to ground non-mental intentionality in unconscious intentionality, thus

---

[14] In some discussions of these matters, the term "interpretationism" is used to mean something like what I here call (following Goldman) "rationality theory." Obviously this should not be confused with the interpretivism I am defending here. The latter accounts for intentionality in terms of interpretation. The former offers an account of how interpretation works.

[15] These are: theory; simulation; rationality; theory + simulation; simulation + rationality; theory + rationality; theory + simulation + rationality.

[16] I expand on the mechanics of charity-based ascription of non-phenomenal intentional states in Kriegel (2010b).

offering a two-step derivation of non-mental intentionality from phenomenal intentionality. For example, an interpretivist could hold that non-mental intentionality derives from speaker intentions, as per familiar Gricean intention-based semantics. These speaker intentions are unconscious, and therefore derive their own content (according to interpretivism) from conscious interpretation. This would require the Gricean account to apply not only to linguistic representation, but indeed it has recently been argued that the Gricean account applies just as well to depictive representation (Abell 2005; Blumson 2006).[17] On the emerging view, all intentional content derives ultimately from phenomenally intentional content, though it may derive from it in several stages. I am attracted to this view.

Having clarified the nature of interpretation, let us consider the nature of an ideal interpreter. I said that an ideal interpreter is one who exercises the intentional stance perfectly under all conditions, but more can be said. For starters, we may construe an interpreter (in general) as any subject capable of entering interpretive states, that is, states of ascribing content to something. How to characterize what makes an interpreter ideal is not a simple matter. One option is virtue-epistemological: an ideal interpreter is a well-informed interpreter who exhibits (to the highest degree) all the epistemic virtues that bear on the production of interpretive states. Another option is teleofunctionalist: an ideal interpreter is a well-informed interpreter whose mechanisms responsible for the production of interpretive states always function exactly as they are supposed to. The best characterization for our present purposes, however, is to simply construe the ideal interpreter as an epistemic agent parachuted into the world (so to speak) with no knowledge of the facts we are appealing to her to fix, but complete knowledge of all other facts (as well as perfect reasoning capacities). That is: our ideal interpreter is one who approaches an interpretive task with (i) complete knowledge of all the non-intentional facts and all the phenomenal-intentional facts, (ii) no knowledge of any other facts, (iii) the capacity to draw every valid deductive inference and every justified non-deductive inference, and (iv) the capacity to avoid drawing any invalid deductive inference and any unjustified non-deductive inference.[18] This, if anyone, is an ideal interpreter.

---

[17] This would take care of the derivation of the intentionality of paintings, photographs, etc., as well as the intentionality of traffic signs and other forms of symbols that combine linguistic and pictorial representations. If there are non-mental representations that are neither linguistic nor pictorial, nor based in stipulative conventions (which are also, and more straightforwardly, derivative from intentions), then the interpretivist would need to either show that they too can derive from Gricean intentions, or else provide an altogether new account of how they derive their intentional content from conscious interpretation.

[18] This may have to be further tweaked, given that facts described as concerning unconscious intentionality may turn out to be reducible to facts describable in non-intentional (e.g. neurophysiological) terms. It could be insisted, of course, that such facts do not qualify as non-intentional facts, on the principle that a fact qualifies as intentional if there is an intentional description of it (and regardless of whether there is also, in addition, a non-intentional description of it). But alternatively, we could modify the characterization of the ideal interpreter by making explicit reference to the description under which the ideal interpreter knows the facts it does.

Having now clarified the nature of interpretation and the ideal interpreter, let us next consider the nature of ideal conditions. Let us say that a condition K is ideal relative to a subject S and a task T just in case S can, under C, perform T the most competently that S can perform T. Given this construal of ideal conditions, and the above construal of the ideal interpretation, it would seem that any conditions are ideal relative to the ideal interpreter and the task of interpretation.[19] However, it may be worthwhile to insist that the conditions relevant to the formulation of interpretivism are conditions of forced choice: the ideal interpreter must either assent to "x has C" or dissent from it—suspending judgment is not an option.

Note that an ideal interpreter, because ideal, would also (correctly) assign content to phenomenally intentional states.[20] So (A) holds not only of unconscious items but also of conscious items. However, the reason it holds is very different in each case. With *conscious* intentionality, the ideal interpreter *tracks* intentionality. With *unconscious* intentionality, s/he *constitutes* intentionality. There is something akin to a Euthyphro Dilemma here: does the ideal interpreter assign content C to item x because x has C or does x have C because the ideal interpreter assigns to it C? With conscious intentionality it is the former, with unconscious intentionality the latter. Crispin Wright (1992) claims that such a dilemma applies to all biconditionals of this form, and when the biconditional is supposed to capture a genuinely response-dependent property, it must hold *a priori*. If so, we should probably modify (A1) as follows:

(A2) Epistemically necessarily, for any unconscious item x and intentional content C, x has C iff there are a possible conscious item y, a possible ideal interpreter N, and possible conditions K, such that (i) y has the content $<x$ has C$>$ and (ii) x is such as to elicit y in N under K.

In this formulation, I use epistemic necessity as a formally well-behaved gloss on aprioricity. Roughly, p is epistemically necessary iff p is true in every centered world, i.e. in every possible world considered as actual.[21]

It is also important to note that (A)–(A2) do not require in any way the existence of an actual interpreter, let alone an ideal one. They insist that an unconscious item must have the *disposition* to elicit the right interpretation in the right interpreters, but not that

[19] It may be thought that since the ideal interpreter is defined in terms of the *capacity* to draw inferences, and capacities can be inhibited, that there are some sub-ideal conditions for the ideal interpreter's execution of its interpretive function, namely, the conditions under which the relevant capacity is in fact inhibited. If so, we would need to specify in the response-dependent biconditional that the response is elicited in other conditions, conditions under which the interpreter's capacity to draw inferences is not inhibited.

[20] If this is not the case, and the ideal interpreter may sometimes ascribe to a phenomenal state a content different from the one the state carries in virtue of its phenomenal character, then the problem I discuss in this paragraph does not arise. It may be thought that another problem arises, namely, that there is tension between the interpretation-based ascription of content and the phenomenally based ascription. But this is not really a problem, since interpretivism put forward here is not an account of phenomenal intentionality, only of non-phenomenal intentionality. So any interpretation-based ascription is not constitutive of the content of phenomenal states.

[21] For more on epistemic necessity, see Chalmers (forthcoming).

the disposition must be *manifested*. The non-existence of ideal interpreters only means that the relevant disposition cannot be manifested, not that it is not present.

There may be cases where there is no single best interpretation of some item. In those cases, one ideal interpreter would ascribe to an item content C_1 and another would ascribe to it content C_2. In such circumstances, (A) entails that the item's content is indeterminate as between C_1 and C_2. But this kind of content indeterminacy should be extremely infrequent, and to that extent harmless—it is not the kind of corrosive indeterminacy threatened by inscrutability worries. For there is no reason to suppose that in standard cases there is more than one best interpretation. Crucially, since the ideal interpreter knows all the phenomenal-intentional facts, it knows that ordinarily I consciously think of rabbits rather than undetached rabbit parts, and would therefore interpret my relevant *unconscious* states as about rabbits, not undetached rabbit parts. Such an interpretation would make better sense of the cognitive, inferential interactions among my various intentional states, some of which are conscious and some unconscious.

Our interpretivism about unconscious intentionality would bring in its train all the hallmarks of the more standard, global type of interpretivism we find in Dennett, Davidson, and others. For example, interpretivism often goes hand in hand with *holism*, the view that contents cannot be assigned to individual items but must be assigned to whole groups at once. This is because creatures' behavior admits of several coherent interpretations in which changes in the assignment of content to one item are compensated for by changes in the assignment of content to another item. For example, a student who shows up in the wrong room on the day of the exam may be interpreted either as (i) believing that the exam is in (what is in fact) the wrong room and desiring to take the exam or (ii) believing that the exam is in (what is in fact) the right room and desiring not to take the exam. This kind of holism certainly characterizes the interpretation of behavior caused by unconscious mental states—indeed, we may suppose that our student's beliefs and desires are unconscious. Thus, interpretivism about unconscious intentionality, as captured in (A2), results in holism about unconscious content.

A related doctrine often associated with interpretivism is that massive error and irrationality are *a priori* impossible. This is because when several coherent interpretations are available, competent selection among them appeals to a principle of charity. For example, if your interlocutor points at your new laptop and says "congratulations on your new capsicum," it is possible to interpret her as either (i) desiring to congratulate you on a new pepper and believing that the word "capsicum" means pepper or (ii) desiring to congratulate you on a new laptop and believing that the word "capsicum" means laptop. A competent interpreter would always opt for the second interpretation, even though both accommodate the data equally well, because (presumably) it is the more charitable interpretation. The combination of holism and the employment of the principle of charity then tends to undermine the ascription of erroneous and/or irrational contents to other items in the relevant web of unconscious items, with the result that sweeping error and irrationality are ruled out *a priori*.

Another doctrine often associated with interpretivism is a kind of irrealism or instrumentalism about intentionality. According to such instrumentalism, intentionality is a useful fiction: the practice of intentional ascription is useful for the conduct of everyday life, but does not strictly speaking issue in true descriptions of what actually goes on in the world. At the same time, while ascription of unconscious intentionality is certainly useful, and moreover its existence cannot be appreciated independently of its usefulness according to interpretivism, it does not follow that it is a *fiction*. In fact, a common form of argument reasons from usefulness to truth via inference to the best explanation (Fodor and Lepore 1993). The issues raised by this question are too involved to address here, but let me go on the record expressing my preference for a non-instrumentalist reading of (A2). After all, the response-dependent property is fully integrated in the natural order, is publicly accessible, etc.[22]

This, then, is the interpretivism about unconscious intentionality that I propose. What motivates the view to me is that it is vastly preferable to the alternative accounts of unconscious intentionality one can find in the literature. I argue for this in detail in Kriegel (2011: ch. 4), where I consider three alternative accounts, which I call *potentialism, inferentialism,* and *eliminativism.* According to potentialism (Searle 1991, 1992), an unconscious state has the intentional content it does in virtue of potentially having the phenomenal character it potentially does, and has intentional content at all in virtue of potentially having phenomenal character at all. According to inferentialism (Loar 2003; Horgan and Graham 2009), what makes an unconscious state have intentional content is that it is inferentially or functionally integrated into a cognitive system in which some intentional states are phenomenally conscious; what makes it have the specific intentional content it does, rather than another, is that it plays the specific inferential or functional role it does, and not another, within that cognitive system. According to eliminativism (Strawson 2008, Georgalis 2006), meanwhile, there simply is no unconscious intentionality. The considerations bearing against these accounts are many and varied, but strikingly, all three appear to get wrong the extension of unconscious intentionality. They leave us with less intentionality than we are antecedently inclined to think there is. Potentialism cannot account for the intentionality of unconscious states that are not even potentially conscious, such as visual states in the dorsal stream (Davies 1995; Horgan and Kriegel 2008). Inferentialism cannot account for the intentionality of inferentially insulated unconscious states, as well as of zombie states. And eliminativism cannot account for *any* antecedently plausible instance of unconscious intentionality. For details, see Kriegel (2011: ch. 4).

---

[22] The view could be interpreted as a kind of "response-dependent realism," akin to the kind of view McDowell (1985) has been pushing in meta-ethics, where moral properties are construed as secondary qualities, but this is taken to be a form of realism. There are legitimate questions as to whether this is genuine realism and if so in what sense, but in any event, the view is more realist in spirit than Dennett's.

My claim is that interpretivism returns the right results in all cases in which it seems antecedently that we should count a certain unconscious state as intentional. Importantly, there is something principled in the way interpretivism manages this. The reason is that what makes it desirable to count something as in the extension of intentionality is not accidentally related to what makes it the case that interpretivism returns the result that it is a case of intentionality. There are two kinds of fact that make it desirable to count a given state as intentional: (i) that it is so treated by cognitive science and (ii) that it is so treated by folk psychology. Certainly in the former case, but probably also in the latter, what makes it desirable to count the state as intentional is that it is explanatorily beneficial to do so. But whenever it is explanatorily beneficial to treat a state as intentional, an ideal interpreter would do so, and therefore interpretivism would ratify the state's status as intentional. Thus, it is no accident that interpretivism returns the independently desirable results in the above cases and would probably do so in other cases. The only way it could fail to do so is if there were unconscious states to which we have independent reasons to ascribe intentionality but for which it is explanatorily useless to do. In all likelihood, however, there could be no such states: unlike phenomenally intentional states, we have no first-person acquaintance with unconscious intentional states; our only reason to believe in them is that doing so is theoretically or explanatorily profitable from the third-person perspective.

In the assessment of scientific theories, it is common to distinguish empirical and theoretical virtues: the empirical virtues concern accounting for the data, the theoretical virtues concern parsimony, simplicity, unity, clarity, elegance, conservatism, etc. It is natural to think that a similar distinction applies to philosophical theories, where the independently desirable results play the role of data, such that returning those results is the empirical virtue (or "quasi-empirical," if we prefer).[23] It is clear from the above discussion that interpretivism is more (quasi-)empirically virtuous than its competition.[24] It is, in effect, massively *confirmed*, whereas alternative accounts are often enough *disconfirmed*.

3 Cognitive phenomenology

The most phenomenologically impressive experiences we undergo are visual experiences and somatic experiences: color perception and pain/pleasure, in particular, are often phenomenologically overwhelming. But there is a variety of milder phenomenologies we often experience. For starters, other perceptual phenomenologies, such

---

[23] One reason to treat this particular test—consistency with intuition and existing scientific practice—as (quasi-)empirical is that it is a familiar thought in philosophical methodology that in the same sense in which empirical theories face the tribunal of experience, philosophical theories face the tribunal of intuition and of existing scientific practice. A philosophical theory does not make contact with any other sorts of data. The only data for philosophical theorizing are judgments produced either "intuitively" or on the basis of "our best theory of the world."

[24] In Kriegel (2011: ch. 4), I argue that interpretivism is also more theoretically virtuous.

as olfactory and proprioceptive phenomenology, can be quite subtle and unimposing, as can the phenomenology of sufficiently mild background moods.

Indeed, some phenomenologies may be so unimpressive that it becomes controversial whether they exist. There are many examples of this, but the one I will focus on here is what is often referred to as *cognitive phenomenology*. The idea is that there is a distinctive phenomenology involved in having an occurrent thought, which moreover is not just the phenomenology of the imagery accompanying the thought, but is proprietary to occurrent thoughts.[25] To say that this phenomenology is proprietary, or *sui generis*, is to say that it does not reduce to some other, already familiar (perceptual or somatic, in particular) phenomenology.

It is, of course, controversial whether such proprietary cognitive phenomenology exists, but several authors have recently argued that it does (Goldman 1993; Strawson 1994; Peacocke 1998; Siewert 1998; Horgan and Tienson 2002; Kriegel 2003b; Pitt 2004; Klausen 2008; Tennant 2009).[26] The view that it exists admits of several grades (Kriegel 2003b). The strongest claim would be that every type of occurrent thought has its own cognitive phenomenology, such that the cognitive-phenomenal character of believing that p is different from that of believing that q (whenever $p \neq q$). A weaker claim would be that cognitive phenomenology varies with attitude but not with content, such that believing that p is phenomenally different from desiring that p but not from believing that q.[27] The weakest claim is that there is a single cognitive-phenomenal character shared by all conscious cognitive states. Proponents of PIRP typically assert the strongest of these claims. And so they should: the more phenomenology there is, the more phenomenal intentionality there is, and the more plausible it becomes that all intentionality derives from phenomenal intentionality.[28]

In the literature, there are three main argumentative strategies that have been wielded by way of defending the existence of cognitive phenomenology: arguments from phenomenal contrast, arguments from phenomenological overwhelm, and arguments from first-person knowability.

In arguments from phenomenal contrast, two overall conscious episodes of a subject are presented, such that (i) it is intuitively clear that there is an overall phenomenal difference between the two, and (ii) the best explanation of this difference is that one of the two episodes exhibits a cognitive phenomenology that the other does not. Perhaps the best-known instance of this argumentative strategy is Strawson's (1994) contrast of the overall experiences of a French speaker and a non-French-speaker when

---

[25] It is not part of this claim that there can be no phenomenally unconscious occurrent thoughts. The claim is merely that, in addition to those, there are also phenomenally conscious occurrent thoughts.

[26] For defenses by more historical figures, see Husserl 1900 and Moore 1953.

[27] This view could be naturally augmented by the claim that there are also differences in the phenomenal intensity of attitudes: believing that p with great conviction is phenomenally different from believing that p with some doubt in one's heart.

[28] At the same time, it is important to note that (PI) can turn out to be true even if there is no such thing as cognitive phenomenology at all. Thus, cognitive phenomenology is unnecessary for PIRP, though it would be greatly helpful, so to speak.

they listen to the news in French. Strawson argues that there is a phenomenal difference between their overall conscious episodes, and that the difference is best accounted for in terms of an element of understanding-experience present only in the French speaker's stream of consciousness.[29]

In arguments from phenomenological overwhelm, the contrast between two episodes is replaced with a single episode, clearly cognitive in nature, whose phenomenal character is supposed to be overwhelming in the way that approximates the phenomenological overwhelm involved in visual and somatic experiences, and due to which they are unquestionable instances of phenomenality. Perhaps the best-known instance of this argument is based on the sudden and acute onset of an experience of grasping something. Consider the following passage (Mangan 2001; Chudnoff forthcoming):

A newspaper is better than a magazine. A seashore is a better place than the street. At first it is better to run than to walk. You may have to try several times. It takes some skill but it is easy to learn. Even young children can enjoy it. Once successful, complications are minimal. Birds seldom get too close. Rain, however, soaks in very fast. Too many people doing the same thing can also cause problems. One needs lots of room. If there are no complications it can be very peaceful. A rock will serve as an anchor. If things break loose from it, however, you will not get a second chance.

This passage elicits mostly puzzlement, until one is told that it is about *kites*. Once informed, one typically undergoes the acute onset of the grasp experience of which I speak.[30]

In arguments from first-person knowability, it is pointed out that the knowledge we have of some of our occurrent cognitive states is the kind of knowledge we have only of our phenomenally conscious states, from which it is inferred that these cognitive states must be phenomenally conscious.[31] Thus, Pitt (2004) argues that we have an immediate, non-inferential knowledge of some cognitive states (as well as their contents), and that only phenomenally conscious states are knowable in this way.

---

[29] For other arguments of this form, see Peacocke (1998), Horgan and Tienson (2002), Kriegel (2003b), Pitt (2004), and Chudnoff (forthcoming).

[30] Similar arguments are presented in Goldman's (1993) and Mangan's (2001) discussion of tip-of-the-tongue phenomenology, Siewert's (1998, this volume) and Siewert's (this volume) and Chudnoff's (forthcoming) discussion of intellectual Gestalt shifts. The tip-of-the-tongue experience is familiar to most of us and is claimed by Goldman and Mangan to involve a distinctively cognitive phenomenology. Siewert's delayed understanding concerns experiences in which we suddenly understand a piece of text we have been rereading and trying to understand for a while (imagine suddenly thinking of kites on your own when reading the above passage). Intellectual Gestalt shifts, meanwhile, concern experiences in which a phenomenon is construed one way but is suddenly reinterpreted another way; Siewert (this volume) illustrates this with an entertaining exchange he heard in Miami on an unbearably hot day, in which one woman said to the other, "I am so hot," and the other responded, "you don't have to brag about it."

[31] Schematically, the argument proceeds as follows: we have a special, immediate access to our cognitive states (and their contents); only to conscious experiences (and contents) can we have this kind of special access; therefore, our cognitive states (and their contents) are conscious experiences (and experiential–intentional).

He concludes that there is a phenomenal character proper to cognitive states (and their contents).[32]

Opponents have tended to be unmoved by these considerations, claiming that there are better explanations of phenomenal contrast, phenomenal overwhelm, and first-person knowability than the supposition of cognitive phenomenology. Frustratingly, the disagreement often seems to devolve into a seemingly verbal matter rather quickly. Both sides agree that cognitive states can exhibit some special feature F, but disagree on whether F is a phenomenal feature, and it is unclear in what way the issue goes beyond whether one is willing to apply the term "phenomenal" to F.

Under these conditions, progress would require first and foremost that a characterization of phenomenality be devised which is antecedently neutral and does not prejudge the question of the existence of cognitive phenomenology. In Kriegel (2009: ch. 1), I have suggested that phenomenal consciousness is best characterized as the "explanatory-gap-able property." More specifically, I suggested that we fix the reference of "phenomenality" with the following rigidified definite description: "The property P, such that, in the actual world, there is (the appearance of) an explanatory gap between physical properties and P."[33] Any species of the genus P would then qualify as a phenomenal property. (For fuller development of this criterion of phenomenality, see Kriegel MS.)

Although I cannot expand on this here, it seems to me that an argument could be erected for cognitive phenomenology which would work with this characterization. This would involve conceiving of a world in which subjects have no perceptual, somatic, or emotional phenomenology and claiming that the worry captured by the explanatory gap nonetheless appropriately arises for this world. There are conditions involving congenital absence of perceptual phenomenology, such as blindness and deafness, as well as conditions involving congenital absence of somatic phenomenology (e.g. congenital analgesia) and of emotional phenomenology (e.g., perhaps, in certain forms of autism).[34] We can certainly envisage a person suffering from all these conditions at once (Kriegel 2003b, MS), and can therefore conceive of a world where everybody does. The proponent of cognitive phenomenology would then make

[32] An earlier argument of a similar form is developed by Goldman (1993) and recently endorsed by Lycan (2008).

[33] I add a parenthetical mention of appearance because it is not meant to be built into this characterization of phenomenality that the explanatory gap is unbridgeable. Since some people hear the term "explanatory gap" as committing to the impossibility of bridging, and others as committing to the impossibility of a priori bridging, whereas I do not mean to characterize phenomenality in a way that commits to the existence of such an unbridgeable gap between it and physical property, I add the reference to an appearance.

[34] The renowned high-functioning autistic Temple Grandin reports (Grandin 1996) experiencing only four types of emotion: joy, sadness, fear, and anger. Subtler emotions are unfamiliar to her experientially, though she has managed to understand their nature in a purely intellectual, bloodless manner. This is an instance of congenital *restriction* of one's emotional phenomenology. We can readily envisage someone suffering from congenital *absence* of such phenomenology.

the following substantive claim: it is rationally appropriate to feel the pull of the explanatory gap for that world. This claim suggests that the explanatory-gap-able property is instantiated in that world, and therefore that phenomenality is instantiated. Since perceptual, somatic, and emotional phenomenalities are *not* instantiated, it follows that there must be a non-perceptual, non-somatic, and non-emotional phenomenality. One could then argue that the best candidate for this non-perceptual, non-somatic, and non-emotional phenomenality is cognitive phenomenality. This would be again not a demonstrative argument, but an argument from inference to the best explanation. Its advantage over the previous kinds of argument is that it would not be as susceptible to devolution into verbal dispute.

I develop this sort of argument in more detail elsewhere (Kriegel MS). Here, I will *assume* the existence of (proprietary or *sui generis*) cognitive phenomenology, and will concern myself rather with its relation to unconscious intentionality. I want to argue that unconscious intentionality is grounded ultimately in a certain type of cognitive phenomenology, namely, the cognitive phenomenology of conscious interpretation.

4 Interpretivism and cognitive phenomenology

In this final section, I argue that an upshot of interpretivism is the proposition sloganeered in the title: cognitive phenomenology is the basis of unconscious content. The argument I will present is this:

1) Interpretivism entails that all unconscious content is ultimately grounded in conscious interpretation;
2) The content of all conscious interpretation is grounded in the phenomenal character of conscious interpretation;
3) The phenomenal character of all conscious interpretation is a kind of cognitive phenomenology; therefore,
4) Interpretivism entails that all unconscious content is ultimately grounded in a kind of cognitive phenomenology.

I have already defended the first premise—that was the mandate of §2. This section defends the second and third premises.

Within NERP, there is no reason to believe the second premise. But the premise is an essential—perhaps *the* essential—tenet of PIRP. The focus of this paper has been on the nature of *unconscious* intentionality within PIRP. The other half (if you will) of a PIRP-ish theory of intentionality concerns the theory of *conscious* intentionality. There are several options here too, but they all have in common that the intentionality of phenomenally conscious states is grounded in those states' phenomenal character.

It is not at all clear how the relevant grounding is to be cashed out, though it is natural to appeal to a certain relation of metaphysical dependence. The relation is surely anti-reflexive and transitive,[35] but it could be legitimately construed either as *asymmetric* or as *anti-symmetric*. The anti-symmetric interpretation would entail that the phenomenal character of a phenomenally intentional state does not depend on the state's intentional content, whereas the asymmetric interpretation would not have this entailment—it would be compatible with both one-way and two-way dependence. One could make this difference explicit by subscripting "metaphysical dependence." Another device would be to construe metaphysical dependence as asymmetric and then explicitly distinguish two grades of the grounding thesis: a strong conjunctive thesis claiming that the intentional is grounded in the phenomenal and the phenomenal is not grounded in the intentional, and a weak thesis consisting merely of the first conjunct of the strong thesis. An intriguing version of this weaker thesis would be an *identity* thesis: the intentional property and the phenomenal property are one and the same. In this thesis, it is clear that there is no primacy of the phenomenal over the intentional within phenomenal intentionality. If one hears "grounding" as implying primacy, this weaker thesis would not cast the intentional as grounded in the phenomenal. But for present purposes, let us hear "grounding" as uncommitted on the primacy of the phenomenal to the intentional, and committed only regarding this: there is no primacy of the intentional to the phenomenal (as there is in standard intentionalist theories of phenomenal consciousness). With this stipulation, it is clearly a central tenet of PIRP that the intentional content of phenomenally conscious states is grounded in the phenomenal character of those states.

Naturally, this applies also to the intentionality of phenomenally conscious interpretive acts. Such acts, being phenomenally conscious, have phenomenal character. Moreover, it is plausible, though not uncontestable, that there is some phenomenal commonality among them. Just as there is a phenomenal commonality among all gustatory experiences as of bitter things, which is the phenomenology of bitterness, and a subtler phenomenal commonality among all conscious thoughts about the number *pi*, which we may call the *pi* phenomenology, so probably there is a phenomenal commonality among all conscious acts of intentional ascription, which we may call *interpretive phenomenology*. This is not trivial: every phenomenally conscious state that occurs on a Wednesday has a phenomenal character, but there is no Wednesday phenomenology, because there is no phenomenal commonality among Wednesday experiences. But it appears to be the case that whenever phenomenally conscious states have an intentional commonality they also have a phenomenal commonality (though, again, this is not beyond rational doubt).[36] Thus, the fact that there is an intentional commonality among conscious interpretive acts, in that they all ascribe an intentional

---

[35] So (a) there is no x which metaphysically depends upon itself, and (b) whenever some x metaphysically depends on y and y metaphysically depends on z, x metaphysically depends upon z.

[36] This is not to say that the intentional commonality underlies the phenomenal commonality rather than the other way around. In fact, it is not to comment at all on the order of explanation, or order of constitution, between the intentional and phenomenal commonalities.

property to something, suggests that there is a phenomenal commonality among them as well.[37] That is, it suggests that there is such a thing as an interpretive phenomenology. What the proponent of PIRP would typically claim is that this interpretive phenomenology grounds the intentional content of phenomenally conscious interpretive acts. She would, in other words, assert the second premise of the argument with which I opened this section.[38]

It is not easy to say anything particularly illuminating about the nature of interpretive phenomenology. An involved phenomenological analysis may excavate interesting aspects of this phenomenology, but short of fully engaging in such analysis, there is not much to do beyond point out the intentional commonality interpretive phenomenology grounds: what it is like to interpret someone as believing that it is sunny is just the someone-believes-that-it-is-sunny what-it-is-like.

Even without a comprehensive analysis of interpretive phenomenology, a case can probably be made that all interpretive phenomenology is cognitive. There are three main views about which kinds of mental state are phenomenally conscious interpretive acts. One view is that all conscious interpretive acts are beliefs, or judgments, or thoughts. On this view, to interpret someone as believing that it is sunny is to believe/judge/think that they believe that it is sunny. A second view is that some interpretive acts can be perceptual: one can *see* that someone believes that it is sunny; at the very least, *some* intentional states are such that one can just *see*, or otherwise *perceive*, that someone is in them. A third view is that interpretation involves rather some kind of *sui generis* attitude, the attitude of interpreting that *p*, e.g. that someone believes that it is sunny.

The first, "cognitive" view seems to me the most plausible. The third, "sui generis" view seems unmotivated: it is unclear what explanatory work cannot be done by any familiar attitude that a new kind of attitude should be posited. Certainly, the burden of argument should be on those who wish to posit the unfamiliar "interpretive attitude." As for the second, "mixed" view, it would only be well motivated if there were clear examples of perceptual interpretive acts. I think it is fairly clear that the case of interpreting someone to believe that it is sunny is not such an example—it is difficult to envisage in what way a person could perceive another to believe that it is sunny.

There may be other, more tempting cases, of course. Thus, perhaps one can just *see* that one's friend is smelling something funny, say by seeing a particular facial

---

[37] Here, too, none of this prejudges either the order of explanation or the order of constitution between interpretive content and interpretive phenomenology. As I argue immediately in the text, for the proponent of PIRP the order goes from phenomenology to content: conscious interpretive acts have their interpretive content because of their interpretive phenomenology.

[38] It may be objected that this would work only if cognitive phenomenology is individuative in Pitt's (2004) sense, that is, if there is a different kind of cognitive phenomenology for every type of conscious cognitive state. My response is to simply accept the objector's claim and subscribe to the claim that cognitive phenomenology is individuative. As indicated in §2, this is not mandatory for holding that there is such a thing as cognitive phenomenology. But I accept the objector's claim that it *is* mandatory for holding that cognitive phenomenology is the basis of unconscious intentionality.

contortion of one's friend. In this case, one's visual experience ascribes to one's friend an intentional state, namely, an olfactory experience as of a foul odor.

If the first view is the right one, and interpretive acts are always cognitive, it would seem to follow quite straightforwardly that interpretive phenomenology is a variety of cognitive phenomenology, since all phenomenally conscious interpretive acts are construed as cognitive states (beliefs/judgments/thoughts). More interestingly, plausibly this is the case even if the second, "mixed" view is the right one. For it is plausible that the phenomenology of any perceptual interpretive acts is a composite of sensory and cognitive phenomenologies. Observe that our example of such a perceptual interpretive act involves seeing that a friend is smelling something funny *by* seeing a facial contortion. Arguably, the phenomenal character of seeing the facial contortion exhausts the purely sensory component of the overall experience's phenomenal character. What one sees *by* seeing the facial contortion, the phenomenal component that goes beyond seeing the contortion, is a kind of non-sensory phenomenology. Moreover, it is hard to see what kind of phenomenology such non-sensory phenomenology could be if not cognitive phenomenology. It is certainly not a somatic or emotive phenomenology. Nor does it seem to be a conative or agentive phenomenology. This leaves cognitive phenomenology as the only natural candidate for understanding this non-sensory phenomenology involved in perceiving someone to smell something funny.

This treatment of such perception requires a conception of perceptual phenomenology as potentially comprised of two components, a sensory-phenomenology component and a cognitive-phenomenology component.[39] It is no part of this conception that the two components must be neatly factorizable. It may well be that perceptual phenomenology consists in a phenomenal fusion of the two components that does not allow for neat separation of their individual contributions. Nonetheless, to the extent that the phenomenal character of a perceptual act comprises this cognitive element or contribution, it is a kind of cognitive phenomenology. My contention is that perceptual acts lacking this kind of cognitive-phenomenal component, such as perceptual experiences of facial contortions, do not have interpretive phenomenology. The only mental acts that exhibit interpretive phenomenology are acts with cognitive phenomenology, and moreover, it is in virtue of their cognitive phenomenology that they exhibit interpretive phenomenology. In other words, their interpretive phenomenology is a kind of cognitive phenomenology.

It may be worthwhile to distinguish the emerging picture of perceptual interpretive acts from a certain historical conception of perception. According to this historical view, perceptual experiences are composites of sensation and belief: to perceive

---

[39] Of course, the view does allow perceptual experiences with sensory phenomenology only. Perhaps a perception of a facial contortion is a case in point: an experience with a purely sensory perceptual phenomenology. But the point is that, in addition to such experiences, this conception allows also for more sophisticated perceptual experiences, ones whose phenomenology comprises a cognitive element.

something is to (roughly simultaneously) sense something and believe something. The view suggested here is different. It does not posit two numerically distinct states, a sensation and a belief, but rather allows a perception to be a single unitary state. At the same time, it has some continuity with the historical view, inasmuch as it finds structure in the perceptual phenomenology of that unitary state. This structure casts perceptual phenomenology as a composite of two kinds of phenomenology, sensation-like and belief-like.[40] In any event, the emerging picture portrays perceptual interpretive acts as exhibiting a composite phenomenology comprising a sensory component and a cognitive component, with their interpretive phenomenology being part of the cognitive component, that is, being a form of cognitive phenomenology.

Beyond its natural appeal, this picture is further supported by the fact that our example of a perceptual interpretive act is one of seeing *that*, therefore one of a *propositional attitude*, though a perceptual propositional attitude. As Klausen (2008) argues, the phenomenal character propositional attitudes have *qua* propositional attitudes is always a kind of cognitive phenomenology, and this applies to perceiving-that: insofar as one's perceiving is propositional, one's experience's phenomenal character is cognitive.[41]

I conclude that both on the first view of conscious interpretive acts, as always purely cognitive, and on the most plausible reading of the second, "mixed" view, according to which some interpretive acts are perceptual, interpretive phenomenology is a kind of cognitive phenomenology. This is the third premise of the argument at the opening of this section.

This completes my preliminary case for the reasoning that grounds unconscious intentionality, via conscious interpretation and interpretive phenomenology, in cognitive phenomenology. I do not pretend to have offered a thorough defense of this argument here. Rather, my aim has been to sketch the case for each of its premises. My hope, however, is that this section has made it *prima facie* highly plausible that an upshot of interpretivism about unconscious intentionality is that unconscious intentionality is ultimately grounded in cognitive phenomenology.

5 Conclusion

Cognitive phenomenology may be at the basis not only of unconscious intentionality, but also of conscious intentionality. For another question within PIRP concerns the phenomenal signature of intentionality: what phenomenal feature, if any, transforms

---

[40] In a way, then, the difference between the view presented here and the historical view is the difference between making a claim about states and making a claim about properties of states. Also, the view presented here is uncommitted on the issue of factorizability, whereas the historical view is committed.

[41] On some understandings of what it is for a state to be "cognitive," this may be a conceptual truth— namely, in case having propositional content is sufficient for qualifying as cognitive. However, even if we use another criterion for being cognitive, it strikes me as substantively true that perceptual propositional attitudes have a cognitive phenomenology (see, again, Klausen 2008).

phenomenal *character* into phenomenal *intentionality*. On some views, that feature may turn out to be a kind of cognitive phenomenology as well (though presumably a different kind from interpretive phenomenology). One such view is Strawson's (2008): there is a subtle phenomenal feature whereby the mind *takes* something to be thus-and-so, and this *phenomenal taking* is a kind of cognitive phenomenology present in every conscious experience endowed with intentionality.[42,43] Personally, I am not persuaded that phenomenal taking is this key feature; but someone who were, or who identified some other cognitive phenomenology as the key to phenomenal intentionality, and who also adopted interpretivism about unconscious intentionality, could claim cognitive phenomenology as the basis of both phenomenal and non-phenomenal intentionality, hence as grounding all intentionality.

I have not argued for this stronger claim, though I am somewhat sympathetic to it (see Kriegel 2011: ch. 5). My main aim here has been to present the interpretivist approach to unconscious intentionality within PIRP, indicate what the case for it is, and argue that it ultimately grounds unconscious intentionality in a kind of cognitive phenomenology, since the intentional content of conscious interpretation is grounded in interpretive phenomenology, which is a kind of cognitive phenomenology. If all this is right, cognitive phenomenology is the basis of unconscious content.[44]

References

Abell, C. (2005). "Pictorial Implicature," *Journal of Aesthetics and Art Criticism*, 63: 55–66.

Blumson, B. (2006). "Resemblance and Representation," PhD Dissertation, Australian National University.

Bourget, D. (Forthcoming). "Consciousness is Underived Intentionality," *Noûs*.

Brentano, F. (1874). *Psychology from an Empirical Standpoint*. Edited by O. Kraus. English edition L. L. McAlister. Translated by A. C. Rancurello, D. B. Terrell, and L. L. McAlister (1973). London: Routledge and Kegan Paul.

Chalmers, D.J. (Forthcoming). "The Nature of Epistemic Space," in A. Egan and B. Weatherson (eds), *Epistemic Modality*. Oxford and New York: Oxford University Press.

[42] Thus, every phenomenally intentional state has a phenomenal character that involves phenomenal-taking as a component, which is a cognitive component of its phenomenal character, and it is in virtue of this cognitive component that the state is intentional. This may raise the objection that certain animals and neonates may be robbed of intentionality. There are probably reasonable responses to this objection, but a full discussion would take us too far afield.

[43] Similarly, according to Georgalis, the essential subjectivity of conscious intentional state, in virtue of which they are such, is a "non-sensory" feature. Under certain assumptions (which Georgalis may or may not accept), this could be taken to mean that this essential subjectivity is a kind of cognitive phenomenology.

[44] For comments on a previous draft, I am indebted to David Chalmers, Nicholas Georgalis, Michelle Montague, David Pitt, two readers for OUP, and especially Tim Bayne. For very helpful conversations, I would like to thank George Graham, Terry Horgan, and Amie Thomasson. I also benefited from presenting the paper at a conference at the University of Bern, and would like to thank the audience there, in particular Michelle Montague, Philippe Keller, Sebastian Leuggers, Gianfranco Soldati, and Galen Strawson. The paper was partly written during a research fellowship at the University of Sydney, to which I am greatly indebted.

Child, W. (1994). *Causality, Interpretation, and the Mind*. Oxford: Oxford University Press.

Chudnoff, E. (Forthcoming). "Intellectual Gestalts," in T. Horgan and U. Kriegel (eds), *Phenomenal Intentionality: New Essays*. Oxford and New York: Oxford University Press.

Davies, M. (1995). "Consciousness and the Varieties of Aboutness," in C. Macdonald and G. Macdonald (eds), *Connectionism: Debates on Psychological Explanation* (Vol. II). Oxford: Blackwell.

Dennett, D.C. (1971). "Intentional Systems." *Journal of Philosophy* 68: 87–106.

——(1981). "True Believers," in A.F. Heath (ed.) (1987), *Scientific Explanation*. Oxford: Oxford University Press. Reprinted in Dennett.

——(1987). *The Intentional Stance*. Cambridge MA: MIT Press.

——(1988). "Evolution, Error, and Intentionality," in Y. Wilks and D. Partridge (eds), *Sourcebook on the Foundations of Artificial Intelligence*. Albuquerque NM: New Mexico University Press.

——(1990). "The Myth of Original Intentionality," in K.A. Mohyeldin Said, W.H. Newton-Smith, R. Viale, and K.V. Wilkes (eds), *Modeling the Mind*. Oxford: Oxford University Press.

Dretske, F.I. (1980). "The Intentionality of Cognitive States," *Midwest Studies in Philosophy*, 5: 281–94.

——(1981). *Knowledge and the Flow of Information*. Oxford: Clarendon.

——(1988). *Explaining Behavior*. Cambridge MA: MIT Press.

Fodor, J.A. (1990). *A Theory of Content and Other Essays*. Cambridge MA: MIT Press.

——and E. Lepore (1993). "Is Intentional Ascription Intrinsically Normative?" in B. Dahlbom (ed.), *Dennett and His Critics*. Oxford: Blackwell.

Georgalis, N. (2006). *The Primacy of the Subjective*. Cambridge MA: MIT Press.

Goldman, A.I. (1989). "Interpretation Psychologized," *Mind and Language*, 4: 161–85.

Goldman, A. (1993). "The Psychology of Folk Psychology," *Behavioral and Brain Sciences*, 16: 15–28.

Grandin, T. (1996). *Thinking in Pictures*. New York: Vintage.

Grice, H. (1957). "Meaning," *Philosophical Review*, 66: 377–88.

Harman, G. (1987). "(Non-Solipsistic) Conceptual Role Semantics," in E. Lepore (ed.), *New Directions in Semantics*. London: Academic Press.

Horgan, T. and G. Graham (2009). "Phenomenal Intentionality and Content Determinacy," in R. Schantz (ed.), *Prospects for Meaning*. Amsterdam: de Gruyter.

——and U. Kriegel (2008). "Phenomenal Intentionality Meets the Extended Mind," *Monist*, 91.

——and J. Tienson (2002). "The Intentionality of Phenomenology and the Phenomenology of Intentionality," in D.J. Chalmers (ed.), *Philosophy of Mind: Classical and Contemporary Readings*. Oxford and New York: Oxford University Press.

——, ——, and G. Graham (2004). "Phenomenal Intentionality and the Brain in a Vat," in R. Schantz (ed.), *The Externalist Challenge: New Studies on Cognition and Intentionality*. Amsterdam: de Gruyter.

Horst, S.W. (1996). *Symbols, Computation, and Intentionality*. Berkeley and Los Angeles: University of California Press.

Husserl, E. (1900). *Logical Investigations I*. J.N. Findlay (trans.) (1970). London: Routledge.

Johnston, M. (1989). "Dispositional Theories of Value," *Proceedings of Aristotelian Society*, 63: 139–74.

Klausen, S.H. (2008). "The Phenomenology of Propositional Attitudes," *Phenomenology and the Cognitive Sciences*, 7: 445–62.

Kriegel, U. (2003a). "Is Intentionality Dependent upon Consciousness?" *Philosophical Studies*, 116: 271–307.

——(2003b). "Consciousness as Sensory Quality and as Implicit Self-Awareness," *Phenomenology and the Cognitive Sciences*, 2 (2003): 1–26.

——(2007). "Intentional Inexistence and Phenomenal Intentionality," *Philosophical Perspectives* 21: 307–40.

——(2009). *Subjective Consciousness: A Self-Representational Theory*. Oxford: Oxford University Press.

——(2010a). "Interpretation: Its Scope and Limits," in A. Hazlett (ed.), *New Waves in Metaphysics*. London: Palgrave-Macmillan.

——(2010b). "Intentionality and Normativity," *Philosophical Issues*, 20.

——(2011). *The Sources of Intentionality*. Oxford and New York: Oxford University Press.

——(MS). "Cognitive Phenomenology: From Analysis to Argument."

——and T. Horgan. (Forthcoming). "The Phenomenal Intentionality Research Programme," in U. Kriegel (ed.), *Phenomenal Intentionality: New Essays*. New York: Oxford University Press.

Loar, B. (1995). "Reference from the First-Person Perspective," *Philosophical Issues*, 6: 53–72.

——(2003). "Phenomenal Intentionality as the Basis for Mental Content," in M. Hahn and B. Ramberg (eds), *Reflections and Replies: Essays on the Philosophy of Tyler Burge*. Cambridge MA: MIT Press.

Lycan, W.G. (2008). "Phenomenal Intentionalities," *American Philosophical Quarterly*, 45: 233–52.

McDowell, J. (1985). "Values and Secondary Qualities," in T. Honderich (ed.), *Morality and Objectivity: A Tribute to John Mackie*. London: Routledge and Kegan Paul.

McGinn, C. (1988). "Consciousness and Content," in *Proceedings of the British Academy*, 76: 219–39. Reprinted in N.J. Block, O. Flanagan, and G. Güzeldere (eds) (1997), *The Nature of Consciousness: Philosophical Debates*. Cambridge MA: MIT Press.

Mangan, B. (2001). "Sensation's Ghost: The Non-Sensory Fringe of Consciousness," *Psyche*, 7.

Millikan, R.G. (1984). *Language, Thought, and Other Biological Categories*. Cambridge MA: MIT Press.

Moore, G.E. (1953). "Propositions," in his *Some Main Problems of Philosophy*. Oxford: Routledge.

Peacocke, C. (1998). "Conscious Attitudes, Attention, and Self-Knowledge," in C. Wright, B.C. Smith, and C. Macdonald (eds), *Knowing Our Own Minds*. Oxford: Oxford University Press.

Pitt, D. (2004). "The Phenomenology of Cognition; or What Is It Like to Think that P?" *Philosophy and Phenomenological Research*, 69: 1–36.

Searle, J.R. (1991). "Consciousness, Unconsciousness, and Intentionality," *Philosophical Issues*, 1: 45–66.

——(1992). *The Rediscovery of Mind*. Cambridge MA: MIT Press.

Siewert, C. (1998). *The Significance of Consciousness*. Princeton NJ: Princeton University Press.

Strawson, G. (1994). *Mental Reality*. Cambridge MA: MIT Press.

—— (2005). "Intentionality and Experience: Terminological Preliminaries," in D.W. Smith and A. Thomasson (eds), *Phenomenology and Philosophy of Mind*. Oxford and New York: Oxford University Press.

—— (2008). "Real Intentionality 3: Why Intentionality Entails Consciousness," in G. Strawson, *Real Materialism and Other Essays*. Oxford: Oxford University Press.

Tennant, N. (2009). "Cognitive Phenomenology, Semantic Qualia, and Luminous Knowledge," in P. Greenough and D. Pritchard (eds), *Williamson on Knowledge*. Oxford: Oxford University Press.

Wright, C. (1992). *Truth and Objectivity*. Cambridge MA: Harvard University Press.

On the Phenomenology of Thought

Joseph Levine

1 Introduction

Phenomenal consciousness is usually captured by Nagel's (1974) phrase "what it's like." A phenomenally conscious experience is the kind of state there is something it is like to occupy, and the phenomenal character of the experience is precisely what it is like. One way to put it is this. Phenomenal consciousness involves two fundamental components: subjectivity and qualitative (or phenomenal) character. There being something at all it's like to have an experience manifests subjectivity. Subjects of experience are the entities *for whom* the experience is like what it's like. Qualitative, or phenomenal character is the complex of features presented to the subject of experience. That subjectivity at all should exist in the world is, to my mind, itself a major puzzle, independently of the puzzles that surround the particular features presented to us as phenomenal characters.

The standard examples of phenomenal states involve sensation, and maybe emotion too. Feeling pain, seeing red, tasting salty, and perhaps also feeling angry or sad, are thought to be examples of states with phenomenal character. Mental states that lack phenomenal character are all those states, including non-occurrent beliefs and desires, that are classified as unconscious. But what about occurrent cognitive states? I now consciously, occurrently believe that I am typing on my computer, that the sun is shining (for a change), and I'm also wondering what's for dinner tonight. I certainly seem to be conscious of these thoughts; or, to be more careful, I certainly am consciously thinking these thoughts. (Just what it is I am conscious *of* while occurrently thinking that P is yet to be decided.) But do these cognitive states possess phenomenal character? Is there something it is like to be having these thoughts?

Let us call the doctrine that these questions have an affirmative answer "CP," for "Cognitive Phenomenology." CP has been strongly defended by a number of philosophers[1], and also denied by others[2]. My aim in this paper is twofold: first, I want

---

[1] See Goldman (1993), Horgan and Tienson (2002), Pitt (2004), and Siewert (1998).
[2] See Lormand (1996) and Nelkin (1989).

to distinguish various possible versions of CP, ranking some as stronger than others; second, I want to examine the standard arguments in favor of CP and see just which versions of the thesis they support. I will conclude that though the standard arguments do make plausible at least a relatively weak version of CP, they do not support stronger versions.

2 Two arguments for CP

There are two basic pro-CP arguments I want to consider: what I'll call "the self-knowledge argument" and "the phenomenological argument." The first appeals to phenomenal character as the only, or at least the best, explanation of how we have the particularly intimate knowledge of our conscious cognitive states that we do. The second appeals to our own experiences to demonstrate the existence of cognitive phenomenology.

Let's consider the self-knowledge argument. Of course, I have a multitude of beliefs and desires at any one moment, and clearly, in one sense I am not aware of them all at once. These are the unconscious cognitive states. But when I make one of them conscious—when I consciously entertain a thought—I am automatically, it seems, aware that I am thinking it. What's more, this immediate awareness of what I'm occurrently thinking constitutes knowledge. If I know anything, it seems, I know what I'm now consciously thinking. So what can explain this sort of self-knowledge?

The CP advocate answers that we know what we're thinking by experiencing the phenomenal character of consciously thinking it. Just what this means, and how it explains what requires explanation here—indeed, just what it is that requires explanation here—are all issues I will take up in some detail as we proceed. For now, I just want to get the arguments on the table.

The phenomenological argument is best seen as a reply to a standard anti-CP ploy. Consider again my occurrent thought that the sun is shining. If I take stock of what it's like for me now, what do I find? Of course there are all the sensory states with their phenomenal characters. But when it comes to the thought itself, one might argue, all the phenomenal character there is to be found is that which belongs to the auditory and visual imagery connected with the thought—the sound of "inner speech" and perhaps some visual images as of the sun shining, etc. Of course, no one doubted that imagery of this sort possessed phenomenal character (unless you were skeptical of phenomenal consciousness in general, a view we're not considering here), so if CP is a substantive thesis, it has to entail the presence of phenomenal character that goes beyond such imagery. But, the objection goes, there isn't any such phenomenal character to be found.

In response, the CP advocate points to phenomena like ambiguities, the difference between rehearsing a sentence in a language one doesn't understand and "hearing" it in inner speech when one does understand it, the moment of "getting" what a garden path sentence means, and the like. The general idea is this. If all phenomenology is sensory phenomenology, then there shouldn't be a difference in what it's like to have the very same sound sequence imagined in your head when it means one thing rather than another, or nothing at all. For instance, as a young boy I was taught various blessings in Hebrew which I learned to recite at the proper times without understanding what they meant. As I got older I learned quite a bit of Hebrew, and now when I say, or imagine one of these blessings I know what it means. (Alas—I liked them better when I didn't know what they meant.) The CP advocate will ask: Isn't there clearly a difference in what it's like to hear the blessing in your head when you understand it from what it's like when you hear it without understanding? If so, then this difference is attributable to the phenomenal character of the grasping of the thought or content in question, and not merely that which comes with the sound of the words that express that content.[3]

So these are the two principal pro-CP arguments I want to consider. In order to evaluate the arguments, it's helpful to specify in a little more detail what the anti-CP position is. While obviously there are lots of different views one might have on the nature of occurrent thought, or any thought at all, I am going to take the following as our "null hypothesis," the default anti-CP position. Let's call it "NPFR," for "Non-Phenomenal Functional Representationalism." On this view, as on any functionalist-representationalist view, the mind is a representational system, with representational states embodied in physical configurations in the brain. Thinking is a matter of tokening certain "mentalese" sentences and processing them in various ways. The different attitudes are constituted by different functional relations to the relevant mentalese sentences, and the different contents toward which one can take an attitude are determined by the semantic properties of the mentalese sentences. These semantic properties are determined by causal or nomic relations to the world, and also (perhaps) by functional relations among the sentences themselves. What NPFR adds to standard functionalist-representationalism is this stipulation: While there is (or may be) phenomenal character experienced as a result of occupying certain perceptual states, there is no corresponding phenomenal character experienced as a result of occupying even occurrent cognitive states. What distinguishes occurrent from non-occurrent cognitive states is completely exhausted by functional features, such as whether or not a certain sentence is currently tokened in a certain location. So the question now is whether the two arguments, either singly or together, show that NPFR is wrong.

Before proceeding to look at the arguments in detail, a note about terminology is in order. Notice that I framed NPFR in terms of a thought's being "occurrent" or "non-occurrent," not "conscious" or "unconscious." The problem is that for some (see Pitt, this volume), the term "conscious" is appropriate only for states that have phenomenal character. Obviously, CP would be vacuous on this view if it applied only to "conscious" thoughts. Others, notably Block (1995), distinguish "access conscious-ness" from "phenomenal consciousness," and thus could frame the question as whether

---

[3] Siegel (2007) calls this form of argument "the method of phenomenal contrast."

any access-conscious thoughts are also phenomenally conscious. On Pitt's understanding of "conscious," the null hypothesis is that thoughts are themselves never conscious, only their sensory accompaniments. On Block's understanding of "conscious," the null hypothesis is that access-conscious thoughts are never phenomenally conscious. I will try to stick to the neutral characterization of our target phenomena as "occurrent thoughts" in what follows. As we will see below, however, the issue is not purely a matter of terminology, but has substantive consequences as well.

3 Evaluating the two arguments

The following lengthy quote from Pitt (2004) presents the self-knowledge argument and also serves to fill out CP somewhat in the process:

Normally—that is, barring confusion, inattention, impaired functioning, and the like—one is able, consciously, introspectively, and non-inferentially (henceforth, "Immediately") to do three distinct (but closely related) things: (a) to distinguish one's occurrent conscious thoughts from one's other occurrent conscious mental states; (b) to distinguish one's occurrent conscious thoughts each from the others; and (c) to identify each of one's occurrent conscious thoughts as the thought it is (i.e. as having the *content* it does). But (the argument continues), one would not be able to do these things unless each (type of) occurrent conscious thought had a phenomenology that is (1) different from that of any other type of conscious mental state (proprietary), (2) different from that of any other type of conscious thought (distinct), and (3) constitutive of its (representational) content (individuative). That is, it is only because conscious thoughts have a kind of phenomenology that is different from that of any other kind of conscious mental state that one can Immediately discriminate them from other kinds of conscious mental states; it is only because type-distinct conscious thoughts have type-distinct phenomenologies (of the cognitive sort) that one can Immediately distinguish them from each other; and it is only because a conscious thought that p has a phenomenology that constitutes its (representational) content that one can Immediately identify it as the thought it is. Hence (the argument concludes), each type of conscious thought has a proprietary, unique phenomenology, which constitutes its representational content. (pages 7–8, emphasis in original)

According to Pitt, CP (his version of it) involves three elements: that cognitive phenomenology is *proprietary*, *distinctive*, and *individuative*. That it's proprietary means that it involves its own kind of phenomenology; it's not sensory in any way. That it's distinctive means that there is a different one for each thought. These two features are fairly clearly explained in the quote. But what it means to say that the phenomenal character of an occurrent thought "constitutes its representational content" is not so clear, and I will return to it below. For now, however, I just want to evaluate the general argument that we must appeal to CP to explain what Pitt calls our "Immediate" knowledge of what we're occurrently thinking.

Pitt goes through a number of possible alternative explanations, finding them all wanting. The alternative I want to consider specifically is the one that naturally follows from NPFR, our null hypothesis. What it is to have knowledge of what one is thinking is to token a mental representation—a mentalese sentence—that expresses the fact that one is thinking what one is thinking. What makes this Immediate knowledge, in Pitt's sense, is the fact that this sentence tokening is not the result of an inferential process, but rather an immediate causal result of the first-order thought state itself (together with some functionally characterizable internal monitoring process). It's because of the reliability of the relevant process yielding the higher-order sentence expressing the fact that one is thinking a certain content that it counts as knowledge. If this explanation is adequate, then we don't need to appeal to the thought's phenomenal character to explain how we know—Immediately—that we're thinking it.[4]

Pitt considers this alternative, but presents two objections to it. I'm not awfully sure that I understand his objections, so I'm going to quote him and then provide my interpretation. If I'm right, it will turn out that the objections don't succeed. The first objection is captured in the following passage:

> But to think that *t* is the thought that *p* while *t* is occurring—even because *t* is occurring—is not to *identify it* as the thought that *p* in the sense at issue in this paper. Introspective identification of occurrent conscious thoughts is analogous to perceptual identification of objects and introspective identification of sensations: it is a form of knowledge *by acquaintance*. Such identifications have the canonical form *this [that] is (an/the) F*; they require simple acquaintance, in the relevant mode, with the object identified. That is, the object identified—"this"—must be *experientially discriminated by the perceiver from its environment*. And, as pointed out above, this requires that the object appear to one in some determinate way, and that one be attending to it. One cannot, say, visually identify a thing as a dog (see that it is a dog) unless one has an attentive discriminative visual experience of it—that is, unless one *simply sees* it (in the sense of section 2). Merely to think *this animal is a dog* when a dog is within visual range and is causing one to have a visual experience of it and to think that it is a dog, is not to *see that* it is (visually identify it as) a dog. Likewise, merely to think that *s* is a pain when *s* is a pain, is occurring, and is causing one to think that it is a pain, is not to *feel* that it is (introspectively identify it as) a pain. And merely to think that *t* is the thought that *p* when *t* is the thought that *p*, is occurring, and causing one to think that it is the thought that *p*, is not to *grasp that t* is (introspectively identify it as) the thought that *p*. (page 19, emphases in original)

I find this passage quite interesting for what it suggests concerning how to think about just what phenomenal character is, and I will return to this theme below, when I distinguish the various versions of CP. But for now, I just want to see what force this objection has against the advocate of NPFR. As far as I can tell, not much. The reason is that so much is packed into the notion of Immediate self-knowledge that it appears to beg the question. This is the point, mentioned above, where what seemed merely a terminological issue becomes more substantive.

---

[4] See Nichols and Stich (2003) for an account along these lines. Nelkin (1989) also endorses a view like this, though he explicitly refrains from committing himself to the claim that meta-beliefs formed this way constitute knowledge.

Pitt characterizes "Immediate" self-knowledge as "conscious." If by "conscious" one only means "occurrent," or "access conscious," then there's no harm in it. But if one insists that our "conscious" knowledge of what we're currently thinking is a matter of perceptual-like acquaintance—comparable to how I know what I'm seeing or feeling—then I guess it must involve phenomenal character. This is tantamount, however, to just describing it as phenomenally conscious. But then we don't need to appeal to phenomenal character to explain this kind of knowledge, since the alleged explanandum is already described as a phenomenal state. If, on the other hand, we refrain from building phenomenal character into the description of the kind of self-knowledge we're trying to explain, then Pitt's objection seems to disappear. After all, it certainly seems as if one can hold a position to the effect that we have immediate (perhaps not "Immediate" if that entails perceptual-like appearance) knowledge of what we're thinking—it's just, as it were, magically available to us, in that we don't discern any process of discovery or inference—without there being anything like a phenomenal appearance, as we have with sensory experience. To demand an explanation of this richer, appearance-like knowledge is, as I said, to beg the question.

The second objection is captured in the following passage (t' is the higher-order thought to the effect that first-order thought t has the content p):

> ... t''s consciousness is supposed to make the content of t Immediately knowable. But this is because the content of t' is that the content of t is p. Hence, if the consciousness of t' is not sufficient to make its content Immediately knowable—i.e. to make it Immediately knowable that it says that the content of t is p—then it is not sufficient to ground Immediate knowledge of t's content. Hence, conscious occurrence of t' must, if it is to be sufficient to ground Immediate knowledge of the content of t, be sufficient to ground conscious knowledge of its own content as well. Since the theory under consideration denies this, it is false. (page 20)

I don't think this objection works either. To say why, I need to introduce a distinction between *implicit* self-knowledge and *explicit* self-knowledge. Explicit self-knowledge is what we have when we explicitly formulate a metacognitive thought, such as "I believe that San Francisco is a beautiful city." Someone asks me, say, if I believe San Francisco is beautiful, and I reply that yes, I do. This seems to be one of those special, first-person ways of knowing what I believe. I don't have to infer it from observing my behavior, and it certainly doesn't seem as if I wait to see what inner speech goes through my head and then interpret that and infer what I believe. I just seem to know.

What I'm calling "implicit" self-knowledge, however, is not the result of any explicit formulation or reflection. Rather, it's the knowledge that seems to come with the very thinking of the thought itself. (Perhaps it's not really apt to call this "knowledge" of what I believe; that might be only appropriate to say of the explicit self-knowledge case. But I'm going to continue to use the term "implicit self-knowledge" for ease of exposition.) As I think, and let's imagine this involves some inner speech, I understand what it is I'm "saying to myself," and in that sense know what it is I'm thinking. No explicit metacognitive proposition has been formulated. I think to myself, as I gaze at the view from Dolores Park, "This sure is a beautiful city." As I think it, it seems, I know what it is I'm thinking. This kind of knowledge is implicit self-knowledge.

Now the objection in the last passage quoted seems to assimilate these two forms of self-knowledge. The problem is supposed to be that unless I Immediately know the content of t' I can't Immediately know the content of t itself. But, on the NPFR account, Immediately knowing the content of t' would require yet another thought, t'', and then we're off and running. But that's not the right picture. On NPFR one gets implicit self-knowledge for free. All that's required is that one thinks in one's language of thought, mentalese. To implicitly know what one is thinking is just to think it with understanding. But it's a mistake to view thinking with understanding as a matter of interpreting one's own thoughts. No, one just thinks them. If they have the requisite semantic properties, then that's all there is to it.

Explicit self-knowledge, on the other hand, does involve formulating another thought—a thought to the effect that one is having the first-order thought. But for that to work, all we need is for the subject to token a higher-order representation that means that the lower-order representation has content p. Here, the subject is explicitly reflecting on what she believes (thinks, desires, etc.) and does assign an interpretation. But doing this—thinking, interpreting, etc.—is, on NPFR, just a matter of tokening the relevant mentalese sentences with the right semantic properties. We can put it this way. To know (explicitly) is just to occupy another cognitive state, and that, on this theory, is just to token the right representation in the appropriate circumstances. To explicitly know thought t's content is to think another thought, t', whose content is that the content of t is p and is itself implicitly known. On NPFR, it's tokening and processing sentences all the way down.[5]

Let's turn now to the phenomenological argument. We are asked to reflect on various possible experiences and see if we find that there is a difference in what they are like. So, imagine that you are having a certain course of visual and auditory imagery. Keeping that sensory/imagistic phenomenology constant, imagine two scenarios: one in which you are saying a sentence you understand to yourself, and another in which you don't understand it. If you think there's a difference in what the two experiences are like for you, then that difference—given we've held the sensory/imagistic phenomenology constant—must be attributable to the phenomenological contribution of grasping (or not) the relevant content.

---

[5] In Pitt (this volume) and personal communication, Pitt objects that the sort of implicit self-knowledge I attribute to the subject—i.e. just understanding what she's thinking by tokening, in functionally appropriate circumstances, the relevant sentence of mentalese—doesn't capture what it is to consciously know what one is thinking. Again, I agree, so long as one understands "consciously" in as rich a fashion as Pitt does. But then the anti-CP advocate will deny that we have such conscious self-knowledge in the first place, and so therefore there's nothing of the kind to explain. I will return to the question of just how to characterize the explanandum below.

Of course, one possible line of reply is that in such cases the sensory/imagistic phenomenology is not actually held constant. To see what I mean, consider the debate over perceptual modularity. Fodor (1983) and Pylyshyn (2001) defend a strong modularity thesis on which there is no cognitive penetration from higher cognitive processes into the deliverances of the visual module. An alleged counterexample to this thesis is the Gestalt switch phenomenon, the "duck–rabbit" being one of the best well-known examples. The point is that deciding to see it as a rabbit—a higher-level conceptual process—clearly affects how it appears, what it looks like. Hence, there seems to be genuine cognitive penetration from above.

There are a number of ways to defend the modularity thesis against this sort of example, but one way in particular, mentioned by Pylyshyn (2001), is relevant to our case. Pylyshyn discusses research that shows that when you decide to see the figure as a rabbit, say, rather than a duck, your eyes actually focus on different points in the figure from where they focus when you intend to see it as a duck. In a sense, the higher-level process is influencing the way it looks, but not by direct cognitive penetration. Rather, one's decision affects the precise character of the stimulus presented to the eyes, which then, in a strictly bottom-up fashion, produces a difference in how the figure looks.

Whether this move works for all examples of Gestalt switches I don't know. But it seems to me a similar move could be made by the advocate of NPFR in response to the phenomenological argument. That is, one might argue as follows. When one understands a sentence performed in inner speech—or understands it as read one way rather than another—this affects the prosody, or some other perceptually manifested feature of the imagined sound stream. So the difference in what it's like between understood inner speech and non-understood inner speech might just be a sensory difference after all. When you understand what you're saying to yourself—or understand it this way rather than that way—you actually say it differently, and this is the phenomenological difference you detect. It's not a direct phenomenological reflection of grasping the content, of the understanding itself.

I don't know how far this move can go in accounting for the phenomenological data. I'm inclined to think it's a promising avenue to explore, but in the end I doubt it can do all the work needed. For now, I propose to concede to the advocate of CP that the phenomenological argument does establish that at least some version of CP holds. But which version? How should we understand CP, and what do the two arguments—the self-knowledge argument and the phenomenological argument—tell us about the nature of cognitive phenomenal character? This is the topic of the next two sections.

4 Distinguishing stronger and weaker versions of CP

At the beginning of the paper I characterized phenomenal character as what it is like to occupy a mental state when there is something it is like to occupy it. So the phenomenal character of a pain state is the precise way that pain feels, and the phenomenal character of a visual sensation is the precise way things in one's visual field look. While this combination of a very general, and rather abstract characterization of phenomenal character (the "what" in "what it's like") with specific sensory examples suffices to provide substance to the notion when dealing with sensory experiences, it would be nice to have something more to say if we are to attribute phenomenal character to cognitive states. True, we can say that there is something it is like to occurrently believe that p, and the phenomenal character is just what it's like. But given that sensory phenomenology constitutes the only really uncontroversial example of phenomenal character, it would be helpful to find some more concrete characterization of the phenomenon that might plausibly capture both sensory and cognitive phenomenology.

I don't have anything precise to offer in this regard, but it seems to me that the following helps to flesh out the notion somewhat. In fact, what I have in mind is closely related to David Pitt's remarks, quoted above, concerning the relation between phenomenal character and acquaintance. To be phenomenally conscious, I want to say, is to be "appeared to." It is for the conscious subject to be experientially presented with a determinate object (or objects) with determinate qualities. I think this is the notion that Kant was after when he spoke of "intuition." Intuitions for Kant, as I understand it, are what provide the understanding with the concrete, singular material to which to apply concepts. Phenomenal character, then, is not just "what it is like," but more fundamentally, it's "what is presented" in experience.[6]

With this, admittedly still vague, characterization of the phenomenal in mind, there are two, orthogonal distinctions I want to introduce concerning the notion of cognitive phenomenology; both distinguish between a weaker and a stronger version of CP, though along different dimensions. The first distinction can be described using the Kantian terminology just introduced. On the one hand, one might hold that all phenomenal experiences, all intuitions, involve what Kant called a "sensory manifold," the forms of which are Space and Time. On this view, while all phenomenal character is essentially sensory—involving the distribution of sensible features (color, shape, sound, etc.) in space and time (or sometimes only in time)—cognitive states make a distinctive contribution to the precise phenomenal character experienced. The idea is that what one is currently thinking/believing/desiring affects the way a particular sensory manifold appears, so for two experiences with identical purely sensible features but different thoughts, the subjects will experience the two sensory manifolds in different ways. However, all phenomenal character is grounded in sensory

---

[6] This characterization of phenomenal character assumes a kind of representationalism about phenomenal character, though not of a reductionist variety. The alternative is to view phenomenal character as a kind of "mental paint," an intrinsic quality of experiential states that has no inherent intentional or representational features. Since both I and the CP advocates discussed in this paper reject the mental paint view, it's safe to set it aside without argument for present purposes.

phenomena, so that cognitive states can only be consciously experienced through their effects on what sensorily appears to the subject.

One might put it this way. On this version of CP, which I'll call "impure CP," cognitive phenomenology is a matter of one's sensory experience being cognitively inflected. What one is thinking changes the way what one is perceiving (imagining, etc.) appears to one, but in the end all phenomenology involves the appearance of some sensorily presented object and its qualities. So, on this view, when you visually experience something you recognize it has a different "look" from the one it has when you don't recognize it, as does speech you understand have a different "sound" from the one it does when you don't understand it. But it's still the case that the only way to phenomenally experience a cognitive content is through its effect on some sensory presentation.

On the other hand, one might claim that there is a phenomenology of pure thought, a doctrine I'll call "pure CP." That is, independently of any sensory phenomenology, and not strictly through its effect on one's sensory phenomenology, there is just something it is like to think a thought with a certain content. Now, given my characterization above of phenomenal character as involving the presentation of some object and its qualities, how would this apply in the case of purely cognitive phenomenology? Here's one way to put it, and, again, I think this fits fairly well with Pitt's characterization of cognitive phenomenology when he describes it as a kind of acquaintance: the content of a thought is presented to the subject thinking it—it appears to the subject—but in a non-sensory way. Perhaps this is what Kant had in mind when he speculated about the possibility of "intellectual intuition," the concrete, singular presentation of a purely cognitive, conceptual object.

Between pure CP and impure CP, which position is Pitt defending? I'm inclined to think it's pure CP, since the notion of a "distinctive" cognitive phenomenology seems to fit that position better.[7] However, since on the impure version the admixture of cognitive content creates distinctions among sensory phenomenal characters that wouldn't exist otherwise, one can imagine calling that contribution a kind of "distinctive" phenomenology as well, even though it can't, as it were, stand on its own. But whichever version Pitt intended, what interests me here is which version is supported by the two arguments, the self-knowledge and phenomenological arguments. Before turning to that question, though, let me introduce the second distinction.

The question on which this distinction turns is whether cognitive phenomenology shares with sensory phenomenology a feature I'll call "transparent content." What I mean is this. When I have a conscious visual experience of, say, a ripe tomato sitting on a kitchen counter, a proper characterization of what it's like for me to have this experience makes essential reference to how the space around me appears. Round shapes and red colors constitute the look, and there doesn't seem to be any space, as it

---

[7] I think this also fits Siewert's defense of the claim that what he calls "noniconic" thought has phenomenal character.

THE PHENOMENOLOGY OF THOUGHT   113

were, between what it's like for me and how the world is being presented to me. This characterization of visual phenomenology of course coheres with my account of phenomenal character at the beginning of the section.

If cognitive phenomenology has transparent content (call this CPTC), that means that what the cognitive state is about, what it's representing, constitutes the "look" as it were of the cognitive state. What appears to me when phenomenally experiencing a belief, say, is the belief's content, how I'm believing the world to be, in just the way that what appears to me when I see a ripe tomato is how I'm visually experiencing the world to be. If cognitive phenomenology has transparent content, then it can serve the epistemological function Pitt assigns it; it can acquaint me with what I'm thinking.

Suppose, however, that cognitive phenomenology lacks transparent content—let's call this having "opaque content" (CPOC).[8] What would that mean? I can imagine two alternatives. The first is the "mental paint" view of cognitive phenomenology.[9] On this position, it turns out there is just something it is like to believe that *p*, but what it's like is an intrinsic feature of the believing experience and has no essential connection—though presumably a causal one—to the content believed. While I don't see any outright inconsistency in holding a mental paint view of cognitive phenomenology and rejecting it for sensory phenomenology, it's hard to see what motivation there would be for doing so. In particular, the idea that phenomenal character is a matter of how something determinate appears to a subject is inconsistent with the mental paint account, so adopting the mental paint view for cognitive phenomenology would mean abandoning the general account of phenomenal character presented above.

The second alternative preserves the idea that phenomenal character is "presentational" in nature. However, rather than presenting a content, what is presented is one's own mental state; on a representational theory of mind, what is presented is the underlying mental representation that is the immediate relatum of the cognitive attitude in question.[10] The picture I have in mind is this. Consider again the anti-CP position mentioned earlier, on which there is no cognitive phenomenology at all, but instead only conscious awareness of sensory experiences associated with inner speech, imagery, and the like. The opaque content version of cognitive phenomenology I'm imagining here allows that there is more than the sensory experience of inner speech and imagery, but claims that this something more is still analogous to the sensory phenomenology of inner speech in that it is a kind of cognitive "hearing" of underlying mental representations. Just as I am presented with auditory imagery of spoken

<hr/>

[8] I realize that by using this terminology I am inviting confusion between this distinction and the one between extensional and intensional contexts. However, the metaphorical character is significantly similar in both cases. With extensional contexts, where substitution of co-referentials is allowed, the idea is that we somehow see directly through the representation to the object itself. Opaque contexts are those in which we can't see through the representation. I mean something similar here, except that the metaphor is being taken a little more seriously in my use of the transparent/opaque distinction than it is in the standard use concerning extensional and intensional contexts.

[9] See note 6 above.

[10] Hence, the appropriateness of the term "opaque," as noted in footnote 8 above.

speech when thinking out loud, I can also be presented with cognitive imagery of underlying speech when consciously thinking. Whether it's genuine inner speech, or non-sensory experience of a conscious occurrent state, all conscious thought, on this view, is a matter of being presented with what's going on in one's own mind.

We now have two apparently independent dimensions along which to distinguish versions of CP: pure vs. impure, and CPTC vs. CPOC. This gives us four possible versions of CP altogether. Now as I see it, pure CP is a stronger hypothesis than impure CP, since the latter restricts the realm of the phenomenal to the sensory, though allowing fine distinctions in phenomenal character that have a cognitive source. Cognitive phenomenology, on impure CP, must always find a sensory manifold on which to appear to the subject, whereas it is often experienced independently of sensory phenomenology on pure CP.

Similarly, CPTC—the idea that fairly abstract, non-sensible contents can be objects of direct acquaintance—seems a stronger position than CPOC, the view that all cognitive phenomenology adds is a conscious acquaintance with our own mental representations. One can see this from the characterization of CPOC above, and its relation to NPFR, the null hypothesis that there is no cognitive phenomenology at all. On the latter view, phenomenology is about how our senses present the world to us. It is restricted to those features that the senses can depict.[11] So while there is a sense in which we are directly, consciously acquainted with colors and shapes, say, we are not so acquainted with non-sensible properties. It's not that our thoughts don't represent mind-independent reality on this view; it's not a matter of skepticism. Sure, we think, and in that sense we cognitively grasp mind-independent contents. But the point of denying cognitive phenomenology is to restrict our conscious access to the sensory manifestations of our mental representations; to leave us consciously behind the veil of inner speech and imagery.

CPOC maintains the veil that separates us from our cognitive contents, it just allows that we have a kind of phenomenological access to underlying representations that are not sensorily manifested.[12] The veil in question is not constituted only by our sensory

[11] Of course, which worldly features the senses can depict is controversial. A standard empiricist view would restrict the senses to depicting clearly sensible properties such as colors, shapes, textures, motion, etc. Siegel (2006) argues for a more expanded range of properties. How her view concerning the contents of sensory experience relates to the debate over cognitive phenomenology is an interesting question, but one I can't address in this paper.

[12] Now of course there is considerable controversy over just what a content is. I would like to avoid dealing with that issue if at all possible, just acknowledging that one basic division between theories of content is between Russellian and Fregean views. For Russellians, contents are something like states-of-affairs, actual components of the world (or constructed out of such components). On the Fregean view there is an intermediary between the mind, and representations generally, and the states-of-affairs that constitute truth conditions. Contents are senses, or modes of presentation of states-of-affairs. The idea that we have "Immediate" access to contents, that contents appear to the conscious subject, seems to make more sense on a Fregean view of content than on a Russellian one, but the issues here are complex. Anyway, as I said, I can't go into the extremely difficult question of what a content is in this paper, so I'll leave the matter with just one more brief comment on Fregean contents.

presentations, but also by non-sensory ones; the point is, however, a veil exists on both positions. CPTC, on the other hand, claims that we have as much acquaintance with the actual content of our thought as we do with the content of our sensory experiences. Clearly, then, CPTC is a greater deviation from NPFR than is CPOC.

What I want to do in the next section is return to the two arguments, the self-knowledge and phenomenological arguments, and determine which of the versions of CP—pure or impure, TC or OC—they support. Just what do these arguments buy us in the way of cognitive phenomenology? I will argue for two claims. First, the phenomenological argument only buys you the weaker alternative of both distinctions, namely, impure CPOC. Second, understood in the way we have so far, the self-knowledge argument buys you very little at all, since, as I argued above, NPFR, without appeal to any cognitive phenomenology, can explain the relevant self-knowledge. However, understood another way, it's possible it gets you at least impure CPTC. Whether or not it does depends on figuring out just what it is we know about what we're thinking "from the inside," and I conclude with some very inconclusive, speculative remarks on that topic.

5 Which version is supported by the two arguments

So let's turn to the phenomenological argument. Remember, it enters the dialectic as a response to someone who claims not to notice anything but sensory phenomenology in her stream of consciousness. The argument addresses this objection by noting many circumstances—whether it be ambiguous sentences or visual figures, the difference between rehearsing a sound sequence in one's head while understanding and not understanding, or many other such examples—in which the cognitive state one occupies makes a difference to what hearing, seeing, or otherwise sensing something is like. I mentioned above that there are moves to be made by the advocate of NPFR in reply, but I myself think there is something to the phenomenological argument. The question is, what does it buy you in the way of cognitive phenomenology?

When it comes to the distinction between pure and impure CP, it seems obvious that this argument can't support more than impure CP. After all, all the examples

The comment is that on at least one conception of mode of presentation (MOP) this difference between CPTC and CPOC that I'm emphasizing now disappears. The idea is this. If we think of a MOP as what explains how we can be ignorant of identities, how we can rationally believe that Hesperus appears in the evening but Phosphorus doesn't, then on a representational theory of propositional attitudes we can identify MOPs with mentalese representations. Venus, the object, is presented to me one way by thinking of it with my mentalese equivalent of "Hesperus," and another way by thinking of it with my mentalese equivalent of "Phosphorus." The point is that, for the representationalist, there is no reason to posit some entity, a sense, that is distinct from the mentalese word and is presented to the mind when thinking of the object using that word. The MOP can just be the word itself. It "presents" the object by referring to it. End of story. If we take this view of Fregean content (which, admittedly, is a very deflationary account of content), then both CPTC and CPOC allow that we have Immediate access to content. (I thank Louise Antony for making this point in discussion.)

involve ways of experiencing visual appearances, sound streams, and the like. The argument is addressing someone who doesn't find anything but sensory phenomenology in her conscious life, and it pushes her to notice distinctions among these sensory appearances that can only be accounted for by appeal to cognitive penetration.[13] Fair enough. Still, this doesn't get us anything like pure CP. It's still possible, for all this argument demonstrates, that the only way for a cognitive content to make itself appear to a conscious subject is through affecting the way some sensory manifold appears. That's impure CP.

How about CPTC versus CPOC? Here too, I think the phenomenological argument only buys you the weaker version, CPOC. What we can tell from the difference between what it's like to see Hebrew script, say, with understanding and what it's like to see it without understanding, is just that: that there is a difference in what it's like. For all that's manifest to us, merely by noting this difference, what we are responding to is the difference between the representational states we're occupying in the two circumstances. I'm not making the move here that's sometimes made by saying that the only phenomenological difference noticed in such cases is a general feeling of understanding, as opposed to a feeling of puzzlement. On that view, which an advocate of NPFR might accept, there is a kind of emotional phenomenal character added to the strictly sensory one, but nothing that is either distinctive or individuative of the cognitive state involved in understanding the script. No, I'm allowing that the cognitive state contributes in a way that is distinctive of cognition and specific to this cognitive state. But what makes this cognitive state the state it is may very well be the identity of the representation that constitutes it. Yes, we understand, and grasp what the script means, but what it is, on this view, to understand what something means is to token a representation that means what the script means. We now add that there is something distinctive that it is like to occupy such a state.[14]

So far I've argued that the phenomenological argument itself only supports impure CPOC, the weakest of the versions of CP that we've seen. Let's turn now again to

---

[13] Using this term of course brings to mind Fodor's (1983) modularity thesis. In fact, these sorts of examples must be explained away on his view in one way or another. One possibility, discussed by Fodor, is that they represent post-modular processing. The other possibility, also discussed by Fodor, is that certain conceptual representations are available within the perceptual modules. Notice that if we go with this line, then there ought to be a clear distinction between those thoughts capable of penetrating sensory appearances and those that can't. I can't go into this here, but it seems to me that there are such limits, and therefore the phenomenological argument can't show that there is cognitive phenomenology for all occurrent thoughts.

[14] Charles Siewert, present when an earlier version of this paper was delivered at Cal State LA, objected that what he is aware of when understanding a sentence is its content—what it means—not any mentalese sentence. I'm not sure I totally understand his objection, but if I do understand him correctly, I think there are two replies to make. First, "aware" in this context is opaque. What I mean is that what I am aware of is not presented as a mentalese sentence, but as what the public language sentence means. However, what might be the case for all that is that one's state of understanding just is tokening the right mentalese sentence in the right way. The awareness here, the phenomenal character, just is the conscious reflection of this representational state. We never get closer to content than that.

Second, the consideration Siewert brings up might be a reflection of one of the two ways of taking the self-knowledge argument mentioned above. In that case, I'll address it below.

the self-knowledge argument. If the question is whether we can account for how we have non-inferential, immediate, and reliable knowledge of what we're thinking, then I think the discussion in section 2 above demonstrates that no version of CP is necessitated by the phenomenon of self-knowledge of content. Our null hypothesis, NPFR, does fine. However, I do think there is another way to think about self-knowledge, a conception on which the connection to CP, and indeed to CPTC, is much stronger.[15]

Here's one way of getting at what I have in mind.[16] Consider Cartesian skeptical scenarios and their relation to knowledge claims. We all think we know all sorts of things about which Cartesian skeptical doubts can be raised. I know I'm typing on this computer now. But, the skeptic interjects, really, "for all I know" I'm really a brain in a vat. Does this entail that I don't know I'm typing on the computer? Well, I'm no epistemologist, but I will go out on a limb and say I still know it. Yes, it's subject to skeptical doubt. There is a clear sense in which everything could be as it is with me, epistemically speaking, and yet I'm a brain in a vat. I can't definitively rule it out. Yet, for all that, most of us would agree that I do know I'm currently typing on my computer.

Let's call such knowledge "dubitable" knowledge. I can doubt it, it makes sense to doubt it, I know what's being proposed when the doubt is presented, but I still know it nevertheless. Is there "indubitable" knowledge? Well, what's happening with me phenomenally—or, at least, some aspects of it—seems like a pretty good candidate. I'm now feeling a pain, or seeing red. It just seems an essential constituent of my epistemic position that I am having these experiences. I find it hard to even understand the skeptical doubt that I'm supposed to entertain here, if there is one. Yes, I might be a brain in a vat and none of what I see or hear or taste is real, but that doesn't touch my having certain auditory, visual, and gustatory experiences. Skepticism just doesn't get a grip here.

If we grant that conscious experience gives rise to at least some indubitable knowledge, then certain consequences follow. I have myself appealed to indubitable self-knowledge of phenomenal character to argue against externalist representational theories of phenomenal character.[17] Briefly, the argument goes like this. If phenomenal character were determined by the external, referential content of visual representations, then we could encounter Frege-cases, where two visual representations, say, pick out the same color, even though they look different. So long as phenomenal content

---

[15] It's very possible that the conception of self-knowledge I'm about to describe is what Pitt had in mind when speaking of an acquaintance-type relation. I still maintain that in the context, his appeal to acquaintance was question-begging; indeed, even at the end of the day it may be, as we'll see below.

[16] I owe a debt to Terry Horgan for valuable discussion of this conception of self-knowledge and its role in the cognitive phenomenology debate. See also my discussion in Levine (2001) and Horgan, Tienson, and Graham (2006).

[17] See Levine (2003a and 2003b). But also see Levine (2008), where I endorse a version of representationalism.

isn't identified with, or supervenient on, external content, there's no problem. But if the external content determines the phenomenal character, and the two visual representations pick out the same color, then how can they look different? That there is a phenomenal difference seems like a good example of indubitable knowledge, and my argument is that externalist representationalism cannot account for this.

Suppose we turn now to knowledge of content. Is this indubitable knowledge? Consider the Swampman hypothesis.[18] On some theories of content—especially teleo-semantic views, but maybe causal-covariational accounts as well—SwampJoe, my molecule-for-molecule duplicate that just appeared as a brain in a vat in deep space (just to make the case as strong as possible), doesn't genuinely think, or represent with his cognitive states, as his mental representations do not possess semantic properties. Now, I want to say this. That I'm not SwampJoe is something I know, but not indubitably. There is a clear sense in which I can coherently entertain the hypothesis that I am SwampJoe. But, initially at least, I want to say that I really can't entertain the hypothesis that I'm not thinking—I mean, really thinking—in just the way that I can't coherently entertain the hypothesis that I'm not phenomenally conscious right now. But if that's right—if indeed we have indubitable knowledge that we're thinking and what we're thinking—doesn't that cry out for explanation? It doesn't seem as if NPFR can provide that explanation. After all, the only clear example we have (if one goes this far with us "qualia freaks") of indubitable knowledge is what is presented to us phenomenally. What's more, both NPFR and CPOC, remember, put us behind the veil of representation, with no direct acquaintance with contents.[19] But then the argument that thought content must be presented phenomenally, and that its phenomenal presentation is the basis for our cognitive access to it, becomes compelling. Hence, we have an argument for CPTC.[20]

So whether we can get CPTC out of the self-knowledge argument—indeed, given my criticisms of the argument above, whether we get any version of CP out of it—depends on what kind of knowledge we're talking about. If we do indeed have indubitable knowledge—if I can tell without possible doubt from the inside that I'm genuinely thinking, with genuine content—then I would be inclined to accept that this somehow must be a matter of phenomenal access. The problem is, unlike with the case of sensory knowledge, I don't really know how to evaluate the claim to indubitable self-knowledge of content. Suppose there were a creature that only had a non-conscious computational mechanism superimposed on a phenomenally conscious sensorium. Would it be any different for that creature than my conscious life is for

[18] I discuss the implications of Swampman in Levine (1996).
[19] But see note 12 above.
[20] But notice this doesn't give us an argument for pure CPTC over impure CPTC. It could still be that contents can only be phenomenally revealed to us through sensory vehicles.

me?[21] Can I really tell, in that particular skepticism-repelling, indubitable way, that I'm *not* that creature? I have to admit that I just don't know.

For what it's worth, here's how things seem to me phenomenologically. I don't feel that I have any special access to *what* I'm thinking about, other than by way of the representations I use to express it. Of course, the advocate of CP will press the phenomenological argument to show that I can make finer distinctions phenomeno-logically than those provided by the range of sensory representational vehicles I can experience. But the phenomenal distinctions argument doesn't apply to the language of thought, where all ambiguities that are distinguishable in thought are captured by distinct representations. So I don't really see how I have any more direct, or firmer grasp of what I'm thinking than that it's whatever I'm currently representing in thought.

However, *that* I'm thinking, that my thoughts are really about something, and not meaningless formal objects, does seem apparent to me in that special way. I am, to borrow a phrase that was popular among presenters at a conference I recently attended, "just emoting" here, not arguing. I don't really know if one can have indubitable knowledge that one is thinking without indubitably knowing what one is thinking.[22] But if you can, then I think you still don't get CPTC. For which content one is entertaining is determined by the semantic content of one's mental representations, and all one has to think with are one's representations. We're still behind the veil, on this view, but it's just that it's phenomenally apparent to us that something is on the other side.[23]

Emoting aside, I want to conclude as follows. Dubitable self-knowledge of content is consistent with NPFR, and so with no cognitive phenomenology at all. Indubitable self-knowledge very well might support CPTC, though whether we have such self-knowledge of content is itself dubitable. The phenomenological argument, on the other hand, does support at least one version of CP, namely impure CPOC. Though this is the weakest of the versions surveyed here, it is still a version of CP—by my lights, anyway—so in the end I do come down, though not heavily, on CP's side.[24]

---

[21] To forestall a possible misunderstanding here, let me say this. Horgan and Tienson (2002) argue that consideration of phenomenal duplicates supports CP. They claim that it's hard to imagine two creatures with identical phenomenal streams who nevertheless are consciously thinking distinct thoughts. I take this to be a version of the phenomenological argument, which I have already accepted. However, what's at issue now is whether this consideration also supports CPTC. I don't see that their argument does that.

[22] Interestingly, Dretske (2003) seems to argue for the reverse, though he wouldn't endorse my notion of indubitable knowledge. Still, he thinks we have a kind of epistemic guarantee of what we're thinking, so long as we are in fact thinking anything at all, though no such guarantee that we satisfy that condition. There are passages in Siewert's (1998) discussion that seem to rely on a distinction between knowledge that thought is going on and knowledge of precisely what is being thought that might support this idea.

[23] I suspect that this position as stated cannot be maintained, but that something like it can so long as we come up with the right theory of content. Material for another project.

[24] I want to thank Louise Antony, Terry Horgan, Michelle Montague, David Pitt, Georges Rey, Charles Siewert, Kelly Trogdon, and the audience at Cal State LA, where an earlier version of this paper was presented, for comments on an earlier draft and very helpful discussion.

References

Block, N.J. (1995). "On a Confusion about the Function of Consciousness," *Behavioral and Brain Sciences*, vol. 18, 227–47.

Dretske, F. (2003). "Externalism and Self-Knowledge," in S. Nuccetelli (ed.), *New Essays on Semantic Externalism and Self-Knowledge*. Cambridge, MA: MIT Press.

Fodor, J.A. (1983). *The Modularity of Mind*. Cambridge, MA: Bradford Books/MIT Press.

Goldman, A. (1993). "The Psychology of Folk Psychology," *Behavioral and Brain Sciences*, vol. 16, 15–28.

Horgan, T. and Tienson, J. (2002). "The Intentionality of Phenomenology and the Phenomenology of Intentionality," in D. Chalmers (ed.), *Philosophy of Mind: Classical and Contemporary Readings*. Oxford: Oxford University Press.

——,——,and Graham, G. (2006). "Internal-World Skepticism and the Self-Presentational Nature of Phenomenal Consciousness," in U. Kriegel and K. Williford (eds), *Self-Representational Approaches to Consciousness*. Cambridge, MA: Bradford/MIT Press.

Levine, J. (1996). "SwampJoe: Mind or Simulation?" *Mind and Language*, vol. 11, no. 1, March, 1996, 86–91.

——(2001). *Purple Haze: The Puzzle of Consciousness*. New York: Oxford University Press.

——(2003a). "Experience and Representation," in Q. Smith and A. Jokic (eds), *Consciousness: New Essays*. Oxford and New York: Oxford University Press.

——(2003b). "Knowing What It's Like," in B. Gertler (ed.), *Privileged Access: Philosophical Accounts of Self-Knowledge*. Burlington, VT: Ashgate Publishing.

——(2008). "Secondary Qualities: Where Consciousness and Intentionality Meet," *Monist*, vol. 91, no. 2.

Lormand, E. (1996). "Nonphenomenal Consciousness," *Noûs*, 30: 242–61.

Nagel, T. (1974). "What Is It Like to Be a Bat?" *The Philosophical Review*, vol. 82, 435–50.

Nelkin, N. (1989). "Propositional Attitudes and Consciousness," *Philosophy and Phenomenological Research*, vol. 49, no. 3, 413–30.

Nichols, S. and Stich, S. (2003). "How to Read Your Own Mind: A Cognitive Theory of Self-Consciousness," in Q. Smith and A. Jokic (eds), *Consciousness: New Philosophical Perspectives*. Oxford: Clarendon Press.

Pitt, D. (2004). "The Phenomenology of Cognition, Or What Is It Like to Think that P?" *Philosophy and Phenomenological Research*, LXIX, no. 1.

Pylyshyn, Z. (2001). *Seeing and Visualizing: It's Not What You Think*. Cambridge, MA: Bradford Books/MIT Press.

Siegel, S. (2006). "Which Properties are Represented in Perception?" in T.S. Gendler and J. Hawthorne (eds), *Perceptual Experience*. Oxford: Oxford University Press.

——(2007). "How Can We Discover the Contents of Experience?" *The Southern Journal of Philosophy*, vol. xlv, 127–42.

Siewert, C. (1998). *The Significance of Consciousness*. Princeton, NJ: Princeton University Press.

The Phenomenology of Particularity

Michelle Montague

1 Introduction

Almost everyone agrees that we perceive individual physical objects, and almost everyone agrees that we perceive them *as* individual physical objects—as discrete, numerically distinct, as particulars. Even those who claim that there are no physical objects, or that there is only one,[1] can hardly deny that we *seem* to perceive particular individual objects—chairs, tables, and people, i.e. that we have perceptual experience that has the *character* of being experience of individual particular objects. It is part of the *experiential qualitative character* of many of our perceptual experiences, to put it in other words, that they are experiences of individual particular objects. This is part of the *phenomenal character* or (experienced) *what-it's-likeness* of many of our perceptual experiences, whether or not they are in fact veridical experiences of individual particular objects in the world.

It is this fact about the character of our perceptual experience—the fact that perceptual experience exhibits particularity when purely phenomenologically considered—that is my present concern. I will refer to it variously as the 'particularity of perception', the 'phenomenological particularity fact', the 'phenomenology of particularity', or 'phenomenal particularity'. It is a distinctively phenomenological fact, and it is as remarked something that can be exhibited as much by a non-veridical (e.g. hallucinatory) experience as by a veridical experience. In recognition of this point I will use the expression 'perceptual experience' in such a way that it applies equally to hallucinatory experience and veridical experience: on these terms, then, there can be *perceptual experience* without genuine *perception*, where genuine perception implies detection of a genuinely existent external object, just as there can be a pink-elephant experience without a pink elephant.

Is the particularity of perception philosophically interesting? Does it raise a genuine philosophical problem, and if so, what is it exactly? Part of it, I think, is this. We seem

---

[1] E.g. Parmenides, Spinoza, and a considerable number of contemporary physicists and cosmologists. For a recent philosophical statement of the view, see Horgan and Potrč 2008.

to perceive particular physical objects. But 'Twin Earth' style thought experiments encourage the idea that there is a fundamental sense in which the perceptual content of perceptual experience must be thought of as essentially and wholly general in nature, rather than particular. In discussing Twin-Earth style thought experiments, I propose to use the phrase 'general content' to cover all content that is shareable across experiences in such a way that the *content* of two experiences can be said to be exactly the same while the (external) *objects* of those experiences differ.[2] Given this 'generalist' view of content, the problem of particularity can be stated as follows: if the content of perceptual experience is general content, how do we account for the experiential, qualitative character of particularity, and how do we do so in a phenomenologically satisfactory manner?

What about a 'particularist' account of content, according to which the perceptual content of a genuine perception is in some sense 'object-dependent'—so that one can't give an adequate specification of its content without reference to the actual physical objects it is a perception of? Does it do any better? No. Just as simply stating that we do in fact perceive physical objects, or stand in causal relations to them, does not account for the phenomenology of particularity, so too simply stating that perceptual content is object-dependent does not account for the phenomenology of particularity. Appealing to a supposed object-dependency of perceptual content does not give a satisfactory *phenomenological* account of phenomenal particularity because it doesn't explain why particularity is a phenomenal feature of perceptual experience.[3]

In what follows I will try to clarify what I mean by 'giving a satisfactory phenomenological account of a phenomenological fact', and explain how we know when we're giving one. In sections 2–5 I will argue that both paradigmatic generalists about content and paradigmatic particularists about content fail to account for the phenomenological particularity fact (whether or not they are trying to account for it).[4] The generalists fail not because the content of perceptual experiences is not general, but because they have not isolated the correct general feature of content to account for the phenomenological

---

[2] By 'object' I will always mean 'physical object'.

[3] One may object that the mere fact that one is in perceptual contact with an object does explain the phenomenological fact. After all, according to 'representationalists' like Tye, the phenomenal character of a perceptual experience is determined by that experience's 'representational' properties, i.e. the properties of the object that are represented. According to these accounts, however, the object qua object of an experience, considered independently of its properties, does not play any role in determining the phenomenal character of that experience (see e.g. Tye 2009: 258). So, the question that remains for the particularist is, what about the object, if not the properties of the object, is accounting for phenomenological particularity? It is doubtful that many particularists will wish to appeal to haecceities or bare particulars.

[4] Among generalists about content (typically called 'internalists' about content) I am counting McGinn (1997), Davies (1992), and Horgan and Tienson (2002). Among 'particularists' about content (typically called 'externalists' about content) I am counting Evans (1982), Martin (2002a, 2002b) and McDowell (1986). Martin's case is slightly complicated by the fact that he claims to be offering an account of phenomenal particularity that a generalist about content could accept (see e.g. 2002b); but I'll argue that in the end, the account he articulates is particularist.

particularity fact. The particularists fail because they don't give a *phenomenological* account of the phenomenological particularity fact at all.

In section 6 I will present the core of my own theory of mental content, and in particular perceptual content, and show how it succeeds in giving an adequate phenomenological account of the phenomenological particularity fact. I will argue that the feature of perceptual content that accounts for the phenomenology of particularity is in fact general in form. There is a distinctive feature of the (general or phenomenological) content of perceptual experiences, which I will call *object-positing*, or *taking as object*. *Object-positing* is a fundamental category of perceptual experience, a basic structural element of perceptions and perceptual experiences in general. Moreover, *object-positing* is best seen as a matter of what philosophers now call *cognitive phenomenology*, a kind of phenomenology distinct from sensory phenomenology. That *object-positing* is a matter of cognitive phenomenology is a central point in the overall cognitive phenomenology debate, precisely because *object-positing* is central to human *perceptual* experience. So, the phenomenon of cognitive phenomenology cannot be restricted to occurrent thoughts such as *judging that 2+2=4* or *judging that temperance is a virtue*; it has an indispensible role to play in accounting for perceptual experience as well. Finally, I will argue that although *object-positing* is a wholly phenomenological matter, it is nevertheless an essential part of what secures external reference to the objects of our perceptions.

2 Generalists about content

Generalists typically begin with a notion of content that is explicitly meant to capture the phenomenological aspects of perceptual content. McGinn, for example, defines perceptual content as 'how the experiencer represents the world as being' (1997: 49). Davies writes that 'perceptual content is a phenomenological notion—it concerns how things seem to the subject' (1992: 25). Horgan and Tienson claim 'sensory-experiential states have intentional content inseparable from their phenomenal character' (2002: 520); that is, there is a kind of intentionality—which they call 'phenomenal intentionality'— that is constitutively determined by phenomenology alone. All of these notions of content share, as their starting point, a characterization of content *from a subject's point of view* or in terms of *what it is like for a subject*. But while McGinn and Davies are explicit about their definitions of content being generalist, it's only implied by Horgan and Tienson's account.

Generalists typically express their position on content with the following kind of claim:

[1] two experiences can have exactly the same perceptual content but different objects.

The central idea is that different subjects who are 'phenomenal duplicates' of each other can share the same perceptual content across experiences of distinct objects.[5] This

---

[5] Subject A is a complete phenomenal duplicate of subject B if and only if A's total experience is phenomenologically identical to B's.

idea is expressed in a variety of ways. McGinn considers the example of seeing a book. He characterizes the perceptual content as 'has an experience of a book with such and such a character', and claims that numerically distinct books could 'fit' this content for the same subject or for different subjects.[6] Davies expresses the same point by claiming that two distinct objects can seem phenomenologically indistinguishable to a subject. Finally, Horgan and Tienson ask us to imagine phenomenal duplicates situated differently (e.g. one in the actual world, one in a Twin world, and one a disembodied Cartesian soul), all having a sensory experience as of a crooked picture hanging on the wall in front of them. Based on the sensory phenomenology alone, they claim, we can determine how things have to be with them in order for each experience to be accurate.[7] For each duplicate, there has to be a crooked picture hanging on a real wall in front of them in real space. So, each phenomenal duplicate's experience shares what Horgan and Tienson call *narrow truth conditions*.[8]

The next claim is that if [1] is true, if two experiences can have the same perceptual content with different objects, then

[2] a (singular) term referring to the object of experience (if any) cannot be used in specifying the perceptual content of whichever experience is in question.

Consider two experiences with the same perceptual content on the terms of [1]. If a singular term were used to refer to the object in specifying the content of one of those experiences, it would be impossible for the experiences to have identical perceptual content while having distinct objects of experience; contrary to [1]. So, assuming that either general terms or singular terms must be used in specifying the content of perceptual experience, we can conclude that, on this conception of content,

[3] only general terms can be used in specifying the content of experience.

It's no good to argue that we do in fact use singular terms such as 'that' to refer to the objects of experience, as in 'I see that book'. The argument just given is not meant to show that we can't use singular terms for this purpose, only that they can't be used if our goal is to fully and accurately capture the perceptual content of the relevant perceptual experience.

I have couched [2] and [3] in terms of general and singular terms, but the same point can be made in terms of existentially quantified content. Davies says, 'we can take perceptual content to be existentially quantified content. A visual experience may present the world as containing an object of a certain size and shape, in a certain

---

[6] Each of these phenomenologically identical experiences with different objects can be fully veridical.

[7] For more on this point see Siewert (1998).

[8] Horgan and Tienson's account of phenomenal intentionality is much more complex. For example, it involves a discussion of certain presuppositions that must be in place given a particular sensory experience. However, I can ignore these complexities for my purposes. There is also more to be said about truth conditions, which I will come back to in section 5.

direction, at a certain distance from the subject' (1992: 26). In Horgan and Tienson's terms: since for phenomenal duplicates there is a respectable sense in which the locations they inhabit have to be the same in order for their experiences to be accurate, the content of their experiences must be existentially quantified content.

3 The phenomenological particularity fact

A significant problem with the generalist account of perceptual content is that although it is motivated by phenomenological considerations, it seems to ignore a fundamental phenomenological fact—the phenomenological particularity fact—the fact that it seems to us that we perceive particular objects. How can content of the type generalists have thus far appealed to, which is completely general in nature, provide sufficient materials with which to give an account of the phenomenological particularity that is undeniably a part of perceptual experience?

The problem can be seen in the following way. Since Russell, philosophers have been keen to isolate a kind of thought—which we now call *de re* thought or *singular thought*—that is distinct from so-called *general thought*. The idea is that *de re* thought is in some sense more intimately connected to objects than general thought. If we accept a Russellian view of definite descriptions, for example, there is a fundamental difference between thinking about the tallest man in the jungle via a definite description and thinking about him because one is directly acquainted with him via perception.[9] In the first case, the tallest man in the jungle is isolated by means of quantifiers and properties, whereas in the latter case there is a kind of direct contact with the man. It is sometimes said that in perception the subject is *en rapport* with the object in question, whereas when deploying a definite description the subject engages in a process of narrowing or whittling down to a single object via quantifiers and properties. If Horgan et al. are right about how to characterize the content of perceptual experience, then in perceiving the object of perception the subject isolates—makes unique demonstrative contact with—the object of perception by using only general features of the object, the object's properties. In representing the content of perceptual experience as purely general in this way, the distinctive way in which perception isolates the object of perception is left out, and so in turn the phenomenology of particularity is left out.[10]

There is clearly a semantico-logical difference between descriptive/general thought and singular thought. My contention is that even if the generalists are right about all perceptual content being general content, the content of perceptual experience cannot simply be a matter of properties being used to isolate objects, because this misses out the

---

[9] For an interesting discussion on the difference between how general thoughts and singular thoughts are about their objects see Evans (1982: 128).

[10] Appealing to tropes—particularized properties—does not solve the problem of particularity. Even if trope theory were the correct metaphysical account of properties, there would still be the phenomenological fact that a particular physical object is presented to the subject in a given perceptual experience and this fact would not be captured by listing the tropes one is presented with in that particular experience.

phenomenological or presentational difference between general and singular thought.[11] An adequate account of this presentational difference requires reference to the phenomenological feature of phenomenal particularity.

It may seem that particularists about content should do better than generalists, when it comes to explaining the phenomenological particularity fact. And it is true that particularists have quite rightly pointed out the necessity of acknowledging the phenomenology of particularity. For example, Martin says:

When I look at a duck in front of me, I am not merely presented with the fact that there is at least one duck in the area, rather I seem to be presented with *this* thing in front of me, which looks to me to be a duck . . . It looks to me as if there is a particular object before me . . . Hence we should expect a theory of sensory experience which aims to give an adequate account of the phenomenology to accommodate and explain how such experience can indeed be particular in character (2002b: 173).

Although the phenomenology of particularity is explicitly acknowledged, I'll argue that particularists such as Evans and McDowell, and even Martin, who attempts to square general content with the phenomenology of particularity, do not adequately address the phenomenology of particularity.

4 Particularists about content

With Evans, McDowell introduced the idea that the content of a perception can only be determined with reference to the object the perception is of. According to Evans and McDowell, physical objects are in some sense 'constituents' of the contents of (veridical) perceptions. That is, veridical perceptions are object-involving in such a way that the content of a veridical perception cannot occur in a perceptual experience in the absence of the relevant objects. So hallucinations and qualitatively identical veridical perceptions cannot possibly have the same content. Using 'content' in the wholly externalist way, and putting an internalist conception of content into scare quotes, McDowell says of hallucinations that 'these 'contents' could not yield answers to the question what it is that someone thinks; there is really no reason to recognize them as contents at all' (1986: 165). According to Evans, when we see an object 'there is a kind of thought we sometimes have, typically expressed in the form "This F is G", and we may aim to have a thought of this kind when, in virtue of the absence of any appropriate object, there is no such thought to be had'.[12]

[11] At this point, one may suggest that generalists could appeal to temporal indexical items and egocentric spatial relations between the subject and the objects of experience, in order to explain how the subject makes demonstrative contact. The question is: do these features help in accounting for phenomenal particularity? It seems not. Moreover, locating objects in egocentric space already assumes one has isolated particular objects, which in turn assumes an account of phenomenal particularity.

[12] Evans (1982: 46). The question of how to describe the mental episode one would have if one were having a hallucination that was qualitatively identical to a veridical perception is left open by Evans, as well as the exact sense in which a physical object is a constituent of a veridical perception. I'll leave both of these issues aside for the time being.

Clearly Evans and McDowell would reject premise [1] of the argument considered in section 2: two (veridical) experiences cannot have identical content if the objects of those experiences differ. If external objects are essential to determining the content of perceptual experiences, and if two experiences have numerically distinct objects, it follows that those experiences have different content, whatever else they may seem to have in common.

On the one hand, taking phenomenal particularity (the phenomenological particularity fact) seriously may move one to accept this kind of externalist theory of content. That is, the fact that a subject is presented with a particular object in a given perception may seem to be the *reason* why the content of the perception can only be specified relative to the relevant physical object. Although McDowell does not talk in these phenomenological terms, his motivation for object-dependent modes of presentation seems similar: object-dependent modes of presentation are the only way to account for the object-directedness of intentionality.[13] On the other hand, the notion of content introduced by Evans and other externalists seems to moves us further away from a phenomenological conception of content. On their view, the essential factor for determining a perception's content is *not* how things seem to a subject, but an external-world object.[14]

We seem to be in a bit of a conundrum. Twin-Earth style thought experiments appear to support the intuition that perceptual content is general, purely qualitatively specifiable in an internalist way, and this seems to be clearly so when it comes to phenomenological content, even if there is more to be said about content in general. At the same time, it now begins to seem as if the phenomenology of particularity, the phenomenological particularity fact, may support an externalist conception of content.

This remains to be seen. What is clear, I think, is that neither generalists nor particularists can adequately explain the phenomenological fact with the resources so far available. It is as remarked unclear how one can derive the phenomenological particularity fact from the kind of content the generalists have offered. And even if the phenomenological particularity fact were to support an externalist conception of content, it would be equally unclear how claiming that content is object-dependent could explain anything about the phenomenology of perceptual experience. What is so far missing, what is really needed, is a 'from the inside' account for why it seems to us that we perceive particulars—of what it is for it to seem to us that we perceive particulars.

5 Martin and Burge

I will now consider Martin's attempt to square the generalists' claim that the content of perceptual experience is general with the fact that perceptual experience has a distinctive phenomenology of particularity.[15]

---

[13] See his 1986 criticisms of McGinn's so-called 'two-factor' view.

[14] It is interesting to note that Evans was not at all concerned with the phenomenology of particularity—the issue does not even arise for him.

[15] Martin (2002b). It should be noted that part of Martin's project in this paper is precisely to resist any inference from the phenomenological particularity fact to an externalist conception of content.

To begin, I'll introduce a bit of Martin's terminology. He distinguishes between *phenomenal nature* and *phenomenal* or *qualitative character*. 'Qualitative character' is meant to capture similarities and differences of *content* that can exist across distinct experiences irrespective of their actual objects. Determining qualitative character requires abstracting away from the objects of perception to identify the ways in which two or more experiences are qualitatively alike or different. Considering two experiences of qualitatively indistinguishable yellow ducks, Martin says: 'The content of sensory experiences is context insensitive: distinct sensory episodes which could have occurred at different times, or with the presentation of distinct objects, possess the same content' (2002b, pp. 191–2). So, Martin's qualitative character is essentially equivalent to the generalists' general content, and I think it is crucial to point out here, for reasons that will become clear below, that Martin has reserved the term *content* for qualitative character.

As mentioned above, however, Martin also quite rightly recognizes that perceptual experiences possess phenomenal particularity. In speaking of what he calls a perceptual experience's '*phenomenal nature*', he aims to capture the idea that experience typically presents particulars, or a particular, as such and he asserts that *what an experience is like* cannot be understood independently of this (phenomenological) fact. Perceptual experiences phenomenologically present particular objects, and an account of the phenomenal nature of an experience registers this fact: 'we can't understand what an experience is like independent of its subject matter. The phenomenal nature of a given experience is a matter of what is presented to the subject and the manner in which it is presented . . . the phenomenal nature of experience is, at least in part, the presentation of a subject matter' (ibid: 186). It should be clear, then, that Martin is using 'presentation' in a phenomenology implicating sense.

Martin then goes on to characterize an experience's phenomenal nature and an experience's content (its qualitative or phenomenal character) as unrepeatable and repeatable features of that experience respectively:

Once we reflect on the way in which an experience has a subject matter, the presentation of a particular scene, then we need a way of making room for the essentially or inherently particular aspects of this as well as the general attributes of experience. We need to contrast the unrepeatable aspect of its phenomenology, what we might call its *phenomenal nature*, with that [which] it has in common with qualitatively the same experiential events, what we might call its *phenomenal character* (ibid: 193–4)

It seems, then, that although experiences of numerically distinct objects can share *qualitative characters*, on Martin's terms, they cannot share *phenomenal natures*: if two experiences have different objects, then they have distinct phenomenal natures, even if they have identical qualitative characters: 'one may claim that what it takes for an entity to be an aspect of the phenomenology of experience is just that it be among the presented elements of that particular episode. Such an experience could be entirely qualitatively identical with another experience involving a distinct object and yet still differ in its phenomenal nature solely in this respect' (ibid: 187).

Pointing out that perceptual experiences have phenomenal natures, i.e. that they present particular subject matters, clearly registers the fact that perceptual experiences of particular objects have a phenomenology of particularity. But what can be said about phenomenal natures? To answer this question, and thus to give an account of phenomenological particularity, Martin purports to offer a Burgean account of the content of perceptual experience (see Burge 1993). I'll argue, however, that the account Martin offers is not Burgean, and is arguably inconsistent with Burge's view. I'll argue that the account Martin does offer collapses into an Evans/McDowell style of account. I'll begin with a brief presentation of Burge's account.

Burge conceives of a truth condition of a perceptual experience 'as a requirement that has to be met for the Intentional state to be veridical' (1993: 196), rather than as what would fulfil the requirement, i.e. an object or a state of affairs. He also accepts the strategy of giving an account of the intentional content of a perceptual experience in terms of conditions of satisfaction or truth conditions. The content of a particular perceptual experience, then, is (essentially) the requirement a state must meet in order to be veridical. (In what follows, I will use the terms 'truth conditions', 'conditions of satisfaction', and 'correctness conditions' interchangeably.)

According to Burge, the content of a perceptual experience essentially involves a demonstrative element, but he says over and over again that the contribution of the demonstrative element to a perceptual experience's content is not object-dependent.

the Intentional content does not include any physical object that is actually picked out: the content is a demonstrative application of something of the form 'That F is G'. Sometimes a demonstrative content fails to pick out any objects. And sometimes, even when it does, it [the content] can be individuated independently of that object. The satisfaction conditions require that there be *a* relevant demonstrated object if the Intentional content is to be true (ibid: 196; my emphasis)

to be *de re*, a thought should both contain a primitive demonstrative element in its content and involve successful reference through a demonstrative element to an object or *re* . . . [but] the two requirements for being a *de re* thought are separable. It is possible for an applied demonstrative element to fail to have a referent. Since thoughts are individuated in terms of their contents, some demonstrative thoughts are not *de re*. Moreover, since some demonstrative token applications that in fact have a referent might have failed to have had one (if the contextual circumstances had been different), some thought tokens that are in fact *de re* are not essentially *de re* (ibid: 208).

The first conclusion we can draw from these quotations is that a veridical perception of a red round ball, for example, and a subjectively indistinguishable hallucination of a red round ball can share the same content. In one circumstance a token application of the intentional content has a referent, and in a relevantly different circumstance a distinct token application of that same intentional content fails to have a referent. Since these two experiences are distinct tokens that share the same content, Burge must have content types in mind when he says distinct experiences can share a content. A veridical perception of a red round ball and a subjectively indistinguishable hallucination of a red round ball share a content type in such a way that when that content type is tokened in one circumstance the result is a *de re* perceptual experience and when tokened in the relevantly different circumstance the result is a hallucination (a non *de re* perceptual experience).

Now, if it's possible that a *de re* perceptual experience could have failed to have had a referent, had the circumstances been different, I think we must also conclude that it is possible for that applied demonstrative element to have had a different referent from the one it actually has had the circumstances been different. There seems to be no legitimate way to restrict the variation of circumstances, vis-à-vis a particular intentional content type, to circumstances that would result in a hallucination, while excluding circumstances in which there is a different real object. When Burge says that 'the satisfaction conditions require that there be *a* relevant demonstrated object if the Intentional content is to be true', the indefinite article plainly allows for this second possibility.

On Burge's account, then, at least three perceptual experiences may share the content type [that F is G].[16] In circumstance 1, the content type is tokened and it refers to object a, and a is F and G. In circumstance 2, the content type is tokened and it fails to refer because the perceptual experience is a hallucination. In circumstance 3, the content type is tokened and it refers to object b, b≠a, and b is F and G. In cases 1 and 3 the content types are true (or veridical), and in case 2 the content type is false. It follows, on his account, that the truth conditions (or correctness conditions) associated with content types are object-independent. If a content type can be made true (or veridical) by distinct objects, the truth (or correctness) conditions cannot be object-dependent. What is not object-independent is whether a content type when tokened is true; but this is trivial.

Let's now turn to what Martin offers as an account of the phenomenology of particularity and ask: is it Burge's? In explicating phenomenal natures, Martin begins by introducing the idea that perceptual experiences have correctness conditions, and he explicates correctness conditions by considering the case where one has two experiences of qualitatively indistinguishable but distinct ducks. According to Martin, the correctness conditions for these two experiences will be distinct because correctness conditions can only be determined relative to a context.

---

[16] The notation [that F is G], and its use of a predicate expression 'F' to characterize the demonstrative element, is Burge's.

The content of sensory experiences is context insensitive … distinct sensory episodes which could have occurred at different times or with the presentation of distinct objects [can] possess the same content. But content can be context-insensitive without its correctness conditions being so: for the content may determine a correctness condition relative to context. (Martin 2002b: 191–2)

So, according to Martin, the content of two qualitatively identical experiences can be the same while those experiences have distinct correctness conditions, because it is possible that the objects of those experiences are different.

We can already see that this is not Burge's account. According to Burge, and as he himself states, the *truth* or *veridicality* of a particular thought or experience depends on a particular object, but the correctness or truth conditions do not. In other words, same content type delivers same truth conditions; what is context-dependent is simply whether that content type is true (veridical) or false (non-veridical). As Burge (ibid: 211) says, 'The satisfaction conditions require that there be a relevant demonstrated object if the Intentional content is to be true'. So Martin is not appealing to Burge's theory to account for the phenomenology of particularity. I will therefore continue to refer to the theory Martin does articulate as 'Martin's account'.

We can now ask of Martin's account: does the claim that the content of a perceptual experience determines correctness conditions only relative to a context move us forward in explaining the phenomenology of particularity? Martin seems to think that the idea of correctness conditions gives us a way of understanding the *repeatable* and *unrepeatable* features of perceptual experience, which in turn elucidates the phenomenology of particularity. The phenomenal or qualitative character of an experience is a *repeatable* feature of that experience; it can after all be shared with other experiences. But the subject matter of a perceptual experience—where this is meant to capture the phenomenology of particularity—is an *unrepeatable* feature of that experience. And what better candidate for an unrepeatable feature of a perceptual experience of a physical object than the physical object itself?

In summary, although the qualitative character of a perceptual experience is determined by that experience's intentional content, and is shareable across experiences, Martin emphasizes the idea that there is a phenomenology of particularity involved in perceptual experience. Perceptual experience presents a particular subject matter: this is what is meant to capture the phenomenology of particularity. But Martin makes a further claim about the phenomenology of particularity, that it is an unrepeatable feature of experience, and the obvious candidate for this unrepeatable feature are physical objects themselves. He says:

In order to do justice to the intuition that the very object one is perceiving is an aspect of the phenomenology of one's experience, we must recognize that such objects figure within any adequate specification of the particular phenomenal nature of the experience one has at a time, and this is reflected in giving the truth conditions of how things are presented relative to that context. (Martin 2002b: 196)

So, physical objects are introduced via truth conditions, which, according to Martin, are context dependent.

There are a number of problems with Martin's account, which I'll briefly state here and return to in section 6.

[a] Ultimately, Martin appeals to physical objects themselves to explain phenomenal particularity, and in so far as this is an attempt to explain the phenomenological particularity fact, it is no different from an Evans/McDowell style of approach. (He uses the word 'content' differently, which masks the similarity to the Evans/McDowell account). In short, Martin conflates the fact that a perceptual experience, when veridical, is of a particular object and the fact that it *seems* to a subject that she is perceiving a particular object.

[b] In using *content* in the way he does, to designate the qualitative character of experience, Martin has it that what he calls the *subject matter* of a particular experience, what the experience is of, is not part of the *content* of that experience.

[c] As far as I can see, according to Martin, hallucinations do not have a subject matter—they do not present a particular scene. If the phenomenal nature or subject matter of an experience is ultimately explained in terms of physical objects, and hallucinations are perceptual experiences that lack physical objects, hallucinations do not have subject matters.

The main problem with Martin's account is that although it registers the phenomenological particularity fact, and registers it as part of what he calls an experience's 'phenomenal nature', it does not provide a satisfactory phenomenological solution. He does not actually say anything substantive about the phenomenology of particularity itself.

Indeed, although Horgan and Tienson use different terminology, they can agree with most of what Martin says. In section 3 I introduced Horgan and Tienson's conception of what they call 'narrow truth conditions' for sensory experiences. On their account, the experiences of phenomenal duplicates looking at qualitatively identical crooked pictures share narrow truth conditions. However, Horgan and Tienson also acknowledge that there is a sense in which the truth conditions for those experiences are different. The accuracy of each duplicate's experience will also depend on the particular picture he is looking at, and these pictures are numerically distinct, and in this sense the truth conditions for each experience differ. These are appropriately called 'wide truth conditions'. It looks as if Horgan and Tienson's narrow truth conditions are Martin's qualitative character, and their wide truth conditions capture the essential idea behind Martin's phenomenal nature.

One of the main differences between these views concerns the question of whether to countenance two kinds of truth conditions, and perhaps correspondingly two kinds of content. Does the qualitative character of a perceptual experience alone determine a set of truth conditions, as Horgan and Tienson suppose, or is Martin right to think that truth conditions or correctness conditions can only be determined relative to a context? I'm not sure what the right answer to this question is, but it seems we still do not have an adequate account of phenomenal particularity. I now turn to my own proposal.

6 Object–positing and cognitive phenomenology

Any adequate approach to the notion of perceptual content must have a phenomenological component, even if phenomenological content is not the only kind of content that perceptual experiences have. Let us say—it should hardly be controversial—that the *total* content of any particular experience is *everything* that one experiences in having the experience, everything one is aware of in having the experience. The question is then, What does one experience? What is one aware of?

Well, if I see a green tree, then, plainly, I have experience of the tree, I am aware of the tree. I may also then be aware of the ambient temperature, the hills behind, certain grasped opportunities for action with respect to the tree and many, many other things in the world. But my awareness also has certain phenomenological features: it is also, and of course, something that has, essentially, a certain experiential qualitative character, given which there is, in a familiar phrase, 'something it is like' for the subject of experience to have it. This is part of what I experience in having the experience. A wholly externalist understanding of the phrase *what I experience* is as inadequate as a wholly internalist understanding of it.

All perceptual experiences involve *sensory* experience, whether exteroceptive (e.g. visual, olfactory, auditory) or interoceptive (e.g. experience of pain, hunger, nervousness, bodily movement), and many take the word 'phenomenology' to cover only the qualitative character of sensory experience. It is, however, clear that there is more to perceptual experience, phenomenologically, i.e. experientially, than merely sensory phenomenology. There is more to perceptual—visual—experience (as) of a green tree beside a beach ball than there is to having merely sensory experience of the array of colours that would be recorded by a photograph taken from where one is. I will express this by saying that in any perceptual experience there is non-sensory phenomenology, which I will call *cognitive phenomenology*, as well as sensory phenomenology. One part of it, for example, is seeing the tree *as a tree*, or seeing the duck–rabbit figure as a duck (or as a rabbit). One can't give a full account of the phenomenological character of the experience without referring to facts such as these.

The question of how much falls under the heading of cognitive phenomenology is a huge philosophical topic, which I cannot hope to address here. For now, let me simply say that it is the fact that the subject possesses and applies the concepts that he does apply, in the having of that experience, that principally determines the cognitive-phenomenological content of the experience. In these terms, my question is whether the cognitive phenomenology of an experience extends beyond—or behind—the deployment of everyday particular concepts such as TABLE and CHAIR. I'm going to propose that it also includes certain extremely fundamental concepts that are basic to almost all of our thought and perception, and, in particular, contribute essentially to the account of the phenomenology of particularity.

The main mistake of the particularists considered here is the way in which they attempt to tie the phenomenology of particularity to actual physical objects. What is true of almost all ordinary perceptual experience is that it *seems* to us that a particular object is perceived (or that several particular objects are perceived). It is part of the phenomenology of the experience that a particular object is perceived (or that several particular objects are perceived). This is what I have called the 'phenomenological particularity fact'. Martin and other proponents of Evans/McDowell-style accounts mistakenly look for something unrepeatable (non-general)—particular physical objects —to explain the phenomenological particularity fact. This cannot be right, however, for the simple reason that phenomenological particularity also occurs in hallucinations.

I think this simple fact should lead us to conclude two things:

[i] we have a strong reason not to look to physical objects in seeking to give an adequate account of the phenomenon of phenomenological particularity;

[ii] phenomenological particularity is actually a general feature of content. Nearly all perceptual experiences have as part of their general (phenomenological) content something like the following: that there is a/some particular item being represented—there is a presentation of a *this thing*. The *this thing* feature is a general feature since it can be shared by many different perceptual experiences.

What we need, then, is to square the fundamental (internalist) generality of perceptual content with the phenomenon of phenomenological particularity in a way that respects the claims made in [i] and [ii]. We need an account that allows us to treat perceptual experiences and hallucinations in a uniform manner with respect to the phenomenological particularity fact. A Martinian approach, by contrast, will have to give a different kind of account of phenomenological particularity in the case of hallucinations.

Martin gestures towards an explanation of the content of hallucination, an explanation which is again based on Burge's account of *de re* thought. Burge accounts for *de re* thoughts in terms of what he calls their 'nonconceptual, contextual' relations. The property of a thought's being a *de re* thought about an object consists in the subject's standing in 'an appropriate nonconceptual, contextual relation to [the] object'. '*De re* beliefs', he says (and the point presumably applies equally to *de re* thoughts), 'are about predication broadly conceived, dealing with a relation between open sentences (or what they express) and objects'.[17] (Burge does not use 'nonconceptual' to mean a kind of representational content as it is often used today; here it just means contextual.) So, in the case of hallucination, according to Martin, the content of the experience would be given in terms of open sentences, e.g. x is red and x is round:

> For hallucination and perception to warrant the same explanation we only require that they be of the same qualitative kind: this is captured by the common, object-independent content . . . Such an experience can share the very same intentional content with the [veridical] perceptual experience, since that content, in being given in a manner analogous to an open sentence, is object-independent.[18]

Again, this account of hallucination is inadequate at the crucial point because it leaves out phenomenal particularity, which can be just as present in a hallucination as it is in a typical veridical perception. And since Martin takes phenomenal particularity so seriously in the case of veridical perceptions, we should expect that he would take it just as seriously in the case of hallucinations.

My alternative account of the phenomenology of particularity begins with the proposal that many of our perceptual experiences (and thoughts) involve, as part of their basic structure, a bare demonstrative *thought-form* which can be represented as

[that (thing) —]

where the blank is typically filled by 'is F', for some property F. In fact, overcoming Evansian scruples about straightforwardly attributing thoughts, rather than thought-forms, in the absence of concrete things that the thoughts purport to be about, I propose that such experiences involve, as part of their basic structure, a bare demonstrative *thought*

[that (thing) —]

The claim, then, is that a full description of the content of many *perceptual experiences* reveals them to involve (quite literally) a *thought*—a bare demonstrative thought, at the very least; and that it is not necessary that the bare demonstrative [that thing] refer in order for the instantiation of the bare demonstrative thought-*form* to count as a bare demonstrative *thought*.[19]

Consider, for example, my seeing a brown cow. It's plausible that I have several ways of reporting what I see:

[I see a brown cow]
[I see something brown just over there]

---

[17]   Burge 1977: 343.

[18]   Martin 2002b: 196. Martin doesn't go all the way with Burge in accepting that certain *de re* thoughts could have failed to be *de re*. But this kind of move is precisely what gives Burge's account a chance of accounting for the phenomenology of particularity.

[19]   In this respect, my account is similar to Burge's (1993) account. However, as will become clear, I go on to develop the account differently.

Of course, some reports will be closer to a full description of my visual experience, and the latter report is ultimately based on, included in, or derived from my experience of a brown cow.[20] The point is that if I see a brown cow, it is plausible that this perception necessarily includes or entails the bare demonstrative thought [that thing —].[21] Since in this case I do see an individual physical object (and indeed a brown cow), the demonstrative thought is true. But this *kind* of entailment between the full perceptual experience and the bare demonstrative thought exists even if the demonstrative thought is not true. For example, if I am suffering from a hallucination of a brown cow that is indistinguishable from a veridical perception of a brown cow, my hallucination also entails (because it involves) a demonstrative thought of the form [that thing —], although the demonstrative thought is not true because [that thing] fails to refer to, fails to be about, an external object.

My suggestion is that many *perceptual experiences*, veridical or not, entail these types of demonstrative thoughts. The idea then is that demonstrative thoughts involving bare demonstratives such as [that thing] manifest a fundamental category of our thinking and indeed our experience in general—the category *object*.[22]

It seems clear that our thinking is structured in such a way that it is fundamentally *object-positing*.[23] The default setting is *object-positing* or taking-as-object. The bare *object-positing* feature of thought may then be filled in with other concepts and sensory properties to produce the experiences of objects we commonly have.

This fundamental category of thought—the category object—which typically makes our experiences *object-positing* is what accounts for the phenomenology of particularity. *Object-positing* delivers the *this-object* of perceptual experience. Even more strongly put, *object-positing* is the experiencing of a *this-object*. Experiencing this kind of *thisness* is a matter of being presented experientially with an identifiable and usually persisting unity, and this is just what *object-positing* does.

It is clear that very young children identify objects as continual existing unified entities, and it seems plausible that animals do too, and this object-identification seems to be done in the absence of concepts of objects—concepts of rabbits, tables, and chairs—of the sort ordinarily possessed by adult human beings. So, the kind of phenomenology involved in *object-positing* is less specifically conceptual than that involved in, say, seeing a chair as a chair. So too, it doesn't seem quite right to say that *object-positing* necessarily involves identifying an object specifically *as an object*, because this presumably would require the possession of the concepts of unity and

[20] I am being intentionally vague about the exact relationship between the perceptual experience as of a brown cow and the bare demonstrative thought *that thing is brown*. I will speak loosely of 'entailment'.
[21] It is the presence of the bare demonstrative [that thing] that makes the thought as a whole count as a bare demonstrative thought, even though it has the non-bare content [brown].
[22] I have been moving fairly freely from talking about perceptual experiences to talking about bare demonstrative thought-forms 'entailed' by these experiences. Given the bare structure and content of the bare demonstrative thought-forms I am concerned with, I think this move is unproblematic.
[23] See e.g. Spelke (1990) and Carey and Xu (2001).

persistence.[24] *Object-positing* is a matter of cognitive phenomenology, in the sense that it involves a kind of taking that is fundamentally related to, and is indeed a necessary part of, more specific takings, like taking something *as a dog*. The taking in basic *object-positing*, though, is less conceptually specific. However, it is more than a bare [this] taking, or a bare [that] taking, for these may occur in response to undifferentiated experience of red across the whole visual field, say; it is a [this thing] or [that thing] taking.[25]

This is a wholly phenomenological account of the phenomenological fact, as promised. It does not give any role to actual objects. It is clear that the phenomenology of particularity is part of many of our perceptual experiences (it is of course as much a feature of experience of seeing many particular things as it is of seeing one particular thing), and the idea is that this phenomenology is the manifestation in experience of the *object-positing* structural feature that is fundamental to our existence as mental creatures. Kant may be appealing to a similar idea in his *Duisburg'sche Nachlass* when he considers taking the 'transcendental object = *x*' as one of his fundamental categories. The idea is that our having and deploying the concept OBJECT is a necessary condition of our having what Kant calls 'experience', by which he means experience which has the phenomenological character of being experience of an objective order of things distinct from the subjective order of our experiences; on this view, the concept OBJECT is something general in form and is not empirically given.[26]

We need some theoretical account of the phenomenology of particularity. This phenomenology is something experienced in having perceptual experiences. It is part of our conscious awareness, and therefore part of the content of such experiences. It occurs in veridical perceptions and hallucinations alike. Since sensory phenomenology on its own is incapable of accounting for particularity, we must look to cognitive phenomenology. Cognitive phenomenology expands the scope of phenomenology, in particular the phenomenology of *perception*, beyond sensory phenomenology, and has so far focused mainly on ordinary concepts such as PINE TREE, but it seems that it can be expanded to include certain basic structural elements of our thought such as the feature of *object-positing* or taking-as-object.

---

[24] It may be that one can see something *as an object* without having the exact concepts of unity and persistence, but some concept of an object must be in place, just as some concept of a dog must be in place if one is to see something *as a dog*.

[25] [This thing] taking should also be distinguished from what may be involved in perceiving an individual property or a natural kind. The latter case obviously involves much more than a [this thing] taking, whereas the former case is akin to an undifferentiated experience of red. Another interesting case is that of seeing or hallucinating a distinctive pattern of lights, which are taken as particular but not persisting. This case may be plausibly described as perceiving (or hallucinating) objects, which exist only for very short periods of time.

[26] See Walker (1978: 106–7). It may be, though, that the supposed necessity of the idea of the transcendental object (= x) is simply the necessity of the idea that there exists something which stands over against experience, and doesn't include the idea of object particularity.

7 Phenomenological particularity and reference

At this point, one may object that in perceiving a particular object (given that we do in fact perceive physical objects), there is more than a general phenomenological *this thing* involved. If one is seeing a dog, for example, one's perception is of *this very object, this actual concrete dog*. This is true, and it is also true that a substantial part of the account of how and why this is so can be given in non-phenomenological terms, appealing centrally to certain sorts of causal connections that must hold between this dog and my present perceptual state. But, first, this is not any sort of objection to the present account of perceptual experience, according to which we need to recognize a purely phenomenological fact, i.e. the phenomenological particularity fact.

Secondly, and more dramatically, it seems that the phenomenological particularity fact is a necessary part of the explanation of how my perception can in fact be a perception of this very dog. Focusing on the kind of object perception I am concerned with here, as opposed to perceptions of undifferentiated expanses of red, given any perception of any object whatever, it is the experience of a *this thing* that the perceptual experience involves—the *object-positing* feature of the perceptual experience— that makes it possible for that particular experience to secure external reference to that particular object. It is not just the right external connections that must be in place. The *object-positing* must also be in place. To *perceive* a particular object (given appropriate causal connections), we need an aspect of *experience* to deliver that particular object, and this is precisely what *object-positing* does. In the absence of *object-positing* it is quite unclear how my experience of this object, this dog, for example, gets to be an experience of this dog at all. If we could somehow subtract the *object-positing* feature from the total (phenomenological) character of my dog-caused experience while somehow leaving everything else in place, phenomenologically speaking, and while also leaving all the external connections in place, we would not have something that counted as a perception of this very dog. The subtraction is hard to imagine, because the *object-positing* feature is part of the basic fabric of the experience, but we can perhaps get some idea of it by imagining the visual case, and supposing that the subtraction leaves only the complex array of colours (we can't subtract the *object-positing* without subtracting the concept DOG, because it is built into DOG). The basic point, in any case, is this: that if there is nothing in the *character of experience* which is a this thing-ness, we cannot be said to *perceive* a particular object, rather than merely *be causally affected by* a particular object.

One could object that non-conceptual creatures like bees perceive objects, and so object-perception must be possible without cognitive phenomenology, which is closely tied to concepts, even if only to very primitive concepts.[27] It's very unclear to me what to say about the sense in which bees perceive objects and in what sense this may or may not be similar to the way we perceive objects. Of course, it's an empirical

[27] I'd like to thank an anonymous referee for making this point.

question, but it may be that bees only strictly perceive colour contrasts, for example. One could then say that bees strictly perceive colour contrasts and perceive objects only in a derivative sense; they perceive objects in virtue of perceiving colour contrasts. But this is no objection to the present account, because we perceive more than colour contrasts when we perceive objects. We perceive whole, unified objects, and in order to account for this phenomenon we need *object-positing*.

In conclusion, any satisfactory general theory of the content of perceptual experience must give a satisfactory theoretical account of the phenomenological particularity fact. There is no denying that it is a fundamental experiential aspect of perceptual experience. Although the generalists I have considered here are not wrong about phenomenological perceptual content being general, none of them have isolated the correct general or shareable feature to account for the shareable feature of phenomenal particularity. As for the particularists I have considered here, even those who explicitly acknowledge the particularity phenomenon in question fail even to come close to giving a satisfactory account of it. The general feature of content that, I have argued, accounts for phenomenal particularity is what I have called *object-positing*. It is a structural feature of the perceptual experiences I have been concerned with here, which is consciously manifested as an experience of *this thing*. And *object-positing* not only accounts for phenomenal particularity; it also plays an essential role in explaining how perceptions manage to be perceptions of particular objects. For perceptions cannot be perceptions of particular objects at all unless they display the feature of phenomenal particularity.[28]

References

Burge, T. (1977). 'Belief De Re', *Journal of Philosophy*, 338–62.
——(1993). 'Vision and Intentional Content', in R. v. Guhck and E. Lepore (eds), *John Searle and his Critics*. Oxford: Basil Blackwell.
Carey, S. and Xu, F. (2001). 'Infants' knowledge of objects: Beyond object files and object tracking', *Cognition*, 80: 179–213.
Carruthers, P. (2005). 'Conscious experience versus conscious thought', in *Consciousness: Essays from a Higher-order Perspective*. Oxford: Oxford University Press.
Davies, M. (1992). 'Perceptual Content and Local Supervenience', *Proceedings of the Aristotelian Society*, 92: 21–45.
Evans, G. (1982). *The Varieties of Reference*. Oxford: Clarendon Press.
Horgan, T. and Potrč, M. (2008). *Austere Realism: Contextual Semantics Meets Minimal Ontology*. Cambridge, MA: MIT Press.

[28] I'd like to thank Tim Bayne, Uriah Kriegel, Terry Horgan, Maja Spener, Galen Strawson, and audiences at the Philosophical Institute of the Czech Academy of Sciences, the University of Oxford, the Phenomenal Intentionality workshop at the University of Arizona and the University of Bern.

Horgan, T. and Tienson, G. (2002). 'The intentionality of phenomenology and the phenomenology of intentionality', in D. Chalmers (ed.), *Contemporary Readings in Philosophy of Mind*. Oxford: Oxford University Press.

Martin, M.G.F. (2002a). 'The Transparency of Experience', *Mind and Language*, vol. 17 no. 4: 376–425.

——(2002b). 'Particular Thoughts and Singular Thought', in A. O'Hear (ed.), *Logic, Thought and Language*. Cambridge: Cambridge University Press.

McDowell, J. (1984). 'De Re Senses', *Philosophical Quarterly*, 34: 283–94.

——(1986). 'Singular Thought and the Extent of Inner Space', in P. Pettit and J. McDowell (eds), *Subject, Thought, and Context*. Oxford: Clarendon Press.

McGinn, C. (1997). *The Character of Mind*. Oxford: Oxford University Press.

Pitt, D. (2004). 'The Phenomenology of Cognition, or *What Is it Like to Think that P?*' *Philosophy and Phenomenological Research*, 69: 1–36.

Siewert, C. (1998). *The Significance of Consciousness*. Princeton: Princeton University Press.

Smith, D. (1989). *The Circle of Acquaintance: Perception, Consciousness and Empathy*. Dordrecht and Boston: Kluwer Academic Publishers.

Spelke, E.S. (1990). 'Principles of Object Perception', *Cognitive Science*, 14: 29–56.

Strawson, G. (1994). *Mental Reality*. Cambridge, MA: MIT Press.

——(2008). 'Real Intentionality 3: Why Intentionality Entails Consciousness', in his *Real Materialism and Other Essays*. Oxford: Oxford University Press.

Tye, M. (1995). *Ten Problems of Consciousness*. Cambridge: MIT Press.

——(2000). *Consciousness, Color and Content*. Cambridge: MIT Press.

——(2009). 'Representationalist theories of Consciousness', in B. McLaughlin, A. Beckerman, and S. Walter (eds), *The Oxford Handbook of Philosophy of Mind*. Oxford: Oxford University Press.

Walker, R. (1978). *Kant: The Arguments of the Philosophers*. London: Routledge and Kegan Paul.

Introspection, Phenomenality and the Availability of Intentional Content

David Pitt

1 Credo

I believe there's a phenomenology—a "what it's like"—of occurrent conscious thought. I believe this because I believe that *any* conscious state necessarily has phenomenal properties. Further, I believe that the phenomenology of occurrent conscious thought is *proprietary*: it's a *sui generis* sort of phenomenology, as unlike, say, auditory and visual phenomenology as they are unlike each other—a *cognitive* phenomenology. I believe this because I believe that the conscious occurrence of any of the more familiar sorts of phenomenal properties is neither necessary nor sufficient for the occurrence of conscious thought. I also believe that the phenomenal character of a conscious occurrent thought (type) is *distinctive*: that is, distinct thought types have distinct cognitive phenomenal properties. I believe this because I believe that distinct conscious occurrent thoughts are introspectively discriminable not only from other types of conscious states, but from each other. Finally, I believe that the phenomenal character of a conscious occurrent thought (type) is *individuative*: that is, in virtue of its having the phenomenal properties it has, it's a *thought* (as opposed to some other kind of mental state) with a specific *intentional content*. I believe this because I believe that we're able to identify our occurrent conscious thoughts as the thoughts they are, consciously, introspectively, and non-inferentially, and that phenomenal properties are the only properties of occurrent conscious states that are so identifiable. In fact, I believe that the cognitive phenomenal character of an occurrent conscious thought *is* its intentional content. I believe this because I can (fear of psychologism turns out to be irrational), and because it provides for a simpler account of content: the intentional content of a conscious thought is like the sensational content of a conscious pain—they are the states they are not because of their relational properties, but because of their intrinsic phenomenal nature.

Amen.[1]

I will call the view that there's a proprietary, distinctive, and individuative phenomenology of occurrent conscious thought the *phenomenal intentionality of thought thesis* (PITT, for short). Not many people believe PITT. But skepticism about it seems to me more often based on prior theoretical commitment, or overreaching confidence in the explanatory resources of contemporary Naturalism (what Charles Siewert (this volume) calls "the tyrannizing anxieties and ambitions of mind–body metaphysics"), than on unbiased reflection upon our conscious mental lives, or careful evaluation of the arguments in its favor.

In this paper I consider three more reasoned lines of resistance to PITT, the first advanced by Joe Levine (this volume), the second taking its cue from extrospectionist views of self-knowledge, and the third stemming from concerns about introspective availability of intentional content. I argue that none of these challenges constitutes a serious threat to the thesis that the intentionality of thought is proprietarily phenomenally constituted.

I begin, however, with a new argument for cognitive phenomenology.

2 The individuation of conscious states

For all *non*-cognitive kinds of mental states, sameness and difference *within* consciousness are entirely phenomenally constituted. The various modes of conscious *sensory* experience, for example, are, *qua* conscious,[2] constituted by their proprietary kinds of phenomenology. Conscious *visual* experiences, *qua* conscious, share a particular kind of phenomenology that makes them *visual*, and distinguishes them from conscious experiences in all of the other modes. What it's like to have a conscious experience of yellow is the same, *qua* visual, as what it's like to have a conscious experience of green (or of any other visible property), *qua* visual, and it's the visual kind of phenomenology that makes them both, *qua* conscious, visual experiences. To be a conscious visual experience is to be conscious in the visual way—to have conscious visual phenomenology. Any conscious experience that has this kind of phenomenology is, necessarily, a conscious visual experience, and no conscious experience that lacked it could be a conscious visual experience. There's a proprietary visual mode of conscious experience, and it's phenomenally constituted.

Likewise, there's a proprietary kind of conscious *auditory* experience, and it's also phenomenally constituted. A conscious experience of the sound of thunder is, *qua* conscious, of the same general kind as a conscious experience of the sound of a C minor triad; and their sameness *qua* conscious *auditory* experiences is due to their

---

[1]   I provide more detailed arguments for these claims in Pitt (2004) and Pitt (2009).

[2]   That is, *as manifested in consciousness*—as opposed to, say, as caused by, or realized in, different sorts of brain states, or as occurring on a Thursday.

shared auditory phenomenology.[3] Any conscious experience that has this kind of phenomenology is, necessarily, a conscious auditory experience, and no conscious experience that lacked it could be a conscious auditory experience. There's a proprietary auditory mode of conscious experience, and it's phenomenally constituted.

The same is true of all the other kinds of conscious sensory experience (olfactory, gustatory, tactile) we are capable of, as well. Each is, *qua* conscious,[4] constituted by its own general kind of phenomenology (olfactory, gustatory, tactile), and differs from all the others in virtue of its phenomenal kind. A conscious experience of the sound of thunder is different from a conscious experience of the smell of burning hair, in part because of the intrinsic differences between auditory and olfactory phenomenology. Sameness within the various modes of conscious sensory experience, and the differences between them, are phenomenally constituted.

Further, differences within the various modes of conscious sensory experience are also phenomenal differences. A conscious experience of the smell of burning hair is of a kind different from a conscious experience of the smell of fresh basil, in virtue of their differing olfactory phenomenologies: what it's like to smell burning hair is different from what it's like to smell fresh basil. They differ as kinds of conscious olfactory experiences because of their distinctive phenomenologies. A conscious experience of the taste of sugar is different from a conscious experience of the taste of salt, in virtue of the difference in their distinctive gustatory phenomenal properties. It's the difference between sweet and salty phenomenologies that makes them different types of gustatory experiences.

Finally, the phenomenology of a conscious experience makes it the kind of conscious experience it is. Differences in kinds of phenomenology between and within the various modes of conscious sensory experience make them different kinds of conscious experiences; but what individuates a conscious experience, *qua* conscious, is also its phenomenal character. A conscious experience of the feel of an unshaved chin is different from a conscious experience of the feel of polished marble, in virtue of their differing tactile phenomenologies. But it's also the case that a conscious experience of the feel of an unshaved chin is the particular kind of experience it is because of its phenomenal character. Nothing that felt like *that* could be a conscious experience of the feel of polished marble, and, necessarily, any conscious experience that feels like that is a conscious experience of the feel of an unshaved chin. No conscious experience that lacked thundery auditory phenomenology could be a conscious experience of the sound of thunder, and any experience that has it is, necessarily, an experience of the

---

[3] I intend definite descriptions used in characterizing experiences to be rigid designators of particular kinds of experience, regardless of their causes ("the sound of thunder" in "an experience of the sound of thunder" designates a particular kind of auditory experience, whether or not it is caused by the relevant atmospheric phenomenon).

[4] I'll try to stop saying this (though I'll continue to mean it).

sound of thunder. Likewise for the visual experience of green, the olfactory experience of the smell of burned hair, the gustatory experience of the taste of salt, etc.

Similar considerations could be adduced with respect to all of the further determinates of these determinable sensory experiences, as well as all of the other familiar kinds of conscious experience, e.g. somatic, proprioceptive, emotional, etc. They're all, *qua* conscious experiences, individuated and identified by their proprietary, distinctive, and individuative phenomenologies. To *be*, in consciousness, is, for these kinds of experiences, to be *phenomenal*. A conscious experience can't occur unless some phenomenal property is instantiated, and *which* phenomenal property is instantiated determines which kind of conscious experience (up to maximal determinateness) has occurred. In short, in all of these cases, consciousness *supervenes on* phenomenology: difference in consciousness entails phenomenal difference, and sameness in phenomenology entails sameness in consciousness.[5]

Now, that these principles of phenomenal individuation should be applicable to all kinds of conscious states (*qua* conscious) *except* conscious thoughts is, at the very least, improbable. Given that they apply across such a wide range of so radically different kinds of states of consciousness, surely the burden of proof falls on anyone who claims that conscious thinking is exempt. Why should it be so different?

Furthermore, if conscious thoughts don't have proprietary, distinctive, and individuative phenomenologies, then they would have to be conscious in some way *other than* phenomenally. But what could that be? How could a state be conscious—i.e. be *manifest* in, or *appear* in, consciousness—without being conscious (or *appearing*) in some *way* or other? And what could such *ways* be if not phenomenal properties? Again, minimally, the burden of proof is on anyone who would claim that there can be consciousness without phenomenality.

The only attempt I know of to make such a case is Lormand (1996); but Lormand's efforts are unsuccessful. (My reasons for thinking so are given in Pitt [2004: 23–24].) Moreover, claiming that conscious thoughts are "access" conscious without being "phenomenally" conscious won't help here, since to be available for conscious use is not *per se* to be *in* consciousness. (See also page 151, below.) And to say that something is *in* consciousness is not *per se* to say that it's phenomenal. Even if it's necessarily the case that conscious states have phenomenal properties, it's *not* the case that consciousness and phenomenality are *identical* (that "conscious" and "phenomenal" have the same *meaning*). They're not the same property. If they were, then phenomenality *sine* consciousness would be impossible (which it isn't), and Lormand's claim that some conscious states lack phenomenality would be *prima facie* incoherent (which it isn't. It's incorrect, and necessarily so; but it's not obviously contradictory).

---

[5] Which is not to say that phenomenality entails consciousness. Given that phenomenality without consciousness is possible (as I believe it is; see Pitt MS1), to say that sameness of phenomenology entails sameness in consciousness is to say that *if* two experiences are phenomenally identical, then *if* they're conscious they're type-identical conscious experiences.

Further, since consciousness is a *unitary* (non-determinable) property, if phenomenality were identical to it, then all conscious states would be phenomenally identical. But they're not: phenomenality is a *determinable*.[6] So it can't be the same property as consciousness. Hence, the claim that some thoughts are conscious is not, in this context, trivially question-begging. It's not *trivially* true that conscious thoughts have phenomenal properties, since it's not trivially true that conscious states in general have phenomenal properties (cf. Pitt 2004: note 4). And the claim that some thoughts are conscious is not just the claim that some thoughts are phenomenal in thin lexical disguise.

Thus, if conscious cognitive states (thoughts) constitute their own general kind—if they differ from all other kinds of conscious mental states—then they must enjoy their own proprietary sort of phenomenology. Pains are not tastes, sounds are not smells, visual experiences are not moods, in virtue of having different proprietary phenomenologies. Hence, if thoughts are not pains or tastes or sounds or smells or visual experiences or moods or . . . , then they must have a proprietary mode of conscious existence—a proprietarily *cognitive* phenomenology. If they *are* different sorts of conscious states, then, *qua* conscious, they must be *phenomenally* different.

But conscious thoughts *can't be* identified with any other sort of conscious states (the most plausible candidate being conscious verbal imagery), since it's possible for any such to occur in the absence of thought. (Thinking is *not* the same as producing internal sentence tokens, as anyone who has read Derrida should be able to tell you.[7]) Thoughts are states of a different kind from all others. Hence, there must be a proprietary phenomenology of *cognition*—a proprietarily cognitive way of appearing; a phenomenology that makes a state cognitive, as opposed to visual, auditory, olfactory, somatic, proprioceptive, etc.

And if there are different types of conscious thoughts, then each distinct type must have its own unique mode of conscious existence. Thus, the phenomenal properties of distinct thought types must be sufficient to distinguish them from each other (as well as from all other kinds of conscious states), just as the phenomenal properties of different smells or sounds or color experiences must be sufficient to distinguish them. If a conscious thought t is to *be* a different thought from a conscious thought t', then t and t' must have distinctive cognitive phenomenal characters.

Finally, since in general conscious states are the states they are in virtue of their proprietary and distinctive phenomenologies, the cognitive phenomenology of

---

[6] I don't think phenomenal properties are determinates of consciousness, since I think phenomenality doesn't entail consciousness. Phenomenality is necessary, but not sufficient, for consciousness. (Thanks to Declan Smithies for pressing me to get clear on this.)

[7] And, speaking of Frenchmen, in virtue of *what* do I and Jacques think the same thought when I inwardly utter "Paris is beautiful but boring" and he inwardly utters "Le Paris est beau mais ennuyeux"? Presumably it's our *meaning* the same thing (i.e. intending to express the same thought) by our utterances. But our utterances are different; so, meaning is not the same as uttering. *Qua* conscious, then, meaning and inner-uttering must be phenomenally different.

a conscious thought must be individuative as well. A conscious thought is a thought, and the thought that it is, in virtue of its distinctive cognitive phenomenology. Moreover, if thought types are individuated by their contents, then thought contents are cognitive phenomenal properties. Each thought that $p, q, r, \ldots$, where $p, q, r, \ldots$ are different contents, has a proprietary, distinctive, and individuative phenomenal character that constitutes its intentional content (see Pitt 2009). Not, as I argued in Pitt (2004), because this is the only way we can *know* what they are, and discriminate them from each other in introspection (though I still think this argument is sound), but because, *qua* conscious, this is the only way for them to *be* what they are, and to be different from one another and all other kinds of conscious states. In consciousness, *esse est pareo*.

3 Hey Joe

In his contribution to this volume, Joe Levine maintains that the argument from self-knowledge in Pitt (2004) doesn't establish that there's a proprietary phenomenology of cognition, since the kinds of self-knowledge it's introduced to explain can be explained without it. He begins his critique by making a distinction between *implicit* and *explicit* self-knowledge of thought. Implicit self-knowledge

is not the result of any explicit formulation or reflection. Rather, it's the knowledge that seems to come with the very thinking of the thought itself.... All that's required is that one thinks in one's language of thought, mentalese. To implicitly know what one is thinking is just to think with understanding. (Levine, this volume: 108–9)

Explicit self-knowledge, in contrast,

is what we have when we explicitly formulate a meta-cognitive thought, such as "I believe that San Francisco is a beautiful city." (ibid: 108)

and is explicable in terms of

the reliability of the relevant process yielding the higher-order sentence expressing the fact that one is thinking a certain content. (ibid: 107)

He maintains that implicit and explicit self-knowledge, so construed, are all we need to explain self-knowledge of thought, and that neither requires a special phenomenology of cognition. One implicitly knows that one is thinking that p by tokening a mental representation whose content is that p, and explicitly knows that one is thinking that p by tokening a mental representation whose content is that one is thinking that p.

I think the distinction between implicit and explicit self-knowledge is very useful; but I don't think it can explain self-knowledge of conscious occurrent thought if it's understood in Levine's terms. For one thing, mere occurrence of a mental state can't constitute *conscious* implicit self-knowledge unless the occurrence is itself conscious, and consciousness requires phenomenology. Even if there's some sense (though

I rather doubt it) in which mere occurrence of a mental representation whose content is that *p* counts as implicit knowledge that one is thinking that *p*—i.e. that the computational system "knows" which representations are being tokened—this in itself doesn't explain how *I* can implicitly know what *I'm* consciously thinking. You can't have implicit conscious knowledge of what you're thinking in virtue of tokening an unconscious mental representation. Levine's account doesn't seem to allow for there to be an *epistemic* difference between conscious and unconscious thinking. Any occurrence, conscious or not, of a mental representation counts as implicit knowledge of it, and any occurrence of a meta-representation of it counts as explicit knowledge of it. So it seems that consciousness makes no difference to what I can know about what I'm thinking (unless Levine is advocating a higher-order theory of consciousness, on which thinking about a thought *makes it* conscious; which I don't think is the case). But it does make a difference. There's a perfectly good sense in which I *don't* know what I'm thinking, believing, fearing, desiring, etc. if it's unconscious, and I *do* come to know it when it becomes conscious. Surely Freud wasn't wrong about *that*.

Moreover, without characteristic phenomenal differences among occurrent conscious states, implicit self-knowledge couldn't be discriminative—that is, you couldn't be implicitly consciously aware *that* you're thinking, or of *what* you're thinking. Implicit knowledge of conscious experience requires implicit individuation of experiences, which, in consciousness, is purely phenomenal. (I'll say more in support of this claim below.) One can't consciously implicitly know what one is experiencing unless the experience is implicitly discriminated in consciousness from all others. Hence, there must be a proprietary, distinctive, and individuative phenomenology of conscious thoughts if one is to have implicit conscious knowledge of them.

Of course, Levine maintains that we simply *don't have* conscious implicit knowledge of the contents of our thoughts. And I suppose this is why he doesn't offer a competing, non-phenomenal explanation for it. Indeed, he seems to concede that such knowledge would require a distinctive phenomenology of content, and, hence, that to suppose that we have it begs the question against opponents of cognitive phenomenology. He claims that "[i]f we grant that we do have acquaintance with the contents of our thoughts in the way Pitt claims we have, then that just is granting the reality of C[ognitive] P[henomenology]" (Levine MS: 20).

I don't think the claim that we're acquainted with the contents of our thoughts begs the question. In Pitt (2004) I characterized such acquaintance as direct, non-inferential conscious knowledge of what we're consciously thinking. This does not, *per se*, presuppose phenomenology. It does need an explanation, however, and I provided an argument that the only available one requires a proprietary phenomenology of content. Though some have tried to show that consciousness and, presumably, conscious acquaintance don't require phenomenology, I think this position is untenable. And I considered what I took to be the most promising non-phenomenal account, based on a reliabilist–computationalist theory of knowledge and belief (of the kind

Levine appears to favor), and argued (as I do here) that such theories can't ground an explanation of direct access to conscious contents.

Claiming that it's question-begging to affirm direct introspective knowledge of what we're consciously thinking *because* it turns out that the only explanation for it appeals to cognitive phenomenology, is like claiming that it's question-begging to affirm direct introspective knowledge of what we're consciously feeling because it turns out that the only explanation for it appeals to somatosensory phenomenology. It's plausible only if you've already decided that the phenomenology in question doesn't exist. It's not question-begging to maintain that what's required in order to explain a capacity we have in fact exists. And it does seem to me to be non-tendentiously, almost platitudinously true that we can have non-inferential conscious knowledge of the contents of our occurrent conscious thoughts—of what we're occurrently consciously thinking—and, hence, that providing an alternative explanation for it is a far better (though in the end doomed) strategy for resisting cognitive phenomenology than denying its existence. The connection between conscious acquaintance and phenomenology is very close. But this doesn't make it question-begging to assert it. It only makes it scandalous that it has been overlooked in the case of conscious thought.

I understand the implicit–explicit distinction as it applies to conscious knowledge as the distinction between acquaintance *as* knowledge—or "acquaintance-knowledge," as I'll call it—and knowledge *by* acquaintance; and I maintain that the mechanism by which beliefs about one's conscious experience are formed is in at least some cases not computational or automatic. Acquaintance-knowledge of a mental state consists simply in its conscious occurrence. (One can't be acquainted with (directly aware of) unconscious mental states.) In undergoing a conscious experience, one has implicit knowledge of what one is experiencing (though not, *per se, that* one is experiencing it), and of what the experience is like. If I've tasted uni, then I know what uni tastes like (what it's like to taste uni), even if I didn't know it was uni I was tasting. Knowledge *by* acquaintance of a mental state, on the other hand, is knowing *that* one is in it, and requires application of concepts and formation of beliefs. If, after my first, innocent taste of uni, someone tells me that it was uni I ate, then I can know that I'm tasting (or have tasted) uni, and that I know what uni tastes like.

Moreover, neither sort of knowledge can be reduced to the other; and knowledge by acquaintance (knowledge-*that*) of conscious experiences presupposes acquaintance-knowledge (a form of knowledge-*what*) of them.

When Mary leaves the Black and White Room, she comes to know what it's like to see red when she experiences it. In having the experience of red, she acquaintance-knows what seeing red is like. If she's re-imprisoned (poor thing) and her memory fades, then she'll no longer have this kind of knowledge—she'll no longer know what it's like to see red. Further, Mary's first experience of red would not constitute implicit knowledge if it weren't conscious, since if it weren't conscious it would make no difference to *her* (she couldn't be said to be acquainted with it). If her color experiences upon her release from the Black and White Room were unconscious, she would notice no relevant changes in her experience, and could not be said to have learned anything new. She still would not know what it's like to see red, or any of the other colors. And if her experience of red were not phenomenally different from her experiences of the other colors, her implicit knowledge could not be said to be of what it's like to see *red*, as opposed to another color.

Knowing what it's like can't be reduced to any form of knowing that. Knowing what it's like to see red is not knowing that seeing red is like *this* (or that *this* is what it's like to see red), where an instance of a phenomenal property is the referent (or perhaps a constituent[8]) of the concept THIS, since one may have an experience of red, and thus acquaintance-know what it's like to see red, without being able to categorize it conceptually—i.e. without being able to think that one is experiencing *red*, or that *this* is what it's like to experience *red*. This may be because one lacks the appropriate concept (which may be because it's not in the human repertoire), or because one doesn't know how to apply it to one's experience. As Nida-Rümelin (1995) has shown, Mary could know what it's like to see red without knowing that it's red she is seeing, if she's trapped in the Technicolor Vestibule—that place between the Black and White Room and the Wide Chromatic World, where there are colors but no familiar objects from which she could infer which color is which.

Of course, once she's out of the Technicolor Vestibule, Mary can also have explicit propositional knowledge of her psychological states: she can know *that* she's seeing red. But this presupposes acquaintance-knowledge of what it's like to see red. She can't introspectively know *that* she's seeing red if she doesn't know *what* seeing red is like. Knowledge by acquaintance of conscious states presupposes acquaintance-knowledge of their distinctive phenomenologies. Mary's experience of red must be (implicitly) discriminated from other experiences; and she must apply concepts to it and form a belief about it in order to know that she's having an experience of red.

So the (revised) argument from self-knowledge is this: Immediate knowledge-that of conscious thought requires knowledge-what, and knowledge-what requires distinctive phenomenology. Knowledge-what consists in simply the conscious occurrence of the thought.[9] (This is what I called simple (non-epistemic) introspection in Pitt (2004), though

[8] Some philosophers maintain that demonstrative "phenomenal concepts" have sample experiences embedded in them, and are thus partly self-referential (see, e.g., Chalmers 2003). Before she has experienced red, Mary can't have this sort of concept, and so can't know that red looks like *this*. I prefer a view on which concepts and sensations are kept separate, so that the thoughts Mary might have in the Technicolor Vestibule (the brightly colored antechamber containing no recognizable objects that she is released into before getting out into the world (see Nida-Rümelin 1995))—*I wonder if red looks like this* (demonstrating a red patch) and *I wonder if red looks like this* (demonstrating a green patch)—have the same conceptual content, but different truth conditions due to the different referents of "this." (I defend a general account of demonstrative and indexical concepts along these lines in Pitt, Forthcoming.)

[9] Hence, my view is not committed to the regress Levine charges it with (this volume: 108–9). One has implicit knowledge of the second-order thoughts whose occurrence constitutes explicit knowledge of the contents of first-order thoughts.

I now think it *is* epistemic in the sense that it constitutes a kind of knowledge. It's just not conceptual or doxastic.) One has implicit knowledge of the second-order thoughts whose occurrence constitutes explicit knowledge of the contents of first-order thoughts. I don't, and I don't think I ever did, "assimilate these two forms of self-knowledge," as Levine (this volume: 109) suggests—though initially I didn't think of implicit occurrence as a kind of self-*knowledge*. Immediate knowledge-that consists in beliefs about one's mental states formed on the basis of conscious acquaintance with them, which is just their conscious occurrence. One *recognizes* what one is thinking—just as one recognizes what one is hearing or smelling or seeing—and applies the relevant concepts and forms the relevant beliefs. The recognition is neither conceptual nor inferential, and the formation of the relevant beliefs, while of course conceptual, isn't inferential either.

No doubt Levine would still consider all of this question-begging, since he maintains that we can be "as it were, magically" (this volume: 108) aware of our occurrent conscious thoughts (i.e. (I suppose) we're privy to the results of a computational process, but not to the process itself), without invoking "phenomenal appearance, as we have with sensory experience" (*id.*). A conscious thought occurs; a mechanism that can register which thought it is causes me to believe that it's that thought (tokens a mentalese sentence that expresses the fact that one is thinking it), and if the mechanism is reliable, the belief will count as knowledge. There's no work here for a proprietarily cognitive phenomenology to do.

But it's not the case that we *always* "as it were, magically" know what we're thinking or feeling—that the belief about our experience just pops into our head. We often *recognize* what we're thinking or feeling, *identify* it on the basis of its recognizable properties, and self-ascribe it. We make *voluntary judgments* about the contents of our consciousness on the basis of recognition of their distinctive phenomenologies. We're consciously aware, not just *that* we're in a particular conscious state, but *of* the state itself. Sometimes I come to have a belief about what I'm experiencing on the basis of attending to it and recognizing what it is. *This* is the kind of self-knowledge the argument in Pitt (2004) is concerned to explain. Maybe there's a reflex "I'm in pain!" that pops into my head when something hurts me. But I can also, so to speak, browse around in my conscious mind (selectively attend to the contents of my consciousness) and attend to things that are there (the song that's been in my head all day, the ringing in my ears, the thought that I'm condemned to be free). I may or may not form the thought that I'm in any of these states; but if I do, it seems that I can do it *voluntarily*— just as I might absent-mindedly (thoughtlessly) be looking at an orange flower, and then think to myself: "That's an orange flower." The seemingly automatic belief-forming mechanism story can't explain this.

The issue between Levine and me here is not whether or not there are conscious experiences, or whether or not we can have introspective knowledge of their occurrence and nature. We seem to agree on this. Our difference concerns, rather, *how* beliefs about experience are formed. Levine is claiming that they're *always* formed by a reliable, automatic belief-forming mechanism. My claim is that, whether or not there are beliefs about experience formed in this way, we can *also* voluntarily form beliefs about our conscious experiences on the basis of active introspection, and that this presupposes that we have some way of identifying and distinguishing them from each other, *qua* conscious. But the only properties of conscious experiences that can serve to distinguish them *qua* conscious are phenomenal properties (because these are the only intrinsic properties that conscious experiences as such can have). So, given that it's possible to gain self-knowledge of thought in this way, there must be a distinctive phenomenology for thoughts—a *cognitive* phenomenology. The activity of an automatic belief-forming mechanism can't, *qua* automatic, explain this sort of self-knowledge.[10]

Moreover, even in cases where a computational mechanism spontaneously informs me what state I'm in, by producing a thought about it in the appropriate way, there's *still* a need for distinctive cognitive phenomenology. For, unless I know what the mechanism has "said"—if, so to speak, the message that has magically appeared on the "belief-board" isn't legible, or I don't know what it means—I won't know what state I'm in. (Especially if the message is in *mentalese*, which no one can read.) Levine suggests that I rely on an (in the context) unduly "rich"—i.e. phenomenal, hence question-begging—conception of consciousness in the argument in Pitt (2004). But the alternative is to suppose either that thoughts are never conscious at all, or that they're only ever *access* conscious. The first disjunct is a non-starter. On the second, for a thought to be conscious is just for it to be *available for use* in control of reasoning and behavior. But it's difficult to see how a thought could actually *be used* in *conscious* control of reasoning and behavior without the user being conscious of its content in a *non*-access sense (i.e. without being *acquainted with it*). And I can't see how *that* could be explained if all cognitive consciousness were access consciousness. Non-inferential introspective awareness of the contents of conscious states requires phenomenology. Even if the meta-cognitive belief is implicit—its mere occurrence on the belief-board constituting implicit knowledge of its occurrence and content—there's still a need for a distinctive cognitive phenomenology. As argued above, implicit conscious knowledge requires individuative phenomenology. Implicit knowledge that I'm consciously thinking that *p* (and not that *q, r, s,* ...), like implicit knowledge of any other sort of conscious mental state, requires a distinctive phenomenology. So the automatic belief-forming mechanism story doesn't really provide an alternative to the phenomenally based account. It doesn't explain everything that needs to be explained.

Levine (MS) accepts that differences in phenomenology are in general necessary for introspective discrimination, but he maintains that introspective discrimination of

---

[10] It would, I think, be very odd to suppose that all of our knowledge of our conscious occurrent *sensory* states is automatic, since this would render the phenomenology of such states irrelevant to our knowledge of them—we would come to know that, for example, we're hearing the dinner bell *in the absence of conscious auditory phenomenology*. It seems much more plausible that one recognizes the sound of the dinner bell, and on that basis comes to believe that the dinner bell has rung.

thoughts is not discrimination of their *contents*—so there's no need to postulate a cognitive phenomenology. He suggests that thoughts are instead "indexed" by properties of underlying mental representations that have nothing to do with their contents, and distinguished in direct introspection in virtue of those properties. We have access to contents only indirectly, through their representations. Phenomenal contrast in the case of, for example, thinking different readings of an ambiguous sentence such as "I'm hot" is nothing but the contrast between tokening distinct sentences in mentalese which represent (unambiguously) the two readings, but do not "wear their contents on their sleeves." The contents of our thoughts are not individuated in experience, only their mentalese vehicles. There is a phenomenology of cognition, but it's not cognitive; it's a kind of linguistic phenomenology, where the relevant language is the language of thought.

I don't know if mentalese tokens have distinctive phenomenal properties. I rather doubt it, since they're supposedly subpersonal, computational entities. But, be that as it may, I don't see that Levine's account can explain knowledge of what we're thinking. We have direct conscious access to (unambiguous) mental representations of contents, which are individuated in consciousness by their phenomenal features. Presumably, implicit conscious awareness of these features provides the basis for explicit conscious discriminating beliefs about them. But we don't have this kind of direct access to the contents themselves. Levine writes:

> Our only access to content is through thinking, but thinking is a matter of employing representations. There's no way, as it were, to use phenomenal awareness to directly get behind our mental representations to the contents themselves. (Levine MS: 19)

This is, I suppose, because contents are not consciously tokened along with the representations that express them—contents aren't intrinsic phenomenal features of mental representations. We nonetheless do have implicit knowledge of them, however. According to Levine, "[t]o implicitly know what one is thinking is just to think it with understanding" (Levine, this volume: 109)—that is, to token a mental representation with understanding. But what's involved in tokening a mental representation with understanding? I don't see how it could be simply tokening a representation that *has* a content. If I'm to think it *with understanding* I have to know, either implicitly or explicitly, what that content is. But here I think Levine is faced with something like a dilemma. If mere tokening of a representation is to count as *implicit* knowledge of its content, then that content must be tokened along with the representation, as an *intrinsic* feature of it. Implicit understanding is implicit knowledge of content, and implicit knowledge of content is simply occurrence of an *intrinsically* contentful representation. Now, computational accounts generally deny that contents are intrinsic features of mental representations; and I suspect Levine agrees.

But if content is extrinsic, then one can't have implicit knowledge of it simply by tokening a representation of it—any more than one could have knowledge of the meaning of a sentence simply by inscribing it. Knowledge of content in this case would have to be explicit. But how would this be achieved? By automatically tokening a representation that attributes content to it? Presumably this would have to involve *understanding*, at least implicitly, the attribution. If I don't know what I've explicitly attributed to the representation, then I don't have explicit knowledge of its content. But if our attribution is another mentalese token, and we don't have implicit understanding of *its* content, then we'd have to have explicit knowledge of it. And this would require still another meta-representation, which would also have to be understood. (Is it getting regressive in here, or is it just me?) Which would land Levine back in the intrinsic soup. He now owes some sort of account of intrinsic contents. We've already seen that he thinks contents aren't *phenomenal* or *syntactic* features of representations. So what, then, could they be? I'm clueless.

4 Representationalism and self-knowledge

A different line of resistance to PITT takes its cue from *representationalist*[11] views of self-knowledge. On more or less traditional views, self-knowledge of the qualitative content of perceptual experience is achieved through introspection, which is a kind of *inner sense*, directed at experience itself. The sensational content of perceptual experience is the qualitative properties (qualia) it instantiates, and one comes to know how one is experiencing through inner acquaintance with them. On representationalist views, on the other hand, self-knowledge of experiential content arises from a kind of extrospection: *deferred perception*. One comes to know what the content of one's perceptual experience is by focusing *outward*, on its objects and their properties. The qualitative content of perceptual experience is a kind of *representational* content, which is in part constituted by the external qualitative properties it represents. Knowing *what it's like* to see a clear sky at noon is not a matter of inspecting one's experience and finding a blue quale there, but of observing the sky and seeing that it is blue. Given that the sky looks blue, you can conclude that you are representing it as such. In describing what it's like, one describes not a property of one's experience, but a property of the object of one's experience—*the sky*. The blue is relevant to the characterization of the qualitative content of the experience because the experience *represents it*, not because it *instantiates it*: one's experience of the sky is no more blue than one's *thought* about it is.

(Motivation for such views comes from the alleged "transparency" of perceptual experience (when we attempt to inspect our experience, we find only extramental objects and their properties), from broadly physicalist scruples (qualia are mysterious, non-physical things whose relation to the brain is, at best, problematic: there's nothing

---

[11] Of the *reductive* variety. See, e.g., Byrne (2001); Dretske (1995); Harman (1990); Lycan (1996); Tye (1995, 2000). See Chalmers (2004) for the distinction between reductive and non-reductive representationalism.

blue in your brain when you are looking at the sky), and from certain epistemological worries.[12])

Thus, were one to argue that experiences must instantiate phenomenal properties because we come to know *how* we're experiencing by examining experience itself, and hence that the properties that constitute how we're experiencing must be there to be detected, the representationalist would counter that self-knowledge of experiential content can be otherwise explained. It's not based on inner sense, and there are no mysterious inner qualitative properties of experiences to be discovered.

Now, one might think that a similar strategy could be adopted in opposition to PITT. In Pitt (2004) I argued that, though it may not be readily apparent to some, there in fact *must* be a phenomenology of cognition, if a certain kind of introspective knowledge of content is to be accounted for. I maintained that if thoughts are to be distinguishable *to inner sense* from each other and from other kinds of mental states, then they must have their own proprietary, distinctive and individuative qualitative character. They must "show up" (appear) in consciousness in unique ways. But if the inner-sense view of knowledge of the contents of occurrent conscious states has been discredited, then the argument, which depends upon it, is fatally weakened: I haven't provided a reason to believe in cognitive phenomenology.

I think reductive representationalist theories of the qualitative content of perceptual experience founder on the twin hazards of dreams and hallucinations; though I won't argue for this here.[13] Rather, I want to try to show that extrospectionist theories of self-knowledge of perceptual content and propositional attitudes in fact do not succeed in explaining how it is that we can know that we're experiencing, believing, or desiring, and that in any case there's no plausible way to extend them to cover knowledge of intentional content.[14] Thus, what might seem like a good strategy for thwarting PITT doesn't get off the ground.

Extrospectionist theorizing about self-knowledge of propositional attitudes takes its cue from Evans, who (interpreting a remark of Wittgenstein's) writes (1982: 225):

---

[12] Michael Tye (2000: 46) argues that "[t]o suppose that the qualities of which perceivers are directly aware in undergoing ordinary, everyday visual experiences are really qualities of the experiences would be to convict such experiences of massive error. That is just not credible. It seems totally implausible to hold that visual experience is systematically misleading in this way."

On the contrary, I would argue, if visual experience were *not* systematically misleading—if it didn't present itself as something it's not (namely, external reality)—it would be *useless*. Transparency is an illusion made necessary by the facts that what experience is supposed to represent is external to the mind, while experience itself is internal. Perceptual experience cannot present itself as what it *is* if it's to be a naively believable guide to what it's *not*.

[13] Proponents are reduced to talk of representation of uninstantiated universals and objects in non-actual possible worlds, neither of which seem to me to be representable in the right sort of way, or to have the right sort of properties. (What is *deferred perception* of such things?) I develop these considerations further in Pitt (MS2).

[14] I'll use the phrase "intentional content" to refer to the contents of cognitive/conceptual states such as thoughts, beliefs, and desires. Some philosophers think that non-conceptual states have intentional content as well; but I won't be discussing such states in these terms here.

[I]n making a self-ascription of belief, one's eyes are, so to speak, or occasionally literally, directed outward – upon the world. If someone asks me "Do you think there is going to be a third world war?," I must attend, in answering him, to precisely the same outward phenomena I would attend to if I were answering the question "Will there be a third world war?"

Evans's view has recently been developed by Richard Moran, in his book *Authority and Estrangement*.[15] Moran generalizes Evans's claim, and couches it explicitly in terms of transparency:

With respect to the attitude of belief, the claim of transparency tells us that the first-person question "Do I believe P?" is "transparent" to, answered in the same way as, the outward-directed question as to the truth of P itself. (Moran 2001: 66)

Here, as in the case of perceptual experience, one determines the contents of one's mental states by looking *outward*. If you want to know if you believe that justice is a virtue, don't look into your mind, but consider *justice* and its relation to *virtue*.

Now, Alex Byrne (2005) has argued persuasively that Evans–Moran-style views, on which self-knowledge of belief is achieved by a process akin to decision-making, can't be the complete story.[16] As Byrne points out, there are many cases in which, when asked what one believes, one *already knows* the answer, and, therefore, doesn't have to *figure it out*:

Consider the question "Do I live in Cambridge, Massachusetts?" or "Do I believe that Moran is the author of *Authority and Estrangement*?" These questions can be answered transparently, by considering the relevant facts of location and authorship, but I do not need to make up my mind. On the contrary, it is already made up. (Byrne 2005: 85)

Byrne concludes that transparency, *per se*, "does not show that knowledge of one's beliefs is in general a matter of making up one's mind" (*id.*). He then goes on to develop an extrospectionist account of self-knowledge which, he claims, avoids the Evans–Moran limitation and explains both *privileged* and *peculiar* access to one's own intentional states.[17]

On Byrne's view, one comes to know what one believes by applying to oneself (or at least *trying to* apply to oneself) the *transparent* epistemic rule BEL (Byrne 2005: 95):

(BEL) If *p*, believe that you believe that *p*

In order to establish the truth of the antecedent, one considers whether or not *p*, where *p* is, typically, not a proposition about oneself or one's mental state. One looks outward

---

[15] I'm indebted in this section to Byrne's discussion of Moran's views in Byrne (2005), from which I've also taken the Evans and Moran quotations.

[16] Martin (1998) has objected along similar lines. (See also Gertler 2003/8.)

[17] Beliefs about one's own mental states are *privileged* in that they're more likely to yield knowledge than beliefs about the mental states of others, and *peculiar* in that they're acquired in a way one couldn't acquire beliefs about the mental states of others.

to determine the status of p, and recognizing it to be true, applies the rule and believes that one believes that p.

But how is it that considering whether or not it's the case that p, where p concerns facts not about oneself but about a mind-independent world, can support attributions of mental states to oneself? This is the "puzzle of transparency." As Byrne puts it (*id.*), it seems that "surely [BEL] is a *bad* rule: that p is the case does not even make it *likely* that one believes that it is the case." Here one seems to be in the same situation with respect to oneself as one is with respect to others. BEL, it would seem, is just as bad as BEL-3 (Byrne 2005: 96):

(BEL-3) If p, believe that Fred believes that p

Determining the truth value of p won't help at all in coming to know what Fred believes.

Byrne claims that the solution to the puzzle of transparency lies in the fact that "[o]ne is only in a position to follow BEL . . . when one has recognized that p. And recognizing that p is (inter alia) coming to *believe* that p" (*id.*).[18] That is, the only conditions under which BEL can be applied to yield self-knowledge are those in which the that-clause of its consequent is true: one must *recognize that p*, where recognizing that p entails *believing* that p. Hence, BEL is *self-verifying*. p may be a mind-independent fact, but that one recognizes that p is not; it's a psychological fact about oneself, and as such justifies a psychological conclusion. In making *cognitive contact* with the fact that p, one licenses the inference to an explicit self-attribution of a psychological state—in a way that making cognitive contact with p would not license attribution of a psychological state to someone else. Given that one is in the proper circumstances—the circumstances of recognizing that p—one is justified in applying the rule and inferring (the that-clause of) its consequent.

But now it seems BEL is no longer *transparent*. For, in order to *apply* it, you have to *know that* you're in the proper circumstances. It's one thing to *be* in the proper circumstances—for there to be a justification for the application of BEL; but if you don't know that you are—if you don't know that you have such justification—then you have no reason, no motivation, for applying the rule. Byrne likens application of BEL when one recognizes that p to application of the rule of necessitation ($p \rightarrow \Box p$) "whenever one is in circumstances in which the rule applies—whenever, that is, one is confronted with a proof whose initial premises are axioms" (Byrne 2005: 95). But just as you would

---

[18] Simply *entertaining* the proposition that p is not sufficient, since one can think that p without believing it. Suppose someone says, "George W Bush was the greatest American president." You, shocked, think: *George W Bush was the greatest American president. I don't believe that.* (You probably had to think it to understand what was said in the first place. Clearly, however, you don't have to believe what someone says in order to understand it.) This isn't paradoxical. The thought: *p. I don't believe that p* is paradoxical only if it's assumed that the initial p is an (inner) expression of a belief. (Likewise, the *sentence* "p. I don't believe that p" isn't paradoxical. If "p, but/and I don't believe that p" is paradoxical, it's (I would argue) because "but" or "and" somehow imply that the first utterance of 'p' is an *assertion*. Not all utterances of declarative sentences are assertions, however, though that might be the default assumption.)

have no reason to infer $\Box p$ from p unless you knew that p was occurring in a proof whose initial premises are axioms (why not infer q as you would if p appeared in a proof below a line on which p appeared, under assumption of q?), you would have no reason to infer that you believe that p from the recognition that p unless you knew that you recognized that p. In the absence of such knowledge, you'd have no more reason to apply BEL to yourself than you'd have to apply BEL-3 to Fred.[19] But knowing that you recognize that p is knowing that you're in a psychological state; and so BEL is not transparent.[20]

Moreover, given that recognizing that p is, as Byrne notes, *inter alia*, believing that p, knowing that one is in a position to apply BEL is *already* knowing that one believes that p. But that's what's supposed to be achieved by the application of BEL. Byrne claims that "the puzzle of transparency is solved by noting that BEL is self-verifying" (Byrne 2005: 96). But the puzzle is not solved, since one is not really looking outward after all. Additionally, the explanatory value of the theory is lost, since application of BEL presupposes the knowledge it's supposed to generate: the theory is viciously circular.[21]

It might be objected that one need not recognize that one is in proper circumstances for application of BEL in order to apply it and come to know what one believes, because its application is *automatic*: whenever you're in the circumstances of recognizing that p, some mechanism that implements BEL is activated, and forthwith you believe that you believe that p. Simply being in the proper circumstances *is* sufficient to trigger the relevant mechanism; it's not necessary that you consciously recognize that you are, or self-consciously apply BEL, in order for application of BEL to yield self-knowledge. My objection relies on an *internalist* conception of justification, which is not inevitable.

But the sorts of cases Byrne is trying to explain are not automatic. He's concerned with a process in which one *considers* how things are, *applies* BEL, and *concludes* that one believes that p—a conscious, voluntary process of coming to know what one believes. (Note that the consequent of BEL is an *imperative*—an instruction to *do* something, and

---

[19] Of course there can be a reason to apply a rule that one is not aware of. But such lack of awareness would prevent one from applying it. The fact that a crane is about to drop a Steinway D on the street right where I'll be in ten seconds is a reason for me to cross the street. But if I don't know this—if I don't know that I'm in a situation in which the rule "If you're about to be crushed by a concert grand falling from a crane, cross the street. Quickly." is applicable—in the absence of some other motivation, I won't cross the street; I won't apply the rule. I will, in a perfectly ordinary sense, *have no reason to.*

[20] Or, more precisely, BEL′, which makes explicit the conditions one must be in in order for application of BEL to yield self-knowledge, is not transparent:

(BEL′) If you recognize that p, believe that you believe that p

BEL itself is transparent, in that its antecedent is neutral (contains no psychological terms); but Byrne's solution to the puzzle of transparency entails that BEL cannot be transparently *applied*.

[21] Though I've focused on Byrne's account, I think these problems arise for any theory (including extrospectionist accounts of perceptual self-knowledge; more on this below) that relies on transparency. The general problem is that external facts are only relevant when they're cognized, and one must know the *way* in which they're cognized in order to draw any inference about one's psychological state. But knowledge of the way in which they're cognized is what the inference is supposed to yield.

that this is something one may *try* to do and *succeed in* doing.) Surely this is one way to come to know what one believes. Whether or not there's a mechanism of the other kind, its operation cannot explain such a process.

Moreover, mechanizing the inference doesn't obviate the transparency and circularity problems. Given that the mechanism needs as input not just the content that p, which could be believed, doubted, hoped, etc., but, again, the *mode* in which it's cognized, the rule it implements would have to have the form of (something like) AUTO-BEL':

(AUTO-BEL') If that p is recognized, dump a token of 'I believe that p' into the belief box

the antecedent of which is not about the world—the fact that p—but about the psychological state of recognizing that p. Hence, even if the inference is automatic (and/or unconscious), the implemented rule isn't transparent: its antecedent refers to a psychological state.[22]

Further, whether the inference is voluntary or automatic, the conditions under which the rule is applicable must be represented somewhere in the system. If there are a number of such mechanisms, each putting out a different kind of attitude with potentially the same content (belief that p, fear that p, hope that p, ...), they'll each require information about the mode in which the content is cognized—whether it's built into the rule explicitly, as in AUTO-BEL', or encoded somewhere "upstream" in some kind of input sorting mechanism, or otherwise represented. Without this information, the system won't "know" which routine to run, any more than a conscious, voluntary user of the rule. So the automated account is just as circular as the voluntary one: it requires that in order to come to know what you believe, you must already know (be in possession of information concerning) what you believe.

It might be countered that the "knowing" of the subpersonal system and the knowing of the believer are sufficiently different to render the account non-circular. The state the automaton is in is not a psychological state—it's *not* the very state the believer comes to be in when the routine is run. But whether or not the state is properly called psychological, it must carry information in some form about content and attitude if it is to play a role in the causation of the second-order belief. And this is sufficient to render the account circular.

Analogous non-transparency and circularity problems afflict Byrne's (Fullerton) extension of his model to self-knowledge of what one *desires*. Byrne suggests that self-application of the transparent rule DES explains how one comes to know one's preferences:

(DES) If ϕing would be desirable, believe that you want to ϕ

[22] I owe this point to Charles Siewert, in conversation.

This rule is supposed to be transparent because the judgment about the desirability of ϕing is a judgment about ϕ, and not about oneself.[23] However, as in the case of BEL, in order to have reason to *apply* DES (and not simply to *be in a position to* apply it), you'd need to know that you were in a position to apply it. This is, again, what the puzzle of transparency shows us is required. DES is as bad as DES-3:

(DES-3) If ϕing would be desirable, believe that Fred wants to ϕ

You'd need to know that *you believe that* ϕing would be desirable in order to know that you want to ϕ, just as you'd need to know that Fred believes that ϕing would be desirable to conclude that he wants to ϕ. And this is a fact, not about ϕing, but about you, and what you believe. So DES is not a transparent rule.

Moreover, given the intimate connection that, according to Byrne, obtains between judging that ϕing would be desirable and wanting to ϕ, the account suffers from circularity as much as the account based on BEL. Byrne maintains that the relation between judging that something would be desirable and wanting to do it is, though not *necessary* (like the relation between recognizing and believing), close enough to make DES "strongly reliably self-verifying" (Byrne MS). However, if this is so, then the fact that one must know that one believes that ϕing would be desirable in order to be justified in applying DES is sufficient to render the account circular. You can't conclude that you want to ϕ unless you know that you believe that ϕing would be desirable; and believing that ϕing would be desirable is sufficiently close to wanting to ϕ that knowing that the former is true is *already* knowing that the latter is true.

The same sorts of problems would confront an effort to apply this approach to self-knowledge that one was merely *thinking*—as opposed to believing, desiring, etc. Suppose I come upon you, frowning and staring off into space, and ask: "What's up? Why so glum?" and you answer, "I was just thinking about inner-sense and Byrne-style extrospectionist accounts of self-knowledge of belief." ("Poor you," I think.) How is it that you knew what you were doing—that you were *thinking* about something? Should we say that you applied the transparent epistemic rule TNK?

(TNK) If p, believe that you are thinking that p

But there's no more reason to suppose that TNK can be transparently and non-circularly applied than either BEL or DES. In order to *be in a position to* apply TNK, you must be thinking (merely entertaining the proposition) that p; but in order to have *reason* to apply TNK (to do what its consequent tells you to do), you must know that

---

[23] Of course if it were the case that something is desirable if and only if one desires it, DES itself (not just its application conditions) would be circular, since it would be equivalent to DES':

(DES') If you desire to ϕ, believe that you desire to ϕ

This construal of desirability is controversial, however. Suppose it therefore incorrect for the purposes of this discussion.

you're in that position. Hence, you must know that you're thinking that p in order to conclude that you're thinking that p.

Comparison of BEL and TNK is telling. Given that their antecedents are *the same*, it's imperative that one know what *kind* of cognitive contact one has made with the content of the antecedent. Otherwise, one wouldn't know which rule to apply, and which consequent to detach.

Further, TNK lacks a feature that gave BEL (and DES) whatever initial plausibility they may have had. For if one takes BEL's antecedent to record the result of an act of looking outward to determine *the way (non-mental) things are*, there would seem to be a fairly direct route to the conclusion that what the antecedent records is something one *believes*. Your answer to the self-posed question "How is it with the world?" expresses how you take the world to be; and how you take the world to be is what you believe. BEL formalizes this connection between answers to world-directed questions and knowledge of what one believes; so if you believe BEL[24] you can apply it to yourself and come to know what you believe. What's doing the work here is the close connection between how one takes things to *be*—what one takes to be *true*—and what one *believes*. But it's hard to see what features of the extra-mental world, and, hence, of one's stance with respect to it, could be used to ground knowledge of what one is (merely) thinking. Mere thinking is a *neutral* (non-committal) propositional attitude—if it's even a propositional attitude at all. In either case, in merely thinking, there's no question of the truth or falsity or desirability of what one thinks, no way in which one is taking the world. There's no *stance* to correlate with properties of extramental reality; there's no objective correlate (the way things *are*, the way they *ought to be*, the way they're *not*) of a propositional attitude (belief, desire, disbelief) for the extrospectionist to exploit here.

It's no surprise, then, to find Dretske (an *éminence grise* of contemporary extrospectionism) despairing of finding an explanation of privileged knowledge that one is thinking what one thinks. Dretske doesn't deny that we can have privileged knowledge both of *what* we're thinking and *that* we are thinking it. But he argues that while the former has a straightforward explanation, the latter does not:

> We have privileged and exclusive access to our own thoughts through acquaintance with their propositional content.... [but] there's nothing we're aware of in thinking that indicates we're thinking. We're aware of what we think...but thought content is evidentially worthless." [Dretske MS; see also Dretske 2006]

And he can't see where else one might look to find a basis for an explanation:

> If our mode of contact with our own thoughts doesn't give us a reason to think we're having these thoughts, what does? I haven't found anything – at least nothing one has privileged access to .... [*id.*]

---

[24] Belief in BEL is what Dretske (1994) calls a *connecting belief*.

I would like to think that these remarks evince some sensitivity to the problems just discussed for extrospectionist theories of self-knowledge of thought. (There's nothing *out there* for the extrospectionist to appeal to.) Though Dretske's stated reasons for his position are different. Thinking, he says, is not like being hungry:

When you are hungry there's (often enough, anyway) something you are aware of, something you feel, that indicates you're hungry.... When you think, though, there's nothing you're aware of, nothing you feel, that indicates that you're thinking. [*id.*]

I, of course, would beg to differ with this assessment. There's an introspectively detectable proprietary phenomenology of occurrent, conscious thinking: it's the phenomenology of occurrent, conscious *thoughts*. One knows what one is thinking, and that one is thinking it, in the same sort of way one knows what one is hearing, and that one is hearing it. Hearing has a distinctive phenomenology, such that when you're consciously experiencing it, you can know what you're hearing, and that you're hearing it. And the same is true (or so I would maintain) for thinking.[25]

Hence, the extrospectionist's failure to explain self-knowledge of thinking is due, I would argue, to not allowing for a distinctively *cognitive* kind of phenomenology. But I think the immediate cause of Dretske's impasse is the lack of an objective correlate of (mere) thinking that would allow the extrospectionist to extend his model.

Byrne (forthcoming) has proposed a different account of self-knowledge of thinking. He claims that one can come to know that one is thinking that *p* by trying to follow the transparent epistemic rule THINK-THAT:

(THINK-THAT) If the inner voice says that *p* and *p*, believe that you are thinking that *p*[26]

Byrne argues that since there's no such thing as an inner voice (to admit that there is would be to accept that there's "a shadowy inner world of . . . auditory images" (Byrne, Forthcoming: 20)), THINK-THAT can't in fact be successfully followed. However, one may still *believe that* there's an inner voice (a "harmless delusion"), and that it has said that *p*; and Byrne claims that thus *trying* to follow THINK-THAT is "very likely" to yield knowledge that one is thinking that *p*.

Now, Byrne rejects THINK*:

(THINK*) If you inwardly speak about *x*, believe that you are thinking about *x*

---

[25] There are of course problems lurking here. (For example, how does one know that one is *experiencing* something at all?) I think they have solutions (see below); but given what he says about hunger, Dretske seems to be as saddled with them as PITT.

[26] THINK-THAT combines BEL with THINK:

(THINK) If the inner voice speaks about *x*, believe that you are thinking about *x*

It's not clear to me why the clause "and *p*" is needed here, since *p* need not be true, nor need one believe it, in order that one simply think that *p*.

and would, presumably, also reject THINK′:

(THINK′) If you inwardly say that *p*, believe that you are thinking that *p*

on the grounds that they're not transparent, since their antecedents mention mental states. But I don't see how changing "if you inwardly say that *p*" to "if the inner voice says that *p*" solves this problem. Presumably, it's one's *own* inner voice that's at issue; and, even if there really is no such thing, THINK-THAT requires that one *believe that* there is, and, hence, is still ostensibly about the rule follower's mental state (the imaginary state of speaking inwardly). So, THINK-THAT is not transparent.

Further, application of THINK-THAT requires both that one take the inner utterance to be meaningful, and that one know what the inner voice has said. This is built into THINK-THAT (if the inner voice says *that p*), but if it's the (pretend) *utterance* that one defers to in coming to know what one thinks, Byrne isn't really entitled to this. One can't take an utterance, whether inner or outer, to be a mere string of vocables if it's to provide evidence of *thinking*. And one must assign a particular meaning to an utterance if it's to provide evidence of the *content* of the thinking. In short, the inner utterance must be *understood*.[27] But understanding the inner utterance is just thinking what it means, and so already involves thinking that *p*. Thus, given that one must in general know that applicability conditions hold, the account of self-knowledge of thinking based on THINK-THAT is viciously circular.

A further problem for extrospectionist theories of self-knowledge of intentional states is how to account for knowledge of *content* itself. In order to successfully apply a transparent epistemic rule, one must know not only what one's *attitude* toward the antecedent is, but what its content is as well.[28] Knowledge of *both* is required in order to justify self-ascription of the attitude of the consequent. If I don't know that it's *p* that I recognize or think (or *φ*ing that I find desirable), I won't be justified in concluding that it's *p* that I believe or think (or *φ*ing that I want to do). Knowledge of content is built in to BEL, DES, and THINK-THAT. But one might just as well wonder how one knows what the contents of one's thoughts, beliefs, and desires are. BEL and DES are focused on the attitudinal components of their respective state types, as evidenced by the fact that their application conditions presuppose knowledge of propositional

---

[27] What if the inner voice says, "You can take that stock to the bank!"? Shall I conclude that I'm thinking that I can take a farm animal to a river, or that I can count on shares of ownership in a company paying dividends? (Cf. note 4.)

[28] In fact, I'm skeptical of immediate introspective knowledge of propositional *attitudes* such as belief and desire, since I think a functionalist account of believing is correct (and functional properties are not introspectable), and since (for familiar Freudian reasons) one can be wrong about what one believes or desires. It seems to me more plausible that one can have immediate introspective knowledge of *acceptance* (or affirmation—*seeming* to believe) or *attraction* (*seeming* to desire), and that these sorts of "quasi-attitudes" are *prima facie*, but defeasible, evidence for what one's proper attitudes are, and that they have characteristic phenomenologies. (Note that in Pitt (2004) I argued that there's a phenomenology of conscious *thought*, not of belief.)

content, and are stated in terms of what's true or desirable. They don't provide any explanation of how it is that one knows the contents of one's intentional states.

So, presumably, we would need some other sort of rule to apply in order to explain how one knows that one is recognizing or thinking that p (and not that q), or that one wants to ϕ (and not to ψ), and we would need to specify the conditions under which such a rule would be applicable. Using BEL and DES as models, a rule of the form CONT seems a likely proposal:

(CONT) If χ, then believe that the content of your intentional state is that p[29]

where χ is the non-psychological object one looks to, and the conditions under which one is to apply CONT specify the property of this object that indicates that it's the content of one's intentional state. But what should the object be, and what's the relevant property? In the case of BEL, the object is (as the use of a propositional variable indicates) a *proposition*, and the property that indicates that one believes it is *truth*: if you ask yourself how things are with the world, and you judge that p is a *fact* (a true proposition), then it's reasonable to conclude that you believe that p. (In the case of DES, the object is ϕing and the property is desirability.) So it seems clear that we ought to replace χ with p: the object of a thought (as of a belief) is a proposition. But what of the conditions for application of CONT? What property is such that judging the proposition that p to have it would give one reason to infer that the content of one's intentional state is that p?

Given that propositions *are* intentional contents, it would seem that one would have to judge that it *is* the proposition that p. That is, one would simply have to identify it as the proposition it is. But this assumes that propositions have properties that we are able to detect, and on the basis of which we can discriminate them (just as, on the extrospectionist view, knowing the *sensory* content of one's perceptual experience assumes that one can discriminate its objects in terms of their properties). So, according to the extrospectionist, what sort of access could we have to propositions and their properties?

Dretske (MS) maintains that it's *acquaintance*:

...our point of contact with our own thoughts is through their content: what it is we're thinking. We have a privileged and exclusive access to our own thoughts through acquaintance with their propositional content.

Hence, to think (merely entertain) a thought is simply to be acquainted with its content, and acquaintance with a content entails awareness of its distinctiveness.

Now, one might well wonder how one could be *acquainted with* (what is presumably) an abstract object (as well as how one could be *exclusively* acquainted with it, given that it's public). Dretske dismisses such qualms—too quickly, in my view. (He says that being acquainted with a proposition is simply knowing the content of one's

---

[29] Assuming, *arguendo*, that desiring to ϕ is desiring that one ϕ.

thought. But this is unhelpful, given that knowledge of content is explained in terms of acquaintance with a proposition.) If there's to be a plausible extrospectionist account of knowledge of content along these lines, we're owed some sort of explanation of our access to propositions and their properties. In the case of perception, we have our sense organs and their causal transactions with the physical world: we know how we're experiencing (representing) things by inference from their perceived properties, which we can distinguish with our selectively sensitive sensory apparatuses (or so the extrospectionist story goes). Should we say then that we have a special faculty that allows us to peer into Platonic Heaven, and to pick out a particular abstract object, distinguishable to our gaze from its co-inhabitants? A naturalist would of course reject such a view; and naturalism is the *raison-d'être* of representationalism.[30] So I'm not sure what Dretske has in mind here, or what sort of story an extrospectionist could tell about acquaintance with propositions.[31]

My own view is that acquaintance with the intentional contents of one's thoughts works in the same way as acquaintance with the sensational contents of one's sensory experiences. Experiences in general instantiate and are individuated by phenomenal properties. One experiences a phenomenal property when it's instantiated in one's conscious experience, and one is acquainted with the phenomenal properties one consciously experiences.

Acquaintance with thought content works in the same way. Intentional contents are cognitive phenomenal types. To think that *p* is to token a phenomenal type that *is* the content that *p*. (See Pitt 2009.) One is thus acquainted with intentional contents when they're tokened in one's experience. Such acquaintance counts as a kind of knowledge. One knows *what* one is thinking in being consciously acquainted with it. Such acquaintance-knowledge can also be the basis for a kind of knowledge-*that*— knowledge *by* acquaintance. One can know *that* one is thinking that *p* in virtue of recognizing the token of the individuative cognitive phenomenal type that *p*, applying the appropriate concepts (*thought, that p*, etc.), and forming a belief about it.[32] Cognitive phenomenology can also be used to explain knowledge of *thinking*. One knows *which* sort of psychological state one is in by being acquainted with a proprietary sort of

---

[30] Naturalists are not, *per se*, nominalists. The program of "naturalizing content" is inaptly named. It's the *expression relation* between contents and brain states that's the target of this program, where contents are almost universally taken to be mind- and language-independent abstract objects (propositions). (See, e.g., Fodor 1990: note 6.) Equally, it's the *acquaintance relation* between contents and brain states that must be naturalized. No spooky extra-sensory powers of discernment, whether of abstract objects or immaterial qualia, are to be sanctioned. (Still, you might wonder why someone who countenances abstract objects would balk at other sorts of immaterials.)

[31] Here's a story that I think won't work. I know that I'm thinking that the sky is blue because I see that the sky is blue. Propositions are property complexes, and property instances can be detected in perception. But, first, how, on this account, is the thought that the sky is blue to be distinguished from the perceptual state of seeing that it is blue? And, second, not all thought is about what's perceivable. What of my thought that justice is a virtue? (In short, Empiricist theories of thought are inadequate.)

[32] Concepts that one may have to *acquire*. (Hence the developmental phenomena Dretske (MS) discusses.)

phenomenology, and *that* one is thinking on the basis of such acquaintance-knowl-edge.

I close this discussion of extrospectionism by noting that non-transparency and circularity problems of the sorts discussed above affect extrospectionist theories of self-knowledge of *perceptual* (experiential) content, as well. For notice that the puzzle of transparency arises as much for such theories as it does for extrospectionist theories of knowledge of thought, belief, and desire. PER is, ostensibly, as bad as BEL:

(PER) If x is F, then your experience is representing x as F

for, of course, that x is F constitutes no reason at all to believe that anyone is experiencing anything. And, as in the case of BEL, the presumptive remedy would be to specify conditions under which application of PER would yield knowledge of perceptual content. The obvious suggestion is that it be the case that it (perceptually) *seems to you* that x is F. But then the same problem arises in the application of PER as does for BEL. In order not merely to *be* in the circumstances that license application of PER, but to *have reason to apply* PER, one would need to know that x seems to one to be F. And, again, knowing how something seems is knowing something, not about an external object, but about one's experience of it. So PER is not transparent. Moreover, knowing that x seems to one to be F is already knowing that one perceptually represents it to be F (or, at least, is as close as finding ϕing desirable and wanting to ϕ are); so applying PER requires that one already have the knowledge its application is supposed to deliver.

I conclude, therefore, that extrospectionist theories of self-knowledge pose no serious threat to PITT.

Which is not to say that PITT is without problems. In the remainder of this paper I discuss one in particular that strikes me as, *prima facie* anyway, potentially serious.[33]

5 The introspective availability of intentional content

Here's the worry. You might think that any phenomenal property of an occurrent conscious state is, at least potentially (you might have to attend to it, really hard, for a long time, repeatedly), available to the individual who's in it. That is, you might think that there can be no *phenomenal* feature of a conscious experience which is *in principle* introspectively undetectable. Conscious phenomenology *is* the introspectable: it's the *surface* of our minds; the only point of direct contact we have with ourselves; the very *substance* of consciousness. And just as you might think that we ought to be able to perceive all the perceivable features of the surfaces of external objects (the only points of direct perceptual contact we have with *them*), you might think it equally tautologous

[33] Thanks to congregants Charles Siewert and Terry Horgan, as well as the infidel Joe Levine, for very helpful discussion of the issues in sections II through IV. I'm especially grateful to Joe for the care he has taken in understanding, and challenging, my view.

that we ought to be able to introspect all the introspectable features of occurrent conscious states. We might not be omniscient with respect to our minds; but we ought to be (something close to) omniscient (in principle) with respect to our *conscious* minds. And if you thought all of this, you might wonder how it could be that the intentional content of an occurrent conscious thought could be identified with its phenomenal character, when in fact we're pretty *lousy* at identifying the contents of our thoughts—because in particular we're pretty lousy at identifying the contents of their constituent *concepts*.

I take myself to be consciously thinking, for example, that I know that Hell is other people.[34] Well, if the intentional content of the thought is cognitive-phenomenal, and it's compositional, then it's determined by the cognitive-phenomenal content of its constituent concepts. In particular, the content of the concept KNOWLEDGE is cognitive-phenomenal. So, if I can know introspectively that I'm thinking that I know that Hell is other people, I ought to be able to know introspectively what the content of the concept KNOWLEDGE is. And if that content is just a kind of conscious phenomenology, all on the inner surface, so to speak, I ought to be able to determine introspectively what it is. But I can't say what the content of the concept KNOWLEDGE is. Indeed, maybe *no one* can. Likewise for all the other concepts that confound our efforts at understanding: TRUTH, JUSTICE, RIGHTNESS, LOVE, etc.

In sum, if there are conceptual contents that are introspectively unknowable, then it can't be that the contents of concepts, and, hence, of thoughts, are phenomenally constituted: PITT must be wrong.

An easy response to the problem is to claim that it requires that concepts be *analyzable*, and that (didn't we learn this way back in 1951?) there's no such thing as an analysis of a concept. The ostensibly problematic concepts are *primitive*. Indeed, *all* lexical concepts are semantically primitive. Their introspective recalcitrance isn't philosophically interesting at all; it's just what you'd expect. An analysis of thoughts into their conceptual constituents is all the analysis there is: knowing the content of your thought that you know that Hell is other people requires knowing the content of its constituents (namely: I; KNOW; [THAT]; HELL; IS; OTHER; and PEOPLE); but knowing the content of each of its constituents doesn't require knowing the contents of *their* constituents, since they don't have any.

I don't much like this response, myself. I'm rather partial to conceptual analyses, definitions, and their kin. (Primarily because I'm compelled by intuitions like *"the present king of France is male" is analytic, "female sister" is redundant, "false knowledge" is contradictory, "male sibling" and "brother" are synonymous*, etc.; because I think explanations of these facts in terms of the analysis of concepts are the most satisfying; and

---

[34] Maybe it's just other philosophers.

because I'm not afraid of apparent counterexamples like "black" and "sheep") So I'd prefer another way of addressing the objection. Here are a few possibilities.

In fact, it's not clear that *all* the contents of conscious experience must be *equally* available to the experiencer. Introspective knowledge requires introspective *attention*, and the capacities for conscious experience and introspective attention to it are distinct. Perhaps it is, then, not implausible that the *resolving power* of introspective attention might be insufficient to discern all the fine-grained details of conscious experience. There might be features of our conscious experience that we simply can't make out introspectively—just as there might be details of a visually represented scene that we can't quite make out, no matter how closely we look. Our *experience* is fully determinate in its details, but *reporting* all those details requires a fineness of discernment—of *attention*—that we just don't have.

Or maybe the *scope* of introspective attention is limited—it's like a kind of inner *foveating*, where (at least) the finer details of what's beyond the center of attention aren't accessible, hence not reportable (as the unattended ticking of a clock, the song stuck in one's head, the road one's driving on). Perhaps there are sectors of the field of conscious experience that are simply out of the neurologically determined range of the "inner fovea" (just as we can't see what's behind us merely by turning our eyes). So then it could be that when one can't say what the complete content of one's concept is, it's because one isn't—or perhaps *can't be*—focusing on the whole thing at once.

I don't find either of these suggestions very plausible. For one thing, it doesn't seem that inability to discern beyond a certain fineness of grain, even if we have such a limitation, is the problem in the case of concepts like KNOWLEDGE and JUSTICE. There seem, rather, to be substantive pieces missing. Supposing that knowledge is *F* justified true belief, it seems unlikely that *F* is some fine detail of the concept JUSTIFIED TRUE BELIEF that we simply can't make out. It seems like something more substantive is missing—a constituent of the same level of grain as JUSTIFIED, TRUE, and BELIEF.

Yet, it's also hard to believe that the missing piece is missing from our understanding because, though it's of the same scale and grain as the others, and equally conscious, we simply can't "foveate" on it, and so can't say what it is. Why can't we redirect our attention to a constituent presently unattended to? For sure, you can't see what's behind you *merely* by moving your eyes: their *in situ* range is limited. But you can resituate them. You can turn your head. And if you also turn your body, you can access all 360 degrees of the visual scene (not to mention looking up and down, underneath and above, etc.). Can't we similarly direct our inner attention all over the place, as it were scouring our conscious inner landscape? It seems odd—that is to say, unmotivated—that there should be places we can't look that just happen to be where we find ourselves at a loss with respect to KNOWLEDGE, TRUTH, JUSTICE, and the rest.

So let's try something else. Maybe in cases of incomplete accessibility one is *consciously* entertaining only *part* of the concept the relevant term expresses in one's language, the rest being unconscious, and hence introspectively inaccessible. This is different from the previous strategy, according to which the whole concept is conscious, but you just can't discern a part of it. In this case there's nothing to consciously introspectively attend to. Part of the concept is, as it were, "submerged."

But this doesn't seem very plausible either. *Why* should the submerged pieces be submerged? It's not like we're *repressing* them, because they're so dangerous or sexy that we feel guilty for thinking them. It might be difficult to analyze a conscious concept— just as it might be difficult to become aware of all of the rich detail of a conscious experience of, say, hearing a mass by Josquin or tasting an old Bordeaux. But that's not because these experiences have deeply buried unconscious features that you'd need a psychoanalyst's help to disinter. Discernment is typically something that must be *acquired*. But acquiring discernment with respect to one's conscious experiences is not a matter of making conscious what was unconscious. Maybe it's a matter of becoming more sensitive to what's already there. Or maybe it's a matter of having a new and different experience in response to the same stimulus. In either case, it doesn't seem likely that it's a matter of making conscious what's unconscious.

Here's the strategy I'm partial (but not entirely committed) to. Suppose that there is, in English, this word "knowledge," and that it has a socially (i.e. non-individually) determined meaning, and that this meaning is *F justified true belief*. Well, in that case, if you don't know what *F* is, and, hence, you don't know what "knowledge" means, then *you can't have any KNOWLEDGE thoughts*—because *you don't have the concept KNOWLEDGE*. You might *say*, "I'm thinking that I know that I'm condemned to be free," and your *words* might *mean that* you're thinking that you know that you're condemned to be free. But if knowledge is *F* justified true belief, and, long and hard as you try, you simply can't say what *F* is, then you're *not* thinking that you *know* that you're condemned to be free. That might be what your *words* mean, but it's not what's in your head. What you're consciously thinking is what you can report; so if what you can report is just that you truly, justifiedly believe that you're condemned to be free, then that's all you're consciously thinking. And if that's not sufficient for thinking that you *know* that you're condemned to be free, then your self-attribution is wrong.

In general, if the intentional content of a conscious thought is phenomenally constituted, and if introspection has equal access to phenomenal properties of all conscious states, then what you couldn't discover by introspection *is not (consciously) there*. And if it's not there, then you're not consciously thinking it. If it's the case that one can't think that one *knows* that *p* without having the concept *F*, and you can't discover the concept *F* in your conscious experience, then you're not consciously thinking that you know that *p*. You're consciously thinking something else. (And if you can *never* consciously entertain concept *F* together with the concepts JUSTIFIED, TRUE, and BELIEF, then you can never consciously think that you know *anything*.)

It might be objected that Burge has shown us that we can possess concepts we don't completely grasp (ARTHRITIS, SOFA, and the like)—hence, *a fortiori*, that we can possess concepts that we don't completely consciously grasp. You can very well be thinking that you know that Hell is other people even if you can't say what knowledge is, provided you're a member of a linguistic community in which the words you utter to express your thought—in particular, in this case, "know"—have a determinate meaning. Conceptual content is socially determined, and what's social is by definition not in any one individual head; so you shouldn't expect to automatically have *introspective* access to the contents of your thoughts. If you've *internalized* the socially determined content (i.e. made it completely explicit to yourself), then you can access it introspectively. But if you haven't, then you can't. So if you can't say what the content of the concept KNOWLEDGE is, it's not because you don't *have* it, and, hence, that you're not thinking that you know that you're condemned to be free; it's because you haven't internalized (made explicit to yourself) its content.

In response, I maintain that you *can't* possess concepts you don't completely grasp. Burge is a very subtle and resourceful philosopher, and has argued for his anti-individualist thesis in subtly different ways on different occasions. I don't have the space here to examine all of them; but it does seem clear to me that the most influential presentation of the thesis, the one that almost everyone cites in defense of their allegiance to the basic tenets of externalism—the one in "Individualism and the Mental" (cited 1,369 times to date, according to Google Scholar)—is fatally flawed. In brief, the problem is this. The lynchpin of the anti-individualist argument in that paper is the thesis that belief attributions it's intuitively *natural* to make to individuals, based on their sincere avowals, ought to be construed as literally true, all things equal. Hence, if someone (call him Art) sincerely utters the sentence "my arthritis has spread to my thigh," we who are in the know about where one can and can't (as a matter of *conceptual* necessity) have arthritis will nonetheless describe him as believing that his *arthritis* has spread to his thigh. We describe his conceptual error using *our* words, with the contents they have in *our* linguistic community; and since this is the overwhelmingly *natural* way to describe his mistake, we take it to be literally true. But if it's literally true, then Art has our concept ARTHRITIS (he can't have ARTHRITIS beliefs without it), in spite of his misunderstanding of it.[35]

The intuitive power of Burge's thought experiment derives from the observation that it's—pretheoretically, innocently, commonsensically, overwhelmingly—*natural* to describe errors such as Art's using the very words the ascribee doesn't completely understand, without supposing that we're using them with anything but their ordinary meanings for us. I think there's little doubt that this is correct. But the principle that what's intuitively natural in this way should be taken to be *literally true* is not. There are too many cases where what's powerfully intuitively the correct way to describe what

---

[35] Burge's (1979: 91) parenthetical comment that he's "not convinced" that someone who believes that "orangutan" is a word for a fruit drink and says "An orangutan is a fruit drink" shouldn't therefore be taken to *mean that* an orangutan is a fruit drink and *think that* an orangutan is a fruit drink is, I believe, strong evidence that the argument for anti-individualism in this paper is based on the principle that the intuitively natural way to describe someone's mental state, on the basis of the words they use (even mistakenly), is literally true. (Burge has since come to reconsider the emphasis he places on belief *ascriptions* in this paper (see Burge 2007), and has changed his mind about the orangutan example (personal conversation).)

someone believes, in full knowledge of his conceptual confusion, and without intending that our words have nonstandard meanings, *can't* be construed as literally true, and where it's clearly *not* our intention that it be so construed. Here's just one.

Little Simone is taken to the zoo, having been told that, among other fun things, she'll get to ride a big escalator. (It's the Bronx Zoo. (I seem to remember there being a long escalator up from the subway.)) After passing a number of cages containing large animals, Simone asks, excitedly: "Which one's the escalator? When do I get to ride it?" It seems entirely natural to describe Simone as having mistakenly believed that escalators are animals. This is a perfectly intuitive way to describe the mistake she made. "Ha, ha, ha!" we say, "Simone thinks elevators are animals! Isn't she *cute*?" (We routinely describe children's errors in this way: "When she was little, Lotta thought garter snakes were something you wear!"; "As a child, Linus thought guerillas were monkeys!") But surely we don't think that Simone was thinking that *escalators* are *animals*: "Really?" the tone-deaf philosopher asks. "You're saying that she thought that mechanical stairways for the vertical transport of pedestrians are biological entities of the *Kingdom Metazoa*?" "Well, of course not," we reply. "She obviously doesn't know what an escalator is. She wasn't thinking *that* at all!" Well, if she wasn't thinking *that*, then what exactly was her *conceptual* error? We don't mean to be attributing to her either so sophisticated, or *conceptually incoherent* beliefs. Even though on a *literal* interpretation of what we say, this *is* what we're doing. We use our words with their literal meanings, but we don't intend what we say about Simone to be *literally* true of her.

But isn't it equally obvious that Art doesn't know what arthritis is? And that, *therefore*, in describing his error we don't mean to be attributing to him the (by our lights) *contradictory* belief that a disease that can't occur in his thigh has spread to his thigh? So why isn't this a reason *not* to take our description to be literally true of him? And this in spite of the fact that it's intuitively entirely natural to describe his error using the very word he doesn't understand? It remains intuitively natural to use the very words the confused have used *even when it's perfectly clear that we don't think that what we say is literally true of them*. So the fact that it's intuitively natural to describe Art as believing that his arthritis has spread to his thigh tells us nothing about whether or not he has *our* concept ARTHRITIS. We certainly don't *mean to say* that.[36]

If a concept is a thing with constituents, and you don't possess all of the constituents, then you don't possess the concept. So if KNOWLEDGE has more constituents than JUSTIFIED, TRUE, and BELIEF, but those three are all the constituents you possess, then you don't possess the concept KNOWLEDGE, and you can't think that you *know* anything. And if you can't think that you know anything, then it's not surprising that you can't introspectively know that you think you know anything. The content is

---

[36] I develop a sustained critique of Burgean anti-individualism in Pitt (MS3) (eventually finding the root of all content externalism to be the false identification of thinking with inner-speaking).

not there to be introspected. If you were really consciously thinking it (and it's not primitive), then you ought to be able to say what it is.[37]

I think that it might, in fact, not often be the case that we're *saying* exactly what we're *consciously thinking, if* what we say is a matter of what the words we utter mean in the language we speak. Lexical understanding is a patchy and idiosyncratic affair. Do you *really* know what *all* of the words you use mean? (What, for example, is the precise difference in meaning between, say, "atrocious," "execrable," and "rebarbative"?) I think I can tell you what at least some of the words I use mean *to me*—which of my concepts *I* use them to express. I'm not so sure I could quote *Webster's Third* on any of them, however. (By "atrocious," "execrable," and "rebarbative" I think I probably just mean *very bad.*)

Maybe most of us don't have cognitive lives nearly as articulated as our vocabularies would suggest. And maybe we don't have nearly as much in common with each other, cognitively, as our shared language would suggest. We get by in communication and interaction provided the differences in the contents of our thoughts aren't sufficient to derail whatever projects we may have going, or want to begin, with others. But each of us is in his own little semantic bubble, blissfully unaware that we're by and large talking past each other.[38]

The way past the objection I've considered thus has far-reaching consequences, some of which may seem unacceptable. We often, perhaps typically, don't *think* what we *say*, and don't *say* what we *think*; nor do we often agree in what we think, even if we agree on what words we ought to use to express it. I don't find any of this very disturbing. In fact, I'm inclined to think that *linguistic meaning*—conceived of as a fixed, mind-independent assignment of unique semantic values to expression types of a language, which all speakers get hooked up to in the same way in virtue of shared intentions to obey certain conventions, or in virtue of happening to have grown up in a place where by and large people tend to make the same kinds of noises—is a will-o'-the-wisp. This is not to say that my words as I use them don't have meanings for me, derived from the thoughts and concepts I use them to express. (Nor is it to say that the concepts I express by my words don't have constituent structures that are accessible to me in conscious introspection, *or* that you and I *never* think or say the same thing.) Indeed, it's *because* my words as I use them have meanings that derive from the thoughts and concepts I use them to express that it's at best an idealization to speak of a unique, determinate, shared system of linguistic meaning for a community of speakers.

---

[37] It *is* pretty weird that we can know that we don't know what knowledge is. If we don't have an analysis of knowledge, then how do we know when we get it wrong? What are we comparing candidate analyses to when we see that they come up short? Are our intuitions responsive to a complete but inaccessible (because unconscious?) analysis? (It's a paradox of analysis. If you can tell when you've gotten an analysis right, then you must already know what the analysandum means; in which case the analysis is pointless. On the other hand, if you can tell when you *haven't* gotten an analysis right, then, again, you must already know what the analysandum means; in which case it's a mystery why you can't get the analysis right.)

[38] Maybe this wouldn't be too hard for a philosopher to accept.

I think this is a consequence of taking seriously the idea (which I take very seriously) that linguistic intentionality is derived from cognitive intentionality. If cognitive intentionality is phenomenal, and phenomenal properties are not intersubjectively accessible, then knowledge of shared intentional content (and, hence, shared linguistic content) becomes (though not impossible) problematic. Though what you *say* you think provides me with evidence of what you do think, the possibility that the way I construe the evidence—the content I assign to your utterance—is not the content of your thought is a live one.

Perhaps there's an innately determined, shared system of *cognitive* contents. (I'm eager to believe that there is, just as there's an innately determined, shared system of *sensory* contents.) But the *communication* of such content, which is necessary for the construction of objectively evaluable systems of linguistic meaning, is problematic.

So, on the internalist theory of meaning I'm defending here, language is a much bigger mess than one might have hoped. Maybe any ostensible "language" (English, Spanish, Tagalog) is too big a mess to succumb to one set of theoretical generalizations. Indeed, some linguists have said that there really is no such thing as English, Spanish, or Tagalog (from either a syntactic or semantic point of view), but only collections of more or less similar dialects—or perhaps even idiolects. For my own reasons, I think this is probably right. We ought not to assume that an individual's apparent competence with a given set of syntactic-phonological types is an indication that he has internalized the same unique, determinate system of linguistic meaning as anyone else who is apparently competent with that same set of syntactic-phonological types.

Ite Missa Est.

References

Burge, T. (1979). "Individualism and the Mental," in P.A. French, T.E. Uehling and H.K. Wettstein (eds), *Midwest Studies in Philosophy, Vol. IV*. Minnesota: University of Minnesota Press.

——(2007). "Postscript to Individualism and the Mental," in *Foundations of Mind*. Oxford: Clarendon Press.

Byrne, A. (2001). "Intentionalism Defended," *Philosophical Review*, 110: 49–90.

——(2005). "Introspection," *Philosophical Topics*, 33: 79–104.

——(Forthcoming). "Knowing that I am thinking," in A. Hatzimoysis (ed.), *Self-Knowledge*. Oxford: Oxford University Press.

——(MS) "Knowing What I Want," Talk with PowerPoint (distributed), 39th Fullerton Philosophy Symposium, Cal State Fullerton, April 30, 2009.

Chalmers, D. (2003). "The Content and Epistemology of Phenomenal Belief," in Q. Smith and A. Jokic (eds), *Consciousness: New Philosophical Perspectives*. Oxford: Clarendon Press.

——(2004). "The Representational Character of Experience," in B. Leiter (ed.), *The Future for Philosophy*. Oxford: Oxford University Press.

Dretske, F. 1994. "Introspection," *Proceedings of the Aristotelian Society*, 94: 263–78.

——1995. *Naturalizing the Mind*. Cambridge, MA: The MIT Press.

——2006. "Representation, Teleosemantics, and the Problem of Self-Knowledge," in G. Macdonald and D. Papineau (eds), *Teleosemantics*. Oxford: Clarendon Press.

——(MS). "I Think I Think, Therefore, I am—I Think," Text of talk delivered at the 39th Fullerton Philosophy Symposium, Cal State Fullerton, April 30, 2009 (subsequently revised and renamed "Awareness and Authority: The Structure of Self-Knowledge").

Evans, G. (1982). *The Varieties of Reference*. Oxford: Oxford University Press.

Fodor, J.A. (1990). "A Theory of Content, II," in *A Theory of Content and Other Essays*. Cambridge, MA: The MIT Press.

Gertler, B. (2003/8). "Self Knowledge," *Stanford Internet Encyclopedia of Philosophy*, http://plato.stanford.edu/entries/self-knowledge/.

Harman, G. (1990). "The Intrinsic Quality of Experience," in J. Tomberlin (ed.), *Philosophical Perspectives 4: Action Theory and Philosophy of Mind*. Atascadero: Ridgeview Publishing Company, 31–52.

Levine, J. (MS). "What Is Cognitive Phenomenology, and Do We Have It?", presented at APA symposium on cognitive phenomenology, December 2010.

Lormand, E. (1996). "Nonphenomenal Consciousness," *Noûs*, 30: 242–61.

Lycan, W. (1996). *Consciousness and Experience*. Cambridge, MA: The MIT Press.

Martin, M. (1998). "An Eye Directed Outward," in C. Wright, B. Smith, and C. Macdonald (eds), *Knowing Our Own Minds*. Oxford: Oxford University Press.

Moran, R. (2001). *Authority and Estrangement*. Princeton: Princeton University Press.

Nida-Rümelin, M. (1995). "What Mary Couldn't Know: Belief About Phenomenal States," in T. Metzinger (ed.), *Conscious Experience*. Exeter: Imprint Academic.

Pitt, D. (2004). "The Phenomenology of Cognition, Or, *What Is It Like to Think That P?*", *Philosophy and Phenomenological Research*, 69: 1–36.

——(2009). "Intentional Psychologism," *Philosophical Studies*, 146: 117–38.

——(Forthcoming). "Indexical Thought", forthcoming in U. Kriegel (ed.), *Phenomenal Intentionality: New Essays*. New York: Oxford University Press.

——(MS1). "Unconscious Intentionality," http://www.calstatela.edu/faculty/dpitt/Unconscious/Intentionality.pdf

——(MS2). "The Paraphenomenal Hypothesis," http://www.calstatela.edu/faculty/dpitt/PH.pdf

——(MS3). "The Burgean Intuitions," http://www.calstatela.edu/faculty/dpitt/The%20Burgean%20Intuitions.pdf

Tye, M. (1995). *Ten Problems of Consciousness*. Cambridge, MA: The MIT Press.

——(2000). *Consciousness, Color, and Content*. Cambridge, MA: The MIT Press.

——(2009). *Consciousness Revisited*. Cambridge, MA: The MIT Press.

The Sensory Basis of Cognitive Phenomenology[1]

Jesse J. Prinz

Most research on consciousness has focused on sensory experiences, but some authors believe that consciousness outstrips the senses. They claim that we can be conscious of cognitive states that are not reducible to sensory or even verbal imagery. If they are right, theories of consciousness that have been developed to explain how perceptual states become conscious may not be adequate for explaining all aspects of consciousness. This would be a major setback for those of us who have invested in theories of perceptual consciousness with the hope that these theories can explain consciousness in general. If cognitive phenomenology outstrips perception, some theories of consciousness (including a theory I have defended elsewhere) are incomplete. This concern would be abated if it could be shown that cognitive phenomenology has a sensory basis. That is what I attempt to do here.

I will begin by clarifying the distinction between theories that restrict consciousness to perceptual states (restrictivism) and those that are more inclusive (expansionism). Then I will present my preferred form of restrictivism, arguing that even high-level perceptual states and motor commands are inaccessible to consciousness. After that I will explore ways in which restrictivists can rebut leading arguments for expansionism. I will not argue that cognition cannot be conscious, but rather that the felt qualities of our thoughts can be completely accommodated by appeal to concomitant sensory imagery.

1 Restrictivism and expansionism

It was once widely assumed that every mental state is conscious. It's obvious to see why this was so: unconscious mental states simply went unnoticed. By the turn of the twentieth century, people were increasingly recognizing the possibility of unconscious

[1] I am grateful to Tim Bayne and two anonymous referees, who pressed me on important points.

mental states. This shift was heavily influenced by Freud's theory of repressed desires, and gained further traction from the failure of introspectionist psychology. In the early twentieth century, behaviorists railed against consciousness quite generally, and, in the mid-century, Chomsky argued that we comprehend language using unconscious rules. In the contemporary climate, it would be more than a bit eccentric to suggest that all mental states are conscious. But there remains considerable disagreement about which mental states are candidates for consciousness.

I will be defending the view that all consciousness is perceptual—what I'll call restrictivism. The contrasting view, expansionism, says that consciousness outstrips perception. These simple formulations are a good starting place for understanding the distinction, but there is an important clarification in order. As stated, the restrictive/expansive contrast implies a sharp separation between the perceptual and the non-perceptual, but there are distinguished philosophical traditions that deny any such distinction. Classical empiricists, like Locke and Hume, claimed that all mentality is perceptually based: concepts are stored copies of percepts, and thoughts are combinations of concepts. On this view, thought is couched in a perceptual code. Thus, for a classical empiricist, the restrictive/expansive distinction seems to break down. Empiricists are technically restrictivists, in that they say all consciousness is perceptual, but there is nothing especially *restrictive* about this restrictivism, since, for them, all cognition is perceptual too. Moreover, it would be misleading to say that empiricists cannot be expansionists simply in virtue of their perceptual theory of thinking. Imagine one empiricist who claims that only low-level perception is conscious, and another who says our most cognitively sophisticated thoughts can be conscious. Clearly the latter is more expansive than the former, but, on the definition above, neither qualifies as an expansionist. I myself happen to think classical empiricism is a plausible theory of the mind (Prinz 2002), so I would prefer to define the restrictive/expansive distinction that blocks a trivial inference from empiricism to restrictivism.

To provide such a definition, it will be helpful to distinguish vehicles, content, and qualities. *Vehicles* are the token particulars that have representational content. The vehicles in this sentence are orthographic marks on a page, and the vehicles in the head are mental representations. Empiricism is essentially a thesis about vehicles: it says that the vehicles used in thought are copies of the ones used in perceptual systems. The *content* of a vehicle, as I will use the term, is what that vehicle represents. For example, vehicles in the visual system may represent things like shapes and colors. If empiricism is right, visual vehicles can represent other properties too, like objects, or natural kinds, or even highly abstract properties, such as numbers. The *quality* of a vehicle is how it feels when it is conscious—what philosophers sometimes call phenomenal character. A red representation and a blue representation in the visual system have different content and different qualities—they feel different when they are conscious.

Now we need just one more piece of machinery to define restrictivism and expansionism. Let us say that the content of a vehicle is *sensory* just in case that vehicle represents some aspect of appearance. A content is *non-sensory* if it transcends appearance; i.e. if there can be two things that are indistinguishable by the senses, one of which has the property and the other of which does not.

With these distinctions in hand, let's adopt the following definitions:

Restrictivism is true if and only if, for every vehicle with qualitative character, there could be a qualitatively identical vehicle that has only sensory content.

Expansionism is true if and only if some vehicles with qualitative character are distinguishable from every vehicle that has only sensory content.

Notice two things about these definitions. First, I am not committing to the representationalist thesis that there is a one-to-one mapping between qualitative character and representational content. These definitions apply only to states that represent (vehicles), and leave open the possibility that non-representational states may have qualitative character. If restrictivism is true, there can also be states that are qualitatively alike but representationally different. Second, the definition of restrictivism is compatible with the view that perceptual states can represent non-sensory properties. Restrictivism says only that having non-sensory content does not introduce phenomenal qualities absent from sensory representations. Put differently, restrictivism is the view that content that goes beyond appearance has no direct impact on quality.

Restrictivism has probably been a default position for many, until recently. Some authors have argued that we don't even experience external features of the world, but only experience how the world affects our senses. Humphrey (1992) puts this in terms of Thomas Reid's sensation/perception distinction; he locates consciousness at the level of sensation and says that sensations represent "what is happening to me" rather than "what is happening out there." A somewhat more generous and typical view says that we experience *superficial* features of the external world, so that, in vision for example, we experience colors, shapes, and spatial relations (e.g. Peacocke 1983; Dretske 1995; Tye 1995; Lormand 1996). Some authors have also claimed that we can also experience objects (Clark 1993), and others have suggested we experience action affordances (Gibson 1979; Noë 2004). The crucial thing about these views is that they deny, implicitly or explicitly, that the quality of experience goes beyond these aspects of appearance.

Expansionists argue that consciousness is more encompassing. Siegel (2006) argues that we can experience natural kind properties, even though being a natural kind goes beneath the surface. Pitt (2004) argues that, for any thought that we can know we are thinking, there is a distinctive conscious quality, even though two distinct thoughts may represent states of affairs that look alike. Siewert (1998) has argued that there can be unverbalized, imageless thoughts. Expansionist views are also implied by Dennett (1991), whose cerebral celebrity theory of consciousness implies that just about anything in the neocortex can become conscious, and Searle (1992), whose Connection Principle says that every mental state is potentially conscious. (Searle's view is a bit hard to interpret, since he defends the Connection Principle by arguing that many unconscious brain states do not qualify as mental, rather than arguing that every unconscious brain state can be conscious.)

When looking at this debate, it is easy to get the impression that the main issue is whether *concepts* or *thoughts* can be conscious. I have intentionally defined expansionism and restrictivism to avoid this impression. Restrictivists can allow conscious concepts and thoughts as long as they are encoded in sensory vehicles and have no qualities above and beyond their sensory qualities. Restrictivism is neutral about what can be *represented by* a conscious experience, but it is restrictive about what qualities our conscious experiences have. Some formulations in the literature are potentially mis-leading in this respect. Siegel (2006) presents the debate as turning on what is "represented in experience." This formulation is acceptable only if we define "repre-sentation in" (in contrast to "representation by") as a technical term for those aspects of content that have an impact on phenomenal qualities. Siewert (1998) presents the debate as turning on whether "phenomenal character extends to conceptual activity." This is acceptable only if "extends to" means that conceptual activity has phenomenal character above and beyond sensory activity. The debate I am interested in is not about whether conceptual activity can feel like something to a subject, but whether it feels different than sensory activity. For this reason, I've resisted adopting Siewert's (2009) terms exclusivism and inclusivism, which are defined in a way that blurs this distinction. That said, I think Siewert's excellent arguments clearly pertain to restrictivism and expansionism as I have defined these terms, and I will turn to them below.

2 Perceptual consciousness

Let me now briefly sketch the brand of restrictivism that I will be defending. Else-where, I have presented empirical arguments for a theory of perceptual consciousness that builds on the work of Jackendoff (1987). Jackendoff begins by observing that perceptual systems are hierarchically organized. At the earliest stage (the low level), they respond to local stimulus features without integrating them into coherent wholes; at the next stage (the intermediate level), feature integration takes place; and, then, at a final stage (the high level), perceptual systems abstract away many details from the prior stage, and produce stimulus representations that remain invariant across multiple vantage points. In vision, for example, there is a progression from edge-detection, to contour detection, to structural descriptions that remain constant across changes in size in the visual field and viewing angles. Jackendoff's conjecture, which I endorse, is that consciousness arises at the intermediate level. In vision, we experience stimuli as bounded wholes from a specific vantage point, occupying a specific size and position within the visual field (cf. Marr 1982, on the 2.5-D sketch). Within sound, we experience bounded words, rather than isolated syllables, and we experience their volume and other specific acoustic qualities (for example, the voices of particular individuals are experienced differently). Within smell, we experience whole fragrances, not their chemical components (Livermore and Laing 1998), and we experience their intensity, location, and specific character (for example, distinct red wines are experienced differently, even if they are both recognized as red wine).

If the intermediate-level theory is right, the neural correlates of perceptual consciousness are restricted to those brain areas that implement perceptual processing at a level of abstraction that lies between local feature detectors and the abstract representations that play an active role in object recognition. This claim is highly specific about where consciousness arises, and contrasts with more permissive views, which say that any state within our perceptual systems can be conscious. I have defended this theory of perceptual consciousness elsewhere (2002; 2005). My goal here is to defend an even more controversial hypothesis: the claim that all consciousness is perceptual consciousness, and hence located at the intermediate level of our perceptual systems. Thus, if concepts or thoughts can have an impact on experience, it is only by altering these relatively rudimentary perceptual representations (for more on this, see Prinz 2007).

Many will balk at this. The intermediate-level view may seem overly restrictive even if we hold off on the question of cognitive phenomenology. I want to nip that concern in the bud. If I can't even establish that the intermediate-level view is sufficient for *non-cognitive* phenomenology, I won't stand much of a chance when it comes to explaining alleged cases of cognitive phenomenology.

There are five ways in which non-cognitive phenomenology is frequently said to outstrip intermediate-level perceptual phenomenology. Let me briefly consider each, because the resources introduced here will come in handy when we turn to conscious thoughts. First, some people think that we have experiences corresponding to high-level perceptual representations. This is the level at which object recognition is normally achieved. For that reason, it seems obvious to some that when we see a chair, for example, we experience its chairness, not just a bounded contour from a particular point of view. But this intuition can be easily accommodated on the intermediate-level theory. Intermediate-level representations of chairs *are* representations of chairs, in two senses. First, they may represent chairs according to prevailing theories of intentional content (for example, they may have the function of being reliably caused by chairs). Second, they correspond to the way chairs *appear* to us. Thus, to "look like" a chair is to look the way things look when we have one of these intermediate-level representations of a chair. This echoes an old chestnut in the philosophy of perception. It's a familiar point that an experience of an elliptical shape can look like a perfect circle, because perfect circles look elliptical from certain angles. It's a mistake to infer a circular experience from the presence of an experience of something that looks circular. Likewise, it's a mistake to infer an experience with the intrinsic structure of a chair from the fact that we experience chairs, as such. Against this reply, the critic might say that there is a phenomenal change that takes place when we come to recognize that something is a chair, after first failing to recognize it, and this change must be explained at the high level. But this move is problematic. For one thing, on the rare occasions when we fail to recognize a chair immediately, it's usually because the image is difficult to parse (e.g. the contours of the chair are obscured); when this happens, top-down information can affect phenomenology indirectly by altering the images at the intermediate level. For another thing, it's entirely unclear what the experience of a high-level representation would be like. It would have to capture what chairs are like in a viewpoint invariant way—the intrinsic structure of chairs, rather than a chair viewed from some angle. The brain may have representations like this, but, crucially, there is no experience that has that character.

Second, the intermediate-level view might be challenged by arguing that some perceptual constancies are consciously experienced but not encoded at the intermediate level. For example, look at a vertical line, and then bend your neck over as far as you can. You will notice that the line continues to appear perfectly vertical. Within the visual system, some high-level and, more surprisingly, low-level brain structures represent objects as they are objectively oriented regardless of body position, but intermediate-level representations change with body position (Sauvan and Peterhans 1999; McKyton and Zohary 2007). This might lead some to believe that the intermediate level cannot be the correlate of experience. When you tilt your head, vertical lines look vertical, even though they are represented at an angle in the intermediate level. But, I submit, this may be an illusion. As with the elliptical circle, looking vertical does not entail that there be a vertical object in experience. Looking vertical can be a matter of having an appearance that is perpendicular to the appearance of the ground. We also experience verticality by the fact that visual experiences co-occur with the somatic experience of gravity and body orientation (Yardly 1990). When we tilt our heads, the column is *visually* experienced as tilted, but the overall experience presents the column as emerging vertically from the center of gravity. But these other senses do not completely make up for the visual tilt; it is well known that judgments of verticality are systematically skewed in the direction of our head position when we bend our necks (ibid). Color constancies can be explained as well. When a colored surface changes illumination conditions, as when a shadow is cast, we can recognize that it's the same color. But this ability may not reflect a phenomenological constancy: when lighting changes, people report phenomenal changes (Reeves et al. 2008). Instead, the constancy reflects an inference about the objective color, an inference that can go wrong or vary without corresponding changes in the phenomenology. To confirm this, look at a white wall under shadowy conditions and imagine being told the wall is actually pale gray. This change in the belief about the objective color does not seem to alter experience of the perceived color.

Third, the intermediate-level view has difficulty explaining what Noë (2004) calls the experience of presence in absence. Suppose you see a ball. The intermediate-level representation depicts only one surface, leaving the far side of the ball completely absent. Yet, we are aware, in some sense, that the ball is a perfect sphere. There is a phenomenological experience, Noë claims, corresponding to the far side of the ball, even though the intermediate-level representation leaves it out. If you share Noë's phenomenological intuition, you might think this undermines the intermediate-level theory of consciousness, but Noë's own explanation of the phenomenon points to a way out. Noë favors an enactive theory of perception, according to which the visual system picks up on sensorimotor contingencies; we literally see how the ball would appear were we to move around it. I do not endorse enactivism (see Prinz 2006a; 2008), but there is good evidence that visual perception *causes* motor responses that correspond to the actions that visual objects afford (Tucker and Ellis 1998; Chao and Martin 2000). If you see a ball, you might prepare a grasping motion, and—because of unconscious high-level visual representations that extract the volumetric structure of the ball—the grasp you prepare will be appropriate for a full sphere, rather than the mere hemisphere that happens to be visible. If you consciously experience your body preparing such a grasp, your experience will capture the sphericality of the object. For me, unlike Noë, sphericality is not part of the visual experience at all, but it is part of the total experience that includes both vision and covert bodily actions.

This explanation of how we experience presence in absence brings us to a fourth objection to the intermediate-level view. It seems we often have experiences of our motor actions, such as grasping a ball, but motor actions are not perceptions, so it cannot be the case that all consciousness resides within perceptual systems. This objection supposes that there is motor phenomenology. But that may not be the case. It is possible that we experience action by perceiving real or anticipated changes in our bodies. When we grasp, there is a motor command, but also a kinesthetic experience of our hand muscles clenching, a tactile experience of the surfaces that our hand takes hold of, and a visual experience of our hand taking on a new configuration. Indeed, neuroimaging studies that explore the phenomenology of action, again and again show activation in areas of the parietal cortex that are associated with action perception, rather than mere activations in the motor cortex (Blakemore and Frith 2003). It is plausible that motor systems have no phenomenology.

Finally, consider emotions. If there is anything that we can consciously experience, it's our emotions. But most people assume that emotions are not perceptual states, and it follows from this assumption that consciousness cannot be limited to intermediate-level perceptions. The problem with this objection is that it is based on a false assumption. Emotions are perceptions. They are perceptions of changes in our respiratory, circulatory, digestive, musculoskeletal, and perhaps endocrine systems (James 1884; Damasio 1994). I have defended this view at great length elsewhere, and won't repeat the case here (Prinz 2004). I have also argued that the conscious experience of emotions resides at an intermediate level within systems that perceive bodily changes. When we feel afraid, we experience a pattern of bodily change that integrates more local changes (a racing heart, goose bumps, respiratory arrest) that are specific to our current physical position. If this is right, emotion fits neatly into the intermediate-level story.

These brief remarks will not satisfy every critic, but I hope they serve to show open-minded readers that the intermediate-level theory of consciousness has resources to explain a broad range of perceptual experiences, and that apparent counter-examples are more easily accommodated than might initially appear. It will be the burden of the remaining sections to show that this theory can accommodate *all* aspects of phenomenology.

3 Resisting expansion

Expansionists claim that cognition contributes something to phenomenology over and above perception. More formally, I defined the view as entailing that there can be cognitive mental states that have phenomenal qualities that differ from every possible state that has purely sensory content. Expansionists try to make their case by devising examples where cognitive phenomenology seems to outstrip anything sensory. I will survey putative examples here and offer restrictivist reconstruals.

3.1 Conceptual consciousness

The question of whether concepts can contribute to phenomenology depends, of course, on what concepts are, and that is a Big Question, beyond the scope of this chapter. I will begin by offering a few remarks about what I take concepts to be, and then turn to conceptual consciousness. My own views about concepts are not universally shared in philosophy (far from it!), but they are ostensibly conducive to expansionism, so, assuming that I am right about concepts, I may be biasing the case in favor of expansionism and against restrictivism, rather than conversely. Since I will defend restrictivism, I am, in effect, making my own chore harder. Moreover, the strategies I offer to block expansionist theories of conceptual consciousness can be adapted to any other theory of concepts.

As already noted, I am partial to concept empiricism, according to which concepts are acquired by storing records of percepts. This alone does not entail that concepts can be consciously experienced. There is good reason to think that we store high-level perceptual representations in long-term memory, not intermediate-level representations (Prinz 2002). That would explain why our powers of discrimination are far greater than our powers of recall (Raffman 1995). If concepts are acquired by storing percepts, then concepts may be encoded in a high-level perceptual format that is not consciously accessible, if the intermediate-level theory is right. But I think concepts *can* be conscious, because, in occurrent acts of conceptualization, we use the high-level representations that are stored in long-term memory to construct temporary mental images of what our concepts represent (Martin 2007). These temporary images can be conscious because imagery can be generated using intermediate-level representations (Slotnick et al. 2005). I think we should regard images generated from long-term conceptual memory as occurrent tokens of the stored concepts used to generate them. Thus, I think that concepts can be conscious, and, in this sense, there is such a thing as cognitive phenomenology. But it doesn't necessarily follow that expansionism is true, because it doesn't follow that conceptually generated images are qualitatively different from purely sensory images.

I think that the images generated from stored concepts inherit semantic properties from those concepts (Prinz 2006b). So an image of a walrus represents that natural kind, and an image of an electron circling a proton represents these particles. But I think these images also retain their sensory content. I endorse a Lockean notion of *double reference* according to which images represent *both* "real" natural kinds with unobservable essences and their "nominal" appearances (Prinz 2002). But simply, images refer to their conceptual contents *by means of* representing sensory contents. A mental image represents walruses by representing how they look, and an image represents subatomic particles by representing swirling circles. Thus, the brand of restrictivism that I favor says that the phenomenal qualities of an image derive entirely from its nominal content, not its real content. A little reflection (homework for the reader) will show that this formulation is a special case of restrictivism as defined earlier. That earlier definition is defined more generally so as to avoid any commitment to the doctrine of double reference.

To refute this story, the expansionists would need to show that real content contributes phenomenal qualities that are not already associated with the nominal content of an image. For example, the expansionist might try to show that my image of a walrus differs phenomenologically from a perceptual experience someone might have the first time she saw a walrus, not knowing what it was. Siegel (2006) implies that this is the case when she proposes that we can experience natural kinds as such, but I am highly dubious. I don't think we *experience* natural kind properties when we apply concepts to our percepts.

As a preliminary, it's worth noting that perception is not normally dependent on conceptualization. The phenomenology of object perception can remain undisturbed after incurring profound deficits in conceptual knowledge. Research on semantic dementia, associated with degeneration of the anterior temporal lobe, shows that individuals can continue to perceive normally once they have lost category memory (Patterson et al. 2007). For example, when shown a picture of a duck, a semantic dementia patient won't be able to recognize it, and when asked to reproduce the picture from memory, she might produce a bizarre chimera with duck-like features and four legs. But the same patient would have no difficulty matching the duck picture with a duplicate or even matching it with pictures of the same duck at different orientations. This suggests that perception and conceptualization are somewhat autonomous activities.

In response, expansionists will hasten to note that conceptualization *can* influence perceptual experience. Consider the phenomenon of seeing-as. When we interpret ambiguous figures they seem to transform experientially. The most famous case is Jastrow's duck-rabbit. Does the experience change when we see the duck-rabbit as a duck and then switch to seeing it as a rabbit? Introspectively, the answer seems to be yes, and this might be taken as evidence for the existence of cognitive phenomenology that goes above and beyond sensory phenomenology. But the shift in experience can easily be explained in other ways.

For one thing, when we interpret an image as of a duck, we gain access to duck knowledge stored unconsciously in long-term memory, and some of this knowledge may bubble forth in the form of mental imagery. It is possible, for example, that when construing the duck-rabbit as a duck, viewers faintly imagine a duck's body and other features. Research has shown that black-and-white images of familiar objects are misperceived as being faintly colored in appropriate ways (Hansen et al. 2006), and animal names to prime auditory imagery of animal sounds (Orgs et al. 2006). And of course, picture recognition generates the production of verbal labels, so when seeing a duck-rabbit as a duck, the word "duck" is probably heard in the mind's ear. In addition, conceptualization can lead to perceptual distortions that make the object look prototypical or easier to discriminate from others (Goldstone 2004). Linguistic labels can also have that effect: labeled ambiguous pictures are recalled as having label-consistent disambiguating features (Carmichael et al. 1932) and labeled ambiguous facial expressions cause label-consistent unambiguous emotional contagion (Halberstadt et al. 2009). Conceptualization can also affect the allocation of attention to the features most relevant to the operative interpretation (Aha and Goldstone 1992). There is evidence for this in the case of the duck-rabbit; those who interpret the image as one animal, fail to notice when the portion corresponding to the face of the other animal is altered (Chambers and Reisberg 1985).

These findings show that conceptualization can influence perception in dramatic ways: there are shifts toward prototypicality, verbal labeling, generation of associated images, and allocation of attention to category-relevant features. This may look like evidence for expansionism, but that would be a bad inference. Crucially, none of these effects requires postulation of distinctively cognitive phenomenology. In principle, someone who had no concept of ducks could, with careful contrivance, have a perceptual experience akin to the one that we have when we interpret a duck-rabbit as a duck. The top-down effects all involve the imposition of further sensory information or an allocation of attention to sensory features. There is nothing essentially cognitive in the resulting unambiguous image. Thus, we can fully account for the phenomenology of placing an ambiguous image under a concept without assuming that conceptualization introduces non-sensory features.

3.2 Imageless thoughts

Let's move now from concepts to thoughts. In some ways, this step should be trivial since thoughts are said to be combinations of concepts. I have claimed that concepts can be conscious by means of sensory images that have no distinctively cognitive phenomenal qualities. If so, the same may be true of thoughts. We can render a thought conscious by forming an image of what it represents. I think such images have no distinctively cognitive phenomenal qualities. Expansionists demur. They claim that the phenomenology of thought outstrips the sensory. One way to argue for this is to find thoughts that lack associated imagery but are nevertheless available to consciousness.

A century ago, imageless thoughts were a major topic of debate in psychology. Introspectionists like Wilhelm Wundt and Edward Titchener had claimed that all thoughts were imagistic, and the psychological science should consist in eliciting subjective reports about the images that occur during cognitive tasks. This view was challenged by Oswald Külpe in Würzburg, who claimed that thought could be imageless. He based this conclusion on studies by his colleague Karl Marbe in which subjects were asked to assess which of two weights was heavier. Marbe's subjects often reported having what he called *Bewusstseinslage*, or conscious attitudes—feelings such as vacillation, hesitation, and doubt—but no images. Titchener quickly challenged the results, saying that his subjects reported kinesthetic images when he tried to replicate the study, and the accompanying epistemic attitudes can, we will see below, be explained in emotional terms.

The debate did not end there, however. The issue was taken up again by George Stout, one of the early editors of *Mind*, who coined the term imageless thought, but later denied that such things can exist (see Angell 1911). The greatest champion of imageless thoughts was R. S. Woodworth of Columbia University, whose arguments anticipate much of the contemporary discussion. Woodworth acknowledged the limitations of Külpe's arguments and tried to improve on them. In his experiments, he would ask people to answer questions and then report on any images they formed. For example, he asked, Which is more delightful, the smell of a rose or its appearance? What is the difference between similarity and congruity? and What substances are more costly than gold? Many people reported that they were arriving at answers without use of imagery. For example, in response to the question about what costs more than gold, one woman answered "Diamonds," and said, "I had no visual image of the diamond; the thought of diamonds was there before the sound of the word" (1906: 704).

These Woodworth experiments will not move the restrictivist. It's easy to suppose that his subjects are simply wrong about their own mental states. The woman may well have visualized diamonds, despite her insistence to the contrary. Indeed, the failure of introspection on cases just like this led to the end of introspectionist psychology. Titchener's subjects always reported images, and Woodworth's did not, suggesting that introspectionist results could not be replicated in a way that science demands. Modern measurement techniques now suggest that Titchener's subjects were more likely right. The mere reading of a word spontaneously prompts mental imagery (Chao et al. 1999), so the woman who claimed she thought "Diamonds" without imaging them was probably mistaken.

Woodworth may have realized this, and he did not rest his case entirely on introspection. He has other arguments for imageless thoughts. One of these anticipated an argument in Dennett (1969) by 60 years. In 1907 Woodworth's colleague Edward Thorndike had asked students to visualize the front of Columbia's library, but even those who reported having vivid images were unable to report simple facts like the number of columns. Woodworth (1915) suggests that people may be wrong to think that their images are copies of experiences, and he hints that maybe when people take themselves to be using images, they are actually relying on stored descriptions, which leave out details that would be apparent in any genuine picture. The argument threatens those who claim that conscious thoughts are always imagistic, by showing that even when people are instructed to use imagery and report using imagery, they may be relying on something else entirely. But opponents of imageless thought need not give in so easily. They can explain the uncountable columns in several ways: images may be blurry, they may omit details just as vision does, and they may fade too rapidly to accurately report. Forming an image is often easier than inspecting it; if you look at a cage, you may see it vividly but have difficulty counting the bars.

Woodworth (1906: 707) suggests another argument for imageless thought when he notes that, "The thought of the object is not the image, for the image may change while the same object is thought of." This is a bit like Descartes' argument that we can be aware that an object is the same piece of wax even as it is melted and deformed, suggesting that we have an idea of wax that goes beyond imagery. Woodworth takes this a step further, adding that the idea of an object "is as substantial an element of thought as the image, and there is no absurdity in the notion that it may be present alone." Once we grant that ideas transcend images, we should suppose they can exist without images.

This is an ingenious argument, but it can be rejected. First, the connective tissue that helps us recognize that successive images are images of the same object may be entirely unconscious. Reflecting on Descartes' example, it's far from clear that there is anything in consciousness that can qualify as a representation of wax as such as we watch a piece transform. Moreover, we don't need to postulate a single object representation that united the successive images of wax. We can just as easily suppose that the mind tracks the object by its continuous spatiotemporal trajectory—something infants readily do with no regard to structural continuity (Xu and Carey 1996). By tracking objects in this way, we store knowledge of how they change, and we can use memory traces of object transformations to recognize two things as the same, even if they look different. We do not need some constant mental item to recognize that successive images correspond to one object; rather, observers can use knowledge of permissible transformations to treat successive images as belonging together.

Woodworth's most powerful argument for imageless thought draws attention to the fact that some thoughts represent facts that are difficult to represent imagistically. As an example, he offers his own recollection that a speaker at a meeting was exaggerating, and that the speaker was acting in his capacity as chair of a committee (Woodworth 1915). Since these features have no characteristic appearance, Woodworth concludes that the memories are not entirely imagistic. But this claim neglects the possibility that the relevant features were present in the form of verbal imagery. We might say to ourselves in silent speech that the speaker was exaggerating or serving as chair.

I suspect that verbal imagery can explain every instance of conscious thought that cannot be accounted for by appeal to images of the contents of our thoughts (what I will sometimes call simulations). Inner speech is incessant and implicated in many aspects of cognition (Hurlburt 1990; Carruthers 2002a; Morin 2005). It is also known to be underwritten by the brain mechanisms involved in speech production and, importantly, perception (Shergill et al. 2001). Given the conspicuous presence of silent speech in the stream of consciousness, it seems likely that we often come to know what we are thinking by hearing inner statements of the sentences that we would use to express our thoughts.

I don't mean to suggest that words alone constitute *understanding*. Comprehending that someone is the chair of a committee, for example, involves a complex set of norms and expectations, such as the expectation that the chair will lead the discussion, and a granting of permission to do so. These things may affect phenomenology. For example, if someone who isn't chair tries to take control, witnesses may feel annoyed or outraged. But, the totality of these complex expectations and norms will not be brought fully into consciousness at each moment. The verbal label ("that person is chair") can serve as a mental shorthand, consolidating a complex concept into a single sound ("chair"). Words serve as placeholders for ideas that cannot be experienced all at once, and, through habit, inner speech becomes a way of registering complex thoughts in consciousness. Thus, the claim here is not that verbal imagery constitutes thought comprehension, but only that, as a matter of fact, verbal images are often the way thoughts present themselves to us in consciousness, as a kind of shorthand.

This commonsense suggestion is effective against some recent arguments for expansionism. One of the most ambitious recent arguments owes to David Pitt (2004). He notes that we often have conscious access to what we are thinking. We know the content of our thoughts, and we can distinguish one thought from another and from non-cognitive mental states. Pitt uses these claims to infer that thoughts must have a characteristic phenomenology. He thinks this phenomenology outstrips mere imagistic simulations (because, e.g., thoughts often have contents that are more fine-grained or abstract than the images that might happen to co-occur with them). The argument is clever, but there is a natural reply: we know what we are thinking by means of verbal imagery. The impression that we can distinguish one thought from another and from other mental states can be easily explained on the assumption that we identify thoughts by inner speech. Sentences can be distinguished from other forms of imagery, and distinct thoughts can be distinguished verbally, even when they might be visualized in similar ways (compare "The cat is on the mat" and 'The mat is under the cat'). The claim, again, is not that words constitute comprehension, but that they are handy bookkeepers that tell us what we are thinking under conditions when imagining thought contents in some other way might be difficult or inefficient. Pitt, of course, anticipates this verbal imagery reply and offers a rejoinder, which I will take up in the next section. For now, let us settle on the conclusion that alleged examples of *imageless* thoughts either rest on dubious appeals to introspection, or can be explained by supposing that cognitive phenomenology often takes the form of verbal imagery. The proponent of expansionism must show that verbal images are not up to the task.

3.3 Languageless thoughts

I have just been suggesting that some seemingly imageless thoughts may actually be cases in which we lack imagistic simulations of what our thoughts represent, but have verbal imagery of the words we would use to express them. Expansionists are dubious of this claim. In this section I want to consider several arguments that they have levied against efforts to equate cognitive phenomenology with inner speech.

The first argument that I will consider comes from Pitt (2004). As we just saw, he argues for expansionism by noting that people have conscious awareness of what they are thinking. Conceding this, I suggested that such awareness characteristically takes the form of verbal imagery. Pitt is not convinced. He notes, first, that we have immediate acquaintance with our thoughts in a non-inferential way. We don't need to extrapolate what we are thinking by experiencing something else. Pitt then notes that thoughts cannot be *constituted* by sentences. After all, words have their meanings arbitrarily (see also Woodworth 1906: 706). If consciousness of thoughts is direct and sentences aren't thoughts, then it follows that the conscious experience of thoughts can't be an experience of sentences.

Both premises in Pitt's reply can be challenged. The claim that we have non-inferential access to our thoughts is surely right at some level: phenomenologically, it doesn't seem that we figure out what we are thinking by an act of inference. But it doesn't follow that we are directly acquainted with our thoughts. We might be directly acquainted with sentences, and simply treat them as if they are thoughts without trying to infer what they mean. On this suggestion, sentences *stand in for* thoughts, and we are so habituated to this that we feel as if we are experiencing thoughts themselves. Alternatively, one can challenge Pitt's second premise, and say sentences do not merely stand in for thought, but actually constitute thoughts. When we produce sentences in silent speech, they issue forth from unconscious representations that correspond to what those sentences mean (these are perceptual representations if empiricism is true). Sentences inherit their truth conditions from the unconscious ideas that generate them. So produced, these sentences are not arbitrary marks, but rather meaningful symbols. If we define a thought as a mental state that represents a proposition, then mental sentences qualify as thoughts (see also Carruthers 2002b).

Expansionists sometimes resist the equation of thoughts and inner speech by arguing that, under some circumstances, we become conscious of a thought before becoming conscious of a corresponding sentence. Woodworth (1906: 704) makes this case by appeal to the phenomenology of conversation, where, he claims, we become aware of our thoughts before we find the words to express them. A modern version of this argument has been put forward by Siewert (1998), who draws attention to the fact that thoughts sometimes suddenly occur to us in a way that doesn't seem like the inner rehearsal of words or construction of images. His favorite example is the sudden realization, while driving to work, that he left his briefcase at home.

Woodworth and Siewert want us to believe that we experience such thoughts in an immediate way prior to any images or sentences. They both call on examples where thoughts come unbidden and quickly: the steady flow of conversation, a sudden realization. But these examples will not convince restrictivists. First of all, from introspection alone it's far from obvious that there is any conscious thought prior to the sentences we utter in rapid conversation. We simply hear ourselves replying to our interlocutors. And in the case of sudden realizations, it's far from obvious that the phenomenology outstrips imagery and inner speech. While driving to the office, one might anticipate, with faint dread, a day of grading papers; this involves formation of an imagined scenario, in which one retrieves papers from a briefcase; that simulation triggers a recalled image of the briefcase standing by the front door at home; a panicked glance confirms that the briefcase is not in the car; this prompts the expletive, "Damn! I left my suitcase." I don't think Siewert has identified a clear case of a thought that appears unbidden in consciousness without accompanying imagery.

Unsurprisingly, Siewert does not rest his case for expansionism on introspective intuitions about a forgotten briefcase. He offers a battery of powerful arguments against the allegation that inner speech can explain the phenomenology of thought. The arguments all have a similar form: he generates cases in which we change our interpretation of a word or phrase, and suggests that, when this happens, there is a corresponding change in phenomenal qualities (Siewert 1998; 2009; see also Pitt 2004; Siegel 2006). For example, Siewert invites readers to repeat a word until it becomes meaningless, suggesting that this will alter the phenomenology. Or consider the change that occurs after learning the meaning of a word in a foreign language; *eichhörnchen* is just a funny sound until we know it's the German word for squirrel. Siewert also treats us to lovely examples of lexical ambiguities, as in "I hope the food's not too hot for you," which we might interpret as a warning about temperature before realizing that the meal is very spicy. There are also cases of syntactic ambiguities, or sentences that are difficult to parse. Pitt (2004) gives us the garden path sentence, "The boat sailed down the river sank," which seems ungrammatical at first, but then gets resolved by treating "sailed" as a noun modifier rather than a main verb. In each of these cases, the very same words give rise to distinct phenomenology, suggesting that phenomenology cannot be exhausted by inner speech.

This is a clever argumentative strategy, and the introspective intuitions are robust. But committed restrictivists need not surrender. In each of these cases, changes in interpretation may be accompanied by changes in associated imagery. When we repeat a word, we go from imagining what the word represents to focusing on the way the word sounds. When we learn the meaning of a foreign word, we can imagine its referent, along with sentences we might utter in response to that word. When we shift from one meaning of an ambiguous sentence to another, we alter images and action plans (it's useless to blow on spicy food). When we hear garden path sentences, we experience confusion, and then, on parsing them, there can be a change in imagery. When "sailed" is construed as a main verb in "The boat sailed down the river sank," we might visualize a boat that first glides down a river and then sinks; but when "sailed" is interpreted as part of the noun phrase, we might omit the gliding part, and just imagine a boat sinking.

The examples fail because they do not rule out the possibility of changes in non-verbal imagery. The examples would work only against the person who claimed that verbal imagery *exhausts* cognitive phenomenology. But that position is not plausible. Evidence from short-lived episodes of aphasia clearly demonstrates that conscious thought continues in the absence of speech. For example, Lecours and Joanette (1980) describe a patient who was able to locate a hotel, and order food at a restaurant during an episode of transient aphasia. There is also little reason to deny that some infraverbal animals have conscious thoughts, as when a chimpanzee figures out how to pull termites out of a hole using a slender stick. On any plausible restrictivist view, the phenomenology of thought is underwritten by both verbal and non-verbal imagery. Thus, expansionists face the difficult challenge of having to find cases in which the phenomenal character of a thought transcends both of these rich sources.

That challenge is very difficult to meet. I can think of no examples that are even plausible. For any pair of thoughts that differ phenomenologically, there always seem to be sensory features that distinguish the two. If you doubt this claim, try the following exercise. Visualize a baseball bat while saying the word "bat" in silent speech. Now try as hard as you can to interpret that word as representing the flying mammals. It's not easy, and, if you are like me, success comes only by visualizing one of the animals alongside the baseball bat and binding the word in attention to that image. If you suppress imagery of the animal (or associated verbal descriptions), your inner utterance of the word "bat" cannot take on any phenomenal character that would lead you to experience it as denoting anything other than the vividly visualized piece of sporting equipment. Consistent with this, Lee and Federmeier (2006) measured brain activity as they presented subjects with ambiguous words, like "duck," which can be interpreted as a noun or a verb. When primed to interpret "duck" as a noun, activity in posterior visual areas was detected, and, when interpreted as a verb, there were frontal activations consistent with motor imagery. Here, imagery may be recruited to disambiguate words, just as earlier we saw how words might disambiguate imagery (e.g. "The mat is under the cat").

If this picture is right, inner speech and non-verbal imagery are mutually supporting resources that can each pick up for the other's limitations. Words can help us experience very abstract thoughts or thoughts that arise too quickly to simulate in imagination. They can also disambiguate images, allowing us to think of Tweedledee, when a visual image appears equally just like Tweedledum. Non-verbal images help us to disambiguate words and simulate what our words represent. For most of us, both elements are constant components of conscious thought.

3.4 Attitude differentiation

I have been suggesting that cognitive phenomenology can be exhaustively accommodated by the phenomenology of inner speech and sensory simulations of what our thoughts represent. These resources provide a powerful mix, but there is still one thing that they leave out. Inner speech and simulations give phenomenal coloring to the *contents* of our thoughts, but they do not encompass the *manner* of our thoughts. They reveal what we are thinking, but not how. In philosophical parlance, thoughts are propositional attitudes, and we can have different attitudes toward the same content. We can believe that something is the case, desire it, doubt it, or fear it. These attitudes are often distinguishable in consciousness. When asked whether a particular candidate will win an upcoming election, we can immediately recognize whether we are confident, dubious, or terrified. In all cases, the inner speech and associated visualization may be the same, but the attitude differs in palpable ways.

In the late nineteenth century, members of the Würzburg school of psychology regarded this as evidence for an imageless component in conscious thought. Attitudes correspond to Marbe's *Bewusstseinslage*. Recently, Peacocke (2007) has also suggested that attitude differentiation raised trouble for the view that all consciousness is perceptual. But restrictivists have an obvious resource for explaining the phenomenology of conscious attitudes: they can appeal to accompanying emotions.

In some cases, it's quite obvious that emotions contribute to the phenomenology of the attitudes. Take fearing. The thespian who feels that she will forget her lines certainly experiences an emotion, and that emotion is (as suggested earlier) clearly felt in the body. Stage fright is manifest through butterflies in the stomach, shallow breath, perspiration, and a racing heart. Likewise for other emotional attitudes, as when we are elated, annoyed, or sad that something is the case.

Emotions may also explain the phenomenology of desire. This is most obvious in the case of basic drives such as hunger and lust. When I desire that dinner be served soon, I may feel a hallow hankering in my gut. But even more cognitive desires may be accompanied by felt emotions. If I want it to be the case that my candidate wins, I will feel nervous anticipation, and the thought of victory will instill delight, while the thought of defeat will usher in waves of despair. On experiencing any of these fluctuating feelings, I may report that I desire a victory. There is no one feeling of desire, but rather a family of anticipatory emotions.

Belief might seem a hard case. It's not obvious that it feels like anything to believe that grass is green above and beyond the visualization of that proposition. But I actually think many beliefs come along with attitudinal feels. We can feel confident or certain. It's like something to have a hunch or to suspect that something is the case. There are also emotions of doubt: uncertainty, incredulity, hostile dismissal. My suspicion, though highly speculative, is that all of these states are felt as emotions, which, like other emotions, are constituted by bodily expressions. We knit our brow in doubt and pound our fists in confidence. Further evidence for this proposal comes from the simple fact that doxastic attitudes can be expression through intonation; we can vocalize the difference between an assertion, an interrogative, and even a tentative speculation. These speech sounds exemplify differences in bodily states.

Doxastic feelings belong to a larger category of epistemic emotions (Prinz 2007). They belong to a class that includes curiosity, interest, awe, wonder, familiarity, novelty, puzzlement, confusion, and surprise—all of which can give rise to corresponding propositional attitudes. With the exception of surprise, these have been woefully neglected in recent research, though they were once widely discussed. For example, Descartes (1649/1988) lists wonder as a basic emotion. In contemporary psychology, epistemic emotions are largely ignored, but there is a growing literature on one interesting example: the feeling of knowing (Hart 1965). Memory researchers have noted that sometimes people clearly recall a prior stimulus, and sometimes they can't recall experiencing it, but they have a feeling of knowing that it was there. This is sometimes called metamemory—a memory that something is in memory. The feeling of knowing is a sense of assurance that arises without vivid recall. I conjecture that the feeling of knowing is an emotion. If so, it may be implemented, like other emotions, in brain circuits that are involved in body perception (cf. Woody and Szechtman 2002). There has been no empirical exploration of the link between feeling of knowing and bodily perception, but fMRI studies reveal that it is associated with action in ventro-medial prefrontal cortex, which is a main player in embodied emotional responses (Schnyer et al. 2005).

In making these claims, I am not trying to suggest that attitudes are nothing but emotions. Each attitude may correspond to a complex functional role, making distinctive contributions to decision making. Their subtle workings may unfold in time outside the spotlight of consciousness. My claim is only that we may be able to distinguish some of these attitudes phenomenologically in virtue of accompanying emotions. Those who claim that attitude differentiation is incompatible with restrictivism must show that attitudes can be distinguished without felt emotions, which, I have suggested, can be characterized as perceptions of bodily states. This is largely uncharted territory, but the emotional account of felt attitudes has enough initial plausibility to defuse the objection from *Bewusstseinslage*.

4 Restrictivists' revenge

The vast majority of consciousness research has focused on perceptual experience, and, even more narrowly, on vision. In recent years, that has started to change. There has been a welcome tide of interest in the phenomenology of thought. That interest has spawned an outbreak of expansionism. Restrictivists might try to stave off expansion by denying that cognition has phenomenology, but that's an unpromising course, because there are both theoretical reasons for thinking we have conscious thoughts (deriving from empiricism) and strong introspective evidence. I have been arguing that restrictivists should resist expansion in another way. We should try to explain the phenomenology of thought by appealing to inner speech, simulations of what thoughts represent, and emotions. These resources can all be characterized as forms of sensory imagery, and they are rich enough, I've argued, to accommodate introspective evidence for conscious thoughts.

In making this case, I have been on the defensive, blocking expansionist arguments for distinctively cognitive phenomenology. By way of conclusion, I want to go on the offensive by offering a diagnosis of expansionism, and a reason for being skeptical about the expansionist program.

First, the diagnosis. Those who still think that phenomenology outstrips the sensory may be subject to a family of introspective illusions. We often think that introspective access to our conscious states is perfectly accurate, but this is not the case. Having an experience and reporting what it's like are two different things, and the latter can be prone to errors. We saw some examples of this when I was discussing the allegation that noncognitive consciousness outstrips the intermediate level. People who think that perceptual consciousness resides at a high level may be mistaking experiences that represent such properties (an elliptical experience represents roundness) for experiences that have corresponding phenomenal quality (a round experience). People who think we are conscious of certain constancies (such as vertical lines) are mistaking unconscious identification of permissible transformations for a constancy in experience. People who think we *see* features that are present in absence are mistaking one kind of experience (touch) for another (vision). People who think we are aware of our motor commands are mistaking the effects of those commands (somatosensory states) for their causes. People who deny that emotions are perceptions are misinterpreting the mental states that constitute our emotions (bodily experiences) as mere effects.

I think the same kinds of errors may lie behind the impression that there is distinctively cognitive phenomenology. When Siegel says we can have experiences corresponding to natural kind properties, she may be mistaking experiences that represent such properties for experiences that have corresponding phenomenal quality. When Woodworth says that consciousness of an object can remain constant as our image of the object changes, he may be mistaking unconscious identification of permissible transformations for a constancy in experience. When Siewert says that the experience of a word changes when we shift interpretations, he may be mistaking one kind of experience (associated imagery) for another (alleged cognitive phenomenology). When Peacocke says that we experience propositional attitude types, he may be mistaking the effects of those attitudes (emotions) for their causes (functional roles). When Pitt says we can't distinguish thoughts by inner speech, he may be misinterpreting mental states that constitute thoughts (silent sentences) as mere effects.

Of course, these authors provide arguments for expansionism. I am not trying to say that they are simply confused. I am merely suggesting that there are introspective illusions that may bolster the intuitive plausibility of expansionism. For some people, expansionism seems *obvious* and that fact needs to be explained. The explanation on offer here is that introspection is subject to certain kinds of illusions, which lead us to posit features in experience that are not actually there. If we guard against these illusions, the impression that phenomenology outstrips the sensory may subside.

Let me end with a challenge to the expansionist. If expansionism is true, there are phenomenal qualities over and above sensory qualities. When we add up our sensory simulations, inner speech, and emotions, there is a phenomenal remainder. If this were the case, I think it should be possible to experience that remainder *without* the concomitant imagery. Siewert (2009) tries to resist this commitment, saying that the proponent of distinctively cognitive phenomenology need not deny that all conscious thoughts have imagistic components. But this strikes me as cheating. After all, the components of *sensory* consciousness can all be experienced in isolation. We can see any given color on different objects or covering a formless *ganzfeld*. Shapes, sounds, and smells can all be recombined, and, when conditions are right, experienced without other conscious qualities, as under conditions of intense focal attention. If there were distinctively cognitive phenomenal qualities, then there is no reason to suppose that they are different in this respect. We should be able to experience them in isolation. The stipulation otherwise is *ad hoc*. So, in the end, the expansionists' case may depend on their ability to come up with a clear example of a cognitive experience that occurs without any sensory experiences, or at least without sensory experiences that are related to the cognitive act. The examples that dominate in this literature are fairly easy to deflect, because the restrictivist can always pin the phenomenology on clear and present sensory states. I have encountered no compelling example of an imageless, dispassionate, languageless, conscious thought. If there were cognitive phenomenology, examples should be abundant, just as we can readily bring before the mind an endless range of contours and melodies. The elusiveness of purely cognitive qualities leads me to think they are an illusion, and we should content ourselves with the minimal posits of restrictivism.

References

Aha, D. W. and Goldstone, R. L. (1992). "Concept learning and flexible weighting," *Proceedings of the Fourteenth Annual Conference of the Cognitive Science Society*. Hillsdale, New Jersey: Lawrence Erlbaum Associates: 534–9.

Angell, J. A. (1911). "Imageless thought," *Psychological Review*, 18: 295–322.

Blakemore, S.-J. and Frith, C. (2003). "Self-awareness and action," *Current Opinion in Neurobiology*, 13: 219–24.

Carmichael, L. P., Hogan, H. P., and Walter, A. A. (1932). "An experimental study of the effect of language on the reproduction of visually perceived form," *Journal of Experimental Psychology*, 15: 73–86.

Carruthers, P. (2002a). "The cognitive functions of language," *Behavioral and Brain Sciences*, 25: 657–719.

——(2002b). "Conscious thinking: Language or elimination?" *Mind and Language*, 13: 457–76.

Chambers, D. and Reisberg, D. (1985). "Can mental images be ambiguous?" *Journal of Experimental Psychology: Human Perception and Performance*, 11: 317–28.

Chao, L. L., Haxby, J. V., and Martin, A. (1999). "Attribute-based neural substrates in posterior temporal cortex for perceiving and knowing about objects," *Nature Neuroscience*, 2: 913–19.

——and Martin, A. (2000). "Representation of manipulable man-made objects in the dorsal stream," *Neuroimage*, 12: 478–84.

Clark, A. (1993). *Sensory Qualities*. Oxford: Oxford University Press.

Damasio, A. R. (1994). *Descartes' Error: Emotion, Reason and the Human Brain*. New York, NY: Gossett/Putnam.

Dennett, D. C. (1969). *Content and Consciousness*. London: Routledge and Kegan.

——(1991). *Consciousness Explained*. Boston: Little, Brown and Company.

Descartes, R. (1649/1988). "The passions of the soul," in J. Cottingham, R. Stoothoff, and D. Murdoch (trans. and eds), *Selected Philosophical Writings of René Descartes*. Cambridge: Cambridge University Press.

Dretske, F. (1995). *Naturalizing the Mind*. Cambridge, MA: MIT Press.

Gibson, J. J. (1979). *The Ecological Approach to Visual Perception*. Boston: Houghton Mifflin.

Goldstone, R. L. (2004). "Believing is seeing," *American Psychological Society Observer*, 17: 23–6.

Halberstadt, J., Winkielman, P., Niedenthal, P., and Dalle, N. (2009). "Emotional conception: How embodied emotion concepts guide perception and facial action," *Psychological Science*.

Hansen, T., Olkkonen, M., Walter, S. and Gegenfurtner, S. (2006). "Memory modulates color appearance," *Nature Neuroscience*, 9: 1367–8.

Hart, J. T. (1965). "Memory and the feeling-of-knowing experience," *Journal of Educational Psychology*, 56: 208–16.

Humphrey, N. (1992). *A History of the Mind*. New York, NY: Simon and Schuster.

Hurlburt, R. (1990). *Sampling Normal and Schizophrenic Inner Experience*. New York, NY: Plenum Press.

Jackendoff, R. (1987). *Consciousness and the Computational Mind*. Cambridge, MA: MIT Press.

James, W. (1884). "What is an emotion?" *Mind*, 9: 188–205.

Lecours, A. R. and Joanette, Y. (1980). "Linguistic and other psychological aspects of paroxysmal aphasia," *Brain and Language*, 10: 1–23.

Lee, C. L. and Federmeier, K. D. (2006). "To mind the mind: An event-related potential study of word class and semantic ambiguity," *Brain Research*, 1081: 191–202.

Livermore, A. and Laing, D. G. (1998). "The influence of chemical complexity on the perception of multicomponent odor mixtures," *Perception and Psychophysics*, 60: 650–61.

Lormand, E. (1996). "Nonphenomenal consciousness," *Noûs*, 30: 242–61.

McKyton, A. and Zohary, E. (2007). "Beyond retinotopic mapping: The spatial representation of objects in the human lateral occipital complex," *Cerebral Cortex*, 17: 1164–72.

Marr, D. (1982). *Vision: A Computational Investigation into the Human Representation and Processing of Visual Information*. New York: W. H. Freeman.

Martin, A. (2007). "The representation of object concepts in the brain," *Annual Review of Psychology*, 58: 25–45.

Morin, A. (2005). "Possible links between self-awareness and inner speech: Theoretical background, underlying mechanisms, and empirical evidence," *Journal of Consciousness Studies*, 12: 115–34.

Noë, A. (2004). *Action in Perception*. Cambridge, MA: MIT Press.

Orgs, G., Lange, K., Dombrowski, J.-H., and Heil, M. (2006). "Conceptual priming for environmental sounds and words: An ERP study," *Brain and Cognition*, 65: 162–6.

Patterson, K., Nestor, P. J., and Rogers, T. T. (2007). "Where do you know what you know? The representation of semantic knowledge in the human brain," *Nature Reviews Neuroscience*, 8: 976–87.

Peacocke, C. (1983). *Sense and Content*. Oxford: Oxford University Press.

——(2007). "Mental action and self-awareness," in Brian P. McLaughlin and Jonathan D. Cohen (eds), *Contemporary Debates in Philosophy of Mind*. Oxford: Blackwell, pp. 358–76.

Pitt, D. (2004). "The phenomenology of cognition, or, what is it like to think that P?", *Philosophy and Phenomenological Research*, 69: 1–36.

Prinz, J. J. (2000). "A neurofunctional theory of visual consciousness," *Consciousness and Cognition*, 9: 243–59.

——(2002). *Furnishing the Mind: Concepts and their Perceptual Basis*. Cambridge, MA: MIT Press.

——(2004). *Gut Reactions: A Perceptual Theory of Emotion*. New York: Oxford University Press.

——(2005). "A neurofunctional theory of consciousness," in A. Brook and K. Akins (eds), *Cognition and the Brain: Philosophy and neuroscience Movement*. Cambridge: Cambridge University Press, pp. 381–96.

——(2006a). "Putting the brakes on enactive perception," *Psyche*, 12: 1–19.

——(2006b). "Beyond appearances: The content of sensation and perception," in T. S. Gendler and J. Hawthorne (eds), *Perceptual Experiences*. Oxford: Oxford University Press, pp. 434–60.

——(2007). "All consciousness is perceptual," in B. McLaughlin and J. Cohen (eds), *Contemporary Debates in Philosophy of Mind*. Oxford: Blackwell, pp. 335–57.

——(2008). "Is consciousness embodied?", in P. Robbins and M. Aydede (eds), *Cambridge Handbook of Situated Cognition*. Cambridge, UK: Cambridge University Press.

Raffman, D. (1995). "On the persistence of phenomenology," in T. Metzinger (ed.), *Conscious Experience*. Paderborn: Imprint Academic, pp. 293–308.

Reeves, A. J., Amano, K., and Foster, D. H. (2008). "Color constancy: Phenomenal or projective?", *Perception and Psychophysics*, 70: 219–28.

Sauvan, X. M. and Peterhans, E. (1999). "Orientation constancy in neurons of monkey visual cortex," *Visual Cognition*, 6: 43–54.

Schnyer, D., Nicholls, L., and Verfaellie, M. (2005). "The role of VMPC in metamemorial judgments of content retrievability," *Journal of Cognitive Neuroscience*, 17: 832–46.

Searle, J. (1992). *The Rediscovery of Mind*. Cambridge, MA: MIT Press.

Shergill, S. S., Bullmore, E. T., Brammer, M. J., Williams, S. C. R., Murray, R. M., and McGuire, P. K. M. (2001). "A functional study of auditory verbal imagery," *Psychological Medicine*, 31: 241–53.

Siegel, S. (2006). "Which properties are represented in perception?" in T. S. Gendler and J. Hawthorne (eds), *Perceptual Experiences*. Oxford: Oxford University Press.

Siewert, C. P. (1998). *The Significance of Consciousness*. Princeton, NJ: Princeton University Press.

——(2009). "Consciousness and conceptual thought," in T. Bayne (ed.), *The Oxford Companion to Consciousness*. Oxford: Oxford University Press, pp.167–8.

Slotnick, S. D., Thompson, W. L., and Kosslyn, S. M. (2005). "Visual mental imagery induces retinotopically organized activation of early visual areas," *Cerebral Cortex*, 15: 1570–83.

Tucker, M. and Ellis, R. (1998). "On the relations between seen objects and components of potential actions," *Journal of Experimental Psychology: Human Perception and Performance*, 24: 830–46.

Tye, M. (1995). *Ten Problems of Consciousness*. Cambridge, MA: MIT Press.

Woodworth, R. S. (1906). "Imageless thought," *Journal of Philosophy*, 3: 701–8.

——(1915). "A revision of imageless thought," *Psychological Review*, 22: 1–27.

Woody, E. and Szechtman, H. (2002). "The sensation of making sense: Motivational properties of the 'fringe'," *Psyche*, 8: 20.

Xu, F. and Carey, S. (1996). "Infants' metaphysics: The case of numerical identity," *Cognitive Psychology*, 30: 111–53.

Yardly, L. (1990). "Contribution of somatosensory information to perception of the visual vertical with body tilt and rotating visual field," *Perception and Psychophysics*, 48: 131–4.

A Frugal View of Cognitive Phenomenology

William S. Robinson

I take it as a premise that others have the same phenomenology that I do—not, of course, in detail, for we may differ in powers of discrimination, training, attention, and in our emotional and intellectual reactions upon learning of the same set of circumstances. But I take it that all physiologically normal people have the same categories of phenomenology, and a similar range of variety in each category. And if something is a normal aspect of some recurring circumstance for some of us, it is at least usual for everyone.

It seems to me to be a consequence of this assumption that differences in views about cognitive phenomenology must be due to differences in accuracy of description or differences in reasoning. In this paper I will address both sources of difference, but I want to begin with the first.

Proponents of relatively liberal views of cognitive phenomenology have their impressive cases of what I will call "sudden realizations," e.g. switches from not understanding to understanding, or from one interpretation to another. I know what cases they are talking about, and my phenomenology is at least sufficiently like theirs that I think I understand why they say what they do about these cases. I feel the plausibility of what they say. But I think there are also some impressive cases that suggest a more frugal view, and it is these with which I shall start.

I say "more frugal." As will develop, I recognize phenomenology that is additional to what is included in standard empiricist accounts. I shall explain these additions, and distinguish them from other additions that I do not believe to be needed for an adequate account of my own experience. So, I expect there to be doubters of what I have to say from both sides—the more liberal and the downright stingy.

But enough of preliminaries. Let us get down to cases.

1 Cases in support of a frugal view

1.1 Certain occasions of daydreaming

I confess to having nodded off during a lecture or two. These occasions have not been altogether simple. Between full alertness and full loss of consciousness, there have been intermediate periods. Naturally, I can only recollect what these intermediate periods were like, but the following is what my memory tells me about them.

As usual, as I begin to listen to a speaker on one of these occasions, I carry on an internal monologue of commentary about what I expect next, unanswered questions that I want to ask after the talk, objections, comparisons to what others have said, and promising relations to things I am working on that I want to remember to follow up on later. But later on, there is a point at which I will "come to" and tell myself I am falling asleep, and that what I have been saying to myself for the last few seconds is nonsense. The impressive part of these experiences is that the latter, nonsensical part of my internal monologue is just like the rest—until, that is, I "come to." There I was, just silently talking to myself in the usual way and—in the moments just before "coming to"—not understanding a thing. Not understanding anything because there was nothing to understand, just utter confusion. On these occasions, I can recall a few words and an image or two, but the images are unrelated to the words and the words are just gibberish.

The conclusion that seems compelling to me in the light of recollection of the occasions just described is that there is no experience of understanding. There is recognition that what I was just now saying to myself is nonsense, but before the recognition there was no difference between telling myself that nonsense and telling myself the sensible things I tell myself when I am normally alert—no difference, that is, other than in the words I was inwardly saying and the images I was having. There is an absence of any sense of discord in both cases, but no presence of anything that distinguishes the sensible parts from the nonsensical part.

One can, of course, say that a sense of understanding can be illusory, so it is present in both the alert and confused phases, and the difference is the non-phenomenological difference between veridicality and non-veridicality (of the experience of understanding). I agree that this view is open as a dialectical possibility. But as far as what seems to be present (for a few moments before the recognition of the confusion) in my phenomenology, there is just the telling of things to myself in my inner speech without any further inner speech that classifies some of it as confused or nonsensical, and without any phenomenological sign of passing from understanding to its absence.

It may aid clarity to put the point a little differently. When I look back upon cases of the kind I am describing, I remember, of course, the moments when I recognized that I had lapsed into confusion. *These* moments have something phenomenologically distinctive. But I have no natural tendency to think that there was anything distinctively different that distinguishes the few moments *before* the recognition from the longer, more alert stretch that preceded those few moments—except, of course, that just after I recognized my confusion, I judged the last few words, but not the earlier ones, to be nonsensical. The last few words were, so to speak, said in the same tone of voice as the earlier ones.

It may be suggested here that I am only failing to find what is not being claimed anyway—that is, it may be suggested that a sense of understanding is not the kind of thing that could be regarded as any sort of marker or distinguishing feature that is a sign of understanding. Perhaps such descriptions of a difference would be thought to be limited to differences that are "sensory" in character; and it may be denied that the difference between understanding and not understanding is "sensory."

But I am not placing a filter on what might count as the difference that I am saying I am unable to find, that would let through only what is sensory or something like what is sensory. At least, I am not aware of employing any such filter. The impressive part of what I am attempting to point to here is that my post-recognition judgment is that I had run off the rails of sense completely unawares (until, that is, I "came to"), and there isn't *anything*—sensory or not—that was different (except that my later words are judged, *after* "coming to," to be nonsensical).

1.2 Cases of complete involvement

There I am working out a Sudoku. This cell has to be a 2 and let's see, then the only place the 7 in this row can go is in *that* cell, . . . and so on. Since I spend a lot of time thinking about things like cognitive phenomenology, I may have an intrusive thought, along the lines of asking myself what was going on, mentally speaking, just now. The answer seems to be what I just reported, and nothing else.

Again, it is possible that I don't notice the sense of understanding what I was saying to myself because I am looking for the wrong sort of thing—e.g. some sensation that is always there when I am absorbed in a task and completely undistracted. But the way it seems to me is that there is nothing going on except my inner speech and some spatial and kinesthetic imagery (relating to where I should look next for a possible solvable cell). If I believe what seems to be in my consciousness, there just isn't anything else.

1.3 Overt speaking

I trust it will be conceded that I usually understand what I am saying. But when I am speaking about ordinary things, or about philosophical matters other than philosophy of mind, there just doesn't seem to be anything accompanying my words that has to do with understanding. There is sometimes some imagery, or internal commentary on my style or whether my interlocutors look like they are following what I'm saying, and so on. But that is it.

Again, one can say I am just missing something, or looking for the wrong thing. The plausibility of that, however, must depend on further argument. It doesn't *seem* that I am leaving anything out of account, and so, my natural tendency is to think there isn't anything phenomenological that I am leaving out.

2 Difficulties for a frugal view

The appearance that nothing phenomenological has been left out in the description of these cases can be overruled if we encounter difficulties in articulating what we should say in other cases. Let us examine some of these.

2.1 Stage fright

I confess to having been nervous the first time I read a paper at a national conference. One symptom was that somewhere in the middle of it, I asked myself how I was doing. There followed a strange few moments in which, while continuing to read my paper, I wondered whether my asking myself how I was doing was affecting my delivery, judged that it was not, opined that it soon would if I didn't stop asking these questions, and admonished myself to get back to concentrating on the subject matter of my paper. During this (fortunately brief) period, I was also aware that while the words were continuing to come just as planned, I had no idea what I was saying. (A similar experience of what might be called "empty sounds" can sometimes be produced by excessive repetition of a word.)

One natural way of describing this case would be to say that the normal sense of understanding what we are saying was briefly lost. In its place, there was something else, a sort of eerie anxiety and a hyper-attentiveness to the auditory shape of one's words, and then after a brief time, a return of the normal sense of understanding.

This description implies that there is a normal sense of understanding. But need we accept it? We need not. What is clear is that there is a contrast. But that contrast can just as well, it seems to me, be described as a contrast between the presence of the eerie anxiety and hyper-attentiveness to one's words, and the absence of these things. Their absence is not replaced by a presence of anything except the words that are continuing to come, imagery of the ordinary kind one has while speaking, and perhaps some non-anxiety producing inner speech relating to what one is going to do next, or noticing nods of apparent agreement or frowns of potential objectors.

In trying to decide between these descriptions, it may be tempting to reason in the following way. (1) When we are not in the strange state I just described, we understand what we are saying. (2) Our sayings occur at particular times, and are different at different times. Therefore, (3) our understandings of what we are saying are occurrences that take place at particular times and differ among themselves at different times.

I do not find this reasoning convincing. We understand what we are saying if we can explain it, give coherent paraphrases, recognize the relevance of objections, and so on. We can usually do these things, so we usually understand what we are saying. Adding occurrent understandings that track what we are saying contributes nothing explanatory, and so they are not needed. The reason occurrent understandings do not contribute anything explanatory here is that the explanations, paraphrases, and responses to objections depend on abilities that are exhibited in performances that spread over significant periods of time. Occurrents are just not the right kind of thing for explaining abilities for temporally extended performances.

A related formulation with the same difficulty is this. During my waking hours, there is always something phenomenologically present. When I am thinking, speaking, or reading, I am usually doing so with understanding. So, usually, when I am thinking, speaking, or reading, there is a phenomenology of understanding.

But the premises do not justify this conclusion. There being something phenomenological *while* understanding does not imply that it is correct to describe that phenomenology as a phenomenology *of* understanding. People who understand what they are saying, or what is being said to them, are people who do not experience a problem with what is being said. They may be uneasy because of the content, they may have strong emotional reactions to it, but they are not experiencing frustration or anxiety about taking in what is being said. Images may accompany the words; if so, they seem to flow without effort or problem, even in cases where the content of the images is disturbing. There is normally a lot going on, phenomenologically, in a person who understands, and this accompanying phenomenology is normally intimately connected with what is understood. But, evidently, this fact does not imply that there is a particular part of the phenomenology that deserves the label "phenomenology of understanding," nor does it imply that there is a part of the phenomenology that deserves the label "phenomenology of understanding *p*," where *p* is some proposition. Our ability to say something rather general about the complex relations in the phenomenology of *a person who understands* cannot legitimately be taken to imply that there is a phenomenology of understanding *per se*, or a phenomenology of understanding particular propositions.

There is another possible source for the view that a phenomenologically present sense of understanding accompanies my speech (whether overt or inner). Let us begin with overt speech, and the obvious fact that I always know it is I who am speaking (when I am doing so). Of course, I hear my own voice—I know, for example, that it sounds different from what I hear when I listen to a recording of my voice. But I do not *just* hear myself and recognize who is speaking from the voice quality, as I do recognize others who are out of sight by their voices. Instead, whenever I recollect what I have said, I recollect myself as *speaking* it. And it is the same with my silent inner speech: when I recall my inner speech, I recall *saying* things to myself, not merely inwardly hearing my inner words.

I am, fortunately, not subject to "hearing voices" or having the sense that someone else is saying something to me in my inner speech. But I believe I can, with some effort, imagine what it would be like to have that happen. I am aided in this by the (very) few occasions on which I have given overt answers to questions students have asked me, while inwardly telling myself that I didn't know that I knew this. I experienced something like surprise at what I was saying. I can imagine this happening in my inner speech (although I cannot recall its ever having done so), and I am inclined to think that if it did, I *might* have the sense that my inner speech was being delivered by someone other than myself.

Since I can imagine this peculiar state of mind, I am inclined to think that in recollections of inner speech, there is a phenomenological component of inwardly affirming what one is saying to oneself. And I also think that it would be easy to think of this phenomenologically present sense of inner affirmation as a sense of understanding what one is saying. But I think that would be a mistaken description. The first case I recalled in section I ended in a stretch of absence of understanding, but the sense of affirmation of what I was saying to myself was equally present through the sensible and nonsensical stretches.

Allowing a phenomenological sense of affirming may bring in its train a suggestion that there is also a phenomenology of doubting or wondering. I do not think, however, that this is right. I may inwardly say that I doubt that *p* or that I wonder whether *q*. These are as much affirmations as are inward sayings that I believe that *p* or want that *q* (to become the case). The doubting and wondering are, so to speak, in what is said, not in some accompaniment to that. Of course, there are apt to be accompaniments; but these do not seem to me to be phenomenologies of doubting or wondering *per se*. Instead, they are accompanying emotions. For example, coming to doubt something one has believed for some time may be accompanied by distress or sadness, especially if one has used it as a basis on which to act or support other beliefs. Wondering whether something might be true could be accompanied also by sadness, or by joy, depending on whether one would be distressed or pleased if what one wonders might be true turned out to be true.

In other cases, the doubt or wonderment might concern something of only a passing moment. In these cases, emotions are not likely to be present; and correspondingly, such cases do not suggest a phenomenology of doubting or wondering, over and above occurrences of words or phrases like "perhaps" or "it may be that . . ." in one's inner speech. Similarly, conviction or yearning have a phenomenology, in that strong emotions accompany them. If you merely believe there is beer in the fridge, you may just go and get one.

2.2 Sudden realizations

The literature of cognitive phenomenology is replete with sudden realizations.[1] There are several kinds. One may suddenly realize one has forgotten something, or suddenly realize that there is another interpretation that makes what one has just said an unintentional pun. One may suddenly realize what someone else is talking about, after having been puzzled for a few moments. Many jokes depend on suddenly realizing what a scene implies. Garden path sentences lead to a sudden overturning

---

[1] See, e.g., Horgan and Tienson (2002), Pitt (2004), Siewert (1998), and Strawson (1994). There is more to be said about particular cases of sudden realizations than I shall say here. I have provided further detail about some of these cases, and related phenomena, in Robinson (2005).

of what one had thought was going to be their point. ('Fatty weighed two hundred pounds of grapes', Goldman 1993.) Center-embedded sentences of depth three often sound as if they could not be grammatical, until one suddenly "gets" what they mean.

These are common experiences for me and, I assume, for nearly everyone. What can the issue be about them? It seems to concern the appropriateness of the following alternatives.

Liberal: There is a conscious, occurrent, phenomenologically present understanding that does not consist in anything imagistic and is not a change in emotional state. (Where "imagistic" includes words in inner speech, and sensory imagery of any kind, but most usually visual or kinesthetic.)

Frugal: Everything that is occurrent and phenomenologically present in such cases is either imagistic or a change in emotional state.

The frugal view agrees with the liberal view that there is a clear difference in our phenomenological state before and after a sudden realization. It locates the difference in differences of imagistic and emotional materials. It disagrees with the liberal view in holding that no further kind of phenomenological element occurs at the moment of sudden realization.

A key task for the frugal view is to give an account of how the liberal view can seem so plausible if there is no such further phenomenological component in a sudden realization. I will give this account, then add some explanations and comments.

What happens *at the moment* of sudden realization is just what is in the frugal account. Very soon after that moment, one may (a) act in a way that is appropriate to what has just been realized, and/or (b) state, in inner or overt speech, what has just been realized. When the action or the statement is made, it seems appropriate to what has just happened. It may then seem very natural to think of this sense of appropriateness as arising from a match between what is done or said, and something that just occurred in consciousness. But, natural though it may seem, there being such a match does not follow from the occurrence of a sense of appropriateness of the later events. That sense of appropriateness is a phenomenological occurrence, and its nature does not entail any account of its causes.

Does the frugal view say that the sense of appropriateness is illusory? Yes and no. Yes, because, according to the frugal account, there was not anything *in consciousness* to which the action or statement is appropriate. But also, no, because there was a change in one's brain that has put one into a condition that does lead to the action or statement.

Let me put this a little more fully. The frugal account holds that a sudden realization, whatever one goes on to say about it, is an effect of changes in one's brain. (With this much, I think everyone will agree.) This change is *at least* a change in the categorical basis of one's dispositions. E.g. if you don't get a joke, you may be disposed to say things like "I don't see what's so funny about that," or simply "Hunh?" After you get it, it would generally be best not to explain it; but if there were reason to do so, you might repeat a key word (one, perhaps, on whose ambiguity the joke depends), or you might observe that this is a joke that could not be told in a certain context, and so on. And your comments after you have gotten the joke might be quite appropriate to its meaning (and so, your comments would show, to anyone who might have doubted, that you did understand the point of the joke).

If you were to say, a short while later (at T2), that what you are saying at T2 is appropriate to, or "fits," or "expresses" what you understood at the moment you got the joke (i.e. at T1), you would be right if you meant that what you are saying at T2 is an effect of a change in your brain that occurred immediately before you started laughing. But it doesn't follow that there was anything *in your consciousness* at T1 that "matches" what you are now saying, or to which what you are now saying is related by the relation of "fitting" or "adequately expressing," and that is additional to occurrences at T1 that were imagistic items such as a (very) few words in inner speech and/or visual or kinesthetic imagery, and emotional changes such as the oncoming of the particular joy associated with getting a joke.

This account incurs a debt that I will shortly identify and try to discharge. But first, I want to note one important theoretical—i.e. non-phenomenological—reason for preferring the frugal account. Namely, the frugal account avoids a debt that must be paid, sooner or later, by the liberal account. On the liberal account, there is something in consciousness that occurs very rapidly, but to which an action or a statement is appropriate. This raises the question: How can an action or a statement, which occupy a time on the order of several seconds, be appropriate to, or fit, or express, a phenomenological occurrence that allegedly took place in one second or less? E.g. how could "Oh, damn, I've left my office key at home" fit or express a very brief occurrence? I am skeptical that these questions can have an answer. It would seem that the brief event would have to have a phenomenologically apparent internal structure that is comparable to what is said afterward, but this internal structure is not a structure of words. (These take time to say, even in inner speech; and liberal accounts do *not* say that brief events in sudden realizations consist of inner speech, only conducted very fast; nor do they say that these events have spatial complexity.) I am at a loss to know what the elements of such a structure could be, or what might be the phenomenologically available "material" or "medium" in which they could occur. Let us call this "the structure problem" for the liberal account.

The debt that the frugal account incurs is that it invokes a sense of appropriateness between what is said soon after a sudden realization and something that happens at the moment of realization. There are two questions here: Isn't this sense of appropriateness a significant addition to the frugal account? and How does it arise?

The answer to the first question is yes. But this addition is not an objection to the frugal account, because the sense of appropriateness comes *after* the sudden realization. It must do so, since it is a sense of appropriateness of the statement of what is said to have been realized, or of an action that makes sense only in light of what was realized, and these come a little later than the sudden realization itself. So, the frugal account of what happens in a sudden realization is not undercut, even though the full account must recognize a (slightly) later addition. This addition is a genuine phenomenological occurrence. I do not know how to describe it except to say what I have already said; but I think it must be recognized also by those who offer a liberal account. For, otherwise, it would not appear natural to regard the later statements or actions as expressions of what came at the moment of sudden realization.

The answer to the second question is that I do not know. But I am not surprised that the sense of appropriateness should occur. That is because there are what seem to me to be *similar* phenomena elsewhere. One of these is found in work led by Daniel Wegner, another is a well-established result of processing fluency. I will briefly summarize the sense of these results.

Wegner and colleagues have manipulated the degree of control that subjects have over certain events.[2] They have also contrived to manipulate the time at which the thought of a certain action occurs. The details of the method of these manipulations are very complex and I will not attempt to summarize them here. The result claimed by Wegner and his colleagues is that a sense of control depends on the timing of the thought of the action. If the thought comes immediately after, or 30 seconds before the action, subjects will not feel in control; if it comes 5 seconds before the action, subjects report some sense of control, even when they had none. Similar results, in a study of very different design, have been obtained by Linser and Goschke (2007).

A different sense—namely, a tendency to "recognize" words (i.e. classify them as having been on a previously studied list, when they were not on it)—has been established by many researchers as an effect of processing fluency.[3] In this case, a simple manipulation is possible, namely, priming a test word, either with itself or an unrelated word, where the prime is brief (e.g. 34 ms) and masked before and after. The brevity and the masking prevent any conscious recognition of the primes, but self-primed non-studied words are more likely to be taken to be "recognized" by subjects than non-studied words that are primed by unrelated words.

The work on feelings of willing is both relatively new and controversial. The work on manipulation of recognition is better established and robust, but it too is not directed toward the feeling of appropriateness of reports of sudden realizations. There are many cases in which apparently small differences of psychologists' instructions have reliable effects on experimental outcomes. So, we should be cautious in relating the work just described to our present case. It is not possible to claim that there is experimental work that is directly supportive of the frugal account that I have been proposing.

At the same time, there is enough plausibility in the described results to support a limited claim that we cannot rule out the frugal account's proposal: namely, that the ease with which we state what we have realized, or act upon what we have realized,

---

[2] See Wegner (2002) and Wegner and Wheatley (1999).
[3] For a recent study, and references to previous studies, see Westerman (2008).

may give rise to a feeling that what we are saying or doing is appropriate to something that has gone before. It is evident in such cases that the appropriateness is not due to our recalling something from memory, that happened hours, days, or longer ago. So, it is natural to attribute the appropriateness of what we are saying or doing to something else—something that has just happened. And, in a sense, we would be correct—that is, we would be correct if we were to think that what we are saying or doing just after the sudden realization is an effect of a very recent change in our neural organization. The only mistake, according to the frugal view, would be to make the quite natural error of attributing the appropriateness of our saying or doing to something that had just taken place in our consciousness. There was conscious auditory imagery of a few relevant words, perhaps, and perhaps also some relevant visual or kinesthetic imagery; and there were emotional changes. So, there was a lot going on in consciousness that can be cited as relevant co-effects of our neural change, and can be rightly interpreted as reliable (but not infallible) signs that what we are now saying and doing are effects of the same neural change that caused the imagery and emotions. But there is no need to add a nonimagistic and nonemotional conscious sudden understanding. And if we do not add it, we do not have to solve the structure problem.

The sense of appropriateness of what we go on to say after a sudden realization is not a sensation. By that, I mean that it is not the sort of thing that can occur just by itself, independently of being the appropriateness *of* something (namely, of what we go on to say we realized, or of some action we do in light of what we realized). Moreover, it is the meaning of the sentence or the point of the action that we think is appropriate to what we have realized, not the accent or loudness with which we say it, or particular movements involved in executing an action. So, there is an aspectual element to our sense of appropriateness. This aboutness and aspectuality make our sense of appropriateness unlike the sensations of traditional forms of empiricism, and thus may be resisted by proponents of what I would call stingy accounts.[4] But this addition seems nonetheless distinct from the sense of rapid understanding that is often proposed in accounts I would classify as liberal.

There are other non-sensory experiences, and one of them may seem to support an objection to what I have been saying about our sense of appropriateness (i.e. our sense of appropriateness of what we go on to say or do to something that has very recently occurred. Since there is no other kind of sense of appropriateness that will be mentioned in this paper, I will henceforth omit repetition of this explanation). This is the feeling of familiarity that we sometimes have when we see a person we know in an unexpected context. This feeling is sometimes expressed in words such as "I know I've seen that person before, I just can't think where." This feeling is likewise not a freestanding sensation but an experience that is directed on a particular face;

---

[4] I have explained these non-sensory experiences somewhat more fully in Robinson (2006). See also Mangan (2001).

and it is aspectual, i.e. directed upon this face, not on its eyes or nose, or merely on its being a face.

When we have a feeling of familiarity that does not immediately dissipate, we are likely to judge that we have in fact seen the face before, and we are likely to regard the feeling of familiarity as a ground for the judgment. There is no question here of regarding it as a conclusive ground, but it does seem to be a good reason to judge that we have previously seen the face. This fact suggests an objection: if we rightly take the feeling of familiarity as a good indicator of previous acquaintance (with a certain face), why should we not regard our sense of appropriateness as a good indicator that we have just had a (very) recent conscious occurrence to which it actually is appropriate?

There are, however, two differences between these cases, and these seem to me to be sufficient support for treating them differently. (1) The sense of familiarity does not concern a relation of a present feeling to an episode of consciousness. If we do succeed in, as we say, "placing" the face, we remember where we have previously encountered its owner. We may (or may not) visualize a scene where we have previously seen the face, but we do not have the sense that we succeed in placing the face by recalling a particular episode of consciously viewing that face. But the (in my view unjustified) inference to a sudden understanding does concern a relation between one's later report of what was understood (or action taken on its basis) and an alleged episode in one's consciousness. (2) There is nothing in the context of the feeling of familiarity that raises an analogue of the structure problem for sudden understandings.

2.3 Fragmentary inner speech

Our inner speech is often somewhat fragmentary, or not fully grammatical. But we understand what we say to ourselves, and we do not feel that we have to ask ourselves for clarification (as we might very well have to do if someone else were to exactly reproduce their inner speech for us). It may seem natural to suggest, therefore, that we have accompanying, occurrent understandings of our inner words that fills them out, so to speak, i.e. that are conscious carriers of the more complete meanings that our fragmentary inner linguistic productions express only partially.

Related cases that we should keep in mind in this discussion occur on those occasions when we overtly say such things as "I don't know how to say what I've just thought, but I'll try"—where this is followed by some overt words, which may be followed in turn by "That's actually pretty much what I had on my mind" or else "I'm afraid I am expressing this very badly."

I have little to add to what I have already said, except to apply it to this case. We have our inner speech and we have accompanying visual and kinesthetic imagery, and sometimes emotional feelings. Most of the time, there is no sense of frustration about not being clear and no sense of confusion about what we mean. We just go on talking to ourselves. If we have gone on in this way for some time, we may make a retrospective judgment that we understood what we were saying to ourselves, just as we may express a sense of satisfaction about what we have overtly said, for example, in answer to some question. Adequate ground for such a judgment lies in our not having had any moments where we said to ourselves that we were not making sense, or were not clear, and in our not having had any emotions of disappointment or embarrassment about what we have been saying.

Sometimes, however, it may happen that we say something to ourselves, inwardly or overtly, that is immediately followed by an inward comment to this effect: "Wait a minute, that's not right." We may also have an emotion of distress or frustration. On these occasions, we often try another formulation. We think of ourselves as trying to say what we said again, only better this time.

But what can this mean? We *did not* say something satisfactory, and we do not want to say *that* again. Must I not really mean that we want to say what we *meant*? And, if that is so, must there not be a "something I meant" that was phenomenally present, and that we realize was not adequately expressed by our words?

That is ever so natural a way to describe the cases I have in mind. But, on reflection, it seems to me that all that actually occurs is that we say something further to ourselves, and then we are satisfied—or we are not. If we are satisfied, we go on. It is extremely tempting to say that we are satisfied because we now realize we have properly expressed what we thought. But this is an unnecessary hypothesis, and eschewing it enables us to avoid having to explain how a structured sentence can correspond to an unstructured phenomenon, or a structured phenomenon that occurs rapidly and without an apparent medium of elements. The alternative, more frugal, account is that we feel satisfied because we do just go on, without any sense of frustration or puzzlement.

If we are not satisfied with a second or third formulation, it is again tempting to say that these new formulations fail to match something we very recently had in our consciousness. But the ground we actually, phenomenologically have is dissatisfaction with the new formulations. It is an inference that we have dissatisfaction because of failure to match a previous, conscious phenomenon. The frugal account says that this inference is not required for an adequate account of what we actually know to be in our consciousness.

Our failed formulations do fail to match something—namely, a still later formulation that is one we are satisfied with. This later satisfaction consists (a) in our simply going on—i.e. it is one that is *not* followed by any inner comment on its inadequacy, or any negative emotion about what we have, at last, found to say. And in many cases, our successful formulation may also be followed by (b) an emotion of relief, or a kind of joy in having surmounted an obstacle. Such an emotion is appropriate: there *was* an obstacle, as is evident from our returning to successive formulations. It is only a certain description of the nature of the obstacle that the frugal account rejects; namely, the supposition that there was a failure to match a conscious, occurrent understanding of a meaning.

It may be objected that I have described only cases in which we are not sure what we think, and that there are other cases in which we know what we think and merely have difficulty in articulating it. These latter cases, it may be thought, would require a different description from the one I have just given.[5]

I do understand the difference in these cases, but I think the difference lies only in different judgments of confidence that may accompany what I have described. In the former kind of case, we are not confident, and so we will be only mildly frustrated if a problem occurs to us immediately after an attempt to say what we think. If we aren't satisfied after a few such efforts, we may be content to give up and declare that we are not sure what to think. In the latter kind of case, we positively expect (rightly or wrongly) to be able to produce a sentence that satisfies, and if we fail to do so, we may experience considerable frustration. But the actual succession of events—formulations, followed by re-formulations, which are followed by further problems, or else no problems, relief, and satisfaction—is the same in both cases.

There is another kind of sense of confidence that may appear to be a phenomeno-logical element that lends support to a liberal view. This is a sense of confidence in what one says, either inwardly or overtly. Even when we are speaking overtly, and are willing to be taken as asserting what we are saying, we may have a sense that part of what we say is evident and hardly subject to challenge, while other parts of what we say are risky—we do believe what we are saying, but we have the feeling that we are sticking our necks out, or we have a sense that we are preparing for challenge. Now, it may happen, in the cases where we reject some formulations before finding one with which we are satisfied, that when we come to the last, satisfactory one, we also utter it with a sense of confidence that was absent in our failed attempts. It seems to me that this sense of confidence might seem to be a good fit with the idea that we are matching a very recent conscious understanding. But it also seems to me that the hypothesis of matching is an unexplanatory addition. What is phenomenologically evident is only the sense of confidence.

The gain in simplicity that the frugal view affords is, of course, not a demonstrative argument against the view that there is a phenomenological understanding that was present, but failed to get expressed in our early attempts at formulation in words. But it has significant advantages. It avoids the need to explain how such phenomenal understanding could have appropriate structure, and it appeals only to relatively uncontroversial phenomenological materials. That is, I take it that even proponents of the liberal view will agree that the phenomenological materials to which I have appealed actually do occur. If these agreed materials are sufficient to explain the phenomena, we have no ground for additions.

---

[5] I thank Michelle Montague for calling attention to this difference.

2.4 Interpretation of images

Just as we may hypothesize phenomenologically occurrent understandings to fill out our fragmentary inner speech, we may hypothesize them to resolve the ambiguity inherent in visual imagery. For example, an image of a building with pillars might very well be an image of a bank, but it might be an image of a courthouse. We generally have no difficulty in knowing what we are imaging. Doesn't this show that we have a consciously occurring understanding of our images?[6]

Since my answer should not be surprising, I will be brief. So long as things are going well, alternative interpretations never occur to us. There is an absence of any sense of ambiguity, and our images simply succeed one another. If, as is usual, there are words along with our images, they will relate to one interpretation rather than another—e.g. they will be about banks, money, vaults, security, and the like, in one case, or trials, laws, judges, and so on in another. We just go on confidently. If a question is later raised, we may recall the images and the words, and we can give reasons for saying we took an image to be of a bank rather than a courthouse, or conversely.

How did we know which interpretation we were using? The question did not arise and we did not do anything to find out or come to know. We just did go on in a certain way. The reasons we can give are retrospective reasons that are based on recollections of what was in our consciousness before any question arose. If, as may happen, an ambiguity does occur to us, the only ground we have for resolving it is to give these retrospective reasons.

2.5 An objection inspired by Quine

This brief discussion of images may give rise to a dissatisfaction based on discomfort with Quinean indeterminacy.[7] The argument behind the dissatisfaction is this. (1) Quine has shown that no third-person investigation can establish that my "rabbits" means rabbits and not, e.g., sets of undetached rabbit parts. (2) But I know what I mean by "rabbits." Therefore, (3) I have access to what I mean by "rabbits" that is not available from any third-person perspective. (4) If what I mean by "rabbits" were determined only by some unconscious event, then I would have access to what I meant only by methods that could, at least in principle, be used by others, i.e. that could be understood from a third-person point of view. Therefore, (5) my access to what I mean by "rabbits" must be through a conscious understanding of what I mean. (6) The frugal view denies such conscious understandings. Therefore, (7) the frugal view should be rejected.

---

[6] Perceptually ambiguous figures such as Necker cubes, duck/rabbits, and vase/twin faces figures depend on unconscious mechanisms of spatial attention or figure ground resolution. They do not seem to me to raise a suspicion of a need for a cognitive phenomenology in the way that the bank/courthouse example does, and so I forego further discussion of them.

[7] My comments on Quinean indeterminacy are inspired by Graham et al. (2007).

Evidently, if premise (1) is rejected, the rest of the argument collapses, and so does not offer a reason against the frugal view. So, I shall not go into the reasons for (1); I shall simply concede it to the proponents of the objection for the sake of argument.

I do, however, doubt whether (1) and (2) imply (3). To support that they do imply (3), we would have to have an argument that overcomes the point of what I take to be Quine's answer to similar worries. Namely, we do not in fact have "access" to what we "mean" by "rabbits," but there is a powerful source for the illusion that we do, namely, the true but unhelpful fact that, of course, our "rabbits" means *rabbits*, and our "sets of undetached rabbit parts" means something different. Where there is just one rabbit, there are many undetached rabbit parts; and, we may be tempted to intone, our "one" means *one*. But, of course, Quine's argument applies to "one" just as much as any other term. What's definite is that we have no sense of ambiguity or difficulty when we use words that are familiar to us. But that is just because we use our words with ease. The truth of "our word 'W' means W" cannot show that we have a special phenomeno-logical determiner of what it is about.

This response might be resisted by the following line of thought. Suppose I see a rabbit in the yard; let us call it "Hoppy." It does seem possible for me to think of Hoppy as a set of undetached rabbit parts. If I do that, I might say, "There's a complete set of undetached rabbit parts out in the yard"—but is there any difference other than my words? There could be; e.g. perhaps I have an image of Hoppy with lines drawn across the neck, between torso and limbs, and between torso and tail. If I count Hoppy as one, and do not have an image with such lines, I'm thinking of it as a rabbit; if I have an image with lines and say the parts are many, I'm thinking of Hoppy as a set of undetached rabbit parts.

Imagery of this kind is not helpful here, because the lines need not indicate separation of the parts. They could just as well be a way of emphasizing the unity of the rabbit that is spread out over distinguishable regions of space—a way of attending to the fact that the one rabbit *has* parts. Of course, I can say which way I am taking them (perhaps in my inner speech). Evidently, this will not introduce any determinateness if linguistic reference is not already taken to be determinate.

This remark may seem to conflict with what I have recently said about images, but it does not. We know that we are having an image of a rabbit, just as we know we are having an image of, say, a bank. How do we know that? We do not do anything to come to know it and we have no special piece of evidence. We just go on with other images, or words about rabbits. Retrospectively, we can say our image was of a rabbit (rather than a set of undetached rabbit parts) because we talked (inwardly or overtly) about *rabbits*—and what we mean by "rabbits" is different from what we mean by "set of undetached rabbit parts." But by now it should be evident that this is no advance. The invocation of images does not get us beyond the triviality that "rabbits" means rabbits.

If an alleged occurrence of phenomenologically present understanding is proposed as introducing determinateness over and above the triviality that "rabbits" means *rabbits*, it encounters the same problem that pertains to images. Namely, it can always be asked what settles the interpretation of that bit of phenomenology. If an alleged bit of phenomenology is supposed to introduce determinateness because it intrinsically suggests "rabbits" (rather than "sets of undetached rabbit parts") as its correct expression, no progress will have been made, since we will still need some answer to what "rabbit" refers to that gets beyond the trivially true "It refers to rabbits."

In sum, it will not do to just assume that we have a source of definiteness of interpretation that gets beyond " 'W' means W" and then propose phenomenologically present understandings as the best candidate for that source. Instead, it would need to be explained how such understandings could introduce definiteness. It is not evident how this is to be done.[8]

3 Conclusion

When we think about the kinds of questions with which this paper is concerned, we are often in a special state of mind. We may describe cases of not understanding in words that we understand, and inwardly comment on the fact that we understand *these* words that we are now using. In such moments, we are thinking about our present words and contrasting our situation with remembered misunderstandings or absences of understanding (such as hearing words in a language we do not speak, or the sense of empty words described above). We are thus aware that there is a difference between our present situation and those we are remembering.

Philosophers are generally aware of pitfalls of introspection, and so it is unlikely that anyone will infer that we are always comparing understanding and absence of understanding, even when we are not attending to our doing so. But more subtle possibilities are available. For example, there is often a sense of confidence in what we are saying, and we easily recall whether we asserted a view (with or without full confidence) or merely mentioned it as a view to be considered. It is not beyond possibility that these phenomenological elements could lead us to think that there is something present whenever there is no difficulty in understanding; and it is a short step from that to the view that words that we understand are accompanied by occurrent, conscious understandings of them.

The frugal view I have been recommending rejects the outcome of such an inference. It does not, however, depend on this particular suggestion as to the source

---

[8] Strawson (2008: 296) raises a particular form of the problem of definiteness, namely, the "stopping problem": What stops a thought, perception, or image at an ordinary thing (e.g. a rabbit) rather than at some other place in a causal series, such as neural events in the perceptual system, retinal image, or light waves one meter from the eye? His view is that this problem can be solved only by appeal to cognitive experiential qualitative content. However, (1) Strawson admittedly does not offer an account of how such content enables us to stop (see pp. 300–1); and (2) I do not see why we cannot account for such determinateness as there is by appeal to our beliefs about what we are thinking about, seeing, or imaging—where, of course, the account of beliefs must not appeal to cognitive experiential qualitative content. For elaboration of this evidently sketchy last remark, see Robinson (1988: chs. 3 and 4, and 2005).

of more liberal views. It says, instead, that there are many things in our consciousness, and that there may be many paths that seem to lead to accepting a phenomenology of cognition that recognizes conscious, occurrent understandings. Besides confidence and the assertive character of most of our inner and overt speech, the frugal view recognizes a sense of appropriateness of our later formulations to something earlier (while regarding it as partially misleading), and many emotions, including a particular kind of joy associated with relief from the frustration of not understanding, and emotions (positive or negative) associated with changes in how one interprets a situation or a remark. Perhaps some will even say this is not frugality at all. But appropriateness of the term aside, there would seem to be many reasons why we might be under the impression that there is more than the frugal view allows.

As earlier explained, denial of a phenomenology of understanding is not denial that we understand what we inwardly or overtly say while we are saying it. Nonetheless, those who propose a liberal view of cognitive phenomenology may feel that something is missing. They may feel that if the frugal view were true, there could be no difference between empty words and our ordinary words. The frugal view accounts for this difference with items that are present in the empty words cases that are normally absent. But this may be felt to be inadequate, on the ground that no mere absence could correspond to so valuable a thing as understanding what one is saying.

In sum, the frugal view responds to this feeling by (a) supplying many occurrent aspects of what is in our consciousness and (b) by pointing to the structure problem in liberal accounts. I have been arguing that these matters carry significant weight. But I do not think they carry the day by themselves. The frugal view also needs (c) directly phenomenological support. This, I believe, is provided by the cases at the beginning of this paper. What these show, I believe, is that when we speak (inwardly or overtly) with understanding, when we are not attending to issues in cognitive phenomenology, we really are just going on in the absence of any sense of question, puzzlement, confusion, ambiguity, or frustration.

References

Goldman, A. I. (1993). "The Psychology of Folk Psychology," *Behavioral and Brain Sciences*, 16: 15–28.

Graham, G., Horgan, T., and Tienson, J. (2007). "Consciousness and Intentionality," in M. Velmans and S. Schneider (eds). *The Blackwell Companion to Consciousness*. Oxford: Blackwell, pp. 468–84.

Horgan, T. and Tienson, J. (2002). "The Intentionality of Phenomenology and the Phenomenology of Intentionality," in D. J. Chalmers (ed.). *Philosophy of Mind: Classical and Contemporary Readings*. Oxford: Oxford University Press.

Linser, K. and Goschke, T. (2007). "Unconscious Modulation of the Conscious Experience of Voluntary Control," *Cognition*, 104: 459–75.

Mangan, B. (2001). "Sensation's Ghost: The Non-sensory 'Fringe' of Consciousness," *Psyche*, 10(1).

Pitt, D. (2004). "The Phenomenology of Cognition, Or, What Is It Like to Think That *P*?", *Philosophy and Phenomenological Research*, 69: 1–36.

Robinson, W. S. (1988). *Brains and People: An Essay on Mentality and Its Causal Conditions*. Philadelphia: Temple University Press.

——(2005). "Thoughts Without Distinctive Non-Imagistic Phenomenology," *Philosophy and Phenomenological Research*, 70: 534–61.

——(2006). "What is it Like to Like?" *Philosophical Psychology*, 19: 743–65.

Siewert, C. (1998). *The Significance of Consciousness*. Princeton: Princeton University Press.

Strawson, G. (1994). *Mental Reality*. Cambridge, MA: MIT Press/Bradford.

——(2008). *Real Materialism and Other Essays*. Oxford: Oxford University Press.

Wegner, D. M. (2002). *The Illusion of Conscious Will*. Cambridge, MA: MIT Press/Bradford.

——and Wheatley, T. (1999). "Apparent Mental Causation: Sources of the Experience of Will," *American Psychologist*, 54: 480–91.

Westerman, D. L. (2008). "Relative Fluency and Illusions of Recognition Memory," *Psychonomic Bulletin and Review*, 15(6): 1196–200.

On Behalf of Cognitive *Qualia*

Christopher Shields

1 Introductory phenomena and some problems pursuant to them

Some cognitive states seem to seem some way. When I am curious about whether *p* is true, I am in an experiential state rather unlike the experiential state I am in when I doubt that *p* is true. What is it like to be curious? I might say that it is like being intrigued or that it is like having a mental itch; but already, then, I am characterizing the quality of curiosity, and assuming, as I do, that there is something which is *what it is like to be curious*, or, less cumbersomely, that *curiosity is a certain way*. I am assuming, that is, that curiosity has a qualitative feel. Further, since it is one of the propositional attitudes, curiosity is a cognitive state.[1] Hence, when I ask what it is like to be curious, I am equally assuming that some cognitive states are qualitative, and so that there are cognitive no less than perceptual *qualia*.

More tendentiously, suppose I suspect that some of my fellow patrons in the Bodleian Library in Oxford are zombies. I wonder about them. Suppose, further, that I decide that yes, they really are zombies. What will happen, I wonder, when they

---

[1] There seems to be no non-tendentious way of characterizing cognitive states positively. Some philosophers are content with the negative characterization that cognitive states are those mental states which are both non-perceptual and non-emotive. If, by contrast, we want to say more positively that all of the propositional attitudes qualify, then in addition to beliefs, we may also have to add, depending upon our theoretical inclinations, desires and even, for an increasing number of theorists, the emotions. If we restrict the domain somewhat by limiting cognitive states to those propositional attitudes which are themselves truth-evaluable, then we seem to miss *inter alia* doubt and curiosity (my doubt may be well motivated or not, but it is not itself true or false; it is the thing doubted which is true or false). Since such states are neither perceptual nor emotional, then if they fail to be cognitive in the relevant sense, we need some further category in our taxonomy, and some further question as to whether states in that category are qualitative. Two observations: (i) if it is impossible to provide a defensible positive taxonomy of an exclusive class of mental states as cognitive, then still less will it be possible to deny that cognitive states are qualitative; and (ii) it will be serviceable and appropriate for the purposes of this paper to accept as cognitive the very states which cognitive psychologists introduce as paradigmatically such, including, e.g., belief and memory. For if these prove to be qualitative, then the question of a crisp taxonomy recedes. Mainly, I limit myself to a consideration of those propositional attitudes which are plainly non-emotive and non-perceptual. In this I follow most detractors of cognitive *qualia* in relying on an essentially negative characterization.

hear a joke? What will happen, that is, to them? As I can see, when they hear the punch line, they smirk and give a chuckle, just like any ordinary non-zombie. I wonder, though: do they find this joke humorous? Does anything tickle their funny bone? I am not sure, because I am not sure whether finding a joke funny is something a zombie could do, even though it can evince suitable finding-funny behaviour at expected finding-funny moments. When I wonder about this, I am curious about whether zombies can find humorous the same states of affairs I find humorous, and then I find myself drawn by that familiar mental itch to investigate the truth of a certain proposition or to answer a certain question: can a zombie have a genuine sense of humour, or is a sense of humour incompatible with zombiedom? The experiential state I am in at this moment of wondering seems to me to be the same experiential state I am in when I am drawn to investigate altogether distinct propositions whose truth values I do not know, for example, whether the national debt in America in the 1990s rose at a pace faster than did the national debt of Germany during the Weimar Republic, or whether triangles, if they exist, can differ *solo numero*.

I do not know the answers to these questions, but I am drawn to investigate them. Although ranging over different contents, there seems a familiar and more or less constant phenomenology across them all, and this is the feeling of curiosity. Sometimes I am curious when nothing important to me turns upon the question of whether a given proposition is true, is false, or is neither true nor false; at other times the eventual determination matters to me a great deal. In either case, however, when I find a proposition somehow intriguing, I am drawn to investigate it. My own sense of the phenomena, as a matter of report rather than argument, is that the mental state I am in when I am curious would not be the state that it is had it lacked the qualitative character I have just indicated. That is to say, however, that the mental state of being curious is essentially qualitative. Or at any rate, it *seems* to me to be qualitative, and essentially so. So, it seems to me that there are cognitive *qualia*.

For a variety of reasons, philosophers have displayed a surprising reluctance to countenance cognitive *qualia*. In this paper, I investigate this reluctance and argue that reasons given for doubting the existence of cognitive *qualia* are uncompelling. Because most hesitation in this regard derives from an optimism about the prospects of handling the propositional attitudes within a broadly cognitive psychology, I also consider the upshot of the existence of cognitive *qualia* for the so-called hard problem of consciousness,[2] namely, the problem of capturing the nature of experience, or, more precisely, of characterizing phenomenal consciousness, in some suitably neutral third-person way. I show that although the existence of cognitive *qualia* does not make the hard problem any harder, it does show that the hard problem has a more expansive sweep than has been hoped by the proponents of cognitive psychology.

---

[2] Following Strawson (1994) and Chalmers (1995).

I proceed in five stages. I begin with a series of contrasts intended to sharpen current debates about the existence of cognitive *qualia*. It turns out that the debates are more or less tractable depending upon where one stands with respect to these contrasts (§ I). As partial proof of this point, I next turn to an argument routinely advanced for doubting the existence of cognitive *qualia*: the variability argument. Although, as I contend, this argument fails in all its objectives, it may prove more or less seductive depending on how we characterize its intended target, and this is best ascertained by reference to our initial sets of contrasts (§§ II and III). Further, although I am partly sympathetic to those who maintain that we cannot argue for the existence of *qualia* of any kind but must rely instead on naked ostension,[3] I do think we can offer three kinds of parity argument for the existence of cognitive *qualia*. Each of these parity arguments takes the same general form: any reason we have for supposing that various non-cognitive states are qualitative counts equally as a reason for supposing that cognitive states are qualitative (§ IV). I conclude with a brief consideration of the ramifications of our admission of cognitive *qualia* for cognitive psychology (§ V). Although it is not my main interest here to chart these ramifications, whether deleterious or beneficial, it is worth at least appreciating that the hard problems of consciousness have not been winnowed from the easy problems of consciousness in the ways that some detractors of cognitive *qualia* have supposed—if, indeed, there are any easy problems of consciousness.

2 Cognitive *qualia*: Contrasts and contentions

We began with the suggestion that there is something which it is like to be curious. When I am curious as to whether there is non-carbon-based life somewhere in our vast universe, or again, more abstractly, whether non-carbon-based life is even a possibility in any imaginable universe, then the state I am in has a perfectly familiar phenomenology. Being curious as to whether there is non-carbon-based life in the universe is unlike hoping that this is so, or fearing that this is so, or dreading that this is so. Being curious as to whether p is also more like wondering whether p than it is like believing that p, since being curious carries no feeling of conviction; and it is also more like being intrigued whether p than it is like merely entertaining that p for the sake of argument, since instances of curiosity characteristically carry with them a sensed drive to discover. It is hard to characterize this (putatively) qualitative state intrinsically, beyond saying that it is that familiar feeling of curiosity, and harder still to offer ground-up arguments for its existence; but as a phenomenal matter, it seems an easy matter to ostend it, and the same holds true for a host of other cognitive states: wondering, hoping, believing, remembering, anticipating.[4] There is, in fact, nothing remarkable or

---

[3] So Block (1980).

[4] Much of Horgan and Tienson's (2002) brief for what they call PI (the Phenomenology of Intentionality), the view that 'consciously occurring intentional states have phenomenal character that is inseparable from their intentional content', takes this form. While I am in sympathy with their general view, I am disinclined

tendentious about ostending the feelings associated with any of these cognitive states: like other qualitative states, cognitive *qualia* are perfectly mundane, easily recognizable experiences, the denial of whose existence should require very special pleading indeed. Cognitive *qualia* are, in identifiable and repeatable ways, *feelings*: there is something which it is like to be puzzled or pleased, and something else which it is like to be curious or confounded. Since these states are also among the propositional attitudes, we evidently unreflectively regard some propositional attitude states as experiential states; in this way, we accept the existence of cognitive *qualia*.

Precisely what we are accepting when we acknowledge the existence of such feelings is, however, a further and more contentious matter. In fact, there is nothing obvious or innocent about the postulation of cognitive *qualia*—if, at any rate, we are to characterize this thesis robustly enough.[5] To begin, if we regard the existence of cognitive *qualia* as immediately obvious upon a moment's reflection, then we should be given pause by those who just as earnestly deny their existence altogether. Consider the following two perfectly plain and evidently sincere denials. First, Tye, speaking of two cognitive states sometimes alleged to be qualitative, namely, beliefs and memories:

It seems to me not implausible to deal with these cases by arguing that insofar as there is any phenomenal or immediately experienced felt quality to the above states, this is due to their being accompanied by sensations or images or feelings that are the real bearers of the phenomenal character.[6]

Nelkin is still more confident and dismissive:

There are propositional attitudes, and we are sometimes noninferentially conscious about our attitudinal states. But such consciousness does not *feel* like anything. A propositional attitude and consciousness about that attitude have no phenomenological properties.[7]

It is noteworthy that these two denials take markedly different forms. Tye at least nods to the phenomena by conceding that there may be feelings associated with cognitive states, but denies that these feelings belong to the states themselves; instead, he contends, they must belong to distinct, non-cognitive states, however closely tied those states may be to their allied cognitive states. Nelkin, by contrast, simply denies the phenomena altogether. No propositional attitude feels like anything at all.

We should in the first instance accept these denials for what they seem to be: non-doctrinaire, non-polemical reports that where we friends of cognitive *qualia* find something to report about our experiences, others find nothing, or at least nothing

---

to accept the philosophical morals they infer from its truth. There further seems to me to be a non-trivial question about what non-separability amounts to. I make some recommendations of my own in this regard by adverting to the more familiar language of essential and accidental instrinsicality.

[5] See, e.g., Strawson (1994) for a relatively robust formulation.

[6] Tye (1995: 4).

[7] Nelkin (1989: 430). Cf. also Carruthers (2005). Bayne (2009) characterizes the impulse towards 'phenomenal conservatism', as he aptly calls this stance.

intrinsic to the states we take ourselves to be describing. Moreover, it bears stressing that the first denial affirms the existence of *qualia* only for some range of mental phenomena. That is, someone with Tye's orientation is not a qualia-denier *tout court*, a *quiner* as for instance Dennett claims to be,[8] but rather what I will call a *demi-denier*. As a clear and forthright demi-denier, Tye allows perceptual *qualia*, and supposes that he owes the world a reductive account of them; but he thinks that nothing is owed in the case of cognitive *qualia*, since there simply is no phenomenon for which an account is needed. At most, one would need to explain away the appearance of cognitive *qualia* by locating the subjects of the qualitative characters outside the narrowly cognitive realm.

The situation with respect to cognitive *qualia* is thus rather distressing: some philosophers of goodwill point to a phenomenon which they take to be more or less obvious and uncontroversial, while their colleagues of equal goodwill inspect what these philosophers indicate and find them to be pointing to a mental vacuum. The suggestion thus lies near that the champions of cognitive *qualia* and their detractors are arguing at cross purposes, or are at least talking past one another. At any rate, one hopes that this is so, since otherwise, the debate regarding cognitive *qualia* quickly devolves into an unproductive stalemate, with one side ostending an item of phenomenal consciousness which the other simply claims not to experience. It is as if one psychologist characterized proprioception as the *introceptive sense of the orientation of one's own limbs in space* only to be rebuffed by another psychologist who insisted, with no polemical intent, that she has never experienced any such sensation and that she accordingly denies the existence of proprioception altogether. It would be a bit difficult to know the way forward for these two.

One way forward in the realm of cognitive *qualia* is to draw two related contrasts. We may do so by borrowing an example from Tye. Suppose someone describes the memory of her first kiss as sweet. In the face of this report one might, without drawing any immediate substantive conclusions, identify two aspects of her memory event (m), which we will introduce as a mental episode occurring on New Year's Eve, 2000: (i) the content (c) of this memory, the kiss she experienced at some earlier time, let us say New Year's Eve, 1988; and (ii) the feeling that the memory (m, not its content) is sweet. There seem to be two aspects of m here: its content c, and its character, the *quale* q. Having drawn this distinction, one might in principle move to any of a number of different substantive theses, by relating the features c and q of m as follows:

Single- v. Two-State Solutions:

Single-state: there is but one state, the memory m, which has as intrinsic properties both the intentional property *having-content-c* and the qualitative property *being-q*.

Two-state: the memory m has the intrinsic property *having-content-c*, but the memory report alludes also to *an associated but distinct state, n*, which is the bearer of the qualitative property q;

---

[8] Dennett (1988).

presumably *n* is a state directly related to *m*, perhaps because the existence of *m* causes the existence of *n*, or, more narrowly, because *m*'s having *c* causes *n*'s being *q*.

Tye seems to articulate a two-state solution, whereas Nelkin has advanced a no-state solution. I will be arguing for a single-state solution, which itself might be characterized in a weaker and a stronger form:

Accidental v. Essential One-State Solutions:

Accidental: there is but one state, the memory *m*, which has as an essential property *having-content-c*, but also happens to have, as an accidental intrinsic property, *being-q*.

Essential: there is but one state, the memory *m*, which has as *essential* intrinsic properties *having-content-c* and *being-q*.

Armed with just these two pairs of distinctions, some headway becomes possible.

To begin, given these distinctions, one can sharpen the debate about the existence of cognitive *qualia* as follows. Cognitive *qualia* deniers, like Nelkin, simply deny the phenomena outright. (NB that such cognitive *qualia* deniers need not, though might, join Dennett in denying the existence of *qualia* altogether; in what follows, I will address only those who do not, that is, those who affirm the existence of some qualitative states, but who deny that there are any cognitive *qualia*.) Cognitive *qualia* demi-deniers, like Tye, admit that there are *qualia* in the neighbourhood of various contentful states such as memory, but deny that these *qualia* are intrinsic to those states, let alone essential to them. These kinds of deniers contrast with different kinds of affirmers. Amongst the cognitive *qualia* affirmers, some allow that various cognitive states are intrinsically qualitative, while denying that they are essentially so; others insist that the contentful states in question are not only themselves intrinsically qualitative, but that it is essential to those states being the states they are that they be qualitative. I will advance the stronger, essentialist version of the one-state solution.

This framework, I suggest, helps to explain at least one source of disagreement between our philosophers of goodwill: they are wrangling about the bearers of the *qualia* associated with cognitive states. It also helps, I argue, to disarm some arguments against the existence of cognitive *qualia*.

3 An argument against cognitive *qualia*: The variability argument

Moving forward with the example of memory, let us consider Tye's primary argument against cognitive *qualia*, which I will call the *variability argument*. I should say, however, that in calling this Tye's argument, I do not mean to suggest that it is his alone, or even his originally. On the contrary, it is an argument one very frequently encounters in this area. It is just that Tye offers an exceptionally clear and direct formulation of it, and thus provides an especially helpful focus for our discussion.

Let us then focus more minutely on our memory report. Rebecca reports, on New Year's Eve, 2000, that the memory of her first kiss, which transpired on New Year's Eve, 1988, is sweet. On the basis of this report, we may say:

(1) The memory of Rebecca's first kiss is sweet.

On its surface, (1) is a simple, monadic predication, on a par, for example, with:

(2) The pain in Rebecca's knee is sharp.

Just as sharpness characterizes the qualitative character of her pain, so sweetness characterizes the qualitative character of her memory. Without having qualitative character, her pain could not possibly be sharp. Should one then equally hold that her memory could not possibly be sweet without its having a qualitative character?

Tye thinks not. When canvassing the kinds of mental states he understands as phenomenally conscious, he includes, as distinct types: (i) perceptual experiences, such as hearing a trumpet play; (ii) bodily sensations, for example, feeling a pain or a hunger pang; (iii) emotions and felt reactions, including love, fear, and jealousy; and (iv) felt moods, such as happiness and depression.[9] He then pauses to ask:

Should we include any mental states that are not feelings and experiences? Consider my desire to eat ice cream. Is there not something it is like for me to have this desire? If so, is not this state phenomenally conscious? And what about the belief that I am a very fine fellow? Or the memory that September 2 is the date on which I first fell in love? Is there not some phenomenal flavor to both of these states? In the former case, some phenomenal sense of pride and ego, and in the latter some feeling of nostalgia?[10]

As we have already seen, he thinks not, because he believes that in all such cases 'insofar as there is any phenomenal or immediately experienced felt quality . . . this is due to their being accompanied by sensations or images or feelings that are the real bearers of the phenomenal character'. If one will '[t]ake away the feelings and experiences that happen to be associated' with these sorts of states, one will find that 'there is no phenomenal consciousness left' (Tye 1995: 4). Tye here offers a version of *the variability argument*.

Before we state the argument, however, we should note Tye's fairly tendentious way of reporting the phenomena. He says that he wishes to know whether mental states that are 'not feelings and experiences' belong on any list of phenomenally conscious states. The answer to that question ought to be analytic: no. Plainly, no non-felt, non-experiential state is a state of phenomenal consciousness. That there is a question to be asked at all in this arena stems from the fact that some desires and some beliefs—as well as a host of other non-perceptual, non-emotive states—certainly seem to feel some way. I know how it feels to desire something ardently; and I know how it feels to struggle to remember the name of an old acquaintance when I meet her on the

---

[9] Tye (1995: 4).   [10] Tye (1995: 4).

street (especially when she remembers my name with an expectant smile). Our question about the existence of cognitive *qualia* cannot be trivially reduced to the question of whether some states which are not feelings or experiences qualify as states of phenomenal consciousness; for the states we are considering are—or at least certainly *seem* to be—experiential.

Tye tacitly acknowledges this when allowing that some desires and beliefs sometimes 'happen' to have feelings and beliefs associated with them. In urging that it is a matter of happenstance that any given memory has an associated feel, Tye has already characterized the situation so as to ease his way into the variability argument. Perhaps, he implies, a memory of my first love might happen to carry along with it wistful pinings for simpler times in my life; but it need not have. So, these experiences pertain not to my memory as such, but are instead merely occasioned by my memory. This shows, one might infer, that any phenomenal states associated with my memory are not intrinsic to the memory itself, and belong, if anywhere, to states discrete from the memory itself. After all, urges Tye, I might have had precisely *the same memory* with *different* associated feelings altogether. I might rather feel bitter or angry or hurt. This shows, Tye concludes, that it is not my memory which has qualitative character. If I try to transfer the phenomenal character onto the memory itself, I have erred: memory states are not themselves intrinsically experiential at all. They are devoid of qualitative character.

This sort of variability argument is uncompelling. To see why, it is necessary to appreciate first that it admits of at least two formulations. In its first and simplest formulation, the argument attempts to show that no cognitive state is *intrinsically* qualitative. That is, in this first version, it is intended to refute the cognitive *qualia* affirmer who maintains the *accidental one-state solution*, that is, the friend of cognitive *qualia* who believes that cognitive states are intrinsically but not essentially qualitative. In this first formulation, the variability argument is plainly unsound, because it relies upon an obviously false premiss. Even so, the argument admits of a second formulation, which attempts to refute only the stronger affirmative thesis, the one-state solution, according to which cognitive states are not merely intrinsically but essentially qualitative. On this formulation, the variability argument is at least not obviously unsound. In its second formulation, however, it features a premiss which is tendentious at best. In fact, I shall argue, upon closer inspection, the situation with respect to the second formulation collapses into the situation which obtains for the first: it too features a false premiss and so is unsound. In either formulation, then, the variability argument fails.

The core idea of the variability in any formulation is this: the intentional content of my cognitive states may be held fixed while any associated qualitative states are varied; hence, the cognitive states themselves are not intrinsically qualitative. If there are any qualitative properties in the neighbourhood at all, they belong not to the cognitive states but rather to closely associated affective states, e.g. emotional states or bodily sensations, which are the genuine bearers of qualitative character. The argument, then, in its first and simplest formulation is as follows:

(1) Every cognitive state is intentional.

(2) For any given cognitive state, it is possible to alter its qualitative character without altering its intentional content.

(3) If (2), then no cognitive state is *intrinsically* qualitative in character.

(4) So, no cognitive state is *intrinsically* qualitative in character.

(5) If (4), then there are no cognitive *qualia*.

(6) Hence, there are no cognitive *qualia*.

We grant (1); (2) seems correct, at least for the kinds of cases which Tye considers; so we may grant it for the present.[11] Inescapable trouble, however, begins with (3).

(3) claims that the possibility of variability is sufficient for a quality's being non-intrinsic to an intentional state. It should, however, be immediately clear that this is false. The Washington Monument, the white marble obelisk in Washington D.C., might one day be painted pink in order to celebrate the legalisation of gay marriage in the United States. Then it would be the same monument, but the same monument with a different colour. If (3) were correct, we would need to conclude that the Washington Monument is not *now* intrinsically white; yet clearly it is now intrinsically white. Hence, something is amiss with (3).

The irremediable problem with (3) is now easy to state. If (3) were correct, then only essential properties would be intrinsic; for it is always possible to vary non-essential intrinsic properties without threatening the identity of the bearer of those properties. So, (3) is simply false. It is on a par with insisting that since you might hold my gender fixed while altering my eye colour, I cannot be both intrinsically male and intrinsically blue-eyed. Yet I am.

So far, this is enough to see that (3) is false, and obviously so. It relies upon a principle which no one could support. The problem with (3) can also be made clear when we apply it to other sorts of mental states, states whose qualitative character we are disinclined to deny. Imagine someone who has his leg badly broken in a skiing accident. He remains in the hospital for a few days. During his early days in hospital, his pain is, he reports, throbbing, sharp, excruciating. Towards the end of his stay, he speaks of his pain as having abated somewhat. All along, his pain is a source of discomfort. So, one might conclude, the state which is a source of discomfort to him at first has the property of being excruciating and then later has the property of being simply unpleasant. Since its intrinsic character has changed, one must conclude, if (3) is true, that the pain could not have been excruciating but then abate somewhat. Yet it was and it did.

This example brings out still more clearly what is wrong with (3): it relies upon the thought that so long as I can vary the properties of some diachronic continuant in one way while holding some other properties fixed, the variable properties cannot be

---

[11]   Horgan and Tienson (2002) offer what is in effect a spirited attack on (2), though they do not formulate what I am calling the variability argument (cf. n. 4 above). For the present, I am neutral about the force of their contentions, since my aim is to point out that the variability argument fails even if (2) is granted. I return to (2) below, however, and argue for reasons other than Horgan and Tienson's that it is tendentious at best.

intrinsic properties of that subject. The same point could as well be made in non-temporal, counterfactual terms. In its elementary version, the variability argument relies upon the thought that I could not hold some intrinsic properties fixed while counterfactually altering others. This is false in general, and so false in the domain of the mental. Still, it suggests how (3) might be rewritten so as to avoid this obvious problem.

Perhaps (3) should be understood not in terms of intrinsic properties, but rather in terms of a subset of intrinsic properties, namely, those which are essential. This would permit us to rewrite the argument as directed against the thesis I actually maintain, the *single-state essentialist solution*, according to which cognitive states are not only intrinsically but also essentially qualitative. The enhanced variability argument holds:

(1*) Every cognitive state is intentional.
(2*) For any given cognitive state, it is possible to alter its qualitative character without altering its intentional content.
(3*) If (2*), then no cognitive state is *essentially* qualitative in character.
(4*) So, no cognitive state is *essentially* qualitative in character.
(5*) If (4*), then there are no cognitive *qualia*.
(6*) Hence, there are no cognitive *qualia*.

As written, the argument is hopelessly flawed, since (5*) is plainly false: a state may be intrinsically ϕ without being essentially ϕ. So, taken as a general argument against the existence of cognitive *qualia*, the enhanced variability argument already fails.

That said, in the current dialectical context, it is really (3*) which is at issue. Its general form is now, I concede, correct. If some ϕ thing may be made non-ϕ without threatening its existence, then that thing is not essentially ϕ. So, if one really can alter the qualitative character of some cognitive state without threatening its status as a cognitive state, then that state is not essentially qualitative. Can one?

This question is really in fact directed at (2*), the bald assertion that for any given cognitive state, it is possible to alter its qualitative character without altering its intentional content. Let us revert once again to Tye's memory example. Suppose the memory of Rebecca's first kiss is pleasant for her. It is not at all obvious that one could vary the qualitative character of her memory and *have it remain the same memory*. A claim to the contrary is question-begging at best, and, I suggest, actually false: if her memory were bitter rather than sweet, then it would not be, or would not obviously be, the same memory. (Again, to be clear, we are at present focusing on m, the episode of her remembering, and not the character of the event remembered.) Of course, it would have the same content c, though what is at issue in the present context is precisely whether sameness of content is sufficient for sameness of memory m. Suppose, for example, that at some point subsequent to her first kiss, which had been pleasant enough for her at the time, it came to her attention that the boy who had bestowed it upon her did so only because her mother had paid him handsomely to do so. Of course, the content of the memory would be the same: it would be the kiss of New Year's Eve, 1988. From that it does not follow that the bitter memory would be the same memory as the pleasant memory she had before she learned the unhappy truth about the original event. Indeed, this seems to be the very point at issue. So, even overlooking the other problems already identified in this argument, we should be unmoved by the variability argument, even in its revised formulation.

We can see this more clearly, and more clearly to the detriment of the revised variability argument, if we move away from Tye's memory example towards other cognitive states. Consider, for instance, the case with which we began: curiosity. Suppose Fernando is curious as to whether p, where p is the proposition *that Uruguay has won the World Cup in football*. According to ($2^\star$), it is possible to alter the qualitative character of this instance of curiosity without altering its intentional content. Yet for ($2^\star$) to have any hope of supporting ($3^\star$), this must be possible without bringing it about that Fernando is no longer curious as to whether p. Yet that seems plainly false: if Fernando comes to develop feelings of doubt, or hope, or disbelief, or indifference, with respect to p, and is thus no longer drawn to investigate its truth, then he is no longer curious. It is hardly the case, then, that one could alter the qualitative character of his curiosity while holding its propositional content fixed without threatening its status as an instance of curiosity. Quite the contrary, if his mental state lost the relevant qualitative character, then we would also for that very reason lose our grounds for treating Fernando's relation to p as an instance of curiosity.

Taking all that together, any reason to suppose that ($2^\star$) might be true is also a reason for thinking that ($2^\star$) provides no grounds for ($3^\star$); and without ($3^\star$), we have no reason to doubt that (at least certain) cognitive states are essentially qualitative. So, the enhanced variability argument gives us no reason to deny that cognitive states may be essentially qualitative, and indeed, on the contrary, some reason to conclude that they must be.

Summing up the discussion thus far, then: the variability argument was initially introduced to show that cognitive states are not intrinsically qualitative. Thus construed, the argument is a non-starter. Perhaps, though, its supporters were really after another point, that cognitive states are not essentially qualitative. The argument so construed also fails. Hence, in neither version does the variability argument establish that cognitive states are not qualitative. Therefore, despite its undeniable popularity, the variability argument fails to establish that we cannot hold what the phenomena recommend, namely, that some cognitive states have qualitative character.

4 What went wrong?

Despite what I regard as its obvious shortcomings, the variability argument has enjoyed a widespread appeal. This is a matter which calls for some explanation. There are, of course, various genetic explanations, having to do with people's hopes and motivations in the realm of cognitive psychology. These may range from the salutary to the peculiar; but they are not my current focus. Rather, I mean to investigate, briefly, why, when it is so poor an argument, the variability argument could be thought to have such philosophical appeal. For a consideration of this question will lead naturally to a discussion of what parity cognitive *qualia* may have with other forms of *qualia*.

Judged from a sufficient distance, the variability argument trades on the indisputable fact that every cognitive state can be taxonomized in terms of its propositional content. That is, cognitive states, like all intentional attitudes, can be thought of as *p-states*, where a p-state is a state with a specifiable propositional content. Since it is (evidently) understood that every cognitive state is essentially a p-state, it is easy to conclude that it is not *also* essentially another kind of state, a *q-state*, a state with a discernible qualitative character. At any rate, this conclusion follows easily from the general principle that no mental state can be essentially both a p-state and a q-state. This assumption, though false, is easily made.

The problem with the variability argument can now be put in more general terms, and these terms can help explain why even those sympathetic to the phenomena have felt constrained to adopt some manner of two-state solution. Allow that when I entertain whether a given proposition *p* is true, I am in a certain mental state, an *m-state*, where being an m-state is to be neutrally characterized with respect to whether it might or might not be a qualitative state. (We are taking it as given that *some* m-states are q-states. That is, in the current discussion, we are not accepting any form of complete *qualia* eliminativism.) If we believe that a given m-state is essentially a p-state, we may conclude, without further consideration, that it is therefore not essentially a q-state. Indeed, on the other side, we may equally be inclined to conclude that since a given state is essentially a q-state, it is therefore not also essentially a p-state. (This is, after all, what a fair number of Humeans have thought about the emotions.) We are not entitled to this quick conclusion, however, in either direction. For it is entirely possible that one and the same m-state be *both* essentially a p-state *and* essentially a q-state. Any assumption to the contrary, that m-states can be at most essentially and exclusively either p- or q-states leads, I think, to the unsustainable conclusions we have identified.

Cognitive states, I maintain, are states which are essentially both contentful *and* qualitative. That is, when I doubt that you are truthful, my m-state is *both* a p-state and a q-state. From this perspective, the revised variability argument gained some specious plausibility only from the fact that the original variability argument held the p-state-feature of an m-state fixed, while varying its q-state-feature. But also from this perspective, we can appreciate more precisely the shortcomings of the variability argument. It was supposed to establish the theses, in first its weaker and then its stronger form (where the subscripts denote intrinsic and essential predications), that:

$$\neg \Diamond \exists x_m (P_i x \ \& \ Q_i x),$$
$$\neg \Diamond \exists x_m (P_e x \ \& \ Q_e x)$$

Without a general principle to the effect that no m-state could be essentially taxonomized under non-equivalent, discrete sortals, no such variability argument can succeed.

The variability argument itself provides no such general principle. Nor, if any of the arguments of the next section succeeds, could it. For the principle is false.

5 Parity arguments

I have indicated that I regard it as difficult to argue positively *ab initio* for the existence of cognitive *qualia*. Still, one can do more than point and invite one's interlocutors to reflect on their own mental lives. In particular, for at least some sceptics, argumentation is possible. For our purposes, sceptics appear in two guises, already indicated: demi-deniers and those cognitive *qualia* deniers who eschew the full-scale eliminativism of Dennett. To refresh, not every cognitive *qualia* denier is a quiner: some would eliminate the phenomena as pertains to cognitive states, even while acknowledging the existence of other qualitative states, characteristically perceptual or sensational. Demi-deniers both acknowledge the existence of the qualitative character of at least some mental states, and are prepared to acknowledge that there may seem to be qualitative states in the neighbourhood of the cognitive, but for theoretical reasons opt for a two-state solution in the face of the phenomena. While they deny cognitive *qualia* per se, regarded as intrinsic states with propositional content, they tolerate closely associated qualitative states, connected at best causally to phenomenologically blank cognitive states. In their different though related ways, I contend, these theorists find themselves in an unstable and untenable situation with respect to cognitive *qualia*. Left by the wayside in what follows are only those radical eliminativists, the quiners, who deny that any mental states *ever* manifest qualitative features; but we have not been hoping to engage the fringe.

Accordingly, my general strategy is to show that those who accept the qualitative character of some mental states, including the perceptual or sensational states, but who reject the qualitative character of cognitive states, do so only incorrectly. Thus, my arguments are *parity* arguments: if one has reason to accept the qualitative character of some mental states, then one has equal reason to accept them in the case of the cognitive. Complete eliminativism about the qualitative is, I allow, a stable, if un-tenably radical view; non-quining eliminativism and demi-denial are, by contrast, unstable views, and so ought to be rejected. In sum, I argue that since cognitive *qualia* have all the hallmarks that other, non-cognitive qualitative mental states have, it follows that from the standpoint of the qualitative, cognitive *qualia* are on a par with other kinds of qualitative states. This result invites either undifferentiated acceptance or wholesale elimination of the qualitative. Such a result, of course, a *qualia* quiner could gladly champion.

The parity arguments I have in mind are three: (i) a *seeming seeming argument*; (ii) a *determinability argument*; and (iii) an *argument from willing*.

(1) *Seeming Seemings*: I seem to be able to imagine that the puddle before me lacks oxygen. I seem, consequently, to be able to imagine something which many hold to be necessarily false, namely, that it is possible for water to lack oxygen. How can this be?

Beyond the now familiar point that bare, low-grade imaginability does not by itself entail possibility, lies a diagnosis of what has gone wrong in those cases in which we seem to imagine the impossible. The diagnosis is that what I take myself to be imagining may not be exactly what I am in fact imagining.

More exactly, suppose I describe myself as imagining that it is possible for water to lack oxygen. When asked why I should think such a thing, I respond that I am at present picturing a puddle at my feet, supposing that it contains water, and further imagining that the puddle is made up of some oxygen-free stuff. When my scientific essentialist friend, whose views on metaphysical necessity we may grant for the present purpose, points out that I am evidently describing myself as imagining that there is something which is *identical* with H_2O, and so which in every possible world in which it exists *is* H_2O, is somehow also such that it possibly lacks oxygen, I backpedal. I paraphrase: I was only imagining myself to be in the perceptual situation in which I find myself when I am in front of a puddle. That is, I imagine myself to be in a perceptual state qualitatively indiscernible from the state I am in when I perceive water. I imagine myself, for example, to be standing before an impression in the concrete just after it has rained and gazing down into some clear liquid. What I am imagining is that *that clear stuff lacks oxygen.* That clear stuff, which looks a lot like water, is not water—not, at any rate, if it lacks oxygen; and it really is possible that some clear liquid might lack oxygen. That much, indeed, is actual.

For our present concern, what is important about these sorts of situations is that the putative imaginability can be paraphrased away. Paraphrase is possible. A story can be told. It is easy to make sense of my mistake: I thought that I was imagining water without oxygen, but in reality I was imagining some other clear water-like stuff which lacked oxygen.

Now we may compare this situation with another. I imagine myself to be consciously entertaining a proposition p, perhaps the proposition *that 'transmogrify' is a nonce* word. I do not believe this proposition, but neither can I trace the etymology of this word. So, I come to entertain the possibility that it is a nonce word. I now step back and reflect in a second-order sort of way on my entertaining of that proposition. I think of that entertaining as seeming a certain way to me: it seems to me, I claim, that entertaining is like a kind of non-committal considering. Now, if the non-quining eliminativist were correct, it should be possible for me to paraphrase away that seeming. For though it seems to me that my cognitive state seemed a certain way to me, this must be false, and necessarily false, since it is not possible for the m-state in question to be both a p-state and a q-state.

This, I maintain, cannot be done. Or, in any case, it cannot be done any more for the cognitive states than it can for other uncontroversially q-states, like being in pain. (To be clear: in what follows I am not worried about the question of whether I can be mistaken as to whether I am in pain, but rather with the more attenuated question of whether I can be mistaken about a pain's seeming to seem a certain way to me.) Now, the non-quining eliminativist might wish to argue that I am somehow confused when

I report, for instance, that my being perplexed about a certain proposition *p* seems a certain way to me. This is, however, difficult to credit. Evidently, if something seems a certain way to me, then it involves, well *seeming*. Whereas I might in principle be wrong about *how things seem* to me, unless I am a quiner, there is no route to my being wrong *that things seem* to me in general. So, the non-quining eliminativist has no recourse for paraphrase.

Matters are more complex with the demi-denier. The demi-denier credits the seeming: he agrees that things do seem a certain way to me. He then hastens to relocate the qualitative feature in a second, associated state, evidently on the grounds that it is known *a priori* that the cognitive state itself cannot be intrinsically qualitative. Hence, the two-state solution.

One may respond in two phases. First, there is no need of a two-state solution, because there is no problem in need of solving. There would be a problem if—as the demi-denier allows—there were a qualitative feature in need of a home *and*—as the demi-denier wrongly assumes—its home could not be where it seems to be, namely, in the cognitive state in question. The reason for maintaining the second conjunct of this supposed problem, recall, was just the now discredited variability argument. So, there seems to be no problem in search of a two-state solution.

Moreover, and more importantly, the demi-denier's commitment to a two-state solution does in fact raise a difficult and delicate problem about the individuation of mental states, namely, the question of how fine-grained a mental state should be individuated. The source of this problem is as follows. The demi-denier allows that some cognitive states seem to seem some way, and even credits their seeming seemings. Still, he wishes to re-describe what seems to be the case. He seeks not to paraphrase away the seeming itself, but rather the seeming subject of that seeming. To make this slightly more manageable by way of illustration: it seems that curiosity, a propositional attitude, seems to seem a certain way (I have said mine seems like a mental itch), but since we are, according to the demi-denier, committed to the belief that a p-state cannot seem any way, we must find some other associated subject to underlie the q-state, the mental itchiness. Which subject might that be? One is inclined to ask: what other state *could* it be, if it is not the state of curiosity itself? If it is not the very state of being curious which seems the way curiosity seems, then what are the other candidate bearers?

However that question is to be addressed, in the current dialectical context, one need not meet the difficult question about mental state individuation given rise by the demi-denier's re-description head-on. Indeed, one *should* not address it, in as much as it is held to arise only in the case of cognitive states and not perceptual or sensational states. Here, however, we are modestly demanding only parity for all of the mental states which seem to seem some way. Thus, whatever the grain of individuation we adopt for cognitive states which seems to be qualitative, such evidently will be the grain for other, uncontroversially qualitative states such as perception and sensation. To illustrate, we may agree that perceiving green is an information-bearing state. It is, in this regard at least, not a qualitative state. So, one might wish to hive off the qualitative character of perception, and locate in some other non-information-bearing state, on the grounds that nothing could be both information-bearing and qualitative. Now, I see no reason at all why one should wish to proceed in this way. That is not, however, my present point, which is rather, that there is parity between the cognitive states and the non-cognitive states as regards the question of fine-grainedness of individuation. If for some reason one wishes to be ultra-fine-grained about individuation conditions across the full spectrum of mental states, then her doing so remains open at least as a theoretical possibility. Then, however, two- or several-state solutions would reign over all. Parity recommends not that states be individuated in some way or other, but only that all m-states be treated on a par as regards their individuation conditions. No reason has been given for treating different qualitative states differently, by taking some to be individuated thick-grainedly and others fine-grainedly. On the contrary, seeming seemings seem the same across the sweep of the mental.

The demi-denier is thus in an important respect unlike the non-quining eliminativist. Yet both encounter the same instability, and for much the same reason: whatever inclines them to grant qualitative features in one domain of the mental should equally incline them to grant it in others, and to do so in like fashion.

Their joint situation thus recommends the following argument. It seems to me that some of my p-states are also q-states. Hence, it seems to me possible that some of my p-states are also q-states. Yet, if I am wrong about that—if what seems to me to be the case is not and *could not* be the case—then there must be some rephrasal strategy available to me. Now, such a rephrasal strategy is possible for p-states which are also q-states only if it is possible for q-states which are not also p-states. Looking in the direction of non-quining eliminativists, no such strategy is available. Looking in the direction of demi-deniers, such a strategy is available only if it occasions unmotivated and unwanted fragmentation of uncontroversially qualitative states. Hence, rephrasal strategies lead either nowhere or to the wrong destination. So, both non-quining eliminativism and demi-denial are unstable, and ought to be rejected.

Consequently, any attempt to paraphrase away the qualitative by moving towards increasingly fine-grained mental states in the end devolves into a shell game which relocates the phenomena without explaining them away. The purport of the present argument is that paraphrase is possible or not possible equally across the full range of the seemingly qualitative. This is to say, then, that paraphrase is possible in all cases in the same way and to the same degree: either not at all or only to ill effect.

(2) *Intensity and Determinability*: Some pains we describe as sharp, others we describe as intense, and still others we describe as dull or diffuse. The reason we are able to do so stems from two facts about the qualitative character of pain. The first is that pain states admit of degree. One and the same pain can be more or less intense. The second is that being painful is a determinable qualitative character of pain states, one admitting of a range of determinants beneath it. Every pain state, whether throbbing, or acute, or

mild, is also painful; but not every state of pain is throbbing, or acute, or mild. It is plausible to suppose that these are ways of being in pain, and that being in pain is a determinable qualitative property of a certain sort. Moreover, it seems plausible to suppose that the range of potential determinants is categorically constrained by the nature of the determinable in question: it will not do to describe my hunger pain as gaudy, or as enchanting, or as winsome. Like other determinables, qualitative determinable properties admit of only a fixed range of categorically appropriate determinants.

Now, I also describe some of my qualitative cognitive states in much the same way. My belief that *p* might be fervent or weak, or it might be a bit shaky at the moment. Similarly, my suspicion is acute, or it is slight, or it is a bit uncomfortable. Then again, my curiosity is intense, or mild, or burning to the point of being distracting. In all of these cases, I treat the qualitative character of my cognitive state as admitting of degrees; and I also allow that there are ways of being curious. In this sense, unsurprisingly from my perspective, the qualitative character of my p-states behaves like the qualitative character of my non-p-states. For they are all equally q-states.

This situation recommends the following two arguments. The first is direct.

(1) It is possible for the qualitative character of my p-states to admit of degrees and to act as determinables act only if they are also q-states.
(2) The qualitative character of my p-states admits of degrees and acts as determinable qualitative states act.
(3) Hence, my p-states are genuinely q-states.

Of course, the eliminativist shrugs, and simply denies (2).

This does not seem open to the demi-denier. A second formulation brings this out a bit more clearly, by being a bit more indirect. It simply seeks to establish parity:

(1) The qualitative character of some of my p-states (i) admits of degrees, and (ii) behaves like a determinable under which fall various qualitative determinants.
(2) In this respect, the qualitative character of my p-states behaves like the qualitative character of my non-p q-states.
(3) The only or best explanation of (2) is that the qualitative characters of p- and non-p mental states are qualitative in the same way.
(4) Hence, the qualitative character of p- and non-p mental states are qualitative in the same way.

Once again, the total eliminativist is happy with this result. Indeed, he happily embraces the conclusion. All of my m-states, he says, are qualitative in exactly the same degree: not in the least.

Evidently, both the non-quining eliminativist and the demi-denier must deny either (2) or (3). A denial of (2) seems to implicate both in a further denial of the phenomena: sometimes my curiosity is intense, and sometimes it is waning. Presumably, then, only

(3) is open for questioning. But a wedge between my various q-states now seems like special pleading. We have already seen that there is no principled reason for supposing *a priori* that some of my m-states cannot be both p- and q-states. Absent any such argument, the only remaining approach would need to be piecemeal, explaining why each p-state which is also a q-state only seems to admit of degrees, or only seems to admit of a constrained range of determinants under a determinable. The motivation for such an approach escapes me; the likelihood of its success does not.

(3) *Willing and Qualia*: It is often remarked that we are somehow passive before the qualitative properties of our experiences. If this stew tastes salty to me, then this *quale*, seeming salty, characterizes my experience. If the sky seems azure to me, then this *quale* too seems a character of my experience. It seems difficult to fathom, but in the vast literature on *qualia*, the obvious connection between this kind of passivity in experience and the inefficacy of the will is rarely made explicit. Though I would not say it is a defining feature of the qualitative, I would want to insist that it is altogether characteristic of *qualia* that it is not open to the subject experiencing them to make them disappear at will. Although I can will myself, with some success, to forget experiences after I have had them, and I can will myself to move out of the states in which I am as I experience them, I cannot will myself to remain in a given qualitative mental state while not continuing to experience its qualitative character. I cannot will myself to continue consciously experiencing the heat of the fire without also experiencing this state as qualitatively hot. Nor indeed can I will myself not to experience this Zinfandel as jammy if this is how it seems to me at the moment. My will is impotent in the face of the phenomenal.

Notice that this is not a point concerning the difficult matter of incorrigibility. I fully allow that I can mistake, for instance, the sensation of a pin pricking my skin for a freezing sensation. Rather, the point is that if an experience feels sharp to me now, I cannot will it not to feel sharp even as I experience it. Perhaps, if I am a Stoic sage I can bring myself not to care about how things seem to me at the moment; but in not caring about how things seem to me at the moment, the things about which I do not care evidently seem a certain way to me.

Thus, there seems to me to be a general fact about *qualia*: if I am now in an occurrent conscious state with qualitative character q, I cannot now will myself not to experience q without also bringing it about that I am no longer in that state.

For instance, when I am tasting *Trockenbeerenauslese* and experiencing it as sweet, then I cannot will myself to experience it otherwise while I am in that experiential state. Similarly, and by parity, when I am curious, my curiosity may now seem to me fierce or mild. If so, it will not seem to me merely to be a random fierce or mild state, but a fierce impulse or a modest inclination to investigate the truth of a certain proposition. When I am in this state, I am incapable of willing it to seem other than it does. I may be able to will myself to diminish my curiosity, or to set it aside altogether; but I utterly fail if I try to will myself now, while remaining in this state, to make it seem other than it does.

This connection between willing and *qualia* recommends the following argument:

(1) When someone is in an uncontroversially qualitative state, say a perceptual state, she is incapable of willing that state to lose its qualitative character.

(2) When someone is in a cognitive state which also seems to have qualitative character, she is incapable of willing that state to lose its qualitative character.

(3) The only or best explanation of this parallelism is that the p-state is no less qualitative than the uncontroversially q-state.

(4) Hence, there is every reason to conclude that our p-states are no less qualitative than our non-p q-states.

The uncompromising eliminativist denies (1), on the grounds that there are no uncontroversially q-states. The rest of us accept (1), as long as we acknowledge the impotence of will in these circumstances.

If enough has been done to motivate that principle, the non-quinean eliminativist and the demi-denier may turn to (2) or (3). (2) is an assertion which I will not undertake to defend, except to say that it is admitted as part of our initial phenomena, and to invite the critic to attempt to will himself not to be in a state of seeming to be drawn to investigate some state of affairs the next time he finds himself curious about something. (3) is then the last recourse. The best way to deny (3) is to offer another explanation which is better than the one I have offered. I cannot myself envisage any such explanation which does not implicitly invoke radical eliminativism.

6 Conclusion

Some cognitive psychologists intent on naturalizing the mind have hoped to cordon off the cognitive attitudes from the hard problem of phenomenal consciousness.[12] Their thought was that if the cognitive states could be functionalized or otherwise handled within the confines of a suitably physicalist framework, then that would leave only the problem of addressing the qualitative character of perceptual experience and bodily sensation. Perhaps, then, their further thought was that these problems could be addressed by treating the qualitative character of such experiences within a representational theory of mind: if perceptual and sensational *qualia* could be shown to be representational states, they would no longer pose any problem for a naturalized theory of the mind. The job, at last, would be complete.

When they have relied upon the variability argument for the first part of their campaign, these cognitive psychologists have failed to advance their strategy. If this result seems unsurprising, then that is due at least in part to their transparent methodo-

---

[12] In addition to Tye, an especially clear example of this strategy can be found in Dretske (1995).

logical integrity. Rather than adopting a stridently eliminativist stance towards *qualia* in general, such cognitive psychologists have displayed an admirable willingness to attend to the phenomena—however diaphanous they may be—of phenomenal consciousness. That is, these cognitive psychologists have wanted to take the data of phenomenal consciousness seriously in some domains at least, and so have not gone the expedient way of the unapologetic quinean eliminativist. When they go part of the way, however, they must go all of the way or decide to backtrack and go nowhere at all. Every consideration to be adduced for non-cognitive *qualia* tells equally on behalf of cognitive *qualia*. At any rate, this follows if at least one of the parity arguments I have offered is compelling. I believe that all three are perfectly sound; and I note, in closing, that my belief in this regard feels a certain way to me: firm.[13]

References

Bayne, T. (2009). 'Perceptual Experience and the Reach of Phenomenal Content', *Philosophical Quarterly*, 385–404.

Block, N. (1980). 'Troubles With Functionalism', in N. Block (ed.), *Readings in Philosophy of Psychology*, Vol. 1. Cambridge, MA: Harvard University Press, 268–305.

Byrne, A. (2001). 'Intentionalism Defended', *The Philosophical Review*, 110: 199–240.

——(2004). 'What Phenomenal Consciousness is Like', in R. Gennaro (ed.), *Higher-Order Theories of Consciousness: An Anthology*. Amsterdam: John Benjamins, 203–25.

Carruthers, P. (2005). 'Conscious Experience versus Conscious Thought', in *Consciousness: Essays from a Higher-Order Perspective*. Oxford: Oxford University Press, 79–97.

Chalmers, D. (1995). 'Facing up to the Problem of Consciousness', *Journal of Consciousness Studies*, 2(3): 200–19.

Dennett, D. (1988). 'Quining Qualia', in A. J. Marcel and E. Bisiach (eds), *Consciousness in Contemporary Science*. Oxford: Oxford University Press, 42–77.

Dretske, F. (1995). *Naturalizing the Mind*. Cambridge, MA: MIT Press.

[13] I first began thinking about the topic of this paper some years ago in a seminar at Stanford on naturalizing the mind led by Fred Dretske. He would, I expect, be unsympathetic to the primary contentions of this paper. Even so, I owe to Dretske, a philosopher of admirable clarity of mind and sympathetic intellectual honesty, my initial framework for approaching these issues. During the course of that seminar I also had especially fruitful conversations with Güven Güzeldere, for which I remain grateful. Earlier drafts of this paper were presented to audiences at The University of Colorado at Boulder, Yale University, and University College, Dublin. Many members of those audiences provided stimulating objections and suggestions. I remain cognizant of revisions effected in the face of especially instructive observations made by Daniel Stoljar, Luc Bovens, Paul Studtmann, Jessica Wilson, Graham Oddie, Troy Cross, Robert Adams, and Rowland Stout. More proximately, Tim Bayne and Michelle Montague have kindly given me detailed comments which have helped me to clarify the main contentions of this paper considerably, as have two anonymous readers for this volume, both of whom offered astute and extremely helpful criticisms. Reading some of Bayne's work has also proven cautionary for me: he is right, I fear, that some issues regarding phenomenal *qualia* recede from view even as we bring them into focus. That acknowledged, I remain optimistic that progress is possible, and I am accordingly grateful to all these critics for their intellectual generosity.

Horgan, T. and Tienson, J. (2002). 'The Intentionality of Phenomenology and the Phenomenology of Intentionality', in D. Chalmers (ed.), *Philosophy of Mind: Classical and Contemporary Readings*. Oxford: Oxford University Press, 520–33.

Kriegel, U. (2002). 'Phenomenal Content'. *Erkenntnis*, 57, 175–98.

——(2007). 'Intentional Inexistence and Phenomenal Intentionality', *Philosophical Perspectives*, 21: 307–340.

Langsam, H. (2000). 'Experiences, Thoughts, and Qualia', *Philosophical Studies*, 99: 269–95.

Levine, J. (2001). *Purple Haze: The Puzzle of Consciousness*. Oxford: Oxford University Press.

Loar, B. (2003). 'Phenomenal Intentionality as the Basis of Mental Content', in M. Hahn and B. Ramberg (eds), *Reflections and Replies: Essays on the Philosophy of Tyler Burge*. Cambridge, MA: MIT Press, 229–58.

Nelkin, N. (1989). 'Propositional Attitudes and Consciousness', *Philosophy and Phenomenological Research*, 49: 413–30.

Strawson, G. (1994). *Mental Reality*. Cambridge, MA: MIT Press.

Tye, M. (1995). *Ten Problems of Consciousness*. Cambridge, MA: MIT Press.

Phenomenal Thought

Charles Siewert

1 Introduction

Does consciousness—that is, *phenomenal* consciousness—embrace both sensory experience and conceptual thought? We may feel embarrassed to ask such a question. Shouldn't it be introspectively obvious what's in consciousness? But surprisingly perhaps, simple reflection on our own mental lives leaves some stubborn disagreements. That will seem less astonishing if we find we lack a clear, shared interpretation of the issue, and approach it against a complicated background of varying, unarticulated influences. What underlies the lack of agreement here may, in fact, be so obscurely complex, or so entrenched, that a consensus will never be reached. But we should not avoid the question on that account—unless we simply want to avoid philosophical disputes.

To face the issue we need some initial grip on the relevant—phenomenal—notion of consciousness. We may start with Ned Block's formulation, which expresses the now common idea that the phrase 'something it's like' aptly conveys what we're after here: "What makes a state phenomenally conscious is that there is something it's like to be in it" (Block 2002). And just *what* that "something" is—what it is like for you to be in a given state—is said to be its "phenomenal character."

The notion of phenomenal consciousness is also commonly explained by appeal to sensory examples. Its feeling painful to you when you have a toothache, something's looking somehow to you when you see its color or shape—these are prototypical phenomenally conscious states. And the *phenomenal character* of pain consists in its feeling to you just as it does to be in pain; that of vision, in its looking to you as it does when you see colors and shapes.

But what is the significance of using *sensory* examples? Notoriously, it can be very unclear just how far to extend the use of a concept beyond paradigms. Should we conclude that phenomenal consciousness is *exclusively* a sensory affair? When you doubt that something is so, or wonder whether it is, when you think about what to do, or consider reasons for or against a claim, when you try to remember why you've come into the kitchen and recall you were looking for the pliers—you engage in conceptual thought. Do such episodes—and not *merely* their sensed expression or some concurrent imagery—belong to phenomenal consciousness? Are they as much a part of this as the experiences of hearing a thud, seeing a spiral, tasting some chocolate, or feeling an ache? Is there something it's like for you to think just as there is something it's like for you to sense? This is the gist of the issue.

Perhaps reliance on sensory paradigms would not leave this issue unsettled, if we had a relatively settled understanding of what it means to speak of there being "something it's like" to be in a state. But we don't. I will return to this crucial point.

Another problem here is that it is not immediately obvious how to get the right conceptions of the *sensory* and the *conceptual* to set up a discussion. We do not want to start by assuming too much—too theoretically loaded or ambitious an understanding of these notions. And we do not want simply to stipulate that the sensory can never *also* be conceptual. I propose we initially frame the issue as follows. Let's classify as "conceptual" such cognitive activity we enjoy that is (or can be) expressed in language, and requires capacities for voluntarily making inferences, classifications, and analogies. Next let's call "sensory features" those features whose possession is found in the activity of various standardly recognized perceptual modalities (vision, hearing, etc.) along with bodily feelings of pain and pleasure, cold and warmth, and kindred sensations, together with whatever analogs of these there might be in imagery (visualization, hearing words or music "in one's head," etc.). Finally, let's call "*merely*" sensory features those whose possession by a subject during a time is insufficient for the occurrence at that time of some conceptual activity.

Plausibly, there are merely sensory features. For it is plausible that, for example, colors, shapes, positions, movements, distances, and sizes, can *appear* somehow to a being who simply cannot voluntarily *classify* colors, shapes, etc., in a sense that requires the capacity to make *inferences* and *analogies* relevant to understanding these classifications, or who at least is not *then and there* so classifying them. But if this is mistaken, and there are in fact *no* "merely sensory features" in this sense, or if there are, but we (normal human adults) at least typically don't have them (because even our sensory experience is—not just linked—but "permeated" with conceptual activity[1]), then all (or most) instances of phenomenal sensory features with which we are familiar from our own experience will already involve the exercise of conceptual powers, and so it will be unavoidable to include conceptual activity in phenomenal consciousness. I do not wish to deny this. But the specific way of including conceptual activity that I will discuss and defend here is neutral with respect to this idea that the sensory is conceptually permeated or "loaded." On the view I'll present, whether or not our sensory features are *merely* sensory, phenomenality should be granted to the occurrence of conceptual activity that is found in *thinking* about something, even when what

---

[1] I take this way of putting it from McDowell (1994).

we are thinking about is not sensorily apparent or imagined. That, roughly speaking, is what I will call an "inclusive" view of phenomenal consciousness.[2] It seems fair to say that such a view is advocated in, for example, Goldman (1993), Horgan and Tienson (2002), Pitt (2004), Siewert (1998), and Strawson (1994). The opposing view, which *excludes* conceptual thought from phenomenal consciousness, I will call "exclusivism." This can be found, for instance, in Georgalis (2003), Jackendoff (1987), Nichols and Stich (2003), Robinson (2005), Tye (1995, 2000), and Wilson (2003).

The issue needs much more refinement. But why should we even care about it? What's at stake? Considerations of length do not permit me to go into detail. Suffice it to say that whether or not phenomenal consciousness is understood inclusively has consequences for what one will take to be a viable candidate *explanation* of it (since some explanatory frameworks assume an exclusively sensory view of consciousness). The issue also bears on what resources one has for understanding the role of phenomenal consciousness in *self-knowledge*. Further, it affects one's view of the kind of *value* consciousness has, and how that is related to the value and respect we should accord human beings. Finally, it provides a crucial test of our ideas about how to address apparent disagreements in which divergent "introspective" judgments about pervasively shared aspects of experience seem to be involved.[3] Does further first-person reflection have a role in forming a reasoned response to such controversies? Does philosophy?

2 A plea for historical self-consciousness

Though an answer to the question I am raising has serious implications, it does not always get a serious hearing. Since I believe it should be taken seriously, I want to start with some remarks about historical background that may help with this. Thirty years ago or so, many philosophers concerned with what is now often called "phenomenal consciousness" would likely have just assumed that the issues here had to do entirely with "sensory qualia" of some sort—sensations of pain and after-images of color being standard examples. From their standpoint, to be "inclusive" would be to suggest— bizarrely—that there is, for instance, a *"belief quale"*—where this means that much as it feels somehow to be in pain, it *feels* somehow to hold a belief—that there is perhaps an "instrinsic," "ineffable," "felt quality" to belief. And they would see this as pretty obviously absurd. They would admit that activities of *thought* and *understanding* are not guaranteed by sensory experience and imagery alone. But they would say there is a special "qualitative" sense of "consciousness" confined to the sensory domain.

---

[2] Note that my issue leaves to the side the question of whether there might be some way to reduce conceptual thought to the activation of complex *dispositions* for, or *operations upon*, merely sensory features. Prinz (2002) proposes and defends such a theory.

[3] Schwitzgebel (2008).

However, we should wonder a little at the fact that, a *hundred* years ago or so, philosophers concerned with consciousness also would likely have found *this* perspective puzzling and strange. What happened in the interim? Was there some philosophical discovery that consciousness, in a certain sense, is inherently sensory?

Let's go back a little over a century to see how "consciousness" is disambiguated in Husserl's *Logical Investigations*. Husserl there ([1900/01] 2001, V § 2) canvasses three concepts. One concept of consciousness, he says, is "inner perception." Another identifies consciousness with intentional mental acts generally. The remaining sense he introduces pertains to the "stream of consciousness." This includes whatever is *experienced* by someone—in the (internal accusative) sense in which an experience can itself be experienced—e.g. one experiences a sensation. Husserl rejects the idea that all experiences that are conscious in the "stream" sense are objects of some kind of "unbroken activity" of ongoing reflective judgment, such as is included in what Brentano calls "inner perception." And he thinks that non-intentional ("uninterpreted") sensations (of color, for example) belong to consciousness in this same ("stream") sense. Now then: if you purport to identify a concept of consciousness that distinguishes *being conscious* from *being the object of higher-order judgment, and* say that *non-intentional sensations* would be conscious in this sense, *and* characterize what is conscious as *occurrent* and *experienced* at a personal level, it may well seem that what you're talking about is none other than what some of us today would call phenomenal consciousness.

But now notice: if Husserl would be happy to include sense experience and imagery in this "stream of consciousness," he is far from *confining* it to this. He says: "In this sense, percepts, imaginative and pictorial representations, acts of conceptual thinking, surmises and doubts, joys and griefs, hopes and fears, wishes and acts of will etc., are . . . 'experiences' or 'contents of consciousness.' " Thus the sort of consciousness recognized by Husserl, most plausibly regarded as phenomenal, is supposed to be found in a rich variety of mental activities—spanning sensory experience, imagery, emotions, volition, and all sorts of conceptual thought. There is no hint at a sense of consciousness that would cast all conceptual thought into *un*consciousness. A little earlier than Husserl, William James (1890) similarly employs a notion of consciousness embracing all sorts of thought: James' famous "stream of consciousness" is a "stream of *thought*" in a very liberal, inclusive sense of "thought." And James' and Husserl's near contemporary, G.E. Moore (1962: 72), does not hesitate to include in consciousness the event of understanding what we say, as we say it: ". . . [S]omething happens in your minds— some act of consciousness—*over and above* the hearing of the words, some act of consciousness which may be called understanding their meaning." And Moore regards it as a matter of "Common Sense" that "acts of consciousness" include not only seeing, hearing, feeling, and imagining, but also *thinking* and *believing* (the latter being for Moore an event of judging some proposition) (ibid.: 16, 281–3).

The contrast between this late nineteenth-/early twentieth-century way of thinking about consciousness and that which came to inform much philosophy in the latter half of the twentieth century becomes evident, if we consider the position of a philosopher who, directly and indirectly, has had a considerable impact on this, Gilbert Ryle. In his (mid-century) *The Concept of Mind*, Ryle remarks he can find no use for the phrase "stream of consciousness," unless perhaps it refers to a "series of *sensations*," sensations which, by their very nature, are incapable of being correct or incorrect, and manifest no quality of intellect or character (1949: 203–5).

Ryle, working relentlessly to dispel what he saw as the "Cartesian Myth" of a mind as the "ghostly" locus of hidden occurrences, continually strove to *exteriorize* the mind by interpreting mental concepts in terms of public, observable performances and dispositions to these, while shrinking down as much as possible the class of mental events eluding this treatment. If there are some it is hard to *behaviorize* in this way (e.g. sensations, and words and tunes "heard in one's head"), they represent only the fading shadow of the Cartesian ghost. If Ryle cannot completely dry up the "stream of consciousness," he is determined to reduce it to a trickle. For only then, Ryle seemed to think, can we hope to neutralize the threats the dualist legend would otherwise invite: a hopelessly mysterious nexus of mind and matter, and an insoluble problem of other minds. Thus the private mental life that previous philosophers, novelists, and psychologists had imagined so rich and significant becomes, in Ryle, an impoverished sensory residue, to be contrasted with what really matters—publicly displayed qualities of intellect and character. And the sense of "consciousness" at work in James' and Husserl's "stream" talk is attached to the former, belittled side of this contrast. Ryle's "logical geography" crucially influenced seminal writings in the materialist philosophical tradition of the 1950s that emerged in his wake (those of U.T. Place and J.J.C. Smart), as the subject that came to be known in university curricula as "Philosophy of Mind" was established.[4]

From roughly this time on—due in no small measure to the impact of Ryle, as well as to influential interpretations of the later Wittgenstein—it became commonplace for philosophers to contrast the sensory with the conceptual, or sentience with sapience, or sensed qualities with propositional attitudes, while conceiving of the first member of these pairs to comprise some special "qualitative" domain, perhaps marked with

---

[4] Place (1956), citing Ryle with approval, starts from the idea that both "cognitive" concepts (e.g. knowing, believing, understanding) and "volitional" concepts (wanting, intending) are suitably analysed in terms of behavioral dispositions. But he then worries that this still leaves what he calls an "intractable residue of concepts clustering around the notions of consciousness, experience, sensation and mental imagery" that must somehow be fit into the materialist worldview in *another* fashion. (And here "the identify theory," with its consciousness/lightning analogy, comes to the rescue.) Smart (1959) announces that he takes Place as his point of departure. And, with a sympathetic nod to what he sees as Wittgenstein's and Ryle's noble (if failed) efforts to subject talk of pain to "behavioristic analysis," he sets himself to warding off any form of mind/body dualism, and completing a view of ourselves as nothing but "physico-chemical mechanisms." This means vowing not to accept the reality of anything "irreducibly psychical," even in the face of those few remaining, stubborn metaphysical hold-outs: "states of consciousness"—that is to say, "sensations." Place's and Smart's articles, with their Rylean "sensory residue" conception of consciousness, sustained by its role in the fundamental project of vindicating a materialist vision, provided the pervasive background against which subsequent functional and causal accounts of mind (and criticisms of them) emerged.

a special sense of "consciousness" and strongly associated with ill-articulated doctrines of "ineffability" and "intrinsic-ness," a domain that potentially poses a distinctive challenge for behavioral or functional accounts supposedly well suited to intellect, belief, and desire.[5] The surface plausibility of this framework was also perhaps bolstered by schooling in empiricism's doctrines of sensible qualities and copy-like ideas, together with standard critiques of these—critiques that fault them *not for impoverishing consciousness*, but for failing to account for linguistic *meaning, belief, and concepts*.

It is true that, as the "cognitivist revolution" consolidated, it came to seem intellectually respectable, even obligatory, to embrace a very unRylean (but now physicalized, "ghost" free) picture of the mind, buzzing with "inner processes" awaiting theoretical discovery. To that extent, the behaviorist mentality waned. Still, these "inner states" were to be thought of "functionally" or "computationally." And construing them thus seemed to preserve a radically limited conception of experience similar to Ryle's—but with the difference that the old behavior–dispositional construal of the intellection lying outside experience gave way to a functional or computational one. Thus the idea survived that something distinctively *sensory* exemplifies some special *sensory notion of consciousness*, to be set over against the arena of intelligence—or as it came to be called, the information-processing aspect of mind.

This history has led many who have been educated in Anglophone philosophy since the 1950s to find familiar an account on which the mind divides into some "qualitative" aspect that is purely sensory, and some behavioral/functional aspect, home to intelligence and the use of concepts. One may reject this bifurcated picture in various ways. But one lives still largely in thrall to it, if one rejects it on the grounds that the second behavioral/functional aspect of mind is all there really is to it, since the first "qualitative" aspect turns out to be either reducible to some special province of the second, or illusory and eliminable.[6] Insofar as one's grasp of "phenomenal" talk is rooted in the first of these purported aspects, in associated use of the jargon of "qualia," and in certain ways of engaging with classical empiricism, one may be inclined to think that "consciousness" in one sense just *means sentience*, or, in any case, an exclusivist view is likely to seem "natural." Introductory lectures and textbooks that take for granted some version of the framework I've described, and the canonical status of writings that have instituted it, promote a philosophical formation that can make an inclusivist alternative seem bafflingly eccentric, the kind of idea an ambitious graduate student would be well-advised to treat with casual scorn.

---

[5] This can be seen in Wilfrid Sellars' (1956) stark contrast between "sentience" and "sapience," which places intelligence, understanding, and reason all on the latter side, while leaving the former to mysterious sensory "qualia." Richard Rorty (1979), having come of age under Sellars' and Quine's tutelage, embraces this sort of dualism, and pronounces the notion of mind an arbitrary amalgam of sensation and intentionality, whose spurious sense of unity is to be blamed on (who else?) Descartes—whereupon the "Cartesian" sensory remnant is rhetorically bludgeoned into insignificance before being eliminated. Putnam (1981), though with more indifference than hostility towards sensations, perpetuates a similar dualism.

[6] Tye (1995, 2000) I would regard as illustrating the former attitude, Dennett (1991) the latter.

However, it is not inevitable to mix rejection of classical empiricist views about meaning and concepts with retention of a Humean view of consciousness as comprised of cognitively primitive sense experiences (of shape, color, flavor, etc.) and the images formed of them. Hume may have been wrong *both* in trying as he did to extract all thought and meaning from a meager, flattened-out experiential basis, and in viewing consciousness in narrowly sensory terms. And the fact that James, Husserl, and Moore would have agreed on this suggests such a stance does not depend on holding either eliminativist or reductionist attitudes toward consciousness (since they did not). Further, we should consider that the tendency to recognize there is more to *mental* life than sensory activity and imagery, but to reserve *consciousness* in some sense (flagged with "phenomenal") exclusively for what is merely sensory, comes as the relatively recent product of a certain intellectual history. And it's hardly clear that what *explains* that history provides *justification* for this picture. Did Ryle really show that the stream of consciousness is as meager as he makes it? If some now find something in the neighborhood of a Rylean view natural, that may only reflect their inheritance of an under-examined mindset dominated by theoretical agendas that emerged, mid-twentieth century, in philosophies steeped in a particular reception of British Empiricism, and driven by a certain strategy of militant anti-Cartesianism.

But if I am right about how the exclusivist's picture of consciousness can hold one captive, we should not expect to avoid it simply by prompting "intuitive" reactions to questions like: "Does *your* conceptual thought have phenomenal character?" If your intellectual upbringing primes you to expect any phenomenally conscious state to be highly similar to sensations or after-images, such general and direct appeals to introspection will only confirm exclusivism. On the other hand, if you are suspicious of this heritage, and your interpretation of "phenomenal consciousness" does *not* hinge on a close resemblance to its sensory paradigms, you may find James, Husserl, and Moore to have had a properly inclusive attitude, and see the dubious legacy of Ryle and Hume in shrunken conceptions of experience. For an inclusivist like me, the variations in sensory appearance that the exclusivist admits into phenomenal consciousness are but species of a broader genus of *ways of seeming*, including also its seeming to one as it does to *think* and *understand*—in a univocal, phenomenal sense of "seems."

My challenge, then, is to recreate an alternative to the maps that sustain exclusivism. Setting aside talk of "intrinsic, ineffable qualities" as obscure and prejudicial, I will explain what I mean by "phenomenal consciousness" so that this applies appropriately to sensory paradigms, though in doing so I neither preclude nor assume, but facilitate a recognition, of phenomenal thought—while holding at bay the tyrannizing anxieties and ambitions of mind–body metaphysics. As background to my efforts, I urge a reconsideration of—and a wary self-consciousness about—the historical situation from which our question arises. Nothing dictates that we see an exclusivist conception of consciousness as natural, sensibly cautious, or commonsensical. It is just a perspective that has only lately become entrenched in certain segments of philosophical culture, entitled to no default authority. We should approach it skeptically, and open our minds to understanding phenomenal consciousness in a way that does not tie it inextricably to the merely sensory, a way we may find as broadly inclusive as conceptions of consciousness in James, Husserl, and Moore, without ignoring developments since their day.

3 How to interpret "What it's like"

One development we must not ignore concerns the way in which the phrase invoked at the outset, "what it's like for someone," has gained prominence as a marker of *phenomenal* consciousness. In the past, I have not relied on this to introduce the notion of phenomenal consciousness, explaining it instead by means of paradigms (its looking somehow to someone), and contrast cases (blindsight).[7] But while that certainly does not rule out an inclusive view, some may take it to tie phenomenal consciousness to sensory exemplars so tightly that they cannot include thought within it. For this and other reasons, I want in this section to come to terms with the use of "what it's like" talk to convey a grasp of the notion of phenomenal consciousness.

To tell my story, I want to show how it emerges in response to a difficulty with Block's formulation, quoted earlier: "What makes a state phenomenally conscious is that there is something it's like to be in it." That formulation might be taken to imply that, if there is something it's like to be in a given type of state, then any instance of that type is guaranteed to be a phenomenally conscious state. But this seems dubious. Suppose that I tell you I ate a durian fruit. You may intelligibly respond, "Hmm, I've never eaten durian—*I wonder what it's like*." Similarly, you might say: "I wonder what it's like to weigh over a 1000 lbs." It seems there is something answering to such expressions of curiosity. There was indeed something it was like for me to eat durian. And there is something that it is like to weigh over 1000 lbs—something it's like *for* a 1000 lb-plus person. But if that's right, then it is problematic to say that the fact that there is something it is like for one to be in a given state makes it phenomenally conscious. For I don't think we should say that *eating a durian* and *weighing over 1000 lbs* are themselves phenomenally conscious states—in the way in which *tasting* a durian or *feeling like* one weighs over 1000 lbs are. Or rather, that should not be a result so cheaply won. On the face of it, Block's dictum seems to spread phenomenal consciousness around too readily.

Now you may say that there is something it's like for one to *eat* a durian, but only in *a different sense* from that in which there is something it's like to *taste* durian. And it's only this second sense that makes something a genuine phenomenally conscious state. That seems reasonable. But it remains unclear how the senses differ, and they do not seem *unrelated*. For there seems to be "something that it's like" to be in a type of state—something it's like for the one who is in it—in the sense *somehow* relevant to

---

[7] Siewert (1998).

phenomenal consciousness, if it is a type of state, about which it is sensible to express what we might call a *subjective curiosity*. By this I mean: a type of curiosity that can be satisfied only by occupying, either actually or imaginatively, the position of a subject of that state, that is, by "adopting the subject's point of view." For example: you wonder what it's like to *taste* durian, and the satisfaction of your curiosity seems to require that you either taste durian yourself, or somehow be able to imagine tasting durian. But the problem is, much the same could be said of *eating* durian. You wonder what it's like to eat durian, and the satisfaction of your curiosity seems to require you either eat some durian yourself, or can somehow imagine doing so. So again: the application of this idiom seems too unrestricted to elucidate phenomenal consciousness, and to be of much use in addressing controversies about it, where its *extent* is precisely what's at issue.

You may think a remedy is ready to hand. You might want to alter Block's dictum to something like this:

What makes a state phenomenally conscious is that it is a *mental* state, and there is something it's like to be in that state.

Thus, eating a durian is disqualified from being a phenomenally conscious state, because (intuitively) eating is not a *mental* state. But for several reasons this solution is unsatisfying. For brevity I will speak only of the reason most directly pertinent to the current issue, the controversy over phenomenal thought.

The suggested revision does not equip us to understand that controversy. For even those who say that phenomenal consciousness is ultimately a merely *sensory* matter can accept that there is something it is like for one to be in the mental state of engaging in evidently conceptual thought. They may say: "When I think about the financial crisis (say) *I hear myself speaking*—either out loud or in imagination—and *that* is sensory experience of a sort. And perhaps this is also accompanied by various other sorts of *sensory imagery*. And maybe this is coincident with certain bodily feelings, which I interpret as anxiety. Inasmuch as there is something it is like for me to be in this accompanying complex sensory state, there is something it is like for me to think about the financial crisis."

But inclusivists will not be content to say that conceptual thought is phenomenally conscious just insofar as *something else accompanies* it, and there is something *that* is like. For an inclusivist, conceptual thought does not merely borrow its "what it's likeness" from some concomitant state of mind, distinguishable from it in kind, any more than does sense-experience. So it is not enough to say that what makes a state phenomenally conscious is that it is a mental state, and there is something it's like to be in that state. That would fail to distinguish mental states whose "what it's likeness" is merely *derived from* those that *do not need to derive it* in the same way.

Now I think we *can* get our understanding of "what it's like" into decent shape, so as to use it to address the question of phenomenal thought. We can start by rendering this critical (derived/non-derived) contrast a little more precise with reference to the durian example. We may observe: if eating durian is something with respect to which we can correctly claim, and sensibly desire, knowledge of what it's like, this is only insofar as we tacitly assume this *comes with something else that confers that status*. I can know what it's like for me to eat durian, and you can wonder what that's like, just because, besides eating a durian, there is something distinguishable from that going on, something to which eating durian is not strictly essential, which I subjectively know and you are curious about—for example, something's *tasting* a certain way to me, or its consistency and texture *feeling* somehow to me, as I eat it.

The point can be generalized. Suppose you know what it's like to have some feature Φ, because you know what it's like to have certain *other* features to which Φ is inessential, and because certain *further* conditions obtain, which don't themselves require any additional knowledge of what it's like for one to have some feature. If you know what it's like to have Φ only in this way, you know what it's like *only derivatively*. And if there is no other way to know what it's like to have it, there is only derivatively something it's like for one to have it.

But what does it mean to say there's "something it's like for one" to have such features? This needn't be a primitive notion. We can say: there is something it's like for one to have Φ just when it is a feature suited for a certain kind of *subjective knowledge or curiosity*. That is to say, it is a feature of which one can either correctly *claim to have*, or sensibly *want to have* a knowledge *of what feature it is*, which requires one have or can imagine having that very feature.

Now this is *not* just to say it is the sort of feature whose *instances are introspectively knowable* by the person who has them. The "subjective knowledge" of features invoked is specifically a knowledge *of what features they are*—where this "what feature" knowledge is not just the same as knowledge *that a feature has this or that particular instance*. Let me illustrate. Suppose you say that some car has that "new car smell" (knowing well what it's like for something to smell that way). I, for my part, wonder *how that smells*. In this case, the knowledge that I *want* and that you *claim* is not simply the knowledge *that some car smells that way to you*. In some sense I already know that it smells that way to you. If there is a sense in which I *don't* know this, it is because there's a sense in which I'm still wanting a knowledge of *what that way of smelling is*. This missing knowledge is the sort of "what feature" knowledge that subjective curiosity longs to possess.

Now notice, this "what feature" knowledge also should not be equated simply with *introspectively* knowing that the feature has a particular instance. It is true that *by* introspectively knowing this—e.g. that some car smells that way *to me* (i.e. that way new cars smell)—I can know *what* way of smelling *that* is. But this introspective knowledge is then a *means* to satisfying one's desire for knowledge of *what feature this is*, a desire that one might seek to satisfy by other means: namely, by *imagining* having the feature (e.g. imagining tasting durian, or imagining the smell of a new car).

Note further that this sort of knowledge is not *theoretical* knowledge. It does not consist in the ability to *explain*, e.g. what that way of smelling to someone consists in. And note, finally, that this knowledge is not just an ability to respond to the presence of the feature. The sheer fact that a creature can respond to an itchy feeling (for instance) by (e.g.) scratching, is not enough for it to *know what that feeling is*. What one wants when one is curious about what it is to feel a certain way is not just the ability to respond somehow to that feeling. All this yields the following proposal:

There is something it's like for one to have a feature Φ, just when one can either correctly *claim to have*, or sensibly *want to have*, a certain sort of knowledge *of what feature Φ is*—i.e. a sort that is both:

- *non-theoretical* (i.e. it doesn't require one be able to explain what having Φ consists in), and
- *subjective* (i.e. it *does* require one have or be able to imagine having Φ).

There is non-derivatively something it's like for one to have Φ just when Φ is not suitable only for *derivative* subjective knowledge or curiosity of this kind. That is: it's not the case that one has this sort of subjective "what feature" knowledge of Φ, if and only if there are some *other* features to which Φ is inessential, of which one has such subjective knowledge (and additional conditions hold, which require no subjective "what feature" knowledge).

This gives us a grip on "what it's like" talk that will allow us to frame the issue of phenomenal thought. For now we can see this in terms of the question of whether there is non-derivatively something it's like to engage in conceptual thinking, something it's like that isn't entirely derivative from what it's like to have concomitant sensory features.

But we may now wonder: does this help us zero in a bit more on what a phenomenally conscious state is, and what phenomenal character is? And how should we connect our conception of this with the distinction between derivative and non-derivative "what it's like"? I would propose the following:

A state is phenomenally conscious just when it is an instance of a phenomenal feature.

A feature Φ is phenomenal, just when *necessarily*, there is non-derivatively something it's like for one to have Φ. That is: Φ is inherently or essentially suitable for non-derivative subjective knowledge or curiosity regarding what feature it is.

Instances of phenomenal features Φ and Ψ—phenomenally conscious states, i.e. experiences—*differ in phenomenal character* (and these *features* differ *phenomenally*), just when what it's like for one to have Φ differs from what it's like for one to have Ψ. That is to say: these features differ in a manner suitable for non-derivative subjective knowledge or curiosity. (E.g. what it's like for you to feel dizzy differs from what it's like for you to feel thirsty just in case these two (phenomenal) features differ in such a way that you can correctly claim to have, or sensibly want to have, a subjective, non-theoretical knowledge of what that manner of difference is, which is not derivative from other such knowledge.)

By this standard, I take it we can interpret various appearance words—"look," "smell," "taste," "feel," "sound,"—so as to count its looking, smelling, etc., various ways to people as phenomenal features. At the same time we can allow that there can be something it's like to have certain *other* features (and one may know or wonder what it's like to have them)—features such as eating durian, weighing over 1000 lbs, flying through the air, being near the epicenter of a massive earthquake—without just assuming illegitimately that these are themselves phenomenal features. For we may want to say that there is something it's like for one to have these features only *derivatively*, in virtue of *other* features that occur with them, of which one can have or desire subjective knowledge. Or: what it's like for one to have the first is entirely derived from what it's like for one to have the others. And this would disqualify the first set from being phenomenal features.

Further, on my account, we can allow that there may be features there is non-derivatively something it's like for one to have, which—because this status is not *essential* to them—still aren't bona-fide *phenomenal* features. This bears significantly on the present topic. Suppose we grant that some type of (conceptual) thinking can go on in either a phenomenally conscious form, or a non-phenomenal form. We might then say that *in some cases* there is something it's like for one to think in this sense, and in some cases not. But we might suppose that where there is, what it's like to think cannot be derived from what it's like to have some further feature, to which thinking is inessential. For we may suppose that, when there is something that it's like for us to think, *what* it's like is not entirely *derivative* from the merely sensory, and actually thinking is essential to this phenomenal character of thought. And yet, we may allow that thinking *in the generic sense* is not itself a phenomenal feature, because it can occur, even when there is nothing that it is like for it to occur.

In the present context, my interpretation of "what it's like" talk, and my associated conceptions of phenomenal consciousness and character display the following advantages. First, I make use of this "what it's like" talk widely held to be key to getting at phenomenal consciousness, but without simply relying on a brutely intuitive or ostensive grasp of this locution. Second, my interpretation of it allows me to count as "phenomenal" cases that *should* be so counted, if *any* should be, without illicitly assuming a verdict on more controversial cases. I leave open that (at least some) conceptual thought might be phenomenally *unconscious*, and, at the same time, that there might be (at least some) form of conceptual thought that is genuinely phenomenal. Third, the conception of phenomenality I deploy makes no assumptions about whether or not phenomenal character is "exhausted by" some proposed physicalist or functionalist characterization of its nature. This initial *neutrality* is surely desirable, when we set out to address the question of phenomenal thought. Finally, I think it counts in favor of my approach that it takes into account something we have seen is essential to framing that question adequately—namely, the difference between there being something it's like to be in a state *derivatively* and *non-derivatively*.

4 What the issue is

To apply the preceding conception to the issue at hand, we need to see a bit better where inclusivists and exclusivists can find common ground. We can agree that, not just generally, but on this or that *occasion*, we take or understand what we hear or read, say or write, in this way or that. That is, there is such a thing as *occurrent understanding*. To make this stand out: consider the difference between, on the one hand, reading some text (either to yourself or out loud) while attentive to its meaning, following what is being said, understanding it in a certain way, and, on the other, reading it *without* following it, without ongoing understanding, so that you need to restart at the beginning, concentrating on the meaning.[8] And if you can in this way either follow or fail to follow the meaning of your own *recitation*, you can occurrently understand your own *spontaneous* speech. (There's no reason to think that the *spontaneity of your speech* should destroy the *occurrentness of your understanding*.) And the occurrent understanding of speech can be said to be a way of thinking, in the sense that requires *conceptual* abilities, as glossed earlier. So, *occurrent understanding is a form of episodic conceptual thinking*. We may also point out: we are often engaged in episodic conceptual thought such as is involved in (for example) *trying to think of the answer* to a problem or in *supposing* that or *wondering* whether something is so, or in *doubting* that it is so, or in *considering reasons* for doubting it, or *concluding* it is so—whether or not such thought is audibly or visibly expressed. Finally, we can agree that ongoing differences in *the ways we think or understand* are subjectively discernible to us. Not only can we judge with warrant, in a distinctively first-person way, how things look, sound, feel, and smell to us, it is also subjectively discernible to us how we're thinking or understanding from one time to the next. (I intend here to leave quite open just *what* distinguishes this "first-person way.") All this we can accept without yet speaking explicitly of the phenomenal character of such thinking/understanding, or of what it's like for one to understand occurrently.

Against this background, we can see the issue of phenomenal thought as turning primarily on two questions. First there is what I'll call the question of *Reducibility*. Suppose there is only derivatively something it's like for us to think and understand as we do, because knowledge of what it's like is *entirely derivative from* knowledge of what it's like to possess concurrent, separable sensory features—i.e. ones whose possession at that time is insufficient to guarantee anything about our thinking and understanding as we then do. Then knowledge of what it's like to think and understand in the manner we do is *reducible to* this knowledge of separable sensory features. This is the thesis of Reducibility. If you say yes to Reducibility, you are exclusivist; if you are inclusivist, you say no.

Second, there is what I'll call the question of *Variation*. Do significantly many subjectively discernible differences in ways of thinking and understanding constitute

---

[8]   When I speak of an occurrent understanding of an utterance, of course I do not intend to imply that this is always a *correct* understanding of the utterance as meant by the speaker (or of its meaning in the language). I am just saying that the utterance is then *taken* in a certain way, *understood in a certain way*, whether or not this coincides with speaker or sentence meaning. As it would be too cumbersome to make this qualification explicit every time, I will often omit it, trusting the reader to supply it as needed.

differences in *what it is like for us* to have the experience we do? If you are exclusivist, you say no to Variation; if you say yes, you are inclusivist.

To affirm Variation is to deny Reducibility. Now you could coherently deny both Reducibility and Variation. And admittedly, I have left it undefined whether you would then be inclusive or exclusive. But it does not matter much to me how we extend my labels to such a position; what I am most interested in here is the sort of inclusivism captured by the combination of Irreducibility and Variation.

Framing the issues as I propose allows us to understand questions about the phenomenal character of thought as follows. If Reducibility is false, then the phenomenal character of one's occurrent thought and understanding is not "exhausted by"—there is "more to it than"—the phenomenal character of sensory experience separable from it. And since there is (non-derivatively) something it's like to *think and understand*, there is *inherently* something it's like for one. Then there is, let us say, some *cognitive* phenomenal feature. And if Variation is true, then there are significantly *many* phenomenally differing cognitive phenomenal features. In that case, the phenomenal character of cognition, of conceptual thinking, is *rich*. Questions will then arise about just how this relates to *what* is understood or thought—questions about *content*. I will come to these. But right now let's focus on the questions of Reducibility and Variation.

Seeing the issue of "inclusion" in these terms allows us to avoid certain prejudicial ways of framing it. Occurrent conceptual thought is typically (maybe sometimes even necessarily) *unified* with either sensory or imagery experience. Occurrent differences in ways of thinking are often, in some sense, *intimately bound to* experienced differences in verbal expression, whether silently imaged or publically perceptible. As I *think* differently, I *speak* differently—and I experience this speech. But someone might suppose that to confirm inclusivism, we need to find, *alongside* both our sense experience of speech and verbal imagery, *and* hitherto subjectively discerned differences in ways of thinking/understanding expressed in it, something *additional*, which one may also always find humming along all on its own, utterly disentangled from utterances sensed or imaged, and phenomenally just the same whether or not it "accompanies" experienced or imaged speech. Perhaps one will imagine that we need to find sensory and cognitive phenomenal features occurring as distinctly and autonomously as, say, visual and auditory appearances do, if there really are cognitive phenomenal features to be discerned.

But these would be false assumptions. For we can now see that the inclusivist does *not* require that, *in addition* to the ongoing differences in ways of thinking and understanding that you already discriminate in first-person reflection, there is a phenomenal *something more* we should look for. Rather what you're asked to consider is that some such reflectively recognizable variations in one's manner of thought and understanding *are themselves phenomenal differences*, whether or not you think of them *as such*. Furthermore, it forms no essential part of the inclusivist picture to suppose that words are merely the "clothing of thought," needed for public appearances, which might just as well be shed in the mind's privacy, where phenomenal cognition can nakedly frolic. No, as far as the inclusivist is concerned, it may very well be that *thought needs talk*, in various ways. To approach the issue fairly, all this needs to be clear.

5 A case for being inclusive

Now I will give three distinct though closely related arguments for being inclusive. I do not think such matters should be decided in a single blow. We should consider a variety of relevant issues from a number of angles. Indeed, I think further arguments for inclusiveness need to be examined beyond those I will express here. However, for reasons of length I will confine myself to these three—linked by their common focus on the *experience of understanding language*.

Let me first say something about the burden of proof. Struck by the broader agreement that at least sensory appearances and imagery count as phenomenal, one may be tempted to think the burden rests on those who also somehow include conceptual thinking. And (one might think) if this burden is not met, we should default to exclusivism. I would disagree. First, generally: the mere fact that group A is inclined to extend a classification more generously than group B does not, by itself, show that A owes us more of an argument or is on shakier ground than B. (Maybe group B is unreasonably *stingy*.) Second, more specifically to the case at hand: a hesitation to be inclusive does not necessarily reflect higher epistemic standards. It may, for example, come from assuming (mistakenly, as we now see) that we can apply the notion of phenomenality only in virtue of close similarity to sensory paradigms.[9] Or one may decide the matter based on misconceived, misleading, or gratuitous tests— such as whether one is inclined to say there is a "qualitative feel" to belief,[10] or whether, beyond the subjectively discernible variations in how one understands one's words, one can detect, alongside this, some further, phenomenal "extra."[11] Or one may mistakenly think inclusivism assumes that our conceptual thinking can or does have no need at all of verbal expression.[12] Or that it requires we have a certain view about *concepts*—that they are introspectible objects, rather than abilities.[13] Or (relatedly) one may take an inclusive view to hold that we have some appearance-like "acquaintance" with the *contents* of our conceptual thoughts, that these are thus "presented" to us, yielding a "cognitive phenomenology" that is "pure" of any sensory presentation.[14] However, we can now see that the version of inclusivism I ask us to consider assumes *none* of this, and is not threatened by their doubtfulness, though it has been assumed otherwise. There is this additional reason why the occurrence of cognitive phenomenal

---

[9] Georgalis (2003).
[10] Nichols and Stich (2003: 198).
[11] See Robinson (2005: 253): ". . . a further phenomenological something."
[12] Jackendoff (1987: 289–91). (I respond to Jackendoff's arguments here in Siewert (1998: 361–2).)
[13] Putnam (1981: 17, 20–1). Note: the inclusivist view is fully compatible with the idea that to have a concept is to have an *ability*.
[14] See Levine, this volume.

features is more controversial than the occurrence of merely sensory ones. For if we admit that there is something it's like to have sensory features, the idea that there might only *derivatively* be something it's like to have them can get no traction. For whether these be "merely" sensory features, or "conceptually loaded" ones, they will pretty clearly sometimes occur in the absence of any *candidates to consider* as that from which their "what it's likeness" can be derived or "borrowed." By contrast, in the case of what it's like to think and understand, it's not clear that we're ever lacking such candidates—namely, concomitant sensory features.

The overall point here is: all the just mentioned factors might explain the greater ease with which the phenomenality of sense experience is admitted. But they do not *justify* exclusivism. And if occurrent thought and understanding *should* be segregated from phenomenal character, that is not a result we get by default. With this in mind, I would like you to consider some arguments for being inclusive.

5.1 Argument (i): The elusive duplicate

Here is a passage from Thomas Jefferson:

Every difference of opinion is not a difference of principle. We have called by different names brethren of the same principle. We are all Republicans, we are all Federalists. If there be any among us who would wish to dissolve this Union or to change its republican form, let them stand undisturbed as monuments of the safety with which error of opinion may be tolerated where reason is left free to combat it.

Reading this in the midst of an article, and with a contemporary reader's diet of flat contemporary prose, one might well not quite follow at first what Jefferson is saying in the last sentence, and find one needs to come at it again with more attention to its meaning before one gets it. (I confess I had to re-read it when I came across it.) If this example does not work for you, others should be easy to encounter, especially if you read philosophy—or if you just crack open your Shakespeare.

In such cases we find the sort of contrasts earlier introduced—contrasts between reading *while following what one is reading* (understanding it to mean something as one is reading it), and reading *without following the meaning* (or only partly "getting it") because one is not concentrating adequately. Now ask yourself: is what it's like for you to read a passage without understanding it different from what it's like to then re-read the same passage and understand it in a certain way? I will assume you can answer this question affirmatively, on the interpretation of "what it's like" talk earlier explained. You can correctly claim to have (and someone could sensibly want to have) a subjective, non-theoretical knowledge of what the manner of difference in question is, non-derivative from other such knowledge. The question will be whether *that* difference is a difference in separable *sensory features*—whether what it's like for you to read with understanding is reducible to what it's like to have some concurrent merely sensory features that could occur in the absence of understanding.

What it's like to understand should not be conceived of merely negatively. The phenomenal difference with which we're concerned does not consist entirely in the fact that one *lacks* in the understanding case some *feeling of confusion* one has in the uncomprehending case, so that what it's like to read comprehendingly is just what it's like to read *without* following the meaning—except in the semantically deficient case, there's *phenomenally* an addition: a certain feeling. The experience of re-reading a passage, this time with understanding—the experience of "getting it"—is a *positive phenomenon*; it is not just the experience of saying words to yourself without simultaneously feeling confused or frustrated.[15]

If this is not already obvious, consider a bit more closely what we might mean by speaking here of "feelings of confusion." First, if such feelings are supposed to be *merely sensory* experiences of some sort (perhaps the feeling of knitting one's brow, or perhaps something similar to somatic flutterings of anxiety), they do not *invariably* or even *usually* coincide with the experience of not following what one is reading. Often I'm reading along and I simply realize that I didn't get what I just read, and ceased to follow the meaning, and so am prompted to re-read it—but without having experienced any discernible sensory disturbance. Even so, what it's like to have the experience of not "getting it" is different from what it is like to get the meaning, when I do, upon re-reading. Now if *this* sort of "not getting it" experience counts as a "feeling of confusion," then it includes some sudden (generally unverbalized) *realization* that you didn't understand what you just read. And if you admit this, then you admit there is something it's like to be struck by a thought, where no sensory reduction is to be had. (A willingness to call such realization a "feeling" in no way shows its merely sensory status.) But, if one admits this, then it would be arbitrary to exclude from phenomenal consciousness the way one understands the sentence when one *does* get it, so as to maintain a purely negative view of what it's like to understand.

But suppose you don't admit that you know what it's like for it to occur to you that you didn't get what you just read in such circumstances. Still, you shouldn't maintain the purely negative view. For notice that when understanding a passage requires intense concentration, one can read it while *refraining from any such effort*, and thereby experience a lack of comprehension. But in such cases, one doesn't in any sense *feel confused or frustrated* (nor, for that matter does one always concomitantly experience some distinctive somatic sensation). The experience of "not following" when one *refrains from even trying* is not an experience of *confusion or frustration* (which presupposes some effort or interest in comprehension). But still, what it's like to read without following the meaning differs from what it's like to read while following the meaning. And where there is no *feeling of confusion* involved in the former (nor any supposedly

---

[15]   This is partly in response to Robinson (2005). He suggests, in effect, that we sometimes should reduce the phenomenal character of understanding to the absence of a "feeling of frustration"—though he also adds a positive element: a "feeling of relief" when the frustration goes away. In this connection, see also Pitt's (2004) remarks about the experience of "bewilderment," which my points here are meant to supplement.

special somatic feeling), and what it's like not to understand is held to involve no concurrent *realization that one isn't following*, then no *positive* experience of incomprehension remains, about which we can propose: "there's nothing more to what it's like for me to understand, beyond the absence of *that*." On the contrary, what it's like to read *without* understanding will need to be seen in terms of the absence of what it's like to read *with understanding*.

Let's now return to the question of Reducibility, approaching this via the case of durian. It is plausible that what it's like to eat durian derives entirely from what it's like to have other features, having to do with the way durian tastes and smells, and how it feels in one's mouth. This is because it seems to us that actual durian eating could be absent, though *what that was like would remain the same* (because the right taste, smell, and feel were still there). This could happen if we ate cleverly engineered *fake* durian, or (perhaps) if we vividly *hallucinated* or *dreamed* we had a meal of durian. But suppose this weren't the case. Suppose there were just no conceivable way that, in the absence of eating durian, what it's like for one to have what remained would be just the same as what it's like for one to eat durian. Then what it's like to eat durian would *not* be entirely derivative from what something else was like. For there wouldn't *be* a "something else" that preserved what this was like for one, whose presence could serve to endow durian eating with its phenomenal character.

Apply this to the case of thought and understanding. It is not now disputed that there is positively something it's like for one to think and to understand what one is saying, hearing, or reading as this happens—any more than it's disputed there is positively something it's like to eat durian. What's disputed is whether this derives entirely from what it's like to have concomitant, separable sensory features, as Reducibility requires. If it does, then in every case we should be able to find some sensory features that exactly duplicate what it's like for us to read comprehendingly, but in the absence of any way of understanding what is read, much as we could duplicate what it's like to eat durian without actually eating genuine durian.

Can you find such features? You could try, by comparing *actual* cases where you read a given text without comprehension and then you re-read it *with* understanding. But this won't support Reducibility, unless you sincerely judge that what two such actual experiences of that text are like for you is just the same. And I doubt you will find this. I think you will admit that in actual cases, when you read a passage you do not understand or follow, what this is like for you differs from what it is like to read it again, this time following it, understanding it. Since comparisons of *actual* experiences of reading do not support the judgments of phenomenal sameness needed to warrant Reducibility, for this you need to conceive of a *hypothetical* case, constructed by first isolating some sensory features present in the case where you understood, and then *subtracting in imagination your occurrent understanding of what's written*. And once you do that, then it needs to be clear to you that what it would be like for you to have this *hypothetical experience of uncomprehended text* would be just the same as what it is like for you to have your *actual experience with understanding*. Then you could reason: since what it's like would be just the same if you simply duplicated the appropriate sensory concomitants, the fact that there is something it's like to understand is derived entirely from its association with these.

But by appeal to what separable sensory features could we hope to construct in thought *totally semantically clueless* phenomenal duplicates of our actual comprehending selves? These sensory features would need to differ from those found in the actual cases of reading without comprehension, where what it's like for one to read admittedly differs from what it's like to read the same text comprehendingly. But they must be only *subtly* different, for they would also need to be found in the ordinary case of reading that very same text *with* understanding.

Will they perhaps involve some *sensory imagery*? But what would this be—perhaps: my aurally imagining (saying "to myself") the words I'm reading? That suggestion won't work for those who say they don't utter words to themselves when they read silently. But while I'm *not* such a person, and do say the words to myself, I also do this when I don't follow what I'm reading. Is the separable sensory element then perhaps *extra-verbal* imagery that supposedly always coincides with what it's like to read with understanding? But when I don't understand what I read, and then go on to a second, more successful try, I do not find this does always (or really, even usually) coincide with the sudden upswell of imagined shapes, smells, colors, or noises. (And even if it just happens to do so, I don't get the requisite sameness judgments, if I try to imagine an analogue of myself, whose uncomprehending mind is filled with sensory, extra-verbal images stripped of all relevant conceptual interpretation, when the passage is re-read.)

Does reading with understanding perhaps then always involve an enhanced appearance of the details of shape and position of the letters or words? But equally detailed experience of shape and position will readily be found in a *phenomenally different* case without understanding. (The words of Jefferson's text and their placement on the page appeared to me quite clearly when I didn't follow the meaning.)

Is there then perhaps some distinctive way of experientially *grouping* the words, with a certain rhythm, or saying them to yourself with a certain intonation, which is notable in the actual experience of reading comprehendingly, but could also be found in reading without understanding, such that when I imagine what *that* would be like for me, I find it to be just the same as what the first, actual case is like for me? I find I can, in actuality, read along, quite *fluidly grouping words as a competent speaker/reader of the language*, without just then *following the meaning* of the text—and what *that* is like for me is, again, *different* from what it's like when I re-read it, this time following the meaning. (This is especially clear where I'm reading text in a foreign language, in which my competence is *minimal*—when it is all too easy for me to read along fluidly with little or no understanding.) And while re-reading a passage with comprehension may sometimes involve saying the words to oneself with a certain emphasis or intonation, I can also do this without understanding, and often enough I re-read such passages without any such exaggerated stress when understanding them. The upshot is, when I try to imagine reading a text as *fluidly* as I do with understanding, but now *without understanding* it, it does *not* seem to me that what this would be like for me is just the same. For again, what I am asked to imagine is not clearly discernibly different from actual cases of reading without understanding—where what *that's* like is *not* phenomenally the same as reading with comprehension.

Perhaps I should consider: one can experience what one reads as *syntactically well formed* in a certain manner—as grammatically "parsed"—even if one doesn't understand it. Would that give us the desired segregation of conceptual activity from phenomenal character? The suggestion would be this: "Take the sentence you experience with ongoing understanding, and in imagination subtract any occurrent understanding of what it means, leaving only a grasp of grammar. Now do you judge that what *that* would be like for you is just the same as what it is like for you to read the same passage comprehendingly?"

What I am here asked to imagine as hypothetical is again something I already *approximate* in actual experience—because sometimes when I read along without (entirely) following the meaning, this does not (as near as I can tell) involve any snag in getting the mere *syntax* of the passage. I am reading a text aloud, and suddenly it occurs to me I haven't been following; still I recognized the sentences as well formed. But when I re-read with understanding, again, *what that is like for me is different.* (And surely it wouldn't change things—I wouldn't get a judgment of phenomenal *sameness*—if somehow I managed to imagine away every *trace* of semantic understanding from the case in question.)

Perhaps I should try to make the comparison where there is, on neither side, a deficit in attention to the meaning of the text. Maybe I should consider actual cases where I experience a sentence as well formed grammatically, but do not understand it as I read it, though not through lack of semantic attention—because in this instance I simply have *no understanding of many of the terms involved.* Then by analogy with this I could try to construct a relevant hypothetical case. A familiar example to work with would be the opening of Lewis Carroll's "Jabberwocky": "Twas brillig, and the slithy toves/ Did gyre and gimble in the wabe;/ All mimsy were the borogroves,/ And the mome raths outgrabe." So the hypothetical I am being asked to imagine is that what I actually read with understanding becomes for me "Jabberized"—I experience it *merely phonologically and syntactically*, as I at least *come close* to doing with the opening lines of Carroll's poem.

But to the extent I can imagine what that would be like, I certainly do *not* get a clear judgment of phenomenal sameness. If anything, I imagine experiencing a disturbing alienation from the meaning of what I speak and hear. And this takes on a nightmarish quality, as I realize that the exclusivist view implies that if my reading were to become *routinely* Jabberized, *what that would be like for me would be the same as my actual experience of reading.* And that doesn't seem right at all. Of course, it is fun to read a poem like "Jabberwocky." But the thought of what it would be like for my experience of reading *generally* to become Jabberwocky-like is horrifying. Or I might at least say: all reading would become horrifically *boring*—even if it were still accompanied by imagining lots of uninterpreted shapes and sounds.[16] In any case, I find again I cannot carry out the relevant hypothetical construction in a way that secures the judgments of phenomenal sameness required for Reducibility. Are you are confident you *can* do this?

We must not hastily conclude that we have done this, based on a tendentious or cursory consideration (as, for example, in Putnam 1981). And we must take care not to confuse conceiving of a case where understanding is defective or partial, with conceiving of a case where understanding is *totally absent*.[17] The issue here is certainly *not* whether we might or do sometimes "feel like we understand" something better than we do. The issue is: do we find, once we contrast the experiences of reading with and without understanding, that we can construct a hypothetical case of reading, utterly devoid of understanding, which yields the right judgments of phenomenal sameness? If not, then we should reject the Reducibility thesis.

But if this is rejected, can't we still reasonably deny Variation? One may propose that the additional aspect of what it is like to think and understand is *not* constituted by the subjectively discernible ongoing variation in our manner of thinking and understanding, but by something else. However, we should accept this proposal, only if there is some other reasonable candidate for this something else. *Is* there? One might suggest: here there is, not a separable *sensory* experience, but a *non-sensory* experience of understanding—a perhaps more or less homogeneous "understanding-feel"—separable from the varying ways of understanding one's words as one speaks. And that non-sensory "understanding feel" exhausts the more-than-sensory aspect of phenomenal character found in the cases under discussion.[18]

But is it really clear to you that there is, subjectively distinguishable both from your occurrently understanding a phrase *in a certain way* as you read it, and from the *experience of words* comprising it, always *something else* that occurs, and that this additional component, together with some separable sensory one, exhausts what it's like to read comprehendingly? Suppose that is *not* clear to you. Then at least: there clearly *are* occurrent variations in ways of thinking and understanding. And since that is all that clearly *remains* to serve as the aspect of what it is like for you to read comprehendingly that isn't exhausted by separable sensory features, you should just default to view that this does constitute part of the phenomenal character of experience.

[16] Galen Strawson has suggested in conversation that something like this point could be converted into an argument of its own: we can see that understanding is included in phenomenal character, because otherwise reading would be intolerably boring.

[17] Putnam (1981) invites us to imagine being hypnotized into having a "feeling of understanding" as we utter words in a language we don't in fact understand at all. But this approach to the challenge is flawed in several ways, as I argue in Siewert (1998: 293–6), where I also discuss the importance here of the distinction between partial understanding and total incomprehension.

[18] Somewhat similarly, Robinson (2005) confines the phenomenal character of understanding to a generic "feeling of familiarity." But "familiarity" won't do here, since you can cease or fail to follow the meaning of a passage whose words nonetheless are quite familiar to you. And then when you do understand, the phenomenal difference does not involve a sudden injection of some hitherto absent sense of familiarity.

Maybe you are tempted to endorse this idea of a separate, non-sensory "understand-ing-feel." Then consider again what it's like for you to read a particular passage comprehendingly. Now suppose what it was like for you to read it then were just what it was like for you to read *without* understanding. In that case, wouldn't you *think* you were *not* understanding what you were reading? And so you would *not know* what you were understanding what you were reading to say? This seems right. For other-wise, why are you prompted to *re-read* the passage, when what it's like for you is what it's like to read without following what's being said?

But consider: if how you varyingly understood what you were reading lay strictly outside of what it was like for you to read, this would seem unintelligible. For first: in that case, in order to know how you are understanding what you are reading, you'd need to know *much more* than what it's like for you to read comprehendingly on that occasion. (Especially, if we're assuming the "understanding feel" is uniform: for that at most could yield the mere knowledge you are *understanding something somehow*.) But now, anything additional, which you would need to know and which would be available for you to know—about how you understand a given phrase—would *already be enough to do the job by itself*. For what is available for you to know is what specifically you are taking utterance "u" to mean. But if you already know *that*, you already know you are understanding "u." There is no gap in your semantic knowledge that would need to be filled by *also* knowing you were having some accompanying phenomenal tinnitus-like "buzz of understanding." That would tell you nothing you didn't already otherwise know; it would just be *epistemically superfluous*. But we granted earlier that knowing what it was like was not epistemically superfluous. For we said we wouldn't know we were reading with understanding in a given case, if what it was like for us to read then were no different than what it is like for us to read without comprehension: we'd think we didn't understand.

By contrast, phenomenal character *can* be relevant to knowing how one is under-standing utterances, provided we admit that one's way of understanding is inseparable from what it's like for one to read with understanding. For, in that case, in the absence of phenomenal character, one wouldn't know how one was understanding what one was reading, for this reason: the manner of occurrent understanding itself would then be absent.

Argument (i) can now be summed up like this. What it's like to read a passage *with* understanding positively differs from what it's like to read the same passage *without* understanding. This difference will be reducible to a merely sensory phenomenal difference, only if we can isolate separable sensory features in each such case of understanding, and imagine having them in a hypothetical case *without* understanding, in which we find what that would be like is *just the same*. But efforts to identify these separable sensory features and secure the relevant judgment of phenomenal sameness do not pan out. So *Reducibility is rejected*. The acceptance of Variation will follow, if we can subjectively discern no good candidate to serve as the occurrent additional aspect to phenomenal character, other than variable ways of understanding. Some might suggest there is, separable from this, an "understanding experience" that serves as the sole locus of phenomenality. But it's hardly clear that such a separate experience *is* subjectively discernible, whenever there is something it's like to read comprehendingly. And if we insisted on confining phenomenal character to some such factor, we would render unaccountable the fact that we take ourselves not to understand what we are reading, when what it is like for us to read is what it is like to read uncomprehendingly. Thus *Variation.*

5.2 Argument (ii): Delayed understanding

Now consider this sort of case. I meet a friend, and she asks me, "Did you bring the book?" For a moment I am at a loss as to what book she's talking about—and then I realize in an instant what book it is. (It is: *A Supposedly Fun Thing I'll Never Do Again*, by David Foster Wallace, which I had said I would lend to her.) But I didn't *say* the title, even to myself, even partially, in the moment of realization, nor did I visualize the cover of the book. Though I needn't, I *might* have said, a moment after realizing what she meant, "Oh, *that* book." But that comes after the fact. Now I know what it's like for me to realize suddenly what was meant on such occasions. So there *is* something it's like. And this is not merely what it's like for a separable sensory "confusion experience" to *go away*. For even if we construe the experience of being momentarily "at a loss" in terms of some such sensation, once it dissipates I might be struck by no positive realization, and what *that's* like for me differs from what it's like to *have* the realization. But now: there's also no separable sensory feature I have, concurrent with the realization, of which I have subjective knowledge that might reasonably serve as a candidate from which to derive the knowledge of what it is like to realize what was meant. Thus, there is a change in phenomenal character, but no relevant coincident change in sensory features separable from the advent of understanding. And so Reducibility is rejected.

This argument cannot be evaded by saying: "What it's like here is merely what it's like to experience the *onset of a disposition* to make and experience certain *sounds* in response to *others*". (For instance, to someone's 'What book?' I am disposed to utter, '*A Supposedly Fun Thing*, etc.') But what sounds I am disposed to utter depends on what I would take them to *mean*. Without that link to understanding, I would lack such phonetic dispositions. And so what it's like to understand here would not in this manner be confined to sensory features, severed from understanding.

This sort of case differs from that in argument (i). Here my realization of what was meant did not come through some sort of repetition (e.g. re-reading) with greater attention to the meaning (as in the Jefferson example). Notice too that here, something like the earlier "parsing" suggestion for how we are to construe the phenomenal character does not even get a foothold. One cannot suggest that the phenomenal difference between not getting what was meant and getting it is limited to some purely syntactical grasp, peeled away from one's semantic understanding—for there is just no new grammatical grasp to get.

However, the same basic argument could be reformulated in cases where the delayed understanding does occur after reiteration of the sentence, and there are "parsing" problems—the sort of examples Pitt (2004) and Horgan and Tienson (2002) use to support inclusivism—of "machine gun" and "garden path" sentences. (An example of the former (in Horgan and Tienson): "Dogs dogs dog dog dogs." An illustration of the latter (in Pitt): 'The boy the man the girl saw chased fled.") Here one usually does need re-readings or re-hearings before one can make sense of these sentences (and there is something that it's like for one to do so). The experience is something akin to recognizing a visible pattern or form to which one had been oblivious. But these are not just cases of sensory figure/ground organization. Nor is it merely a matter of experiencing a certain rhythm or pattern of stress or intonation. For while saying the sentences with a certain rhythm, stress, or intonation can *help* one to recognize the meaning, one can also say or hear them in that way and still not "get it." But then when one *does* get it, there is a difference in what that is like. And that is not just the departure of some positive, separable sensory, "confusion feeling," which anyhow is not present in every case (if indeed it ever occurs at all). Further, if someone should here raise the suggestion that the phenomenal difference noted is in some sense *merely* syntactical, the response would partly parallel what I said in connection with argument (i). That proposal implies that if our grasp of what we read were to become "Jabberized," what it's like for us to read it would be just the same. But that is not a consequence we should find acceptable.

Another point to bear in mind: the fact that one can or does *sometimes* image something relevant at the time of understanding (the book cover, the face of David Foster Wallace, a bunch of dogs) should not detain us. What's crucial is simply that *sometimes* this sort of delayed understanding occurs *without* the advent of such imagery (just as *undelayed* understanding does). And yet I know what it's like for this understanding to occur, even at such time as no reasonable candidate for a reduction of what it's like to a detachable sensory element presents itself. (Note: beware here of what we might call "the Hume effect."[19] Once you *ask yourself* if you imagined dogs, you find yourself *now* imagining a bunch of dogs. And you take this to show that you *were* imagining dogs before. This kind of slip should not prevent us from recognizing that, often enough, there is a phenomenal difference between (first) not understanding what's meant by an utterance and (then) understanding it in a certain manner, even though *at that time* no image pops up in one's mind.)

At this juncture similar issues arise as before about the move from rejecting Reducibility to accepting Variation, and similar arguments are available. Will someone say that what it is like to "get it" is phenomenally just the same regardless of what is "got"

---

[19] You ask yourself whether you form an image of a horse when you speak and think of a horse, and by so asking *prompt yourself to picture a horse*—forgetting that commonly enough when you speak or hear of horses you don't *then* visualize any horses. I call this the Hume effect because I think it accounts for the appeal a Humean image theory of meaning can have to those coming to it (and the issues) initially.

(or even, perhaps, whether *anything* is got)? I myself do not discern any experience meeting that description, always occurring in addition to the *specific way of understanding* I take myself to have on this or that occasion. In the moment when I realize what book she meant, it is not as though I am aware of two distinct things: (a) my occurrently understanding her to mean a specific book by "the book," and (b) a (more-than-sensory) "feeling" of understanding her to mean *something* by "the book." And if I were to insist otherwise, and confine phenomenal character to (b), then I would have the epistemic problem again. Consider: I wouldn't have known what book I took her to mean, had there been nothing it was like for me to realize she meant *A Supposedly Fun Thing I'll Never Do Again*. That is, if what it was like for me at that moment were no different from what it would have been like for me to be just then *utterly devoid of thought*, I wouldn't have believed I was getting what she meant at all. But this seems unaccountable, on the hypothesis that what it was like for me would have been just the same regardless of what I thought she meant. For then the most the presence of that phenomenal character could get me would be knowledge that *I am understanding her to mean something or other by that phrase*. But what more is subjectively discernible that I would need to know to get more specific knowledge, or to confirm the accuracy of the "understanding signal"? It is simply: the specific way I took her to mean the phrase. But this additional thing would be enough *on its own* to do the job of giving me knowledge that I understood her to mean something by her utterance, without the need of any separate "phenomenal indicator." By contrast, if the way I understand what she's talking about is itself *part of* what it's like for me to understand it, the relevance of the latter to knowledge of the former is restored.

Argument (ii) comes to this. Sometimes there is a delay in one's understanding a given utterance, and when one does understand, no relevant, coincident, separable sensory change occurs. If you know what it is like for you to experience such a delayed understanding, then there is something it's like to understand occurrently, even when there is no sensory feature detachable from understanding to which that is reducible. Moreover, the specific way one understands on such occasions will be a phenomenal feature, and different ways of understanding will differ phenomenally, unless phenomenal character can be confined to some "understanding experience" that remains invariant regardless of what is understood. But the claim that there always occurs, at the relevant time, some such distinct, subjectively discernible experience, separable from one's specific way of occurrently understanding, not only is highly dubious in itself, but renders unaccountable how the phenomenal character of understanding could matter to one's knowledge that one understood what was said in a certain way. Finally, once *some* subjectively discernible differences in ways of occurrently understanding are admitted into the phenomenal realm, it would be arbitrary not to make the admission *general*. It would be absurd to suppose that having been *delayed* is essential to making different ways of understanding phenomenally different. Variation then ensues.

5.3 Argument (iii): Interpretive switch

My last argument concerns cases—not where you go from *not understanding* a phrase to *understanding* it, but—where you switch from understanding it in *one* way to understanding it in *another*. So, consider this conversation overheard, on a sweltering day in Miami.

A says: "I am *so hot*."
B responds: "Well, okay, but you don't have to brag about it."

Many punning attempts at humor illustrate this experience of alternatively resolved ambiguity—where getting the joke involves some sudden interpretive switch. Of course, efforts at humor need not be involved. You may hear someone say, "I think I've got a virus," and switch from thinking he says he's coming down with something to taking him to mean *his computer* has a problem—or vice versa. The question is, in these cases, do you know what it's like to switch from one interpretation to the other? If so, then is there always some difference in how the words sound or look to you, or some difference in accompanying imagery or bodily feel, which you can conceive of independently of the difference in meaning or interpretation involved, and to which you might reduce the phenomenal difference in question? If not, then again, we have phenomenal differences involved with conceptual understanding that can't be segregated to some separable sensory features.

Again, here we may consider the potential gap between denying Reducibility and affirming Variation. Maybe someone will say that in these cases there is just a homogeneous (though admittedly non-sensory) "switch" experience—but no phenomenal difference between understanding "hot" or "virus" in one way, and understanding them in another. Again, I myself find in my experience no separately distinguishable phenomenal "switch" indicator, apart from the very change between interpretations itself. And there is a problem with such a suggestion in any case. If that were true, then there would be no difference in what it is like to switch in one direction rather than another. For example, what it is like first to understand "virus" as *biological infection*, then as *computer problem*, would be exactly what it is like first to take it to mean *computer problem*, then *biological infection*. But I can tell the difference between what it's like to resolve these ambiguities in one order rather than another. So the premise is mistaken.

If you balk at that, then consider again the epistemic issue. Had it not been like what it actually *was* like for me to switch interpretations, had my experience not had that phenomenal character, I would not have thought the switches (e.g. from biological to computer virus, from temperature-hot to sexy-hot) occurred—and I wouldn't have known they did. But if all that were going on *phenomenally* here was some uniform non-sensory "Switch!" experience, the most I would get from this was that *some switch or other* is going on. What *more* is there then available for me to know that I would need to add to get knowledge of *what switch it was*? There seems to be nothing available to appeal to here but the *varying occurrent understanding itself*. But that would leave *what it's like* to switch interpretations epistemically otiose. But it isn't. Best then to include phenomenal character in the varying ways of understanding comprising the switch. But if we include *these* ways of understanding, then it would be arbitrary to exclude others. It would be absurd to suppose an occurrent way of understanding is phenomenal only if it's involved in a "switch." And now we've gone all the way, from rejecting Reducibility to accepting Variation.

6 Phenomenal variation and thought content

Suppose, in response to my arguments, one says,

"I grant that there are *phenomenal* differences that occur as we think and understand that are not reducible to *sensory* differences. And I grant that some more-than-sensory differences in the ways we think and understand occurrently involve *conceptual capacities*. But I deny *that the two classes of difference overlap*. For the former (phenomenal) differences are not, even in part, differences in *what* one thinks or in *what* one understands an utterance to mean—they never constitute differences in *thought-content*."

This would be to try to open a gap between differences in how we think and understand, recognized as phenomenal, and any difference in the *content*, and by doing so, to open a gap between the phenomenal character of thought and thought itself. The suggestion is: while *something* more than sensory is included in the phenomenal, my inclusivism mistakenly identifies this with differences in ways of thinking and understanding essentially tied to conceptual activity, defined in terms of a grasp of semantics, of thought content.

But I think this proposed gap is not real. For I still do not find subjectively discernible differences available, identifiable with the phenomenal differences that occur as we think and understand, but distinguishable from differences in ways of thinking and understanding, where these are characterized in a manner essentially tied to conceptual capacities—and thus to differences in what is thought/understood (differences in content). *For I have no satisfactory way to identify these phenomenal differences without speaking in ways that imply there is something thought or understood.* When I think of what, specifically, it was like for me to understand the passage from Jefferson, I have no recourse but to speak of *what I understood it to mean*, repeating the very words I read, or others I take to mean the same. When I think of what it was like for me to realize what book my friend meant, I speak in those very terms—of what it was like for me to realize *what I understood her to mean*. When I conceive of the phenomenal character of my interpretive switch, I speak of what it was like for me to switch from understanding "hot" to mean *high in temperature* to *sexy*, i.e. in terms of a difference in *what I understood* the expression to mean. What I don't seem to have then, is a grasp of these specific phenomenal differences in terms that allow me to detach them entirely from genuine thought or understanding, or to attach them will-nilly to quite different ways of thinking/understanding.

Here one might object: even where there are no sensed or imaged differences in familiar natural language utterances to which I can reduce phenomenal differences in ways of understanding, still there are perhaps hidden, coinciding differences in *brain language* "utterances"—the tokens of the "language of thought," which are typed purely syntactically, independently of any thought-content they might express or encode. And perhaps then I can think of the phenomenal differences in "ways of understanding" I've been discussing "contentlessly" as nothing but covert differences in brain writing.[20]

But first, even granting this notion of correlated "brain writing," I still don't know how to think of *which* neural inscriptions I am allegedly discerning in given cases, if not (for example) as: *the brain writing that coincides with what it's like for me to take "hot" to mean sexy*. So I actually still *haven't* been given what is wanted here: a manner of identifying what it's like for me to think the thoughts I do that separates them from having thought or understood something. Moreover, even if the imagined correlations were made, that would not show that I can conceive of someone for whom what it is like is just what it is like for me, *but who understands nothing by the words he hears or imagines*. And that is still what is called for, if we really want to justify segregating phenomenality from semantics.

Now I may perhaps conceive of a phenomenal duplicate whose head contains the same "writing" as mine. But that isn't enough. What I would still need to do is to identify what it's like for me to think and understand in a way that enables me to project the *very same phenomenal character* as I subjectively discern in my own case into the life of a hypothetical thoughtless subject whose head is filled with the same writing. That is, I would again be seeking the "semantically clueless phenomenal duplicate" of Section 5 above. I cannot find him, merely by *understanding the proposition* put to me that my phenomenal character consists in something such a thoughtless subject might have (e.g. the detection of meaningless brain writing), or by simply *stipulating* this to be so. That would do nothing to alter the fact that once I have made myself aware (as in Section 5) of the contrast between what it's like for me to speak with and without understanding, I don't see how what it is *actually* like for *me* to speak, and what it *would* be like for some *imagined mindless other* to speak, could always be *just the same*. For I lose my grip on the very phenomenal contrast I am being asked to conceptually export to another, and I am no longer clear that this is indeed "the *same* phenomenal character" I am exporting, when told that it must be drained of all difference in thought and understanding, leaving nothing but Jabberized chatter.

But what about the "externalist" idea that subjects must have the right connections to their environments to enjoy thought content? We may think that gives us what we need to radically divorce phenomenal character from genuine thought. However, this

---

[20] In discussion (and later in a draft of his paper for this volume he has kindly shown me), Joseph Levine has proposed something like this strategy for giving me the "content-less" grasp of what it's like for me to think/understand that I say I lack here.

would be unwarranted. If I have difficulty conceiving of a literally thoughtless phenomenal duplicate of myself, then just adding that he is to lack my environmental embedding does not help matters. If I *assume* the truth of content externalism, my conceptual difficulty here might lead me to infer that having the right environment is essential for the phenomenal character of thought. But the radical separability of thought and phenomenal character certainly doesn't follow. And the thought experiments crucial to arguing for externalism do not warrant such a separation. *At most* they show only that some ways of identifying thoughts would distinguish two subjects content-wise who were phenomenally the same. They do *not* show that my phenomenal twin might conceivably be *utterly bereft* of thought, or *utterly dissimilar* to me in what he was thinking.

Take, for example, the standard (H_2O) externalist thought experiment Putnam made famous: a (chemically uninformed) subject on Earth is thinking that *there is water in a glass*, while another, similarly ignorant and phenomenally type-identical subject (on "Twin Earth") is thinking (not this, but) that *there is twater in a glass*. ('Twater'—we assume—names a Twin Earth substance superficially similar to, but microstructurally quite different from, Earth's H_2O.) Even if we accept the attribution of distinct thought contents, this does not show that one of the subjects might be devoid of thought. Furthermore, attribution of distinct thought contents leaves it open that two such subjects may still be significantly cognitively similar. We might say that the conception one has of *water* is no different from that the other has of *twater*. And having what they share would be enough to make someone a thinker of thoughts. So acceptance of this Twin Earth-style scenario does not show that phenomenal character is insufficient for some kind of thought content. Similar considerations hold, I believe, for the kind of social externalism defended by Tyler Burge.

These points could also be developed so as to allow that where there is phenomenal invariance through a difference in "singular thoughts," still there is genuine phenomenal *thought*. The phenomenal character of my thought, actual and dispositional, cannot on its own make it true that I am thinking of the one and only *Brasilia* (whereas my twin is thinking of the equally charming *Twin Brasilia*). Still, it is enough to make it true that I am in some way *thinking*, and enough to *contribute* significantly to making my thought a thought of Brasilia. And the essential contribution of the (extra-phenomenal) *context* to fixing the reference and truth conditions of my thoughts still leaves the role of phenomenal character in meaning dramatically different from the role that belongs to those merely *formal* characteristics of a symbol or image that constrain its *interpretation* in a way compatible with radical reinterpretation, or with the total absence of meaning. The way the phenomenal character of thought constrains what it can be about is not like *that*. Further, I see no reason not to speak of the part of what is thought that is fully determined by phenomenal character as a kind of thought *content*, even if the truth of attributions of content (e.g. "I think that Brasilia is the capital of Brazil") are not determined by phenomenal character alone, independently of extra-phenomenal context.

None of this runs afoul of what I said earlier about phenomenal character and self-knowledge. What it's like for me to realize what book my friend was speaking of when she said "the book" may not by itself make it the case that I was then thinking of a book by (the one and only) David Foster Wallace. But it can still play a crucial part in my knowing what I took her to mean. And it's not an objection if we say something extra-phenomenal is needed to yield the full content of the thought—my being in the right *context*, living on the David Foster Wallace planet, not his twin's. For it's not the case that I would then need to have knowledge of extra-phenomenal facts that would turn out to render my knowledge of what it's like for me epistemically otiose. To know that I'm thinking of David Foster Wallace on a given occasion, I just need to know what it's like for me then to think as I do, and actually to be in that context in which the expression I am prone to give of my thoughts would be correctly interpreted to refer to David Foster Wallace.

Let me be quite explicit about this: inclusivists are not necessarily anti-externalists about content. We could consistently hold that having the "right" brain-environment links is strongly necessary (and not just contingently causally required) if a brain is to belong to a subject of genuine conceptual thought. We can even hold that there are differences in thought content due to environmental differences that do not supervene on phenomenal differences. We may, however, wish to speak of a kind of thought content that does supervene on phenomenal differences in any case: "phenomenal content." Nonetheless, acceptance of inclusivism in the sense and for the reasons discussed here is compatible with various forms of content externalism. So they should not be taken to refute it.

7 Conclusion

The disagreement over phenomenal thought stems from a number of global and complex differences rooted in varying historical legacies, different implicit "logical geographies," and the extensive obscurities and subtleties involved. So it is not realistic to expect a ready consensus. Certainly it would be naïve to suppose it could be achieved by simple appeal to introspection. But that needn't make us despair of critical examination, nor need it make us abandon first-person reflection altogether.

To justify a view of these matters, we need to take care in how we configure our framework for thinking about them. This is a complicated business. Ways of thinking can become entrenched because one is interpreting key terms and questions in ways that restrict what one can take seriously. And the need to sustain a certain conception of mind, or a relation to the history of relevant discussions, may set one's thoughts inexorably along certain paths. Part of what is necessary then is to make explicit an interpretation of crucial notions that will help us to formulate our questions carefully and without prejudice, and to raise awareness of intellectual history in a way that frees up thought, and makes us alive to alternatives. And all this needs to be done while minimizing controversial assumptions.

I claim to have made here just such a reasoned case for the view that if we shut conceptual thought out of consciousness, we diminish our experience significantly. While I have made use of first-person reflection, I have done so in the context of arguments. I have not resorted to mere assertion, nor made brute appeal to "intuitions of cognitive phenomenology." The arguments are not to be blithely dismissed, and can be fairly assessed only with patient reflection on the sorts of cases discussed, as we encounter them in our lives, in the light of relevant distinctions.[21]

References

Block, N. (2002). "Concepts of consciousness," in David J. Chalmers (ed.), *Philosophy of Mind: Classical and Contemporary Readings*. Oxford: Oxford University Press.

Dennett, D. (1991). *Consciousness Explained*. Boston: Little, Brown and Company.

Georgalis, N. (2003). "The fiction of phenomenal intentionality," *Consciousness and Emotion*, 4: 243–6.

Goldman, A. (1993). "The psychology of folk psychology," *Behavioural and Brain Sciences*, 16: 15–28.

Horgan, T. and Tienson, J. (2002). "The intentionality of phenomenology and the phenomenology of intentionality," in David J. Chalmers (ed.), *Philosophy of Mind: Classical and Contemporary Readings*. Oxford: Oxford University Press.

Husserl, E. ([1900/01] 2001). *Logical Investigations*. J. Findlay (trans.). London: Routledge.

Jackendoff, R. (1987). *Consciousness and the Computational Mind*. Cambridge, MA: MIT Press.

James, W. (1890). *The Principles of Psychology*. Cambridge, MA: Harvard University Press.

McDowell, J. (1994). *Mind and World*. Cambridge, MA: Harvard University Press.

Moore, G.E. (1962). "Propositions," in *Some Main Problems of Philosophy*. New York: Collier Books.

Nichols, S. and Stich, S. (2003). *Mindreading: An Integrated Account of Pretence, Self-Awareness, and Understanding of Other Minds*. Oxford: Oxford University Press.

Pitt, D. (2004). "The phenomenology of cognition or what is it like to think that p?", *Philosophy and Phenomenological Research*, 69: 1–36.

Place, U.T. (1956). "Is consciousness a brain process?" *British Journal of Psychology*, 47: 44–50.

Prinz, J. (2002). *Furnishing the Mind*. Cambridge, MA: MIT Press.

Putnam, H. (1981). "Brains in vats," in *Reason, Truth and History*. Cambridge: Cambridge University Press.

Robinson, W.S. (2005). "Thoughts without distinctive non-imagistic phenomenology," *Philosophy and Phenomenological Research*, LXX: 534–61.

Rorty, R. (1979). *Philosophy and the Mirror of Nature*. Princeton: Princeton University Press.

---

[21] I would like to express my gratitude for feedback from audiences for presentations of this material at: The California Phenomenology Circle, The University of Arizona, The University of Fribourg, Rice University, and The 2008 Consciousness and Thought Conference in Dubrovnik. I would particularly like to thank for helpful feedback: Baruch Brody, David Chalmers, Frank Hoffman, Terry Horgan, Uriah Kriegel, Joseph Levine, Jesse Prinz, David Pitt, David W. Smith, Ron MacIntyre, Farid Masrour, Kevin Mulligan, Matjaž Potrč, Martine Nida-Rümelin, Susanna Siegel, and two anonymous reviewers for Oxford University Press.

Ryle, G. (1949). *The Concept of Mind*. Chicago: University of Chicago Press.

Schwitzgebel, E. (2008). "The unreliability of naïve introspection," *Philosophical Review*, 117/2: 245–73.

Sellars, W. (1956). "Empiricism and the philosophy of mind," *Minnesota Studies in the Philosophy of Science*, 1: 253–329.

Siewert, C. (1998). *The Significance of Consciousness*. Princeton: Princeton University Press.

Smart, J.C.C. (1959). "Sensations and brain processes," *Philosophical Review*, 68: 141–56.

Strawson, G. (1994). *Mental Reality*. Cambridge, MA: MIT Press.

Tye, M. (1995). *Ten Problems of Consciousness*. Cambridge, MA: MIT Press.

Disagreement about Cognitive Phenomenology

Maja Spener

1 Introduction

It used to be orthodoxy in the philosophy of mind that our mental states divide into those that are intentional and those that are qualitative (e.g. Block 1978). Intentional states are states which are directed at something or which, as it is also sometimes put, have a subject-matter. Standard examples of intentional states are propositional attitudes, such as beliefs and desires. By contrast, according to the orthodox assumption, qualitative states are non-intentional. These states are not in the business of having a subject-matter; they have no intrinsic directedness onto something. On the orthodox picture, qualitative states instead provide a phenomenological awareness constituted by what it is like to have the state itself; they are merely 'raw feels' or sensations. Standard examples of qualitative states include bodily sensations such as pains and tickles, emotions, and moods. Philosophers have since challenged the orthodox distinction. The first round of attack consisted in defence of the claim that at least some qualitative states also have intentionality. It now has become standard to hold that the phenomenal character of some or even all qualitative states is intimately bound up with intentionality (e.g. Tye 1995).

More controversially, the orthodox assumption has been challenged from the opposite direction: some philosophers have claimed that, when consciously entertaining them, intentional states such as beliefs and desires also have a phenomenal character. Call this 'the phenomenology of thought thesis'. One can endorse the claim that conscious thought is like something, but hold that the phenomenology involved is of familiar kinds. Perhaps, with Hume, one thinks of thoughts as faint copies of images and so the phenomenology involved in entertaining a conscious thought is similar to imagistic phenomenology we know from various kinds of imagination. Call this 'the weak phenomenology of thought thesis' (weak thesis, for short). By contrast, one might hold that the phenomenology involved in having a conscious thought is distinctive, in particular, that it is non-sensory and non-imagistic. Call this 'the strong phenomenology of thought thesis' (strong thesis, for short).[1]

The debate concerning the phenomenology of thought is marked by severe disagreement about how best to characterize a given conscious thought on the basis of introspective reflecting upon it. In this paper I focus on the fact of this introspection-based disagreement—in particular, on its epistemic import for participants in the debate. How ought these philosophers respond when facing such radical disagreement about the deliverance of introspection?

Recently, disagreement itself has become a renewed focus of interest among epistemologists. The main question concerns the epistemic significance of disagreement with apparently well-qualified others: how ought one to respond when confronted with disagreement where, on the face of it, partners in disagreement are epistemically symmetric? At one end of the spectrum are views which say that typically, the epistemically appropriate reaction is to be conciliatory towards one's disagreeing partner ('Conciliationism'): disagreement with apparently well-qualified others should cause one to be less confident than before in what one originally believed, or even to suspend judgement about one's original view (e.g. Christensen 2007; 2011). On the other side are views which say that typically the appropriate reaction is to remain steadfast ('Steadfastness'): disagreement with apparently well-qualified others allows that one maintain one's level of confidence in what one originally believed (e.g. Kelly 2005).

As we shall see, certain structural features of the introspection-based disagreement about the phenomenology of thought seem at first glance to favour a Steadfast response. Moreover, Steadfastness is also implicit in how participants in the debate typically respond to the disagreement. In this paper I argue that despite initial appearance to the contrary, we should be Conciliationists in the case of the introspection-based disagreement about cognitive phenomenology. The fact of disagreement about the deliverance of introspection in the debate about cognitive phenomenology should lead participants to be less confident—or even to suspend judgement—in their own introspection-based claims. If that is right, then *to the extent* that the debate about the phenomenology of thought is carried out by appeal to introspective evidence, this constitutes a serious epistemological concern. At the very least, if Conciliationism is the epistemically appropriate response, non-trivial reliance of introspective evidence in the debate comes under pressure.

---

[1] Defenders of the strong thesis are, e.g., Strawson (1994), Horgan and Tienson (2002), Pitt (2004), Siewert (1998). Robinson (2005) is perhaps a defender of the weak thesis. Opponents of the phenomenology of thought thesis are, e.g., Lormand (1996) and Tye (1995).

2 Disagreement about what conscious thought is like

The main issue discussed by philosophers interested in the topic of cognitive phenomenology is whether the strong thesis is true. This is an issue about the existence of a certain kind of phenomenology, namely, a distinctive non-sensory, non-imagistic phenomenology of thought. Most philosophers in the debate agree that there normally is phenomenology present when one is having a conscious thought. To use the what-it-is-like terminology, there is a sense in which everyone agrees that normally, there is something it is like for one when one is having a conscious thought. If I tell you to consider the thought that there are ripe pears in the warden's garden, you will most likely have some sort of image of a garden, of pears, of a warden and perhaps you even imagine the scent and taste of ripe pears. But opponents of the strong thesis argue that this much does not force them to say that the conscious thought itself has a distinctive phenomenal character or any character at all. Instead, an opponent might say, insofar as there is something it is like to have a conscious thought, this is because the conscious thought is accompanied by all sorts of imagistic and sensory associations and feelings, none of which are part of the thought itself. And while these accompanying mental phenomena all have qualitative characters—there is something it is like to have them in virtue of their qualitative nature—the conscious thought itself does not (e.g. Tye 1995: 4). A different sort of opponent (a defender of the weak thesis) might say that even though there is something it is like to have a conscious thought in its own right (which is not merely due to accompanying qualitative states), there is nothing distinctive about this phenomenology. Rather, she might hold, the phenomenal character of thought is of a familiar sensory or imagistic kind (perhaps Robinson 2005).

Thus, philosophers in the debate tend to agree that there is phenomenology present in having a conscious thought. They disagree about two aspects of such phenomenology: what kind of phenomenology it is—whether sensory or non-sensory, imagist or non-imagistic—and about the location of the phenomenology—whether it is attributed to the thought itself, or to certain feelings, sensations, perceptions and images which accompany the thought.

Philosophers attempting to settle this question often appeal to introspective reflection on what it is like to have the thoughts in question. Those that do, use what I call an 'introspective method'. Typically, they first provide an introspection-based description of what it is like to have a certain kind of conscious thought and on the basis of this description they then argue that the thought in question has, or fails to have, a distinctive non-sensory, non-imagistic phenomenology.[2] These philosophers assume that there is introspective evidence which provides grounds to

---

[2] This methodological approach is explicitly acknowledged in some places, e.g. Horgan and Tienson (2002); Robinson (2005: 536).

type certain aspects of phenomenology and to attribute them to one kind of state rather than another. In addition, and by appeal to the same introspective evidence, they also frequently accuse their opponents of getting the phenomenology wrong and thereby mis-typing and mis-attributing phenomenal character.

The widespread use of such introspective methods is reflected in the fact that a considerable part of the debate about the strong thesis proceeds by phenomenological description and re-description of cases. Consider the following two examples of this back and forth. Charles Siewert, an influential defender of the strong thesis, seeks to provide an instance of cognitive phenomenology by drawing attention to the phenomenon of having a seemingly complex thought in a very short period of time.

Somehow this thought of my philosophical preoccupations and parenthood, and an analogy between their effects, rather complex to articulate, occurred in a couple of moments while I approached the cashier, in the absence of any utterance. I think you will, if you try, be able to recognize examples from your own daily life, similar to these I have mentioned, of unverbalized noniconic thought. . . . [In these cases] thought occurs, wordlessly, without imagery, condensed, and evanescent. If you agree that you have such unverbalized noniconic thoughts, and the way it seems to you to have them differs from the way it seems to have imagery and sensory experience, then you will agree that noniconic thinking has a phenomenal character distinct from that proper to iconic thinking and perception. (Siewert 1998: 277–8)

In response, William Robinson denies that Siewert has aptly characterized the phenomenology of this sort of case:

My own introspection leads me to believe that I have had experiences of the kind that Siewert means to be indicating; I am denying only that the proffered phenomenological account matches anything in my experience. What then is my positive account of what happens on such occasions? What I believe occurs is a few words in subvocal speech (we might call them 'key words'), perhaps a rather vague sense of a diagrammatic sketch, and perhaps some pictorial or kinaesthetic imagery. There is also usually a feeling of satisfaction, something I might express by saying I'd thought of something particularly interesting. There is also a confidence – which may or may not prove to be justified – that I can go on to say something now that I could not have said before this occurrence and that will be the verbalization of an interesting claim, description, observation, etc. (Robinson 2005: 554)

The second example of phenomenological description and re-description concerns the tip-of-the-tongue phenomenon. Alvin Goldman uses it to make a case for the strong thesis:

When one tries to say something but cannot think of the word, one is phenomenologically aware of having requisite conceptual structure, that is, of having a definite . . . content one seeks to articulate. What is missing is the phenomenological form: the *sound* of the sought-for word. The absence of this sensory quality, however, does not imply that nothing (relevant) is in awareness. Entertaining the conceptual unit has a phenomenology, just not a sensory phenomenology. (Goldman 1993: 24)

In response, Eric Lormand holds that Goldman is getting the phenomenology of the case wrong. Lormand cites Ray Jackendoff's phenomenological account of the tip-of-the-tongue phenomenon:

Jackendoff provides the seeds of a response to Goldman's argument. Jackendoff uses the tip-of-the-tongue phenomenon to "demonstrate" that "conceptual structure is excluded from [phenomenological] awareness" (1987: 290). He distinguishes the aspects of what the experience is like into a soundless "form" and an "affect" of effort, so that "one feels as though one is desperately trying to fill a void" (1987: 290, 315). Neither of these aspects seem attributable to nonsensory attitudes. Jackendoff attributes soundlessness not to propositional attitudes or conceptual structures but to "an empty set of brackets" in a sensory, phonological representation (1987: 291). I think this is roughly right; there is something sensory that having the "void" is like, akin to what *hearing silence* (as opposed to being deaf or asleep) is like. Although Jackendoff provides no account of the feeling of effort, I also see no reason to describe *it* as nonsensory or to attribute it to Goldman's propositional attitudes and conceptual structures; there is something sensory that the feeling of effort is like, namely, what *feeling physical effort* is like. I conclude that our attitudes themselves are never p-conscious, although there may often be something it's like when we have them, due to accompanying [sensory phenomenal] states. (Lormand 1996: 247)

These examples illustrate a tendency among philosophers to assume that introspection yields data about the phenomenal character of conscious thought which is relevant to theorizing about it. Introspection is routinely taken to deliver phenomenological data in support of views about whether or not a given aspect of what it is like for one to have a conscious thought is non-sensory, non-imagistic, or distinctive to the thought itself. There is some fluidity among users of introspective methods about how exactly they conceive of the evidential support provided by introspective data. Strictly speaking, there are different kinds of introspective methods, depending on the precise role that introspective data plays in acquisition of a given view (see Spener 2011 for discussion). Some—e.g. Tienson and Horgan (2002)—directly read off their view from the introspection-based phenomenological data. Others use introspective data together with an inference of some sort (e.g. inference to the best explanation, *a priori* inference, or inference from simplicity). All these require additional reasoning with additional premises, and the role of introspective data in grounding a view can be greater or lesser depending on the contribution of the additional premises.

Notwithstanding, most philosophers in the debate about cognitive phenomenology typically argue in a manner which treats introspection-based data about phenomenology as significant and forceful grounds on which to base a view about the strong thesis. Not all do so to the same extent and they sometimes have other, non-introspection-based arguments in favour of their view as well. But as the quotations above show, introspective evidence about the phenomenal character of conscious thought is considered highly relevant. For some, the source of that conviction lies in the assumption that we have very good introspective access to our conscious phenomenology. Introspective judgements about conscious phenomenology are sometimes even held to be especially reliable (Horgan and Tienson 2002: 10). Whatever the source, though, introspective evidence is usually taken to have some authority over theorizing about cognitive phenomenology—introspective evidence is a kind of evidence that can only be denied at great cost to the plausibility of the theory offered (see, e.g., Pitt 2004: 26).

As we have just seen, the very same philosophers who use introspective evidence in their theorizing, also fiercely disagree about what introspection reveals concerning the phenomenal character of conscious thought. Yet they also largely conduct the debate as if the disagreement they face has no epistemic significance. But are they right to do so? Before arguing that participants in the debate ought to pay more attention to epistemological concerns arising from the fact of introspective disagreement itself, I will set out the basic issue of the epistemic significance of disagreement and the main views about it in the next section.

3 The epistemic import of disagreement: Conciliationism vs Steadfastness

Suppose my friend and I, after examining the same body of evidence E, disagree about thesis T. I judge T is true and she judges T is false. How should I rationally respond to our disagreement? It depends on what I take to be the likely explanation of our disagreement: in particular, on my opinion as to who is most likely to have made a mistake. If I consider myself most likely to be wrong in my assessment of E, I ought to revise my belief that T is true and join my friend in believing that T is false. I would come to accept my friend to be an epistemic superior in this case, perhaps because I realized some epistemic advantage on my friend's part, say that she had additional evidence or was better at appreciating E, or because I became aware of some deficiency on my part, e.g. some erroneous reasoning. If, on the other hand, I consider my friend most likely to be in error, it is appropriate for me to continue in my original belief about T. I would hold myself to be an epistemic superior in this case based on some epistemic advantage on my part or some epistemic deficiency on hers. If, however, I consider us both equally likely to have made a mistake, I also ought to revise my original belief about T. In holding us both equally likely to be wrong in our assessment of E, I acknowledge that there is an epistemic symmetry between us giving neither of us an epistemic advantage. The rational reaction to this acceptance of symmetry in our respective epistemic situations is that I revise my original belief about T to reflect a much lower level of confidence, perhaps even suspending judgement altogether.

In the literature on disagreement, discussion turns on whether there are cases of disagreement that genuinely mandate the third assessment. The focus is on instances of disagreement where disagreeing partners count as 'epistemic peers'. That is, to the best of their knowledge they are both equal in access and exposure to salient evidence, in intelligence, freedom from bias, etc. Furthermore, they do not know of any special circumstances (e.g. intoxication, fatigue, humour, mischief) that would undermine epistemic peer-hood on the occasion. Proponents of the two main views mentioned in the introduction, Conciliationism and Steadfastness, differ in their evaluation of whether or not these cases of disagreement feature a genuine epistemic symmetry and hence require appropriate revision of belief. More precisely, they differ on how to evaluate the epistemic significance of the fact of such disagreement itself. Let us consider a concrete example (see Christensen 2007):

Meteorology: Suppose I am a meteorologist and I am provided with up-to-date weather data by the top meteorological institutions. I am trained to use this data to make weather predictions by applying certain models. On the basis of the data supplied today and application of the models I am familiar with, I am 55% confident that it will rain tomorrow. After I have come to this conclusion I talk to my meteorologist friend. She has received the same training I have, she has considered the same data I have and no more, she uses the same models that I do, etc. We both have equally extensive and good track records in making predictions. However, she is only 45% confident that it will rain tomorrow.

My friend and I are epistemic peers but now we disagree. What evidential status, if any, does this fact have? A popular defence of Steadfastness holds that in typical cases of this kind, the disagreement itself provides me with evidence which breaks the tie in my favour. The thought is roughly this. Having done my best to interpret the data and apply the models on this occasion, I am 55% confident that it will rain tomorrow. So on my view, the evidence supports my level of credence in the proposition that it will rain tomorrow and it does not support 45% credence in that proposition. So while I acknowledge that my friend in general is an epistemic peer, I have some evidence that on this particular occasion she has made a mistake. This supplies me with a tiebreaker, a relevant difference between us to show that her belief is to be trusted less than mine (see Kelly 2005). I am therefore rational in continuing in my 55% credence that it will rain tomorrow.

Defenders of Conciliationism agree that in the above case I have some evidence that my friend has made a mistake. But they also think that the fact that my friend, who is in general as reliable as I am, disagrees with me gives me some evidence that I have made a mistake on this occasion. While the disagreement between us is evidence that at least one of us has made a mistake, it is neutral between who has made it and therefore the rational reaction is to adjust my level of credence towards my friend's. Conciliationism involves the acceptance of the following principle:

Independence: An assessment of my disagreeing partner's belief about T in order to decide about whether to respond to the disagreement by adjusting my original belief about T must be independent of my reasoning employed in coming to my original belief about T.

According to Independence, any reasonable assessment of the disagreement, especially the assessment of who is more likely to have made a mistake, must be independent of the particular instance of reasoning giving rise to the disagreement itself. That is, I cannot use my 55% credence that it will rain tomorrow, or the reasoning supporting this belief, to explain the disagreement between my friend and me in terms of her mistake. Conciliationists point out that that would simply beg the question (Christensen 2007: 15ff).

The Conciliationist response in Meteorology strikes me as very plausible. In general, my sympathies lie with Conciliationism, but I am not arguing the general case here. But even if one assumes that Independence is well motivated in general—as I do in this paper[3]—this leaves open whether Conciliationism is the epistemically appropriate response to the introspection-based disagreement about cognitive phenomenology. On the face of it, at least, the partners in disagreement in that debate are epistemic peers. In responding rationally to the fact of disagreement about the deliverance of introspection, should they revise their original introspective beliefs about what their conscious thoughts are like, perhaps by becoming less confident about their claims, perhaps even by suspending judgement in them? Or does the fact of their disagreement with apparently well-qualified others carry no epistemic weight in this debate and therefore have no significant impact on these philosophers' own epistemic situation?

The latter response—Steadfastness—is in line with how many participants argue in the context of the debate about the strong thesis. As we have seen, they engage in introspection-based description and re-description of what their conscious thoughts are like and continue in their respective beliefs in the face of disagreement with their opponents. They also typically use their introspective claims to ground their views about the strong thesis—as noted, some more directly than others. Insofar as they are using an introspective method to argue for their view about the strong thesis, they are steadfast in responding to the introspection-based disagreement they are confronted with.

Steadfastness, they might add, also seems the intuitively correct view of the introspection-based disagreement. Notice that initial intuitions about the right reaction to disagreement in Meteorology are not especially strongly in favour of a particular reaction. In such cases, showing that one's account yields at least a plausible intuitive take is enough. Independence and the charge of begging the question are then a matter of further argument. However, there are cases where intuition seems overwhelmingly and strongly to point in one direction only (i.e. either revision or continuation of one's original beliefs). *Prima facie* these cases provide support for one side and count against the seemingly counter-intuitive side. In particular, there are putative cases—those involving initially high rational confidence—where intuitive assessment seems to go overwhelmingly and strongly in favour of continuing with one's beliefs. The introspective disagreement about cognitive phenomenology seems to be a case of just this

---

[3] For criticism of Independence see Kelly (2005; 2010), for defence see Christensen (2011).

kind. The epistemically appropriate response therefore seems to be to remain steadfast in one's original beliefs. I will set this out in detail in the next section.

4 High confidence cases

The salient kinds of disagreements that provide *prima facie* intuitive support for Stead-fastness are ones where one has a very high degree of rational confidence in what one originally believes. The initial high rational confidence is thought to trump evidence that one might have made a mistake flowing from the disagreement itself. Intuitively, it would be more rational to continue in one's original belief on these occasions, rather than revise it in light of disagreement with an epistemic peer. Let me illustrate this with two examples. (See Christensen 2011 and Lackey 2010, respectively. I have changed the details of Lackey's example, though.)

Careful Checking: Suppose I regularly eat with my friend at a certain restaurant. The two of us always split the bill and both calculate the shares. In the past, my friend and I have done equally well, and I believe she is as smart and capable as I am when it comes to calculating bills. On this occasion, neither of us has had any alcohol, we both seem as alert and sharp as usual. But, because there is time available, I not only calculate our shares in my head, I also do so on paper and then I do so on my pocket calculator. Then I check every calculation again. Every time, I arrive at the conclusion that our shares are £20 each. Meanwhile, my friend has finished her calculations and she claims the shares are £18 each.

Boat Perception: Suppose I am sitting with my brother on the bank of a river having lunch on a bright, sunny day. I have lived with my brother my whole life and I have not had any reason to think that he or I are visually or cognitively impaired in any way. I point to a sail boat I see sailing by very closely and I say: 'Look at that beautiful boat.' He sincerely replies that there is no boat out there.

In each of these cases, there is a strong intuition that I should not change my original belief in the face of my disagreeing partner's dissent. Given my extremely conscien-tious manner of calculating and re-calculating my conclusion in Careful Checking employing several different procedures, including a pocket calculator, I should be extremely confident in my belief that our shares are £20 each. Against the back-ground of such a meticulous method, changing my belief merely in light of my friend's dissenting opinion seems unwarranted and at odds with my original high rational confidence that we each have to pay £20. Similarly, in Boat Perception my confidence in the proposition that there is a beautiful boat sailing by should be very high. This is not because of some meticulous method of calculation that I deliberately employ which has as the conclusion that there is a beautiful boat sailing by. My belief is grounded in my visually perceiving the boat in maximally good perceptual condi-tions: all is well with me; the boat is huge and right there in front of me; it's the middle of a bright, sunny day, etc. To doubt my own eyes merely because my brother disagrees would seem unwarranted and at odds with the high confidence with which I originally held the belief that there is a beautiful boat sailing by.

So in both of these cases it seems rational to continue in my original beliefs rather than change them in the light of disagreement with epistemic peers. And, defenders of Steadfastness will point out, the symmetry-breaker that tips the epistemic balance in my favour is the fact that I am highly rationally confident in what I believe. If that is right, however, my reason for preferring an explanation of the disagreements with my friend and my brother in terms of the greater likelihood of their mistake is not independent of the belief at issue or the reasoning at work in acquiring it. According to defenders of Steadfastness, in cases like Careful Checking and Boat Perception the appropriate epistemic response involves rejecting Independence, and with it a Conciliationist response.[4]

It very much looks as if disagreement about cognitive phenomenology shares the key feature with the above sort of cases. Here, too, the partners in disagreement hold their respective views about the strong thesis with high confidence. High or even very high confidence is typically considered to be part and parcel of introspective judgements about one's current phenomenal consciousness.[5] Given this, the high confidence with which introspective beliefs are held can also be thought to trump any evidence that oneself might have made a mistake flowing from the disagreement itself. The rational reaction in the face of such disagreement seems to be to continue in one's original introspective beliefs, fairly unmoved by the conflicting introspection-based views of others.

Conciliationists have a reply to the challenge posed by Careful Checking and Boat Perception, but it concedes that, based on the initial strong intuition, the rational response in these cases is to continue in one's original beliefs. They argue this intuition can be accommodated without violating Independence (Christensen 2007: 202–3; 2011). Key to this reply is the notion of personal information (Lackey 2010). In Careful Checking, for instance, I am justified in being highly confident in my original belief because I know that it is extremely unlikely that someone who is generally mathematically competent as I am and who goes through all these different ways of calculating the bill would come up with the same wrong result every time. Moreover, it would be extremely unlikely for this to be true of two people—hence, I am also justified in Careful Checking to believe that something unusual is going on explaining the disagreement. Normally, remote chances become more likely in this instance, e.g. that someone might after all be intoxicated, cognitively malfunctioning, joking, tired, distracted, etc. The Conciliationist's thought is that with

---

[4] Proponents of Steadfastness use this to undermine Independence itself and Conciliations more generally, of course.

[5] Accepting this much does not involve accepting that introspective judgements about one's conscious experience are infallible. Many philosophers hold that we have excellent, albeit fallible, first-person access to our own current conscious experience. For dissenting voices see, e.g., Schwitzgebel (2008) and Spener (MS).

respect to all these possibilities, I am in a much better position to rule them out for me than for my friend because I have access to personal information about me in a way I do not about my friend. Combined with my high rational confidence that the bill comes to £20, I now have a good reason to think that the greater likelihood of mistake lies with my friend and this breaks the epistemic symmetry between us in my favour.

None of this undermines Independence, for the explanation does not rely on the particular reasoning employed by me to acquire my belief that the bill comes to £20, nor does it rely on that result itself. It is based solely on considerations regarding the kind of reasoning employed in Careful Checking, independently of its particular application and the substance of the disagreement. Thus the tiebreaker—which allows for an explanation in terms of my friend's mistake and which thereby accommodates the strong intuition that the rational response to our disagreement is to hang on to my original belief—respects Independence.

The above reply is focused on defending Independence and Conciliationism more generally. As we saw, it involves conceding that cases of high confidence typically involve continuing in one's original beliefs. In this paper I am only concerned with the epistemically appropriate reaction to the introspection-based disagreement, however, whether licensed by Conciliationism or Steadfastness. It looks now that both of them give the same verdict and, if so, that seems strong confirmation that in the introspection-based disagreement, participants should hold steadfast in their introspective claims.

But I think this is false, doubly so: Conciliationism and Steadfastness do not give the same verdict in this case and the epistemically appropriate response is not to hold steadfast in one's introspective beliefs in the disagreement.

Notice, first, that the introspection-based disagreement about cognitive phenomenology does not allow for the above Conciliationist reply. This is because here, the notion of personal information cannot play the role of tiebreaker that it does in Careful Checking and Boat Perception. Unlike the latter cases, the introspection-based disagreement about cognitive phenomenology is not the work of a moment. Quite the opposite: participating philosophers have repeatedly sought debate with each other about the strong thesis and they have written papers expounding their views. This process takes considerable time. Presumably, their introspective beliefs are the result of repeated, careful, and sustained introspective efforts. Moreover, the debate involves more than two participants and has spanned more than one generation of philosophers and psychologists. In view of this, participants in the disagreement cannot reasonably appeal to an asymmetry in access to personal information to drive an explanation of the disagreement in terms of the greater likelihood of the other side's mistakes. It would be ridiculous to claim that all the disagreeing partners happened to be intoxicated, cognitively malfunctioning, joking, or inattentive at crucial junctures.

However, a more systematic explanation involving some sort of persisting blunder, such as an ingrained theoretical bias of some kind, of the other side in effect involves downgrading partners in disagreement to epistemic unequals to begin with. For, the latter are unable to introspect properly in a more general sense. Their theoretical bias leads them to systematically misjudge what their conscious thoughts are like. This is a different response altogether, not based on appeal to personal information and unusual circumstances, but on rejecting the introspection-based disagreement as a salient case of *peer* disagreement.[6]

In the next section I argue that the introspection-based disagreement is best accounted for in terms of a different Conciliationist reply—one which gives the verdict that the epistemically appropriate reaction for participants is to change their original introspective beliefs.

5 Conciliationism about introspection-based disagreement

The reason that the Conciliationist reply to Careful Checking and Boat Perception is not available in the introspective case is that these cases must be—despite superficial similarities—treated rather differently. In particular, the high confidence that goes with introspection-based views about cognitive phenomenology does not drive a forceful intuition mandating against belief revision in the face of disagreement. Let me explain this.

Consider the high confidence involved in Careful Checking and Boat Perception. Why am I justified in being extremely confident that our shares are £20 and that there is a beautiful boat sailing by? The ultra-high confidence involved in these cases is rational because it is embedded in the extremely high confidence we have in the general reliability of the methods of reasoning and belief acquisition employed in those particular instances. In turn, the latter attitude is justified because we have very good evidence that these methods are generally highly reliable. For example, when we employ these methods on similar occasions, most times we meet with agreement from our epistemic peers. Normally, ordinary perceptual judgements that we make are not subject to controversy. And, normally, when a competent person carefully calculates, re-calculates, and cross-checks her mental arithmetic on paper and with a pocket calculator she arrives at the same result that equally competent others have arrived at. Furthermore, the beliefs acquired by these methods are usually open to confirmation by other means. So, for instance, if I want to check whether I heard correctly that there is a helicopter hovering above the house I can go to the window and look for it. I could test whether I have figured out correctly how many pancakes to make for everyone at the table to get at least three by using sticks and marbles to represent persons at the table and pancakes and then lining them up. There is thus abundant evidence that the

---

[6] For example, one might cite theoretical bias in favour of reductive views of experience as underlying introspection-based denials of the strong thesis, or theoretical bias in favour of grounding intentionality in phenomenal character as leading to introspection-based endorsement of the strong thesis. These are ways to deal with introspection-based disagreement by users of the introspective method, but this sort of explanatory strategy faces some tough question about the soundness of the introspective method (see Spener MS).

methods of reasoning and belief acquisition at work in Careful Checking and Boat Perception are in general highly reliable. They are tried and tested, and have an excellent track record.

But if this sort of evidence grounds the rationality of high confidence in those cases, the introspection-based views giving rise to the disagreement about cognitive phenomenology are not on a par with them. For the track record of introspection is not exactly glowing. There is a longstanding controversy surrounding most uses of introspection in philosophy and psychology, and one will find little evidence that introspection generally inspires agreement on similar occasions of use. In addition, an array of empirical studies showing that we are not very good at introspecting various other mental aspects only serve to undermine, not build confidence in the general reliability of introspection (see e.g. Schwitzgebel 2011). Furthermore, in contrast to the methods of reasoning and belief acquisition involved in Careful Checking and Boat Perception, introspective judgements about conscious phenomenology cannot be confirmed by other means. At present, at least, we do not have any recognized successful way to collect data about phenomenal consciousness other than by introspection.[7] While there are various scientific approaches to conscious aspects of the mind, they all face the notorious gap between physical and phenomenal properties (Levine 1983).

In short, introspection has a bad track record. Considered alongside the methods of reasoning and belief acquisition employed in Careful Checking and Boat Perception, there is no analogous grounding of high rational confidence in its general reliability. In turn, there is no analogous grounding of high rational confidence in introspective judgement on a given occasion. For the high confidence attending introspective beliefs about conscious phenomenology is not rational *by the standards* of Careful Checking and Boat Perception. But then we have been given no reason to concede that there is any intuitive pressure in favour of continuing in one's original introspection-based beliefs when faced with disagreement about cognitive phenomenology.

So what can we say about the high confidence attending introspective judge-ments—is it a mere psychological habit accompanying these judgements with no rational basis? A full answer goes beyond the scope of this paper, but I nonetheless want to make some brief comments. Despite its bad track record, a wholesale rejection of high confidence introspective judgements as irrational seems wrong. Perhaps there is a (limited) class of introspective beliefs that would meet with almost universal agreement among epistemic peers. The widespread agreement could then be held to warrant a high level of confidence in these judgements.[8] Another source of rational grounding for high confidence in (at least some) introspective judgements

---

[7] For discussion see Hurlburt and Schwitzgebel (2007).

[8] It is harder than one initially might think to come up with examples. But maybe introspective judgements of a very general nature could inspire sufficient agreement to warrant high confidence. For discussion see Bayne and Spener (2010).

might be found in the asymmetry between third- and first-person judgements about one's own mind. Discussions of the contrast between first- and third-person access to one's mind centre on notions of privileged access, certainty, etc., and it is common to hold that one's introspective judgements enjoy a higher level of certainty than third-person judgements about one's mind. It seems right, for instance, that I ought to be much more confident in my introspective judgement that I have a visual experience of a boat before me than the person next to me ought to be in her judgement that I have a visual experience of this sort. When it comes to the asymmetry between first- and third-person access to one's own mind, a high degree of confidence in introspective judgements about one's current conscious states seems justified. What this suggests is that the rationality of high confidence might be dependent on the context of inquiry. Standards of evidential support often shift with changing questions and interests. The reasonable level of confidence invested in a given claim might be high when uttered in casual conversation, but much lower when stated in the witness box of a court of law. Similarly, it might be rational for me to be highly confident in my introspective judgement that I am consciously thinking that a beautiful boat is sailing by even though my friend, who is observing me closely, tells me that I do not have such a conscious thought at all. But this does not mean that it is rational for me to be highly confident in my introspective judgement that conscious thought involves a *sui generis* phenomenology even though my friend, on the basis of her own introspective judgement, claims that it does not.

Once it is established that the introspection-based disagreement is different in this way from Careful Checking and Boat Perception, it can be dealt with straightforwardly and effectively along Conciliationist lines. For a participant in the debate does not have any good reason to tip the epistemic balance in her favour. More specifically, she has no reason such that it is more likely that her partners in disagreement have made a mistake, where that reason respects Independence. As we saw, appeal to personal information cannot do the job here. And, given the poor track record of introspection, one cannot be rationally confident of the general reliability of introspection. Thus, an independent reason to think of oneself epistemically superior cannot be supplied on that count either.

If that is right, then the epistemically appropriate reaction to the introspection-based disagreement participants in the debate about cognitive phenomenology find themselves faced with is to be conciliatory. Participants ought to adjust their own introspective beliefs in the light of the conflicting beliefs of others.

6 Conclusion

What is it for participants to adjust their own introspective beliefs in the light of conflicting beliefs of others? Such an adjustment involves lowering one's confidence in what one believes on the basis of introspection about what conscious thought is like. How much less confident should one become? I have no worked-out view on this matter. But, given the sustained and often radical nature of the introspection-based disagreement, severely reduced confidence, or suspension of introspective judgement altogether in some cases would seem to be an epistemically responsible way to proceed.

This point holds independently of whether one side of the dispute actually happens to be correct in their introspective judgements. As long as the epistemic situation is symmetric in the way described above, the rational reaction to the disagreement they face is to revise one's original introspective beliefs in some way to reflect a lowered confidence or even suspension of judgement.[9] It certainly would be wrong to simply continue in one's introspection-based views while facing disagreement from apparently well-qualified others unless one has an additional source of support for these views.

It does seem clear that participants in the disagreement about the strong thesis do not take proper account of the epistemic import of their introspective disagreement with others. As the examples of phenomenal description and re-description illustrate, participants' insistence on their own introspective characterization in the face of conflicting ones from others frequently amounts to introspective foot stamping. Further, they also tend to appeal to these introspective claims in arguments about the strong thesis, where often, they function as key premises. To the extent that this is so, there is little genuine acknowledgement that their arguments are considerably weakened by the fact of introspection-based disagreement itself.

This above point does not rule out that participants in the debate about cognitive phenomenology could get themselves in an improved epistemic position where disagreement between them ceases. Indeed, one motivation of Conciliationism about disagreement in general is that by requiring the rational accommodation of evidence that one has made a mistake, disagreement is an opportunity of epistemic self-improvement. Disagreement is a sign of our fallible cognitive nature and the beliefs of others can serve as checks on our cognition (Christensen 2007). On this conception, the goal is to get into a better epistemic position, once one has had time to adjust and improve, and reconsider one's evidential base in the light of others' disagreement.

But the opportunity for epistemic self-improvement in the case of introspection-based disagreement about cognitive phenomenology is of an altogether less hopeful kind. According to a compelling assumption, reliable methods of inquiry tend to produce agreement. Disagreement indicates an epistemic deficiency of some sort.[10] An explanation of the disagreement should show what or who is epistemically blameworthy—it should show why the method of inquiry employed did not produce agreement in this case. Thus, among other things, disagreement produced by a given method of inquiry raises questions about the reliability of that method itself. As we saw,

---

[9] This is not to say that a rational difference between a right and a wrong side (if there is one) might not show up somewhere in one's epistemic assessment of the overall situation (see Kelly 2010 and Christensen 2011 for relevant discussion of the general case).

[10] Assuming, of course, that there is only one maximally rational response concerning a given set of evidence.

in the case of the introspection-based disagreement about the strong thesis, we lack positive evidence to show that introspection is generally reliable and if anything, we have evidence from empirical science and from other uses of introspection in psychology and philosophy to the contrary. Moreover, the circumstances of the introspection-based disagreement about cognitive phenomenology—the fact that disagreement is spread out over time and individuals—prevents plausible *ad hoc* explanations in terms of failure to respond correctly to the evidence by one side of the disagreement only. We cannot appeal to special circumstances like adverse lighting conditions or too much caffeine in this case. A very likely cause of epistemic deficiency thus seems to be introspection itself—at least when it comes to introspection as a source of beliefs about what conscious thought is like.

If that is right, we ought to be very cautious in using an introspective method to argue for or against a view about cognitive phenomenology. The opportunity for epistemic self-improvement flowing from rational accommodation of evidence provided by the introspection-based disagreement about cognitive phenomenology consists, perhaps, in recognizing the severe limitation of introspection. We can improve our epistemic standing by restricting as much as possible use of a method of inquiry for which we have good evidence that it is unreliable.[11]

References

Bayne, T. and Spener, M. (2010). 'Introspective Humility,' in *Philosophical Issues*, 20(1): 1–22.

Block, N. (1978). 'Troubles with Functionalism,' *Perception and Cognition: Minnesota Studies in the Philosophy of Science*, 9: 261–325.

Christensen, D. (2007). 'Epistemology of Disagreement: The Good News,' *Philosophical Review*, 116: 187–217.

——(2011). 'Disagreement, Question-Begging and Epistemic Self-Criticism', *Philosopher's Imprint*, 11(6).

Goldman, A. (1993). 'The Psychology of Folk Psychology', *Behavioral and Brain Sciences*, 16: 15–23.

Horgan, T. and Tienson, J. (2002). 'The Intentionality of Phenomenology and the Phenomenology of Intentionality', in D. Chalmers (ed.) *Philosophy of Mind: Classical and Contemporary Readings*. Oxford: Oxford University Press: 530–3.

Hurlburt, R. and Schwitzgebel, E. (2007). *Describing Inner Experience? Proponent Meets Skeptic*. Cambridge: MIT Press.

Jackendoff, R. (1987). *Consciousness and the Computational Mind*. Cambridge: MIT Press.

Kelly, T. (2005). 'The Epistemic Significance of Disagreement', in J. Hawthorne and T. Gendler Szabo (eds), *Oxford Studies in Epistemology, Vol 1*. Oxford: Oxford University Press: 167–96.

---

[11] I am grateful to audiences at Cardiff University and St Hilda's College, Oxford, as well as to Tim Bayne, Michelle Montague, and two anonymous referees for helpful comments.

Kelly, T. (2010). 'Peer Disagreement and Higher-Order Evidence', in R. Feldman and T. Warfield (eds), *Disagreement*. Oxford: Oxford University Press: 111–174.

Lackey, J. (2010). 'A Justificationist View of Disagreement's Epistemic Significance', in A. Haddock, A, Millar, and D. Pritchard (eds), *Social Epistemology*. Oxford: Oxford University Press: 298–325.

Levine, J. (1983). 'Qualia and the Explanatory Gap', *Pacific Philosophical Quarterly*, 69: 222–40.

Lormand, E. (1996). 'Non-Phenomenal Consciousness', *Noûs*, 30: 242–61.

Pitt, D. (2004). 'The Phenomenology of Cognition, or What is It Like to Think That P?' *Philosophy and Phenomenological Research*, 69(1): 1–36.

Robinson, W. (2005). 'Thoughts Without Distinctive Non-Imagistic Phenomenology', *Philosophy and Phenomenological Research*, 70(3): 531–64.

Schwitzgebel, E. (2008). 'The Unreliability of Naïve Introspection', *Philosophical Review*, 117: 245–73.

——(2011). *Perplexities of Consciousness*. Cambridge: MIT Press.

Siewert, C. (1998). *The Significance of Consciousness*. Princeton, NJ: Princeton University Press.

Spener, M. (2011). 'Using First-Person Data', *Journal of Consciousness Studies*, 18(1): 165–79.

——(MS). 'Phenomenal Adequacy and Introspective Evidence'.

Strawson, G. (1994). *Mental Reality*. Cambridge: MIT Press.

Tye, M. (1995). *Ten Problems of Consciousness: A Representational Theory of the Phenomenal Mind*. Cambridge: MIT Press.

Cognitive Phenomenology: Real Life

Galen Strawson

I will now utter certain words which form a sentence: these words, for instance: Twice two are four. Now, when I say these words, you not only hear *them*—the words—you *also* understand what they mean. That is to say, something happens in your minds—some act of consciousness—*over and above* the hearing of the words, some act of consciousness which may be called the understanding of their meaning.

G. E. Moore (1910–11: 57)

... let me see if I can doze off 1 2 3 4 5 what kind of flowers are those they invented like the stars the wallpaper in Lombard Street was much nicer the apron he gave me was like that something only I only wore it twice better lower this lamp and try again so as I can get up early Ill go to Lambes there beside Findlaters and get them to send us some flowers to put about the place in case he brings him home tomorrow today I mean no no Fridays an unlucky day first I want to do the place up someway the dust grows in it I think while Im asleep then we can have music and cigarettes I can accompany him first I must clean the keys of the piano with milk whatll I wear a white rose or those fairy cakes in Liptons at 712d a lb or the other ones with the cherries in them and the pinky sugar 11d a couple of lbs of those a nice plant for the middle of the table Id get that cheaper in wait wheres this I saw them not long ago I love flowers ...

James Joyce (1922: 642)

It is sometimes necessary to repeat what we all know. All mapmakers should place the Mississippi in the same location, and avoid originality.

Saul Bellow (1970: 228)

1 Introduction

In recent analytic philosophy, as opposed to the phenomenological tradition in philosophy initiated by Brentano and Husserl,[1] phenomenology has standardly been taken to be restricted to the study of sensory experiences, including mental images of certain sorts, and feelings, including mood feelings and emotional feelings. I'll say that phenomenology so understood is confined to *sense/feeling experience*, or *sense/feeling phenomenology*, bringing under this heading all sensation-mood-emotion-image-feeling phenomena considered (so far as they can be) entirely independently of any cognitive mental phenomena.

There's a lot more to experience than sense/feeling experience. There's also what I'll call *cognitive experience*, or *cognitive phenomenology*. There's meaning-experience, thought-experience, understanding-experience. There is, most generally, everything about experience that isn't just a matter of sense/feeling experience as just defined.

In this paper I'll take 'sense/feeling experience' and 'cognitive experience' to be mutually exclusive and jointly exhaustive terms (some think that there's experience that falls under neither head). It may be that there are no pure cases of sense/feeling alone, or cognitive experience alone, but the distinction may be valid and useful for all that.

In analytic philosophy there is considerable resistance to the idea that anything rightly called 'cognitive experience' or 'cognitive phenomenology' exists. This is remarkable for many reasons, one of which is that it's doubtful that sense/feeling experience ever occurs without cognitive experience in the experience of an ordinary adult human being. Nor do the two things simply co-occur. They're profoundly interwoven, although we can for purposes of philosophical analysis distinguish sense/feeling elements of experience sharply from cognitive elements of experience.

I'm going to argue for the existence of cognitive experience or cognitive phenomenology, beginning with some assumptions and a few terminological remarks. The main action begins in §6.

2 Terminological preliminaries

In origin and full propriety, 'phenomenology' is the name of a theoretical discipline. Phenomenology is the general study, the -ology, of appearances, of the *experiential character* of experiences—the *experiential* or *qualitative* or *what-it's-likeness* character that experiences have for those who have them as they have them. Recently, the term has come to be used for its own subject matter, so that one can now say that phenomenology (original sense) is the study of phenomenology (new sense). This is less than

---

[1] See e.g. Brentano (1888–9), Husserl (1900–01). When I cite a work I give the date of first publication, or occasionally the date of composition, while the page reference is to the edition listed in the bibliography.

ideal, but the innovation doesn't do any great harm. (Something similar happened with 'ontological', which is standardly used where 'ontic' or 'ontical' is more appropriate.)[2]

I assume that experiences (perceptual experiences, conscious thoughts, and so on) are spatially located events, neural electrochemical goings-on that have as such—in having mass, charge, shape, size, and so on—a certain non-experiential character.[3] This non-experiential character is of no concern to phenomenology, which restricts itself to the study of the experiential character of experiences considered just as such: considered without any reference to any part or aspect of the reality of the experiences other than the part or aspect of reality which consists in the existence of their experiential character. Phenomenology also puts aside 'the world', considered as that which experiences are typically experiences of.[4] In this respect, Husserl's slogan '*Zu den Sachen selbst!*'—'Back to the things themselves!'—is very misleading.

I'll use the plural-lacking mass term 'experience' to refer to: that part or aspect of reality that consists in the existence of experiential character considered just as such and nothing else; and I'll use the plural-accepting count-noun 'experience(s)' as I already have, to talk of experiences (plural) as things that we ordinarily take to have properties other than experiential-character properties, e.g. properties attributed by physics and neurophysiology. Experience, then, is the (experiential) what-it's-likeness of experiences.[5]

Examples of experience? Basic examples will do—the experiential character of pain, tasting potatoes, seeing the colour blue, finding something funny. What are these things like? You know what they're like from your own case. This answer, condemned by Wittgensteinians, is exactly right. It doesn't matter if what it is like for you is qualitatively different from what it is like for me, just so long as it is like something for you, as of course it is.[6]

---

[2] I'll treat 'experiential character', 'qualitative character', and 'what-it's-likeness character' as synonymous. Strictly speaking, one should talk of 'experiential what-it's-likeness', because to have any (intrinsic, non-relational) properties at all is to be like something. There's something it's like to be a stone (there's an answer to the question 'What is it like?' asked about the stone); it's just that there's nothing it's like *for* the stone. It's the 'for' that is crucial, and it entails experience or consciousness in this use, just as it does in the old 'for itself'/ 'in itself' distinction. Clearly the same goes for 'qualitative character': strictly speaking, one should talk of 'experiential qualitative' character, because to have any (intrinsic, non-relational) properties at all is *ipso facto* to have qualitative character—to have a certain character, quality-wise. But in philosophy-of-mind contexts like the present one, 'qualitative' is standardly used to refer only to the experiential qualities that the experience has, i.e. the qualities that constitute its having the experiential character it does.

[3] This claim conceals a further assumption, in fact, which is relied on in the next sentence. For if some form of panpsychism is true, as it may be, these supposedly non-experiential properties or qualities of experience are, ultimately, wholly a matter of experiential being (see e.g. Strawson 2008: 7–8). For the purposes of this paper, though, I'll assume that this isn't so.

[4] Although experiences are of course part of the world, and can, furthermore, be about themselves.

[5] It's what many have in mind when they talk about 'consciousness' or 'conscious experience', but the term 'consciousness' has been used in too many ways to be stable. What Block calls 'access consciousness' (1995) is not consciousness at all, as I understand the term.

[6] There's no force in the Wittgensteinian idea that one can't really think that other people have experience if one grounds one's conception of what experience is on one's own case. The idea seems to be that if one's conception of what experience is grounded in this way, then it comes stamped '*mine*' in a

3 Real realism about experience

Phenomenology incorporates all-out realism about experience (experience is its whole subject matter). But by 'realism about experience' I mean *real* realism about experience. The pleonasm would be unnecessary if a number of analytic philosophers hadn't in the last eighty years or so tried, more or less covertly, to 'reduce' the experiential to the non-experiential, continuing to speak of the experiential in a seemingly realist way while holding that, really, only the non-experiential exists.

A good way to convey what it is to be a real realist about experience is to say that it's to continue to take colour experience or taste experience, say, or experience of pain, or of an itch, to be what one took it to be wholly unreflectively—what one knew it to be in having it—before one did any philosophy, e.g. when one was five. However many new and surprising facts[7] they learn about experience from scientists, real realists' basic grasp—knowledge—of what experience is remains exactly the same as it was before they did any philosophy. It remains, in other words, entirely correct, grounded in the fact that to have experience at all is already to know what experience is, however little one reflects about it. I think this way of specifying what I mean by 'experience' is helpful because it guarantees that anyone who claims not to know what I mean is being disingenuous.[8]

When I say that experiences are neural goings-on, I'm not in any way denying the reality of experience as just defined. I'm assuming that materialism is true, for the purposes of this paper. I am, though, a *real* materialist, a realistic materialist, and a real materialist is someone who is fully realist (real-realist, five-year-old realist) about the thing whose reality is more certain than the reality of anything else—experience. I'm an 'adductive' materialist, not a reductive materialist. Adductive materialists don't claim that experience is, in being wholly physical, anything less than we ordinarily conceive it to be. They claim, rather, that the physical must be something more than we ordinarily conceive it to be, if only because many of the wholly physical goings-on in the wholly physical brain are experience, experience as defined above: (experiential) what-it's-likeness.

('solipsistic') way that makes it contradictory or unintelligible to think that other people might have it. But this view is baseless. All one has to do is to think that things might be for others something like it is for oneself, and this 'something like' is extremely accommodating. It covers the supposition that the qualitative character of someone else's experience may be very different from one's own (a common thought among young children). In this case, the other person is still thought of as fundamentally like oneself, simply in having experience at all.

[7] Facts about the 'filling-in' that characterizes visual experience, for example, or about 'change blindness' or 'inattentional blindness'. See e.g. Pessoa and de Weerd (2003), Simons and Levin (1997), Chun and Marois (2002).

[8] This reference to five year olds, in explicating real realism about experience, is sometimes received with hostility. Some doubt whether five year olds have the concept of experience, or a sensation, at all. The way to remove this doubt is to discuss pins and needles or other odd sensations or tastes with them, or indeed with younger children. Certainly six year olds are quite often interested in the question whether others see colours as they do.

Many philosophers think that there's a major puzzle in the existence of experience. But the appearance of a puzzle arises only given an assumption there is no reason to make. This is the assumption that we know something about the intrinsic nature of the physical that gives us reason to think that it cannot itself be experiential. It's not just that this assumption is false. There is in fact zero evidence for the existence of anything non-experiential in the universe. There never has been any evidence, and never will be. What we have instead is a wholly unsupported assumption about our capacity to know the nature of things (in particular the physical), which must be put severely in doubt by the fact that it seems to create this puzzle if by nothing else.

One of the most important—revelatory—experiences a philosopher brought up in the Western tradition can have is to realize that this assumption has no respectable foundation. This experience is life-changing, philosophically, but it comes only to some—although the point is elementary. The fact that *physics* has no terms specifically for experiential phenomena (I'm putting aside the view that reference to conscious observers is essential in quantum mechanics) is not evidence in support of the view that experience doesn't exist. It isn't even evidence in support of the view that something non-experiential exists.[9]

4 Cognitive experience (cognitive phenomenology)

The fact that experience has irreducibly cognitive aspects in addition to sense/feeling aspects was perhaps never questioned throughout the history of philosophy until the advent of analytic philosophy in the twentieth century.[10] It was only that curious and in many respects admirable academic culture (to which I belong) which gave rise to the view I want to dispute,

The Remarkable View that the subject matter of phenomenology (the completely general study of the experiential character of experience) is nothing more than sense/feeling experience as characterized above.

This view achieved such dominance that the phrase 'qualitative character', used to refer quite generally to the experiential character of experience, came to many to sound

---

[9] Among those who have grasped this are Locke, Spinoza, Hume, Kant, Russell, Eddington, Whitehead, and Chomsky; for some discussion, see Strawson (2003). Note that there's no tension between the view that the physical is at bottom wholly experiential and the view that physics and cosmology, and indeed the other sciences, get a very great deal right about the structure of reality.

[10] The British empiricists sometimes suggest that thinking is just a matter of having images, but this isn't a denial of the existence of cognitive experience; it's a theory about its vehicle. When they say that thinking about a chair involves having a visual image of a chair (say), the 'image' they have in mind isn't just a complex colour patch; it's loaded with cognitive content.

synonymous with 'sense/feeling'. In this way, the mistake was built into the words with which the question was discussed.[11]

We can put aside here the remarkable fact that the Remarkable View grew up alongside

The Astonishing View that there's actually no such thing as the experiential character of experience (no such thing as conscious experience, experiential what-it's-likeness, as real realists understand it),

from which it follows that there's really no such thing as the discipline of phenomenology. And we can put aside

The Astonishing Fact that the Astonishing View was for a considerable period of time the dominant view among a significant number who considered themselves, and were by some others considered, to be at the forefront of their subject,

along with its bedfellow

The Truly Incredible Fact that this was part of a movement one of whose openly stated aims—under various names, such as 'behaviourism' and 'functionalism, and now, it seems, 'strong representationalism'—was to reduce the experiential to the non-experiential, i.e. to show that the experiential was, in some way, really wholly non-experiential.[12]

We can put aside the Astonishing and Truly Incredible Facts in order to focus on the Remarkable View: the view that the subject matter of phenomenology is nothing more than sense/feeling experience; the view, in other words, that one can in principle give an exhaustive account of all aspects of human experience, all aspects of the actual character that experience has for us as we have it from moment to moment and from day to day—everything about human lived experience, everything that our lives are to us and for us—purely by reference to sense/feeling experience.

It was because the Remarkable View was prevalent at the end of the last century that I adopted the term 'cognitive phenomenology', rather than simply 'phenomenology', when trying to describe what it is to experience oneself as a free agent, or as a 'self' in the sense of an inner mental presence distinct from the whole human being (Strawson 1986, 1997). The discussion of free will was 'centrally concerned with what one might call the "general cognitive phenomenology" of freedom ... with our beliefs, feelings,

---

[11] The word 'phenomenal' also plays a role, in so far as it's taken to be interchangeable with 'phenomenological', for 'phenomenal' is naturally taken to refer only to sense/feeling phenomena, whereas 'phenomenological' must be taken more widely if it is to have a general use.

[12] Hume's explanation is of a familiar kind: 'Whatever has the air of a paradox, and is contrary to the first and most unprejudic'd notions of mankind is often greedily embrac'd by philosophers, as shewing the superiority of their science, which cou'd discover opinions so remote from vulgar conception. On the other hand, any thing propos'd to us, which causes surprize and admiration, gives such a satisfaction to the mind, that it indulges itself in those agreeable emotions, and will never be perswaded that its pleasure is entirely without foundation. From these dispositions in philosophers and their disciples arises that mutual complaisance betwixt them; while the former furnish such plenty of strange and unaccountable opinions, and the latter so readily believe them' (Hume 1739–40: §1.2.1.1; Selby-Bigge (edn): 26).

attitudes, practices, and ways of conceiving or thinking about the world, in so far as these involve the notion of freedom' (1986: p. v, new edn. p. vi); the aspects of the sense of the self that were under consideration were 'conceptual rather than affective: it is the *cognitive phenomenology* of the sense of the self that is fundamentally in question, i.e. the conceptual structure of the sense of the self, the structure of the sense of the self considered (as far as possible) independently of any emotional aspects that it may have'.[13]

These are wide uses of the term 'cognitive phenomenology' or 'cognitive experience'. I want now to consider something more specific: the experience one has—one could call it 'understanding-experience' or 'meaning-experience'[14]—when (for example) one hears someone speak in a language one understands. I'm going to argue for the reality of cognitive experience understood in this narrow sense.

5 Definition of 'content', 'internal content', 'external content'

I say I'm going to argue for the reality of cognitive experience. I could equally well say that I'm going to argue for the reality of *cognitive-experiential content* as something that exists over and above sense/feeling content. It may seem unwise to introduce another term at this stage, especially one as troublesome as 'content', but I think it will be helpful.

The content of an experience, as I take the term, is *absolutely everything that is experienced in the having of the experience*, everything that is experientially registered in any way.[15] It's everything that the experience is an experience of, where 'of' is understood in the widest possible manner, and, in particular, in such a way that it covers everything that it is like to have the experience, experientially, in addition to whatever external objects the experience may have. So all experience, what-it's-likeness, considered just as such, is mental content. When I look at a tree, the whole experiential being of my experience of the tree is a matter of the content of the

---

[13] (Strawson 1997: §3; see also (Strawson 1986: 92 (new edn. 82)): '"a mental someone" is a good description of one absolutely central way in which we think of ourselves. Here as elsewhere I am concerned only with this fact of "cognitive phenomenology", and not at all with the question of what if anything a "mental someone" could possibly be, factually or metaphysically speaking'.

[14] See Appendix, pp. 316–22. Note that the term 'understanding-experience' is misleading in so far as it implies that one understands correctly, for strictly speaking it is experience *as of* understanding that is in question: misunderstanding is equally a matter of understanding-experience. (To that extent, 'meaning-experience' is a better term.)

[15] Here I follow Montague (2009: 497): 'the content of a perceptual experience is *whatever is given to one in having a particular perceptual experience*. It is whatever is given to consciousness, however this is further characterized. Since I take the phenomenological character of the experience to be part of what is given in the experience, it is part of the content of the experience....' Note that this definition of 'content' is very different from the definition according to which 'the intentional content of an intentional state is just a matter of the "aspect" under which its object is presented' (see e.g. Crane 2006: 4).

experience, just as much as the tree is in being the thing in the world that my experience is an experience of.

Suppose (temporarily and for purposes of argument) that sensation isn't in itself intentional or representational in any way. It certainly doesn't follow that sensation isn't a matter of mental content. It is of course a matter of mental content: it's 'sensory content'. Mental content doesn't have to be of anything other than itself in order to be mental content. All experiential what-it's-likeness is phenomenological content, quite independently of whether or not it can be said to be intentional in any way.[16]

Consider a few of my philosophical 'Twins', my 'Instant Twin' my 'Brain in a Vat Twin', and my 'Perfect Twin Earth Twin'.[17] Our four courses of experience are very different, when it comes to the question what they are of, non-experientially speaking; they have in that sense very different contents. But there's a no less fundamental sense in which they have identical content, simply because they are by hypothesis experientially qualitatively identical: they're of the same phenomenological-content *type*, although they are of course numerically distinct occurrences of content.

May we say that they have different external content and identical internal content? Perhaps—but the internal/external content (or narrow/wide/broad content) distinction is very unclear.[18] This is partly because philosophers have thought too much about trees, mountains, natural kinds, and so on, when characterizing external content, and not enough about other equally concrete, equally worldly items like other people's pains and colour experiences (or indeed their own pains and colour experiences). We can certainly distinguish between phenomenological content and non-phenomenological content, but this distinction doesn't line up neatly with the distinction between internal and external content.

In this situation of unclarity, I propose to *define* 'internal content' as follows:

Internal content is concretely occurring phenomenological content.

It's concretely occurring experiential what-it's-likeness considered just as such. The internal content of an experience is, if you like, the actual intrinsic phenomenological being of that experience.

What about external content?

External content is every other sort of mental content.

It not only includes trees and so on; it can also include mental states, including phenomenological states. Internal (phenomenological) content can itself be external content, for it is part of the world, and can be an object of thought. I can think about

---

[16] Experience of pain is indeed experience *of* pain. Pain or painfulness is (part of) the *content* of the experience, even if it doesn't represent (is not intentionally directed to or at) anything other than itself.

[17] My Instant Twin has by extraordinary fluke just popped into existence, molecule-for-molecule identical to me. Perfect Twin Earth is qualitatively identical to Earth in every respect (the stuff they call 'water' on Perfect Twin Earth is H_2O).

[18] On this point see e.g. Segal (2008: 367).

concretely occurring phenomenological content, yours or mine, for I can think about anything real.[19]

So we can consider internal content, as defined, both as internal content and as external content. We consider it simply as internal content when we consider it as immediately phenomenologically given. When it's thought about (say), it's also external content. The internal/external distinction remains in place; it's robust as defined. For although external content can include internal content (although internal content can be external content), still the phenomenon of a mental episode's having external content is never the phenomenon of a mental episode's having internal content.[20]

My Twins' experiences are of the same internal-content *type* as mine, but they are of course distinct as *tokens* of internal content. My currently occurring two-second experience of red is a clockable portion of internal phenomenological content, but it's also a token of a certain unclockable *type* of internal phenomenological content, and the type itself is a matter of *external* content.[21]

I take it, then, that there is both internal and external content, and that there's a lot more to external content than the kinds of things that are standardly discussed in philosophy of mind (mountains, trees, natural kinds, and so on). As far as concrete external content is concerned, I take it that

[1] one can't specify the content of a mental state like a genuine thought about an object, or a genuine perception of an object, without referring to the object itself.

I'm also happy to endorse a stronger formulation of this view, according to which

[2] the object of such a thought or perception is, quite literally, a constituent of that thought or perception.[22]

[1] and [2] are wholly compatible with the view that there's also internal content, because the internal content of a conscious experience is (as just remarked) simply its occurrent experiential or phenomenological content. The character of this internal

---

[19] I can even think about things outside my light-cone, because I can think about the universe, or everything that exists. One interesting question concerns what to say about internal content if, as many suppose, it is 'self-luminous' or 'self-intimating'—if all awareness somehow comports awareness of that very awareness. Does this mean that all internal content has itself as external content in some way? I think the answer is no, but this is a subject for another time.

[20] This is so even when part of the mental episode's external content is its internal content, as in the case of the conscious thought *this very thought is puzzling*. I argue for this in 'Content—internal and external': internal content is immediately phenomenologically given content *as* immediately phenomenologically given. This may sound rather complicated, but there's nothing obscure about it. The difference between the way in which internal content is internal content and the way in which it can be external content is no more mysterious than the difference between being in pain and thinking about being in pain (the latter difference is just a case of the former).

[21] It must be, given that it's content, because it's not concretely occurring content, and all internal content is concretely occurring content; it is, some would say, an abstract object, which is certainly something external to a mind, something that is not itself a mental item. For a good discussion see e.g. McGinn (1989).

[22] I take it that both versions entail the essential 'object-dependence' of the perception. (Realists about 'abstract objects' can remove the restriction of [1] and [2] to concrete external content.)

content can be fully characterized without any reference to the object the thought or perception is of or about, because it is (*ex hypothesi*) identical to the character of the corresponding experiences of the thinker's or perceiver's Twins.[23]

Plainly, real realism about experience commits one to the existence of internal content, and to the idea that numerically distinct occurrences or 'tokens' of internal content can be qualitatively (phenomenologically) identical—identical in respect of internal-content type. (Every token of internal content is necessarily of some type just in having phenomenological character at all.) I take it to follow that a viable, realistic general theory of mental content, and of perception, must acknowledge the existence of both external and internal content. Certainly any naturalistic theory of mental content must do so, because real realism about experience is the first step in any genuine naturalism.[24]

6 Meaning-experience

Almost all—perhaps all—our daily experience essentially involves cognitive-experiential content, whether we're birdwatching, cooking, or climbing. Cognitive-experiential content is constitutive of our seeing horses, chairs, and so on specifically as horses, chairs, and so on (and equally of our mis-seeing them as rocks, bushes, and so on), for this seeing-as involves something that is essentially over and above sense/feeling content. I'm going to put this point aside until §8, though, in order to focus on the special case of understanding-experience or meaning-experience, or rather, more narrowly, propositional meaning-experience, such as one may have in thinking. More narrowly still, I'm going to focus on propositional meaning-experience involving linguistic representation: the experience of consciously entertaining and understanding specific and expressly propositional contents as a result of hearing certain sounds or seeing certain marks. This is a rather special case of cognitive experience, but it's worth considering because it's a salient case, and because its existence has often been questioned, even by those who may be open to the idea that everyday perceptual experience has cognitive-experiential content.

Consider, then, your reading and understanding this sentence and the next. This comprehending reading—it's going on at this very moment—is part of the course of your experience. More specifically: the semantic or propositional content of the sentences, including this one, is (I submit) playing a large part in determining the overall character, the overall or total lived experiential character, of this particular stretch of the course of your experience; although you're also aware of the page and the print and also, perhaps, rain on the window, wind in trees, birdsong, traffic noise. More

---

[23] Conscious thoughts have phenomenological character (cognitive-phenomenological character) just as perceptions have sense/feeling phenomenological character; this is still to be argued.
[24] On the radical anti-naturalism of what is often today known as 'naturalism', see e.g. Strawson (2006).

specifically still: in reading and understanding the sentences you have cognitive experience, whatever other experiences (e.g. sense/feeling experiences) reading and understanding may cause in you. This cognitive experience is constitutive of your conscious comprehending, and the claim is simply this. It is something that has to be adverted to in a full account of the experiential character of your experience during this time.

To deny this, one must hold that the total lifelong character of our lived experience—everything that life is to us experientially—consists entirely of bare or pure sensation or feeling of one kind or another. It must, for example, be false to say that anguish at someone's death includes *conscious comprehending believing entertaining* of the proposition that he is dead.

I think this is enough to refute the view that there's no such thing as cognitive phenomenology. What is most striking and painful, for ordinary—real—people, in such a case, is the way the conscious comprehending believing entertaining strikes again and again.

Note, though, that to say this is not to say that the causation is as it seems in such a case. It feels as if it is (a) the constantly returning conscious comprehending believing entertaining of the proposition that Louis is dead that produces (b) the repeated physical–emotional shock, but the actual causation may be different. It may be that (c) the sub-experiential, non-conscious representation of the fact of death produces (b) the physical–emotional shock, which triggers (a) the conscious comprehending entertaining of the fact; or it may be that (c) gives rise to (a) and (b) concurrently. What is not in question is the reality of (a).

Leaving this dramatic case, consider the overall experiential character of your current experience right now as you read this. It's not just and wholly a matter of sensation, sense/feeling content, on the experience side, and entirely non-conscious registration of meaning, and corresponding change of dispositional set, on the non-experiential side. Why has this fact become obscure to some philosophers? One reason among many, perhaps, is that it's very hard to pin down the contribution to the overall character of your experience that is being made by your apprehension (perfect or not) of the semantic content of the proposition expressed by a sentence in such a way as to be able to take it as the object of reflective thought. It seems far easier to do this in the case of the phenomenological character of an experience of green. In fact, when it comes to the attempt to represent fully to oneself the phenomenological character of understanding a sentence like 'Consider, then, your reading and understanding this very sentence' it seems that all one can usefully do is rethink the sentence as a whole, comprehendingly; and the trouble with doing this is that it seems to leave one with no mental room to stand back in such a way as to be able to take the experiential character of one's understanding of the sentence, redelivered to one by this rethinking, as the principal object of one's attention. One's mind is taken up with the sense of the thought in such a way that it's very hard to think about the character of the experience of having the thought.[25]

This is true, but it doesn't put the reality of meaning-experience in doubt. It's helpful to consider the parallel between (i) the cognitive experience we have when consciously apprehending a cognitive content and (ii) the sensation of blue we have when looking at a blue object. There's a well-known sense in which we don't, in our immediate live perceptual engagement with the world in everyday life, notice (ii), the sensation of blue considered specifically as such, i.e. as a sensation. Something similar holds in the case of (i): we don't notice cognitive-experiential content considered specifically as such. In case (ii), our experience is that we're simply concerned with whatever blue thing is in question, not the sensation of blue; we experience the blueness simply as a property of the object perceived. In case (i), our experience is that we're simply concerned with whatever cognitive content is in question, not the cognitive experience of it. Both the sensation of blue and the cognitive experience can be said to be 'transparent' or 'diaphanous', given the sense, just expounded, in which we're not aware of them as such in our dealing with the blue object or the cognitive content.[26]

Although there is this parallel, there's also a difference. For we can in the case of the sensation of blue bring it to attention considered specifically as such. In fact, we can do this even as we continue to have live experience of the blue thing, although we don't naturally do so, and although it isn't that easy. It's not so clear that we can do this in the case of the cognitive-experiential content of a conscious thought. At the very least, it's far more difficult to bring cognitive-experiential content to attention for inspection, because of the way in which one's mind is taken up with the cognitive content of the thought in such a way that it's very hard to think about the character of the experience of having the thought.

Some philosophers who call themselves 'direct realists' deny this difference, because they deny that we can bring the sensation of blue to attention considered specifically as such while perceiving something blue. I think they must have failed to engage in the exercises that are, as Reid points out, necessary for anyone who hopes to get anywhere in the philosophy of perception.[27]

---

[25] Compare Papineau: 'where imaginative phenomenal references to *perceptual* states activate "faint copies" of those states, imaginative phenomenal references to non-sensory thought episodes activate those thoughts themselves. When I imagine thinking that the Roman Empire lasted more than seven centuries, I think this very thought, not some faint copy of it' (2002: 221).

[26] The terms 'transparent' and 'diaphanous' come from G. E. Moore, but he is often badly misread. The case he considers is different from the one in the text (see e.g. Van Cleve 2005), and these two terms are I think ultimately ill-advised.

[27] 'It is indeed difficult, at first, to disjoin things in our attention which have always been conjoined, and to make that an object of reflection which never was before, but some pains and practice will overcome this difficulty in those who have got into the habit of reflecting on the operations of their own minds' (Reid 1785: 196; he's concerned with a somewhat different kind of case). There's a brilliant discussion of the 'transparency' of the sensations of touch in Reid's *Inquiry* (1764: §5.2), and his remark (1764: §2.9) about the way in which words heard, read, or mentally imaged are also 'transparent', relative

The term 'direct realism' has recently been put through the mangle, like so many other expressions in philosophy of mind, and no longer has an agreed sense. But we can at least hang on to the point that no sane direct realist, describing what it is to see the blueness of something blue, denies the reality and necessity of having a sensation of blue, where the sensation of blue is considered as an experience of a kind that one could have in the absence of any external object. Direct realism says, correctly, that when I look at something blue I see its blueness, not a representation of its blueness. But to say this is not of course to deny the reality of the sensation of blue; for the having of the sensation of blue is the seeing of the thing's blueness. No blue sensation, no seeing the thing's blueness![28] There's no greater foolishness in the philosophy of perception than to think that one needs to downplay or deny the reality of the sensation of blue (considered as a thing of a kind that one could have in the absence of any external object) for fear that it might somehow get in the way between the subject and the object seen.

There's more to say on this.[29] For the moment, it's enough to note that the same general considerations hold in the case of cognitive experience as in the case of seeing a thing's blueness. No blue sensation, no seeing the thing's blueness. No cognitive-experiential content, no conscious understanding entertaining of a cognitive content.[30]

The last sentence indicates another potential difficulty, when it comes to convincing philosophers of the reality of cognitive-experiential content. Confusion can arise from the fact that the occurrence of *cognitive-experiential* content is a matter of the entertaining of *cognitive* content. In a way, things are simple, because cognitive content and cognitive-experiential content are utterly different things. It's the difference between 2 + 2's being 4 and the concrete event of my consciously comprehendingly entertaining the proposition that $2 + 2 = 4$, or between this postbox's being red and my consciously thinking or perceiving that the postbox is red. But there is also plenty of scope for getting confused.[31]

to our seemingly immediate understanding of their meaning, carries over directly to an account of the transparency of cognitive experience relative to the apprehension of cognitive content. See also Berkeley (1709: §51): 'No sooner do we hear the words of a familiar language pronounced in our ears, but the ideas corresponding thereto present themselves to our minds: in the very same instant the sound and the meaning enter the understanding: so closely are they united that it is not in our power to keep out the one, except we exclude the other also. We even act in all respects as if we heard the very thoughts themselves'.

[28] A blindsighted person may guess a thing's colour correctly, but doesn't see its blueness. So, too, certain sorts of calculating genius always get right answers without understanding what they're doing.

[29] One interesting point is that the 'transparency' of the sensation may be said to remain in place even when and even as one engages in the philosophical exercise of bringing the sensation to attention considered specifically as such.

[30] To say this is not of course to deny that there is such a thing as non-conscious understanding; see Appendix p. 320.

[31] And not just because concretely occurring cognitive-experiential content can itself be cognitive content, like anything that exists, just as any internal content can itself be external content, like anything that exists (see §5).

Having registered this vital point, I'm going to delay discussion of it until §9. For the moment, we have the point that there are respects in which meaning-experience is hard to get at for the purposes of theoretical examination. But suppose we want to give a truly compendious description of the character of the course of your experience, your lived experience, during a ten-second period of time during which (among many other things) you hear someone say 'no one could possibly have had different parents', or 'this sentence is a sentence of English'. We won't—I claim—be able to give anything remotely resembling a complete description of the full character of your experience over that time without citing the fact that you consciously grasped and entertained the thought that no one could possibly have had different parents, or that the sentence you heard was a sentence of English. And by 'the character of the course of your experi- ence' I mean, of course, and pleonastically, the overall *experiential* character of the course of your experience. We have to acknowledge the existence of cognitive- experiential content in addition to sense/feeling experiential content.

You may say this is mere assertion. But to deny it is to hold that we never consciously apprehend meaning. It's to hold that the sense in which we can be said to apprehend meaning or understand something is exactly the same as the sense in which experienceless machines can be said to apprehend meaning or understand something. On this view, we may differ from the machines in having a certain sort of accompanying *feeling* (which must be a purely sense/feeling experience, even if it's correctly phenomenologically characterized as a feeling of *understanding*), but we don't differ from them (in respect of understanding or registering meaning) in that we actually have experience of meaning or of understanding something, whereas they don't. On this view, the total phenomenon of your experience of hearing 'no one could possibly have had different parents', or 'this sentence is a sentence of English' factors neatly and exclusively into (a) pure sense/feeling visual/quasi-auditory/somato- sensory experiential changes in you and (b) wholly non-experiential changes in you which wholly constitute your understanding although they amount to nothing more than differences in the ways in which the occurrence of this understanding changes your behavioural dispositional set.

I'm using undramatic sentences to make the point, rather than sentences like 'The meerkats wore green pyjamas'. This is important, because in talking of cognitive experience, and more particularly propositional meaning-experience, and in focusing on the linguistic case, I'm not concerned in any way with any of the imagistic or emotional or mood-tone experiences that can accompany the understanding of certain words (often in such a way that they can seem to be integral to the semantic understanding). My present aim is to damp down all such accompaniments as far as possible, ideally to nothing, in order to highlight what is then left over, something that is equally real and definite although it can seem troublesomely intangible when we try to reflect about it: the experience that is standardly involved in the mere comprehend- ing of words (read, thought, or heard), where this comprehending is considered completely independently of any imagistic or emotional accompaniments.

7 The argument from interestingness

One way to make the point is to observe that one often reads or hears words or thinks thoughts that are extraordinarily interesting. They're experienced as interesting. Suppose you're interested in what you're reading now. Clearly your being interested must be a response to something in the content of your experience. What is it in the content of your experience that it's a response to? You may be bored by what you're reading now, but you have at some time read a book or listened to words (perhaps on the radio) because the content conveyed by them was completely fascinating. The question, again, is: Why did you continue to read or listen? What was it about the character of your experience that made you continue? Was it merely the sensory content of the visual or auditory goings-on? Obviously not. It was the cognitive-experiential content of your experience as you consciously and comprehendingly registered the cognitive content of the sentences.

The difficulty for those who doubt this is plain. If one wants to give anything like a full account of the experiential or lived character of our experience in merely sense/feeling terms, one has to be able to explain, in those terms alone, how the experience of looking at a piece of paper with a few marks on it, or of hearing three small sounds, can make someone collapse in a dead faint. One has to be able to look at a class of motionless children listening raptly to a story and give a full explanation of the exceptional physiological condition into which the story has put them by reference to nothing more than the auditory experience of the spoken words.

—Not so fast. These people do indeed experience powerful feelings, and this explains their behaviour. And they experience these feelings because the sounds or marks affect them, and because they affect them as things that have a certain meaning, a meaning that it is correct to say that they understand. All this is true. But what we call their understanding is wholly a matter of their non-conscious or sub-experiential processing of the sounds or marks. Understanding, considered specifically as such, has no experiential aspect. All we actually *experience*, strictly speaking, in these cases, are sounds or marks, and then, as a result of the non-conscious processing, we undergo various purely sense/feeling episodes—shock, say, or 'epistemic emotions' such as interest and curiosity. Experience, experience as such, remains wholly a matter of sense/feeling experience.

Let me try this argument.

Premiss 1: if cognitive experience didn't exist, life—experience—would be pretty boring.
Premiss 2: life—experience—is intricately and complexly interesting and various.
Conclusion: cognitive experience exists.

On the no-cognitive-experience view, it seems, experience is utterly without the kind of interest we ordinarily ascribe to it. This is so even if it not only contains terrific basic sensual sense/feeling pleasures, but also many other sense/feeling pleasures, such as the sense/feeling pleasure (or 'epistemic emotion') we may call the *interestedness-feeling*. On the no-cognitive-experience view, we sometimes have the interestedness-*feeling*, but this is wholly a matter of sense/feeling experience, and we're never interested because we consciously grasp or entertain the meaning of something. Why is this? Because *we never consciously grasp or entertain the meaning of anything.* Instead, we (a) non-consciously and sub-experientially register some conceptual content, in a way that is, on the no-cognitive-experience view, and so far as phenomenological goings-on are concerned, no different from the way in which machines can be said to register conceptual content. This then causes in us (b) a certain sort of sense/feeling experience, a certain quantum of interestedness-feeling, say—experience which involves no experience of the specific content of the registered content.

Note that the interestedness-feeling is necessarily generic, because although three equally fascinating propositions *p, q,* and *r,* may be very different, it's their content that differentiates them, and this isn't something that is consciously experienced in any way, on the no-cognitive-experience view. All that is experienced, apart from any quasi-acoustic mental world-images that may also occur,[32] is the interestedness-feeling, and (by hypothesis) *p, q,* and *r* all give rise to exactly the same amount of interestedness-feeling.

One can re-express this by saying that the interestedness-feeling must be monotonic, on the no-cognitive-experience view, in the sense that it is, as a specific type of sense/feeling phenomenon, only ever a matter of more or less. On the no-cognitive-experience view, variety in experience comes only from variety in colours, sounds, and so on, together with variation in the degree of intensity of other feelings such as the interestedness-feeling or curiosity-feeling. This is, certainly, a lot of variety, a great deal of richness of experience, if you like, but these riches are desperate poverty when placed next to the astonishing variety that I and 99.9999999 per cent of humanity know that experience can have and does have on account of the fact that it involves experience of *different thoughts and ideas.*[33]

Consider Lex, who reads and understands 100 great works of literature, and experiences an enormous variety of feelings and emotions. And consider Lux, her sister, who is inexhaustibly fascinated by colours and shapes, and who has, let us suppose, the same rich variety of feelings and emotions on watching an amazing light show, day after day. We can allow that the content of Lux's experience is far from boring, but the dimensions of its possible interestingness (change and movement of colour and shape) are relatively limited. On the cognitive-experience view, Lex's experience is vastly richer than Lux's. It contains more differences than Lux's—by orders of magnitude. But the no-cognitive-experiencers must presumably think the balance is in Lux's favour, for on the basic sensory side, the colour combinations are much more fun and more varied than the black marks on white background, and—on

---

[32] We often think too fast for these to occur, especially when talking to someone else (we then become impatient to reply; see Strawson 1994: 21). In such cases the word-images come when we mentally repeat the thoughts more slowly, after having already entertained or experienced their content.

[33] In reaching this figure, I'm assuming that there are about 200 human beings who genuinely believe that there's no such thing as cognitive experience.

the mood-emotion side—we've supposed that Lux and Lex have similar amounts of surprise-feelings, delight-feelings, and so on, all of which are presumably monotonic in the sense just given.

The no-cognitive-experience view allows that future neuroscientists might take epistemic-emotion readings from Lex's brain and generate matching epistemic emotions in Lux directly, in such a way that Lux experiences them as caused by the light show. Lux's experience is then just as good as Lex's, from the point of view of interestingness, according to the no-cognitive-experience view. If the neuroscientists are well disposed they may also constantly alter Lux's non-conscious dispositional set—ten milliseconds later, say—in all the ways in which it would have been altered if Lux had understood what Lex had understood. But the non-visual experiential difference between them will remain: Lex will have a vast range of terrific experiences that Lux won't have at all.

No-cognitive-experiencers may stress the amazing variety of the types and blends of basic sensory experiences, exteroceptive and interoceptive, that are available to us, and add the amazing variety of feelings that we're inclined to classify separately under the headings of mood and emotion, including epistemic emotions of interest and curiosity and aesthetic emotions of beauty, and so on. The response is the same. This is a lot, but it's little more than nothing when compared with the variety of cognitive experience, the actual experiential richness of human life. The no-cognitive-experiencers can't say that when we read there's an experiential difference between *Hamlet*-content-flavoured interestedness and excitement and *Othello*-content-flavoured interestedness and excitement, or *Catch 22*-content-flavoured interestedness and excitement. There are no such experiential flavours, on their view. At the phenomenological level these works are significant only as powerful causes of interestedness-feelings, sorrow-feelings, and excitement-feelings of greater or lesser degree (apart from being different as sounds or marks). The interestedness experience that they produce must be of the same phenomenological quality, although it may be very differently blended with other emotional feelings in each case.

When Paul Dirac says 'God used beautiful mathematics in creating the world', the no-cognitive-experiencers find sub-experiential processes of understanding in Dirac, sub-experiential processes that fully constitute everything that is correctly called understanding in Dirac and that cause him to have the purely sense/feeling *beauty-feeling*. These processes also put Dirac into a state in which he is, if asked to give an example of a beautiful equation, disposed to give an example by making certain sounds (he might cite the relativistic quantum-mechanical wave equation we know as the Dirac equation or Ricci scalar). So it seems he finds the equation beautiful. He says so, after all. He passes all the behavioural tests. There is, however, no sense in which he has experienced the beauty of the math, the beauty of that particular math, in experiencing the meaning of the math, on the no-cognitive-experience view. For there is no cognitive-experience, no understanding-experience, at all. We do understand things, on this view: that is, sub-experiential processes go on, processes which alter our dispositional set. And we live or experience beauty-feelings, and much else. But we never live or experience meaning. I don't think that this is what it was like to be Dirac, strange as he undoubtedly was.

8 Duck/rabbit

'I don't believe a word of this', says the denier of cognitive experience.

You're a New Age fantasist; worse, you have a nineteenth-century air. And I'd like now to complete my case by saying something about the matter you put aside at the beginning of §6— the matter of the deployment of concepts or other cognitive elements in perception, as when we see something as a dog or a book, say. I'm a reasonable person, and I agree that what you call 'deployment of concepts' is an acceptable name for something psychologically real, a non-conscious, sub-experiential operation that structures the form of our attention in certain ways. Nevertheless, the actual content of experience remains wholly a matter of sense/feeling content. The case of the duck/rabbit figure is exemplary. I'm prepared to allow a sense in which 'what we see' changes; I'm prepared to allow the locution. But there is none the less a fundamental sense in which what we experience phenomenologically speaking remains the same, visually speaking, even as we also have, phenomenologically, something new, a certain kind of shock or jolt feeling caused by the sub-experiential processes that constitute our registration of the change of aspect.

I'm equally prepared to allow that there's something phenomenological that remains unchanged in the duck/rabbit change of aspect (many have an experience which they're inclined to report as an experience of nothing changing, visually, as the figure changes aspect from duck to rabbit). But what good reason could one have to say that, apart from the slight jolt, the total or global phenomenological character of one's experience remains utterly unchanged, as the figure changes aspect from duck to rabbit, and back, and back again? Remember that 99.9999999 of people will flatly disagree with you when you say this. What exactly is the status of your claim that they're wrong—that they're mistaking a mere experiential jolt for a dramatic change in the character of their experience that, on their view, couldn't possibly be adequately characterized without some reference to the notions of duckishness and rabbitishness?[34]

—What if there is after all a visual-phenomenological change? Some hold that something does (or at least may) change purely visually when the aspect switch occurs involuntarily, whatever else happens.

The general response is the same. Many judge that nothing changes 'purely visually' as the figure changes aspect from duck to rabbit, but we can allow that this isn't so, that

---

[34] Ostertag (forthcoming) has a good discussion of an auditory parallel to the duck/rabbit case: one's musical experience changes although one's sonic experience—and sense/feeling experience generally—remains the same (for a different musical case see Peacocke 1992: ch. 3). Robert Frost has a subtle thought about how cognitive phenomenology can affect sensory phenomenology in linguistic cases: 'The sound is everything. The best means of achieving it are vowels consonants verbal accent meter *but the best of all for variety is meaning*. Great thoughts are of value as they supply profound tones' (2006: 364; my emphasis).

there is some such change,[35] while insisting that it will be trivial, indeed probably undetectable, considered apart from the cognitive-experiential change from seeing the figure as a rabbit to seeing it as a duck. There may also be other changes of sense/feeling experiential tone as a result of the visual change (and apart from the jolt), when the switch occurs. So be it. None of these will add up to the experiential change that interests us, the change that can't be adequately characterized without some reference to experienced duckishness and rabbitishness.

On the whole, I think it's better to focus on everyday examples—seeing a car as a car, a cart as a cart, a carrot as a carrot. But since we're on the duck/rabbit case, suppose I've never undergone the aspect switch before. Suppose I've never seen the rabbit, and do so for the first time. I say 'Wow'. Why? On my view, I do so because of a very large and startling change in the character of my experience of the figure.[36] The no-cognitive-experience account of what happens is just this: on the experiential side (which is as always wholly a matter of sense/feeling experience), a feeling of startlement arises to accompany an unchanging (or very subtly changing) visual given, while on the non-experiential side, my dispositional set changes in such a way that I'm now disposed to say things like 'Now I see the rabbit'.

The cognitive experience account I favour allows all that the no-cognitive-experience account allows. It allows, of course, the feeling of startlement; it allows a respect in which the visual given can be said not to change, and also any subtle respects in which it can be said to change. It also allows, of course, the change in non-experiential dispositional set. What it adds is simply this: that the character of my experience changes dramatically, independently of my feeling of startlement, in that I *see the figure as a rabbit*. There is cognitive experience in perception.[37]

This concludes my main argument for the reality of cognitive experience. Husserl would have had great difficulty in understanding why anyone should feel a need to write a paper like this one. I also think it would be a mistake to think that Wittgenstein is on the side of the no-cognitive-experience view—especially when one considers some of the views expressed in Part 2 of the *Philosophical Investigations*.

---

[35] Perhaps as a result of changes in eye focus. Levine (this volume: 110) cites research by Pylyshyn (2001) that suggests that *deciding* to see the duck–rabbit figure in the way in which one is not currently seeing it causes one's eyes to focus on different points of the figure.

[36] I say 'because', but (as on p. 295) I'm not concerned about the precise order of the causation. The 'Wow' could be triggered by a non-experiential realization of the rabbit aspect which slightly precedes the change in the character of my experience.

[37] It's no good trying to avoid this by saying, in Gibsonian phrase, that this is nothing but a change in my 'ecological affordances', if only because there is a phenomenology to awareness of affordances.

9 The relation between cognitive-experiential content and cognitive content 1

Like all experiential content, cognitive-experiential content is (essentially and by definition) wholly a matter of the experiential-qualitative character of experience. But what is the relation of cognitive-*experiential* content, which is a wholly internal matter, to *cognitive* content, actual cognitive content, which is a wholly external matter? What's the relation between

[1] my being in the cognitive-*experiential* state I'm in when I'm looking at or consciously thinking about the River Cherwell flowing under the Humpback Bridge,

and

[2] my being in the *cognitive* state I'm in when I'm looking at or thinking about the River Cherwell flowing under the Humpback Bridge?

I've delayed this important question until now, although it's a potential source of misunderstanding.

I take it that a cognitive state is any state that represents reality in some way, accurately or not. The cognitive content of a cognitive state is the things (and properties) and states of affairs it represents. It's in virtue of its cognitive content that a cognitive state can be true or false. The thoughts that $2 + 2 = 4$, that $2 + 2 = 5$, that Napoleon died in 1821, or 2007, that the River Cherwell is flowing under the Humpback Bridge, that knowledge requires true belief—they're all equally cognitive states. The cognitive content of the thought that $2 + 2 = 5$ includes (for example) the numbers 2 and 5 and the proposition that $2 + 2 = 5$.

So here I am in Oxford, looking at or thinking about the River Cherwell flowing under the Humpback Bridge. The mental state I'm in has both cognitive-experiential content and cognitive content. The two things are quite different, as already remarked (one could say that one is a matter of appearances, the other a matter of reality, but that would be risky). Nevertheless, cognitive-experiential content inevitably occurs when one genuinely consciously entertains or apprehends cognitive content, whether one sees birds and trees and sees them as such, or reads that justice is a virtue, or that all the rivers, lakes, and rain in the world contain only 0.03 per cent of the world's fresh water. We're genuinely consciously conversant with cognitive content only through and in having cognitive experience, just as we genuinely see the blueness of the sky only in having a sensation of blue, the having of which is the seeing of the blueness of the sky.[38]

Is the converse also true? When one is in a state that has cognitive-experiential content one is very often in a state in which one genuinely entertains cognitive

---

[38] I think, in fact, that there's a fundamental sense in which genuine mental cognitive content exists only in occurrent experience, but I won't pursue the point here (see e.g. Strawson 1994: 162–72; Strawson 2005; Gertler 2007).

content, but is this necessarily so? This issue is not important here, and I'll put it aside.[39] Instead, I'll ask two different questions: 'Does same cognitive-experiential content determine same cognitive content?' and its converse 'Does same cognitive content determine same cognitive-experiential content?'

The answer to the first question is certainly No. Consider a couple of my philosophical 'Twins' again, my Instant Twin and my Perfect Twin Earth Twin (see note 17). By hypothesis, they're having exactly the same cognitive-experiential and sensory-experiential experience as I am, qualitatively speaking, as I think about the River Cherwell ('r1') and the Humpback Bridge ('b1'). But my Perfect Twin Earth Twin is thinking about a different river and bridge from the ones I'm thinking about (he's thinking about 'r2' and 'b2'), and my Instant Twin isn't thinking about any actual bridge or river at all. We're all by hypothesis in exactly the same cognitive-experiential state, qualitatively speaking, a state-type I'll call [RB/X], where 'RB' is short for river/bridge experience of the River Cherwellish/Humpback Bridgeish qualitative type, while 'X' marks the precise way in which my Twins and I are now having such experience; but we're all in different cognitive states. Plainly,

[3] same cognitive-experiential content doesn't determine same cognitive content.

The answer to the second question is less obvious. Consider my sister, consciously thinking about the River Cherwell flowing under the Humpback Bridge. She's in the same conscious cognitive state as I am, a state with the same cognitive content, a state of a cognitive-content type I'll call [r1,b1] for short,[40] and we consciously apprehend cognitive content only in having cognitive-experiential content. And yet it doesn't seem to follow that my sister is in exactly the same cognitive-*experiential* state as I am, in being in a state that has the same cognitive content as mine. Perhaps she's in a cognitive-experiential state of type [RB/Y] in being in cognitive-content state [r1, b1]; a state cognitive-experientially similar to mine, no doubt (it's [RB-ish]), but different: not identical (it's Y-ish, not X-ish).

If this can be so, as I think it can, then

[4] same cognitive content doesn't determine same cognitive-experiential content.

My being in this particular token [RB/X]-type cognitive-experiential state, which I'll call '[RB/X1]', using italics and numbers to denote particular instances or tokens of types of states, constitutes my being in this [r1,b1] cognitive-content state, given my causal situation.[41] Given my causal situation, my being in state [RB/X1] constitutes my consciously thinking that—consciously comprehendingly entertaining the thought

---

[39] Can one have cognitive experience without cognitive content because one's conscious thought is in some way incoherent? Well, there will doubtless be elements of cognitive content, even if they don't add up to anything coherent. What about thoughts attributing non-existent properties to non-existent objects? Still cognitive content here, I'd say (see §11 for a point about the 'general propositional form').

[40] It has other content, to do with flowing, and so on, but I'll stick to the river and the bridge.

[41] My Twin on Perfect Twin Earth, contemplating r2 and b2, is in token state [RB/X2].

that—the River Cherwell is flowing under the Humpback Bridge. My [RB/X]-type state [RB/X1] is the vehicle or realizer of my [r1,b1] state. But perhaps my sister is in [RB/Y1], a cognitive-experiential state of type [RB/Y]. It doesn't seem clear that my sister has to be in exactly the same type of cognitive-experiential state that I'm in, when we're both *thinking* about the River Cherwell flowing under the Humpback Bridge, any more than she need be in the same perceptual state I'm in, when we're both *looking* at the River Cherwell flowing under the Humpback Bridge. It seems that this needn't be so even if the scope for variation is very much less, in the case of thought, than it is in the case of perception.

I'll defend this claim further in the next section. Before that I need to put another point in place. When I manage to be in [r1,b1], the cognitive state I fully share with my sister, it's essentially partly because she and I both deploy genuinely world-anchored concepts like the concepts CHERWELL RIVER and HUMPBACK BRIDGE (or THAT RIVER and THAT BRIDGE) and also—let's say—WATER and IRON. I don't, however, share these concepts with my Instant Twin and Classical Twin Earth Twin, who are in cognitive-experiential states ([RB/X3] and [RB/X4]) just like mine.[42] So these concepts (the ones I share with my sister) can't be used in the characterization of my cognitive-experiential content, since that characterization has to be able to represent the fact that I'm the same as my Twins in respect of cognitive-experiential content. But we're surely going to need something very like these concepts to characterize my cognitive-experiential content. At the very least, we're going to need the notion of a *concept**, or the notion of a *concept-aspect*: a notion closely related to our familiar notion of a concept in certain respects, but also sufficiently different from it for us to be able to use it in characterizing the fact that I'm identical to my Twins in respect of my cognitive-experiential content.

What to do? Here's a proposal. Suppose there are 100 Twin Earths. Some are Perfect Twin Earths, some are Classical Twin Earths. On each planet, many people are on their local Facebook—or so they think—and spend a lot of time communicating in English—or so they think—with their friends. In fact, however, they're not on Facebook in the way they suppose. They're on *Intergalactic Facebook*, on which no one ever really communicates with their actual friends, but only with their friends' doubles on other planets. All Intergalactic Facebook messages get mixed up in this way, but no one has any idea that this is so. Everyone seems to understand everyone else perfectly, however, and all arrangements work out fine—marriages and all. Various Instant Twins are also online. Still everything works perfectly.

Intergalactic Facebook English, *IF-English* for short, is the language that is *defined* by the fact of the apparently seamlessly and massively successful communication that takes place among all the billions of users of Intergalactic Facebook. It seems that we can use the terms of IF-English to specify the concepts* or concept-aspects that are suitable for

---

[42]   On Classical Twin Earth, familiarly, the stuff they call 'water' is not H_2O but 'XYZ', and iron, perhaps is 'ABC'. I may of course be said to share WATER and IRON with my Perfect Twin Earth Twin.

use in the specification of the cognitive-experiential content I share with my Twins. I'll call these 'IF-English' concepts or concept-aspects, or 'IFE' concepts or concept-aspects for short. In older terms: IF-English is a language suitable for the specification of narrow content that is as rich as English and isn't limited to sensorily descriptive terms.[43]

—This doesn't really help. In fact it makes things worse, even if it does provide a way of specifying cognitive-experiential content that captures commonalities across Twins. It makes things worse because it cuts you off from the real world. It leaves you locked up in your cognitive-experiential content-world in such a way that you can't really get to be in cognitive states about the real world by being in cognitive-experiential states.

No. We can (must) allow the respect in which this is how we relate to the world, so far as our cognitive contact with it is concerned, without locking ourselves out of reality in any way, or holding that our cognitive contact is in any way indirect. The present proposal may make some people uncomfortable, because they're attracted by a conception of directness of contact with the world that risks going too far by leaving out the fact that what is in question is precisely the phenomenon of *mind*. The idea of our directness of contact with the world is important and valuable; the fact remains—the utterly fundamental fact—that mind relates cognitively to reality by *representing* it. Mind has to represent reality in order to know about it, be in cognitive contact with it. This, though, is no bar to direct realism about thought; exactly the same point holds for direct realism about perception.[44] And one way to express part of what it involves in the case of thought is to say that we make cognitive contact with reality in the particular way we do in conscious thought by deploying a complex IFE-concept-aspect framework that can be well thought of as being insensitive to our actual context in precisely the way that is made vivid by the thought that we could be switched to a world, a Perfect Twin of our own world, and never know. We need to conceptualize our cognition in something like this kind of way for one utterly fundamental philosophical purpose—achieving a full understanding of the nature of mind and representation—even if we also need to think of it in very different ways for other philosophical purposes.[45]

The fact that it's helpful—illuminating—to think of our cognition in this way for one purpose is wholly compatible with the fact that you and I, embedded as we are in this actual world, possess our actual real-world-tied concepts GOLD, WATER, IRON,

---

[43] One might say that what IFE concepts capture is a special, abstract, stepped-back kind of cognitive content (particular-world-independent cognitive content)—so that IF-English is suitable for the expression of what Horgan and Tienson call 'narrow truth-conditions' (see e.g. Horgan and Tienson 2002).

[44] Mental representations are of course parts of reality that can themselves be represented, and a mental representation can represent itself. There are directly self-referential (self-representing) thoughts, and we can as remarked also think explicitly about *everything that exists*—which of course includes our present mental state. (There is also the intriguing fact that all conscious awareness appears to comport awareness of itself.)

[45] It isn't philosophically vulgar, as some suggest, to say that you can't know that you're not a brain in a vat. The claim expresses a deep thought about structure—isomorphism.

HUMPBACK BRIDGE, and so on. It's wholly compatible with a 'Fodorian' picture of concepts as concrete mental particulars 'in the head' that are *constitutively* linked to real-world phenomena, gold, water, iron, and the Humpback Bridge. Nothing in the ideas of cognitive experience and IFE concept-aspects threatens the directness of cognitive contact with the world that we actually have. The full account of mental content is for all that complex, and one of the complexities can be expressed by saying that our Fodorian concepts can also be seen as tokens of IFE concept-aspect types. This is one way to put things, at least.

All very well—but we still haven't got the resources to capture all aspects of commonality of content between my Twins and me. In fact, there's a sense in which IFE concept-aspects aren't really much help. They do capture one aspect of commonality of content between my Twins and me, when we're thinking about the river flowing under the bridge. The trouble is that they also capture a commonality between my sister's Twins and me, not to mention my sister herself, and for that matter everyone else on Intergalactic Facebook. We're all using the same IFE concepts, or rather, we're all using concepts that have the same IFE concept-aspects. But I now need something more, because I want to say that my Twins and I may be cognitive-experientially different from my sister and her Twins, when we all have experience that has the cognitive-experiential character of being conscious thought that *all squares have four sides*, or (of some river or other) that *the river is deep and wide*, or that *justice is a virtue*, and I can't express that difference by reference to IFE concepts, or rather the IFE concept-aspect of our concepts.

10 The relation between cognitive–experiential content and cognitive content 2

Let me go back to the river and the bridge. I've said that my sister and I can be in states that have the same cognitive content ([r1,b1]) while my state has cognitive-experiential content [*RB/X*1] (it's a state of cognitive-experiential type [RB/X]) and her state has cognitive-experiential content [*RB/Y*1] (it's a state of cognitive-experiential type [RB/Y]). In thinking exactly the same thought I'm thinking, cognitive-content-wise, she doesn't have to be exactly the same as I am cognitive-experience-wise. So I've claimed. I've said that this can be so even though she not only deploys the same IFE concepts as I do, but also (given that we're both Earthlings) the same Fodorian concepts. I've answered 'No' to the question 'Does same cognitive content entail same cognitive-experiential content?'. But I need to justify this answer.

I don't think the answer 'No' is easy. I think it remains difficult even after one has travelled through the absorbing philosophical satrapy that makes it hard to see that there is such a thing as cognitive phenomenology, and has come out on the other side restored to the condition in which it's obvious that there's cognitive phenomenology. Nor should one think that appealing to 'Martians' can quickly show that the answer is

COGNITIVE PHENOMENOLOGY: REAL LIFE 309

no, on the grounds that Martians can think about the river flowing under the bridge just as my sister and I do, and so be in states that have exactly the same cognitive content as ours, while obviously not being in states that have cognitive-experiential content anything like ours. For if the Martians' Fodorian river and bridge concepts are the same as ours—and why should they not be?—then it's not clear that there's any more reason to think that their cognitive-experiential content will be different from ours in this case than there is in the case in which we all four think that $2 + 2 = 4$.

Certainly their sense/feeling equipment may be very different from ours; and their thought about the river and the bridge may be accompanied by sensory-experiential content wildly different from normal human sensory-experiential content. But that's irrelevant. Such sensory-experiential content is no part of cognitive-experiential content. Nor is sensory-experiential content connected to cognitive content in such a way that it's plausible to say that the Martians can't in this case have the same river and bridge Fodorian concepts as we do. It's no more plausible to say this than it is to say that they can't have the same concept of squareness as we do; and it's no more plausible to say that than it is to say that the congenitally blind person and the congenitally non-tactile person can't have the same concept of squareness (it is in other words entirely implausible).[46]

The dialectical situation is this, or so it seems to me. We're confronted with the fact that there's something it's like experientially to understand things, to consciously comprehendingly entertain propositions; we're confronted with the fact that there's such a thing as cognitive phenomenology (it's simultaneously obvious and hard to grasp, under certain conditions of philosophical thinking). But it's then very unclear what else or what more to say about particular cases of cognitive-phenomenological experience. So what are we to do? (This, in effect, is where I got to in *Mental Reality*, in the passage reprinted in the Appendix.)

Suppose you and I are both thoroughly competent inhabitants of the world, and that the world is in certain everyday respects as we suppose it to be,[47] and that we both think *iron is a widely distributed element*, or *some rivers are slow and green*, or *all squares have four sides*, and both entertain the same cognitive content. The question, again, is: Do we then have the same cognitive-experiential content? Suppose we focus furiously on the thought to the exclusion of everything else. Do we then necessarily have the same cognitive-experiential content?

I've suggested that we needn't, and almost certainly don't, and that the same goes for my sister and I, looking at—or thinking about—the River Cherwell flowing under the

---

[46] Suppose that states with cognitive-experiential content are always also states with sensory-experiential content. Then it's extremely unlikely that we and Martians are ever in qualitatively identical experiential states. But we may nonetheless be in states that are identical, specifically in respect of cognitive-experiential content.

[47] 'In certain everyday respects' is meant to absorb the possibility that we may be wildly wrong about the nature of matter and space-time.

Humpback Bridge.[48] How can this be? Here's my proposal. When we take concepts to be mental particulars, we can again usefully think of them in two different ways. In fact, we need to do this to get the full picture.[49] On the one hand, we can take it that all human beings who genuinely possess the concept RIVER or GOLD have exactly the same concept, cognitive-content-wise, because there is only one such concept: *the* concept RIVER, or GOLD. On the other hand, we can allow a sense in which we almost certainly don't have exactly the same concept. Concepts conceived in the Fodorian way as concretely existing mental particulars exist inside particular individual mental economies (yours, mine, and hers), which are highly complex systems. And although there is one shining sense in which we do all have the same concept RIVER, or GOLD, there's another sense in which my mental-particular river concept may be said to be different from yours, because of the way it behaves, considered as a mental particular, in my particular mental economy.

This idea closely resembles a key idea in 'conceptual role semantics' (CRS), according to which we all have somewhat different river concepts (or 'concepts*'). But I'm making only a very limited use of it. One can completely reject conceptual role semantics, when giving one's core account of what concepts are,[50] and endorse strong-as-you-like Fodorian–Wittgensteinian externalism about the (actual external) content of concepts, while at the same time allowing that this particular CRS idea is a helpful way of expressing how your and my cognitive-experiential content can be different when we both think that the river is deep and wide. One can stress the point that you and I and my sister can entertain the same cognitive content *because* a Fodorian (or indeed Wittgensteinian) account of the concept RIVER, say, is correct, even as one employs the CRS notion of concepts as a theoretical tool for the purposes of giving an account of how my sister and I can be in different cognitive-experiential states when we're both in cognitive-content state [r1,b1] (she is in [$RB/Y1$], I am in [$RB/X1$]); and, more generally, for the purposes of explaining the difference between cognitive-experiential content and cognitive content.

We have, then, a picture of concepts as mental particulars. They are, so far, straightforward Fodorian concepts, but they have two aspects—CRS concept-aspects and IFE concept-aspects—that need to be highlighted for certain theoretical purposes. The two kinds of aspects serve quite different theoretical purposes. One of the things IFE concept-aspects allow us to do is to register deep cognitive-experiential-content commonalities between my Twins and myself that can exist in spite of our deep cognitive-content differences. CRS concept-aspects, by contrast, allow us to register possible cognitive-experiential-content differences between me and you or my sister that exist in spite of our deep cognitive-content commonalities.

The proposal is that we need to acknowledge both sorts of concept-aspects, in addition to thinking of concepts in a standard externalist way. You may dislike this

---

[48] On this issue see also Pitt (2009).
[49] See Carey (2009: ch. 13).
[50] Even when considering concepts as mental particulars, as here, rather than as abstract entities.

particular scheme, but we have to separate out three distinct aspects of conception in one way or another in order to understand the intimately connected phenomena of mental representation, cognitive experience, and cognition: roughly, the actual-world-free aspect (IFE), the actual-world-bound aspect (Fodorian), and the individual-bound aspect (CRS). There's no conflict between them, although there are vast opportunities for staging conflicts in philosophical debate by favouring one over another.

11 Experiential modalities

How can we introduce theoretical order, once we acknowledge the reality of cognitive experience? I think we need to go beyond the familiar notion of a sensory modality or sense/feeling modality and introduce the essentially more general notion of an experiential modality (Strawson 1994), which we may define by saying that one experiential modality is distinguished from another by the fact that the experiential character of experiences available in the first experiential modality is different in type from the experiential character of experiences available in the second. With this general notion in hand we can say that all the sensory or sense/feeling modalities are experiential modalities, while leaving space for other possible experiential modalities, and, in particular for the experiential modality of conscious thought, the experiential modality in which we have cognitive experience.

How many experiential modalities are there? One can individuate them as finely as one likes. If one wants, one can say that every qualitatively different colour experience involves a different experiential modality. When it comes to counting sense/feeling modalities, however, the best thing to do for most theoretical purposes is to focus on much more general differences of experiential type of the kind that we mark by sorting experiences into tactile, aural, olfactory, gustatory, visual, visceral, vestibular, musculoskeletal, kinaesthetic, and so on. It's a general difference of type that's in question when it comes to the proposal that we need to add the general experiential modality of conscious thought to whatever set of experiential modalities we distinguish under the heading of sense/feeling modalities.

'The experiential modality of conscious thought'. Analytic philosophy of mind may still find the idea difficult, especially given inputs from psychology and neuropsychology, which constrain some philosophers to think that all experience *must* be somehow sensory. For the moment, the most important point to get clear on, perhaps, is the point that there isn't any difficulty, let alone any special difficulty, in the idea that the particular form of the experiential modality of conscious thought that is found in creatures like ourselves is wholly a product of a process of evolution by natural selection, just as the particular forms of the sensory modalities that are found in creatures like ourselves are a product of a process of evolution by natural selection. Any real (realistic) materialist who believes in the theory of evolution must believe that this has happened, because the existence of the experiential modality of conscious thought—of cognitive experience—is an evident fact. It's one of the first pieces of data that any credible naturalism must accommodate. (It's impossible to entertain any naturalist hypothesis—any hypothesis at all—without encountering the datum in entertaining the hypothesis.)

Certainly, a general commitment to empiricism provides no reason to doubt the existence of the experiential modality of conscious thought; although here, as so often, we need to distinguish what one might call 'ontogenetic empiricism', a doctrine about how each individual acquires the ability to think, from 'phylogenetic empiricism', a doctrine about the origin and evolution of the general human capacity to think.

It may be that nothing like the fully developed human form of the experiential modality of conscious thought can evolve until sense/feeling modalities like ours are already well developed. It may be that the former grows out of the latter, or on top of them, in some way. (It's possible that cognitive experience is principally located in early sensory areas of the brain.) Perhaps the former can't exist in nature independently of the latter. Perhaps the latter are in Kant's phrase 'always already' seeded with the former in some way.[51] Questions about these matters are as old as they are important. They are, however, questions of detail, relative to the present concern. None of them touches the point that the existence of the experiential modality of conscious thought is an unbudgeable natural fact. Nor do they cast any doubt on the idea that the experiential modality of conscious thought is a distinct experiential modality, as distinct from each of the sensory modalities as they are from each other. The Buddha puts the point clearly when he distinguishes six principal experiential modalities or *āyatanas*, seeing, hearing, smelling, tasting, touching, and thinking, the last of which is a matter of 'non-sensory mental activity' (Hamilton 2001: 53). All one needs to add to this is a proper recognition of the interoceptive or somatosensory experiential modalities, and of the point that the cognitive-experiential modality is active in almost all if not all adult human experience.

12 The scope of cognitive phenomenology

Occurrent linguistic propositional meaning-experience is a particularly luminous example of the general phenomenon of cognitive experience, although it can seem troublingly elusive when one tries to inspect it directly. It stands out vividly, when we consider hearing and understanding a particular sentence at a particular time, or comprehendingly entertaining a particular thought, because the cognitive-experiential

---

[51] (Kant, 1781–7: A346/B404.) There are old and obvious reasons to be suspicious of the idea of pure or mere sensation, given the entanglement of sensation and cognition in perception. One can register this point while agreeing with Fodor's (1984) rejection of the idea that there is no theory-independent observation, and before one considers the 'conceptualist' view, advanced paradigmatically in McDowell's *Mind and World*, that there is no non-conceptual experience.

feature of the character of experience that then concerns us is expressly figured in consciousness, even as it fights shy of inspection by a distinct act of apprehension.[52] Occurrent propositional meaning-experience (linguistic or not) is, however, only a small part of the overall subject matter of cognitive phenomenology as I understand it. Cognitive-experiential content pervades all experience. I don't suppose undamaged adult human beings are capable of being in experiential states that have no cognitive-experiential aspect. (Bear in mind that cognitive-experiential content can be 'non-thetic', just as sense/feeling content can: that is, it can be truly and irreducibly part of the content of one's experience, something that must be adverted to in any attempt at a full description of the experiential character of one's experience, without being in the focus of attention in any way, and without being easily discernible, even on reflection, as a distinct element in that content.)

Seeking generality, we could introduce the notion of an *experience-determining mental element* or *experience-constituting mental element*, taking it to cover mental elements of any sort that need to be referred to in giving a full description of the character of experience. On the sense/feeling side it applies, obviously, to basic sensory determinants or constituents of the experiential character of experience, e.g. colour-experience and pain-experience. On the cognitive-experiential side it applies—among other things—to mental elements that we may think of first as IFE concepts or concept-aspects, and then (although this goes beyond the strict bounds of the cognitive-experiential) as CRS concepts, and finally as our actual real-world concepts. Note, though, that the term 'experience-determining mental element' applies also, and equally, to cognitive formations that are essentially less precisely delineable, cognitive formations for which words like 'conception' and 'grasp' or 'schema' are more appropriate than 'concept', as indeed are words like 'sense', 'feeling', and 'intuition', all of which have a natural use to characterize distinctively cognitive apprehensions or framings of how things are or seem.

With the general notion of an experience-determining mental element in place, one strategy is to take the notion of a *sense/feeling experience-determining element* or *SF element* as basic for classificatory purposes (one doesn't have to think that instances of pure sensation ever occur in order to adopt the notion) and characterize all other experience-determining elements negatively, at least in the first instance, as *non-sense/feeling experience-determining elements* or *NSF elements* for short. One can then (using the word 'phenomenology' in its original and primary sense) say that

the discipline of cognitive phenomenology is the general study of NSF elements

---

[52] See p. 295 above. By 'expressly figured' I don't mean that it's entertained through the medium of some quasi-acoustic or visual imagery, for although we do engage in a lot of such imagery we can grasp cognitive-experiential content far faster than that, and wholly without imagery; 'thought is quick', as Hobbes said (1651: 1.3). I can't be sure that Hobbes had only conscious thought in mind, but conscious thought can be incredibly rapid in its presentation of contents; for an illustration see Strawson (1994: 18-21).

—whatever they may be.

I've already given central examples of NSF elements in discussing the experience we have in understanding particular propositions and in our general perceptual experience of the world. I'll end with some more general and initially less obvious examples.

[1] Human 'time-consciousness', including what Husserl calls the 'primal-impression-retention-protention' structure of that which is experienced as the present, the living present or *lebendige Gegenwart*, is plainly not just a matter of sense/feeling elements.

Nearly all the experience-determining mental elements that we have to attribute to someone in order to give a descriptively adequate account of the character of their experience of time fall under the heading of NSF elements.

[2] Perceptual experience contains 'positional' information about the location of the perceiver with respect to the things perceived. This is another good example of NSF content; a perceiver's sense of its location with respect to the things perceived isn't just a matter of sense/feeling content. Some have proposed that it isn't conceptual content either, properly speaking, and have called it 'non-conceptual content'. The merits of this suggestion aren't important here; it's enough to note that non-conceptual content so understood is wholly a matter of NSF elements.[53]

[3] In the case of experience of oneself as a self or 'inner mental presence' (see p. 290), the aim is to specify the basic NSF content or framework of such self-experience, to carry out a *phenomenological deduction* or *extraction* of the core content of the complex NSF experience-determining mental element SELF (I'll put names of NSF elements in small capitals). In other work I've proposed that ordinary human self-experience involves the NSF elements SUBJECT OF EXPERIENCE, SINGLE, MENTAL, THING, PERSISTING, AGENT, NON-IDENTICAL WITH THE WHOLE HUMAN BEING.[54]

When one picks out more specific examples like these, the general and overwhelming point arises again: human experience is saturated with NSF elements. The separation of SF and NSF elements of experience is, phenomenologically, utterly artificial. But it remains valid and valuable—essential—for many purposes of analysis.[55]

One may also say that cognitive phenomenology studies the overall NSF *framework* of an experience, where the NSF framework is understood to be something that is live in the content of experience, i.e. experientially represented in some manner, experientially real. A good example of such highly general cognitive-experiential content is what

[53] Peacocke classifies such content as non-conceptual but (nonetheless) intentional (1992: ch. 3).

[54] Note that self-experience can exist, as a form of experience, whether or not selves do, just as pink-elephant-experience can exist whether or not pink elephants do. 'Self-experience', here, is a strictly phenomenological term, a name for an aspect of our experience of how things are that exists whether or not things are that way in fact.

[55] John McDowell, who may be thought to be opposed to such a procedure, writes in correspondence (responding to my use of the phrase 'sensory what-it's-likeness') 'I don't think insisting that our experience is conceptual through and through stands in any tension at all with giving full weight to its sensory what-it's-likeness'.

Montague calls the 'phenomenological particularity fact', the phenomenologically fundamental fact that we not only perceive individual physical objects, but perceive them *as* individual physical objects, as discrete, numerically distinct, as particulars.[56] It's not just a non-phenomenological causal fact that many of our perceptual experiences are experiences of individual particular objects; it's also and crucially part of their phenomenological and in particular cognitive-experiential character.

The same goes for the 'general propositional form', the THIS IS HOW THINGS ARE cognitive formation, in the terms of Wittgenstein's *Tractatus* (§4.5). And 'THIS IS HOW THINGS ARE' seems equally apt as a descriptive name for the fundamental perceptual formation, the 'general perceptual form', relative to which the THIS IS HOW THINGS SEEM formation is a considerable refinement. It's obvious that a compendious description of the character of our experience needs to have a way of recording the fact that structural elements of this rock-bottom and irreducibly NSF kind are fundamentally constitutive of its experiential and in particular cognitive-experiential character. None of this is psychologism (boo) of any sort. It's just phenomenology (hurray): cognitive phenomenology.

Does cognitive phenomenology extend to the study of phenomenological differences between what one might call the 'cognitive attitudes'—between entertaining the thought that p, believing that p, meditating on the fact that p, seeing (intellectually) that p, supposing that p, and so on? On the present terms, this question is the question whether these differences are genuine NSF differences, or whether they are in the end just a subtle variety of SF differences. They certainly can't be excluded from cognitive phenomenology on the ground that cognitive phenomenology is only and exclusively concerned with the ps and qs, as it were, i.e. only with the experiential character of the entertaining or apprehension of p or q. The job of cognitive phenomenology is to study the NSF elements of experience—of experiential character—whatever they are.

13 Envoi

It's strange that the existence of cognitive phenomenology is a matter of dispute. Somehow we've created a form or climate of thought in which this evident, all-pervasive fact can seem hidden from us. When we think theoretically about hearing someone speak, or speaking ourselves, or even about our thinking, it can somehow fail to be apparent to us. It's as if the salience and absorbing character of the activity somehow obscures its own nature.

It's helpful to consider the experience of lying in bed unable to sleep and thinking (consider Molly lying in bed, in the epigraph from Joyce). One's train of thought is in that case a vivid case of cognitive experience. Cioran may exaggerate when he says that 'the importance of insomnia is so colossal that I am tempted to define man as the animal

---

[56] Montague (this volume: 121).

that can't sleep' (1934: 85), but insomnia may confer philosophically valuable information unavailable to instant slumberers. That said, anyone who has ever tried to concentrate on some one thing in meditation, and whose mind has drifted off on some train of thought, and who has become aware of this, has received conclusive empirical proof of the existence of cognitive experience.

There's another simple and infallible way of encountering the phenomenon of cognitive phenomenology in a way that suffices for one to be able to give it its proper place in one's philosophy of mind. Wait until the next time—perhaps a quiet time—when you're thinking silently, and someone says 'What are you thinking about?', and you think back in order to reply. It's not merely that the existence of cognitive phenomenology will be plain to you as part of what you remember, when you review your immediately past experience. It's also that your remembering, considered simply as what is going on in the present moment, will, with the content that it has, itself be an evident instance of the phenomenon of cognitive phenomenology, vividly on display, rather than merely what it usually is—the fundamental weft of all our experience. It will be an instance of cognitive phenomenology that is framed by the particular circumstance of being asked what one was thinking about in such a way as to be vividly apprehended as what it is.[57]

Appendix: Understanding-experience (cognitive phenomenology)[58]

Consider what it is like, experientially, to hear someone speaking non-technically in a language that one understands. One understands what is said, and one undoubtedly has an experience. How do the understanding and the experience relate? Most will agree that the experience is complex, and that it is not merely sensory, not just a matter of the sounds. But they will hesitate if it is suggested there is *experience (as) of understanding*.

Nevertheless, I will now argue that there is such a thing as experience (as) of understanding, or 'understanding-experience' for short, just as there is such a thing as visual experience. Defence of this view should help to illustrate the intended force and extent of my use of the word 'experience'. It needs separate discussion because it may be thought to be deeply dubious, given the recent history of philosophy of mind. Perhaps I should say straight away that I will only be concerned with linguistic understanding, not with experiences like the experience of finally understanding how some machine works or the phenomenology of the *Aha! Erlebnis*.

Philosophers will ask whether there is really such a thing as understanding-experience, i.e. distinctively cognitive experience, over and above visual experience, auditory experience, and so on. Behind their questioning there may lie a familiar doubt as to whether there is anything going on, experientially, that either is or necessarily accompanies the understanding. This question may be asked: does the difference between

---

[57] I'm most grateful to the participants in the Tucson workshop on intentionality in October 2008, and to the editors of this book, Tim Bayne and Michelle Montague, for their comments on this paper. Charles Siewert drew my attention to the passage from Moore which I've quoted as an epigraph.

[58] Reprinted with minimal changes from G. Strawson, *Mental Reality* (MIT Press, 1994) pp. 5–13.

Jacques (a monoglot Frenchman) and Jack (a monoglot Englishman), as they listen to the news in French, really consist in the Frenchman's having a different *experience*?

Well, it may be wrong to suppose that there is any set of experiential phenomena that can be picked out as constituting the understanding on the part of Jacques. This is not part of my claim. Nor is there any suggestion that his understanding is any sort of directed activity, for it is no such thing. It is an entirely automatic, involuntary, and seemingly immediate process. The present claim is simply that Jacques's experience when listening to the news is utterly different from Jack's, and that this is so even though there is a sense in which Jacques and Jack have the same aural experience.[59]

It is certainly true that Jacques's experience when listening to the news is very different from Jack's. And the difference between the two can be expressed by saying that Jacques, when exposed to the stream of sound, has what one may perfectly well call 'an experience (as) of understanding' or 'an understanding-experience', or 'meaning-experience', while Jack does not. Unlike Jack, Jacques automatically and involuntarily *takes* the sounds *as* signs, and indeed as words and sentences, that he automatically and involuntarily understands as *expressing certain propositions* and as representing reality as constituted in certain ways. As a result, Jacques's *experience* is quite different from Jack's. And the fact that Jacques understands what is said is not only the principal explanation of why this is so, it is also the principal description of the respect in which his experience differs from Jack's.

To talk about understanding-experience is to talk about such simple facts as these. It is not to postulate anything suspect or mysterious in the world, because it is to postulate nothing that is not found in these facts. For a being to have understanding-experience is just for things to be for it, in one central respect, as they can be for us, experientially, when we hear utterances that we understand—or think consciously or realize something in silent words. Note that misunderstanding involves understanding-experience as much as genuine understanding does, for understanding-experience is experience *as of* understanding and need not be veridical. It could, as remarked, be called 'meaning-experience', but for now I will stick to 'understanding-experience'.

To talk of understanding-experience, then, is not to commit oneself to the implausible view that there is some single qualitative type of experience that anyone who has understanding-experience must have. It is not to commit oneself to the view that particular qualitative experiences invariably go with understanding particular sentences.

---

[59] In one sense, of course, they do not have the same aural experience, because of Jacques's automatic segmenting of the stream of sound into words, but this is unimportant here. Consider another case in which two English speakers hear a coded message in which nothing but whole English words are used to stand for other English words. One of them is intensely familiar with the code, the other does not know it. Here, the basic aural experience of the two people may be very similar indeed, although one has an automatic and involuntary understanding-experience that the other does not have.

Added in 2010. Opponents of understanding-experience (cognitive phenomenology) tend to jump on this case, which they think they can easily deal with, and ignore other arguments for cognitive phenomenology. The case is good, in fact, and close to a case given by Moore (1910: 57–9; see p. 22 above); but nothing hangs on it.

Nor is it to commit oneself to the view that understanding-experience involves any kind of inner mental theatre.[60] The point is simply this: there is in the normal case something it is like, experientially, to understand a sentence, spoken or read. You have just done so and are continuing to do so. Your doing so is not nothing, experientially. It is part of your current *course of experience*, part of the content of your conscious life, and it is happening now.

This is obvious, but the mood of much recent philosophy of mind may make it seem obscure and worth stressing. I take it that it is compatible *plumber's bill* with any sense in which Wittgenstein is correct to say that 'understanding is not a mental process' and with any sense in which Ryle is correct to say that there need be 'nothing going on' when one understands something.[61] Certainly, understanding is not something one does intentionally. In the normal case, it is something that just happens. There is, to repeat, an automatic and involuntary *taking* of sounds or marks *as* words and sentences that one understands and that represent something's being the case. Understanding-experience is simply such automatic, involuntary, experientially aspected taking of sounds and marks and involves no sort of intentional action. As McDowell remarks, it is just a fact that beings like ourselves can be such that sounds or marks 'impinge on them with content' whether they like it or not (1980: 137). And as William James remarks, 'no word in an understood sentence comes to consciousness as a mere noise' (1890: 1.281). This is a fact about experience.

So something is happening to you experientially, here and now, as you read this sentence. Obviously, there is the visual or auditory experience. In the reading case, there is perhaps a rapid and silent process of forming acoustic mental images. But this is not all, for—*barath abalori trafalon*—one can have all this without the experience of understanding. There is something else that happens—*the mass of the moon is just over one per cent that of the earth*—a certain complex modification of the quality of one's course of experience, and not just of one's dispositional set. In a word, there is understanding-experience, understanding-experience whose very existence is sometimes doubted, perhaps because it has no obvious experiential character that it can call its own. It has no striking experiential feel in the way in which experience in any of the sensory modalities usually does. But this does not show that there is nothing that can be correctly called 'understanding-experience'. Rather, it shows that in certain contexts of discussion, we may still be inclined to appeal to an excessively restricted notion of what experience is.

---

[60] Schopenhauer dealt with this idea in 1819: 'While another person is speaking, do we at once translate his speech into pictures of the imagination that instantaneously flash upon us and are arranged, linked, formed, and coloured according to the words that stream forth, and to their grammatical inflexions? What a tumult there would be in our heads while we listened to a speech or read a book! This is not what happens at all. The meaning of the speech is immediately grasped, accurately and clearly apprehended, without as a rule any conceptions of fancy being mixed up with it' (1819: 1.39).

[61] See Wittgenstein (1953: §154); Ryle (1949); for the insertion of 'plumber's bill' and for the point that it makes about understanding-experience by its unexpected occurrence in a philosophy text, see James (1890: 1.262).

Here it should be noted that understanding-experience, as currently understood, has nothing to do with what Dennett calls the 'phenomenology of comprehension' (1991b: 56–9). He means the various possible imagistic or otherwise sensory-experience-like accompaniments of understanding, and his account of these is generally accurate. 'The Eiffel Tower is going to be dismantled.' Some who hear or read this sentence will form a visual image of the Eiffel Tower. Others will not. Such imaging is not a necessary accompaniment of understanding-experience, nor is it a part of understanding-experience. It is an interesting question whether human understanding-experience always involves experiencing (heard, seen, touched, or imagined) sounds or marks taken as meaningful, especially since understanding-experience occurs as much in the case of conscious thought as in the case of reading or hearing others speak.[62]

To return to the main theme: one cannot separate off all the sensory-experiential aspects of hearing people talk and then say that although there is also understanding going on as one hears them talk, that fact ought not to be adverted to in any way in a full account of what is going on experientially. One cannot say that the difference between Jack and Jacques is just that certain specific changes take place in Jacques's dispositional set (e.g. his dispositions to respond in certain ways to certain questions) that do not take place in Jack's. If that were so, there would be little difference between the case imagined and a case in which both listen to the broadcast in a language that neither of them understands, while Jacques's dispositional set is, unknown to him, altered by direct brain tinkering in just the way that it would have been altered had he understood what was being said. Or, to get closer, there would be little difference between the case imagined and a case in which Jacques has been hypnotized in such a way that (a) he explicitly believes he understands nothing, so that he listens to the broadcast with complete incomprehension, and (b) he nonetheless takes in what is said, so that he can later respond accurately to questions about the matters discussed in the broadcast. To say that these two cases are similar is to leave out something real that is present in the first case and absent in the second, to wit, Jacques's experience of understanding what was said.

Acknowledgment of the reality of understanding-experience is profoundly important in the philosophy of mind (particularly when it comes to giving a correct account

[62] William James may be starting to bridge the gap between understanding-experience and Dennett's 'phenomenology of comprehension' with his talk of 'the halo, fringe or scheme in which we feel the words to lie' (1890: 1.260), but the gap is very large. There are many similar ideas in the philosophical literature, although I am not sure how many of them support the point that I wish to make about *understanding*-experience. Searle (1992: 60) remarks that 'beliefs ... are actually experienced as part of our mental life', and I take it that he means conscious thoughts that are occurrent entertainings of the contents of beliefs. Flanagan observes that 'not all qualia are sensational.... Conscious moods, emotions, beliefs, desires ... have distinct qualitative character' (1992: 64). There is a striking discussion of some aspects of the experience of thought in Jackendoff (1987: see e.g. ch. 15). See also James (1890: 1.245–6); Peirce (1935: §223; quoted by Flanagan 1992: 64); Ayers (1991: vol. 1, chap. 31); and Murdoch (1992: chaps. 8 and 9). See also, more recently, and notably, Siewert (1998); Horgan and Tienson (2002); Pitt (2004).

of intentionality). It needs to be dwelt on, but I cannot think of any other way to bring the point home. It seems simultaneously obvious and elusive. Perhaps it helps to think of watching a film and of how what the actors say is part of one's overall experience, and to compare this with watching an undubbed film in an unknown language.

Once the general point is granted, it may be added that the claim that there is something that can correctly be called 'understanding-experience' is compatible with the view that talk of understanding-experience may not be appropriate in all cases in which it is correct to say that someone has understood something.

The abstractness and colourlessness of philosophical discourse may incline one to think that it does not provide a very good example when one is trying to convey a properly strong sense of the reality of understanding-experience. This is not so, in fact. The understanding of philosophical discourse must be as good an example of understanding-experience as the understanding of any other kind. To think that it may not be is to misunderstand the nature of understanding-experience. There is, after all, and as already remarked, something it is like for you to read and understand these words. It is part of the course of your experience. Nevertheless, philosophy may slip down one's intellectual throat a little too insensibly for one to be convinced, when listening to it or reading it, that there is such a thing as understanding-experience. Perhaps it really does seem that there is in this case a kind of direct absorption of content, of a sort that constitutes understanding, without anything that could be called 'understanding-experience'. I have suggested that this is not really so. Such a view presupposes a naive and unduly restricted conception of the nature, reality, and extent of experience. To try to convince you, in the wake of Ryle and Wittgenstein, of the reality of understanding-experience, let me quote part of the poem 'A Martian Sends a Postcard Home' (Raine 1979).

> Caxtons are mechanical birds with many wings
> and some are treasured for their markings—
>
> they cause the eyes to melt
> or the body to shriek without pain.
>
> I have never seen one fly, but
> sometimes they perch on the hand.
>
> Mist is when the sky is tired of flight
> and rests its soft machine on ground:
>
> then the world is dim and bookish
> like engravings under tissue paper.
>
> Rain is when the earth is television.
> It has the property of making colours darker. . . .
>
> In homes, a haunted apparatus sleeps,
> that snores when you pick it up.
>
> If the ghost cries, they carry it
> to their lips and soothe it to sleep

with sounds. And yet, they wake it up
deliberately, by tickling with a finger.

This poem is full of complicated metaphors. It is useful as an example because failure to understand all the images on a first reading presupposes a prior understanding of the standard meaning of the words, so that there are two levels or waves of understanding-experience. In this case, puzzlement or not understanding is itself a form of understanding-experience.

The main purpose of this piece is to illustrate the complexity and range of our experience by considering the relatively little discussed example of understanding-experience. I have repeated and varied the point because it may be thought particularly suspect. And yet the facts to which it adverts are familiar facts of common life.

Some may still be worried by the elusiveness of understanding-experience. They may be prepared to concede that there is something that may reasonably be called 'understanding-experience', but be struck by the fact that one can't really do anything much with the idea, theoretically. And they may feel that being able to do something with the idea theoretically is a necessary part of genuinely understanding it, philosophically. They may even think that being able to do something with it theoretically is a necessary condition of accepting it as real. I think, in fact, that it's not possible to give a satisfactory general account of intentionality without making use of the notion of understanding-experience or cognitive experience.[63] But we would need to acknowledge its reality even if this weren't so.

There is another pragmatic difficulty with achieving a satisfactory grip on the notion of understanding-experience. Suppose that one hears it put forward and discussed, and concludes that there is indeed something that may reasonably be called 'understanding-experience'. One may still remain uncertain as to whether one really knows what it is. This may now be because one is too close to what one is trying to think about, so that it is like looking at an elephant from three inches away.

I don't think either of these problems is serious. One doesn't have to do anything much theoretically with the notion of understanding-experience. Nor does one have to try to get an impossibly detached perspective on it. What philosophy requires of one is simply that one should acknowledge its reality and bear it in mind when trying to form an adequate general conception of the nature of experience. One needs to have such a conception to stay balanced in the philosophy of mind. One needs to remember that experience is a vast part of mental reality, even if mental reality also has non-experiential parts or aspects.

In discussing understanding-experience, I have focused on reading and hearing others speak. It should be added that the basic phenomenon also occurs when one thinks consciously. In this case too, apprehension of conceptual content occurs and is part of the course and content of one's experience, part of what has to be detailed in

---

[63] I argue for this claim in Strawson (2008b).

attempting to record one's experience as fully as possible. (It's no good just recording the subvocalized words, as becomes evident when one considers the record of the course of experience of a monoglot speaker of a language one does not know.) This may be clearer to insomniacs, who spend long hours thinking in the dark, than to instant sleepers. It is obvious to non-philosophers and obscured by much philosophy. It may be an elusive fact, hard to grip, but it is extremely important. I think, in fact (it is an old thought), that there is a solid and unbudgeable sense in which meaning only really lives—exists—in this experience, however much the experience evades description. One has to take account of this in the philosophy of mind. If this is meaning-psychologism, then we badly need a certain amount of meaning-psychologism.

The mass of the moon is just over one per cent that of the earth, but I'm pessimistic about being correctly understood by philosophers. It's not that the point is not straightforward. It is straightforward, but it is also hard to pin down. The central claim is that the apprehension and understanding of cognitive content, considered just as such and independently of any accompaniments in any of the sensory-modality-based modes of imagination or mental representation, is part of experience, part of the flesh or content of experience, and hence, trivially, part of the qualitative character of experience.

Discussing music in *Culture and Value*, Wittgenstein writes as follows:

> Should I say that understanding is simply a specific experience that cannot be analysed any further? Well, that would be tolerable as long as it were not supposed to mean: it is a specific *experiential content*. For in point of fact *these* words make us think of distinctions like those between seeing, hearing, and smelling. (1948: 70)

This raises a number of problems of interpretation that I will not consider. It is useful to quote it here, because the present point is precisely that we need to allow that a particular case of understanding-experience can involve a specific cognitive experiential content while overcoming the tendency of the words 'specific experiential content' to make us think only of distinctions like those found in sensory experience.

References

Ayers, M. R. (1991). *Locke*, vol. 1. London: Routledge.

Bellow, S. (1970/2007). *Mr Sammler's Planet*. New York: Penguin.

Berkeley, G. (1709/2008). *An Essay Towards a New Theory of Vision*, in D. Clarke (ed.). Cambridge: Cambridge University Press.

Block, N. (1995). 'On a Confusion about a Function of Consciousness', *Behavioral and Brain Sciences*, 18: 227–47.

Brentano, F. (1874/1995). *Psychology from an Empirical Standpoint* (introduction by P. Simons, trans. A. C. Rancurello, D. B. Terrell, and L. McAlister). London: Routledge.

——(1888–9/1982). 'Descriptive Psychology or Descriptive Phenomenology', in *Descriptive Psychology* (trans. B. Müller). London: Routledge.

Carey, S. (2009). *The Origin of Concepts*. Oxford: Oxford University Press.

Chun, M. and Marois, R. (2002). 'The Dark Side of Visual Attention', *Current Opinion in Neurobiology*, 12: 184–9.

Cioran, E. (1934/1992). *On the Heights of Despair*, trans. I. Zarifopol-Johnston. Chicago: The University of Chicago Press.

Crane, T. (2006). 'Introduction: The Mental and the Physical', http://web.mac.com/cranetim/Tims_website/Onlinepapers.html. English version of the introduction to T. Crane, *Intentionalität als Merkmal des Geistigen: Sechs Essays zur Philosophie des Geistes* (trans. M. Wild and S. Ungerer). Frankfurt: Fischer Verlag.

Dennett, D. (1991b). *Consciousness Explained*. Boston: Little, Brown and Co.

Flanagan, O. (1992). *Consciousness Reconsidered*. Cambridge: MIT Press.

Fodor, J. (1984). 'Observation Reconsidered', *Philosophy of Science*, 51.1: 23–43.

Frost, R. (c.1900–c.1960/2006). *The Notebooks of Robert Frost*, R. Faggen (ed.). Cambridge, MA: Harvard University Press.

Gertler, B. (2007). 'Overextending the Mind?', in B. Gertler and L. Shapiro (ed.), *Arguing About the Mind*. New York: Routledge, pp. 192–206.

Hamilton, S. (2001). *A Very Short Introduction to Indian Philosophy*. Oxford: Oxford University Press.

Hobbes, T. (1651/1996). *Leviathan* (ed. Richard Tuck). Cambridge: Cambridge University Press.

Horgan, T. and Tienson, J. (2002). 'The Intentionality of Phenomenology and the Phenomenology of Intentionality', in D. Chalmers (ed.), *Philosophy of Mind: Classical and Contemporary Readings*. Oxford: Oxford University Press.

Hume, D. (1739–40/1978). *A Treatise of Human Nature* (ed. L. A. Selby-Bigge and P. H. Nidditch). Oxford: Oxford University Press.

——(1739–40/2000). *A Treatise of Human Nature* (ed. D. F. Norton and M. J. Norton). Oxford: Oxford University Press.

Husserl, E. (1900–01/2001). *Logical Investigations* vol. 1 (introduction by D. Moran, trans. J. Findlay). London: Routledge.

Jackendoff, R. (1987). *Consciousness and the Computational Mind*. Cambridge: MIT Press.

James, W. (1890/1950). *The Principles of Psychology*, 2 volumes. New York: Dover.

Joyce, J. (1922/1986). *Ulysses*. Harmondsworth: Penguin.

Kant, I. (1781–7/1933). *Critique of Pure Reason* (trans. N. Kemp Smith). London: Macmillan.

Levine, J. (2011). 'On the Phenomenology of Thought', in T. Bayne and M. Montague (eds), *Cognitive phenomenology*. Oxford: Oxford University Press.

McDowell, J. (1980). 'Meaning, Communication, and Knowledge', in Z. van Straaten (ed.), *Philosophical Subjects*. Oxford: Clarendon Press.

——(1994). *Mind and World*. Cambridge, Mass: Harvard University Press.

McGinn, C. (1989). *Mental Content*. Oxford: Blackwell.

Montague, M. (2009). 'The content of perceptual experience', in A. Beckermann and B. McLaughlin (eds), *Oxford Handbook in the Philosophy of Mind*. Oxford: Oxford University Press.

——(2011). 'The phenomenology of particularity', in T. Bayne and M. Montague (eds), *Cognitive Phenomenology*. Oxford: Oxford University Press.

Moore, G. E. (1910–11/1953). 'Propositions', in *Some Main Problems in Philosophy*. London: Allen and Unwin.

Murdoch, I. (1992). *Metaphysics as a Guide to Morals*. London: Chatto & Windus.

Ostertag, G. (in preparation). 'Sonicism and the Face-Value Theory of Musical Works'.

Papineau, D. (2002). *Thinking about Consciousness*. Oxford: Clarendon Press.

Peacocke, C. (1992). *A Study of Concepts*. Cambridge, MA: MIT Press.

Peirce, C. S. (1935). *Collected Papers*, vol. 6, C. Hartshorne and P. Weiss (ed.). Cambridge, MA: Harvard University Press.

Pessoa, L. and De Weerd, P. (2003). *Filling-In: From Perceptual Completion to Cortical Reorganization*. Oxford: Oxford University Press.

Pitt, D. (2004). 'The Phenomenology of Cognition, or What is it Like to Think That *p*?', *Philosophy and Phenomenological Research*, 69/1: 1–36.

——(2009). 'Intentional Psychologism', *Phil. Studies*, 146: 117–38.

Prinz, J. (2011). 'The Sensory Basis of Cognitive Phenomenology', in T. Bayne and M. Montague (eds), *Cognitive Phenomenology*. Oxford: Oxford University Press.

Pylyshyn, Z. (2001). *Seeing and Visualizing: It's Not What You Think*. Cambridge, MA: MIT Press.

Raine, C. (1979). *A Martian Sends a Postcard Home*. Oxford: Oxford University Press.

Reid, T. (1764/2000). *An Inquiry into the Human Mind* (ed. D. Brookes). Edinburgh: Edinburgh University Press.

Reid, T. (1785/2002). *Essays on the Intellectual Powers of Man*. Edinburgh: Edinburgh University Press.

Ryle, G. (1949). *The Concept of Mind*. New York: Barnes and Noble.

Schopenhauer, A. (1819–44/1969). *The World as Will and Representation*, trans. E. F. J. Payne. New York: Dover.

Searle, J. (1992). *The Rediscovery of the Mind*. Cambridge, MA: MIT Press.

Segal, G. (2008) 'Narrow content', in A. Beckermann, B. McLaughlin, and S. Walter (eds), *Oxford Handbook in the Philosophy of Mind*. Oxford: Oxford University Press.

Siewert, C. (1998). *The Significance of Consciousness*. Princeton, NJ: Princeton University Press.

Simons, D. J. and Levin, D. T. (1997). 'Change Blindness', *Trends in Cognitive Sciences*, 1: 261–7.

Strawson, G. (1986/2010). *Freedom and Belief*. Oxford: Clarendon Press.

——(1994/2009). *Mental Reality* (2nd edn). Cambridge, MA: MIT Press.

——G. (1997/1999). 'The Self', in S. Gallagher and J. Shear (eds), *Models of the Self*. Thorverton: Imprint Academic.

——(2003/2008). 'Real materialism', in G. Strawson, *Real Materialism and Other Essays*.

——(2005/2008). 'Intentionality and Experience: Terminological Preliminaries', in *Real Materialism and Other Essays*. Oxford: Oxford University Press.

——(2006/2008). 'Realistic Monism: Why Physicalism entails Panpsychism', in G. Strawson, *Real Materialism and Other Essays*. Oxford: Oxford University Press.

——(2008a). 'Introduction', in *Real Materialism and Other Essays*. Oxford: Oxford University Press.

——(2008b). 'Real intentionality 3', in *Real Materialism and Other Essays*. Oxford: Oxford University Press.

——(2009). *Selves: An Essay in Revisionary Metaphysics*. Oxford: Oxford University Press.

——(in preparation). 'Content: Internal and external'.

Van Cleve, J. (2005). 'Troubles for Radical Transparency', http://www-rcf.usc.edu/~vancleve/.

Wittgenstein, L. (1922/1961). *Tractatus Logico-Philosophicus* (trans. B. McGuinness and D. F. Pears). London: Routledge and Kegan Paul.

——(1948/1980). *Culture and Value*. Oxford: Blackwell.

——(1953). *Philosophical Investigations*. Oxford: Blackwell.

Is There a Phenomenology of Thought?

Michael Tye and Briggs Wright

Recent philosophy of mind has seen various efforts to bridge the gap between two mental phenomena traditionally kept separate: phenomenology and intentionality. Some philosophers have held that phenomenology itself inherently involves intentionality—that the best account of phenomenal character is one that reduces it to a certain kind of intentional content.[1] Others have held that phenomenology is the basis for intentionality—that conscious intentional states generally have phenomenal character and that this phenomenal character is fundamental to their having the intentional content they do. Philosophers in the latter camp have made much of what has come to be called "the phenomenology of thought" or "cognitive phenomenology." From the internalism/externalism debate about mental content, to our capacity to represent non-existents in thought, to issues surrounding the extended mind, the phenomenology of thought has been ushered in as support for various theses.[2]

For all the merits of these vigorous discussions, philosophers who appeal to the phenomenology of thought have overlooked one important point: in the relevant sense, there is no such thing as the phenomenology of thought. Over the course of this essay, we'll explain why.

We proceed as follows. First, we formulate the phenomenology of thought thesis as it has been paradigmatically characterized in the literature, and explain the *prima facie* case against it. Then we examine two recent arguments in favor of the thesis, concluding that they fail to establish it. We close by offering considerations, the import of which is that thought, by its very nature, may not even be suited to have phenomenology in the sense that the thesis demands.

---

[1] E.g. Dretske (1995) and Tye (1995, 2000).

[2] For discussions of the phenomenology of thought in relation to internalism/externalism about mental content see Horgan and Tienson (2002); Loar (2003); Horgan, Tienson, and Graham (2004); and Farkas (2008). See Kriegel (2007) for applications to representation of non-existents in thought. Horgan and Kriegel (2008) consider the extended mind thesis in light of the phenomenology of thought.

1 The phenomenology of thought thesis

Horgan and Tienson (2002) hold that conscious thoughts have a kind of phenomenology that is unique both to the particular content and to the type of state involved.[3] As they put it:

Cognitive intentional states such as consciously occurrent thoughts... are phenomenal *qua* intentional. The overall phenomenal character of such a state comprises both the phenomenology of its specific intentional content and the phenomenology of its specific attitude-type. (Horgan and Tienson 2002: 523–4)

Pitt (2004), aligning himself with Horgan and Tienson (2002), likewise maintains that occurrent tokens of thought have a particular kind of phenomenology that is specific to both the content and the state type:

[W]hat it is like consciously to think a particular thought is (1) different from what it is like consciously to be in any other sort of conscious mental state (i.e., *proprietary*) and (2) different from what it is like consciously to think any other thought (i.e., *distinctive*). That is, any conscious token of a thought-type *T* has a unique phenomenology different from that of any other sort of conscious mental state, and different from that of any other conscious thought. (Pitt 2004: 4)

Combining these claims with the claim (also endorsed by Horgan and Tienson (2002: 520)) that the phenomenology of a thought is constitutive of or individuates its representational content, Pitt arrives at what we shall call '*the phenomenology of thought thesis*':

Each type of conscious thought—each state of consciously thinking that *p*, for all thinkable contents *p*—has a proprietary, distinctive, individuative phenomenology. (Pitt 2004: 5)

Pitt (2004: 6 fn 9) adds that this thesis should be restricted (at least for those who accept externalism for some thought contents) to thought states having a *narrow* content.[4] Horgan and Tienson (2002: 526–7), Horgan et al. (2004: 299), and Horgan and

---

[3] The alleged phenomenology involved in cognitive states is an example of a broader phenomenon discussed by Horgan and Tienson (2002); Loar (2003); Horgan et al. (2004); Kriegel (2007); Farkas (2008); and Horgan and Kriegel (2008) known as *phenomenal intentionality*. We won't discuss *phenomenal intentionality* directly, but our criticisms of the phenomenology of thought thesis bear on phenomenal intentionality, given that the former is an instance of the latter.

[4] The restriction to thoughts with narrow contents is needed since all will agree that Oscar's thought that water is wet has the same phenomenology as the thought that twater is wet undergone by Oscar's molecular twin on twin earth, even though the two thoughts have different contents. This creates further trouble for the phenomenology of thought theorist. For it must now be admitted that we can identify introspectively which wide-content thoughts we have, even though they lack an individuative phenomenology. Why, then, insist, as Pitt does (see section 4 below), that such phenomenology is needed for the introspective identification of thoughts with narrow contents (allowing arguendo that there are such thoughts)? There are only two moves we see open for the phenomenology of thought theorist: deny that there are thoughts with wide contents or argue that we can't know directly the wide contents of our thoughts via introspection. The former move is desperate indeed; the latter unconvincing. For arguments that privileged access and content externalism are compatible, see McLaughlin and Tye (1998).

Kriegel (2008: 351) take this characterization further, adding that the relevant *phenom-enology* itself is narrow. On their view, the phenomenology involved in your thinking that claret is delightful, say, could be shared by a microphysical duplicate of you, regardless of the environment it occupies, or indeed, by a brain in a vat completely disconnected from a claret-laden environment.

In saying that there is no phenomenology of thought, let us be clear about what it is we are opposing. Our main target is the phenomenology of thought thesis stated above. But we also oppose the view that thinking has a proprietary phenomenology. The latter thesis is weaker than the former in that it concedes that it is possible for thoughts with different (narrow) contents to have the same phenomenology. What is crucial to the proprietary phenomenology thesis is that there be something it is like to think—something that is *different* from what it is like to be in any other conscious state.

In opposing the above theses, we might add, we are not opposing the following thesis:

For any conscious thought *t* and any subject *s*, there is something that it is like for *s* when she thinks t.

Nor do we wish to deny that what it is like for a subject to consciously think a particular thought—the thought that Veuve Cliquot Champagne is superior to Korbel, say—is (typically) different from what it is like for that same subject to consciously think a thought with a different content—the thought that Merlot is overrated, for example. So, we also are *not* opposing the following thesis:

For any two conscious thoughts, *t* and *t'*, and any subject, *s*, what it is like for *s* when she undergoes *t* is (typically) different from what it is like for *s* when she undergoes *t'*.[5]

What we deny is that what it is like for a subject when she undergoes a thought is *proprietary* and further *distinctive* and *individuative* of that type of thought.

2   The *prima facie* case against the phenomenology of thought thesis

One might wonder why there should be any resistance to the phenomenology of thought thesis in the first place. The primary source of resistance emerges from introspective unfamiliarity with the kind of phenomenology in question. Consider, for instance, the claim that the relevant phenomenology is *proprietary*—that what it's like to have a conscious thought is unique to thinking. As Lormand (1996: 242–3) has stressed, we typically recognize and are well acquainted with the following Quartet of phenomenological states:

[5] We add the qualifier "typically" for reasons that will become clear below.

   (i) perceptual experiences, such as the visual experience of red and the auditory experience of a loud noise,
  (ii) conscious bodily sensations, such as pains, tickles and itches,
 (iii) imagistic experiences of a non-linguistic sort, such as consciously imaging a familiar object or person,[6]
 (iv) conscious linguistic imagery, as when one thinks "in words."

The phenomenology of these states is not inherently conceptual or cognitive. To be sure, in some cases, concepts are involved in the states but they are not essential to the phenomenology: under an appropriate twin earth-ing of the concepts, the phenomenology remains the same.

Other states having a noteworthy phenomenology, in our view, are primary emotional experiences, such as feeling anger or fear. There is clearly something it is like to feel angry or to feel fearful. These experiences, we maintain, do not have an inherently conceptual or cognitive phenomenology any more than do the states in Lormand's Quartet. Many animals experience primary emotional states, and it is natural to suppose that such emotional experiences lack the sophistication of thoughts and beliefs. And even in the case of human beings, emotional experiences often do not seem to involve thought (nor is a salient belief required). Consider the experience of disgust, to take one obvious example.

We do not deny that emotional phenomenology is a complex topic and one worthy of careful examination.[7] However, for present purposes, we shall not pursue it further. In claiming that there's nothing unique (or proprietary) about what it's like for a subject to undergo a conscious occurrent thought, what we are claiming is that the phenomenology present is to be accounted for in terms of the non-conceptual phenomenology that occurs when one or more phenomenal states from Lormand's Quartet of types is tokened along with, in some cases, the non-conceptual phenomenology of emotion, as understood above. Adding the latter phenomenology to that in Lormand's Quartet, we have then a quintet of phenomenal states. Our view is that the alleged cognitive phenomenology of thought is to be accounted for in terms of the phenomenology of our quintet of states.

From a phenomenological perspective, thinking a thought is much like running a sentence through one's head and/or (in some cases) having a mental image in mind together with (in some cases) an emotional/bodily response and a feeling of effort if the thought is complex or difficult to grasp.[8] For example, when you think that claret is delightful, you may have an experience of sub-vocalized speech (saying to yourself

---

[6] Lormand uses the term "imaginings" in connection with these experiences.

[7] One interesting question is whether the phenomenology of emotional experiences is ultimately reducible to the phenomenology found in the states in Lormand's Quartet. For a discussion of this question, see Tye (2008).

[8] Jackendoff (1987) makes the even stronger claim that sentences are our *primary* means of consciously experiencing our thoughts.

"Claret is delightful"), or you may bring mental images of claret to mind, or perhaps even remember occasions where you had a particularly delightful claret. Further, a feeling of warmth may descend upon you, along with a smile on your lips with an associated facial sensation. The only phenomenology to be found when a thought is introspected is the phenomenology of these and other such states.

In taking this view, we essentially agree with the following remarks Lormand makes with respect to thought phenomenology (though, as noted, we prefer our quintet of phenomenal states to Lormand's Quartet):

[I]n searching for attitude qualia, we must exclude the qualia of concomitant thoughts and imaginings (as well as perceptual experiences and bodily sensations). Excluding what it's like to have accompanying Quartet states, however, typically there seems to be nothing left that it's like for one to have a conscious belief that snow is white.[9] (Lormand 1996: 246–7)

There are similar resources for denying that the phenomenology of thought is *distinctive* in any strong sense. What it's like to think that claret is delightful differs from what it's like to think that spinach is delightful, but the difference can arguably be pinned down to differences of sub-vocal speech, or other sorts of imagery that might go along with thinking the thoughts.

So far, we've only considered intra-linguistic cases. We can further extend this *prima facie* case by considering examples of cross-linguistic phenomenology. The features of a speaker's native language have important consequences for the ways in which speakers think. Boroditsky (1999) argues that linguistic differences between Mandarin and English produce differences in the ways that Mandarin and English speakers think about time. It is reasonable to suppose that associated with these differences are differences in what it's like for Mandarin speakers to think about time and what it's like for English speakers to think about time. Others argue that polyglots often think in different ways given the demands of the particular language in which thinking occurs. Among the relevant demands, Slobin (1987: 435) notes, are those that involve "picking . . . characteristics that (a) fit some conceptualization of the event, and (b) are readily encodable in the language." Thus, one could maintain that what it's like for a polyglot to think a particular thought depends on the particular language in which she thinks, as well as the particular demands made by that language.

There are also more homely differences. It seems plausible to suggest that what it's like to think a given thought is *in general* different for speakers of different languages, or for a polyglot when thinking in different languages. The differences here are largely reflected in the different syntactic and orthographic features of distinct languages. Consider what it's like for an English speaker to think that claret is delightful. Now imagine what it would be like for a Mandarin speaker to think that thought in his native language. The syntactic, phonological, and orthographic differences are striking,

---

[9] For similar remarks, see Robinson (2005: 536–9) and Tye (1996: 422).

and so surely are the phenomenological differences between the subjects thinking these thoughts.

This fact generates a dilemma for the phenomenology of thought thesis. If phenomenology is individuative of thought content, then thoughts with the same content must have the same phenomenology. But the phenomenology is different for the Mandarin speaker and the English speaker when they think the same thought. So, either there is *hidden* phenomenology which is shared in the two cases (in which case it is hard to see why it should count as *phenomenology* at all), or the thesis is straightforwardly false.

Perhaps it will be replied that, on the basis of introspection, the Mandarin speaker knows that he is thinking that claret is delightful, as does the English speaker, and thus there must be a common underlying phenomenology even though there are accompanying phenomenal differences in the two cases connected to the different sub-vocal sentences tokened. This is a simple non-sequitur, however. Even supposing that introspective knowledge of thought content is *based* on phenomenology, itself a highly contentious claim (see section IV), why should not different phenomenologies in different individuals warrant the same introspective belief about thought content?[10]

Alternatively, perhaps proponents of the phenomenology of thought thesis will insist that our intuitions about a lack of a common phenomenology in the above case are misled by the languages themselves. While there certainly are differences in what it is like for English and Mandarin speakers to think that claret is delightful in their respective languages, these differences can be reduced to differences that are associated with the features of their languages. If we ignore or strip away *those* differences, then we'll find the relevant phenomenological similarity.

This, of course, is precisely what we are contesting. In essence, the *prima facie* case against the phenomenology of thought thesis challenges the very notion that there is a specific, unique phenomenology of thinking that p, for each that-p content. Introspection just doesn't readily make available any phenomenal character that conforms to the phenomenology of thought thesis.

Consider the following analogy. There is, to be sure, something that it is like for a subject when he goes sailing. One might enjoy what it's like to feel the breeze against one's face, or to see the sun glisten against the water. There is also something that it is like for a subject when he drinks a beer. One might dislike the taste and grimace or one might down it quickly and with great pleasure. What it is like for a subject when he goes sailing is no doubt different from what it is like for a subject when he drinks a beer. But surely we don't want to posit a specific, unique phenomenology of sailing or of drinking a beer. The phenomenology in each case is ultimately the phenomenology of

---

[10] Just as, for example, the different phenomenologies to be found in the color experiences of normally functioning individuals whose qualia are inverted relative to one another, as they are viewing an object in normal light, warrant in each individual the same color belief with respect to the object.

familiar states like those of Lormand's Quartet[11] and these will vary from individual to individual. Correspondingly, the phenomenology that goes along with consciously thinking a certain type of thought for a certain individual provides no more reason to posit a *unique* phenomenology of thinking that thought type than is provided by the above observations about what it's like to go sailing or have a beer.

Our discussion thus far has given a central role to linguistic features in accounting for the supposed phenomenology of thought. Such a focus is natural given the extent to which we think *in* language. We typically conceive of conscious thought as a matter of hearing a voice—usually one's own voice—as uttering a natural language sentence *in foro interno*.

This focus on language is, however, probably an oversimplification. There is a variety of cases suggesting that a (human) subject's linguistic capabilities outstrip their abilities for thought, and further that a (human) subject's thought can occur without any linguistic imagery at all. We will first briefly survey the relevant cases, and then discuss the implications they have for the phenomenology of thought thesis.

First, consider Ray Jackendoff's (1997: 183–4) discussion of cognitive deficiencies in those with otherwise intact linguistic abilities. Children with Williams syndrome utilize language with advanced vocabulary, and given this fact, they often appear to be abnormally intelligent. However, these children are unable to take advantage of their linguistic abilities in thought. It would be a mistake to think the children can entertain sophisticated thoughts that would mirror their linguistic mastery. These children are intellectually impoverished, in part, precisely because of this gulf between their linguistic and cognitive capacities.

This disconnect between linguistic and cognitive capacities, as Jackendoff notes, is not limited to children. Some adult idiot savants suffer from a similar gap between their linguistic and cognitive abilities. While they are able to master various languages, they fail to display any deep understanding of the languages of the sort that typically manifests itself in thought. Their linguistic abilities outstrip their capacities for thought.

Hermer-Vazquez et al. (1999) have famously shown that, in both children and adults, a subject's linguistic abilities "are indeed actively involved in their ability to solve problems requiring the integration of geometric and non-geometric information" (Clark 2006: 296). While the primary focus of these experiments has been on the ways in which language enables a subject to solve complex problems, it is also worth focusing attention on those subjects whose linguistic resources were not utilized in solving the task at hand. In determining the role of language in solving complex problems, one group of adults was asked to solve a problem while also engaging in a linguistically demanding task (repeating or "shadowing" speech played over headphones), while a second group was asked to solve the problem while also engaging in a

---

[11]   Or better, our quintet.

non-linguistic task (mimicking or "shadowing" a rhythm played over headphones with their hands). As Andy Clark puts it:

The working memory demands of the latter task were at least as heavy as those of the former. Yet subjects engaged in speech shadowing were unable to solve the integration-demanding problem, while those shadowing rhythm were unaffected. (Clark 2006: 296)

The explanation for why the subjects engaged in rhythm shadowing were more successful at solving the task is that their linguistic resources were freely available to cognition. Yet the subjects shadowing speech were also engaged in a particular cognitive task. Given that their linguistic resources were devoted to another task, they were unable to solve the problem. It is reasonable to suggest that their linguistic resources were, while engaged in speech shadowing, unavailable to cognition.

Nevertheless, we can still ask whether the subjects were thinking through the problem. It certainly seems that they were, even though they were unable to solve the problem with much success. It is thus reasonable to say that the subjects were engaged in thought, despite the unavailability of linguistic resources. In thinking, the subjects in these cases were not tokening sentences of a natural language in their heads, given that their linguistic resources were devoted to another task.

There are other more ordinary cases in which it is plausible to suggest that subjects think without enjoying linguistic imagery or tokening sentences of natural languages in their heads. Consider for instance, certain forms of creativity:

Beethoven and Picasso . . . obviously displayed a lot of intelligence and deep thought. But their thoughts were not expressible as bits of language—their intelligence was in the visual and musical domains respectively. (Jackendoff 1997: 184)

To flesh out the example a bit, let's focus on the case of Beethoven. When Beethoven agonized over the close of Symphony No. 9 in D minor, and whether the ending should be choral or instrumental, he was thinking through how the piece of music came together as a whole. Yet it doesn't seem as though Beethoven's thoughts were a matter of tokening various sentences in his head or that they were otherwise characterized by any linguistic imagery. The enterprise of arranging a musical piece in one's head, of thinking through how the piece should fit together, in general appears non-linguistic.

These cases present a gap between thought and language. What morals should we draw from this gap? Some seem to take it as evidence in favor of the phenomenology of thought thesis. For instance, Horgan and Tienson comment:

[N]on-perceptual intentionality does not always involve language and/or auditory imagery. For instance, conscious, unverbalized beliefs about the locations of nearby unperceived objects are just as ubiquitous in human life as is the explicit or imagistic verbalization of one's focal train of thought. Think for example, of cooking, cleaning house, or working in a garage or woodshop. In any such activity, you might spontaneously move to retrieve a needed tool that is out of sight. There is something that it is like to think that a certain tool is just there—in that cabinet, say—but such beliefs are typically not verbalized either vocally or subvocally or by way of verbal imagery. (Your verbal energies might all the while be directed toward ongoing philosophical discussion with a companion, uninterrupted by your selection of an appropriate tool.) You also, of course, frequently have unverbalized thoughts about the locations of objects in distant familiar locations. (2002: 523)

The particular case Horgan and Tienson cite here seems entirely unconvincing. While a subject might be said to count as thinking when engaged in tasks of the sort they describe (as in the speech-shadowing cases discussed above), it is far from clear whether we actually should say that a subject entertains a *thought* manifest to consciousness with the content that the tool is in the cabinet when she moves to retrieve the tool. It is, of course, certainly reasonable to hold that a subject in a case like the one described *believes* that the tool is in the cabinet. That, together with the desire to use the tool, explains why she spontaneously reached in the direction of the cabinet. None of this, however, requires that the subject actually consciously entertain any beliefs or desires, and indeed, it seems to mis-describe totally the case to impute such conscious mental activity to the subject.[12]

Still, it does seem reasonable to grant that in some of the relevant cases there is phenomenology. But the presence of phenomenology in itself does not count in favor of the phenomenology of thought thesis. Linguistic imagery is, as mentioned, but one of a quintet of the phenomenological states to which we can appeal in explaining what it is like for a subject when he thinks a thought. If there is something that it is like for a subject when thinking, and if it does not involve linguistic imagery of the sort charted above, then we maintain that whatever it is like for a subject is exhausted by the non-linguistic members of our quintet. The example of Beethoven seems to fit this model well. One can imagine what it was like for Beethoven as a matter of enjoying auditory imagery of the music, and determining (perhaps in a phenomenologically effortful way involving a variety of bodily experiences and emotions, e.g. feelings of increased blood pressure, tension, tiredness, anxiety, happiness) how best to construct the symphony on the basis of this imagery. Beyond this, it's indeed hard to see what it *could* be like for Beethoven in entertaining the relevant thoughts.

Our position that the quintet exhausts the phenomenology of thought is in tension with a recent claim made by psychologist Russell Hurlburt that some cases of conscious occurrent thinking are wholly unaccompanied by imagery. Hurlburt and Akhter (2008) suggest that empirical work reveals that a wide range of thoughts are "un-symbolized," meaning that they employ *no* sort of imagery, linguistic or otherwise. Their experiment proceeds as follows:

---

[12] After all, in certain ways, what goes on in performing chores can be seen as rather like Armstrong's (1962) famous case of the automatic driver, someone who after a long time of driving seemingly goes on "auto-pilot," in an important sense unaware of the traffic around them.

[A] subject is given a beeper that is carried into the subject's natural environments. At the beeper's random beep, the subject is to pay attention to the experience that was ongoing at the moment the beep began and then, immediately, to jot down notes about that experience. Within 24 h, the . . . investigator interviews the subject about the (typically six) sampled moments from that day. Then the sample/interview procedure is repeated for several (typically five) more sampling days. (Hurlburt and Akhter 2008: 1365)

Their primary reason for thinking that there are unsymbolized thoughts is the subjects' inability to provide any consistent concrete description of the thoughts they were having prior to the beeper's sounding. As Hurlburt and Akhter (2008: 1366) note, subjects often provide several distinct descriptions of the thought they were (allegedly) entertaining before the beeper went off.

We have our doubts as to whether any of this means there are actually any cases of genuinely unsymbolized thinking. First, it may well be that in some cases the subject was not thinking at all. Take a case in which a subject is grocery shopping. When the beeper sounds, the subject may note that she was staring at a row of cereal boxes and judges that she was thinking that she'd like to purchase the cereal on the middle row. It is consistent with this that she wasn't actually thinking the thought she self-attributes. In interpreting her own behavior, she may be attributing thoughts to herself that she was not in fact having.[13] It then wouldn't be surprising that she cannot pin down a single description of what she was thinking, since she is merely interpreting herself as having a thought with a certain kind of content.

Nevertheless, even if the subject is consciously thinking before the beeper sounds, the inability to provide any consistent description of the content of such thoughts does not entail that they had no associated imagery. First, consider the demands of the task that the subject is performing. Having one's attention drawn to the noise of the beeper and to the task of recording one's experiences may have a masking effect, undermining the subject's ability to access the imagistic vehicles for their previous thought contents. Thus, one can consistently suggest that even though there was imagery associated with the conscious thought, the masking effect hinders the subject's ability to access and report it. Second, if the subject is having a thought accompanied by *non-linguistic* imagery, it should not be surprising that she might find it difficult to consistently offer any single description in words that specifically report the exact content of the thought. Hurlburt and Akhter (2008: 1366) note that "subjects who are describing experiences that are in words (inner speech, for example) quickly learn to be quite confident about the exact words, and their reports of those exact words typically stay much more consistent." It stands to reason that subjects whose thoughts are accompanied by linguistic imagery are better at reporting such imagery in words. We should not expect all such imagery, however, to be so readily and consistently reportable. The subject's inability to spell out consistently in words what they were thinking does not,

---

[13] We are indebted here to Peter Carruthers.

as Hurlburt and Akhter suggest, provide any evidence for the claim that no imagery accompanies such thoughts. The imagery could be that of one of the non-linguistic members of our quintet, and the subject's difficulty in consistently specifying the exact content could stem from the non-linguistic nature of the imagery. A picture says a thousand words, but it's not so easy to specify *which* thousand.

In short, if the subjects in Hurlburt's cases are actually thinking, and if there is anything that it is like for them when they have such thoughts, we hold that it can be exhausted by the phenomenology of the non-imagistic elements of our quintet. We remain steadfastly noncommittal, however, about whether the subject thinks in all such cases, and also about whether there is anything it is like for him or her.

We maintain, then, that the onus remains on the defender of the phenomenology of thought thesis to show that there is something that it is like for a subject when thinking that outstrips the quintet of phenomenological states. Thus far, the claim that there is a disconnect between thought and language and the arguments in favor of unsymbolized thinking fail to provide any clear evidence in favor of the phenomenology of thought thesis.

The *prima facie* case against the phenomenology of thought thesis brings into focus a particular sort of demand. If the experience of thinking a certain thought has a phenomenology of the special kind charted above, then what is it? Put up or shut up, we say![14] In the next section, we'll consider one popular intuitive attempt to put up.

3 Understanding-experience and the phenomenology of thought

The *prima facie* case against the phenomenology of thought thesis has it that introspection doesn't reveal the kind of phenomenology that proponents of the thesis endorse. Horgan and Tienson (2002: 522–3), Horgan et al. (2004: 301–2), Pitt (2004: 27–9), and Horgan and Kriegel (2008: 352) claim that there is an uncontroversial experience, the phenomenology of which straightforwardly supports their position.

The experience they have in mind—understanding-experience—was first brought to attention by Galen Strawson (1994: 10). According to Strawson, there is a distinctive kind of phenomenal state that accompanies hearing sentences as meaningful. Consider what it is like for a subject when he hears sentences in a language that he does not understand with what it is like for that subject when he hears sentences in a language that he does understand. Patently, there is a difference. This difference is due to the

---

[14] Our demand is similar to that made by some anti-representationalists regarding particular kinds of experiences. Representationalists hold that phenomenal character is a certain kind of representational content. Certain anti-representationalists (e.g. Block (1996)) put forth examples of experiences with phenomenal character that supposedly lack representational content (e.g. phosphene experiences, or orgasms). The demand on the representationalist is essentially (in Block's words) to "put up or shut up": provide the representational content the relevant experience is supposed to have or concede defeat. (We take the representationalist to have put up sufficiently in these cases, we might add.)

presence of the *experience* of understanding the relevant sentences in the one case and not in the other.

We agree that there is a real phenomenological difference here. But the phenomenology involved does not establish the phenomenology of thought thesis; for it is not at all clear that the phenomenology is *unique* or *proprietary* in the way that proponents of the phenomenology of thought thesis believe. Once again, why suppose that the phenomenology goes beyond that of our earlier quintet of states? When we hear someone speaking in a language we understand, the phonological processing of the sound stream is different from the processing that goes on when we hear someone speaking in a language we do not comprehend. In the former case, the "grouping" of the sound stream is causally influenced by the semantic processing. The result is that the auditory experiences we undergo are different from those we would undergo were we to hear the same sound stream without understanding the language.

In the written case, as we read, it is sometimes phenomenally as if we are speaking to ourselves. We "hear" an inner voice. In this case, there are linguistic (or verbal) auditory images which have the phonological and syntactic structure of sentences in the relevant language. These images frequently even come complete with details of stress and intonation. Depending upon the content of the passage or the speech, we may also undergo a variety of emotions and feelings. We may feel tense, bored, excited, uneasy, or angry. Differences in the images, perceptual experiences, bodily reactions, and emotional experiences we undergo suffice to account for the phenomenological differences between the experience of understanding certain sentences and what goes on when we lack such understanding.

Consider next the case of understanding ambiguous sentences. Here is an example due to Horgan and Tienson (2002, p. 523). Hearing the ambiguous sentence "Time flies," one might hear it "as a cliché about the passage of time ... [or] as a command at the insect races."[15] Hearing it one way, there is a phenomenal difference from hearing it the other way, they claim. We agree. But so what? Isn't the difference easily accounted for by differences in associated linguistic images or auditory experiences having the phonological and syntactic structure of the sentence "Time flies" under each interpretation (and perhaps differences in visual images too—of flies lined up to compete, say, in the latter case but not in the former)? If you doubt this, take it away. Take away *all* the associated images, *all* the relevant perceptual experiences, *all* the experienced bodily reactions (for example, the smile that accompanies an image of flies in a hundred-meter dash), *all* the emotional responses. Do you really think that there is any *phenomenal* difference left? (David Lewis once considered an objection to his version of modal realism which he labeled "the incredulous stare." Our question may be taken to express *the incredulous request* objection to advocates of the phenomenology of thought thesis.)

---

[15] See here also Pitt (2004: 27–8).

There is a further point worth emphasizing. Hearing the sentence "Time flies" as a cliché about the passage of time, one is subject to a thought with a different content from the thought one undergoes in hearing the sentence as a command about timing insects. In each case, one is conscious of the content of one's thought. So, there is a difference in what one is conscious of in the two cases. That, we agree, is indeed obvious. But the phenomenology of thought thesis requires something *much* stronger: that there be a unique phenomenology that goes along with *any* token thought with the one content however it is expressed linguistically, regardless of associated images, etc., and that there be a unique phenomenology that goes along with *any* token thought with the other content, again however linguistically expressed and regardless again of images, etc. As yet, we have been given no good reason whatsoever to grant this claim.

The upshot is that, in our view, understanding-experience provides no firm ground on which to base the phenomenology of thought thesis. The same can be said for other familiar kinds of phenomenology that have gotten considerably less attention: the *vividness* of certain thoughts and their *clarity*. A thought is usually taken to be vivid when it is accompanied by particularly rich imagery. For example, a native Londoner may be able to have exceptionally vivid thoughts about Brick Lane, and at least part of what can make the thoughts vivid is the richness of the imagery associated with them, imagery that comes in part from a capacity to recall aspects of Brick Lane. Nothing about the vividness of some conscious thoughts lends support to the claim that thoughts have a phenomenology of their own that is proprietary, distinctive, and individuative. Likewise for the clarity of a thought. Clarity in some cases may be no more than vividness; in others it is a matter of how the given thought connects with other thoughts at a conscious level. For example, one may come to appreciate the implications of a certain thought, implications that hitherto one had failed to see.

To this, it may be replied that consciousness of a thought and/or its implications itself requires that the phenomenology of thought thesis be true. The relevance of introspective awareness to the thesis we are denying is taken up in the next section.

4 Introspective knowledge and the phenomenology of thought thesis

According to Pitt (2004), without the relevant phenomenology, certain epistemic abilities that we have with regard to our own thoughts would be unaccounted for. Specifically, our knowledge of the contents of our own thoughts and our ability to identify our occurrent, conscious thoughts allegedly require that thoughts have a proprietary, distinctive, individuative phenomenology. Pitt puts the argument, the conclusion of which is the phenomenology of thought thesis, as follows:

(K1) It is possible immediately [i.e. consciously, introspectively, and non-inferentially] to identify one's occurrent, conscious thoughts.

(K2) It would not be possible immediately to identify one's thoughts unless each type of conscious thought had a proprietary, distinctive, individuative phenomenology.

Therefore,

(P) Each type of conscious thought—each state of consciously thinking that *p*, for all thinkable contents *p*—has a proprietary, distinctive, individuative phenomenology.

On behalf of (K2), Pitt claims that our immediate, introspective knowledge of particular thoughts is based upon acquaintance with those thoughts. Without such acquaintance, Pitt maintains, we would not be in a position to come to know the contents of our thoughts. Acquaintance is here to be understood on analogy with what Dretske has called "simple seeing." Pitt comments:

A subject S is introspectively acquainted with a conscious mental particular M (a state, a thought, an image, a feeling, a sensation, etc.) if S differentiates M from its mental environment purely on the basis of *how it is experienced* by S, where a mental particular's being experienced by S neither presupposes nor implies that S has any beliefs about it. For M to be experienced in some way by S is a matter of its qualitative properties—its phenomenology. (Pitt 2004: 9–10)

One obvious initial worry with Pitt's position is that it relies on a perceptual model of introspection. Introspection, for Pitt, is a matter of a subject turning his attention "inward" and experiencing inner mental particulars. In our view, this is a totally implausible model for understanding introspective awareness. But leaving this to one side for the moment, the point we wish to make is that it will not serve Pitt's purposes; for it *mis-locates* the phenomenology. This needs a little explanation.

Consider a case of simple seeing—my seeing a ripe tomato, say. In seeing a tomato, I am conscious of it. It looks red and round to me. What has phenomenal character here is not the tomato—the thing of which I am conscious—but my consciousness of it. Generally, for M to be experienced some way by S is not a matter of M's phenomenology but rather of M causing in S a state with some phenomenology or other. Correspondingly, if introspective awareness of a particular thought, *t*, is like seeing a tomato, what has phenomenal character is not *t* but my introspective consciousness of *t*. So, if the perceptual model of introspective awareness of thoughts is right (something we deny), there is no more reason to suppose that thoughts have distinctive, proprietary, individuative phenomenal features on the basis of our introspective awareness of them than there is to suppose that tomatoes do on the basis of our simple seeing of them.

Pitt insists, however, that in introspecting a thought, there is a phenomenology that belongs to the thought itself:

Thus, the argument is that Immediate identification of a thought is introspective knowledge by acquaintance (primary epistemic introspection) that it is the thought it is, and that this is not possible without simple acquaintance, which itself depends upon the introspected state having phenomenal character. Immediate identification of a particular thought requires Immediate discriminative awareness of its distinctive phenomenology. Since each conscious thought has a distinctive phenomenology, there is something it is like to entertain it; and since there is something it is like to entertain it, it is possible Immediately to identify it. (Pitt 2004: 11)

Our reply is that simple acquaintance does *not* depend upon the thing with which one is acquainted having phenomenal character, never mind having a distinctive, proprietary, individuative phenomenal character. So, even if the perceptual model of introspective awareness were the only viable model, no good reason has been given for accepting (K2).

Furthermore, there are much more plausible alternatives to the perceptual model of introspective awareness anyway. Here is one such alternative. Let us grant that introspective knowledge of what we are occurrently thinking is not baseless. Rather, it is based on evidence that we can introspect. It might be suggested that the relevant evidence here consists in introspective *beliefs* that provide evidential reasons. Intuitively, however, our evidence for believing that we are thinking that P does not consist in further beliefs at all. Intuitively, we have introspective access to certain mental states, and these states are our evidence for our introspective beliefs without providing a propositional justification for those beliefs.

On this reliabilist view of introspective knowledge, introspective beliefs are warranted because of their causal ancestry, which will include the introspected mental states in question. The claim that introspective knowledge is based on evidence is intuitively appealing, we maintain, given the reliabilist reading of "evidence" and not given the reading that construes evidence as beliefs that are evidential reasons.

But what are the relevant mental states that are a thinker's introspective evidence here? A plausible view is that they are simply the occurrent thoughts the introspective beliefs are about. On this view, it is denied that one has introspective access to a particular thought—for example, the thought that there are many shades of red—only *via* one's introspective access to a linguistic and/or visual image. One has direct introspective access to the occurrent thought itself. This is not to deny that there is typically an associated image. The point is that, whether or not there is an image, the occurrent thought that P is one's evidence for the belief that one is thinking that P without being an evidential *reason* for it. On this view, the belief that one is thinking that P is based on the occurrent thought that P. Thus, for individuals who speak different languages, there can be a common basis for their belief that they are thinking that P, notwithstanding the fact that they are subject to very different quasi-linguistic images and thus very different experiences.

On the above account of introspection of thoughts, our introspective access to our occurrent thoughts differs from our perceptual access to our environment. We have visual access to the scene before our eyes by having a visual experience that is (appropriately) caused by the scene. In contrast, we do not have introspective access to our occurrent thoughts by having experiences that are (appropriately) caused by the thoughts. Our introspective access to the thoughts is direct.[16]

In cases involving what Burge (1996) has called "Cogito thoughts," there is a conscious act of recognition. But in the typical case, one's recognition of what one is occurrently thinking does not involve a conscious act (that of consciously thinking to oneself that one is having so-and-so thought). One can recognize that one is thinking that there are many shades of red, for example, when the only occurrent thought one is having is that there are many shades of red. In the typical case, one's recognition of what one is occurrently thinking does not involve a conscious act (that of consciously thinking to oneself that one is having so-and-so thought).[17]

We conclude that Pitt's argument for the phenomenology of thought thesis fails. He does not show that knowledge of thought content requires anything like a proprietary, distinctive, individuative phenomenology. Given the *prima facie* case against the thesis, and the account of understanding experience offered in the previous section, we conclude that the thesis is ultimately unmotivated.

To forestall further arguments in favor of the phenomenology of thought thesis, we shall conclude by arguing for something stronger than the simple claim that in actual fact there *is* no such thing as a phenomenology of thought (in the sense that the phenomenology of thought thesis requires). We shall offer considerations regarding the nature of thought itself that suggest that thoughts *could* not be bearers of the relevant phenomenology.

5 Thought's structure and the phenomenology of thought

Some time ago, Peter Geach (1957) claimed that thoughts do not have the right structure to figure as elements in the stream of consciousness. As Soteriou (2007), commenting on Geach, puts it:

Implicit in the metaphor of the stream of consciousness is the idea that aspects of mind that make up the stream must *unfold* over time in a way that mental states, like belief, do not . . . I take it that Geach thinks that a stream of thought requires (a) succession within an act of thinking a thought and/or (b) the gradual transition from [one] thought to another, because he assumes that a stream of thought would have to be constituted by the occurrence of unfolding, processive states of mind.

---

[16] For related discussions of the disanalogies between perception and introspection, see Shoemaker (1985, 1988, 1994).

[17] For more on introspection of thoughts, see McLaughlin and Tye (1998).

Geach has it that thoughts lack just this sort of structure. They are so lacking because they are not unfolding, processive states. For Geach (1957: 105), thoughts instead have no more "than a loose connexion with physical time."[18]

In the language of persistence, thoughts *endure* (they are wholly present at each moment that they exist), but, unlike processes, they do not *perdure* (or exist over time in virtue of having distinct parts at each moment of existence). Entities with the former sort of structure, on Geach's view, simply aren't the right kinds of things to be constituents of the stream of consciousness.

It is not easy to discern what Geach is getting at, but the idea of his we wish to exploit can be brought out in the following way. Thoughts do not *unfold* over time in the way that an event like a cricket match unfolds. Once one begins to think that claret is delightful, one has already *achieved* the thinking of it. (Thus, Geach's (1957: 104) claim that "unless the whole complex [of a thought] is grasped all together...the thought or judgment does not exist at all.") In thinking that claret is delightful, it is not as though one first grasps the noun "claret," and then the copula "is," and finally the adjective "delightful" in a successive process. Thinking the thought does not unfold in the way that a string of sounds from a piano unfolds in an etude. The whole thought arrives at once.

And yet, one can think that claret is delightful *for some time*, and the experience of thinking that claret is delightful can seem to unfold before one's mind in a processive fashion. What is it that unfolds over time if not the thought? One obvious suggestion is that it is that which accompanies the thought—those various phenomenal goings-on that one's experience of having the thought comprises.

As we've seen, such things include the unfolding of linguistic, phonological, and orthographic images, as well as the mental imagery that might accompany one's thinking the thought. To stick with the claret example, if one is thinking that claret is delightful and images of an especially delightful claret one once enjoyed pass before one's mind, it seems that what unfolds over time is not the thought, but rather the imagery accompanying it. Or, if one suddenly thinks to oneself that one is late for a dental appointment and one sub-vocally tokens some such sentence as "Oh no, it's 2 p.m.—I'm late for the dentist," what seems to unfold is the sentence, not the thought itself. Geach's idea is that the thought associated with the given sub-vocalized sentence itself remains in stasis; even though it endures for the relevant period of time, it does not *unfold* in the processive way that the imagery accompanying the thought does.[19]

These considerations put into a new light a criticism we made earlier of Pitt's defense of the phenomenology of thought thesis. Recall that we noted that Pitt seems to mis-locate

---

[18] Soteriou (2007: 545–7) traces the source of Geach's claim about the structure of thought to his claim that we cannot use thought-related verbs in the continuous past (verb forms of the sort "was thinking"), placing such verbs in Zeno Vendler's category of achievement verbs.

[19] Items that unfold in the right sort of way to be elements of the stream of consciousness are items belonging to the categories of our earlier quintet.

the phenomenology involved in introspection of our thoughts: while Pitt seems to locate the phenomenology with the thought itself, it actually belongs to the *experience* of thinking the thought. Geach's claim provides a new reason for faulting Pitt on this score. Thoughts, given that they lack the relevant processive features, simply aren't suited to be the bearers of the relevant phenomenology.

Perhaps it will be replied that even though thoughts do not have a *processive* phenomenology, still they have a phenomenology of their own that is *non-processive*. But even if this is coherent—clearly something Geach himself would have denied—the fact is that when we introspect, we find no such phenomenology: the phenomenology available to us unfolds in the way explained above. So, the putative constant phenomenology for each thought must be hidden, which (as noted earlier) makes it hard to see why it should count as *phenomenology* at all.

6 Conclusion

At the outset, we noted that in opposing the phenomenology of thought thesis, we are not opposing the idea that there is something that it is like for a subject when he undergoes a thought. What has been suggested throughout this paper is that the relevant phenomenal character, however, is not *proprietary* to thought; nor is it *proprietary, distinctive, and individuative* of tokens of the given thought type. The *prima facie* case against the phenomenology of thought thesis so far stands unimpeached. Moreover, as Geach suggests, thoughts may not even be the kinds of things that have the salient phenomenology or indeed any phenomenology at all.

When looking for a phenomenology of thought, all we find is a phenomenology that is associated with the act of thinking. Such phenomenology, we have argued, provides no good reason to accept the phenomenology of thought thesis.

References

Armstrong, D. (1962). *Bodily Sensations*. London: Routledge and Kegan Paul.

Block, N. (1996). "Mental Paint and Mental Latex," *Philosophical Issues*, 7: 19–49.

Boroditsky, L. (1999). "First-language Thinking for Second-language Understanding: Mandarin and English Speakers' Conceptions of Time," in M. Hahn and S. Stoness (eds), *Proceedings of the Twenty-First Annual Conference of the Cognitive Science Society*. Philadelphia: Lawrence Erlbaum Associates.

Burge, T. (1996). "Our Entitlement to Self-Knowledge," *Proceedings of Aristotelian Society*, 96: 91–116.

Clark, A. (2006). "Material Symbols," *Philosophical Psychology*, 19: 291–307.

Dretske, F. (1995). *Naturalizing the Mind*. Cambridge, MA: MIT Press.

Farkas, K. (2008). "Phenomenal Intentionality Without Compromise," *Monist*, 91: 273–93.

Geach, P. (1957). *Mental Acts*. London: Routledge.

Hermer-Vazquez, L., E. Spelke, and A. Katznelson (1999). "Sources of Flexibility in Human Cognition: Dual-task Studies of Space and Language," *Cognitive Psychology*, 39: 3–36.

Holton, R. (2006). "The Act of Choice," *Philosophers' Imprint*, 6: 1–15.

Horgan, T. and U. Kriegel (2008). "Phenomenal Intentionality Meets the Extended Mind," *Monist*, 91: 347–73.

——and J. Tienson (2002). "The Intentionality of Phenomenology and the Phenomenology of Intentionality," in D. Chalmers (ed.), *Philosophy of Mind: Classical and Contemporary Readings*. Oxford: Oxford University Press.

——, ——, and G. Graham (2004). "Phenomenal Intentionality and the Brain in a Vat," in R. Schantz (ed.), *The Externalist Challenge: New Studies on Cognition and Intentionality*. Amsterdam: de Gruyter.

Hurlburt, R. and S. Akhter (2008). "Unsymbolized Thinking," *Consciousness and Cognition*, 17: 1364–74.

Jackendoff, R. (1987). *Consciousness and the Computational Mind*. Cambridge, MA: MIT Press.

——(1997). *The Architecture of the Language Faculty*. Cambridge, MA: MIT Press.

Kriegel, U. (2007). "Intentional Inexistence and Phenomenal Intentionality," *Philosophical Perspectives*, 21: 307–40.

Loar, B. (2003). "Phenomenal Intentionality as the Basis for Mental Content," in M. Hahn and B. Ramberg (eds), *Reflections and Replies: Essays on the Philosophy of Tyler Burge*. Cambridge, Mass: MIT Press.

Lormand, E. (1996). "Nonphenomenal Consciousness," *Noûs*, 30: 242–61.

McLaughlin, B. and M. Tye (1998). "Is Content-Externalism Compatible with Privileged Access?", *The Philosophical Review*, 107: 349–80.

Pitt, D. (2004). "The Phenomenology of Cognition; or *What Is It Like to Think that P?*", *Philosophy and Phenomenological Research*, 69: 1–36.

Robinson, W. (2005). "Thoughts Without Distinctive Non-Imagistic Phenomenology," *Philosophy and Phenomenological Research*, 70: 534–61.

Shoemaker, S. (1985). "Introspection and the Self," *Midwest Studies in Philosophy*, 10: 101–20.

——(1988). "On Knowing One's Own Mind," *Philosophical Perspectives*, 2: 183–209.

——(1994). "Introspection," *Cambridge Companion to the Philosophy of Mind*. Cambridge: Cambridge University Press, pp. 395–400.

Slobin, D. (1987). "Thinking for Speaking," in J. Aske, N. Beery, L. Michaelis, and H. Filip (eds), *Proceedings of the Thirteenth Annual Meeting of the Berkeley Linguistics Society*. Berkeley, CA: Berkeley Linguistics Society.

Soteriou, M. (2007). "Content and the Stream of Consciousness," *Philosophical Perspectives*, 21: 543–68.

Strawson, G. (1994). *Mental Reality*. Cambridge, MA: MIT Press.

Tye, M. (1995). *Ten Problems of Consciousness*. Cambridge, MA: MIT Press.

——(1996). "Review of Mental Reality," *Journal of Philosophy*, 93: 421–4.

——(2000). *Consciousness, Color, and Content*. Cambridge, MA: MIT Press.

——(2008). "The Experience of Emotion," in *Revue Internationale de Philosophie*, special issue edited by Joelle Proust.

The Phenomenology of Consciously Thinking

David Woodruff Smith

1 The phenomenon of consciously thinking

What does the discipline of phenomenology tell us about the experience of *consciously thinking* something? There lies cognitive phenomenology: the phenomenology of "cognitive" experiences, including conscious thinking, perceiving (sensory-conceptual experience), judging (either self-evidential or inferential), etc. Phenomenology in general I take to be the study of consciousness as experienced from the first-person perspective.[1]

In due course we shall address: (i) the *phenomenality* of consciously thinking, i.e. its "appearing" in consciousness, with a character of "what it is like" to so think; (ii) the *intentionality* of thinking, i.e. its character of being directed through a propositional content or "thought" toward a putative state of affairs; and (iii) the form of *inner awareness* commonly found in thinking, i.e. the character whereby one is immediately aware of one's so thinking.

On my model, these structures will be interlinked, as an act of consciously thinking is *phenomenally* directed *from* the act, *centered* in its subject, *through* its meaning-content *toward* its putative object *with* immediate awareness thereof. Concerning the subject's inner awareness of thinking, we shall consider distinct phenomenological characters factored from this form of awareness: factors including phenomenality, reflexivity, egocentricity, and temporal and spatial sensibility. Here I follow out, for the special case of thinking, the "modal" model of consciousness pursued elsewhere.[2] On this

---

[1] On the assumed conception of phenomenology see Smith (2007), Smith and McIntyre (1982), and Dreyfus (1982), the latter including Dagfinn Føllesdal's seminal 1969 article on Husserl's notion of noema, or intentional content. Other recent accounts of Husserlian phenomenology are Sokolowski (2000), Moran (2005), and Mohanty (2008). Strawson (1994) emphasizes "cognitive experiences" in contrast to sensory experiences; Strawson (2008, 2009) use the term "cognitive phenomenology" for the characterization of cognitive experiences.

[2] See Smith (1986, 1989, 2004, 2005); and Ford and Smith (2006). Compare the studies of self-representational consciousness in Kriegel and Williford (2006) and in Kriegel (2009).

account, we note at the outset, phenomenality is not restricted to sensory experience bearing sensory "qualia".[3]

2 From conscious sensation to conscious perception to conscious thought

It is often assumed, in some circles in philosophy of mind, that phenomenology finds a phenomenal or (better) phenomenological character only in a *sensation* such as feeling toothache or seeing red—and never in an experience of *thinking* something.[4]

Yet everyday perceptual experience is already richer than mere sensation. When I see "that bluish-black raven landing in the Eucalyptus tree in my neighbor's yard," the content of my visual experience is part sensory and part conceptual. Phenomenologically, *what I see*—what is consciously given in my visual experience—is not a mere pattern of color, but a bird, a raven, landing in a tree, in my neighbor's Eucalyptus. This complex of *perceptual meaning* is infused with sensory data, but is far richer in content than a mere sensation as of a bluish-black shape. This sort of content I like to call essentially *indexical* or *acquainting* sense, realized in an intuitive experience of being acquainted with an object, say, where I see "that bird," "that large black raven landing in the Eucalyptus."[5]

Now, surely there are also activities of *conscious thought* which have a phenomenological character that is decidedly conceptual and consciously experienced while out-

---

[3] To hold that consciousness is restricted to sensation, hence that what is conscious in thinking must be some sort of "cognitive sensation" or cognitive "qualia", is to *looking-glass* the very phenomenon of consciousness in the case of thinking. Too much of recent philosophy of mind indulges in this transmogrification, where we pass through the Lewis Carroll looking glass and on the other side find that consciousness itself is morphed into something else. *Consciousness*, including conscious thinking, is thus morphed into either physicalist–externalist information-flow (pressing consciousness outside itself) or empiricist–internalist sensation-flow (squeezing the life-world out of consciousness, leaving only meaningless sensory residue). In either way, *thought* is forever left out of "consciousness," stranded back on the wrong ("Cartesian"?) side of the looking glass. As Galen Strawson defines the Carrollian verb: "to looking-glass a term is to use a term in such a way that whatever one means by it, it excludes what the term means." See Strawson (2005: 43). Cognitive phenomenology, then, pursues *inter alia* the phenomenology of consciously thinking something—not the looking-glassed "phenomenology" of looking-glassed "thinking" (*sans* consciousness).

[4] This sort of view seems to lie behind many discussions of consciousness centered on sensory qualia, often an implicit assumption. See, e.g., Levine (2001: Chapter 6), where qualia are viewed in relation to "the intentional contents of conscious cognitive states." The empiricist tradition, from Locke to Ayer, may lead some philosophers to find pure sensation at the basis of all our conscious experience, whence Ryle (1949) focused on belief rather than on conscious thought. Only recently has consciousness in thinking appeared in the phenomenological horizon again, partly in the wake of various models of consciousness as higher- or same-order monitoring of mental activity. Pitt (2004) argues that there is indeed an experienced character of what it is like to think that p. Thomasson (2005) appraises the relation between consciousness and introspection. Essays in Kriegel and Williford (2006) study higher-order, same-order, and self-representational monitoring. Kriegel (2009) argues for a self-representational model of subjective character.

[5] See Smith (1989) on indexical sense in experiences of acquaintance: as in *seeing* "that bird" and in *inner awareness* of "this very experience" in seeing "that bird." We recur to these forms of phenomenological structure below. Husserl held that a demonstrative pronoun partly expresses such a perceptual content, also called an "intuition-sense," or *Anschauungssinn*.

running sensory qualia. *Perceptual judgment* is one such form of experience, as when I visually judge that "that black bird hovering above me is a *turkey vulture*."

Thus, in seeing the bird overhead, I form a conscious judgment about what I see, that is, a *conscious thought*, grounded in visual evidence, about the object I see. In the unfolding example: I see a large bird, black, circling a tall tree, currently hovering on the updraft. As it tilts this way and that, I judge that it is a turkey vulture. I consciously think, "Oh, that [black bird which I see circling above me] is a turkey vulture." This I *consciously think*. My experience of consciously so thinking has a phenomenological structure or character, for it is quite unlike my experience of consciously thinking, "The gardener is coming today." What it is like for me to experience the vulturish thought is quite different from what it is like for me to experience the gardenerish thought. And the difference is not that the former carries sensory qualia unlike any in the latter. No, the vulturish thought is a sensory-conceptual visual judgment, a certain form of consciously thinking something about the object I am currently seeing: I see "that large black bird" and I think "that [large black bird I see] is a turkey vulture." Notice that we are describing an occurrent conscious mental *activity* or *process* of so thinking, an activity I consciously perform, a process of thinking within which I am aware of my so thinking. This occurrent act of thinking is not a dispositional state of believing, a mental state that is not coursing through my stream of consciousness.... Husserl distinguished between a "*pre-predicative*" experience of seeing an object, as in seeing "that raven," which is a perception with "attributive" and demonstrative content, and the "*predicative*" experience of judging that a perceived object has a property, as in judging "that that is a raven," a judgment with a propositional content (Husserl 1939).

In this example of perceptual judgment, we must distinguish two occurrent experiences, the second presupposing or grounded in the first. I *see* "that black bird," and at the same moment I *think* (judge) that "that black bird is a turkey vulture." My so thinking presupposes my so seeing, and—here is the point—my thinking is itself a conscious mental activity with its own phenomenological character. The character of my so thinking is not itself the character of a sensory experience, but rather the character of consciously thinking. Yet in this case my thinking is itself dependent on a simultaneous experience of seeing—where that underlying visual experience has its own sensory-conceptual-demonstrative character.

And now we are moving beyond conscious sensory experience to forms of conscious thought that are clearly not experiences of pure sensation. We thus distinguish different forms of conscious experience ranging from, say, visual sensation (seeing a black patch) to visual perception (seeing that black bird), to visual judgment or thought (thinking that that black bird [visually presented] is a turkey vulture). Each of these forms of experience has a particular phenomenological character or structure. If it is useful to begin with the "felt" character of sensation, in homing in on structures of conscious experience, we nonetheless move on from there to the experienced character of consciously *seeing* something and then on to the experienced character of consciously *thinking* something about what one sees. Each of these forms of conscious experience in its own way involves sensation, but in the case of consciously thinking about what one sees we begin to separate out the conscious *thinking* from the conscious seeing and the mere conscious sensing.

We thus begin to appreciate the phenomenological character of consciously *thinking* as opposed to consciously *sensing*. And soon we are ready to appreciate the character of consciously thinking something quite divorced from sensory experience. Accordingly, we shall pursue the phenomenology of somewhat different forms of conscious thinking.

3 Three cases of consciously thinking

Let us consider three particular forms of consciously thinking something: (1) a case of thinking about what one is seeing; (2) a case of everyday thinking about current events; and (3) a case of thinking something rather abstract. These three cases will bring out certain familiar ways in which we experience acts of thinking. This familiarity should bring home salient features of our experiences of thinking. Reflection on these features launches a phenomenology of consciously thinking. And that pattern of phenomenological analysis makes the point that, well, there is such a thing as *conscious* thought, with a familiar *phenomenological* character, a character we experience or live through quite naturally in everyday life.

Consider thus:

(1) Case of visual thought:

Walking by a marsh, I see a strange tall bird, and

(1*) I think that, oh, that bird is a great blue heron.

(2) Case of everyday thought:

Reading the newspaper, I look up, and, contemplating the news,

(2*) I think that Obama favors diplomacy.

(3) Case of abstract thought:

Reflecting on a piece of metaphysical theory, contrasting the drift of Whitehead's metaphysics with Aristotle's, I pause, and then

(3*) I think that time is more fundamental than substance.

In characterizing these three cases, we form rudimentary phenomenological descriptions of the three experiences of consciously thinking something. Accordingly, the sentences (1*), (2*), and (3*) are partial descriptions of the three experiences, each characterizing the relevant experience from the subject's first-person perspective. Of course, the first-person perspective is registered in the first-person pronoun at the beginning of each of these sentences.

Much has been made of the logical structure or semantics of sentences reporting propositional attitudes, especially belief (from Frege 1892, 1997 to especially Hintikka 1969). And there have been important studies of first-person belief reports (consider Perry 1979). However, our concern is the phenomenological structure of the experience characterized by such sentences. In an adaptation of Husserlian theory we may understand a phenomenological description such as (1★), (2★), or (3★) as articulating the overall *content*, or phenomenological structure, of the experience described. The overall content of an experience or act of consciousness Husserl called the act's "noema" (from the Greek for what is known or experienced), and that part of the full content that presents the object Husserl called the act's "sense" (*Sinn*). The sense of an act of thinking is a *propositional* content or sense, the "thought" or "proposition" ascribed by the that-clause in (1★) or (2★) or (3★).[6]

For our purposes, accordingly, let us assume that the phenomenological descriptions (1★), (2★), and (3★) articulate in each case the overall *content*, or phenomenological structure, of the experience or act of thinking so characterized. I'll simply speak of content or structure in an experience, remaining neutral here about the ontology of content (*Sinn*, noema, etc.). However, I shall assume a notion of content that carries more structure than is evident in many current uses of the term "content."

Accordingly, in the first case, we observe three basic components in the overall content of the experience (using angle brackets to specify contents): the subject content <I>, the act-type content <think>, and the propositional object-content or sense <that bird is a great blue heron>. Similarly, in the second and third cases, the content includes propositional object-contents <Obama favors diplomacy> and <time is more fundamental than substance>, modified by the subject content <I> and the act content <think>. Beyond these formal observations, observations of phenomenological form in experience, we should reflect on how different these experiences are, as shaped by the context in which they occur. Yet each of these three experiences is an experience of *consciously thinking*. Each is an occurrent cognitive act, experienced by the subject with a certain phenomenological character. Consider thus, in more detail, how these experiences differ. The propositional contents of the three forms of experience *mean* or (as Husserl might say) "*intend*" in quite different ways, yet in each case there is a certain propositional content that is coursing through the subject's mind in a conscious experience of explicitly thinking.

We proceed now in the first person, reflecting on what it is to experience such-and-such an act of thinking.

[6] See Dreyfus (1982), and Føllesdal (1969). For background on this style of phenomenological analysis see Smith and McIntyre (1982), Smith (1989), and Smith (2007).

In the first case I am *thinking* about an object I am *seeing*. Now, the visual presentation of the object is part of my act of perception, wherein I see "that bird," indeed, "that strange tall grayish bird, with long spindly legs and a long neck, standing totally still." My act of thinking is a separate experience, wherein I think that "that bird is a great blue heron." This act of thinking is founded on the act of seeing. But my seeing the bird is one experience, and my thinking about it is a distinct experience. Specifically, the object-contents of my seeing and my thinking are different: one represents the bird, and the other represents a state of affairs about the bird. My consciousness is thus directed quite differently in the visual experience and in the cogitative experience founded on the visual. And of course in the base experience I *see* something, while in the founded experience I *think* something. In both, importantly, I am consciously experiencing something: consciously seeing, and consciously thinking. While my seeing the bird involves both sensory and conceptual content, my thinking that it is a great blue heron has a propositional content. Yet the thinking is just as much a conscious experience as is the seeing. . . . Here is a case of consciously thinking something where the propositional content <that bird is a great blue heron> itself is grounded in, or logically presupposes, the sensory-conceptual content <that bird>. That is, the visual content <that bird> occurring in my visual experience presents the heron in a sensuous-conceptual way. And that content is borrowed, presupposed, by the propositional content <that bird is a great blue heron> occurring in my act of thinking, where that propositional content predicates of the bird its heronesque species. Consciousness spreads here from my *sensuous* visual experience of the heron to my *thinking* about the heron I see.

Now, in the second case I am thinking not about something I see, but about something in the purview of our wider social world—not an individual object (the bird) that is visually present in my immediate surroundings, but rather an individual object (Barack Obama) that is present in my wider cultural surroundings. I have acquired background knowledge about that individual, known to me as "Barack Obama," and I am thinking that "Obama favors diplomacy." Clearly, the predicative content <favors diplomacy> is a conceptual content (non-sensory, to boot). The subject content <Obama> is a particular sort of individual concept: conceptual, and non-sensory, save for associative visual and auditory images stored in my memory; and *singular*, rather than general, i.e. a concept of a specific individual, not of a type (e.g. a politician). How this type of content works is not easy to specify, even though we all regularly use proper names including that of President Obama.[7]

Here is a case of consciously thinking where a propositional content, <Obama favors diplomacy>, is coursing through my mind in an occurrent conscious act of thinking, yet where my experience of so thinking does not concern whatever may be appearing in my current sensory fields. To be sure, I have seen and heard Mr. Obama on

---

[7] See Smith and McIntyre (1982: Chapter 8), for a detailed phenomenological account of such an "individuating" concept or sense, i.e. *Sinn*.

television, and I have read about him in the newspapers (then before my eyes). Yet my consciously so thinking is its own kind of conscious experience: cognitive, cogitative, but not sensory. However the singular content <Obama> may work, it is not a perceptually demonstrative content like <that bird>, sensuously conceptually demonstrating an individual object in my visual field. The point we emphasize here is that I am *experiencing* this act of thinking that "Obama favors diplomacy", quite as *consciously* as I may experience an act of sensory perception in seeing something, say, if I see Obama at a rally. Here, in other words, is an act of thinking which has a "phenomenology" even though it is a distinctly non-sensory and non-perceptual form of experience.

In such a case we should clearly see that cognitive phenomenology outruns the subjective, qualitative, phenomenal character of sensation. For the experience of consciously so thinking involves no sensation (whether visual, auditory, tactile, olfactory, or gustatory). And yet my so thinking is conscious and is experienced with its own phenomenological character, including "what it is like" to so think.

In the third featured case, in the midst of a metaphysical discussion, I find myself thinking that "time is more fundamental than substance." Clearly, this act of thinking is not a sensory experience, nor is it even about a concrete object I might see and form a thought about. Rather, this is the sort of abstract thought one has only in a probing philosophical reflection or discussion. The propositional content or thought <time is more fundamental than substance> can be accessed, used, "thought" only in the lofty heights of philosophical abstraction. Nonetheless, when I think this thought, I am quite consciously so thinking. Indeed, I am thinking this only in the idiom of classical philosophical discourse. For the notion of "substance" here used is that which derives from Aristotle's metaphysics, and the notion of time, while utterly familiar in everyday life, is thematized in discussions launched by the likes of McTaggart, Bergson, and Whitehead. And these philosophical notions I have absorbed from discussions of their writings. And so, I find the thought <time is more fundamental than substance> coursing through my stream of consciousness—that is, occurrently, consciously.

In the foregoing I sometimes use quotation marks to emphasize the content ascribed to the relevant experience, though these "scare" quotes are strictly unnecessary, and then I use angle "quotes" to designate a particular content or sense, the ideal meaning structure itself. Thus, we characterize my experience and its content, in the first person:

I think that Obama favors diplomacy.

Here we describe and ascribe an act of thinking whose content is the thought or proposition <Obama favors diplomacy>, where we may emphasize this content in the act by saying:

I think that "Obama favors diplomacy."

Interestingly, though, language itself seems to play a crucial role in some forms of thinking, and this case is indeed one of thinking "in a language." For the record, this phenomenological observation does not mean that there is a so-called computational language-of-thought, whereby the sentence "Obama favors diplomacy" is encoded in and processed by a computational symbol system running on a biological computer implementing my mentality, namely, the wetware in my brain. Rather, the point here is that my act of consciously thinking seems to process its content garbed in the sentence "Obama favors diplomacy." It's hard to see how I could think precisely that without in some way thinking, as we say so naturally, "Obama favors diplomacy." "What were you just thinking?" I am asked, and I reply immediately, "I was thinking that Obama favors diplomacy." Similarly, where I think that "time is more fundamental than substance," I am thinking in the vernacular of academic philosophy, where the content <time is more fundamental than substance> seems clothed in the garb of philosophical idiom. We leave it an open question when and how language enters into the contents of consciously thinking in general.

4 Phenomenological description of experiences of consciously thinking

In practicing the phenomenology of perception, Merleau-Ponty remarked, the hard thing is to say *what we see*. In cognitive phenomenology, it is equally difficult to say *what we think*.

I'm lost in thought. Someone says, "What are you thinking?" I'm stopped in my tracks, for it's hard to say. Well, I was thinking about the global economy. What was I thinking about it? Well, I was thinking, "Hypercapitalism is a global Ponzi scheme." And now I start to put *words* into my thought, which as it happens was much more vague.... Or, in the earlier example, I was thinking, "That black bird [hovering overhead] is a turkey vulture." And now, really, the words fall short of capturing what I was thinking as I observed the bird's oddly tilting flight.

We must use language to describe (in language!) the character of our experience just as experienced. Such is the practice of phenomenological description, interpretation, and analysis. And yet, language does not adequately capture our experience, in consciously seeing something or, often, in consciously thinking something. The difficulty, I suggest, is not only with catching myself in the act of thinking such-and-such, or pulling up the thought in immediate recollection. The difficulty is partly in *saying*, or putting into words, just what content was in fact in my conscious process of thinking. Within the limits of language, in any event, we do attempt to reveal the structure of an experience *as it is experienced* from the first-person perspective.

In a simple formulation, as above, we construct a *phenomenological description* of an experience, characterizing it in the first person as from the subject's point of view:

I see that black bird hovering above.
I think that that black bird is a turkey vulture.
I think that turkey vultures eat carrion.
I think that all birds descended from dinosaurs.

Here are simple first-person observations of experience: overly simple, but offering a kind of formal prototype of a phenomenological description. We reflect on familiar types of experience and, in further reflection, characterize such experiences roughly in the way that we each would experience them as subject. In this way, we begin to articulate the *phenomenological structure* of the type of experience so described. As we proceed below, we shall amplify such characterizations of mental acts of consciously thinking.

This form of phenomenological description reflects a broad conception of the logic of first-person reports of experience. The form of an experience of consciously thinking is that articulated in this form of sentence:

I think that p.

We shall develop in due course a more complex form of phenomenological description of an experience of consciously thinking something. But initially, we note that the (object-) content of an act of thinking is a thought or proposition <that p>, where the sentence "p" must articulate what the subject is thinking, as it were, from the first-person perspective.[8]

Where I am thinking something that is only captured by a rather specific form of language, and indeed in one language, something not easily translated into other languages, we must say "I am thinking that p," where "p" is the appropriate sentence in the given language. Here we are led into a so-called principle of *disquotation*:

When I say "p," normally I am thinking that p.

Conversely, we have a principle of *thought-quotation*:

When I am thinking that p, normally what I am thinking I would express by saying "p."

That is, where language and thought coalesce, we can move back and forth by quotation and disquotation. Indeed, one way of understanding Husserl's phenomenological method of bracketing follows just these lines. To carry out a phenomenological description of an experience of consciously thinking, bracket the question of the existence of what is thought and attend to the experience of so thinking. Thus, in the first person, where I am consciously thinking that p, in reflection I now bracket the question of the existence of the state of affairs that p and attend instead to my *experience*

---

[8] This form of first-person thought-report adapts the broad logic of propositional attitudes launched by Jaakko Hintikka in e.g. Hintikka (1969). This form of logical analysis was adapted to Husserl's theory of intentionality in Smith and McIntyre (1982). The first-person perspective was developed further in Smith (1989).

of thinking that p. I find, then, that the *content* of my thinking that p is the proposition or thought <p>, which is expressible by "p."[9]

As we practice phenomenological description here, keep in mind that our focus is on occurrent conscious thinking, rather than dispositional believing, which has been so often a focus in twentieth-century philosophy of mind. As we proceed now, we consider first (and rather briefly) the structure of intentionality in thinking, and then we turn (in more detail) to phenomenological features that characterize acts of thinking as *conscious* rather than perhaps unconscious judgments or dispositional beliefs.

5 The intentionality of thinking

From this phenomenological perspective, then, we turn to the basic structure of intentionality in an act of thought. That structure we articulate in the simple form of phenomenological description:

I think that p.

Our three featured cases were described in this form. An act of thought, so described, is *intentional*, a consciousness *of* something—or *that* such-and-such is the case. Following Husserl (in broad strokes), the phenomenological structure of an act of thinking consists in an *intentional relation* among: a person or *subject* (myself), an experience or *act* of thinking, a propositional *content* <that p>, and a *state of affairs* [that p]—if such state of affairs actually exists and satisfies the content. In general, the form of intentionality is that of an intentional relation among subject, act, content, and object—if such object exists and satisfies the content. And in the special case of thinking, the content of the act is propositional in form and so represents a state of affairs, if such state of affairs exists and satisfies the content. . . . Of course, we often think thoughts that happen to be false, e.g. when I think that Pluto is a planet. In such a case there is no existing state of affairs that answers to the act's propositional content, yet the act has its content. If we assume possible as well as actual states of affairs, the act's content represents a merely possible state of affairs. But we need not commit ourselves here to an ontology of possibilia, so we may speak of "putative" states of affairs, meaning that if there exists such a state of affairs that is what the act's content "intends" or is directed toward.

This model of intentionality for thinking assumes a distinction between the content and the object of the act of thought (where such object exists). For Husserl, the content <that p> is a *propositional sense (Sinn)* or simply *proposition (Satz)*.[10] Further, for Husserl,

---

[9] Regarding the "quotation" of phenomenological content, see Smith (2005, 2007) on phenomenological description and bracketing, and see Thomasson (2005) on self-knowledge and bracketing. Quotation marks are used here to indicate the words they enclose and therewith, as we understand the words, the sense or meaning expressed by those words. Here we use angle quotes for contents as opposed to words.

[10] As noted in Smith (2007), Husserl's notion of a *Satz* derives from Bolzano's notion of an objective proposition or *Satz-an-sich* in Bolzano (1837), and is akin to Frege's notion of a thought or *Gedanke* in Frege (1918), though there are differences among these philosophers' theories of such entities.

the act's sense <that p> represents or presents or "intends" the (putative) state of affairs [that p]. The proposition <that p> is true—veridical, satisfied, successful—if and only if the "intended" state of affairs [that p] actually exists. As we would say today, the truth conditions or satisfaction conditions of the proposition are that this state of affairs exists. In the case of my thinking about the bird, the state of affairs intended consists of the bird itself and its species combined by instantiation, that is, the state of affairs [that bird is a great blue heron]. This complex entity, if such complex exists in actuality, is part of the world of nature—not a mere appearance in my fleeting consciousness. Now, the proposition <that bird is a great blue heron> is quite a different entity. This entity is composed of the demonstrative visual content <that bird> and the predicative content <is a great blue heron> combined by the formal relation of predication. For Husserl, like Bolzano and Frege, this propositional content is an objective entity; however, it is not a formation in the world of nature, but rather in the domain of ideal contents or meanings. We need not commit ourselves here to a particular ontology of such "ideal" contents, but let us recognize the distinction between a proposition or thought and the state of affairs it represents.

In the analytic tradition, belief has been widely construed as a relation between a person and a proposition, thus a "propositional attitude," following Russell (in broad strokes). Here our concern is with an occurrent act of consciously thinking something, rather than a dispositional state of believing something. On the familiar Russellian model, then: When I think that p, I am intentionally related to the proposition "that p." But this model proves too simple. What is a proposition? How does it appear in thinking? Does it not differ from the concrete situation or state of affairs it represents—that is, in such a case as we are considering? Familiar cases show that if the proposition "that p" is an objective formation that can be grasped in different ways, then we shall need to distinguish, in Husserlian terms, between the content and the object of thinking. The *object* of my thinking "that p" is an objective structure in the world, sometimes called a *state of affairs* (*Sachverhalt*, literally things-related) or, in a simpler word, a *situation*: say, that Obama won the election. The *content* of my thinking is then better called a "thought" or "proposition," the thought that Obama won the election. Importantly, the content of my thinking—*what* I am thinking ("that p")—is a matter of the *way* I intend the state of affairs, a feature intrinsic or internal to my consciousness. Whereas the object *per se* of my thinking—that toward which my thinking is directed—is the state of affairs itself, a formation in the world external to my consciousness. If you will, the propositional content is the *mode of presentation* of the state of affairs.

In our three featured cases of thinking we face importantly different ways of "intending" the things *about which* the subject is thinking—addressing now not the "intended" states of affairs *per se*, but the things occurring in those states of affairs. The propositional contents of those three acts of thinking are respectively:

<that bird is a great blue heron>,
<Obama favors diplomacy>,
<time is more fundamental than substance>.

How these propositional contents represent objects turns on how certain constituent contents work, how those contents represent objects that play appropriate roles in the intended states of affairs. Thus, the demonstrative visual content <that bird> must designate an aviary being in the visual purview of the subject while thinking that "that bird is a great blue heron." And the individuative personal concept <Obama> must designate or pick out the individual Barack Obama himself, however that works.[11] Then, the abstract concepts <time> and <substance> must designate, well, the worldly forms of time and substance themselves—whatever those entities may be and however our abstract thoughts represent them. Meanwhile, the relevant predicative contents must designate appropriate properties or relations, however they work: the content <is a great blue heron> represents a property of belonging to an aviary species; the content <favors diplomacy> represents an attitude attributable to a person; the content <is more fundamental than> represents a deep ontological relation (hardly easy to explain).

These are beautiful and difficult philosophical problems, part phenomenological, part logical, part linguistic, social, and ultimately metaphysical. Here is not the place to sort out the myriad issues about contents of various types, about propositions, about states of affairs, about relevant conditions of satisfaction, etc. For present purposes, regarding the intentionality of thought, I want simply to note that thinking is intentionally directed in different ways: via various *modes of presentation* of objects of different types in states of affairs of different types. And I want to show, through examples like those above, how really familiar are these phenomena of thought: consciously thinking, with familiar forms of propositional content, presenting or representing various types of objects in various types of states of affairs in the world around us.[12]

---

[11] Compare Smith and McIntyre (1982: Chapter VIII), for a phenomenological, and not strictly externalist, account of how such individuative "de re" intentionality might work, via an individual concept against background beliefs. See further Smith (2004: "Background Ideas.")

[12] In recent decades, philosophers have sometimes worked with a notion of *singular* proposition—notably in the wake of work of Kaplan (1989) on demonstratives and Kripke (1980) on proper names, two types of term that designate a particular individual in a "direct" way, without appeal to description. In one version, a simple singular proposition is composed of an individual and a property, or two or more individuals and a relation—in effect, this entity is a putative "fact" (per Russell) or "state of affairs" (*Sachverhalt* per Husserl and Wittgenstein: see Smith 2002). A person's believing or thinking that "Obama favors diplomacy" might be glossed, then, as a relation of the person to the singular proposition <Obama favors diplomacy>. But this initial gloss proves inadequate, since Mr. Obama can be presented in different ways in so thinking, say, via different individual concepts grounded in differing images or parcels of information gleaned from the media—even if this presentation is "direct" and indeed tied into the name "Obama," which refers "directly." So the traditional Husserlian distinction between content and object of thought raises its familiar head. A person's believing or thinking that "Obama favors diplomacy" must be parsed, then, as a relation between a person, a propositional "guise," and a singular proposition, i.e. better, a putative fact or state of affairs. See Salmon (1986/1991: pp. 104–5 ff). In this way, the neo-Russellian notion of singular proposition or putative "fact" begets the neo-Husserlian notion of the "noematic" propositional guise of a singular state of affairs.

6 The modal characters of thinking consciously

It is easier to say *what* we think than to say *how* we think. What we think is captured in a propositional content <that p>. But how we think "that p" resolves into several phenomenological forms not easily appraised, including the character of thinking *consciously*.

How indeed does a conscious act of thinking differ from an unconscious act or state of so thinking? Well, my *consciously* thinking that p is an occurrent cognitive activity, flowing through my stream of consciousness in a discrete phase of my experience. And I *experience*, or live through, this flowing act in a certain way: with a character of "consciously" thinking that p. Accordingly, our phenomenological description of a conscious thought should take the form:

Consciously I think that p.

What can we say about this additional character <consciously>? What features of phenomenological structure are involved in my thinking's being *consciously* executed—and so experienced?

We have argued, by a series of everyday examples, that there is indeed a distinctive phenomenological character of *consciously thinking* something. Lest it be doubted that there is a separable character <consciously>, we note the sharp experiential difference between normal conscious sight and so-called "blindsight." The latter phenomenon is now well documented, where a subject has no conscious awareness of seeing anything at all and yet can walk down a hallway and sidestep obstacles just as if consciously seeing! (See the video clip at the website, de Gelder 2009.) Clearly, normal visual experience has a character of seeing *consciously*, a character absent in blindsight vision. Similarly, consciously thinking something has a character <consciously>, a character absent in unconscious cognitive activity.... In our time, unconscious thought is well acknowledged, from psychoanalysis to cognitive neuroscience. *Conscious* thought, meanwhile, has been thematized for centuries. But now, at long last, we home in on what characters distinguish a conscious, as opposed to unconscious, act of thinking.

We turn thus to several "modal" characters of thinking, specifically, to what qualifies an act of thought as conscious.

In prior writings I have sought to factor out from the basic character <consciously> several different features. In this "modal" model of consciousness (as I've called it), we distinguish between the *mode of presentation* of the object of consciousness and the *modality of presentation* in the act of consciousness.[13] In the case of consciously thinking something, we would articulate these phenomenological characters of conscious thought in the following form of phenomenological description:

Phenomenally in this very experience I now here think that p.

---

[13] See Smith (1986, 1989, 2004, 2005), typically focused on conscious visual perception.

The overall content of the act of thinking, then, we here articulate as going well beyond the propositional content <that p>. The act's propositional content comprises the *mode of presentation* of the intended (putative) state of affairs [that p]. But, we now observe, there are additional features that comprise the *modality of presentation* in so thinking. These *modal* characters define how the act of thinking is experienced or executed. They are reflected in the *modal content* <phenomenally in this very experience I now here think>. That structure of content we factor into importantly different types of modal content, reflecting distinct types of phenomenological character:

<think> — the act-type character of intentional activity, here that of thinking;
<I> — the egocentric character of the act, its being executed by a subject;
<now> — the temporal character of the act, experienced as transpiring "now";
<here> — the spatial character of the act, experienced as transpiring "here";
<in this very experience> — the reflexive character of inner awareness of the act itself;
<phenomenally> — the phenomenal or "felt" character of the act.

Given our reflections above, it should be uncontroversial that the *intentional* structure of an experience of thinking has (to begin our account) the form articulated in the content:

<I think that p>.

But we now factor that content into the *mode* of presentation <that p> and the *modality* of presentation <I think>. That is to say, my act of thinking is not a bald intending with propositional content <that p>. Rather, the act is one of so intending with the *modal characters* <I> and <think>: intending, if you will, cogitatively and egocentrically through the modal contents <think> and <I>. These two characters are parts of the way the act is executed, and in that sense "modal" characters. (Of course, the metaphysics of self and the phenomenology of self-awareness are famously contested issues, but let us assume we have a story to tell.)

The tricky issues, for present purposes, are those of the further modal characters cited in the modal model of consciousness.

7 The phenomenal character of consciously thinking

The *phenomenal character* of an experience or act of consciousness is the character defining *how it is experienced*: as we say, *what it is like*, what it feels like, for the subject to experience or live through or carry out the act. Such characters have come to be called "qualia," alluding to the felt subjective qualities of experience.

Every conscious experience has a phenomenal character—as we sought to show by varied examples. Every act of consciousness, that is, has a distinctive character of what-it-is-like, whether it be an experience of seeing red, or seeing "that raven," or thinking such-and-such. In particular, we find different phenomenal characters in consciously thinking different things: in thinking that "that bird is a great blue heron," in thinking that "Obama prefers diplomacy," or in thinking that "time is more fundamental than substance." We dwelt above on such acts of thinking, setting them in familiar circumstances, in order to develop a feel, in reflection, for their differing phenomenal characters. The term "qualia" entered the philosophical lexicon as a name for the subjective character of a sensation such as seeing red or feeling pain. But as we broaden our phenomenological horizons, as we explore cognitive phenomenology, we would naturally extend the term "qualia" to cover phenomenal characters in all types of experience. However, I'll usually speak of "phenomenal character," which I find a more suggestive idiom, and one that echoes "modal character."

It is notoriously difficult to describe phenomenal characters. For, strictly, phenomenal character can be *experienced* but not "said." To comprehend a particular phenomenal character, we *must* experience it—we must experience what it is like to live through that type of experience from the subject's point of view. We can then talk with one another about that character by assuming you and I have had similar experiences. But what can we say to define phenomenal character in general?

We may say the phenomenal character of an experience consists in how the experience "appears" in consciousness as it transpires. Indeed, the Greek term "phenomenon" means appearance. Thus, when the light of consciousness is on, an experience "appears" in consciousness. When the light is off, a mental activity transpires without "appearing." The light metaphor is apt.

We must be careful, however, in talking of the "appearing" or "appearance" of an experience in consciousness. This idiom may seem to suggest that phenomenality consists in the *appearance of* the experience to the subject, that is, a *consciousness of* the experience in living through it. But that tendency conflates *phenomenality* with *inner awareness* of experience. Our task now is to distinguish those two types of modal character. We need to see that a conscious experience has a phenomenal character *whether or not* it involves inner awareness. Indeed, its "appearing" in consciousness is a condition of the possibility of inner awareness of its transpiring.

Where recent discussions of phenomenal character have focused on the qualia of seeing red, our present concern is instead the phenomenal character of consciously thinking something. Nonetheless, the case of consciously seeing red offers a vivid inroad into the role of phenomenal character in consciousness generally.

Some philosophers of perception (Dretske 1995; Tye 1995) hold that perceptual consciousness is *transparent*, in the sense that: I see red, i.e. I am visually conscious of red or perhaps of that red robin, but in so seeing I am not *conscious of* my seeing—rather, my visual experience itself is simply transparent. This is an interesting phenomenological claim about perception (bracketing the further externalist views of Dretske, Tye, et al.). In a similar vein, Charles Siewert warns, generally, about the "consciousness-of trap" (Siewert 1998), where philosophers (at least since Locke) have fallen into the trap of thinking that consciousness requires *self*-consciousness, i.e. *consciousness of* consciousness, perhaps in some form of higher-order monitoring. Addressing the transparency intuition (in Dretske, Tye, et al.), Amie Thomasson (2008) concurs that perceptual consciousness is world-directed and so is transparent, involving no awareness of the act of consciousness itself—unless one is paying special attention to one's experience. Interestingly, this claim extenuates her neo-Brentanian one-level model of consciousness (Thomasson 2000). Brentano (1874/1995) argued that an act of consciousness is directed *primarily* toward its object (say, the red robin) and *secondarily*, in "inner consciousness," toward itself. And this analysis, per Thomasson (2000), allows a model of consciousness as structured all within the one act, on one level of consciousness, without any separable higher-order consciousness of the act (on pain of infinite regress). Now, Thomasson (2008) presses this one-level view further, arguing (I take it) that this form of inner consciousness should be effectively dissolved into the "transparent" act of consciousness so that there is in the act no secondary awareness *of* the act itself. And yet, she rightly observes, the act has a phenomenal character!—the character of seeing red or seeing the red robin.

It follows that the *phenomenal character* of such an experience is distinct from the *inner awareness* of the experience. That is the lesson I want to draw from the phenomenon of transparency.

Let us grant that perceptual consciousness is sometimes—but not always—transparent, and yet phenomenal. For such an experience, then, we must distinguish its phenomenality from any form of inner awareness of the experience. The recognition of transparency guides us to this distinction and thus brings phenomenal character itself into focus. . . . We return shortly, though, to the question of inner awareness, which I think is more prevalent than the transparency advocate recognizes.

Perhaps it is equally striking that consciously thinking may be transparent, yet phenomenal. When I am consciously thinking that "Obama prefers diplomacy," my thought is directed toward the putative state of affairs that Obama prefers diplomacy. If truly lost in thought about the sorry state of the world, I may be thinking about Obama policy, but with no particular awareness of the fact that I am so thinking. In such a case, it would seem, my consciously so thinking is transparent. And yet my act of thinking has a phenomenal character—the character of consciously so thinking. For conscious thought as for conscious perception, then, phenomenality is to be distinguished from inner awareness of experience.

There is something else at stake, we should note, in the transparency debate. The so-called "representationalist" model of perception (in Dretske, Tye, et al.) starts with the claim that consciousness in seeing red is transparent, then theorizes that its function is that of "representing" some instance of red in the environment through a causal flow of "information." This externalist transformation of "representation" (a term that used to mean intentionality!) presses the *phenomenal* quality of seeing-red out of consciousness and into physical involvement with the perceived red object itself. And then the subjective phenomenal quality in the *experience* of seeing red is lost, or "looking-glassed," morphed into something else as in Alice's Looking Glass (adopting the idiom in Strawson 2005). This result flies in the face of our experience, leaving a problem for the externalist–representationalist theory of consciousness in seeing red—which began with the phenomenological claim of transparency. Along the way, intentionality itself—consciousness-of-X—is looking-glassed, morphed into a causal flow called "representation".... Back to the phenomenology, then: Thomasson (2008) resists these moves beyond the phenomenology of transparency. Her account would preserve both phenomenal character (the *appearing-red* character in *seeing* the red robin) and a one-level model of consciousness with transparency (perceptual consciousness *sans* awareness *of* that consciousness *per se*). To that end, she pursues a further feature of phenomenal consciousness.

For Thomasson, *consciousness of* that red or that red robin is the basis for subsequent *self-knowledge*, i.e. knowledge about one's own conscious experience in seeing that red (Thomasson 2005, 2008). In place of an occurrent inner awareness of experience (Brentano's "inner consciousness"), then, an act of consciousness carries the seed of one's further knowledge of that experience. On this line of argument, active self-consciousness yields to potential self-knowledge. Still, I would maintain, phenomen-ality, in one's occurrent consciousness, provides the ground of this capacity for subsequent self-knowledge.

That self-knowledge is precisely what Husserl proposed to achieve in phenomeno-logical reflection. And Husserl proposed to achieve this knowledge by his famous method of bracketing: bracketing the surrounding world, here including the red robin and the redness in the robin's breast, in order to reflect on *consciousness of* that red something in the world. Bracketing is like quotation, Husserl observed: the transition from my seeing that red robin to my reflecting on my seeing the robin, is like the transition from my saying "p" to my quoting my saying it, that is, saying "I said, 'p'." (See Thomasson 2005, 2008; Smith 2005, 2007.) Phenomenological reflection pro-ceeds thereby in a separate, further act of reflecting on the given form of experience. Thus, the original experience has its intrinsic phenomenal character, and that character enables us through retention and reflection to appreciate what that character is. Phenomenality—the "appearing" of an experience in consciousness—is clearly a condition of the possibility of subsequent reflection on that form of experience. As the terms themselves suggest: phenomenality grounds phenomenology.

But what of *pre-reflective* awareness of experience? Is there not in our experience, commonly, a form of immediate awareness of our passing experience that is prior to any reflection? If so, that awareness is nonetheless something distinct from the phe-nomenality of the experience—which, we allow, may occur in the absence of such awareness of the experience. Hence, we distinguish phenomenal character from the character of such inner awareness, where it occurs.

8 Phenomenality vis-à-vis inner awareness in consciously thinking

Is it true that conscious experience, in seeing or in thinking or in acting, is essentially or at least typically "transparent," transpiring with *no awareness whatsoever* of the experience? I think not. Transparent consciousness is only one mode of consciousness. By contrast, there are many types of everyday experience that involve awareness of one's experience, and I want to lead our discussion to a certain form of inner awareness, here, in the case of thinking.

Consider the oft-cited case of long-distance driving. I see the road ahead and steer my car around the bend accordingly, all quite consciously. Yet I have little or no *awareness* of my seeing-and-driving as such. I may be lost in thought about personal matters, or even about the metaphysics of substance. Or I may be motoring along on automatic pilot, not thinking about anything as I round the bend in the road. I am seeing and driving consciously—the Highway Patrol officer, perched on his motorcycle at the bend, would be most interested were I driving unconsciously! And my conscious activity has a phenomenal character; we are arousing a sense of that character by describing the activity in familiar terms, reminding ourselves of what it is like. Yet, we are wont to say, I have no particular awareness of my seeing-and-steering at the moment. Here, it seems, is a case of transparent consciousness in driving.

For the sake of argument here, let us allow that there is no awareness of my sensorimotor intentional activity *per se* in such an experience of driving. A more accurate diagnosis would, however, detail the role of *attention* in such cases. Quite typically, we would then find, my seeing-and-driving is not wholly transparent, but rather involves a basic awareness of my activity. It does not come as news to me that I am seeing-and-steering when, for instance, a rabbit races across the road before me and I maneuver my vehicle around it. Thus, we find, I am driving with an inner awareness of my activity. To be sure, my *attention* as I drive along wanders from features of the road to things I am passing by, but does not turn inwardly to my activity itself—to my *seeing* the road, the rabbit, the interior of my car, *feeling* the steering wheel, *turning* the wheel as I avoid the rabbit and round the bend in the road. Yet, my being *aware* of my passing experience in this basic pre-reflective way is not a matter of focusing my *attention* on my experience. . . . So, let us allow that consciously driving along may in some cases be truly transparent, but in other cases may involve inner awareness albeit *sans* attention.[14]

Next consider a case of "long-distance" thinking. Over the course of the morning, I am steadfastly thinking about the problem of phenomenal character. I am thinking even as I type these words. My consciousness is riveted on the problem, the twists and turns of argument, getting the correct phrase (appearing on the computer screen as I think-and-type). In this case, we might well find, I am consciously thinking through a

---

[14] See Ford and Smith (2006) on attention vis-à-vis consciousness.

complex chain of thought, along this bend in the philosophical road, but with *no awareness* of my thinking *per se*. Here, it seems, is a case of transparent consciousness in thinking. Let us allow for such transparency in thinking, in circumstances as described.

Still, cases of truly transparent consciousness are more the exception than the rule. In the course of everyday life I am typically *aware* of my conscious activity, but in a *pre-reflective* way. Indeed, our three featured cases of consciously thinking, in garden-variety circumstances, involve some such inner awareness of experience, prior to any reflection. Only rarely do I perform an act of consciousness wherein I focus attentively on my activity of seeing or thinking or moving bodily, as if looking over my own shoulder at my passing experience. That I can do, with some effort of attention. But the more usual forms of everyday consciousness involve an inner awareness that is quite different, quite distinct from focusing my attention even peripherally on my experience.[15]

Why is it thought plausible to hold that consciousness is typically or even essentially transparent? Why is the character of inner awareness of experience so readily over-looked in making a phenomenological claim of transparency?

The problem, I suspect, is that many who make the case for transparency assume that one's *awareness* of one's experience must be something like a quasi-introspective observation, a self-monitoring of one's experience, whether higher-order or same-order monitoring. And that self-monitoring element, it seems assumed, carries an explicit thematic content that characterizes the base act. The transparency claim then says, rightly enough, that we do not find any such element in ordinary consciousness.

But that sort of explicit, conceptualizing, thematizing, self-monitoring, quasi-reflective form of introspective awareness is precisely what I was trying to avoid in crafting the "modal" model of *inner awareness* in consciousness.[16] Intrigued by views of Brentano and Husserl and Sartre, I sought a well-defined phenomenological form for inner awareness. Indeed, the task is to appraise not only self-*knowledge* but also self-*consciousness*. In the first person: my subsequent knowledge of my experience, in phenomenological reflection, is itself grounded in my ability to *retain* that experience, which is grounded, normally, in my pre-reflective *awareness* of the experience as it transpires. Importantly, knowledge of the experience, gained in reflection and analysis, is a dispositional state, while inner awareness (where it occurs) is an occurrent feature involved in the unfolding experience itself.

We may use the phenomenon of transparency—however frequent or infrequent it may be—to separate phenomenality from such inner awareness. Thus we see that phenomenal character is its own type of modal character, while inner awareness of experience affords its own, distinct type of modal character, to which we turn shortly.

---

[15] Compare Ford and Smith (2006) on peripheral attention to one's experience. Lay (2010) studies an Husserlian account of temporal "background" awareness of one's current experience.

[16] See Smith (1986, 1989, 2004, 2005).

In varying cases of consciously thinking, we should recognize a spectrum of different types of awareness, and levels of awareness. At one end is truly transparent thinking. At the other end is "mindful" thinking, so characterized in the practice of meditation. In such a case, I am consciously thinking "that p," perhaps even deep in concentration, and I am aware of my so thinking, very clearly or mindfully aware. It is not that I am dividing my attention between thinking that p and noticing my so thinking; rather, I am effortlessly aware of my thinking that p, with full attention to what I am thinking. In the middle of this spectrum, by contrast, is a familiar form of consciously thinking where I am immediately aware of my so thinking: in a basic inner awareness that is naturally built into the activity of thinking in such cases. Granted that there are different forms and levels of awareness of thinking, we emphasize that all these forms of consciously thinking, with varying types of awareness (or lack thereof), have phenomenal character.

In point of *form*, we should see that phenomenality pervades the whole phenomenological structure of a given act of consciousness. The *scope* of the modal character <phenomenally>, that is, covers the whole content of the experience, including (where present) the distinct modal character <in this very experience>. Accordingly, in the logical form of the phenomenological description of the experience, the scope of the modal qualifier 'phenomenally' covers all the rest of the characterization:

(Phenomenally) (in this very experience I now here think that p).

And, *mutatis mutandis*, in the *phenomenological form* of the experience so described, the scope of the modal character <phenomenally> covers all the rest of the character of the experience:

<(Phenomenally) (in this very experience I now here think that p)>.

This phenomenological point factors phenomenality out from other modal characters, including inner awareness, which may be involved in consciously thinking, or in consciously seeing. And we should thus see that phenomenality is not limited to the experience of sensory qualia, say, in consciousness of the visual appearance of red in my seeing "that red robin." Phenomenality is the light of consciousness, the luminous character modifying all other parts of the conscious experience—even where consciously thinking "that p" in the absence of any visual sensation. Again, phenomenality is something to be lived, not said.

Now that we have factored out the distinct character of phenomenality, we may look more closely at the further character of inner awareness.

9 The reflexive character of inner awareness in consciously thinking

A traditional view holds that consciousness is eo ipso self-consciousness: a conscious experience essentially involves one's *awareness* of the experience as it transpires. In the case of conscious thought:

When I consciously think that p, in so thinking I am aware of my so thinking.

On such a view, inner awareness of thinking is intrinsic to the *experience* of thinking and part of what makes it a conscious rather than unconscious cognitive activity. In the modal model sketched above, inner awareness takes the form of the *reflexive* modal content <in this very experience>—or, perhaps more simply, <herein>, thus <herein I think that p>.[17]

The traditional view appears in various forms from at least Locke onward. In recent consciousness studies, the issue of self-consciousness has been explored as the question of how the mind (or brain) *monitors* its own process. Is there a higher-order monitoring accompanying the base activity, or a same-order monitoring in a proper part of the experience, or some form of self-representation to be specified, notably as a reflexive awareness in the experience? A better self-monitoring model of consciousness defines a proper "logical" part of the base experience consisting in a self-representational moment of the act of consciousness (per Kriegel 2006, 2009), that is, an ontologically dependent part built into the act itself (per Kidd 2011).[18] In classical phenomenology, self-consciousness was appraised by Brentano, Husserl, and Sartre. For Brentano, an act of consciousness is directed primarily toward its object and secondarily toward the act itself, but this secondary directedness is an "inner consciousness" that is integral to the act, as opposed to an "inner observation" that would step outside the act to observe it in reflection (Brentano 1874/1995). For Husserl, this inner consciousness of consciousness is further resolved into "inner time-consciousness," or inner consciousness of the temporal flow of acts in the stream of consciousness (Husserl 1893–1917/1991). For Sartre, memorably, self-consciousness is *constitutive* of consciousness (of some object), where self-consciousness takes the form of a "pre-reflective cogito" (Sartre 1943/1992, p. 14).

In the modal model I sought to diagnose the form of inner awareness as a modal character with a reflexive content <in this very experience>, wherewith inner awareness is an intrinsic and pre-reflective consciousness-of-consciousness that is in no way a separable reflective observation of the experience. In this way, consciousness of

[17] Again, this account of inner awareness is explored in (Smith 1986, 1989, 2004, 2005), and Ford and Smith (2006).

[18] See Kriegel and Williford (2006) for studies of these options. See Smith (1989, 2005) on reflexivity of inner awareness, and Perry (2001) on reflexivity (2001: 75ff) and indexical content. See Kidd (2011) on the form of contingently infallible self-representation built into an act of consciousness where the act serves as context of indexical reflexive inner awareness—amplifying the "semantics" of this reflexivity.

something is typically, if not "transparent," rather, in Sartre's metaphor, "translucent." Consciousness is typically world-directed, a consciousness *of* something in the world, yet—characteristically—the subject is ipso facto *aware* of that consciousness-of-something. The trick is to see how this inner awareness is built into the act of consciousness without any higher-order monitoring or even a bona fide self-monitoring on the same level. The modal model preserves this status: inner awareness is intrinsic to the act, pre-reflective, non-thematizing (Sartre said "non-thetic"), and by virtue of that awareness the act itself is *translucent*.

As we found above, this inner awareness is to be distinguished from the phenomenal character of a conscious experience. Initially, I assumed, with the traditional view, that inner awareness (*cum* phenomenality) is what makes a mental state conscious and so is essential to consciousness *per se* (Smith 1986, 1989). Subsequently, I recognized, rather, that consciousness comes in more and less structured forms, of which a familiar form is that of our everyday experiences that do involve awareness (Smith 2004). It is this familiar-enough form of awareness that carries the *reflexive* content <in this very experience>, on the model I have proposed.

Why say that this form of *awareness* is characteristically present in familiar types of experience—contrary to the transparency view, which denies any such awareness? If I see a red robin, and someone asks whether I saw a bird, I say, "Why, yes, I saw that red robin." If I am just now thinking that Obama prefers diplomacy, and someone asks what I am thinking ("Penny for your thoughts?"), I say, "Why, I was just thinking that Obama prefers diplomacy." Again, in Sartre's famous example: when I am sitting at the café and counting cigarettes, if someone asks me what I am doing, I immediately reply, "I'm counting these things" (Sartre 1943/1992, p. 13). I am able to reply in this way precisely because in my just-past experience I was *aware* of what I was then seeing, thinking, or doing—aware in a pre-reflective way.

Where there is inner awareness of an experience: my immediate *retention* of a conscious experience is grounded in my intrinsic *awareness* of my passing experience—prior to any recollection or reflection. Not only does the conscious experience ground my subsequent self-knowledge in phenomenological reflection. But, moreover, an intrinsic awareness of the experience as it transpires grounds my retention and any possible phenomenological reflection.

Accordingly, on the modal model, phenomenal character and the reflexive character of inner awareness are distinguished, where phenomenality characterizes the full conscious experience including its intrinsic reflexivity. For the case of consciously thinking, then, we parse these characters in phenomenological description as follows:

(Phenomenally) (in this very experience (I now here think that p)).

The *formal structure* of inner awareness is crucial, avoiding anything like introspective self-monitoring, self-thematizing, etc. The reflexive content <in this very experience> modifies the basic intentional content <I now here think that p>, and the phenomenal content <phenomenally> modifies the rest of the content of the experience. Because the content <in this very experience> is *reflexive*, it does not take a quasi-observational or quasi-reflective position of intending the experience from above, from outside, or even from inside, in some form of separable "noticing" of the experience. If you will, the experience is "self-monitoring," but only if the monitoring is an internal, intrinsic, dependent part of the flowing experience, and—in point of phenomenological form—merely *reflexive*, or self-intimating, in character (in no way descriptive). Not every conscious activity has this form of reflexive inner awareness. But where it does occur, fairly typically in everyday life, it is built into the flow of consciousness itself. In this, Husserl was right: inner self-consciousness is achieved via inner time-consciousness (Husserl 1893–1917/1991). But, nonetheless, the *form* of inner aware-ness is distinct from the *form* of time-consciousness *per se* ("I am *now* thinking that p"). Accordingly, I propose, inner awareness of passing experience is *dependent* on—or supervenient on—but distinct from inner consciousness of the temporal flow of the stream of consciousness (as noted in Smith 2004).

Drawing on the Husserlian analysis of time-consciousness, and commenting along the way on my model of inner self-consciousness, John Drummond (in Drum-mond 2006) parses the form of self-awareness in everyday consciousness so that time-consciousness indeed does the work of inner awareness of passing experience. I have much sympathy for Drummond's account of self-awareness. However, I stress, the form of inner awareness *per se* should indicate the flowing *experience* itself, whereas the form of inner temporal awareness should indicate the *temporal flow* of the experi-ence. Indeed, the temporal flow of consciousness arguably forms a *temporal "back-ground"* of the current conscious experience as experienced (Lay 2010). And so, I propose, we find the distinct temporal content <now> in the overall content:

<Phenomenally in this very experience I *now* here think that p>.

Indeed, we turn, in closing, to a brief look at the sense of spatiotemporality and embodiment in everyday experience—even, my dear Descartes, in consciously think-ing something.

10 The characters of spatiotemporality and embodiment in consciously thinking

In normal perception we are conscious of what we see (or hear, etc.), but in so seeing we are also aware of our spatiotemporal situation and our embodiment. Thus, I turn my eyes, head, and body in a certain way as I look at the bird overhead: while my consciousness is focused on the bird I see, I am also in some way aware of my bodily movement and of my spatiotemporal surroundings.[19] On reflection we should see that

---

[19] This sense of embodiment is detailed in Husserl (1912/1989) and Merleau-Ponty (1943/2003). Following Merleau-Ponty, Noë (2004) takes this embodiment to entail that perception is itself a form of action, a stronger view than we need take.

a sense of spatiotemporal situatedness and embodiment is a normal part of *thinking* as well as perception.

Indeed, in everyday experiences of consciously thinking, we are not simply aware of thinking such-and-such. We are aware of so thinking "now" and "here" and in such a way that "I" am so situated and indeed embodied.

Here and now I am seated by the fire, in my dressing gown, contemplating my thoughts, my being, my life, the universe, and everything. In so thinking, I am in certain ways aware of my body, my spatial location, my temporal being. As the morning passes, I consciously think of various things. Looking out the window, I see a startling sight, a tall, bluish-gray, long-legged, long-necked bird, stalking some sort of prey, motionless; and I think, "That bird is a great blue heron." Later, putting the morning newspaper down, I think, "Obama prefers diplomacy." Still later, getting into my routine of doing some philosophy before noon, I think, "Time is more fundamental than substance."

As I look out the window, I move my eyes, my head, my torso, to gain a good view of the heron. I am aware of my seeing the remarkable creature, so seeing now and here, in my current surroundings, in my immediate *Umwelt* (as Husserl said). And in seeing this fellow spatiotemporal creature, I am aware of my own body in action. Thus we find in the modal content of my visual experience the content <I now here>, that is, in the full content:

<Phenomenally in this very experience *I now here* think that
that bird [*now here* visually before *me*] is a great blue heron>.

My sense of spatiotemporality and embodiment are not explicit themes in my experience. Rather, they are, I propose, parts of the *modal* character of the experience, or how I execute the act of so thinking about the object I see.

As I put down the newspaper, I tilt my head to one side, I say to myself, "Obama prefers diplomacy," and, pausing a moment, I think to myself that Obama prefers diplomacy. In so thinking, I am not acting as if a disembodied spirit, much less as a human being who has lost all sense of proprioception and kinesthesis. Such poor souls exist, but I am not in such a damaged condition. No, I am aware of my so thinking now and here and as I move bodily in so thinking, gesturing as I gently pound my fist on the table. Thus we find the modal content as follows:

<Phenomenally in this very experience *I now here* think that
Obama prefers diplomacy>.

Even in so thinking, then, I have a certain sense of spatiotemporal embodied activity that is, perhaps surprisingly, a bona fide part of the modal character of my thinking about Obama on this occasion.

And even in our third case, the rather ethereal metaphysical thought, we find a sense of spatiotemporal embodiment. As I put down my earmarked copy of Whitehead's *Process and Reality*, raising my eyebrows and nodding my head with a sort of amazed and amused sensation in my breast, I think, by God, he's right, "Time is more fundamental than substance." And in the act of so thinking we find the modal content:

<Phenomenally in this very experience *I now here* think that
time is more fundamental than substance>.

In so thinking I am aware of my spatiotemporal embodied being even as I think about, well, the abstracted forms of time and body! . . . In real life, practicing metaphysics does not leave me disembodied, or feeling disembodied.

It is obvious that in perception and action our experience characteristically involves a sense of embodied, spatiotemporally situated self. And on the modal model this sense of embodiment is part of the modal character of the experience, so that "phenomenally in this very experience I now here see that ball and pick it up in my right hand." What is intriguing is how integrally a sense of embodiment is tied into an experience of thinking, as in the cases just characterized.[20]

The proposal, reflecting on such cases, is that a sense of embodied self situated in space and time is part and parcel of the modal character of thinking. In the modality of presentation, the contents <I> and <now> and <here> indicate these distinct features of the act of thinking. They do so as only indexical contents can.

11 The phenomenological structure of consciously thinking

To outline the key structures of consciousness in an experience of consciously thinking something, that was the task of this essay, an exercise in cognitive phenomenology.

If consciousness is the hard problem in theory of mind, the really hard problem is assaying the different modalities of presentation in consciousness. Especially tricky is divining the several modal characters in consciously thinking. If we address only the propositional content of thinking, we might even miss altogether the "phenomenology" of thinking. No wonder the phenomenon has escaped notice for so long![21]

References

Bolzano, B. (1837/1972). *Theory of Science* (ed. and trans. Rolf George). Berkeley and Los Angeles: University of California Press, 1972. A partial translation of Bolzano's *Wissenschaftslehre*, 1837.
Brentano, F. (1874/1995). *Psychology from an Empirical Standpoint* (ed. Oskar Kraus and Linda L. McCallister, trans. Antos C. Rancurello, D. B. Terrell, and Linda L. McCallister). London: Routledge.

[20] The phenomenology of embodiment in perception is richly appraised in Husserl (1912/1989) and in Merleau-Ponty (1943/2003). The lessons there learnt are here extended even to acts of *thinking*, within the framework of the "modal" characters we have discussed.

[21] My thanks to Michelle Montague for many helpful comments on the penultimate draft, and also to Martin Schwab for important suggestions.

De Gelder, B. (2009). Video clip of blindsight navigation, at de Gelder's website: http://www. beatricedegelder.com.

Dretske, F. (1995). *Naturalizing the Mind*. Cambridge, MA: MIT Press.

Dreyfus, H. L. (ed.). (1982). *Husserl, Intentionality and Cognitive Science*. Cambridge, MA: MIT Press.

Drummond, J. J. (2006). "The Case(s) of (Self-) Awareness," in U. Kriegel and K. Williford (eds), *Self-Representational Approaches to Consciousness*. Cambridge, MA, and London, England: MIT Press, pp. 199–220.

Føllesdal, D. (1969/1982). "Husserl's Notion of Noema," in Dreyfus (ed.), 1982, pp. 73–80. Reprinted from *The Journal of Philosophy*, 1969.

Ford, J. and Smith, D. W. (2006). "Consciousness, Self, and Attention," in U. Kriegel and K. Williford (eds), *Self-Representational Approaches to Consciousness*. Cambridge, MA, and London, England: MIT Press, pp. 353–77.

——(1892/1997). "On *Sinn* and *Bedeutung*," in M. Beaney (ed.), *The Frege Reader*. Oxford and Malden, MA: Blackwell, 1997. German original, 1892.

Frege, G. (1918/1967). "The Thought: A Logical Inquiry," in P. F. Strawson (ed.), *Philosophical Logic*. Oxford: Oxford University Press, pp. 17–38. Translation of the original, "*Der Gedanke: Eine logische Untersuchung*," published in 1918.

Hintikka, J. (1969). *Models for Modalities*. Dordrecht and Boston: D. Reidel Publishing Company.

Husserl, E. (1893–1917/1991). *On the Phenomenology of the Consciousness of Internal Time (1893– 1917)*, (trans. J. B. Brough). Dordrecht and Boston: Kluwer Academic Publishers, 1991.

——(1912/1989). *Ideas* II, i.e. *Ideas pertaining to a Pure Phenomenology and to a Phenomenological Philosophy, Second Book: Studies in the Phenomenology of Constitution* (trans. R. Rojcewicz and A. Schuwer). Dordrecht and Boston: Kluwer Academic Publishers, 1989. Original manuscript dating from 1912, posthumously published in German in 1952. Called *Ideas* II.

——(1939/1948/1973). *Experience and Judgment: Investigations in a Genealogy of Logic* (rev. and ed. L. Landgrebe, 1948, trans. J. S. Churchill and K. Ameriks). Evanston, Illinois: Northwestern University Press, 1973. Originally published in 1939, from a manuscript prepared by Landgrebe in collaboration with Husserl.

Kaplan, D. (1989). "Demonstratives: An Essay on the Semantics, Logic, Metaphysics, and Epistemology of Demonstratives and Other Indexicals" and "Afterthoughts," in J. Almog, J. Perry, and H. Wettstein (eds), *Themes from Kaplan*. Oxford and New York: Oxford University Press, 1989, pp. 481–614.

Kidd, C. (2011). "Phenomenal Consciousness with Infallible Self-representation," *Philosophical Studies*: vol. 152: 361–83.

Kriegel, U. (2006). "The Same-Order Monitoring Theory of Consciousness," in U. Kriegel and K. Williford (eds), *Self-Representational Approaches to Consciousness*. Cambridge, MA, and London, England: MIT Press, pp. 143–70.

——(2009). *Subjective Consciousness: A Self-Representational Theory*. Oxford and New York: Oxford University Press.

——and K. Williford (eds). (2006). *Self-Representational Approaches to Consciousness*. Cambridge, MA, and London, England: MIT Press.

Kripke, S. (1980). *Naming and Necessity*. Cambridge, MA: Harvard University Press.

Lay, C. (2010). *Time to Account for Consciousness*. Doctoral dissertation: University of California, Irvine, 2010.

Levine, J. (2001). *Purple Haze: The Puzzle of Consciousness*. Oxford and New York: Oxford University Press.

Merleau-Ponty, M. (1943/2003). *Phenomenology of Perception* (ed. Colin Smith). London and New York: Routledge, 1945. French original, English translation by Colin Smith, 2003 edition by Routledge.

Mohanty, J. N. (2008). *The Philosophy of Edmund Husserl: A Historical Development*. New Haven: Yale University Press.

Moran, D. (2005). *Edmund Husserl: Founder of Phenomenology*. Cambridge and Malden, MA: Polity Press.

Noë, A. (2004). *Action in Perception*. Cambridge, MA: MIT Press.

Perry, J. (1979). "The Problem of the Essential Indexical," *Noûs*, 13, no. 1: 3–21 (1979).

——(2001). *Reference and Reflexivity*. Stanford, California: CSLI Publications, Center for the Study of Language and Information, Leland Stanford Junior University.

Pitt, D. (2004). "The Phenomenology of Cognition, or What Is It Like to Think That P?", *Philosophy and Phenomenological Research*, vol. LXIX, no. 1 (July 2004): 1–36.

Ryle, G. (1949). *The Concept of Mind*. New York: Barnes & Noble, Inc.

Salmon, N. (1986, 1991). *Frege's Puzzle*. Atascadero, California: Ridgeview Publishing Company.

Sartre, J.-P. (1943/1992). *Being and Nothingness* (trans. H. E. Barnes). New York: Washington Square Press, Simon and Schuster. French original, 1943. Translation, 1956, reprinted 1992.

Siewert, C. (1998). *The Significance of Consciousness*. Princeton: Princeton University Press.

Smith, D. W. (1986). "The Structure of (Self-) Consciousness," *Topoi*, 5 (2): 149–56.

——(1989). *The Circle of Acquaintance: Perception, Consciousness, and Empathy*. Boston and Dordrecht: Kluwer Academic Publishers.

——(2002). "Intentionality and Picturing: Early Husserl *vis-á-vis* Early Wittgenstein," in T. Horgan, J. Tienson, and M. Potrč (eds), *Origins: The Common Sources of the Analytic and Phenomenological Traditions* (proceedings of the Spindel Conference 2001); *The Southern Journal of Philosophy*, vol. XL, supplement 2002, pp. 153–80.

——(2004). "Return to Consciousness," in D. W. Smith (ed.), *Mind World: Essays in Phenomenology and Ontology*. Cambridge and New York: Cambridge University Press, pp. 76–121.

——(2005). "Consciousness with Reflexive Content," in D. W. Smith and A. L. Thomasson (eds), *Phenomenology and Philosophy of Mind*. Oxford and New York: Oxford University Press, pp. 93–114.

——(2007). *Husserl*. London and New York: Routledge.

——and R. McIntyre. (1982). *Husserl and Intentionality: A Study of Mind, Meaning, and Language*. Boston and Dordrecht: D. Reidel Publishing Company.

Sokolowski, R. (2000). *Introduction to Phenomenology*. Cambridge and New York: Cambridge University Press.

Strawson, G. (1994). *Mental Reality*. Cambridge, MA, and London: MIT Press.

——(2005). "Intentionality and Experience: Terminological Preliminaries," in D. W. Smith and A. L. Thomasson (eds), *Phenomenology and Philosophy of Mind*. Oxford and New York: Oxford University Press, pp. 41–66.

——(2008). *Real Materialism and Other Essays*. Oxford and New York: Oxford University Press.

——(2009). *Selves: An Essay in Revisionary Metaphysics*. Oxford and New York: Oxford University Press.

Thomasson, A. L. (2000). "After Brentano: A One-Level Theory of Consciousness," *European Journal of Philosophy*, 8(2): 190–209.

——(2005). "First-Person Knowledge in Phenomenology," in D. W. Smith and A. L. Thomasson (eds), *Phenomenology and Philosophy of Mind*. Oxford and New York: Oxford University Press, pp. 115–39.

——(2008). "Phenomenal Consciousness and the Phenomenal World," *Monist*, vol. 91, no. 2.

Tye, M. (1995). *Ten Problems of Consciousness*. Cambridge, MA: MIT Press.

Author Index

Subject Index

access consciousness, *see* consciousness, access
acquaintance 111–12, 118, 147–8, 150, 163–5,
    187, 339–40
agency 62, 64–9, 73–5, 180, 232–3
    see also phenomenology, agentive
agnosia 42–3
ambiguous figures 43, 48–9, 51, 110, 182–3, 210n
    see also duck/rabbit
aphasia 189
attention 40, 52, 150, 183, 189, 200, 211, 296,
    335, 362
attitudes, propositional, *see* propositional
    attitudes
autism 93

belief 11, 14, 20, 50n, 58n, 68–75, 82–3, 96–8,
    104, 113, 148–70, 190, 212n, 218,
    221–2, 238, 241, 250, 268, 290, 319n,
    330, 333–4, 341, 346, 349, 354, 355
    see also propositional attitudes
blindsight 29, 60–1, 243, 297n, 357

categorical perception, *see* perception, categorical
Chinese Room 70
cognitive-experiential content, *see* experience,
    cognitive
cognitive penetration 109–10
cognitive phenomenology; *see* phenomenology,
    cognitive
conceivability 44–5, 60, 93–4
concepts 16, 38–9, 48, 54, 133, 138, 166–72,
    181, 183, 237, 300, 302, 308–20, 329;
    see also thought, conceptual
concepts, phenomenal; *see* phenomenal concepts
conceptual role semantics 310–11
conciliationism 269, 274–81
consciousness; *passim*
    access 7–8, 41, 53, 58, 63, 66, 105–7, 144,
        151, 287n
    intermediate level theory of 177–81
    phenomenal 2, 7–8, 35–8, 41, 48–9, 53–4,
        80, 93, 95, 103, 105, 216, 219, 221–2,
        233–4, 236–9, 242–4, 247, 252, 290n,
        361
    stream of, *see* stream of consciousness
    temporal structure of 341–3, 365–7
conservative conception of conscious thought 2,
    17, 21–2, 29
    see also exclusivist conception of consciousness,
        frugal conception of consciousness, and

of consciousness restrictive
    conception
content 15–17, 52, 63, 109, 112–14, 122–41,
    152, 154n, 163, 168, 226, 291–5, 304–9,
    349–58
    cognitive 35–7, 52, 112–14, 172, 289, 296,
        304–11
    as opposed to cognitive-experiential
        content, 297, 304–11
    cognitive-experiential; *see* experience,
        cognitive
    conceptual 6, 38–44, 47–51, 250
    external (externalist) 15–16, 47, 80, 117,
        126–7, 133–4, 169, 263–5, 292–4,
        310, 327
    internal (internalist) 15–16, 307, 327–8
    narrow, *see* content, internal
    non-conceptual 6, 29, 35, 38–44, 47–51, 250
    propositional 14, 54, 160, 225–6, 294–5,
        345–51, 354–8
    wide, *see* content, external
content, determinacy of 25, 210–12
content-grounding argument 24–6, 79, 94 -5,
    210–12, 279n
curiosity 191, 202, 215, 229, 244–6, 299–300
    see also epistemic emotions

desire 2, 8, 11, 13–14, 20, 66, 68–9, 72–4, 82,
    88, 103, 109, 159–60, 175, 190, 221–2,
    241, 245, 247, 269, 334
    see also propositional attitudes
direct realism 296–7, 307
Dr. Strangelove 65–7
duck/rabbit 39, 48, 110, 182–3, 210n, 302–3
    see also ambiguous figures

eliminativism 89, 219–20, 233, 241
emotions 14, 17, 93n, 180, 190–1, 202, 208,
    213, 226
    see also epistemic, emotions
entertaining 156n, 159, 228
    see also thinking
epistemic emotions 14, 17–19, 190–1, 215–18,
    229, 299–301
exclusivist conception of consciousness 3n,
    238, 242
    see also conservative conception of
        consciousness, frugal conception of
        consciousness, and restrictive conception of
        consciousness